A History of Modern Latin America

Lawrence A. Clayton
The University of Alabama

Michael L. Conniff
University of South Florida

HARCOURT BRACE COLLEGE PUBLISHERS

Fort Worth Philadelphia San Diego New York Orlando Austin San Antonio
Toronto Montreal London Sydney Tokyo

Publisher	Earl McPeek
Acquisitions Editor	David Tatom
Product Manager	Steve Drummond
Project Editor	Laura J. Hanna
Art Director	Vicki Whistler
Production Manager	Linda McMillan

Cover credit: Mariano Miguel, *La Popa*, 1923, oil on canvas, 41″ × 51″. Gift of The Cuban Foundation. Courtesy of The Museum of Arts and Sciences, Daytona Beach, Florida.

ISBN: 0-15-500253-8

Library of Congress Catalog Card Number: 98-72417

Address for Orders
Harcourt Brace College Publishers, 6277 Sea Harbor Drive, Orlando, FL 32887-6777 1-800-782-4479

Address for Editorial Correspondence
Harcourt Brace College Publishers, 301 Commerce Street, Suite 3700, Fort Worth, TX 76102

Web site Address
http://www.hbcollege.com

Printed in the United States of America

8 9 0 1 2 3 4 5 6 7   018   9 8 7 6 5 4 3 2 1

Harcourt Brace College Publishers

To the memory of William L. Sherman, friend and colleague

Preface

A History of Modern Latin America is a general history of Latin America covering the nineteenth and twentieth centuries. As such, it is largely concerned with the modern period which dates from the Wars of Independence in the early nineteenth century until today. We have written this textbook for college undergraduates taking an introductory course in Latin American history who are most likely first-time readers in the field. A colonial prologue has been included to give students a brief look at the colonial period, but it is only that—an introduction–and not meant to be a substitute for a good colonial text.

Features of the Book

We are old-fashioned enough to know that the story of men and women and how they fared in the past, how they thought, fought, loved, hated, and carried themselves through life is what truly fascinates us. We have, therefore, indulged our love of biographical detail—the flesh and blood of history. A strong narrative style distinguishes *A History of Modern Latin America* from its predecessors of the past two or three decades, which relied heavily on social science jargon and analysis as the medium for presenting Latin American history. This textbook brings to light major interpretations and analysis for the student to consider, but does so with an entertaining and readable literary style too long out of fashion. This certainly reflects upon the wonderful dichotomy of history, equally at home in the social sciences and the humanities.

We begin each chapter with a dramatic moment in time that gives definition to the age or themes treated in that chapter. In some of these action introductions, much of the narrative is authentic, borrowing, if possible, from the actual words spoken or recorded by eyewitnesses. In other instances, we have taken the liberty to imagine a scene and dialogue. Everything either happened, or most certainly could have happened, given what we know of historical circumstances. No other textbook, to our knowledge, has ever employed such an engaging opener to pull the reader into the flow of the chapter.

A History of Modern Latin America weaves together the history of women, minorities, the enduring Amerindian cultures, and the environment to add depth and dimension to the Latin American story.

We have tried to be comprehensive by giving attention to all the nations of Latin America. The biggest and most populous nations—such as Mexico, Argentina and Brazil—take up a significant amount of our attention, but we have highlighted important events in the histories of all nations, from Chile in the south to Cuba in the northern Caribbean.

We have described the major themes of modern Latin American history. From the age of caudillos in the nineteenth century to the revolutionary struggles of the twentieth century, common themes run through the region's history that help to give form and understanding to how and why things happened. We have turned to certain themes—ethnic strife, populism, militarism for example—which have transcended borders and given Latin America its unity of experience, even while an extraordinary diversity marks the region's geography, native people and cultures.

Pedagogical Features

At the end of each chapter, a summary wraps up the major points, providing students with an easily accessible synopsis. A set of questions is included for further probing into the contents of each chapter by both instructors and students. The questions can be used to open discussions on the contents of the chapter, to help summarize and analyze each chapter's principal elements, or as a springboard for emphasizing an instructor's own particular interests.

Boxed inserts of topical readings and primary documents are included throughout the text. These bring the contents to life with vivid descriptions by the historical players and witnesses themselves. They also serve to explain basic concepts (dependency theory, race relations, political alignments) in a format that stands out and brings attention to that particular subject, intrinsically important for a deeper and clearer understanding of Latin American history.

There are over 90 photos and a section of full-color inserts to enhance and enrich the learning experience for the reader. Each photo was specifically chosen to depict the richness of Latin American history.

Each of the five major sections in this textbook are preceded by an introduction to give the reader a sense of the flow of events and their significance in the chapters that follow.

A bibliography of the most up-to-date works is included at the end of each of the five parts, and a general bibliography is included at the back of the book. These works provide students with a place to begin research on individual topics suggested by the more general treatment afforded in the text.

Acknowledgments

We would like to thank the following people for their assistance in the making of this textbook. The idea germinated on a train ride from Manchester to London in the spring of 1982 when William Sherman and Lawrence Clayton talked about a textbook in the style of the one you have before you as "long overdue" in Latin American history. Sherman was to contribute the colonial section, which he began but never was able to finish. We owe Bill Sherman an immense debt of gratitude for giving us a standard of readable, exciting prose—especially as evidenced in the widely read text of Mexican history that he co-authored with Michael Meyer.

At Harcourt Brace, Drake Bush, former history acquisitions editor, encouraged us over the years to keep at it. He never lagged in his enthusiasm for the project and we thank him with much warm feeling. His successor, David Tatom, was equally encouraging in the latter stages of the work. Laurie Runion, developmental editor, organized us and led us to the final stages, while Laura Hanna, senior project editor, Linda McMillan, production manager, Vicki Whistler, art director, and John Ritland, text designer, shepherded the book through production.

Along the way, a number of colleagues read the manuscript or helped in other ways, and we are immensely grateful to them. They include Ximena Sosa-Buchholz, Sandra McGee Deutsch, William P. McGreevey, Pamela Murray, Carleen Payne, Samuel Brunk, Paul J. Dosal, Marshall C. Eakin, and Ralph Lee Woodward, Jr., Felix Angel, Barbara Tenenbaum, Alan LeBaron, Lyman Johnson, Maria Christina Maldonado, and George Ortiz Sotelo.

While this textbook is principally concerned with the founding and evolution of the Latin American nations from the Wars of Independence to the present, we need to reach back and examine the history of the region before then to appreciate fully how things became the way they were. Nothing left a deeper imprint on the early history of Latin American civilization than the conquest, and for this we turn to a moment in 1532 on the north coast of Peru.

Table of Contents

A History of
Modern Latin America

Colonial Prologue

Atahualpa and Pizarro

It was November in the year of our Lord 1532. Earlier Francisco Pizarro had founded a community, San Miguel de Piura, on the coast, and now the small Spanish expedition that Pizarro commanded, 62 horsemen and 106 foot soldiers, marched south and east, deeper and deeper into the heart of the Inca empire toward the city of Cajamarca.

There the Inca Emperor Atahualpa was camped outside the city. Atahualpa had just triumphed in a bloody civil war against his brother Huascar for dominion of the immense Inca empire. The Tihuantisuyo. The Four Corners of the Earth. It stretched from Ecuador in the north to central Chile far to the south.

On November 15, the Spanish force entered Cajamarca. Atahualpa, surrounded and served by thousands of warriors, noblemen, women, and courtiers, stayed in his camp outside the city. A small troop of Spaniards approached Atahualpa. Hernando Pizarro, brother of Francisco, said, "Our governor would be delighted for you to visit him." Fearing nothing from these few, although exotic, strangers, Atahualpa agreed.

November 16, 1532. Atahualpa and a lightly armed retinue of five or six thousand noblemen and warriors slowly moved toward Cajamarca. Pizarro's army, a pitifully small army by comparison, was arrayed for an ambush, hidden in the buildings surrounding the central courtyard. Outside the city, the Indians seemed to fill every space as they joined Atahualpa's procession.

"Are you afraid?" young Pedro Pizarro, brother to Francisco, asked an even younger soldier standing next to him in the shadows. The soldier shuddered involuntarily. "No!" he snapped and then quickly followed, "Yes, by God, aren't you? They sound like a swarm of bees out there," he said, gesturing toward the entrance to the city.

"Yes, Bernardo," Pedro said. "But commend your soul to God. He will see us through." Pedro Pizarro crossed himself, and so did his companion. It fortified them. God would not allow Christians to be overcome by pagans.

Atahualpa, carried on a litter, entered the square late in the after-noon. His people soon filled the square completely, squeezing in and pressing against the walls until there was barely room to move.

The Dominican friar, Vicente de Valverde, approached Atahualpa. "My governor would like you to come and dine with him."

The Inca shot back at the Spanish friar, "Tell your governor to return everything his men have stolen or consumed since they entered my king-doms! Then perhaps we can talk."

Valverde ignored the rebuke and called upon the Inca to submit to God and his emissaries, the Spanish. "It is all in this book," Valverde said, handing Atahualpa a prayer book that he carried with him. Atahualpa took the small book and examined it. The Inca then dropped it onto the ground, angry that the priest had handed him something so strange that seemed to question the Inca's intelligence.

Valverde spun on his heel and turned to Pizarro and his men hidden in the low buildings surrounding the square.

"Make ready!" Atahualpa warned his people, rising in his litter as he watched Valverde run back to Pizarro.

"Oh God, oh God," Valverde cried out as he ran back. "See what this Lucifer has done, Your Honor!" he shouted to Pizarro and the other Spaniards waiting in ambush. "Come out, come out, Christians! Come at these enemy dogs who reject the things of God. I absolve you!" A cannon roared from the top of one of the buildings. It was the prearranged signal.

"Santiago!" the horsemen shouted as they spurred their mounts out of the buildings straight into the mass of Indians around Atahualpa. Ter-rorized by cannons and trumpets, by the brutal assault of the war horses, by the slashing of steel swords and lances, Atahualpa's followers reeled under the onslaught.

Atahualpa's litter bearers were cut down. All around him his subjects died, limbs and heads pierced and severed by Toledan steel, trampled and bludgeoned under the war horses, suffocated as they were crushed up against the city walls until finally the walls collapsed. The Spanish pursued the fleeing, terrified Indians into the night, piercing and slashing them in the surrounding fields until a trumpet finally called them off.

"When will you kill me?" the frightened Inca asked his captors that evening.

"Oh, no, Your Highness," Hernando de Soto answered for the Spaniards. "We fight with force and courage, but we don't kill afterward. That's not right."

"You are our guest," Pizarro added.

"But tell me," Soto inquired of the Inca, "Why did you allow us in so easily, why did you walk into so obvious a trap?"

Atahualpa smiled ruefully. Perhaps they wouldn't kill him after all. "I meant to capture you," he said.

"God was with us, Your Highness," Pedro Pizarro said quietly.

Indeed, the Spaniards and their Christian God had turned the world on its head for Atahualpa and his people. Cajamarca, and the events therein, marked the end of the Inca empire and the beginning of the Spanish empire in Peru. The story of conquest, however, did not begin with Pizarro in Peru. It began in Spain and Portugal hundreds of years before Columbus sailed, and it is to the Iberian civilization that we must turn briefly to comprehend the nature of a people who so remarkably transformed America.

Spanish civilization at the end of the fifteenth century was riding a high crest of military success that culminated in the reconquest of the Moorish kingdom of Granada in 1492. For almost five hundred years, an intermittent crusading-style war had occupied the Spanish people as they fought to rid the Iberian Peninsula of Moors from Africa. These African peoples, worshippers of the prophet Muhammad, or Muslims, swept over and conquered much of Christian Spain in the eighth century. The push west across Africa and then north into Europe through Spain marked the high tide of Islam as it rose first in the Arabian Peninsula and quickly spread east and west.

Then, around the year A.D. 1000, some small Christian kingdoms in the far north along the Cantabrian coast that had survived the Moorish conquest launched a war of reconquest. This "reconquest" of Spain lasted until 1492, when the last Moorish ruler, that of Granada, fell to the besieging Christian armies of Queen Isabelle of Castile and King Ferdinand of Aragon.

The reconquest was a complicated movement that incorporated many elements, some religious, some of a more secular nature. Basically, it colored Spanish society with a very martial complexion. It was a society that looked to the warrior as the embodiment of Christian endeavor and worldly fulfillment. Warrior kings, warrior bishops, knights, and other fighting men were admired as the embodiment of the ideal life—fighting Moors for the ultimate end of reconquering Spain for Christianity. There was, nonetheless, another dimension to this society, more secular and more worldly. This dimension was the goal of enriching oneself through conquest and the acquisition of booty and slaves. Moorish lands and cities, people and property all were legitimate spoils of war, and conquest became a way of life for much of Spanish society.

When Christopher Columbus returned in 1493 to Spain from his first voyage of reconnaissance and discovery, he not only came back with some fantastic news, but also delivered it to a king and queen who presided over a warrior people with a deeply inbred conquest mentality. Spanish energies, for so long invested in the reconquest of Spain, turned to the opening opportunities in the New World. The warriors formerly engaged in the reconquest swarmed over the newly discovered Americas in the sixteenth century, seeking much the same goals they had sought in Spain: fame and fortune through conquest. They found both in abundance in the New World.

The Americas

As a distinguished historian, John Parry, once observed, "America was not discovered by the Europeans, it was truly a meeting of two cultures who had not known each other previously." The native peoples of Latin America—stretched as they were from Tierra del Fuego on the southern tip of South America to the immense spaces of North America to the north—were more diverse in culture, lifestyles, languages, and levels of civilization than the Spanish conquistadors (conquerors) who sailed the Atlantic in the sixteenth century in search of adventure and fortune. When Hernán Cortés and his small Spanish expedition of several hundred men reached the capital—Tenochtitlán—of the Aztec empire in 1519, they marveled at the splendid Aztec capital as they gazed down from the high passes. The Spanish renamed it "Mexico City" during the colonial period.

The various stages of development and culture that had been reached by the native Americans spanned from Stone Age people of the Amazon to the high cultures of Mesoamerica, Mexico, and Peru. The Spanish encountered primitive, nearly naked islanders in the Caribbean and the descendants of astronomers and city builders among the Maya of Central America. It is almost impossible to characterize simply the Indians of Latin America at the time of the European encounter of America because they were as diverse in language, ethnic identity, and political and social organization as all of Europe at the time.[1]

There were perhaps seventy-five million Amerindians in the Americas at the time of the Conquest, twenty-two million of those in Mexico alone, ten to twelve million under the dominion of the Incas and their emperor, Atahualpa, along the Andes, and the remainder in varying proportions from North America—eight million, for example—to lowland South America. They ranged from nomadic hunters and gatherers to people who had domesticated crops and thus developed a sedentary agriculture. The latter, freed from the tyranny of hunting and gathering, built complex civilizations, complete with well-developed religious rituals, political organizations, artisans, and cities in Central America, Mexico, and Peru. The Maya developed a written language; the Incas, an efficient state bureaucracy and empire; and the Aztecs, a formidable war machine. When the Spanish arrived in the late fifteenth century, the stage was set for a meeting between these two peoples—one European and the other American—that not only would be the initiating moment in Latin American history, but also would transform world history.

The Conquest

In the simplest terms, the "Conquest" refers to the subjugation of the Amerindians by Spanish and Portuguese warriors from Europe. It was not only a conquest by arms, but also, from the perspective of the Spanish, a triumph of Spanish religion and civilization over pagan Indian peoples. In respect to a perspective long ignored by historians, the term "Encounter" is sometimes substituted for "Conquest" to reflect a balance in the merits of the cultures and civilizations—one native American and one European—that "encountered" each other in the seminal sixteenth century.

---

[1] See John E. Kicza, editor and contributor, *The Indian in Latin American History: Resistance, Resilience, and Culturation* (Wilmington, Del.: SR Books, 1993), especially the very useful introduction by Kicza.

But no matter how one alters the words, the Conquest devastated the Amerindians and fueled Spain on its rise as a world power.

By the middle of the century, European diseases, harsh demands, dislocation and demoralization from their defeat combined to destroy more than 50 percent of the native Americans. In 1650, censuses in Spanish America recorded that populations had been drastically reduced from levels that had existed at the time of Columbus's arrival. In the Caribbean islands, virtually no Amerindians survived the first hundred years after the Spanish conquest, while in the central valley of Mexico and along the Andean mountains of South America, 80 percent and sometimes 90 percent of the populations had perished.

Early on, the Spanish conquest also meant the conquest of Indian women. Miscegenation (the mixing of racial or ethnic types) occurred on a vast scale, and a new race was born, the mestizos: those children born of unions between Spaniards and Amerindians. They became an increasing percentage of the population, especially in the great Indian population centers of Mexico, Guatemala, Ecuador, Peru, and Bolivia.

Afro-europeans also arrived with the Spanish conquistadors, sometimes as free men, but increasingly as slaves. A generation later their numbers increased dramatically as Spaniards and Portuguese imported hundreds, then thousands, and finally millions of Africans to the Americas during the colonial period to work the fields and plantations of the New World where Amerindians once had thrived before the decimation of the Conquest.

The Spanish fanned out over much of the continent and found what they came looking for during the Conquest: fame, wealth, and power. They established for Spain the beginnings of American empires that gave Latin American civilization its basic character in all the many ways that we measure and describe a civilization, from its religion to its eating habits. Meanwhile, the Portuguese occupied and settled Brazil, gradually forming a unique tropical society and economy. By blending with the Amerindians and African Americans, the Spaniards and Portuguese in the New World also forged the beginnings of a civilization distinct from Africa, from America, from Europe. It was an amalgamation of all three.

The Developing Colony

For a little over three hundred years the Spanish and Portuguese empires in America grew strong. A vibrant society emerged from the Conquest era, dedicated to making this New World experience in colonization work and work well.

At the apex of Spanish civilization in America was the king of Spain. Through his Council of the Indies, he governed the colonies, which were themselves divided into administrative entities called viceroyalties. The viceroyalty of New Spain included all of Mexico, Central America, and the Caribbean, plus some areas of North America and South America, while the viceroyalty of Peru, with its capital of Lima, extended across all of the continent of South America, excluding Brazil, which belonged to Portugal. From Mexico City and Lima, the nobility of Spain was sent to rule these vast domains as viceroys.

Equal in importance to the viceroys, governors, and other secular administrators were the prelates, missionaries, and priests of the Roman Catholic Church, who arrived simultaneously in the Americas with the conquistadors. The Church quickly became—after the government—the most important institution in colonial Latin America and conditioned much of Latin American society in this formative period.

Members of missionary orders spearheaded the Church's evangelization of native Americans in the sixteenth century. Dominicans, Franciscans, and later Jesuits spread the faith rapidly among their new converts, who had suffered a terrible defeat at the hands of the Spanish conquistadors. Were not, then, the Christian gods, or one god, as the friars insisted, better than their own gods, who had failed them so miserably? The answer was a tentative "yes," making evangelization easier for the Christian missionaries. Churches were established, native languages were given grammars to reach better the new converts with the basic holy writ contained in the Bible, and baptisms were made by the hundreds and thousands as Amerindians came under the cross. Many of the Amerindian deities and religious traditions actually survived the evangelization of the Americas. When these were incorporated into formal Church worship, new, syncretized (combined) forms of worship evolved. Catholic saints and an assortment of pre-Christian gods sometimes co-existed in somewhat unusual harmony, a fact that distinguished the Church in the Americas from the stricter, more conservative Church of the Old World.

The "secular" clergy followed rapidly in the wake of the missionary padres. These secular priests and clerics were involved in the day-to-day affairs of parish life and eventually replaced the members of the missionary orders, sometimes labeled the "regular" Church because members of missionary orders such as the Dominicans and Franciscans were governed by a special set of "regulations." The secular clergy was directly under the control of the Spanish and Portuguese monarchs through an arrangement called the *real patronato,* or the royal patronage. This gave the crown immense influence in the operation of the Church in the colonies—such as the right to name clerics, establish churches, and collect tithes—while endowing the Church with the powerful support of the monarchy. The Church prospered not only in a spiritual fashion by converting millions of Amerindians to Christianity, but also in a material way, accumulating vast wealth in property over the length of the colonial period. It was claimed that by the era of independence, the Church—in Mexico, for example—owned half of the real estate in that vast colony.

Later, in the nineteenth century, the Church became a focal point of intense controversy. During and after the Wars of Independence, it was attacked by reformers and liberals who sought to break its power not only as an immense property holder but also as the dominant force in providing education and social services such as hospitals and philanthropy. The Church was also the principal money lender in the colonies, and in dozens of other ways it controlled and fashioned the way that people thought and acted. The Inquisition, sometimes called the police arm of the Church, sought to enforce orthodoxy in both spiritual and secular matters, seeking out and punishing crimes as serious as heresy and treason. Committing bigamy, soliciting women parishioners in the confessional, and other lesser crimes also came before the courts of the Inquisition in its role of spiritual and moral censor and judge of colonial society.

Yet, if one were to take an informal poll of those first approaching Latin America as an object of study, asking them which one word or phrase comes immediately to mind to characterize Spain's colonies in America, it would not be "religion" or the "Church," but rather "silver." Actually, perhaps most people would say something like the "gold galleons," when, in fact, the bulk of precious metal wealth that flowed from the colonies to Spain for over three hundred years was silver, not gold.

With regard to material wealth, Spaniards enjoyed an incredible run of luck in their colonial experience. The Spanish would claim that finding and exploiting in Mexico and Peru the greatest silver mines the world had ever known were acts of divine providence. Spain's European rivals—principally England, France, and Holland—might have viewed Spain's luck in other terms. Whatever the perspective, by the late sixteenth century the silver mines of Zacatecas in Mexico and Potosí in Bolivia (then known as the province of Upper Peru) were on the way to making Spain the envy of all Europe as fleets arrived annually at the port of Seville loaded down to the scuppers with silver. "Vale un Potosí" ("as rich as Potosí") became a common phrase in seventeenth-century Europe, a metaphor for vast and easy wealth.

Around the great silver mines, a complex agricultural and pastoral system developed to supply the workers and the mines with food, leather, and other supplies. These estates became the models for landownership in colonial Latin America: large haciendas owned by a small minority of the Creole (Spaniards born in the New World of Spanish parents; *criollo* in Spanish) elite who represented the top of colonial society's pyramid of power and influence.

As the economic basis of the colonies gradually diversified to include the production of other export products, such as sugar, cacao (chocolate), indigo, and tobacco, for example, the great hacienda system spread throughout Spanish America and Brazil. A great hacienda owned by a Creole family, however, was not the only form of landownership. Some of the regular orders of the Church, such as the Jesuits, became among the richest and most powerful estate builders in colonial America, while in many parts of Latin America, especially in Mexico, Central America, and Peru, Amerindians managed to preserve their communal lands intact in spite of the encroachments of white settlers. Nonetheless, the dispossession of the Amerindians' land by Creoles and mestizos—as well as exploitation in other areas—produced much stress in this colonial society, flaring up in occasional rebellions that grew more pronounced and violent toward the end of the eighteenth century.

The Mature Colony

By the middle of the eighteenth century, we can speak of mature colonies. There was a sense of place and self among colonial Latin Americans that distinguished them from the transplanted Spaniards of the sixteenth century. The conquistadors had sailed to a new land and encountered exotic peoples. Two centuries later, the

Creoles, mestizos, *pardos* and mulattoes (persons born of a union between a black and a white), *zambos* (of unions between Indians and blacks), and other Americans born of the racial mixture of Spaniard, Indian, and African for the most part felt themselves to be "Americans" or "Peruvians," "Mexicans," or "Chileans," for example, relating to the region of their birth much more than to the land of their ancestors. This sense of nationality was more pronounced among the Creole elite and only imperceptibly sensed in those groups largely estranged from power and privilege, such as Amerindians and slaves, for example. While their parochial sense of identity did not stray far from plantation or village, the Creoles were already developing a protonationalism that helped spark the Wars of Independence in the early nineteenth century.

Economically, too, the eighteenth century represented a period of increasing self-sufficiency. While the colonies exported greater and greater amounts of products from field, forest, and mines to European consumers, coincidentally the American colonies of Spain and Portugal also were producing more and more for themselves—textiles, shoes, ships, and myriad other items—that spoke of maturing colonies.

Certain areas of the colonial export economy expanded dramatically in the second half of the eighteenth century. Cattle products from Argentina (salted beef and leather), sugar from Cuba, cacao from Venezuela and Ecuador, indigo (a dye) from Guatemala and Mexico, magnificent woods from tropical Central America, silver from the rejuvenated mines of Mexico, and other products helped double, triple, and sometimes even quadruple trade between the colonies and Europe toward the end of the century. It was a period of rising prosperity.

Coincidental with prosperity came peace. But the times were changing, reflecting perhaps that great passage in the Old Testament book of Ecclesiastes, which begins with "There is a time for everything, and a season for every activity under heaven . . ." and ends with ". . . a time to love and a time to hate, a time for war and a time for peace."[2] New ways of thinking about the world were changing the old order of things. Revolutions in the United States (1776), France (1789), and Haiti (1791) were—by their example and hot rhetoric—helping Creoles of Latin America to fine tune their own sense of aggravation and injustice at being second-class citizens in the Spanish empire. In September of 1810, Mexico's Creoles and Indians rose up dramatically against the old order. The results, in Mexico and across the Spanish empire, changed the course of Latin America's modern history.

Conclusions and Issues

The colonial background to independence was marked by one of the most fascinating endeavors in human history: the making of a new civilization. Previously the American continents had been isolated from the Eurasian and African land masses

---

[2] From Ecclesiastes 3:1–8.

for ages, each part of the world developing distinct plants, animals, peoples, and cultures that often were quite different. With the Columbian voyages, the European and American cultures came together with a great clash. Principal among the European colonizers were the Spanish and Portuguese. They came with their swords and muskets, with their faith and language, with an immense energy to explore, to conquer, to settle.

They encountered an equally diverse Amerindian culture, which the Spanish and Portuguese first conquered and then attempted to "civilize" with European values. The result was the long colonial period that you have just read about. Certainly the Spanish and Portuguese prevailed in political and economic fashions, but in the end an immensely varied culture and people developed in Latin America, a fusion of European, Amerindian, and African peoples.

Over time, the Spanish and Portuguese empires in the Americas produced an incredibly rich cornucopia of wealth for the mother countries. In the Indies themselves, societies developed with the Spanish and Portuguese administrators at the top, but closely paralleled by a Creole elite who shared power and resources. Eventually these Creoles moved to separate themselves from European control, motivated by self-interest, revolutionary models (the American and French revolutions, for example), and the desire to carve out their own destinies.

Discussion Questions

1. Why does the term "Encounter" seem to be an equally valid, perhaps even better, way to describe the period long labeled simply the "Conquest" of the Americas?

2. Why was the Roman Catholic Church so immensely important in the Spanish and Portuguese empires in the Americas?

3. What were some of the elements that gave Latin American civilization a quality or qualities that made it unique?

Part I

Independence and Turmoil

Latin America passed through one of its most important historical episodes in the first half of the nineteenth century. In a tumultuous twenty-year span, from about 1806 to 1826, the old Spanish and Portuguese colonies broke off from the mother countries and became independent nations. The path that each nation followed to independence was often complicated and marked by fits and starts, periods of intense political confusion, sharp military conflicts, interludes of peace, more battles, and by ethnic and political divisions within the revolutionary movements that defy easy or clear analysis.

Basically, leaders—mostly Creoles, but including other castes such as mestizos and mulattoes—in Latin America determined that they wished greater independence and autonomy from Spain. Spain for the most part resisted this wish, and the stage was set for the wars that followed. In some instances, such as in Mexico in 1810, the conflict took on racial overtones that horrified many conservative Creoles. They wanted independence but did not particularly want "freedom" for all Mexicans, which included a vast majority of Indians, blacks and mestizos who were subject to Creole domination.

In South America, Simón Bolívar headed the patriot forces of Venezuela, Colombia, Ecuador, Peru, and Bolivia in the long struggle for independence that began in 1810 in Venezuela and did not culminate until 1826 in Bolivia. From the south José de San Martín led patriot armies out of Argentina to sweep up through Chile and Peru, eventually joining with Bolívar's forces in the liberation of Peru.

Brazil marched to its own drummer. Independence came late and largely as the result of the transfer of Portugal's court to Rio de Janeiro in 1807. Brazil became essentially equal with Portugal under the rule of João VI, and when he returned to Portugal in 1821 he left his son Pedro to govern over a colony—Brazil—that now felt itself the equal of the old mother country. In 1822 Brazil declared its independence and accepted Pedro as its first emperor. The ease with which Brazil became independent contrasted vividly with the long and violent road followed by the old Spanish colonies.

After independence was achieved, a confusing period of political turmoil followed until about mid-century. Multiple experiments with various political forms of government were initiated, from monarchy to republics, but very few were stable or long lasting. What did ensue were periods of dictatorial rule by men styled caudillos, such as Antonio López de "Manga de Clavo" of Mexico and Juan Manuel de Rosas of Argentina, who governed by force but who themselves were vulnerable to the power of other caudillos. Constitutions seemed to rotate almost as rapidly as caudillos in countries such as Peru and Mexico. Political anarchy in turn stifled economic recovery from the independence wars, and to the observer of the 1830s and 1840s, Latin America appeared chaotic politically and stagnant economically.

Yet, even in this period new forces were at work. The wars disrupted the old racial and ethnic structures of the colonial period. Some nations emancipated their slaves during the wars, and by mid-century emancipation was in full swing. Liberals desired to free Amerindians of old bondages such as tribute labor (a form of taxation levied only on indigenous peoples) that long chained them to secondary citizenship. The experiments to elevate Amerindians to equality were, however, marked by as many failures as successes.

Commercially, British, French, and American merchants—among others—were welcomed into the newly independent ports of Latin America, bringing with them not only new wares and merchandise but also new ideas and fashions. It was the beginning of a new dimension in Latin America's relationship with the rest of the world that would truly take off in the second half of the century.

The Coming of Independence

Father Hidalgo's "Grito de Dolores"

The priest Miguel Hidalgo didn't sleep that night. He tossed and turned, troubled and excited by the prospects of revolution.

"Everything is in place, then?" Hidalgo remembered his last conversation with Ignacio Allende, a co-conspirator in the plot to overthrow Spanish rule in Mexico.

"Yes, yes, Father," Allende reassured him. "We rise in Querétaro and San Miguel on the morning of October 2."

"Have you got the arms ready?" Allende asked.

"Not only spears, slings, and machetes, Ignacio, but a band as well," Hidalgo said with a broad smile. He had recruited Juan Garrido, drum major of the band of the Guanajuato battalion of provincial infantry, to the cause of independence. His beloved Mexico would soon throw off the shackles of Spanish tyranny, and it would be done to the roll of drums and the blaring of trumpets! Victory was guaranteed.

Hidalgo went to bed late on the evening of September 15. The plot was set to explode in the face of Spanish tyranny October 2. But Hidalgo couldn't sleep. He rose near midnight and called for his young Indian assistant, Pedro, to fetch him his robes and make some warm chocolate.

The young Indian found Hidalgo in his study writing furiously and with concentration. By one-thirty in the morning, Hidalgo finally wore himself out. He returned to bed and dropped off into a deep sleep. An insistent knocking at the door came from afar, growing louder and louder. Hidalgo was pulled out from the almost hypnotic abyss of sleep, drawn up and up by the knocking. He awoke with a start.

Hidalgo rapidly slipped a robe over his nightshirt and ran down the stairs. Pedro, the Indian servant, cracked the door, but the intruder shoved it open, bursting into the room.

"It's out! We've been betrayed!" Juan de Aldama said as he shoved his way into the foyer. By now, other visitors at the priest's home, including Allende, were coming out of their rooms, hurrying to the foyer where

Aldama, finally sitting and catching his breath, told them all over again, "They know everything!"

A conspirator had gotten cold feet and betrayed them to the Spanish. Even as they spoke, the Spanish were rounding up conspirators. The sentence for treason to the crown was death. The Spanish would not hesitate to quash any challenge to their authority.

A quick council of war convened in Hidalgo's sitting room. It was 2:15 A.M., September 16 in the town of Dolores, in the viceroyalty of New Spain. The conspirators debated over the consequences of the botched rebellion. They all were in danger, but as dawn neared, the fear of the night slowly gave way to the courage that comes with light.

"We must act," Hidalgo finally said with decision. "Not to act is to fail. Let us strike off the yoke of the oppressor and beat it into the ground! To arms!"

"Pedro," Hidalgo called for his assistant. "Sound the chapel bell. The time has come."

Hundreds of supporters, most of them Indians from Hidalgo's parish, heard the insistent pealing of the bell and gathered in the twilight of dawn just as the deep blues and violets of sunrise tinted the horizon to the east. Hidalgo threw open the windows and felt the rush of cool night air and heard the murmurs of the crowd, looking up at him quietly but with conviction. They trusted him.

"*¡Viva el cura!*" one voice said. "Long live the priest!" Others followed with cries of "*¡viva!*"

Hidalgo raised his hands for silence.

"My friends and countrymen," he began. "The moment of our freedom has arrived. The hour of our liberty has struck." The crowd grew silent as he spoke. "We have broken the shackles of tyranny. Neither king nor tributes exist for us any longer. We are a free people, but we have to fight for our liberty. Join me!" Hidalgo's voice roared out over the men. "We will fight for liberty and country."

"*Si, si, mi padre* [yes, yes, Father]," chorused the Indians in approval.

"Our cause is just, and God will protect us," Hidalgo responded. Then, raising his voice again, he claimed for himself the most remembered moment in Mexican history.

"Long live the Virgin of Guadalupe!" the priest cried out.

"*¡Viva!*" responded the throng.

"Long live America!" Hidalgo continued, and, with the roar of the crowd in his ears, finished with, "Long live independence!"

The "Grito de Dolores" ("Cry of Dolores") had been proclaimed. Mexico was on the road to revolution.

But we must recognize that people rarely break easily with the past. The forces of tradition and the safety and comfort of timeworn ways restrain radical thinking,

Father Miguel Hidalgo, Mexican War of Independence hero who set the independence movement into action with his call to arms on September 16, 1810, in his largely Indian parish of Dolores. Each year the "Grito de Dolores" is again renewed by the President of Mexico from the balcony of the Presidential Palace on the broad, central plaza of Mexico City.

preserve old institutions, and discourage exploration of unfamiliar paths to new relationships, be they political, economic, or even social. Thus, for over three hundred years, Spain's colonies in America evolved slowly, stage by gradual stage, with little dramatic change, at least to the eye of the contemporary observer. Life was predictable. Born an Indian peasant, one expected to die tilling the same soil as one's ancestors, passing that legacy on to a sturdy son if God so willed it. Born a Creole, one expected more privileges, perhaps an education at the local college, marriage to a young girl of one's own caste and rank, and a comfortable job in the government bureaucracy. There was constancy to life for man and woman, whether Indian, black slave, mestizo shopkeeper, or Creole aristocrat.

From the late eighteenth century through the early nineteenth century, new forces buffeted this stable world of colonial Spanish America. These forces erupted between 1810 and 1825 in a series of wars and revolutions that shattered Spain's colonial world into pieces and then put the pieces together again as new nations. One of the greatest empires in modern history ended, and a new era of political independence began for the peoples of Latin America—peoples who were, in truth, hardly homogeneous but rather a constellation of different societies.

Causes of the Wars of Independence

Ideas and the Enlightenment

One of the greatest students of revolutions, the historian Crane Brinton, in referring to the French Revolution, wrote: "no ideas, no revolution." In other words, to break with the past, to make a revolution, a people must have an ideology with goals that cannot be fulfilled unless society first changes radically. The desire to achieve these goals must outweigh the risk and trauma of radical change. However, the ideas behind the goals may be largely unarticulated during the early stages of a revolution. When finally formalized, the ideology that emerges may be an *ex post facto* (after the fact) justification of what has already happened. When Thomas Jefferson wrote the American Declaration of Independence in 1776, he, in many ways, was justifying what already had happened. By then the American colonists had broken with the king and Parliament, the Minutemen had engaged the Redcoats in Massachusetts; the Declaration was but the final, legalistic break.

In truth, most revolutions—as in the case of the French and the American revolutions, both of which inspired Latin Americans of the era—embody early concepts and ideas—the ideology—already elaborated and then create momentum by spontaneous acts not necessarily tied to the ideology. The Latin American Wars of Independence were no different.

Ideologically, the Wars of Independence were born in the eighteenth-century Age of Enlightenment, also sometimes labeled the "Age of Reason." New ideas challenged old truths and institutions accepted for centuries in Europe. Some ideas were profoundly subversive, like the notion that the ultimate authority in society resides in the people, not with king or emperor. This idea denied the divine right of monarchs to rule absolutely.

The idea that all people are created equal in nature and possess equal rights furthermore subverted the privileged nobility, whose rank and power derived from birth.

The Church as the guardian of morality and the enforcer of social order came under attack by enlightened philosophers who rejected religious wisdom found in ancient ecclesiastical manuscripts. Instead of an omnipotent god, they envisioned a benign divine presence who had set things in motion but who allowed people freedom to follow their own destinies. This secular trend undermined traditional authority in society.

In science, the new thinkers challenged old knowledge even more decisively. Scientific knowledge had been thought to be complete, immutable and unchanging; it was usually acquired through study of the teachings of Aristotle and his followers. The enlightened scientists, in contrast, studied nature itself for answers to their questions. For example, Aristotelian thinkers "knew" that the earth is the center of the universe. As this was not borne out by scientific observation, it was cast out by enlightened thinkers. They taught inquiring modern men to observe, to classify, to search for rules in nature rather than blindly to accept hand-me-down "knowledge." In sum, new ways of thinking produced new points of view, new frames of reference, and new forms of behavior that challenged the old order.

The Enlightenment in the New World

The Enlightenment had considerable impact in the Spanish colonies, although at first it was more evident in philosophical and scientific thinking than in politics. People like the Mexican Antonio Alzate and the Peruvian Hipólito Unanue were committed to reason and progress as the passwords of a new age. They and others like them fostered scientific investigation in medicine, botany, and agriculture, for example. They saw these as useful tools for building a better society. Universities such as San Carlos of Guatemala became relatively open forums for the discussion and dissemination of the new ways, as did societies of civic-minded citizens, most often called *Amigos del País* (Friends of the Country).

The Spanish crown itself, especially under the enlightened monarch Charles III (1759–1788), encouraged efficiency and the application of enlightened principles in the management of its vast American empire. This had unforeseen consequences for Spain.

Over the years, Creoles had been given access to governmental offices in the colonies from the lowest municipal posts to offices as high as judgeships on the prestigious *audiencias* (high courts with judicial and legislative powers). In the middle and late eighteenth century, the Spanish crown deliberately began to replace Creoles with native Spaniards in many offices to help centralize and streamline the imperial administration. However wise and enlightened this was from the perspective of the Spanish crown, Creoles saw only an insensitive and offensive monarchy.

In this unsettled environment, it was not surprising that other, headier, more politically volatile facets of the Age of Reason fueled the imaginations of a few Creoles. Activists like Francisco de Miranda of Venezuela, Antonio Nariño of Colombia, Claudio Manuel da Costa of Brazil, and Francisco Javier Espejo of Ecuador immersed themselves in the ideas of the political enlightenment and, many years before the eruption of the wars, came up championing the cause of independence and liberty for their homelands. They are called *precursors* (forerunners) of the independence movement. Although few in number, they exercised a disproportionate influence. They forced their fellow Creoles to think in terms defined by the political enlightenment, to look to the examples of the American and French revolutions. To them, the writings of the Baron de Montesquieu on the sovereignty of the people and of Jean Jacques Rousseau on the social contract were clarion calls to action.

Wealthy Creoles were not the only ones dissatisfied with the colonial systems of Spain and Portugal. Across the Caribbean and along the coast of Brazil, African-American leaders, some slave but many free, accelerated plans for uprisings against planters and officials. They sought independence and self-government in order to create societies like those of Africa. The vast new importation of Africans in the late eighteenth century meant that conspirators could recruit veteran soldiers, religious leaders, chieftains, and merchant-kings who enjoyed great prestige among the slave masses. Their uprisings set many islands aflame, and in 1791 the greatest of all the slave revolts, that of Haiti, broke out and forever altered the fate of black people in the Americas. The man who ultimately commanded the victorious Haitian Revolution, former slave Toussaint L'Ouverture, became the most famous black man in the world, both feared and loved by millions.

In the Andean highlands, as well, Indian and *mestizo* laborers and peasants chafed under the oppression of Spanish officials and priests. One especially angry mestizo, José Gabriel Condorcanqui, a descendant of the last Inca king, attempted to redress grievances peacefully through the judicial system. But, pushed over the edge by a long series of abuses of power by Spanish and Creole officials on his people, he took the ancestral name of Tupac Amaru II and led the Great Andean Rebellion of 1780–1783. It was finally put down, and Condorcanqui was brutally executed, but thereafter all Spaniards in the Andes had to remain wary of further rebellions and bloodshed.

Besides leaders such as Toussaint L'Ouverture and Condorcanqui, dozens of others struggled to organize liberation movements. In the end, all of these early conspirators failed individually—most were executed or died in prison—yet paved the way for victory by the next generation of leaders and are much revered in their countries today. Among the most famous precursors were Hidalgo and José María Morelos of Mexico, Francisco Miranda of Venezuela, Claudio Manuel da Costa and Joaquim José da Silva Xavier (the famed Tiradentes) of Brazil, and Antonio Nariño of Colombia.

The Creoles and the Peninsulares

In the end, wealthy white Creoles led the movements to separate their lands from Spain in the Wars of Independence. Besides the ideology of the Enlightenment, other, more gut-level considerations propelled them to action. A diverse set of economic, ethnic, and nationalistic circumstances added to the general level of discontent and frustration among the Latin American population.

Although no one element was more important than another in bringing about the wars, the antagonism and bitter feelings between American Creoles and those Spaniards born in the Iberian Peninsula (*peninsulares*) who came to Latin America either as government administrators or in private enterprise helped ignite the emotional tinderbox that flared in 1810.

For a variety of reasons, Creoles felt abused and offended by the *peninsulares*, who, in turn, tended to be contemptuous of the Creoles. These feelings hardened over the years. Creoles claimed that their legitimate aspirations, not only to hold office, as discussed previously, but also to trade freely, to be full citizens within the Spanish empire, were circumscribed and frustrated by an imperial bureaucracy that invariably favored Spaniards over Creoles. Out of this discontent, a sense of Latin American nationalism began to evolve, a feeling of distinctiveness that the great Peruvian historian, Jorge Basadre, labeled the "*conciencia de sí,*" or national self-awareness.[1]

Creoles and Spaniards

Although the difference in temperament and character between Spaniards and Creoles, and between the different American peoples, was already deeply marked at the end of the seventeenth century, its consequences only began to emerge during the eighteenth. The mutual antipathy between Spaniards and Creoles blossomed forth with unwonted vigor from the beginning of that century onwards.... Spaniards and Creoles were linked by their feelings of loyalty and respect for the king; but they hated one another. In 1748 Jorge Juan and Antonio de Ulloa remarked in their *Noticias secretas de América:* To be a European, or chapeton, is cause enough for hostility to the Creoles, and to have been born in the Indies is sufficient reason for hating Europeans. This ill-will reaches such a pitch that in some ways it surpasses the rabid hatred which two countries in open war feel for one another, since, while with these there is usually a limit to vituperation and insult, with the Spaniards of Peru you will find none. And far from this discord being alleviated by closer contact between the two parties, by family ties, and by other means which might be thought likely to promote unity and friendship, what happens is the reverse—discord grows constantly worse, and the greater the contact between Spaniard and Creole the fiercer the fires of dissension; rancor is constantly renewed, and the fire becomes a blaze that cannot be put out.

(Jorge Juan and Antonio de Ulloa, *Noticias secretas de América*, as quoted in Francisco A. Encina [*Historia de Chile desde su prehistoria hasta 1891*, Santiago: Editorial Nacimiento, 1941–1942], vols. 7–15, which in turn appears on pp. 245–246 of Humphreys and Lynch, editors, *Origins of the Latin American Revolutions*)

Issues of Trade and Commerce

Creole aspirations to independence were also fed by bread-and-butter issues that added to the smoldering jealousy and antagonisms that already marked social and political relations between Creoles and *peninsulares.*

---

[1]Basadre, "La promesa de la vida peruana y otros ensayos," (Lima: Mejía Baca, 1958), in R. A. Humphreys and John Lynch, editors and contributors, *The Origins of Latin American Revolutions, 1808–1826* (Newark: Knopf, 1966), p. 297.

Creoles believed that the Spanish crown and the *peninsulares* unjustifiably favored Spain at the expense of the colonies in matters of trade and commerce. Their dissatisfaction took many forms. In some regions, like those that produced agricultural products for export, the Creole landowners wanted free trade and an end to the system of Spanish monopoly and controls. In other regions, the interior provinces of Ecuador and Peru, for example, where local manufacturers had to compete with imported products, the Creoles wanted more protection. And in regions like Argentina, there were both factions wanting free trade and factions wanting protection. Argentines in the coastal provinces, especially Buenos Aires, produced many cattle products for export and desired free trade; their brethren in the interior produced wines and other products marketed internally and wished to be protected from cheap European imports that undermined their livelihood. Whatever the Spanish crown did was bound to rub someone the wrong way, further eroding loyalties to the monarchy. The friction caused by these commercial differences was increased by the other circumstances that estranged Creoles from *peninsulares.*

The Invasion of Spain

Creole exasperation with overbearing *peninsular* officials was all the greater because Creoles did not see the geopolitical units of the New World as lesser lands subject to a Spanish fatherland. Just as Spain itself was a group of ancient kingdoms (like Valencia, Castile, Aragon, Granada) united dynastically by their allegiance to the same crown, the New World with its various administrative divisions (Guatemala, Mexico, Peru, Venezuela, Ecuador, and so on) was conceived of as a roster of new kingdoms, equal with each other and with their fellow kingdoms in Spain. Each owed allegiance to the crown, and none was subordinate to any other kingdom. Their allegiance to the crown, moreover, was highly personal. That is, it ran from the kingdom to the person of the king, and not to Spain itself. As the nineteenth century dawned, King Carlos IV sat on the Spanish throne. His son Ferdinand was his heir apparent.

In Europe, by 1800 the armies of the brilliant and ambitious Napoleon Bonaparte were on the march, building an empire across the continent. In 1807 and 1808 Napoleon's soldiers overwhelmed Portugal and Spain. A British fleet gathered up the Portuguese royal family and court and whisked them off to safety in Brazil just days before French forces occupied Lisbon. Spain, too, was overrun. Napoleon forced King Charles IV to abdicate in favor of Prince Ferdinand, then removed both to France, where they remained hostage.

Joseph Bonaparte, Napoleon's brother, was crowned king of Spain. The curtain was up on a great drama, the actors were already in place. A usurper, Joseph Bonaparte, sat on the throne of the kidnapped King Ferdinand VII. Spain's new leader and his government lacked legitimacy. What were Spain's colonies to do?

On May 2, 1808, the Spanish people in Madrid rose up spontaneously against the French army of occupation and the French Bonaparte king. This was the opening salvo of a civil war that lasted almost six years, until Napoleon's empire collapsed and Ferdinand returned to Spain. Other Spaniards formed juntas, or committees, to work for the expulsion of the French and to carry on the affairs of state in Ferdinand's name during his exile. The most important of these was the Central Junta of Seville.

The Spanish juntas asked the colonies to join them in resisting aggression. Consistent with their concept of co-kingdoms, the Creoles demanded equality and equal representation. None of these Spanish juntas was willing to concede that.

Local juntas sprang up in the colonies—in La Paz, in Quito, in Santiago, and elsewhere—to consider governing local affairs in the absence of the legitimate monarch, Ferdinand VII. These juntas, largely controlled by Creoles acting through their municipal governing bodies, the *cabildos*, were little disposed to obey self-appointed juntas in Spain that sought to govern the whole empire in Ferdinand VII's absence. When the Central Junta that convened in Spain attempted to legislate and govern the American kingdoms, the Creoles rejected its authority. They would obey the king, but not a group of Spaniards who purported to rule in the name of the king. This was often a ruse, but it maintained a semblance of legality.

In 1810 the Central Junta was replaced by the convocation of a Spanish parliament, the Cortes, which convened in September in the ancient port city of Cádiz. It included representatives from the colonies. The Cortes decreed radical reforms, such as the equality of all Americans, a free press, and abolishment of the Indian tribute (tax paid in coin or kind). But the Cortes, radical and liberal in its makeup and actions, came too late.

Between 1808 and 1810 Creoles of Latin America had responded to the crisis by taking matters into their own hands. Throughout Latin America, they broke with formal Spanish authority usually represented by a viceroy or captain-general who now appeared to stand for the usurper Joseph Bonaparte. The Creoles determined to govern themselves in Ferdinand VII's name and to await his restoration.

But beneath these acts lay the long history of injured Latin American sensibilities. Their dissatisfaction had been given ideological form by the Enlightenment, while the crown and *peninsulares* had thoroughly antagonized Creoles for decades by denying them what they considered their legitimate aspirations. Napoleon's invasion of Spain, by suspending colonial loyalty to the Spanish state, touched off the fuse to the powder keg. Isolated military confrontations soon erupted into war.

For fifteen years the Wars of Independence raged across Latin America from the northern deserts of Mexico to the cold, snowy passes of the Andes Mountains that divide Chile from Argentina in South America. Spain's effort to maintain its rich American empire was overwhelmed by its colonies' fights for autonomy and freedom from colonialism. Spain was pushed violently out of mainland America, and more than half a dozen nations emerged, committed to independence. Portugal, too, was pushed out of Brazil, but the almost peaceful path toward independence in Brazil differed markedly from the long and violent wars of its Spanish-speaking neighbors.

Although independence was the final result throughout the former colonies, each region followed a distinctive path after 1810. Some, like Mexico, exploded in an ethnic and social revolution. Many Indians, angered by centuries of oppression and inspired by the rhetoric and passion of the moment, waged war against not only Spaniards, but also all whites, including the Creoles. In other colonies, like Argentina, the struggle was relatively bloodless, and independence came easily, although deep divisions among the Creoles of that region created unique problems.

Thus, as civil war engulfed Spain after 1808, soaking up its energies, its Latin American colonies took things into their own hands. There was little that Spain could do as Creoles and Spaniards in Latin America jockeyed for position all the way from Argentina to Mexico during this temporary, but crucial, vacuum of power. Matters were complicated by other social, political, ethnic, and economic factors. Perhaps no situation was more complicated than the confusion that reigned in Mexico after 1810.

Mexico: The Powder Keg Explodes

In September 1810 a Creole plot to overthrow the viceroy was revealed, and the conspirators were warned to flee for their lives. But one of them, a priest named Miguel Hidalgo y Costilla, decided to go ahead on his own accord. In the dawn hours of September 16, 1810, he sounded the call for arms at his parish church in Dolores.

Mexico now celebrates its independence on the anniversary of this day. Father Hidalgo's "Grito de Dolores" called on his parishioners, mostly Indians, to overthrow "bad government and the Spanish." He tempered his challenge with the slogan "Long Live Ferdinand VII," professing loyalty to the captive monarch while advocating the overthrow of Spanish government in Mexico. In this, he represented a sentiment that was widespread among Mexican Creoles, who might have risen in his support if not for a major miscalculation. What Hidalgo did not foresee was the smoldering anger of the Indians of Mexico that transformed this initial phase of the Mexican independence movement into an ethnic bloodbath. The Creole leaders of the insurrection saw the Indians rise against *all* white oppressors, Creole as well as Spaniard.

Mexico, in fact, was a nation of unequals. A white population of about one million people dominated the more numerous Indians (about 60 percent of the total population) and castes, or people of mixed racial backgrounds. Violent extremes in wealth and social position characterized Mexico.

"Mexican Inequalities"

Contemporaries clearly described this powder keg. Baron von Humboldt, the German naturalist who traveled through New Spain at the end of the eighteenth century, observed "that monstrous inequality of rights and wealth" that characterized Mexico (quoted in Lynch and attributed to Humboldt). Manuel Abad y Queipo, bishop-elect of Michoacán, identified two groups of late colonial society: "those who have nothing and those who have everything. . . . There are no gradations of man: they are all either rich or poor, noble or infamous."

Droughts and rising food prices added burdens to the Indian population. When Father Hidalgo, who spoke the Indian dialect and sympathized with the plight of his parishioners, issued the "Grito de Dolores," the nearby countryside ignited. Indians and castes flocked to his standard. The beloved Mexican saint, the Virgin of Guadalupe, was adopted as the patroness of the movement, and before long a ragtag army of sixty thousand was sweeping across the countryside on its way to Guanajuato, a major city in the region.

What happened at Guanajuato was burned into the memories of Spaniards and Creoles alike. Hidalgo's army stormed the Alhóndiga, or granary, where the Spaniards and some Creoles had taken refuge, and massacred the defenders. Pillaging and looting ensued as the mob lashed out with a fury aimed at all whites (although Spaniards suffered more than Creoles).

Miguel Hidalgo, Revolutionary

"[There were] two Hidalgos, the symbolic figure and the man," wrote Lesley Byrd Simpson. "Of the two the man is infinitely the more interesting."

Hidalgo was not a great man before he was caught up in the insurrection and placed at the head of it. He had lived for fifty-seven years without achieving more than moderate distinction. He taught Latin, theology, and philosophy for some years at the ancient (1540) College of San Nicolás in Valladolid (Morelia, Michoacán), and rose to be rector of it. His unorthodox teaching and his reading of prohibited books was resented by the faculty, and in 1792 he resigned from the College and accepted the curacy of Colima. Ten years later he was posted to the parish of Dolores, Guanajuato. . . .

Hidalgo loved words and had the power to move people. He certainly thought he had been relegated to the unimportant parish of Dolores because he was a Creole—in which he may have been right. Then, as he saw the better posts in the Church go to men who had no greater recommendation than to have been born in Spain, his sense of injury grew to a bitter hatred of all things Spanish. His personal grievances and the miseries of his country he laid to the diabolism of the gachupines [peninsular Spaniards]. As his phobia matured, he practiced a number of innocent compensations. He read forbidden books; he raised forbidden grapes and pressed out forbidden wine; he planted forbidden mulberry trees and spun forbidden silk . . . [then] the Literary and Social Club of Querétaro . . . offered him an outlet for his forbidden learning and eloquence. He acquired a taste and discovered a talent for conspiracy. The Rights of Man, the Social Contract, and the rest of the intoxicating doctrines of the French Revolution became woven in his mind into a beautiful fabric of the perfect republic, from which gachupines should be excluded.

(Lesley Byrd Simpson, *Many Mexicos*, 4th ed. revised [Berkeley: University of California Press, 1971 (1941)], pp. 209–210)

To the Creoles of Mexico, radical or conservative, pro-Hidalgo or anti-Hidalgo, the Guanajuato massacre signaled an unacceptable direction that the independence movement could not be permitted to take. It threatened their place in society as leaders and put in jeopardy the entire structure of Mexican society, based on the white Creole elite's privileged position. Thus, a great many Creoles and Spaniards alike turned on Hidalgo and his undisciplined army.

As the revolution proceeded, Hidalgo's decrees became more and more radical and threatening. The hated tribute, a centuries-old institution that forced Indians to pay a tax simply because they were Indians, was abolished. Other acts, such as abolishing slavery and allowing his armed followers to slaughter Spaniards in cold blood, further alienated the Creoles of Mexico from the Hidalgo revolt. Perhaps it was inevitable that this first great, spontaneous outburst of desire for freedom and justice was crushed. It was simply too disorganized, and it was certainly too radical to win the support of the more conservative Creole elite. Many of them were certainly in favor of independence, but they were unwilling to yield to the radical demands for social and economic justice of Hidalgo's followers.

By early 1811 the small royalist army near Mexico City, reinforced and supported by Creole militia, stopped Hidalgo's hordes, now numbering eighty thousand, in a decisive battle. Hidalgo retreated, wreaking havoc in Valladolid and Guadalajara. But his army gradually disintegrated under constant blows from the disciplined Spanish-Creole troops. Some months later, Hidalgo himself was captured while trying to escape to the north and was executed.

This first bloody phase of the Mexican Wars of Independence came to an end with Hidalgo's death; but the movement that he sparked was by no means dead. In 1811 another priest (and a far better general), José María Morelos, assumed the leadership of the independence movement and continued pushing Mexico down the road to freedom. Meanwhile, in South America, the greatest Latin American liberator rose in Venezuela like a comet. Simón Bolívar left a trail of brilliance, creativity, and audacity that still inspires the modern people of Latin America.

Conclusions and Issues

The Wars of Independence evolved from a number of internal and external "causes," some related, some independent of each other. At the top of the list were the grievances that Creoles held against *peninsular* Spaniards. Deep-seated hostility between the two classes of rulers ultimately led Creoles to break the three-hundred-year loyalty to the Spanish crown and to move the colonies toward independence.

Other rebellions and revolutions in the Americas either inspired or shocked Latin American Creoles into action in the early nineteenth century. Certainly the American Revolution of 1776 and the French Revolution of 1789, both driven by ideas born in the Age of Enlightenment, encouraged Creoles to emulate their example. On the other hand, the Haitian Revolution of 1791, with its deep-seated racial divisions, horrified Creoles who were accustomed to governing over a subordinate population of Indians and blacks. When Indians and mestizos did join the revolution—such as in Mexico in 1810—they shocked independence-minded Creoles into rethinking the perils of true freedom if it were ever to become a reality.

Finally, the train of events in Spain itself helped precipitate the independence movements. Napoleon's invasion of 1807, the installation of his brother Joseph as the king of Spain, the Spanish resistance, the rise of revolutionary juntas to resist Napoleon, and the convocation of the liberal Cortes in Cádiz all inspired Creoles to take matters into their own hands. It was the beginning of the end of the Spanish American empire.

Discussion Questions

1. A historian once wrote, "no ideas, no revolution." How would you rate or rank the role of ideas among the factors that brought on the Wars of Independence?

2. Why were Creoles and Spaniards so at odds with each other? Does this situation have parallels in other examples of colonial separation from mother countries?

3. How did Hidalgo's "Grito de Dolores" turn into such a nightmare for Creoles, and what was the promise inherent for Mexican Indians?

The Coming of Independence to South America

Josefina and Carmen's War for Independence

"Yes, she behaved so well," Josefina answered Carmen.

The two women spread their ponchos and blankets out on the steeply pitched old cobblestone street of La Paz. It was not quite five in the morning. Fair day.

"Did you see her when she came through the other day?" Carmen asked Josefina. The pair were swaddled in petticoats and ponchos, and each was crowned with an old bowler hat perched at an angle over her thick dark hair, combed into long tresses down her broad back. As they talked, they spread their wares for sale that day.

"She was on a horse!" exclaimed Josefina.

"Poor don Manuel," continued Carmen. "They say the Viracochas hanged him in Villar."

"Yes, but doña Juana will not let him die," Josefina said. They were sorting out the potatoes in little baskets. Some were black and shriveled. Others were small, round, and smooth skinned. There were, indeed, dozens of varieties of potatoes, all neatly displayed for the cagey buyers who would soon be haggling with Carmen and Josefina and dozens of other women who would come down from the hills surrounding La Paz for market day.

"No, she won't," Carmen answered. Doña Juana was Juana Azurduy de Padilla, widow of the recently executed patriot guerrilla Manuel Ascencio Padilla. Doña Juana had taken her husband's place at the head of the band he had led. The war for Bolivia's independence was raging back and forth across the land in 1816. Carmen and Josefina knew about the war firsthand. They also knew that it was market day, and they busied themselves setting out not only their potatoes, but also other fruits and vegetables, the products of their native plateaus and valleys high up in the Bolivian Andes.

Next to them Emiliana, their friend, was surrounding herself with dozens of little bags, each open at the neck for a buyer to see, each filled with medicinal herbs and condiments. Dried llama fetuses shared space with a variety of leaves, beans, powders, and roots, each guaranteed to cure a gut that ailed or heart that was broken, or perhaps to ward off the spirit of a *pishtaco* or *apu,* one of the many minor deities inhabiting the windy, cold spaces of the mountains. Some of them lived on the tops of the freezing, windswept peaks, others in caves and hidden grottoes. It was good to have a cross to kiss, of course, and to thank the little Lord Jesus for being with them, but it never hurt to sacrifice a small vicuña or llama to the spirits of their ancient faith.

Bags of coca leaves from the *yungas,* or lowlands, occupied a prominent place in this marketplace cornucopia of colors, smells, and sounds. Ah, the smells. Cooking fires were setting the kettles and pots to boil. As the lilac shades of twilight slowly gave way to the pink and red hues of true dawn, the smells reminded Josefina and Carmen that they had already been up for three hours, packing their wares and walking down to market in the dark predawn hours.

"You go get some tea, Josefina," Carmen said to her friend. "I'll watch."

Carmen's husband was dead, killed by the guerrillas. Josefina's husband had been drafted into another band. Yet, the two women continued to live pretty much as before, surrounded by their children and relatives in their community. Like doña Juana, who came through on a horse, leading her patriot band, Carmen and Josefina could do pretty much anything that their men did. And more, Carmen thought to herself rather smugly as she nestled in her spot, surrounded by her potatoes and gourds and squashes and radishes and other vegetables. They all were neatly arrayed. She was not a woman given to much introspection. One did not have time for idle dreaming or speculation when life was so demanding. But she was proud of her accomplishments, all arrayed around her in neat piles.

Deep in her petticoat fold, she could feel a few copper and silver coins. She would add a few more as the morning wore on. Life during war wasn't so bad, she reflected. As long as the patriots and royalists, and other half-crazed men drunk with power, stayed away from her community, she was making some money. So many men driven off the land, drafted into the bands, so little being produced. The prices went up, and so did Carmen's profits.

Josefina returned with a kettle filled with maté—coca tea. It was steaming in the dawn, now brightening and sending brilliant shafts of light and shadows down the long, winding street.

"*¡Pucha mamacita!*" Josefina exclaimed as she poured Carmen some tea and turned to settle into her little nest of items for sale.

"What?" asked Carmen.

"General Aguilera put a price on doña Juana's head. And what a price!"

"How much?"

"Five hundred pesos of silver," answered Josefina, sipping her tea, looking down the street at some customers slowly working their way up through the spreads of foods, condiments, coca, women, and children.

"Hmmmm," Carmen let out a soft hum, looking down the same street as Josefina, feeling the few coins in her bag. So much silver. For what? If they caught doña Juana, Carmen thought, they would cut off her head and put it on a pike like they did to poor Vicente Camargo, the caudillo rebel leader of Cinti. Then, of course, would come the payoff. Five hundred coins of silver. So much for a woman. A lot more than for most men, Carmen smirked. She turned to her first customer.

"Señorita, señorita," she said, looking up at the woman who had stopped in front of her spread. "See for yourself, touch it, smell it, señorita," Carmen said, offering a handful of potatoes to her customer. The sun now rose over the red shingled roofs of the houses overlooking the streets, and a ray warmed Carmen. It may be a good day, she thought.

Venezuela

Venezuela, like Mexico, was a country of competing interests. It was complicated even more by radical divisions that included not only Indians, Spaniards, and *mestizos,* as in Mexico, but also many *pardos.* A large body of blacks, both slave and free, played an important role in determining the course of the Wars of Independence in Venezuela.

The basic choice in 1810 in Venezuela, as in Mexico, was nonetheless simple. Should the Venezuelan Creoles bend to the will of the various Spanish juntas or march to their own drummer? When faced with a choice, as they were in 1810, the Creoles chose independence, which was declared on July 5, 1811. By this act, the Venezuelan Creoles, who constituted an aristocracy based on their control of the land and nurtured by their sense of rank and responsibility, took the lead in the Venezuelan Wars of Independence. Theirs was the first country to declare itself fully independent of Spain.

Perceptions and Myths in History

Invariably we are taught to seek the "facts" of history, the names and dates of kings and battles, for example, to find the truth. Indeed, the first step in any search for truth in history is to find those facts, often easily available in books, sometimes lying deeply buried in archives among dusty and forgotten documents, or perhaps in thousands of rolls of microfilm. A full revelation of these facts, woven together and properly interpreted by historians into a narrative, constitutes the truth of the matter. Right or wrong? The answer is both. We cannot study history without the facts, but, strangely enough, men and women often behaved the way they did, not based on the facts as we know them to be, but rather on their perception of the facts. These perceptions could be at odds with the facts themselves, so much so as to conclude that people often behaved irrationally and in response to myths. This makes for interesting history.

For example, the Creoles who fought for independence fully believed that they had been oppressed and deprived over the centuries by a tyrannical Spanish power when, in fact, they constituted an elite with wide influence and wealth in their homelands. But it was convenient and politically necessary to subscribe to the myth of tyranny and oppression to keep alive the spirit and enthusiasm of the Wars of Independence.

Other examples of the dichotomy between fact and myth exist, and the student of history must learn to accept that the motives of people are often veiled and distorted by perceptions that are not always in line with the "names and dates" rendition of history.

But, as the United States had discovered in 1776, it was one thing to "declare" independence; it was another, more difficult thing to make it stick. The radical Creoles who had pushed Venezuela so rapidly toward independence soon discovered the depth of opposition as civil war erupted in 1811. The royalists, as Spanish forces were known during the Wars of Independence throughout Latin America, mounted a determined campaign to crush this insurrection against Spain. Joining the royalists were not only more conservative Creoles, but also many *pardos* and blacks who were disenchanted with the new constitution, revealed in 1811. It essentially disenfranchised the large body of *pardos* by strict voting requirements based on property ownership, and it retained slavery.

Why fight for these Creole landowners, those high and mighty lords of the land who mouthed equality but whose Constitution promised so little? The patriots, or those committed to independence, alienated many groups during the long course of the wars, and many of those groups found comfort and security in the cause of the royalists. In one sense, the wars therefore were as much civil wars as revolutions, and much of the bitterness and ferocity of the fighting can be attributed to this division.

An Ethnic Road Map

The ethnic composition of Latin America was complex in the nineteenth century and has become more so in the twentieth. Unlike relatively homogeneous regions like Southeast Asia, Latin America has attracted migrations of people from all over the globe, in continuous streams. Together they have created a virtual kaleidoscope of ethnic types.

Webster's definition of ethnic is "designating any of the basic divisions or groups of mankind, as distinguished by customs, characteristics, language, etc." For our purposes, we describe below a road map of ethnic types as objectively as possible, keeping in mind the wonderful summation of race in Latin America by the great Cuban poet and nationalist, José Martí: "There are no races. There are only a number of variations in Man, with reference to customs and forms, imposed by the climatic and historical conditions under which he lives, which do not change that which is identical and essential. . ."[1]

These were the basic unions, in and out of wedlock, that took place from the beginning of the Conquest onwards:

Whites and Amerindians =	Mestizos
Whites and Africans =	Mulattoes
Amerindians and Africans =	Zambos

We then have other combinations that could and *did* take place, producing a society of ethnic diversity. And, in each country, different nomenclature emerged that sometimes confounds the observer trying to find some order in the system. In Central America, whites of Spanish descent are often referred to as *ladinos;* in Peru and Bolivia, mestizos *and* Indians are sometimes labeled *cholos;* in Venezuela, mulattoes and zambos sometimes carry the term *pardo,* and the examples multiply if we consider the full range of Latin America, from Cuba to Chile.

What is *important,* however, is to recognize that in modern Latin America, a person's ethnic category is determined as much by culture, language, habits, economic situation, and other non-racial factors, as by skin color. Also, it is easy to pass from one category to another. Indians who dress and act like mestizos and come down from the highlands to work in the cities become *cholos.* Light-skinned mulattoes move easily in the highest circles of society in Panama, the Dominican Republic, and Brazil for example, and they are not stigmatized by their color; they are sometimes thought of as "white." And whites still prevail at the top of society, an inheritance from the Spanish and Portuguese colonial past.

There are other important signposts in this ethnic road map. For example, in Latin America the terms mestizo, zambo, mulatto, pardo, etc. are all employed freely and openly to place people. In the United States, one is white or black; there are no gradations admissible. Indians are Indians, not part-white (mestizos), part black (zambos) as would be the case in Latin America. There is a certain rigidity in the United States, while in Latin American there is much flexibility and fluidity.

A poet friend of ours came north from the Dominican Republic in the 1980s to teach literature on a Fulbright award at an historically African-American college in Alabama. When asked how things were going, he responded: "Well, I didn't know I was black until I came to Stillman College." He was a poet and an esteemed writer in his home country. That he was a light-skinned mulatto was pretty much irrelevant. It had little to do with the position he held in society, or with his own conception of his place in the world.

[1]Quoted in Magnus Morner, *Race Mixture in the History of Latin America* (Boston: Little, Brown & Co., 1967), p. 150.

Latin America
in 1830

Santo Domingo gained its
independence from Spain in
1821. Occupied by Haiti in 1822,
it finally regained its independence
in 1844.

Mexico
City
Veracruz
Cuba–Spanish
Belize–
British
Jamaica–
British
Puerto Rico–Spanish
Trinidad–British
British Guiana was founded
in 1831 by uniting Berbice,
Demerara, and Essequibo.

The United Province of Central
America was dissolved by 1839
Caracas
Surinam–Dutch
Guiana–French
Bogotá
Quito
Guayaquil
Lima
Salvador

❂ Capitals

States with date of independence:

☐ Mexico, 1821

■ United Provinces of Central America, 1823,
joined Mexico, 1823-1839

■ Haiti, 1804

■ Gran Colombia, 1819-1830

▨ Peru, 1821

■ Bolivia, 1825

■ Brazil, 1822

☐ Paraguay, 1811

■ Uruguay, 1828

☰ United Provinces of La Plata, 1816

■ Chile, 1817

São Paulo
Rio de Janeiro
Asunción
Argentine
Confederacy,
1810-1816
Santiago
Buenos
Aires
Montevideo

Patagonia

The complexity of the wars thus becomes painfully apparent. They were not simple wars of independence with sides easily chosen. Blacks, both slave and free, were slow to join with Creole masters; *pardos* were envious of Creoles and reluctant to make a common cause with them to champion independence. The royalists were quick to exploit these deep ethnic and social divisions in Venezuelan society. This complicated independence movement required a leader of remarkably high intelligence and ability—and it found one.

Simón Bolívar, born into a wealthy landowning Creole family on July 24, 1783, has been likened to George Washington for his role in the independence not only of

What Makes a Revolutionary?

What makes a revolutionary? What passion or obsession drives men and women to challenge the traditional nature of things? To question what is accepted as right? To lay down that most precious possession of man, his life, for a cause? For Bolívar, it was not only a zeal both of patriotism and an infatuation with the ideals of the Enlightenment. The inspiration sprang as much from his heart as his mind.

In the following passage he described how he became a revolutionary.

"Listen to this: an orphan and rich at the age of sixteen, I went to Europe after having visited Mexico and Havana: it was then, in Madrid, I fell in love and married the niece of the old Marquis del Toro, Teresa Toro y Alaiza. I returned from Europe to Caracas in 1801 with my wife and I assure you that at that time my head was only filled with the mists of the most ardent love, and not with political ideas, for they had not yet touched my imagination. Then my wife died and I, desolated with that premature and unexpected loss, returned to Spain and from Madrid I went to France and then to Italy. At that time I was already taking some interest in public affairs, politics interested me. . . . I saw the coronation of Napoleon in Paris, in the last month of 1804: that . . . magnificent ceremony filled me with enthusiasm but less because of its pomp than for the sentiments of love that an immense public manifested to the French hero; that general effusion of all hearts, that free and spontaneous popular movement, stimulated by the glories, the heroic feats of Napoleon, made victorious by more than a million individuals seemed to me to be, for the one who would receive such sentiments . . . the ultimate desire to the ultimate ambition of man. . . . what seemed to me great was the universal acclaim and the interest which his person inspired. This, I confess, made me think of the slavery of my country and the glory that would benefit the one who would liberate it." Bolívar swore never to marry again—a promise he kept—and the agony of loss forced him to fill the vacuum with something else. "The death of my wife put me on the road to politics very early; it made me follow the chariot of Mars instead of following the plow of Ceres."

(John J. Johnson, with collaboration of Doris M. Ladd, editors and contributors, *Simón Bolívar and Spanish-American Independence, 1793–1830* (New York: Van Nostrand Reinhold, 1968), who, in turn, draws the passage from Louis Peru de Lacroix, *Diario de Bucaramanga,* edited by Nicolas E. Navarro, translated by Doris M. Ladd [Caracas: Ediciones del Ministerio de Educación Nacional, Dirección de Cultura, 1949], pp. 62–65. Bolívar was born July 24, 1783; married May 26, 1802; wife died January 22, 1803.)

*Simón Bolívar was the Liberator of five countries—
Venezuela, Colombia, Ecuador, Peru, and Bolivia.
Imbued with the ideals of Enlightenment, he took fire
as a young man and devoted his life to freeing his land
from Spanish oppression.*

his homeland, Venezuela, but also of four other Latin American nations: Colombia, Ecuador, Peru, and Bolivia. But Bolívar was unique, whereas Washington shared the limelight with equally brilliant and determined cohorts such as John Adams, Thomas Jefferson, James Madison, and the other "Founding Fathers." Bolívar's comet arched alone into the darkening sky of war in 1810.

Bolívar, the young man, was reared in an atmosphere of privilege, wealth, and learning. From tutors and his own wide reading he was imbued with many of the ideals of the Enlightenment. He was passionately committed to reason, freedom, and democracy, and he borrowed freely from the models of the British and American constitutional systems in elaborating his own goals for Latin America.

As a young man in 1799 Bolívar was sent to Europe to round out his education, and the long experience abroad was both devastating and inspiring. His young wife, whom he adored, died less than a year after their marriage, and the heartbroken Bolívar swore never to marry again. It was a vow he kept, although he never ceased to love passionately and often during his career as "Liberator" of Latin America.

The intensity of his sexuality was easily matched by his intellectual and political genius, sharpened and focused in a Europe dominated by the brilliant French emperor, Napoleon Bonaparte. Bolívar lived in Paris for many years, traveled often, and observed Napoleon as he conquered most of Europe. When Bolívar entered the service of Venezuela in 1810 and was sent as an emissary to London to seek support for independence, one of his first acts was instructive of his nature and his goals. He persuaded Francisco de Miranda, the most important precursor of Venezuelan independence and a confirmed radical, to return with him and lead the movement.

The royalists under the leadership of Domingo Monteverde formed a coalition of Spaniards, conservative Creoles, *pardos,* and blacks that overwhelmed Miranda and the patriots. Even nature seemed to oppose the patriot cause. A devastating earthquake rumbled across Venezuela from the mountains to the coast on March 26, 1812, and royalist clergy were quick to interpret the disaster as a sign from God. When Miranda signed a capitulation in July and appeared to have betrayed the cause, Bolívar had him arrested and let Miranda be taken by the Spaniards. It was the end of the First Republic in Venezuela. Bolívar fled across the border to neighboring Colombia to regroup. Yet, defeat only sharpened the Liberator's resolve.

Far to the south of Venezuela, Creoles in Argentina and Chile also rose up against Spanish authority.

The Southern Cone Movements

The Argentine independence movement was more deeply affected from abroad than was either Mexico or Venezuela. In 1806 a British military expedition invaded the Rio de la Plata region, and on July 27 the English occupied Buenos Aires. This action was part of the greater struggle between England and Napoleonic France, and it set the stage for a brief, successful show of force by patriotic Argentine Creoles.

The Spanish viceroy and wealthy Spanish merchants fled into the interior when the English landed. However, Argentine Creoles organized a patriot army of Creoles, blacks, mulattoes, and some Spaniards and ousted the British in August. Another British expedition followed in early 1807, landing at Montevideo and then attacking across the estuary. It, too, was soundly defeated by the Creole-Spaniard coalition.

Creole pride and nationalism were boosted by the successful defense of Buenos Aires and Montevideo in 1806 and 1807. Some date the true beginnings of Argentine independence to these heroic actions.

After deposing the cowardly Spanish viceroy who had fled before the British attack, the Creoles elevated Santiago Liniers, a French officer in the Spanish service and a hero of the defense of Buenos Aires, to lead the viceroyalty. This act in itself marked the Argentine Creoles as an independent lot who were willing to act on their own behalf in the face of a mother country too weak to protect its colonies. A royalist coup led by the conservative Spanish soldier-merchant Martín Alzaga failed in early 1809, further reinforcing Creole autonomy and self-confidence.

In mid-1809 the Central Junta in Spain, now attempting to govern in the name of Ferdinand VII and to wage war against the French, sent another viceroy to Buenos Aires. But the momentum was clearly with the radical Creoles of Buenos Aires. In May 1810 they forced the issue of power when Buenos Aires received news that the Central Junta had collapsed and that the French were in control of Spain. Led by intellectuals such as Mariano Moreno and backed by Creole militia leaders such as Cornelio Saavedra, the Creoles called a *cabildo abierto,* or open city council, to discuss and to act on the future of the nation. This *cabildo abierto* deposed the viceroy and named a revolutionary junta to govern Argentina.

Although formal independence was not declared until six years later, the province of Buenos Aires, which considered itself the spokesman and leader of Argentina, was now deciding its own destiny. And that destiny reflected many of the ideals and goals of Creoles, such as the determinedly radical Bernardino Rivadavia, whose ultimate goal was total independence.

The new government soon decreed virtual free trade and opened the ports of Argentina to the world. The hallowed relationship between church and state was broken, education was secularized, a free press was encouraged, and other enlightened and liberal measures were decreed. Those who resisted the changes were crushed, some being exiled, others executed.

From 1811 to 1816 the Buenos Aires revolutionaries went through several trying stages, sometimes ruling through juntas and sometimes through triumvirates. Plots and counterplots marked the independence movement. In searching for some consistency three basic trends are apparent: the gradual move toward complete and official independence in 1816; the splintering of the old viceroyalty of La Plata and the emerging of the independent countries of Uruguay, Paraguay, and Bolivia; and the growing rivalry between the city of Buenos Aires and the interior provinces of Argentina, which bequeathed major problems of nation building to Argentina in the nineteenth century.

The struggle between Buenos Aires and the interior provinces, such as Salta, Tucumán, and Mendoza, had many facets. Basically, the interior provinces did not share the worldview of the *porteños,* or citizens of the port city of Buenos Aires, who so dominated the affairs of the new nation.

Porteños looked overseas for their prosperity. They thrived on free trade that included the export of hides, tallow, and other beef products and on the import of goods from Europe, principally England, in the post-1810 period. Trade gave life to Buenos Aires, and Buenos Aires felt that it ruled Argentina.

The interior provinces, on the other hand, marched to a different beat. Traditionally they raised or manufactured simple commodities—sugar, coarse textiles, wine, furniture, draft animals, and livestock—that were marketed locally or to neighboring provinces like Upper Peru, the province of the viceroyalty of La Plata that would emerge as modern Bolivia. Self-sufficiency marked the economic life of the interior provinces.

The stage was set for a confrontation between Buenos Aires, which wanted free trade, and the interior, which resisted. Free trade meant the introduction of cheaper European products—such as textiles—that undermined local economies. *Porteños* tended to be centralists, demanding that the provinces conform to the leadership of Buenos Aires. Provincials tended to be federalists, determined to protect their interests against the metropolis.

Repeated attempts between 1810 and 1820 by the provinces to exert their rights were met by intransigence from Buenos Aires, which as frequently as not dispatched armies to the west and north to bring the recalcitrant provinces to heel.

Superimposed on this rivalry was, of course, the division between patriots and royalists, each one trying to exploit the weakness of the other. Although Argentina's independence was never seriously in jeopardy after 1811, the form that it would take—geographic and political—was hotly debated and fought over for most of the independence period, and, indeed, well into the nineteenth century.

Bolivia

Bolivia was a world apart from Buenos Aires. A country of mountains, high plateaus, and magnificent snow-covered peaks, volcanoes, and steep valleys, it was populated by Indians who were ruled over by a small Spanish-Creole elite. In many respects it was a feudal society, divided between elites who possessed power, privilege, and land and those who served the elites as vassals and peasants. In Bolivia the elite controlled the principal sources of wealth and power, such as vast estates and the lucrative silver mines, while the Indian-mestizo population labored as peons, or peasants, in the service of the rulers. Feudal values—emphasizing the distance between lords and peasants—were not easily changed in such a rigidly organized and conservative society.

Bolivia's patriots, on guard due to pressures from below, were, however, not immune to the liberating influences of the Enlightenment and the rhetoric of independence that inspired the Creoles of Buenos Aires, Caracas, and Mexico City. Beginning in Chuquisaca (modern Sucre) and spreading to La Paz, a revolution led by radical Creoles and mestizos erupted in mid-1809. It called for the liberation of Bolivia from Spanish tyranny, but it failed to gain adherents among the majority of conservative Creoles committed to preserving the social order (i.e., their high positions in society above the Indian and mestizo masses). Several massive native uprisings in the preceding half century—notably the revolt of Tupac Amaru II in 1780, which set the Andes on fire—terrorized the Creoles, and the lessons of Indians and mestizos in rebellion was not lost on the elites. So this early independence movement sputtered and was crushed by royalist forces sent from Peru and Buenos Aires in 1809.

The successful patriot revolutionaries of Buenos Aires instigated the next stage of the Bolivian independence movement. Not content merely with liberating Buenos Aires, they sought to inspire and control the movement throughout the former viceroyalty of La Plata, which included Uruguay, Paraguay, and Bolivia. With this in mind, the first of several liberating expeditions was dispatched from Argentina to Bolivia in late 1810. Initially successful in defeating royalist resistance in the major cities of Bolivia—Chuquisaca, Cochabamba, Oruro, and La Paz—the expedition soon foundered. The *porteños,* led by Juan José Castelli, antagonized the Bolivian Creoles by behaving like conquering overlords rather than companions in independence. Easily defeated by a royalist army, the Argentines pillaged and stole as they beat a retreat from Bolivia.

In 1813 a second invasion from Buenos Aires commanded by Manuel Belgrano struck into the mountains of Bolivia. It, too, was defeated, this time by a royalist army led by the experienced Spanish general Joaquín de la Pezuela. The Spanish, as in 1810, tried to follow up their triumph by marching south into Argentina, but patriot armies pushed them back into Bolivia. In this second major encounter in Argentina, the patriots were commanded by a brilliant soldier named José de San Martín.

Once again, in 1815 an Argentine expedition marched into Bolivia, and once again, after some initial successes, the royalist army, still under Pezuela, threw the

Argentine army out, almost annihilating the *porteño* forces in the process. Aside from a minor raid in 1817, Argentina abandoned the strategy of liberating Bolivia by direct invasion, which had proven disastrous for the *porteño* armies.

What about the Bolivians themselves? They were caught in the crunch of invading armies from Buenos Aires and Lima, each faction bent on dominating Bolivia. The patriot Argentines wished to bring Bolivia under the Argentine republic, whereas the royalist Peruvians wished to keep Bolivia loyal to the monarchy and Spain. Furthermore, Bolivia's rich silver mines were in and of themselves a major prize that both Peruvians and Argentines wished to control.

The Creoles of Bolivia were in the main frightened of the political rhetoric that accompanied the armies from Buenos Aires. The Indians were promised emancipation from forced labor and from payment of tribute; in some instances, the Argentine agents promised land redistribution and other radical reforms. The ruling Bolivian Creoles tended to side with Peruvian royalists who promised social and economic order. Especially frightening to conservative Bolivian Creoles was the guerrilla warfare that had erupted from 1810 to 1816. *Montoneros,* or guerrilla bands of radical Creoles and mestizos, not only plagued the royalists, but also kept the country in a social ferment until a determined royalist effort in 1816 crushed the *montoneros.*

Uruguay

Uruguay, the coastal country on the north banks of the Rio de la Plata estuary, followed a road to independence similar to Bolivia's. Both of these provinces of the former viceroyalty of La Plata were the objects of active intervention from beyond their borders as royalists, patriots, and, in the case of Uruguay, Brazilians sought to influence Uruguayan destinies.

In the case of Uruguay, the proximity to Buenos Aires, right across the Rio de la Plata estuary, was both a stimulant and inhibitor of independence. Uruguay was stimulated by the example of Buenos Aires but inhibited by the determination of Buenos Aires to keep Uruguay within the evolving Argentine nation. The situation was complicated further by the Brazilians, who tried to capitalize on Uruguay's problems and to incorporate that region into Brazil.

Montevideo, Uruguay's capital, was located on the coast of the Rio de la Plata estuary facing the Atlantic Ocean. It was easy to reach from Spain, and, often reinforced by armies from the mother country, it became a focal point of royalist resistance to the Wars of Independence in the Rio de la Plata area. Uruguayan Creoles in search of autonomy or independence for their country were often driven into temporary alliances: sometimes with the patriots of Buenos Aires to oppose the Spanish royalists of Uruguay; sometimes with the royalists to oppose the ambitious Argentines; and sometimes Uruguayan patriots were simply overwhelmed by invading Argentines, Brazilians, and royalists and forced to flee their own homeland. In this era of test and challenge, the gaucho (a cowboy of Argentina and Uruguay) chieftain José Gervasio Artigas emerged as the hero of Uruguayan independence.

Although born to a well-to-do Creole family in Montevideo, Artigas adopted with gusto the semicivilized life of a gaucho smuggler and cattle rustler on the plains of Uruguay near the Brazilian border. Gauchos lived a seminomadic life of cattle droving and herding in South American countries such as Argentina and Uruguay. When the Spanish viceroy in Montevideo declared war on the patriots of Buenos Aires in 1811, Artigas became a celebrated gaucho *caudillo* and a leader of Uruguayan patriots. These Uruguayans issued a call to arms, the "Grito de Asunción," in February 1811, and the war was joined in Uruguay, in this instance with help from the patriots in Buenos Aires.

Pressured hard by the rebel armies, the Spanish viceroy in Montevideo, Francisco Elío, turned to the Portuguese king, then in Brazil, for help in crushing the rebellion. The Brazilians quite willingly dispatched an army because it was an unparalleled opportunity for Brazilian imperialists to extend the southern borders of Brazil all the way to the Rio de la Plata by incorporating Uruguay. Artigas and his supporters, most of them coming from the *estanciero*, or rancher, class of the hinterland, were caught in a squeeze of rival factions from abroad. The Argentines negotiated with the Brazilians, preferring to allow the royalists to maintain control rather than to lose their influence in Uruguay to Brazil. The Brazilians would not be budged, and only English pressure persuaded them to withdraw late in 1811.

With the royalists once more in charge, Artigas and his followers, over four thousand troops and an equal number of civilians, retreated in disgust across the Uruguay River to the province of Entre Rios. The retreat proved to be a turning point in Uruguayan independence. This patriotic and nationalistic act symbolized the rejection of those options being forced by the competing powers from abroad. Although temporarily in exile, the movement gained strength under duress, just as metal is forged by fire.

The pattern of the Uruguayan independence struggle over the next few years was set: Artigas and the patriots maneuvered for control of Uruguay's destiny between Argentines and Brazilians, always fighting off the possibility of a royalist resurgence.

In 1815 Artigas returned to power, but two years later the Brazilians once again struck into Uruguay, determined to conquer the province once and for all. Under the command of the Portuguese general Carlos Frederico Lecor, the Brazilians succeeded this time, ousting Artigas in 1820. The great caudillo took asylum in Paraguay, where he remained for the next thirty years in permanent exile, never to return to his beloved homeland.

Uruguay, like Bolivia, did not become independent until the 1820s after the issue of independence was settled in Peru. After Peru was liberated, Argentina again turned its energies to Uruguay to oust its Brazilian rivals. This struggle in the late 1820s finally produced Uruguayan independence.

The region to the north and west of the Rio de la Plata became known as the "contested lands" because so many diverse factions fought to control it. In fact, national boundaries in this area were not formally established until the 1890s, after decades of skirmishes, invasions, and prolonged wars.

Paraguay

A quick glance at a map of South America shows Paraguay's isolation. Landlocked a thousand miles up the Rio de la Plata river system, it is far from the continent's centers of power and population. Not surprisingly, Paraguay's independence movement developed rapidly and successfully, so that by 1811 Paraguay was effectively free of Spanish control.

In Paraguay, as in other parts of Latin America, a small group of Creole *estancieros* ruled over the large mass of *mestizos* and Indians. The agricultural economy of Paraguay produced tobacco, hides, sugar, and *yerba maté*, a bitter tea popular throughout South America.

The Creoles of Paraguay were moved to action by the events of May 1810 in Buenos Aires, which had directly challenged Spanish authority and triggered crises throughout the former viceroyalty of La Plata. A *cabildo abierto* held in July in the capital of Asunción cautiously decided to tread the middle ground, recognizing the regency in Spain but refusing to accept any relationship with Buenos Aires other than one of "fraternity." The Argentines reacted aggressively and imprudently, dispatching an army under the command of Manuel Belgrano to bring Paraguay under control. Belgrano and his troops were trounced on the battlefield early in 1811. On May 17 Paraguay declared itself independent, and one of the most remarkable caudillos of the century rose in this dawn of the Paraguayan nation. His name was José Gaspar Rodríguez de Francia. By 1814 he was in firm control of the destiny of the nation; in 1815 he had himself appointed "perpetual dictator." Perpetual he was not, but he nonetheless governed Paraguay absolutely until his death in 1840 at the age of seventy-four.

Whereas Paraguay passed rather easily into independence, although under the control of the dictator Francia, Chile, on the southwestern coast of the continent, underwent a turbulent passage, more like that of Mexico and Venezuela.

Chile

The struggle for independence in Chile was long partly because of Chile's location. Located south of Peru—the bastion of royalist power in South America—and west of Argentina—the site of the most successful of the early independence movements on the continent—Chile became a battleground for the patriots of Argentina and the royalists of Peru. But it was neither Argentina nor Peru that triggered the Chilean thrust to independence. The crisis in Spain produced by Napoleon's invasion and the usurpation of Ferdinand set off waves of sympathetic unrest in Chile.

The Creoles of Chile were already predisposed to think of themselves as "Chileans." They had a strong sense of identity with their land and its history. When news of the events in Spain and Argentina between 1808 and 1810 reached Santiago, the major actors in the independence tableau acted according to their self-interests.

The Spanish governor of Chile, a reactionary despot completely loyal to Spain, clamped down on Creole patriots when he heard the news of the May 1810 junta of Buenos Aires. But the Creoles were not to be denied. They manipulated the unsettling circumstances to their advantage and succeeded in calling a *cabildo abierto* for September 10, 1810. Dominated by radical Creoles, this *cabildo abierto* named a junta to govern while a national assembly was called. Spaniards and conservative Creoles were smartly outmaneuvered, and the thread of Chile's destiny was slowly woven into a new pattern.

After the assembly convened in July 1811, a national debate ensued. In the meantime, the junta took some important actions. It organized an army and threw open Chile's ports to trade with all nations—two actions difficult to interpret as anything other than steps on the road to full independence. However, many Chileans were not ready for full and unequivocal independence, preferring to work for autonomy within the Spanish empire. More conservative, they wanted to meet with reformers in Spain who had called a Cortes, or Parliament, to convene to write a new, more liberal constitution.

The true revolutionaries in Chile pushed hard for a complete break with Spain. People like Manuel de Salas, a political economist; José Miguel Carrera, a young member of a prominent family with strong patriotic tendencies; and Bernardo O'Higgins, the son of an Irish-born viceroy of Peru, Ambrosio O'Higgins, were determined to make independence a reality. For example, when the national assembly that convened in July 1811 moved too slowly for Carrera, he led a *coup d'etat* (the overthrow of a government) that reorganized the assembly with more committed revolutionaries. The assembly then turned radical, abolishing the Inquisition, beginning the secularization of education, and passing other measures guaranteed to antagonize Chilean royalists and conservatives.

José Carrera, however, by his highhanded manner, also succeeded in antagonizing other patriots. Twice more he arbitrarily changed the form of government, first setting up a triumvirate and then simply taking charge himself. Powerful families in Chile, envious and distrustful, worked to oust Carrera and his brothers, while other patriots rallied around O'Higgins against Carrera.

O'Higgins emerged as a major figure in this period, a man with an unorthodox background whose military talents and patriotic sentiments marked him as the man of the hour. Born in Chile of a Chilean mother and an Irish father, he was educated in England, where he met the most radical of the revolutionary precursors, Francisco Miranda, who converted him to the cause of liberty and independence. O'Higgins returned to Chile in 1802 and in 1810 joined the revolutionary movement with Martínez de Rozas and others in Concepción. Although he paid lip service to Ferdinand VII and the Spanish liberal Constitution of 1812 (see the following), O'Higgins's devotion to a free and independent Chile coursed deeply through his heart and mind.

In 1813 and 1814, the viceroy in Peru, José Fernando de Abascal, dispatched a series of royalist armies to crush the rebellion in Chile. They succeeded not only because the royalist counterrevolution was itself gaining momentum throughout Latin America after the return of Ferdinand VII to the throne in 1814, but also because the Chileans were divided. When O'Higgins, Carrera, and the patriot army were defeated at the Battle of Rancagua in October 1814, O'Higgins fled with his troops across the Andes and eventually joined the army of San Martín.

Chile was drawn once again into the royalist orbit of Peru. A period of repression and terror ensued between 1814 and 1817 as the Spanish sought to extinguish the embers of revolt. They succeeded only in convincing Chileans even more firmly to forge their own destinies. But they had to await another invading army, this time a patriot army led by San Martín that struck across the Andes from Argentina in 1817.

Colombia and Ecuador

Far to the north, in the viceroyalty of New Granada, the revolutionary movement began in Quito, the capital of Ecuador. The sequence was now familiar. In response to the usurpation of the Spanish throne by Napoleon in 1808, Creoles took the main chance and pushed for autonomy or independence. In Quito this occurred in 1810. A junta of Creoles overthrew Spanish authority. Their victory, however, proved short lived. A violent royalist reaction culminated in the massacre of dozens of imprisoned Creole patriots in August 1810. This harshness prejudiced many against the royalists, but the patriots were extremely factionalized, and the royalists got the upper hand by 1812. Quito did not go free until 1822, when liberating troops marching down from Colombia intervened. Colombia itself fought a long and bitter war before its armies helped to liberate Ecuador.

The revolution in Colombia broke out in 1809, and by March of 1811 a republic had been declared around Bogotá, the capital. Revolutions erupted in the cities of Tunja and Cartagena as well, challenging not only the Spaniards but also the Creoles of Bogotá for leadership of the revolution. While Bogotá sought to monopolize the show, each region and major city jealously guarded its prerogatives and privileges. One revolutionary newspaper lamented that "our revolution seems more like a lawsuit over lands than a political transformation to recoup our liberties."[2] The most celebrated of the revolutionaries, Antonio Nariño, struggled to unify his fellow Colombians, but the attempt was futile. Nariño was captured and exiled to Spain in 1814. Even Bolívar, operating in Colombia in 1814 and 1815, left the continent for exile in Jamaica, disgusted with the extremely divisive Colombians. By 1816, as in Chile, royalists were once again in power, and they dealt brutally with the patriots, executing the captured leaders and exacting a vengeance that only hardened the Colombian resolve to be free.

Peru

The most conservative of all of Spain's kingdoms in the Americas, Peru proved to be the most resistant to revolutionary sentiments. Under the capable administration of its viceroy, José Fernando de Abascal, Peru survived the crises triggered by events in Spain in 1808 with few disturbances.

---

[2] Quoted in John Lynch, *The Spanish-American Revolutions, 1808–1826* (New York: Norton, 1973), p. 239, from Antonio Nariño's *La Bagatela.*

The Creoles of Peru were largely satisfied with their lot and were uninterested in changing their basic position as overlords. Although they may have resented particular Spaniards and aspired to more self-government, they tended to side with the royalists in the preservation of order. This order was put to the test in 1814, however, when an Indian rebellion erupted in the *sierra* (highlands) led by Mateo Pumacahua, a descendant of the Incas.

Before the rebellion was crushed, Pumacahua's troops massacred many Europeans in a particularly murderous rampage through La Paz, the capital of Bolivia. Even Creole and mestizo sympathizers of Pumacahua were repelled by the ethnic violence. Pumacahua was finally captured and executed in 1815, ending an episode that was burned into the minds of Peruvian Creoles.

Ethnic Cleansing and the Wars of Independence

Lest we think that contemporaries invented the term and practice of "ethnic cleansing," it is interesting to note that the intendant [administrator] of Arequipa [in Southern Peru] "exhorted his people to be thankful to their 'liberators' who had freed them from the threat presented by . . . thousands of Indians, mobilized with the object of removing these provinces from the rule of Ferdinand VII, best of sovereigns; then, in satisfaction of their hatred toward the other races, they would exterminate all the other non-Indians of this hemisphere. If this assertion appears exaggerated, direct your imagination towards the village of Sicuani, where the ungrateful and infamous Pumacahua developed his horrifying plans, designed to exterminate every white, beginning with those of Arequipa."

(John Lynch, *Spanish-American Revolutions*, p. 169)

Peru remained a royalist bastion until the 1820s. And it was a formidable one. Between 1810 and 1816, royalist armies from Peru were dispatched south into Chile and Bolivia and north into Ecuador to suppress the revolutions and restore royal order.

To comprehend the behavior of Peruvians in this revolutionary crisis, and indeed of all Latin Americans, one must keep in mind that events in Spain were constantly reverberating throughout the Americas, as Spain itself was convulsed by movements as powerful as those revolutionary forces rocking its colonies across the Atlantic.

Spain

The mother country in 1810 was engaged in a rebellion of another kind: a guerrilla war to overthrow the French usurper imposed by Napoleon in 1808. With the legitimate king, Ferdinand VII, absent, liberals and radicals governed in his place. They called a Cortes in 1810 and eventually produced a new constitution in 1812, all the while fighting a war with the aid of an English army to free their homeland from Napoleon's invaders. During the deliberations for the new constitution, liberals in Spain made common cause with their like-thinking brethren in the colonies. Even Creoles were invited to cross the Atlantic to participate in the Cortes. When the Constitution of 1812 was finally proclaimed, it set in motion a train of reforms, some constitutionally mandated and some produced by the liberal Cortes in power. It abolished the Inquisition, stripped the nobility of many of its privileges and feudal dues, granted freedom of the press, and decreed other reforms that almost transformed Spanish government into a constitutional republic. The new constitution was, however, not popular in the Americas. Among other things, it allowed for only a small representation from the colonies, and many conservative Creoles found the document too liberal for their tastes.

Royalists and patriots in Latin America both were kept off balance by the attempted transition from absolute monarchy to liberal constitutionalism in Spain. Old-line royalists such as Viceroy Abascal in Peru thought the reforms dangerous and foolhardy, although he went through some of the motions of implementing them to placate moderate Creoles in Peru. But the liberal reforms proved short lived.

In 1814 a powerful coalition defeated Napoleon and restored Ferdinand VII to his throne. The latter disavowed the Constitution of 1812 and initiated a conservative restoration that included bringing his Latin American colonies to heel. With fresh, seasoned armies released by the end of the Napoleonic Wars, the royalists reasserted control over the colonies. A period of violent repression, as noted earlier, commenced in 1814 and 1815. By 1816 Spain was once again in charge of most of its American colonies with one notable exception—Argentina. This triumph over the revolutionaries was a testament to Spain's power and the strength of conservative royalism.

Counterrevolution

This Spanish resurgence of arms and initiative was called the "counterrevolution." In Mexico, the restoration of Ferdinand VII came at a most opportune moment for the royalist cause. After Hidalgo was executed in 1811, the revolutionary movement temporarily lost momentum until a brilliant mulatto leader emerged to take up the cause in 1812 and 1813. José María Morelos was born in a humble setting and worked as a muleteer for years before taking up studies for the priesthood. When the revolution erupted, Morelos joined the movement and rose to prominence as a well-organized, intelligent, and temperate leader. A profound Mexican nationalist, he rallied Mexicans of all colors to his cause, calling for equality among his countrymen. Toward this end he declared in 1810 that "all the inhabitants except Europeans will no longer be designated as Indians, mulattoes or other castes, but all will be known as Americans."[3] He decreed the abolition of slavery and of Indian tributes—two stigmas that perpetuated inequality in Mexico, as they did in many other emerging Latin American nations during this period.

Morelos was avidly committed to other liberal principles as well. He abolished the compulsory Church tithe, advocated the seizure of Church lands, and promoted the idea that the land should belong to those who till it. Morelos's program promised a more equal and free Mexico, and the battle to achieve his promises occupied much of Mexican history for the next century.

Morelos, however, fell prey to the counterrevolution. He failed to take Mexico City at an opportune moment in 1813 and spent himself on a long siege of Acapulco, which possessed no great strategic value in the overall war. Furthermore, Morelos was unable to gain the support of Mexico's Creoles. The royalists, reinvigorated by the return of Ferdinand, slowly regained the upper hand in 1815. They captured and executed Morelos on December 22, 1815, and with his death the Mexican independence movement was crushed, not to rise again for several years.

Southeast of Mexico, across the Caribbean Sea, Simón Bolívar and the Venezuelans continued to challenge Spanish authority with passion and increasing violence. After the first republic, called *la patria boba*, or "the foolish fatherland," by Venezuelans, ended in 1812 with a royalist triumph, Bolívar fled to the city of Cartagena and took stock. There he considered the failures and triumphs of the movement, the strengths and weaknesses of its principles measured against reality. He summed up his feelings and conclusions in the Cartagena Manifesto.

In this manifesto Bolívar called for unity above all other considerations if the war for independence was to triumph. Questions of constitutionality, popular elections, and representative government had to be laid aside in favor of prosecuting the war. He was firmly committed to centralism, or central authority, rather than federalism, or the sharing of authority by provinces and states. Latin Americans struggled for most of the nineteenth century to reconcile their deep divisions over centralism and federalism, and Bolívar's perceptions of this future struggle between centralists and federalists proved brilliant.

Bolívar also argued that Venezuela was the key to patriot victory in the viceroyalty of New Granada, while northern South America was in turn the key to the rest of the continent. After issuing his Cartagena Manifesto, Bolívar resumed his military campaign. Reinvigorated by victories in Colombia, he then struck back into Venezuela in 1813. In a brilliant lightning war, Bolívar defeated the royalists and paraded triumphantly into Caracas, his carriage drawn through the flower-strewn streets by adulating young women. It was a hero's welcome that the vain Bolívar, always with an eye for a pretty girl, reveled in. But the festivities and flattery were short lived.

Again, the royalists took advantage of the diversity of Venezuelan society. The patriots had not yet gained the loyalties of *pardos,* blacks, and members of the lower

---

[3]Lynch, *Spanish-American Revolutions*, p. 314.

classes in general, who suspected the haughty Creoles of pursuing only their own interests. And in the plains, or *llanos*, in the south of Venezuela, a brutal and ruthless leader of the fierce *llaneros*—as the cowboys and horsemen were called—arose to fight the Creoles and their patriot cause. José Tomás Boves, a Spaniard, led a mixture of Indian, white, and black *llaneros* into the war on the royalist side and forced Bolívar and the patriots into retreat.

When General Pablo Morillo arrived in Venezuela in early 1815 from Spain with ten thousand veterans of the Napoleonic Wars, the second Venezuelan republic was crushed and Bolívar again retreated into exile.

By 1816 the counterrevolution was almost complete and, with the exception of Argentina, Uruguay, and Paraguay, royal power once again coursed through the Spanish empire in America. But several factors argued against the permanent success of the counterrevolution. First, the fierceness of the wars themselves made reconciliation difficult if not impossible. Too much blood had been shed, too many people executed ruthlessly, too many hard feelings born in the struggle. Second, Creoles had tasted power, and they were unwilling to let go of their dream of self-rule and self-determination. If defeat was bitter, victory had been sweet, and they were determined to retrieve it. Finally, many of the castes in Latin American society—the *pardos*, mulattoes, mestizos—and the blacks and Indians had heard leaders such as Bolívar and Morelos commit themselves to redemption, to freedom, and to equality. Soldiering in the patriot armies produced a new sense of worth and identity that empowered these individuals to claim those promises of their leaders. Yet, although the promises often ran afoul of reality, the expectation of a better, more enlightened and liberal world had been awakened.

Conclusions and Issues

The Wars of Independence opened across South America, from Venezuela in the north to Chile in the south, with a flush of enthusiasm. Declarations, manifestos, open *cabildos*, and other pronouncements marked a departure from the normal course of events. In some countries such as Argentina, earlier events had already established an independent nation in most respects, although a formal declaration of independence did not occur until 1816. In others, such as Venezuela, the declaration came early—July 1811—but the struggle against the royalists was bloody and marked by intense passions.

When Spain was freed from Napoleonic domination in 1814, fresh Spanish armies—veterans of the wars against Napoleon—sailed for the colonies to suppress the rebellions. Making shrewd alliances with conservative Creoles and with many castes who did not relate to the radical, Creole-led patriots, the royalists crushed the patriots from Mexico to Chile. By 1816 it seemed that the fire of the Wars of Independence was snuffed out. Bolívar was exiled, Morelos dead, the patriot cause crushed.

Discussion Questions

1. Why did independence come so easily to Argentina and so slowly to Peru? Are some of the reasons trans-Latin American? That is, do the experiences of Argentina and Peru in this early period represent a uniquely Argentine or Peruvian situation, or did some of the experiences occur in other parts of Latin America?

2. Why did Simón Bolívar become a revolutionary?

3. How did Morelos of Mexico differ in some ways from men such as Bolívar of Venezuela, Artigas of Uruguay, or O'Higgins of Chile? What does this tell us about leaders of the early independence movements?

The Independence Movements: On to Victory

Vicente Guerrero's War for Independence

"Play it again, Paco," said Vicente Guerrero.

"'La Bamba,' don Vicente? Again?" responded Paco, laying his guitar down on his lap for a moment.

"Yes, it is Mexican, Paco," the old revolutionary chieftain Guerrero explained to the teenaged guerrilla who played the Spanish guitar so well. Once again the rapid African beat of "La Bamba" gladdened the little group, isolated in the dark night around them.

They were in the hills near Acapulco. The guerrilla soldiers who followed Guerrero were the last of the revolutionaries. They were a ragged lot. Most of them were young, castes, mulattoes, mestizos, and *zambos,* descendants of Indians, Africans, and whites. "Old man" Guerrero—"El Viejo," they called him affectionately—was in only his thirties, but he was among the oldest of the early revolutionaries. He, too, was a caste, of African and mestizo blood.

It was 1821. Rumors now were flying that others were looking for Guerrero. The spark of independence once again flared. So did the small fire in front of them on this cool night. Guerrero poked it with a long stick. The last of the tortillas had been washed down with a bit of tequila, and Guerrero spoke in an Indian dialect to another of his young followers.

"Pedro, are the mules bedded down well?"

"Yes, don Vicente," Pedro, a Zapotec Indian, responded. "I watered them a bit, and we scrounged some cracked corn from the village."

Few Mexican "revolutionaries" spoke Indian dialects, ate tortillas, drank tequila, or liked "La Bamba" like Guerrero. The men leading Mexico to independence were largely Creoles, bred to enjoy wine, white bread, and the minuet.[1] But men such as Guerrero were more truly

---

[1]My thanks to Ted Vincent's draft of a paper, "Afromestizos in Mexican Politics 1810–1937," given at a conference in Chicago, June 12–14, 1997. Professor Vincent circulated the draft via e-mail to Michael Conniff, who then shared it with me. Vincent is a pioneer in exploring the impact of the African in Mexican history.

"Mexican," their roots in the soil of their land, not looking to Spain or Europe or Africa for inspiration.

"Don Vicente," asked another of the young warriors. "Will you free the slaves when we finally triumph?"

Guerrero paused for a moment to consider. Yes, they would triumph. It was an article of faith with his men. Otherwise they long ago would have faded into oblivion. The hated Spaniards would be cast off, Mexico would be taken over by Mexicans. And the slaves? Thousands and thousands of black slaves? How to reconcile slavery with freedom and independence?

"Yes. We will free the slaves, Paco," Guerrero answered. He had made the pledge to himself many years ago. In 1829, when president, Guerrero abolished slavery in Mexico. On this night, however, cold and lonely in the hills, another round of "La Bamba" and perhaps a last pull on the bottle of tequila to ward off the chill made do before wrapping oneself in a thick blanket and drifting off to sleep. Tomorrow the war for independence continued.

The Wars of Independence and the World

What did the rest of the world know about happenings in Latin America? As the nineteenth century progressed, some parts of Latin America became closely linked to affairs in other parts of the world, principally in Europe and the United States. Indeed, by the twentieth century, the affairs of most Latin American nations became inextricably bound to the ebb and flow of events abroad. But in 1810 the great mass of Europeans and North Americans still knew very little about Latin America. It was a world hidden for three centuries behind a Spanish curtain of dominion and exclusion. All of this changed in the wake of the revolutions.

The two most important nations in this awakening of interest were Great Britain and the United States. English merchants and mariners had long enjoyed profits made by trading illegally with Spain's colonies, and the Wars of Independence promised freer access to new markets. Patriots in Argentina, Chile, and other emerging nations opened their ports to free trade with the English, and the English gladly responded by sending more ships. While England maintained a strong pro-Spanish posture in Europe between 1808 and 1814, as its armies assisted the Spanish in ridding themselves of the French, English merchants openly traded with the patriots in the Americas. It was an awkward but not impossible situation. The student of history soon learns that nations often behave in contradictory fashion to satisfy the self-interests of many competing groups.

From the beginning of the Latin American struggle for independence, the United States was largely sympathetic to the patriot cause. Bolívar and his contemporaries were, after all, committed to the same republican ideals as the United States, and many Latin American patriots looked to the successful American Revolution as their model. Furthermore, many Americans viewed Spain as a degenerate European nation bound to a rigidly conservative monarchy and subservient to the dead hand of the Catholic Church. What better way to trumpet the virtues of the

New World—filled with optimism, equality, and liberty—than to assist the Latin American patriots on their long, tortuous road to independence?

John Quincy Adams on Latin American Independence

The republican spirit of our country not only sympathizes with people struggling in a cause, so nearly if not precisely the same which was once our own, but it is working into indignation against the relapse of Europe into the opposite principle of monkery and despotism. And now, as at the early stage of the French Revolution, we have ardent spirits who are for rushing into the conflict, without looking to the consequence.

(Adams, *Writings*, vol. VI, pp. 275–276, a letter by John Quincy Adams to his father in December 1817 from Washington, D.C.)

However, the United States was not an entirely free agent in its dealings with the revolutionaries. The United States, too, was a relatively new country that had to keep the powerful interests of Europe—especially those of Great Britain—in mind when formulating policy toward Latin America. In 1812 the United States and England went to war, and no clear victor emerged by 1815. Furthermore, in 1815 Napoleon was finally defeated by England and its European allies. The members of this triumphant alliance, among them Austria, Russia, and Prussia, were very conservative and committed to monarchy. So they were quite predisposed to help their brother king, Ferdinand VII of Spain, reestablish control over his rebellious colonies. Although the United States favored the patriot cause, it had to pursue a policy of strict neutrality in these circumstances. James Monroe, serving as secretary of state in 1815, wrote candidly of his bias toward the patriots.

> When it is considered that the alternative is between governments which, if independent, would be free and friendly, and the relations which, reasoning from the past, must be expected from them as colonies, there is no doubt in which scale our interest lies.[2]

Diplomatic, commercial, and cultural relations between the United States and Latin America in this early period were exploratory and uneven because events moved rapidly. Agents from both the United States and the newly emerging republics passed back and forth, some in a formal capacity, others in semiofficial roles, as the two worlds sought to learn more about each other and to exploit their natural self-interests. Patriots and royalists alike were, for example, intensely interested in buying American arms, powder, and foodstuffs such as wheat to keep their armies in the field. Meanwhile, American merchants, from Baltimore, New York, and New England principally, were eager to sell the products of U.S. farms and workshops in exchange for Latin American silver and gold, always in short supply in North America. Yankee merchants did not particularly discriminate between patriots or royalists when it came to finding good markets.

---

[2]Quoted in A. P. Whitaker, *The United States and Latin America*, p. 195, citing Manning, *Diplomatic Correspondence*, vol. I, p. 18. The letter from Monroe to John Adams, then in London, is dated December 15.

One of the earliest U.S. agents to Latin America was Joel Roberts Poinsett, who was sent to Buenos Aires, Chile, and Peru in 1810. Typically, he defended U.S. commercial interests against the English in Buenos Aires, and he involved himself deeply in partisan politics in Chile. Others like Poinsett were dispatched to Cuba, to Mexico, and to Venezuela, while the revolutionaries in Latin America sent such individuals as Diego de Saavedra from Buenos Aires and Telesforo de Orea from Venezuela to the United States to buy arms, flints, and other stores to further the patriot cause.

By 1816, however, a combination of circumstances, among them the low fortunes of the patriot cause due to the counterrevolution and the wariness of the United States with respect to the clout of the powerful European allies of Spain, forced the United States to maintain a public stance of strict neutrality and watchful waiting. The length of that wait to see which side gained a clear advantage would be determined by the patriots themselves. In late 1816 Bolívar was on the move again.

Bolívar Frees Colombia and Venezuela

Before leaving his Jamaica exile to take up arms against the royalists in Venezuela, Bolívar wrote a letter of remarkable candor and penetrating insight into the nature of his people, their aspirations, and their limitations. Frustrated by factionalism among the patriots, he championed a strong central government capable of dealing with crises. Bolívar concluded that his people were not ready for the political freedoms and the democratic, representative style of government that existed in the United States. Instead, they needed strong leadership to overcome all of the handicaps inherited from a colonial system that had deprived the Latin Americans of experience with self-government and free institutions.

In the letter, written in 1815, Bolívar wrote frankly that "events in Tierra Firme [Venezuela and Colombia] have proved that wholly representative institutions are not suited to our character, customs and present knowledge."[3] Bolívar, the young, ardent champion of liberal, representative government deriving its sole powers from the political participation of the people, was becoming Bolívar the older, more experienced military realist, concerned with wielding power efficiently and successfully. It was an important transition that foreshadowed the Latin American dictator who dominated nineteenth-century governments.

Bolívar's "Jamaica Letter"

Bolívar expressed himself candidly on the nature and form that governments should take. "As long as our countrymen do not acquire the abilities and political virtues that distinguish our brothers of the north, wholly popular systems, far from working to our advantage, will, I greatly fear, bring about our downfall. . . . This nation should be called Colombia as a just and grateful tribute to the discoverer of our hemisphere. Its

---

[3]Quoted by Lynch, *Spanish-American Revolutions*, p. 209.

government might follow the English pattern, except that in place of a king there will be an executive who will be *elected*, at most, *for life* [emphasis added], but his office will never be hereditary, if a republic is desired. There will be a hereditary legislative chamber or senate. This body can interpose itself between the violent demands of the people and the great powers of the government during periods of political unrest."

(John J. Johnson, editor, *Simón Bolívar and Spanish American Independence: 1783–1830* [New York: Van Nostrand Reinhold, 1968], pp. 163, 168)

General Simón Bolívar accepting the surrender of Colonel José Maria Barreiro after the defeat of the Spanish Army at Boyacá, August 7, 1819, thereby securing the independence of central New Granada, the heart of modern Colombia.

In late 1815 Bolívar and his ragtag revolutionaries sailed to Haiti, where they were hosted by President Petion. Concerned that the fall of Napoleon and consolidation of the Holy Alliance might lead to European reconquest of the Americas, Petion supported the cause of hemispheric independence. In exchange for Bolívar's promise to emancipate the slaves on the mainland, Petion outfitted the revolutionaries with small boats, stores, and arms. After two unsuccessful attempts, Bolívar finally created a beachhead in the Venezuelan *llanos.*

After returning to the continent in 1816, Bolívar began a five-year campaign to liberate Venezuela and Colombia. The length of this campaign spoke as much for the durability and popularity of the royalist cause as it did for the political and military maneuvering of Bolívar and his allies, like José Antonio Páez, caudillo of the *llaneros,* and a linchpin in the liberation of Venezuela.

Three factors aided Bolívar in this grueling half decade of war. First, he based his campaign deep in the heart of Venezuela's plains, guarded by vast malarial rivers and wide spaces, far from the centers of royalist power in Caracas and the coastal provinces. The *llanos* nourished the patriots in both a physical and spiritual sense, vast herds of cattle providing for the former and the sanctuary and safety of the *llanos* providing the latter. Second, professional English and Irish soldiers, casting about for employment after the end of the Napoleonic Wars, found their way into Bolívar's army, and these legionnaires added a constancy and experience necessary that helped sustain a winning army. Third, Bolívar's genius and charisma held together and inspired a situation of incredible complexity that could call for consummate tact in one instance and ruthless discipline in another.

Nonetheless, by 1819 Caracas and its environs were still beyond Bolívar's reach. The royalist armies under the veteran Spanish general Pablo Morillo had repulsed all of the attacks launched against them by Bolívar and Páez. Bolívar then fashioned a new strategy. He struck audaciously across the Andes into Colombia. The results were spectacular: By boldly switching the main theater of campaign, he surprised the Spaniards in Bogotá.

This lightning campaign fulfilled even the most optimistic of Bolívar's visions. In a harrowing and heroic march across swamps and then twelve thousand feet up into the passes of the Andes, his men suffered terribly, and many perished. But his army defeated the royalists at the Battle of Boyacá on August 7, 1819, and three days later Bolívar entered Bogotá. The viceroy had fled. Colombia was free.

In the next two years Bolívar maneuvered to oust the royalists from his home country. He was helped inestimably when early in 1820 a liberal revolt in Spain stalled reinforcements about to embark from Cádiz to Venezuela. The Spanish sought an armistice, which lasted six months, giving Bolívar a breather.

Bolívar took the field again in 1821, this time carrying the war back to Venezuela, where his campaign triumphed on June 24 at the definitive Battle of Carabobo. Spanish power was now broken across all of northern South America.

Venezuela and Colombia were declared independent as one nation, Gran Colombia, by the Congress of Angostura in 1819. Two years later, a congress met at Cúcuta and wrote a constitution to govern the new nation. The new president of Gran Colombia was, naturally enough, Simón Bolívar.

The Constitution was a mixture of liberal and conservative sentiment so typical of those national charters being written throughout Latin America by the newly independent nations. It abolished Indian tributes, guaranteed civil freedoms, and provided for the gradual abolition of slavery. On the other hand, it mandated a strong president and limited the vote to literate males who owned substantial property. Bolívar, however, did not tarry to govern the new nation. He rode south to liberate Ecuador from royalist control and to incorporate it into the nation of New Granada.

In early 1821 Bolívar's brilliant lieutenant, General Antonio José de Sucre, preceded his commanding officer into Ecuador. Together they forced the royalists to yield by a grand strategy of envelopment. While Bolívar battled through the royalist strongholds of Pasto and Popayán in southern Colombia, Sucre struck at Quito. This campaign culminated on the slopes of the extinct volcano of Pichincha, which overlooks Quito. There, on May 24, 1822, Sucre defeated the royalists and freed Ecuador.

Bolívar proceeded to the coastal city of Guayaquil to meet San Martín, who had sailed up from his campaigns in Peru. The two greatest Latin American liberators met in July 1822. For Bolívar, it was a triumphant encounter, fresh as he was from victory. For San Martín, it was the bittersweet end of a long campaign that had begun in 1814 when he was named general of the Argentine armies. After their meeting, San Martín withdrew from the field and abdicated leadership to Bolívar. But between 1814 and 1822, the brilliant Argentine soldier had matched Bolívar's record with campaigns and victories in Argentina, Chile, and Peru that were no less grand and enduring in the minds and hearts of those people.

Completion of Rio de la Plata's Independence

San Martín's strategy had been simple. After the second defeat of the Argentine invasion of Bolivia in 1815, San Martín had asked to be relieved of his command. Instead, he said, he wanted to be appointed governor of the western province of Mendoza, where he might rest and allow his health to recover.

Taking up his new post, San Martín began secret preparations for a trans-Andean invasion of Chile. He realized that Peru was the center of Spanish control in South America, able to sustain its power using the profits from the silver mines. For this reason, no frontal assault on Lima or the mining district in Bolivia would ever succeed. By the same token, Spanish power had to be destroyed in Peru, or else the other revolutions would never be safe. His plan was to capture Chile by surprise and then send an amphibious expedition to blockade Lima. By late 1816 he had secretly created a new army, the Army of the Andes.

San Martín also had to contend with the near anarchy that prevailed in Buenos Aires. Free of Spanish control since 1811, Argentina was practically independent. Leadership there was marred by politicians' zealous attempts to force Uruguay, Paraguay, and Bolivia to join Argentina. Paraguay and Uruguay resisted and by 1816 were moving down separate roads to independence, while Bolivia remained loyal to the royalist cause. Moreover, various interior provinces in Argentina were unwilling to yield to Buenos Aires's leaders who desired a strong central or unitarian government. The provinces, like Córdoba, Corrientes, and Santa Fe, wanted a loose, federalist form of government, or even outright independence from Buenos Aires.

In the midst of this political chaos, Buenos Aires called a congress in the interior city of Tucumán. This congress formally and finally declared Argentina independent on July 9, 1816. Juan Martín de Pueyrredón was elected director of the new republic, which produced its first constitution in 1819. It provided for a strong central government and favored Buenos Aires at the expense of the provinces. Then, in 1820, several of the provinces revolted against Buenos Aires. Uruguay fell temporarily under Brazilian control while the Brazilians took full advantage of the chaos in Argentina. Paraguay under Francia was already independent. With this background, San Martín launched the heroic task of liberating Chile. It was the first step on the road to the heart of Spanish power in South America—Peru.

San Martín Crosses the Andes and Liberates Chile

San Martín knew that his invasion force would be extremely vulnerable while crossing the Andes. All the passes were above eighteen thousand feet and completely snowbound except during the middle of the summer in January. Even a small defending force could annihilate his troops. His only hope was to keep the exact

General José de San Martín crossed the Andes in early 1817 with a patriot army that surprised the Spanish and helped liberate Chile from royalist control. It was one of the most daring feats of the Wars of Independence.

timing and location of his attack from the Spanish. To do this, he relied on a secret organization called the Lautaro Lodge, based in Buenos Aires. Its members sent money, arms, and volunteers out to Mendoza without revealing the full extent of San Martín's plans. San Martín managed to fashion an army of five thousand, mostly Argentines and Chileans, reinforced with African slaves who were offered their freedom in return for service in the cause of Latin American liberty. San Martín kept this promise, fulfilling one of the noblest aspects of the Wars of Independence.

San Martín, with the Chilean patriot Bernardo O'Higgins in close support, crossed the high, freezing passes in early 1817 at several different points to confuse the royalists. The ensuing campaign proved the genius of San Martín as an organizer and soldier. Exact timing and attention to detail brought his army into Chile with surprise and coordination, while his strict discipline and the devotion of his soldiers kept order and enthusiasm high. San Martín defeated the royalists at the Battle of Chacabuco and rode triumphantly into the capital city of Santiago in February 1817. The royalists rallied in southern Chile, and the campaign continued until April 1818, when another victory on the Plains of Maipo near Santiago finally freed Chile. Leaving O'Higgins in charge, San Martín next turned to Peru.

Fortress Peru—The Last Royalist Bastion

Peru's Creole elite, which held the keys to revolution and independence, were a fickle lot. Not wishing to give up power in any way, they flocked indecisively between both royalists and patriots, searching for a guarantee to their future. The situation called for the highest expression of tact, patience, determination, and cunning. Prepared with all of these qualities, San Martín came in August 1820 at the head of a large expeditionary force of Chileans and Argentines, who were carried on ships of the Chilean fleet and commanded by a former English naval officer, Thomas Cochrane.

Successful warfare along the west coast of South America demanded control of the sea. Cochrane and other English and American officers and sailors provided the backbone of the expeditionary force, which was organized at great financial sacrifice by Chile. It enabled San Martín to transport his army to the Peruvian coast in 1820 and begin his campaign to liberate Peru.

Cochrane's daring and skill at sea seemingly were at first not matched by San Martín's army maneuvering close to Lima. Cochrane wanted to attack Callao and Lima and deal the royalist army a decisive blow. San Martín wished to erode Spanish authority and gradually attract the Peruvian Creoles to the cause of independence. By 1821 San Martín appeared to be successful. He won the allegiance of many Peruvians, who began to assist him and to call for independence. The Spanish, on the other hand, proved intransigent, unwilling to bargain even when San Martín offered to place a prince of Spain at the head of a Peru under a monarchical system of government. San Martín was indeed a monarchist, having viewed the chaos caused by attempts at broadly representative government, but he was totally committed to independence.

Faced with the growing support of the Peruvians for San Martín and blockaded by sea by Cochrane's forces, the viceroy of Peru, José de la Serna, evacuated Lima. San Martín entered in early July and proclaimed Peru's independence on the twenty-eighth. However, independence was not yet won.

The royalist troops still numbered nearly seventeen thousand and controlled the silver mining district. Although they were harassed in the highlands by bands of *montoneros,* they had not been defeated on the battlefield. San Martín's army of liberation, made up mostly of Argentines and Chileans, was chafing at the inactivity that followed the declaration of independence. Cochrane, frustrated by the inability of the San Martín government to pay his crews and keep the navy together, simply left. And many Peruvian Creoles, especially liberals, plotted against the monarchist San Martín. In the face of this general disunity, San Martín sailed up to Guayaquil in 1822 for the famous interview with Bolívar. There he pleaded with Bolívar to give him men, arms, and supplies with which to eradicate the royalist forces. When Bolívar refused, he abdicated his leadership and went into a long exile. He died in Europe in 1850 without ever returning to the continent that he had helped liberate.

Why did San Martín bow out? We will never know for certain, but historians generally agree that San Martín recognized the futility of competing with the charismatic Bolívar. There were other equally compelling reasons. Bolívar would not tolerate monarchy in Latin America, and San Martín could not reverse that deeply ingrained sentiment in the Liberator. Bolívar was at the height of his powers, having just freed Ecuador; San Martín had just left a quarreling, faction-ridden Peru with little hope of enforcing his concept of order on the nation. San Martín suffered from an obscure illness and had become addicted to narcotics to relieve the pain. Without aid from Bolívar, his cause was probably lost.

In a sense, San Martín was the more noble of the two, gracious in defeat, unbowed in the face of a destiny that would have caused a lesser man to abandon his ideals. His example as a man and a leader is rightfully revered by millions of Latin Americans today.

San Martín the Man

"As he approached his fortieth year, San Martín left a vivid impression on his English friend, Commander William Bowles, who described him as 'tall, strongly formed, with a dark complexion and marked countenance. He is perfectly well bred . . . simple and abstemious.' Bowles noted that he was liberal in his instincts, knowledgeable and widely read, with a fanatical devotion to work, yet without personal ambition or acquisitiveness."

(John Lynch, *Spanish-American Revolutions,* p. 138, quoting from Bowles to Croker, February, 14, 1818, in Gerald S. Graham and R. A. Humphreys, editors, *The Navy and South America 1807–1823: Correspondence of the Commanders-in-Chief on the South American Station* [London, 1962], p. 227)

Mexico: Marching to Different Drummers

While Bolívar, San Martín, and their lieutenants completed their pincer movement on royalist Peru, Mexico marched on the road to independence at its own pace. As frequently happened during the Wars of Independence, foreign events triggered changes in the Americas that proved lasting. In this case, the 1820 liberal revolt in Spain set off a reaction in Mexico that finally culminated in its independence. Ironically, the leaders of Mexican independence were conservative Creoles—most unlikely revolutionaries. But an old adage reminds us that politics makes for strange bedfellows, and in this instance the adage was richly and ironically borne out.

In 1820 the Liberals in Spain forced Ferdinand VII to restore the Constitution of 1812 and to call the Cortes, the Spanish parliament, into session. The Cortes proceeded to attack religious institutions, thus striking directly at the vested interests of the Creole elite in Mexico. For example, the Church was forbidden to maintain monastic and hospital orders, the Jesuits were expelled, and many rights, or *fueros,* of the ecclesiastical establishment were stripped away. In the same liberal vein, measures such as enlarging the voting franchise struck at Creole control of political power while other acts undermined their economic status. The result was predictable. Conservative Creoles in Mexico rejected the new liberal reforms and took matters into their own hands.

Mexico had been quiet ever since Morelos's capture and execution in late 1815. A policy of amnesty by Spanish authorities and the tendency of Mexican Creoles to desire tranquillity and social order kept the peace. This delicate balance was upset in 1820 with the liberal revolt in Spain. Mexican Creoles would not accept the unbridled attacks on their privileges, their power, and the Church. Into the act stepped a well-born Creole, Agustín de Iturbide, an ardent Catholic and conservative who had fought against the revolution since 1810. Now he intended to lead the revolution against the liberals in control of Spain.

In late 1820 Iturbide took a royalist army into the field to destroy the last vestiges of a revolutionary band led by Vicente Guerrero. This old fighter had kept the faith with Hidalgo's and Morelos's revolution. Instead of warring on Guerrero, however, Iturbide joined forces with him. He rallied other Creoles to the cause of independence for Mexico under his banner, which he called the Plan of Iguala. If Spain could not guarantee the sanctity of the Church, if Spain could not guarantee the safety and property and privileges and powers of the Creoles, then Mexicans would take matters into their own hands. Iturbide was the instrument of this movement that blossomed into independence.

From Hidalgo's 1810 "Grito de Dolores" to Alvaro Obregón's 1920 Plan de Agua Prieta, revolutionary commanders launched their campaigns with bold pronouncements, usually named for the towns where they began. The most famous plans, in chronological order, were Iguala, Casa Mata, Ayutla, Tacubaya, de la Noria, Tuxtepec, San Luis Potosí, Ayala, Orozquista, Guadalupe, and Agua Prieta. One writer even asserted that much of Mexico's history could be told using these plans.

The Plan of Iguala called for independence under a constitutional monarchy, restoration of the Church and all its rights and privileges, and equal treatment of Creoles and Spaniards in the new nation. Guerrero and other republicans begrudgingly agreed to the plan; at least it promised independence. Perhaps other reforms could eventually be incorporated. On September 28, 1821, they formally declared independence. Iturbide had promised his supporters that as soon as they were victorious, he would recruit a European prince to assume the throne of the independent Mexican empire. He sent off agents to find such a prince, but soon it became clear that no such person was available. With feigned reluctance, Iturbide had himself declared emperor less than a year later. The reign of Agustín I was not, however, destined to last very long.

Iturbide proved unable to cope with the problems that he faced, and, in some instances, that he partly created by his actions. Economic distress in the wake of the wars undermined support from the army. Republicans in the new Congress distrusted the emperor. And Iturbide's almost comic opera trappings of office were repugnant to many.

His Highness, Emperor Agustín I of Mexico

Defining the accouterments of regality took months and at times prompted the most ludicrous debate, such as that concerning whether the motto appearing below Iturbide's bust on the new metal coinage should be in Latin or Spanish.... The greatest preparations of all were made for the official coronation ceremonies in July. ... The efforts were all based on the French model, and the Congress hired a French baroness who had designed the costumes for Napoleon Bonaparte some twenty-two years before.... [After the coronation] the ostentation that engulfed his person helped to reinforce the mystique of his indispensability and to blur the distinctions between the man and the office. The words *Augustus Dei Providentia Mexici Primus Imperator Constitutionalis*, even if they were not understood, sounded enough like the unintelligible locutions of the Sunday mass to inspire awe in the large unsophisticated portion of the citizenry.

(Michael C. Meyer and William L. Sherman, *The Course of Mexican History*, 2nd ed. [New York: Oxford University Press, 1983], pp. 301–303)

When Iturbide suspended Congress, his irritated opponents rose in revolt, rallied by the young commander of the Veracruz garrison, Antonio López de "Manga de Clavo". Iturbide tumbled from power in 1823, and a republican constitution was enacted in 1824. An old revolutionary, Guadalupe Victoria, was elected the first president of Mexico. Mexico was now an independent constitutional republic.

Central America Follows the Leader

Independence came to Central America almost as an afterthought. There was virtually no independence movement until events in Mexico in 1821 forced the issue. Guatemala, the largest of the Central American colonies and the seat of government for the entire isthmus, declared independence on September 15, 1821. Next year the Central Americans' leader joined Iturbide's new Mexican empire as Spanish authority crumbled throughout the Americas. When the union with Mexico proved a failure, Guatemala withdrew, and in July 1823 the United Provinces of Central America became independent of Mexico as well. The United Provinces included the future nations of Guatemala, Honduras, El Salvador, Nicaragua, and Costa Rica.

The principal issues in the new Central American nation, destined to last only to 1838, were largely regional and local. The Creoles "came to blows over Church-State relations, fiscal policies, officeholding, economic planning, trade policy, and general philosophy of government"[4]—everything, it seemed, except independence. Though independence came easily, Central America was in no way spared from the instability and conflict of the 1820s and 1830s that afflicted most of its Latin American neighbors.

Final Patriot Victory in Peru and Bolivia

When San Martín left Peru in 1823, the road to final victory there was opened to Bolívar. Yet even the imperious and commanding Liberator hesitated to take up the challenge of Peru, where quarreling Creole factions in the north and a strong and unbowed royalist army in the south made the road rocky and dangerous. In desperation, the Peruvian Congress called out to Bolívar, who responded to its plea. He traveled to Lima in September 1823, preceded by a portion of his army commanded by the ever loyal and talented General José Antonio de Sucre.

By mid-1824 Bolívar was in charge in Peru, having accepted the title of dictator offered by a Peruvian Congress desperately in need of leadership and unity above all else. Since San Martín had declared Peru independent in 1821, some members of Peru's Creole aristocracy, like the Marquis of Torre Tagle, had changed sides three times, even turning Lima over to the royalists at one time. Bolívar called Peru a "chamber of horrors" where loyalty to independence was regulated by self-interest and where today's Creole patriot was apt to metamorphose into a royalist by morning.[5] Yet his strong hand stayed the centrifugal forces long enough finally to free Peru that year.

Bolívar and Sucre had fashioned a formidable army, using seasoned cavalry drawn from gauchos of Argentina, *huasos* of Chile, and *llaneros* of Venezuela and

---

[4]From the best general work on Central America, by Ralph Lee Woodward, Jr., *Central America: A Nation Divided.* (New York: Oxford University Press, 1976), p. 92.

[5]Quote of Bolívar from Lynch, *Spanish-American Revolutions*, p. 269.

Colombia. The royalists themselves were divided between those who supported the liberal Constitution and the reforms of 1820 and those who supported the absolutism that resulted from the restoration of Ferdinand VII to full power in late 1823. When the patriot army under Sucre and Bolívar met the royalists under General José de Canterac on the high plains of Junín on August 6, 1824, the superb patriot cavalry carried the day. Lances and swords thrust and slashed in the cold, breathless Battle of Junín, where not one shot was fired. The victory at Junín paved the way for one last momentous encounter between royalists and patriots on the continent of South America. On December 8, 1824, Sucre's army defeated Viceroy José de la Serna's royalists at the Battle of Ayacucho. Effective Spanish power on the continent of South America came to an end.

Fresh from his victory at Ayacucho, Sucre traveled to Upper Peru on Bolívar's orders to liberate the highland province, which soon emerged as the independent nation of Bolivia. The royalists had very little choice but to yield to the conquering patriot arms. A battle at Tumusla on April 1, 1825, confirmed the hopelessness of their cause. The royalists capitulated and Bolivia was free.

In July 1825 a Congress convened in Chuquisaca to decide on the country's future. It formally declared independence on August 6 and named the country after the Liberator himself. Bolívar traveled to the new nation late in the year and made a triumphal procession. He then retired to Lima and drew up one of the most extraordinary documents to emerge from the revolutionary period: the Bolivian Constitution of 1826.

In that Constitution Bolívar sought to reconcile his old liberal values with his instincts for order and authority, so severely tested in Peru. At the heart of the Constitution was a president named for life, who controlled the army. Other features included the guarantees of civil rights, a strong, independent judiciary, and ministers responsible to the national legislature. It has been criticized over the years as an awkward instrument, a noble effort striving to provide Bolivia with the foundations for its life as a new nation but combining contradictory and exotic elements into one unworkable instrument.

Bolívar's Bizarre Constitution of Bolivia

The Bolivian Constitution pleased no one. Sucre, the only leader who ever attempted to act under its authority, damned it roundly. Humboldt dismissed it as an inexplicable madness. Scholars have concluded that it united all the defects of all political systems. Víctor Andrés Belaúnde has observed that it took life tenure from absolutism, the demagoguery of electoral assemblies from democracy, and absolute financial centralization from unitarianism. It combined the worst of centralism with the worst of federalism. British constitutionalism was scrapped in favor of Napoleonic despotism or democratic imperialism.

(John J. Johnson, with collaboration of Doris M. Ladd, editors and contributors, *Simón Bolívar and Spanish-American Independence: 1793–1830* [New York: Van Nostrand Reinhold, 1968])

Brazil Follows Its Own Path to Independence

Brazil was a colony of Portugal rather than of Spain, a difference that charted a route to independence quite distinct from that followed by the Spanish colonies.

In 1807 Napoleon's armies, already in Spain, surged across the Iberian Peninsula to Portugal, reaching the capital of Lisbon only four days after crossing the frontier with Spain. The Portuguese could not resist militarily. The French issued an ultimatum to Prince Regent Dom João to surrender, but instead the royal family and the entire Portuguese court immediately fled by sea.

Ships of the British fleet embarked João and fifteen thousand courtiers, bureaucrats, officials, and families and simply ferried the court to Brazil. Rio de Janeiro became the capital of the Portuguese empire in 1808. Six years later, when the queen died, the prince became King João VI in his own right. He declared Brazil an equal kingdom with Portugal, rather than a colony. Brazil was thus spared the brutal transition from colony to independent state that was under way in Spanish America.

Along with the court had come not only equality with Portugal, but also the privilege of freer trade and the rapid elevation of Rio from a provincial backwater to an imperial capital. Its new status warranted new institutions, like a botanical garden, a naval academy, a medical school, a royal museum, the nation's first newspaper, and other accouterments of civilization.

João was happy in Brazil, and his subjects liked him. In 1821, however, he was forced to return to Portugal to preserve his crown, which was being threatened by a new liberal Portuguese Parliament with republican sentiments. He left his son Pedro as prince regent in Brazil. There, a rising nationalism pushed Brazil toward independence.

The presence of the Portuguese court in Brazil between 1807 and 1821 had not been an entirely happy experience for the Brazilians, and even less so for the Portuguese. With the court also came thousands of Portuguese officials, who replaced many native Brazilian administrators and officials because in most matters João favored Portuguese advisors at the expense of Brazilians. Many Brazilians favored transformation into a constitutional monarchy or even a republic. Discontent welled up in scattered revolts, like one in 1817 in the northeastern city of Recife. But the final break was triggered by a crisis brought on by the Portuguese Cortes.

In 1821 the Portuguese Cortes, to reestablish Portugal's primacy over Brazil, effectively restored Brazil to colonial status and ordered Pedro to return to Lisbon. Brazilian Creoles, led by José Bonifácio de Andrada e Silva and by Pedro's wife, Princess Leopoldina, rejected these humiliating measures and urged Pedro to lead the independence movement in Brazil.

Pedro was already thinking along the same lines. Before João had left Brazil, he had counseled his son to do that very thing if Brazil decided on independence. On September 7, 1822, Pedro issued his famous "Grito de Ipiranga." Traveling by the banks of the Ipiranga River, he ripped the Portuguese colors off his uniform, drew his sword, and shouted, "The hour is now! Independence or death!" He then sheathed his sword and continued his journey. The act was the crucial signal. Portuguese garrisons scattered throughout Brazil resisted for a while; but by early 1824 Brazil was free. Lord Cochrane, who had served the Chilean and Peruvian causes of independence, led a Brazilian fleet to fend off a Portuguese attack.

Pedro convened a constitutional assembly in 1823 to write a charter for the new empire. Radicals used the body as a forum to denounce the Portuguese House of Bragança monarchy and to limit the emperor to the role of a figurehead. At that Pedro disbanded the assembly and formed a smaller one to write a constitution more to his liking, which it did in 1824. The new Constitution was very conservative and provoked consternation among freedom-minded Brazilian Creoles. A new republican-inspired revolt promptly broke out in Recife. Although it was crushed, Pedro's regalism and favoritism toward his Portuguese advisors continued to irritate the Brazilians.

Pedro's presence in Brazil nevertheless facilitated the country's relatively peaceful transition to independence and helped set the stage for a unified and politically stable Brazil throughout the nineteenth century. Given the dismal record of chaos, caudillos, and militarism in the rest of Spanish America, it was no small or insignificant legacy to have a ready-made and generally acceptable member of a royal house on the throne of Brazil in 1822.

Recognition and the Monroe Doctrine

The halting but inexorable progress of the Wars of Independence between 1817 and 1824 naturally attracted the attention of the United States. This was the formative period in U.S.-Latin American relations, and much of the future of those relations was foreshadowed by the early intercourse between these two parts of the Americas. Although the United States and Latin America shared the bonds of geography—the Western Hemisphere—and colonial origin—descended partly from European settlers—they were at the same time strikingly dissimilar in other ways, such as ethnic makeup, political and economic institutions, and religious patterns. Much of the history of U.S.-Latin American relations reflected these dissimilarities, which became accentuated as the nineteenth century advanced.

Of the many issues between the United States and Latin America in the early period, none was more significant than that of recognition. The United States wished to encourage the twin virtues of independence and republicanism in Latin America but proceeded deliberately and cautiously so as not to antagonize Spain.

In 1819 Spain had ceded Florida to the United States according to the Adams-Onís (or Transcontinental) Treaty. The United States gave up its claims to Texas, acquired Spain's claim to the Oregon Territory north of the Forty-Second Parallel, and paid Spain $5 million as well. But the ratification process was complicated, and the treaty was not ratified until 1821. Meanwhile Spain's colonies were breaking out in rebellion. While the United States negotiated with Spain, it would have been awkward to recognize the independence of Spain's former colonies. Besides, until 1821–1822, independence had not been clearly won throughout Latin America.

The Wars of Independence were an ongoing process rather than an accomplished fact, and President James Monroe (1816–1824) and his secretary of state, John Quincy Adams, waited until 1822 to recognize the independence of Mexico, Gran Colombia, Peru, Chile, and Argentina. In doing so, they set a precedent of unity and solidarity with their fellow American nations. The United States at this time identified with its sister nations in the Western Hemisphere, comrades in the cause of liberty and independence, all doing battle against European colonialism.

Recognition by the United States came none too soon. Early in 1823 France, backed by a reactionary bloc of European monarchies (the Holy Alliance), marched troops into Spain to overthrow the liberals and to restore Ferdinand VII's conservative, monarchical regime. Many feared that this was the first step toward the restoration of Spain's empire. The specter of French armies crossing the Atlantic to help Spanish royalists crush the newly independent Latin American nations was abhorrent to most Americans and unacceptable to a great many Englishmen as well.

Late in 1823 President Monroe read before Congress a remarkable address, although not much noticed at the time, that set the tone for U.S.-Latin American relations for the next century and a half. The new British foreign secretary, George Canning, helped pave the way for Monroe's address by actively opposing the French effort to restore royalist power in Latin America. Canning and the British cabinet wished to preserve the independence of the new nations, whose open ports and markets welcomed English merchants and English goods. It was certainly not in the English interests to allow a restoration of Spain's monopolistic empire in the Americas, and Canning made his views known to the Americans quite candidly.

The Russian czar, Alexander, also played a role in the formation of the Monroe Doctrine. From their colony of Alaska, the Russians claimed a wide sphere of influence south into the Oregon country—a sphere that challenged U.S. claims in the same region. The establishment of Russian trading posts as far south as California especially provoked the ire of the Americans. They were dead set against a Russian czar who championed despotic monarchy instead of those principles so dear to Americans, the ideals of revolution and republicanism, and a Russian regime that threatened the more practical issues of profits and territorial security.

Monroe, buttressed by the knowledge that the British would use their navy, the greatest in the world, to oppose the French, and feeling the urgency of responding to the Russian threat, elaborated two basic principles in his address to Congress. He declared that henceforth the American continents were closed to future colonization by European powers (the noncolonization principle) and that the American continents and the political systems evolving here were unique and different from the European systems. Consequently, any attempt by the old European monarchies (Spain, France, and Russia, for example) to enforce or expand their systems of government in the New World would be resisted by the United States.

Mr. Monroe's Doctrine

"The American continents, by the free and independent condition which they have assumed and maintain, are henceforth not to be considered as subjects for future colonization by any European Power" (the non-colonization principle) and "The political system of the allied powers (the Holy Alliance) is essentially different ... from that of America.... We owe it, therefore, to candor, and to the amicable relations existing between the United States and those powers, to declare that we should consider any attempt on their part to extend their system to any portion of this hemisphere as dangerous to their peace and safety. With the existing colonies or dependencies of any European power we have not interfered and shall not interfere. But with the Governments who have declared their independence and maintained it, and whose independence we *have, on great consideration and on just principles, acknowledged, we could not view* any interposition for the purpose of oppressing them, or controlling in any other manner their destiny, by any European Power, in any other light than as the manifestation of an unfriendly disposition towards the United States."

(Whitaker, pp. 465–466)

Although the doctrine was specifically written to warn off the Russians and the French, its principles became cornerstones of future U.S.-Latin American relations. The Western Hemisphere was asserted as unique, and the United States vowed to protect the hemisphere's independence and to fend off European interference. Some Latin American nations, such as Colombia and Brazil, officially endorsed the doctrine. Others were negative or coolly indifferent. The *porteño* elites of Buenos Aires, much under the influence of the English, and many Mexicans, who feared the territorial ambitions of their neighbor to the north, had little taste for Monroe's doctrine.

While U.S. recognition of the newly independent Latin American nations marked the near end of the long struggle for independence, the Monroe Doctrine was also the prelude to modern relations between Latin America and the United States. In this new era, Latin Americans, especially Simón Bolívar, took just as much initiative as President Monroe in attempting to define the international relations of the new countries.

Latin Americans sought some unity even as they fought for their independence as separate nations from Spain. This unity traditionally has been labeled "pan-Americanism," and its origins lay in the Wars of Independence period and, very specifically, are associated with the vision of Simón Bolívar. In 1824 Bolívar called for a meeting of all Latin American nations to consider matters of security and possible confederation. Bolívar was acting on the old proverb that "in unity there is strength," and pan-Americanism was the expression of that ideal. After two years of preparation, the delegates gathered in Panama. Bolívar himself did not attend.

The Congress of Panama was notable for two reasons. One, it was the first of many efforts by Latin American nations to act in concert to defend their rights and to provide for international machinery to solve common problems. Two, it failed to accomplish anything in fact because, with the exception of Gran Colombia, no other nation ratified the treaty that emerged from the Congress. One must recall that international treaties and agreements reached at such congresses and conferences ultimately must be ratified at home. In fact, not all Latin American nations had been represented at the Congress, delegations coming only from Mexico, Central America, Gran Colombia, and Peru. Although the United States was invited as well, the Americans were tardy in naming a delegation, arguing over the nature of the Congress of Panama and how much or how little the United States should commit itself to international agreements. One American delegate died en route, and the other discovered that the Congress had ended before he even reached it!

The Congress of Panama was frustrated by the factionalism and jealousies that were then becoming painfully apparent to Bolívar and those who shared with him a vision of pan-Americanism. Yet, Bolívar had initiated the pan-American movement, even if the ideal was difficult to translate into action.

In the next chapter we will analyze the meaning of independence. Latin America strode off into a new world filled with both promise and uncertainty. The promise was in the future and lay with the chance to create new ways of life. Yet, the legacies of the past were not so easily discarded. The uncertainty came from not really knowing how much to keep and how much to discard from a past that had been a source of both strength and discord.

Conclusions and Issues

The "second" half of the Wars of Independence occurred between 1816 and 1826. In many ways, the stage had been set by the "first" half of the wars from 1810 to 1816. The declarations had been made then, the issues clarified, the battles joined, the differences frozen into hatreds by the passions of war. Even though Spain prevailed by 1815 with a few exceptions (Argentina the most significant), the embers of the revolutions were never doused.

From Argentina in the south and Venezuela in the north, San Martín and Bolívar led patriot armies on to victory, meeting in the Ecuadorian port city of Guayaquil in 1822 to determine how to liberate finally the great Spanish royalist stronghold of Peru. And in Mexico, conservative Creoles such as Iturbide persuaded old radical leaders like Guerrero to join them in the final overthrow of Spanish authority.

The United States responded to the Latin American independence movements with support, if not enthusiasm. Recognition was one of the most effective means of support, while the Monroe Doctrine of 1823 expressed both short- and long-term goals of U.S. policy toward Latin America. Bolívar's Congress of Panama of 1826, on the other hand, attempted to formulate a different vision of pan-Americanism—one based on Latin American solidarity and cultural affinity.

At the end of the Wars of Independence, the patriots looked back on their recent achievements with immense pride. They had thrown off a three-hundred-year-old colonial rule and moved the countries of Mexico, Central America, and South America to independence. The legacy of the long colonial rule, and of the often-violent fifteen-year wars, however, was immensely mixed.

Discussion Questions

1. How did Great Britain and the United States differ in their reactions to the Latin American Wars of Independence? In what ways did their reactions coincide?

2. Why did Bolívar evolve into such a dictator in the latter part of his career?

3. Did Monroe and Bolívar share a vision of pan-Americanism? If so, what was it and how was it made evident? What is the contrary view?

The Meaning of War, or the Heritage of Independence

Mr. Tudor and Mr. Bolívar

The Liberator, Simón Bolívar, was not an easy person to understand. William Tudor, first U.S. consul to Peru, had desperately wanted Bolívar to model himself on the noblest incarnation of republican virtue that a North American Yankee could conceive of—George Washington. Yet the evidence seemed to be mounting otherwise.

Tudor's carriage neared Bolívar's estate in Lima, La Magdalena, to celebrate the Liberator's birthday. What had become of the man so dedicated to independence, the slayer of tyranny? Rumor had it that Bolívar's old lieutenant, Antonio José Páez, had offered the Liberator the throne of Gran Colombia. "You should become the Bonaparte of South America," Páez pleaded with Bolívar, "because this country is not the country of Washington."

Was Bolívar seriously contemplating becoming the Bonaparte of South America, Tudor wondered? If so, it would certainly be consistent with the behavior that Tudor had been observing of late. Bolívar behaved more and more each day like a tyrant than a liberator, more like Napoleon than Washington.

At the birthday party the food and the liquor and the conversation flowed freely under the gracious host's proverbial generosity.

"Welcome, Mr. Tudor," General O'Leary, one of Bolívar's Irish aides, said as he took the Yankee's hand and drew him into the loud, buzzing crowd of well-wishers and admirers. "The Liberator is in an ebullient mood this evening, Mr. Tudor. He is on top of the world, sir," O'Leary added.

Indeed, all of Latin America was free. Bolívar was adulated by Lima society. The Protector. The Liberator. At the top of his form. Perhaps the "Emperor," thought Tudor. He saw Bolívar in a knot of admirers. Thin by nature, he seemed even thinner tonight, almost fragile, but with an electrifying power flowing to those around him that seemed irresistible, certainly charismatic.

Toast after toast loosened everyone's tongue, it seemed. The base, almost oriental flattery of Bolívar's sycophantic admirers repelled the bachelor Yankee republican.

Bolívar himself took fire.

"Yes, to liberty, to victory, to independence," he said, each great principle enunciated, followed by a deep swallow.

"To all of you, patriot soldiers without peer. We have outshone Washington and Napoleon. Your fame will live on forever. To Peru! To New Granada! To America!" Bolívar exclaimed. The roar of *"Viva el Libertador"* filled La Magdalena and spilled out into the yards and streets.

Tudor left shortly thereafter, the phrases of base adulation ringing in his ears, the noise of tyranny too much for this reserved republican from Massachusetts.

As the scene dissolves and we return to our narrative, one of the most intriguing questions in modern Latin American history surfaces: the consequences of the Wars of Independence. Bolívar, San Martín, Hidalgo, O'Higgins, Páez, Morelos, and others certainly transformed the political landscape. What else had changed? Was Latin America to be governed by Washingtonians or Bonapartists? Was the choice one between republicans like George Washington or monarchists such as Napoleon Bonaparte? Was there another choice, distinct and Latin American, rather than derivative and coming from North America or Europe?

Some people claim that the wars wrought profound changes, whereas others deny that anything significant changed. As an old Mexican Indian adage claimed, after fifteen years of war and revolution, it was the same tired mule with a different rider. Instead of Spaniards, the Creoles were in control, but little else changed because the Amerindians were still exploited, and the wealth was still in the hands of a powerful white elite.

In fact, a great deal had changed. Or, at the very least, the Wars of Independence had eliminated barriers by destroying many old ties, institutions, and traditions. This cleared the way for changes and experimentation with new institutions and ways. Democratic constitutions replaced the Spanish monarchy. Great Britain took Spain's place as the dominant economic influence. *Caudillos,* often coming to power by force, replaced bureaucrats sent from Spain to govern the people and the land. Slaves were often freed or put on the road to freedom. Change was indeed the password of the era, although not all of the changes were positive.

The Loss of Legitimacy

Among the most obvious results of the wars was the exchange of rule by Spain for self-government. Before, power flowed from the Spanish monarchy; now it flowed from another source: the constitution. This is not a subtle or merely legalistic distinction: It meant that a new political loyalty had to be cultivated to fill the place of the one destroyed by the wars. For a government to be effective and to command the loyalty of its citizens, it has to have legitimacy: It must be accepted as lawful and right. The king was the source of legitimacy in the old system. People believed in and obeyed the monarchy. When it was removed, a new source of legitimacy had to be created to validate the revolutions and the new nations. In almost all instances, constitutions replaced the monarchy, but the flaw in this system was that the people did not trust in nor give their loyalty to constitutions in the same fashion that they trusted and gave their loyalty to the old monarchy.

Constitutions were, after all, but instruments made by humans, perishable and changeable like everything else made by humans. Monarchies were thought to be sanctioned by God and were reinforced by the custom of centuries and by the habit of obedience. Constitutions could be and were altered and replaced with alarming rapidity as the new nations emerged, contributing to a rather bewildering political scene in the years from 1820 to mid-century.

Little stability in government was apparent, prompting even Bolívar to throw his hands up in disgust and claim that chaos prevailed because the good leaders had disappeared and the bad had multiplied.

Competing Political Systems

On another, more theoretical, level, some have speculated that constitutional democracy as it was developing in North America was not workable in Latin America. They argue that the ancient habits of authoritarianism and centralism inherited from Spain could not be supplanted easily by democracy and federalism—principles that the new Latin American constitutions generally embodied. In practice, Latin Americans were more disposed by habit and tradition to seek strong leaders and to govern their new nations with a strong hand from the capitals. The conflict between liberal democracy and Hispanic authoritarianism in the wake of the Wars of Independence may seem to be an abstract, almost philosophical question. However, it is one that should be taken into consideration when accounting for the political instability that followed the wars. The student of history not only learns the sequence of events—the "battles and presidents" approach to history—but also must search beneath the surface for those great issues and more profound causes of the surface events in history. The metaphor of the sea is appropriate. What a shallow knowledge of the oceans one would have based on simply observing and reporting the effects of wind and wave on the surface. The seas take their true character from the tides and currents and life beneath their surface.

Economic Independence

Military victory and political independence were often accompanied by the opening of ports to foreign trade. As Spanish power and influence receded, foreigners

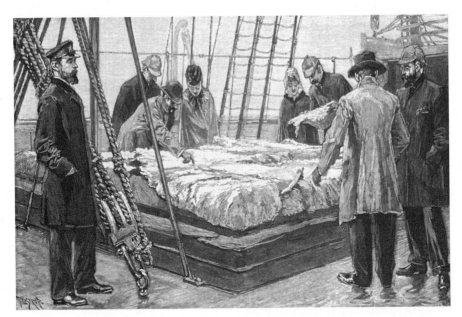

Fur dealers examining pelts at Punta Arenas, Chile, on the Strait of Magellan. The fur trade helped tie the economies of Latin America and Europe into a closer relationship in the nineteenth century.

stepped into the void. Englishmen and Americans eagerly pushed into the ports and provinces of Latin America, bringing with them merchandise to be peddled and capital to be invested, while at the same time seeking the goods of Latin America, principally specie (silver and gold), but also the products of ranches and farms, such as hides and coffee.

The experience of Brazil was typical. When it opened its ports to Great Britain—Portugal's ancient ally and recent savior of the monarchy—trade flourished. Between 1806 and 1818, the annual value of English goods imported into Brazil rose from £1,000 to over £3,000,000, a spectacular increase. English merchants were given preferential treatment, and imports soared. One observer in Rio de Janeiro claimed that more English goods were available in the crowded marketplace of Rio than in London's Cheapside markets. Similar increases occurred in other areas: English imports in Chile jumped from £37,000 in 1817 to £400,000 in 1822, and in Mexico from £21,000 in 1819 to over £1,000,000 in 1825.

English Merchants in Latin America

In 1839 Fanny Calderón was looking out the window of her lodgings on the houses of the main street of Veracruz. They were richer and more elegant than could have been expected in that inhospitable and insalubrious port, and a well-cared-for house drew her attention. 'I find,' she adds, 'it belongs to an English merchant.' Some days later, in the old town of Jalapa, which was little more than 'a few very old steep streets with some large and excellent houses,' she felt entitled to draw a general conclusion: 'the best, as usual, belonging to English merchants.' Twenty years earlier, in Buenos Aires, the representative of the United States government observed that the English merchants had begun to buy the best houses and deduced from this that they were preparing to settle down for a long time. In Pocuro, a tiny Chilean town, an English butcher built himself a house 'which appears palatial in these surroundings, greatly to the admiration of his neighbors.' In Islay, a village on the desert Peruvian coast, which served as a Port for Arequipa, the enchanting house of the English consul stood out against a background of miserable cane huts. Flora Tristán remarked disapprovingly on the somewhat ostentatious luxury of the British merchants throughout Peru, and in Bogotá, when the exceedingly wealthy Arrubla sold his sumptuous house, it was once again an Englishman, the consul, who bought it.

(Quoted from Tulio Halperin-Donghi, *The Aftermath of Revolution in Latin America,* translated by Josephine de Bunsen [New York: Harper & Row, 1973], pp. 44–45)

The leaders of the new nations sought to advance their economies and recover from the wars by attracting capital, new technology, and skilled European labor. Although few of these long-term, substantial goals were accomplished, the phenomenal expansion of the English merchant communities in Latin America in this period did lay the foundation for a more intense period of foreign investment and influence in the second half of the century.

By the early 1820s English merchants throughout Latin America had glutted the market. In Buenos Aires, where over three thousand British lived, the saturated market and political anarchy of the years 1819–1820 left over £1,000,000 worth of English products piled up in the warehouses of Buenos Aires. In Chile, many English merchants living sumptuous lives in Santiago were forced to move to the port of Valparaiso as shrinking profits reflected the glutted market. The Latin American market could absorb just so much English hardware and textiles.

The early and decidedly impressive English presence in the new countries was not limited to merchants. The British, then leading the world in the accumulation of capital as they pioneered the Industrial Revolution, sought other outlets for their money in Latin America. One outlet was lending money directly to the new governments, which were starved for income to pay for the immense costs of war and to rebuild the countries. Loans totaling more than £20,000,000 were made to Mexico, Gran Colombia, Peru, Chile, Argentina, and Brazil during the wars. A large percentage of these loans never reached Latin America, being taken up by commission payments and fees to the banks. For example, while the face value of the bonds sold to generate the Mexican loan was £7,000,000, the bonds sold actually for only £3,000,732, and of this amount, only £2,800,000 actually reached Mexico. Yet, the Mexicans were bound by the obligations of the contract to pay interest on the principal of £7,000,000. The same situation prevailed in all of the other loans made to the new countries. But Latin America, fragile and war torn, simply could not service the immense new debts, and by 1827 all of the loans were in default. A half a century elapsed before English investors would again view Latin America with such unbridled greed and optimism.

The early optimism also persuaded the British to invest heavily in the mining industry of Latin America, with much the same results. Desperate to restore the mines, principally silver, to their prewar production, Latin American leaders, such as José Antonio de Sucre in Bolivia, actively sought British capital and technology in the early 1820s. The British responded with enthusiasm, establishing more than twenty mining companies to develop the languishing mines of Mexico, Peru, Bolivia, Chile, and Argentina. The Potosí, La Paz, and Peruvian Mining Association was typical. Although capitalized at £1,000,000, only a fraction of this ever reached Bolivia. The few British miners who actually traveled to Bolivia and Mexico under these circumstances found immense obstacles, principally the necessity of major work to restore the mines to production after the destruction and flooding and neglect of the war years. Unable to bring massive amounts of capital to bear, unable to introduce the newest steam technologies, and stymied by the vast distances, poor communications, and general lack of labor, the English mining effort collapsed early on.

The lack of capital and skilled labor underscored the failures. Both had fled with the Spanish after the wars, and the dreams of English speculators went aground on hard reality. Local circumstances, such as in Bolivia, where Bolívar freed the Amerindians from the *mita* (tribute labor), exemplified the problems. The mines of Latin America, such a rich source of income during the colonial period, continued to languish until well past mid-century. This financial and economic disaster proved to be one of the most difficult legacies to overcome in the nineteenth century.

New Ways and Old

The Wars of Independence opened the doors to many fresh and novel ways of political, social, and economic thinking, some of which directly challenged a very traditional society. For example, liberals who wished to place the individual at the center of society and to have the individual's "natural" rights (freedom of speech, right to compete, equality before the law) guaranteed by constitutions were resisted, sometimes implacably, by the Church.

The Church was basically a conservative institution in Latin America in the nineteenth century. That is to say, it sought to keep faith with and preserve traditions rather than to alter them in the light of changes precipitated by the Wars of Independence.

The Church had been allied to the Spanish monarchy for three hundred years, and Latin America's transition from colony to nationhood seriously upset this relationship. The Church persistently blocked reforms with its reluctance to share its wealth and power to accommodate to the new, modern society envisioned by liberals.

Throughout Latin America, revolutionaries sought to strip the Church of its power as the arbiter of morality, the educator of its children, the banker to the wealthy, and the philanthropist to the sick, the poor, and the needy. Liberals wished to promote a secular society where the state and/or the individual would ideally supplant the Church. In effect, liberals wanted to eliminate what they considered to be the Church's suffocating, hidebound ways that did not allow for the modernization of society. The stage was set during the 1820s for extreme confrontations later in the century, when the secular Liberals and traditional Conservatives clashed violently over the role and power of the Church in society.

These challenges to the Church advanced at different rates through Latin America. In some areas, such as Brazil, the preservation of the monarchy left the privileges and power of the Church basically intact. In Bolivia, on the other hand, José Antonio de Sucre systematically attacked the Church in the mid-1820s in a typically reformist and liberal fashion.

Sucre, like Bolívar and many other leaders, was thoroughly imbued with the secularism of the Enlightenment. He wanted to strip the wealth of the Church to advance the interests of the new states. And Church resources were considerable.

Thousands and even millions of acres of land belonging to the Church often went untilled or underutilized. The Church owned even more property through its mortgages, and wealthy and not-so-wealthy landowners discovered a convenient way of breaking out of debt by attacking the Church. Large chunks of extremely valuable urban property dedicated to monasteries and nunneries were held by religious orders. Radicals abhorred the secluded, cloistered life of monks and nuns who apparently did nothing to advance the interests of society. That life of contemplation seemed to represent nothing more than self-indulgence and waste. The liberal creed also sought to strip away the Church's traditional role as educator, preferring to champion a secular and public education administered by the state. Public schools would teach children the good liberal doctrines of individualism and constitutionalism and the values of republicanism and free speech—all principles dear to the reformers. The Church and its supporters resisted what they considered to be deranged and ungodly reformers who attacked the very backbone of morality and order as ordained by God. Some of the issues seem arcane and irrelevant to us today—such as the liberals' insistence on secularizing the cemeteries and requiring civil marriage ceremonies—but to Latin Americans of the early nineteenth century, the battle lines clearly divided the forces of good and evil.

Liberals and Conservatives

In studying the history of Latin America one is often faced with terms such as "conservative" and "reactionary" to describe the attitudes of certain people and institutions such as constitutions. On the other hand, "liberals" stand in contrast to "conservatives." What do these terms mean? Sometimes very few specifics are supplied about what it means to be a conservative or a liberal in the nineteenth century. The Chilean Constitution of 1833 is a near-perfect example of a "conservative" instrument. It is often described as authoritarian, centralist, and conservative. Its executive powers—those given to the president—were wide and sweeping, resembling in some ways the broad powers of a monarch. This was certainly "conservative." The Roman Catholic Church was made the official religion, thereby reinforcing the alliance between the Church and state, another old conservative relationship. The right to vote was severely restricted to a small percentage of Chileans—those literate and with property. The drives to provide for "law and order," to preserve the status quo, and to regulate morality were primary ends of conservatives. To be a conservative was, in many ways, to value the forces of tradition and continuity more than those that encouraged change and experimentation.

To be a "liberal," on the other hand, was to esteem change and to champion a number of values and goals that flew in the face of the conservatives. Liberals desired to reduce the power of the Roman Catholic Church and to secularize society, especially education. Liberals wanted more freedom for more individuals, extolling the virtues of a free citizenry who fully participated in the governing of the nation. Liberals wanted free trade. Liberals desired an end to all institutions, such as slavery and Indian tributes, that fixed individuals in unalterable social and economic positions in society.

Yet, for both sides these are not hard and fast distinctions. Sometimes, as we will see later, Liberals acted in astonishingly conservative ways, and vice versa. But these definitions help us to understand some of the passions that marked relations between "conservatives" and "liberals" in the nineteenth century.

Sucre attacked the Church in Bolivia with great vigor and success, setting an example that other Liberals in the nineteenth century would attempt to emulate. He took over collection of tithes, confiscated Church-held mortgages and other income-producing activities, closed all monasteries with less than twelve members, confiscated the estates of the remaining monasteries and put their members on state salaries, did the same to the convents, and, in sum, permanently diminished the power of the Church in Bolivia. It ceased to have a major economic or political influence in Bolivia. By good fortune, this also spared Bolivia from the ravages of religious conflict that engulfed nations such as Mexico, Colombia, and Ecuador later in the century.[1]

Liberals and the Races

Those radicals and Liberals who fought the wars and emerged as leaders in the 1820s and 1830s (not all leaders were liberal or radical, but, like Pedro I of Brazil and Iturbide of Mexico, were quite moderate or conservative in their views) also were dedicated to the proposition that all people should be free of any past restrictions or bondage that limited their ability to act independently in society, in the economy, or in politics. In effect, that meant abolishing slavery and raising the Amerindian to full

---

[1]Herbert S. Klein, *Bolivia: The Evolution of a Multi-Ethnic Society.* (New York: Oxford University Press, 1982, pp. 109–111.)

citizenship in the emerging nations. The long march to this ideal state of equality began during the wars, and indeed many of the forces that pushed for a society free of racial and social barriers were set in motion by the wars themselves. The progress toward this ideal was, nonetheless, very uneven, and it often produced as much hardship and loss for its intended beneficiaries—especially the Amerindians—as progress. Ironically, the Liberal ideal of liberating the Amerindians and assimilating them into mainstream culture often contributed to the destruction of Amerindian ways of life.

The Enduring Indian Nations

The long-range impact of the Wars of Independence on Amerindians was complex. They technically stood to benefit far more than any other group because the Bolívars, the Sucres, the Moreloses, and other leaders elevated the Amerindian to full citizenship within the new nations. The tributes were abolished (only Amerindians had been forced to pay tributes during the colonial period), and Amerindians were promised equality before the law. The words and intentions of the heroes and leaders of the independence era are absolutely clear, powerful, and unambiguous.

Morelos declared in Mexico in 1810 that from then on "all the inhabitants except Europeans will no longer be designated as Indians, mulattoes or other castes, but all will be known as Americans."[2] In Peru, the Congress of 1822 made the following exhortation and promise to the Amerindians: "Noble children of the sun, you are the first object of our concern. We recall your past sufferings, we work for your present and future happiness. You are going to be noble, educated, and owners of property."[3] Others were no less insistent in championing the Amerindians as the great beneficiaries of liberal doctrine brought about by the Wars of Independence.

But well-meaning liberal leaders were confounded by circumstances. Instead of remaking the Amerindians into the image that liberals preferred—that of independent, small farmers, cultivating their own plots of land and developing good democratic and republican instincts—Amerindians failed to make the transition. They fell prey to unscrupulous Creoles and mestizos who took advantage of legislation meant to benefit the Amerindians and instead despoiled them. The case of Gran Colombia illustrates the failure of liberal doctrine with respect to Amerindians.

To enable Amerindians to become small landholders, the old communal system of land tenure in which villages and groups of villages owned land together had to be broken up. The concept of private ownership was foreign to most Amerindians, from Bolivia to Mexico, and the case was no less true in Colombia, where Amerindians had possessed *resguardos,* or community lands, from ancient times.

In 1810 legislation gave the Amerindians individual property rights over their *resguardos,* as well as abolished the tribute. The full implications of this legislation

---

[2]Lynch, *Spanish-American Revolutions,* p. 342.
[3]Ibid.

*On the windswept plateau (altiplano) of Bolivia, Indian women harvest pota-
toes as they have for hundreds of years, testimony to enduring traditions
among the Amerindian populations of Latin America.*

were delayed by the wars themselves, but the principle of private landownership was
again confirmed by the Congress of Cúcuta in 1821. The *resguardos* were abolished,
and individual families were given titles to those lands that they worked. The
process ultimately backfired because the Amerindians were stripped of the protection afforded them by the ancient system of *resguardos* and in turn were made susceptible to the ambitions of whites and mestizos desiring to expand their landholdings. The Amerindians ended up selling their small plots of land over the years
because they were unequipped to survive as small, independent agriculturalists. The
same sad sequence of events swept the Amerindians across Latin America even fur-

ther down the economic scale as they were cheated and despoiled of their ancient lands by the effects of liberal legislation enacted during the nineteenth century.

Even eliminating the tribute, a most obvious stigma of second-class citizenship, proved short-lived in portions of Latin America. In Bolivia and Peru, it was restored in the late 1820s because the new governments simply could not survive without the revenue that the tribute produced.

In effect, although the rhetoric and even the legislation of the Wars of Independence era promised the Amerindians much, great portions of the indigenous population of Latin America continued to live apart from and dependent upon the new rulers. These Creoles, but also some mestizos and mulattoes who had risen to positions of prominence and power through the wars, tended to be liberal in rhetoric but conservative in practice. The Amerindians remained, in a phrase coined during the period of Spanish rule, a "nation within the nations" and did not share in the new power structure.

Imposition of Militarism

The militarism that came to characterize Latin America after the wars was one of the most enduring legacies of the era. A region torn apart by wars for more than fifteen years had learned to depend upon the power of the sword for order and authority in times of great turmoil. From Bernardo O'Higgins in Chile to Agustín Iturbide in Mexico, the man on horseback emerged as the hero, the winner of victories on the battlefield, the writer of constitutions, the guarantor of peace and tranquillity.

He could be a Creole, such as Simón Bolívar, or a mestizo, such as Andrés Santa Cruz of Bolivia. As the new nations emerged, it was the will and power of such men that left an indelible imprint on Latin America.

Conclusions and Issues

As the Wars of Independence formally ended, the formal political changes in the configuration of Latin America were the most evident. Gone were the old Portuguese and Spanish colonial empires. New and independent nations emerged, with a few exceptions: Cuba and Puerto Rico remained Spanish, while most of the islands of the Caribbean continued in the possession of European nations; the Guianas in South America and British Honduras in Central America did not change hands. Mexico, the Central American confederation (Honduras, Guatemala, El Salvador, Nicaragua, and Costa Rica), New Granada (Venezuela, Colombia, Panama, and Ecuador), Peru, Chile, Bolivia, Argentina, Paraguay, Uruguay, and Brazil all became independent, some as constitutional republics, others as monarchies, and some were extremely short-lived. By 1830 New Granada had broken up into three nations, and a decade later the Central American confederation also fell apart, and the five small countries went their separate ways.

With independence came new challenges and new problems. English merchants and miners brought in new wares, new priorities, new monies, and new ideas, disrupting the old economies and traditional ways of commerce. Liberals in Latin America not only courted the English—who, they felt, represented progress and modernization—but also attempted to reinvent Latin American society. They freed the Amerindian from long colonial bondage, attacked the Church as an antiquated, conservative institution equated with antiquated, suffocating, reactionary Spanish rule, and attempted to put into place the high ideals of political equality and economic justice. Through it all, the political disorder caused by the wars argued in favor of strong, military rulers who could enforce a semblance of order in a region adrift in civil strife and anarchy.

Discussion Questions

1. Explain what is meant by the "loss of legitimacy" in the context of the period immediately following the Latin American Wars of Independence.

2. Why was the Roman Catholic Church so reluctant to change, and how did liberals of the early nineteenth century view this reluctance?

3. Would you have been a liberal or a conservative in the politics of Latin America in the 1820s and 1830s? Why?

The Search for Political Order, 1830s–1850s

Mr. Rosas Governs Argentina

"Subordination, that is the key," Manuel Rosas said to his companion while riding slowly along the swampy banks of the Río Colorado near the coast in southern Argentina. They were on General Rosas's Desert Campaign of 1833.

"He is subordinate to you," Rosas continued, "you to me, and I govern in the name of peace and order."

They rode slowly away from what until a few minutes earlier had been an Indian encampment. "Those savages back there," Rosas threw a glance back at the smoldering remains, "they are barbarians. They are not Christians. They ambush us, they kill us, they steal our cattle, they live like animals."

Indeed, the small Indian encampment that had been attacked by Rosas's gauchos earlier that afternoon was hardly recognizable as civilized to the young English scientist then riding by Rosas's side. There had been forty or fifty Indian men, women, and children, ragged, nearly naked really, living off a scraggly herd of horses and cattle. Nearly all were taken or killed. Only the children, as near as Charles Darwin could tell, were spared.

"Why kill them all?" Darwin asked Rosas. It was nearing dusk, but they had another five miles to go before reaching Rosas's main encampment, where his army of five or six hundred gauchos, peons, and friendly Indians were bivouacked.

"I am not killing them all, Mr. Darwin," Rosas answered.

"Very few were spared back there," Darwin answered, casting a glance over his shoulder. Rosas was an imposing man, large, fierce looking, dressed for working like the gauchos on the ranches of Argentina. He demanded and received the loyalty of his gauchos by the power of his personality. He could ride, shoot, break animals, and fight with the best of them, creating the aura that he was the best of them. He was a despot, Darwin thought, but Darwin had to admit that Rosas received the unbounded loyalty of his men.

"No, Mr. Darwin," Rosas said gravely, using the English "Mister" in an unaffected manner. "We did not kill them all. The children were spared to be raised as Christians. The rest were dispatched as a lesson to the others. Once we bring them under control," Rosas continued, "this great pampa will be settled, cattle will prosper, the country will prosper, and we will once again have peace. Then our plains will be free forever and we will secure the foundations of our national wealth.[1]

"We are, as you know, a new nation, Mr. Darwin," Rosas continued. "There has been much lawlessness, at times almost utter dissolution, where little security for lives and property exists." Rosas paused, as if to think carefully. Darwin rode silently alongside, not fearing this fearful man, but admiring him almost as one would admire a force of nature that could be awesome and destructive.

"Before you can have government, you need order and obedience," Rosas said as they slowly drew near the main encampment. It was twilight now, and the haze from the fires roasting the meats curled up through the trees.

Out of the corner of the camp shouting disturbed the peaceful scene. Darwin didn't understand the Spanish, but sharp, angry voices skewered the night. Then it was over just as quickly as it had started. Darwin was startled and looked to Rosas. He wasn't there. All that Darwin saw was the tail end, literally, of Rosas's horse as he and his small retinue plunged toward the fray.

"What happened?" Darwin later asked his interpreter, an older Argentine gaucho who had worked in a British house of trade in Buenos Aires for many years.

"A killing," Patricio the interpreter told Darwin.

"Who? Why?" asked Darwin, the ever-curious investigator of plants and people on this great expedition of inquiry around the world.

"Someone spoke disrespectfully of General Rosas," Patricio answered.

"And?" Darwin asked.

"And another man stabbed him."

"Oh," said the Englishman, looking over toward Rosas's quarters. A murder, thought Darwin.

"What's to be done?" Darwin asked.

"Done?" Patricio asked.

"To the murderer," Darwin said.

---

[1]John Lynch, *Argentine Dictator: Juan Manuel de Rosas, 1829–1852* (Oxford: Clarendon Press, 1981), p. 53, quoting in part from a public letter written by Rosas on behalf of the Desert Campaign.

"Ah, Señor Darwin, he is not a murderer. He defended the honor of General Rosas."

"Yes, of course," said the scientist.

"He is our *patrón*, Señor Darwin. We respect him. He is our leader. You don't speak badly of your leader. He protects us, he gives us jobs, he is one of us. We need to be loyal to the general, not speak disrespectfully of him."

"Rosas is a great caudillo, Patricio?" Darwin half asked, half stated, curious about the relationship between Rosas and his people.

"He is *the* caudillo, Señor Darwin."

The Background and Nature of Caudillos

Politically, the nineteenth century was the age of the caudillo, a term best translated as "Latin American dictator." Caudillos came in all shapes and sizes, ruled over small clans and vast countries, could be ruthless or civil, Creoles or mestizos. It has been said that the first great caudillo was Simón Bolívar, the model of the caudillos who emerged in the 1830s as rulers of the newly independent nations. Bolívar ruled by the force of his personality, identifying another attribute of the caudillo: *personalismo,* or "personalism." Furthermore, Bolívar had been a military man, and virtually all caudillos who governed to the mid-nineteenth century were veterans of the wars like Bolívar: military men—marshals, generals, or guerrilla chieftains—forged into hard men by the campaigns and battles.

One can go back far into Latin American and Spanish history for the origins of the caudillo and of personalism, which can broadly be described as doing things—whether in government or in business—based on friendships rather than principles. An axiom in English provides us with some insight: "It's not what you know, it's who you know."

Even before the Spanish arrived in the New World, great numbers of Amerindian peoples willingly obeyed chiefs and leaders, the *caciques.* During the Conquest and after, this tendency was reinforced by the great conquistadors themselves. What better models for caudillos than the Cortéses and Pizarros? Then, during the Wars of Independence, the strength of personality once more prevailed over principles. Authority issued not from legal, ethical, or moral considerations, but rather from a particular general's ability to protect and defend and provide for the welfare of his soldiers and followers.

Geography also contributed to caudillismo. Latin America was a vast land, sparsely populated, the people separated on their ranches and farms and small towns and hamlets by immense distances. The great haciendas and plantations were ruled by men in patriarchal fashion, dispensing justice and wielding power in the time-honored tradition of the *patrón.* The bonds between the hacienda owners and their retainers and peasants put a premium on personal ties and loyalties. Caudillos often sprang from this hacienda environment, accustomed to personal power, binding their peons and followers to them through ties of kinship.

The Caudillo Phenomenon

The Peruvian historian Francisco García Calderón (1883–1953) described the caudillo phenomenon in rich terms that provide insight from the perspective of Peru, where caudillismo has flourished even to the end of the twentieth century.

"The generals [and early caudillos] imposed arbitrary limits upon the peoples: they were the creators of the history of the Americas; they impressed the crowds with pomp and pageantry, by military displays as brilliant and gaudy as the processions of the Roman Catholic Church, by uniforms, medals, and military order. They labeled themselves Regenerators, Restorers, Protectors. . . .

The individual acquired an extraordinary prestige, as in the time of the Tuscan Renaissance, the French Terror, or the English Revolution. The rude and bloodstained hand of the caudillo forced the amorphous masses into durable molds. Ignorant soldiers ruled; the evolution of the republics was uncertain. There was no history properly because there was no continuity. There was a perpetual repetition caused by successive rebellions. The same men appeared with the same promises and the same methods. The political comedy repeated itself periodically: rebellion, a dictator, a program of national restoration. Anarchy and militarism universally characterized political behavior. . . . The dictators, like the kings of modern states, must defeat local challenges, in the case of the Americas, the provincial generals. Men like Porfirio Díaz [Mexico], Gabriel García Moreno [Ecuador], and Antonio Guzmán Blanco [Venezuela] triumphed. Rebellion followed rebellion until the emergence of a tyrant who dominated the life of a nation for twenty or thirty years. . . .

They represented the new mixed races, traditions, and agriculture . . . these tyrants created a kind of democracy; they often depended on the support of the people, those of mixed races, the Indians, and Afro-Americans, against the oligarchies [prefiguring the populists of the twentieth century]. They dominated the former colonial elites, favored the mixture of the races, and liberated the slaves. . . ."

(Francisco García Calderón, *Latin America: Its Rise and Progress* [New York: Charles Scribner's Sons, 1913], pp. 86–96, from Bradford Burns, editor and contributor, *Latin America: Conflict and Creation: A Historical Reader* [Englewood Cliffs, N.J.: Prentice-Hall, 1993], pp. 64–65.)

The Mexican poet Octavio Paz explained in more lyrical terms this ingredient in the psychological makeup of the caudillo, the man who dominates. "'One word sums up the aggressiveness, insensitivity, invulnerability, and other attributes of the macho: power. It is force without the discipline of any notion of order: arbitrary power, the will without reins and without a set course. . . . The caciques, feudal lords, hacienda owners, politicians, generals, captains of industry . . . are all machos. . . .' "[2]

During and after the Wars of Independence, many caudillos emerged from classes other than the old landed aristocracy. Often they were mestizos who had

---

[2]Hugh M. Hamill, Jr., *Dictatorship in Spanish-America,* editor with introduction (New York: Alfred A. Knopf, 1965), p. 24.

risen through the military ranks. The habit of command was not traditional with them, and they sought to affirm their newly won power and authority by distinguishing themselves from the common man. A new style thus emerged.

It took many forms. In some instances, such as in Argentina and Venezuela, brute physical power characterized the caudillos, men who dominated other men by their strength and energy. Violence and terror often played a part in ensuring their rule.

To guarantee their strength and to demonstrate their power, they often sought wealth, sometimes acquiring it in subtle ways, sometimes simply stripping it away from others. Perhaps the most notorious examples came from the life of Facundo Quiroga, a regional caudillo of Argentina. He terrorized his opponents and competitors into submitting to his will. For example, he bid a ridiculously low sum for the right to collect the tithe and dared any others to bid above him. His critics labeled him a barbarian, and the legacy of Quiroga and others like him endured for many decades.

Later, in other circumstances, more discreet ways to get rich evolved, including influence peddling, monopolies on imports and manufacturing, lucrative contracts for public works from the state, contraband, and the acquisition of the best land through intimidation. In the twentieth century, as will be seen later, members of the Somoza family of Nicaragua exemplified the caudillo tradition, gaining power and expanding their dictatorship at the expense of people, state, honesty, and integrity.

Personalism thrived especially in the Latin American context of family loyalties. Families and dependents not only supported the caudillo, but also expected favors and positions in return. The religious duties of godfathering and godmothering (*compadrazco*) reinforced the cults of *personalismo*. The caudillos would often be godfathers to hundreds or even thousands of children, sealing their alliances even more firmly within this religious institution.

The personality cults that developed around many of the caudillos arose from their need to legitimize their source of power. Because they were not born with the majesty of monarchs and the rights of ancient nobilities, they sought other ways to establish their social and moral superiority, and hence their right to govern in the eyes of their followers. They glorified themselves with monuments, theatrical gestures, and extravagant uniforms and created around them an aura of magnificence.

In Mexico, Antonio López de Santa Anna edified himself in some of the more curious examples of pomp and circumstance. In one instance, he had his amputated leg buried in a solemn ceremony. He created an elaborate etiquette, including yellow coaches with valets in green livery and escorts of lancers in red uniforms and plumed hats, to celebrate his person and his power.

In Venezuela, as historian Robert L. Gilmore noted, caudillismo had a bent similar to that in much of the rest of Latin America. His description of the phenomenon in general, and as it was evoked in Venezuela in particular, is most enlightening.

The caudillos were not without utility and worth. They were essentially unifiers in vast regions where centrifugal forces pulled things apart. Politically, economically, and socially they sought to centralize power and control in their hands and, in

On the Nature of Caudillos

Caudillism as a system of political leadership for the state was an inherently unstable hierarchical arrangement, a structure composed of a network of personal alliances cemented together by community of interest, by force of personality, by ties of friendship and even of family. The scaffolding was enveloped in the brittle stuff of popular acceptance. What stability it possessed was due to the rule of political office and especially of the officer corps of the militia in systematizing relationships among the caudillos. As a political system it imposed limitations on the authority of the caudillo effective in inverse ratio to the degree of dominance achieved by the caudillo over his associates.

Caudillos were the natural leaders of a society whose colonial order was destroyed before the bases for an independent society had taken firm shape. Up to mid-nineteenth century the higher ranking combat-trained beneméritos [patriots], many of whom became members of or reverted to the land-owning upper class after 1825, were the instruments and leaders of rival political groups as a right earned by their part in the making of a nation. They were augmented and, as their numbers were thinned by death or failure, they were replaced by non-veteran caudillos, men who generated their own support, and would in time fight to the top. José Antonio Páez by his virtue and his brilliant career as guerrilla leader, as subordinate to Bolívar, and as Superior Military and Civil Chief of Venezuela, had established by 1827 his personal authority over much of what would be the nation of Venezuela. He became the archetype of the caudillo, perhaps in his own despite. He was never able to eliminate caudillism in Venezuelan society. It has been aptly pointed out that after Páez subdued the rebels of the War of the Reforms in 1835 the Presidents regularly came forth from conflict and were with one or another exception the personification of the guerrillas.

(Robert L. Gilmore, *Caudillism and Militarism in Venezuela, 1810—1910* [Athens, Ohio: Ohio University Press, 1964], pp. 50–51)

many instances, to suppress regional tendencies and to consolidate the integration of their nations as sought by the founders. In the following pages we will examine how the Latin American nations evolved in the age of the caudillos.

Argentina

In 1816 Argentine leaders declared their independence. From then until 1829, when Juan Manuel de Rosas took power, the nation was tugged about by many forces. The port city of Buenos Aires, which had served as the capital of the old viceroyalty of La Plata, attempted to unify the new nation under the leadership of *porteños*. In the 1820s those adhering to this point of view coalesced loosely under the title of centralists (*unitarios*).

On the other hand, the people of the interior of Argentina wished largely to govern themselves autonomously within a loose federation of provinces, and they

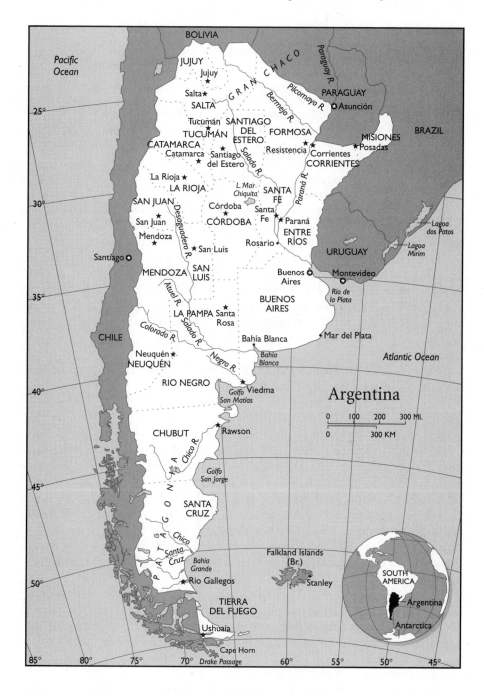

Argentina

evolved into the autonomists (*federales*). The division between the interests of these two groups hamstrung Argentina's development as a nation until well into the second half of the nineteenth century, when Buenos Aires finally triumphed over the provinces.

Between 1811 and 1829 a series of presidents, triumvirates, juntas, congresses, and other political activity confounded the attempts of Buenos Aires to impose its will absolutely. In the course of these two decades, Argentina tried unsuccessfully to keep Paraguay, Uruguay, and Upper Peru (later Bolivia) within the nation, fought a war with Brazil between 1825 and 1828, and finally bowed to the rule of Rosas.

Before Rosas, however, another man who rose and fell from power in the 1820s represented the modern vision of Argentina. Bernardino Rivadavia's program for Argentina struck a responsive chord among some urban, modernizing elements of the population, especially among the *porteños,* who looked beyond their shores for commerce and contacts with the countries of Europe and North America.

Rivadavia was born into a wealthy Buenos Aires family and married the daughter of the viceroy. He fought against the British attacks of 1806–1807 and then joined the conspirators of 1810. He served in several cabinets during the first decade of independence. Later he continued to serve in a number of capacities until the end of his political career in 1827, including serving as president in 1826–1827. He was, in short, one of the founders of the republic and a man of great influence during his career.

An admirer of the English and a believer in the positive influence of foreign contacts, Rivadavia encouraged free trade, foreign investment, and immigration. Irish and Basque sheepherders, English merchants, French shopkeepers, American seamen—they all arrived in considerable numbers during this period, swelling the local population and imparting a more cosmopolitan, outward-looking perspective.

Rivadavia's vision included importing the best of the intellectual influences from abroad and promoting Argentina's own culture. The University of Buenos Aires was founded in 1821, followed by a public library, a museum, and various other literary, scientific, and charitable societies. Rivadavia also sought to separate Church from state by various measures, including the suppression of monasteries and convents. Rivadavia was, in short, a liberal and enlightened thinker, devoted to a modern vision of Argentina. He met implacable resistance from a more conservative and primitive Argentina, an Argentina embodied in the person of Juan Manuel de Rosas.

In a fashion, Rosas was the typical caudillo of the times. Although not a celebrated veteran of the Wars of Independence, such as Páez of Venezuela, Santander of Colombia, or Santa Cruz of Bolivia, Rosas was, in every other way, a magnificent prototype for the Latin American caudillo. Thus, it is well worth considering the man and Argentina as classic examples of caudillos and the lands they ruled in the nineteenth century.

Rosas was above all else a great landowner in a country where land and cattle formed the twin pillars of wealth. The *estancias* were large holdings in the interior of Buenos Aires province, extending eastward and southward into the great plains or pampas. Cattle flourished in this region, and hides and salted or jerked beef became

Argentine cowboys, gauchos, on the cattle-rich pampas of their nation. Primitive and conservative in social customs and culture, they formed the backbone of support for such great caudillos as Juan Manuel de Rosas in the first half of the nineteenth century. Gauchos were romanticized by later generations of Argentines as the soul of their nation.

the principal exports of Argentina in the first half of the nineteenth century, much of the beef destined to feed the slaves of Brazil and Cuba. Between the 1830s and 1850s, exports of hides and salted beef tripled. Tallow—a by-product of the cattle industry—exports increased six times. And wool exports from the growing sheep industry jumped fivefold in the same period, attesting to an even greater growth and dependence upon the pastoral industries in Argentina. Much of the wool was destined for English carpet factories, which were one of the leading engines of the Industrial Revolution then stimulating the production and export of many basic commodities from Latin America.

Rosas inherited several *estancias* and was raised on the land, growing up in the rough-and-tumble society of the gaucho. Rosas was a manager, businessman, entrepreneur, and innovator, but, ultimately, his reputation was based on the image and reality of Rosas, the leader of gauchos. When he first put together a troop of cavalry in 1820 to help Buenos Aires defend itself against provincial armies (the autonomists) challenging the capital's authority, the troop was made up largely of gauchos and peons who worked on Rosas's *estancias*. They owed him loyalty, and in return Rosas protected and rewarded them.

The relationship between Rosas, the *patrón,* and his gauchos and peons, the clients, is described in the accompanying boxed material by John Lynch. It was an extremely important relationship, fundamental to the way society was organized not only in Argentina, but also in many other areas of nineteenth-century Latin America.

Rosas the Caudillo

The relation of patron and client was the essential bond, based upon a personal exchange of assets between these unequal partners. The landowner wanted labor, loyalty, and service in peace and war. The peon wanted subsistence and security. The estanciero [rancher] therefore was a protector, possessor of sufficient power to defend his dependents against marauding bands, recruiting-sergeants, and rival hordes. He is also a provider, who developed and defended local resources, and could give employment, food, and shelter. Thus a patron recruited a peonada. And these individual alliances were extended into a social pyramid, as patrons in turn became clients to more powerful men, until the peak of power was reached and all became clients of a super-patron, the caudillo.

(Lynch, *Rosas*, p. 108)

The key to Rosas's power in Argentina in the 1830s and 1840s was the structure of society, that very society that Rivadavia wanted to change. Society was profoundly conservative, rooted in the countryside and dependent upon the *estancia-saladero* (beef ranching) class for its prosperity. Change was suspect. Foreigners threatened *estancieros'* lifestyles and, ultimately, their control over the country. In their minds, on the other hand, the Church represented stability and order and thus retained a place of prominence and prestige. The *estancieros* felt abandoned by Buenos Aires when their *estancias* and livelihoods were threatened by Amerindian wars as the *estancieros*—such as Rosas—pushed more and more into the frontier regions in search of land. And the provinces especially resented Rivadavia's centralizing measures, such as the Constitution of 1826.

As the 1820s came to an end, Rosas rose to prominence, backed by his gauchos and supported by the *estanciero-saladero* class. He allied with the federalists, but, in fact, evolved into a ruthless caudillo. He was the center of Argentina. The ideological battles between autonomists and federalists faded in significance in the face of Rosas's consolidation of power.

By 1835 Rosas had fought his way to the top, and he remained the supreme caudillo of the caudillos until overthrown in 1852. He divided his world between those who supported him, *rosistas* (Rosas supporters) and those who did not, anti-*rosistas*, and he suppressed the opposition ruthlessly. Terror, violent reprisals, and executions reached their peak in the period 1838–1842. Decapitations became a ritual form of political execution perpetrated by a secret society called the *mazorca*. Rosas was challenged all during his long regime, but only at the high cost of imprisonment, death, or exile. He, in reality, ruled with an undisputed sovereignty, well beyond the constitutional rights and guarantees envisioned by the generation of Argentines who fashioned the independence of the country.

Although Rosas subdued the province of Buenos Aires, he continued to meet resistance to his rule in other areas of Argentina, especially from the province of Entre Rios and its caudillo, Justo José de Urquiza, who eventually led the overthrow of Rosas in 1852. Meanwhile, Rosas's insistent meddling in the affairs of Uruguay provoked crisis after crisis in the 1830s and 1840s, especially with his Brazilian neighbors and the English and the French whose commercial interests were threatened by Rosas's attempt to dominate the Rio de la Plata region. In fact, the French and English on several occasions between 1838 and 1848 blockaded the port of Buenos Aires to force Rosas to yield on several issues—from the treatment of their nationals in Argentina to Rosas's eleven-year attempt to dominate politics in Uruguay.

While Rosas ruled, the old *estanciero-saladero* class drew its livelihood from the continued expansion of the salted beef (charque) business. But the limits of the business were being reached in the 1840s and 1850s. The traditional markets—the slaves of Brazil and Cuba—were on the decline, and overproduction depressed the industry. Furthermore, the developing sheep industry, with its infusion of new immigrants, new business ways, and its encroachment on the *estancias,* pushed Rosas and his followers for change. To condemn Rosas, exiles from abroad, led by such men as Estéban Echevarría and Juan B. Alberdi, joined forces with other anti-*rosistas,* the Uruguayans, and the English and French. A powerful coalition of Rosas's enemies finally coalesced in 1852 and ousted Rosas. Ironically rescued by the British, he went into exile in England and lived the life of an English country squire until his death in 1877 at the age of eighty-eight.

Brazil

After the "Grito de Ipiranga" of September 1822, Brazil became independent from Portugal. Portugal attempted to resist this act, but, in truth, its old colony was too strong and determined. A few skirmishes at sea and battles on land produced far fewer casualties than the Spanish-American wars. That relatively easy transition alone separated Brazil's independence movement from that of most of the old Spanish colonies—such as Mexico, Venezuela, and Peru—which had suffered through long and agonizing wars for independence.

No less significant for Brazil was the accession of Pedro as the first emperor of Brazil in 1822. Pedro was the son of the king of Portugal, a Braganza, and thus *legitimate* royalty. He was accepted as such by most Brazilians, providing for the easiest and most successful transition to independence of all Latin American nations. Furthermore, Pedro accepted willingly the concept of a *constitutional monarchy,* reinforcing his initial acceptance and popularity among Brazilians. The peaceful period of Brazilian independence was, nonetheless, short-lived. Between 1824 and 1831 Pedro managed to antagonize thoroughly his Brazilian subjects, leading to his abdication in 1831.

The basic qualm that Brazilians had with Pedro was his Portuguese birth and his consequent tendency to overlook Brazilian priorities and indulge his Portuguese interests. It began with a constitutional assembly in 1823 that was in the process of writing a constitution too republican and too limiting for Pedro's absolutist leanings. He dissolved that assembly and essentially wrote his own constitution for Brazil in 1824. It gave the emperor broad powers, including the novel one of harmonizing or moderating among the three branches of government. The Constitution indeed lasted until 1889, but in the 1820s, many Brazilian nationalists felt that it endowed their Portuguese-leaning emperor with too many powers because he not only oversaw the executive branch but also exercised the moderating power.

In 1826 Pedro sent an army to Uruguay to counteract Argentine advances in the contested lands. The Cisplatine province—or the *Banda Oriental,* as it was known by the Argentines—erupted into a revolt and declared its allegiance to Argentina. This revolt was led by Uruguayan nationalists (Cisplatine, Banda Oriental, and Uruguay are for all practical purposes the same territory) known as the "Thirty-Three Immortals." Pedro was determined to keep the province, which had long been disputed by the Spanish and Portuguese during the colonial period. The war proved costly and bitter and, in the end, was resolved by a compromise offered by England: Let Uruguay be a free nation, a buffer to stand forever between Brazil and Argentina. Brazilian nationalists felt that Pedro had dragged the country into a frustrating dispute that more reflected old Portuguese aggressions and competition with Spain than the true priorities of Brazil.

Other actions further alienated Pedro from his Brazilian friends who had so enthusiastically supported him in 1822 when he issued the "Grito de Ipiranga." When Pedro's father died in Portugal in 1826, Pedro wished to succeed to that throne as well and to reunite Brazil and Portugal under his rule. Brazilians recoiled at that possibility and told Pedro that in effect he could not have his cake and eat it, too. If he insisted on that course, he would have to give up Brazil. He abdicated his claim in Portugal in favor of his daughter, but he continued to manipulate affairs in Portugal, much to the chagrin of Brazilians.

Even Pedro's libertine habits, which included flamboyant affairs and mistresses, offended Brazilians, not so much because Brazilians were stuffy moralists—they were not—but rather because the peccadilloes were committed by Pedro. In one celebrated instance, Pedro's current mistress, an actress named Ludovina Custodia, was ravished between acts of a performance by the libidinous emperor, who could not resist the temptation. The no-doubt breathless actress was forced to bring her public performance to a close early.

Meanwhile, other Brazilians, especially those in the provinces far away from the capital at Rio de Janeiro, were more or less spontaneously taking their grievances against Pedro into the streets. In Minas Gerais, in Bahia, and in other provinces, riots and revolts were led by a mixture of nationalists, some who were committed to eliminating the monarchy altogether, some who wanted just the end of Pedro's rule, some who were simply anti-Portuguese. When in 1830 the news came that revolutions were sweeping across Europe, challenging the old monarchies and promoting constitutional republics, Brazilians were electrified. Was not Pedro an absolutist? Were not his Portuguese sympathies out of sync with the Brazilian reality? The movement to get rid of Pedro culminated in April 1831. Hoping to at least preserve the monarchy and his five-year-old son's inheritance, Pedro abdicated in favor of his son. A regency was appointed to govern during the boy's minority. Pedro sailed into exile. While still plotting in Portugal, he died a few years later at the age of thirty-six.

Pedro II

The transition from Pedro I to his son, who became Pedro II, was marked by much competition among the different political factions in Brazil, from absolutists to radical republicans. In the end, moderate elements prevailed and preserved Brazil intact until 1840, when Pedro II was declared of age and invested with imperial authority, bringing the regency to an end. However, the decade of the 1830s was marked by scattered rebellions, such as in Bahia in the north and Rio Grande do Sul in the south, which sought more autonomy from Rio de Janeiro and a higher degree of federalism.

In effect, the various rebels found the regents who governed in Pedro II's place from 1831 to 1840 to be overly dictatorial, imposing their wishes and those of the centralists onto regions that wished a higher degree of self-government. The most serious of these rebellions, the War of the Farrapos in Rio Grande do Sul, lasted for ten years and taxed the resources of the empire. In the end, it seemed that the desire of most Brazilians was to see Pedro become the emperor in fact as well as in name. A group of powerful supporters forced the issue in 1840, and Pedro was invested with imperial authority at the tender age of fifteen.

Pedro II's character had much to do with his acceptability to most Brazilians. Brazilian-born, Brazilian-educated, and thoroughly imbued with a strong sense of nationalism by his tutors, he gave no cause to doubt his loyalties and his allegiance, unlike his father before him. Furthermore, he was a serious and highly moral young man who became a dedicated husband and father and was an example that Brazilians took great pride in. After the declaration of his majority in 1840, Brazil moved into a halcyon period of its history, called the Second Empire. It lasted as long as Emperor Pedro II reigned, which was for almost half a century.

While separatism, regional rebellions, and scattered manifestations of provincialism and federalism kept the regents and Pedro II occupied during the 1830s and 1840s, other currents were altering traditions inherited from the long colonial past. None eventually altered Brazil more than the gradual prohibition of the slave trade, which in effect struck at an institution—slavery—that was so intimately associated with Brazil's traditional economic mainstay, the production of sugar and a new crop, coffee.

The basic issue was between the interests of the powerful *fazendeiro* class, and the abolitionist sentiments growing in strength in Great Britain. The *fazendeiros* were committed to slavery as indispensable to their plantation economy, whereas Great Britain, the ruler of the seas, was determined to crush the infamous slave trade with its powerful navy. England in 1826 negotiated a treaty with Brazil that called for abolishment of the slave trade, and Brazil passed a law to that effect in 1831, but it was widely ignored.

As the illegal traffic in slaves continued in the 1830s and 1840s, the English pressured Brazil to truly eradicate it. British warships increased their vigilance off the coasts of Africa and Brazil and often offended Brazilian sensitivities by taking high-handed actions. It was difficult, if not impossible, to withstand the sustained enmity of the world's greatest naval power, and, in truth, there was much sentiment among Brazilians to end the slave trade as well. In 1850 Brazil put real teeth into enforcing the law of 1831, and, together with the vigilance of the English, the trade effectively was snuffed out within three years.

The end of the slave trade coincided with a new era in Brazil. Peace was restored to the land as the quarreling regions accepted the rule of Pedro II. Brazil's territorial integrity was preserved, new forces for the economic development of the country were at work, and prosperity was to become the password for the rest of Pedro II's rule.

Uruguay

Uruguay's eventual independence, finally declared in 1828, resulted largely from its strategic geographic position between Brazil and Argentina. Called the "Banda Oriental" for most of the colonial era because of its location on the eastern bank of the Uruguay River, Uruguay and its greatest independence era hero, José Gervasio Artigas, sought to identify the country's true interests during the long struggle for autonomy and nationhood between 1811 and 1828.

After Artigas was driven into exile in Paraguay in 1820 by Brazilian forces commanded by General Carlos Frederico Lecor, Uruguay was integrated as the Cisplatine province into the Brazilian empire that emerged in 1823. However, neither Uruguayan nationalists nor Argentine centralists were satisfied with the Banda Oriental's incorporation into the new Brazilian empire. In 1825 a band of Uruguayans, the "Thirty-Three Immortals" led by Juan Antonio Lavalleja, invaded their homeland, supported by Argentina. War broke out with Brazil, and it not only rolled back and forth across Uruguay, but also seriously disrupted trade and commerce along the River Plata estuary, especially for British and French merchants whose livelihoods and profits depended upon stability. The British government argued for the creation of a buffer state between Brazil and Argentina, and the two powers, unable to defeat each other, agreed. In 1828 a peace treaty was concluded, and Uruguay emerged as an independent nation, writing its first constitution in 1830.

Uruguay was a small nation, the smallest in South America, with an economy much like Argentina's, dedicated to the cattle industry. Its population, little more than sixty thousand, was made up of Amerindians, blacks who had drifted south from Brazil, and a sprinkling of European settlers. In the 1880s and 1890s its population was swelled by European immigrants. Almost fifty thousand came before the turn of the century, mostly from France, Italy, and parts of Spain such as the Canary Islands, contributing to Uruguay's growing racial homogeneity.

Uruguay continued to be the object of ambitious Argentine and Brazilian rulers, and its growing foreign population almost invited foreign intervention by European powers determined to protect their nationals and their influence in the River Plata region. In the 1830s a civil war between two of its early leaders—both presidents for a time—not only provoked a series of interventions by foreigners, but also caused the formation of Uruguay's two political parties, the *blancos* and the *colorados*, both of which have survived as the principal political parties in modern Uruguay. The *blancos* formed around the leadership of Manuel Oribe, whereas the *colorados* were founded by Fructuoso Rivera. In 1839 the civil war spread as Rosas of

Argentina, the French, and the English all became involved in one form or another, attempting to extend their influence in the Rio de la Plata region. The war lasted until 1852, when a potent coalition of Rosas's enemies, including Brazil and Uruguay, finally combined to overthrow the great Argentine caudillo.

At mid-century Uruguay was only emerging from a long period of internal warfare, aggravated by the near-constant presence of Argentine armies, French or English supporters, naval blockades, and civil war. Naturally the country suffered, and the cattle industry, its basic livelihood, declined. Significant numbers of immigrants from Europe, especially from Italy, were beginning to transform the country ethnically. In the main, Uruguay was still destined for much political strife in the second half of the century.

Paraguay

The story of Paraguay from independence to 1840 is largely the story of one man, Dr. José Gaspar de Francia. He became dictator of the nation in 1814, consolidated his hold in 1820, and thereafter ruled absolutely until dying from natural causes in 1840. His autocratic regime was cloaked in mysticism and dark, secret rule, although he was not simply a ruthless tyrant. He was a complicated man imbued with an intense Paraguayan nationalism and an uncompromising honesty. He certainly was a caudillo of the period, although behaving in some ways differently than those who sprang up in Argentina, Peru, or Mexico, for example. However, he was no less a man who ruled with the iron will of caudillos, and he left an unforgettable mark on his country's modern history.

During a period of intense instability in the Rio de la Plata region, Francia withdrew Paraguay from the international strife and isolated the nation from its neighbors and from foreigners commercially and culturally. A well-educated man, he nonetheless distrusted the Argentines, the Brazilians, the English, and the French. He barred them from Paraguay, and if they entered he arrested and detained them. One of them was the distinguished French botanist Aime Bonpland. Otherwise, Francia interrupted the normal ebb and flow of commerce and diplomacy between Paraguay and the world. Even though Paraguay was isolated in the extreme from the currents of the rapidly changing world about it, Paraguay's independence was guaranteed by Francia's rigid neutrality and xenophobic nationalism. His contributions ran deeper, however, than merely guaranteeing political independence in a region seesawing between the ambitions of the two powers sharing its borders: Brazil and Argentina.

Francia fashioned an internal regime that eliminated the old ruling elite, made up largely of Creoles and Spaniards with a smattering of foreigners. Between 1820 and 1823 Francia suppressed a conspiracy of his enemies from the old ruling class, executed many, drove others into exile, and confiscated their properties. While destroying the traditional elite, he actively fostered a policy of intermarriage among the mestizos who made up the great majority of the population (descendants of the Guarani Indians and Spanish settlers), and they—the common folk of Paraguay—benefited from Francia's policies.

Francia confiscated Church wealth and, combining it with those assets stripped from the old elites, spread it among the people of Paraguay. He redistributed land to the small farmers and ranchers of the nation and forced them to diversify their production away from traditional export crops of yerba mate and tobacco, which had chained the nation to the whims of a marketplace economy controlled by foreigners. By the 1830s Paraguay was self-sufficient in corn, rice, dried manioc, ham, cheese, and other food products. Francia lowered taxes and made his government extremely efficient, an accomplishment that astounds us today. He never had more than one or two ministers and a few secretaries to do the business of government, instead doing most of the work himself—an incredible commitment of one person. He was rigidly honest, sober, and totally dedicated.

He championed the principle that "private interest should be subordinated to the common and general welfare."[3] He practiced this principle with conviction and success. Paraguay in 1840 was on the whole a healthier, more prosperous, and more peaceful place to live than were any of its neighbors.

But there was a price to pay. Francia's successes with Paraguay were achieved at the expense of a total, despotic control that has given Francia the dubious honor of being the model dictator for students of history. When he died in 1840 he left a Paraguay strong and intact, but also subordinated entirely to the will of one man, even when his supporters defended his rule as visionary or successful. It is not surprising then that his successors were caudillos, equally ruthless in their rule. They followed the tradition established by Francia, governing the nation molded by a man known in Paraguayan history as "the Dictator."

Whereas Francia was somewhat of an ascetic, his successor, the corpulent Carlos Antonio López, most certainly was not. A huge man physically with immense appetites, López also was a nationalist like Francia, dedicated to protecting Paraguay in the midst of warlike, bickering neighbors such as Argentina under Rosas. Under López, Paraguay was opened more to the world, and education was improved considerably; the caudillo sought to strengthen his nation. His son, Francisco Solano López, succeeded him in 1862. Within three years Paraguay would became involved in a disastrous war against Brazil, Uruguay, and Argentina that shattered the small nation and left it almost prostrate for the remainder of the nineteenth century.

Chile

Chile has long been thought of as exceptional in Latin America. Following a short period of instability in the 1820s after winning independence, it settled into an era of political stability and economic prosperity that lasted almost to the end of the century. The transfer of power from president to president-elect every five years stood in striking contrast to Chile's caudillo-ridden neighbors. Political order, in turn, helped promote economic development, especially in Chile's mining and commercial sectors, which gave Chile the strength to impose its will on its neighbors and to emerge as a power on the South American continent.

---

[3]Richard Alan White, *Paraguay's Autonomous Revolution, 1810–1840* (Albuquerque: University of New Mexico Press, 1978), p. 99.

A closer look at Chile produces a slightly less dazzling picture. What emerged in the 1830s was an authoritarian form of government that in truth possessed few democratic or liberal elements. It was fashioned by a coalition of the wealthy landowners and merchants, brilliantly led by a man named Diego Portales (1793–1837), and it denied the average Chilean peasants, miners, and stevedores a share of Chile's new wealth and power. In a way, the price of Chile's peace and stability in the nineteenth century was a sacrifice of liberal principles and economic sharing. Yet, Chile's stability stood in such remarkable contrast to that of its neighbors that its history still elicits admiration from students of its past.

To the observer in the 1820s, however, Chile appeared to be no saner a place to live and work than was any other place in Latin America. Chile, too, reverberated to the beat of marching armies as *caudillos* rose and fell in a frustrating parody of government.

Yet, the instability proved short-lived. A liberal constitution written in 1828 provoked a revolt by more conservative elements, which in turn led to the Constitution of 1833, which was to survive almost to the end of the century. It was written by Mariano Egaña, a well-traveled man who served Chile as envoy to England in the 1820s and came away with a tremendous respect for the balance of powers between king, lords, and commoners in that nation. The Constitution that Egaña wrote for his own country reflected that respect, although Egaña was careful to adapt those principles that he so admired to the Chilean reality. Although Egaña wrote the Constitution, the real spirit behind the origins of the "autocratic republic" in the 1830s was Portales.

Born into an upper-middle-class family in 1793, Portales naturally felt a part of the privileged class in Chile. Two of his ancestors had been colonial governors of Chile, and his father enjoyed a royal appointment as superintendent of the mint. Portales went into trade and became a successful businessman. When he plunged into politics in the late 1820s and 1830s, he brought a no-nonsense perspective to bear. He formed a powerful alliance between the Church, the military, and the landowners. They emphasized the absolute necessity for law and order, for fiscal integrity, and for a strong, centralized government. This, in fact, was the type of government that Portales—even though he never served as president—forged in the 1830s.

His attitude toward a government of law and order perhaps was best summarized by a statement attributed to him: "The stick and the cake, justly and opportunely administered, are the specifics with which any nation can be cured, however inveterate its bad habits may be."[4] Portales enforced a strict honesty and efficiency in government, suppressed banditry and disorder in the countryside, and, in effect, paved the way for the economic prosperity and international success that marked Chile's passage through most of the rest of the century. A successful war waged between 1836 and 1839 against Peru and Bolivia, allied in a confederation, heightened Chile's national consciousness and self-esteem. Economic prosperity meanwhile

---

[4]Brian Loveman, *Chile: The Legacy of Hispanic Capitalism* (New York: Oxford University Press, 1979), p. 138.

issued from two vital sectors of its economy: the mines of northern Chile and the great estates of the central valley.

Although silver and gold both were extracted from the arid hills and mountains of Chile's northern desert region, copper became Chile's leading export in the 1830s and 1840s. Chile's mines were so rich that, indeed, by mid-century Chile held first place in world production, a lead that endured until the 1880s. Nitrate exports also increased rapidly after mid-century and helped fuel Chile's rising economic prosperity. The foreign exchange generated by these vital exports in turn promoted political stability during much of the century.

The great haciendas of the central valley also prospered, especially from the export of wheat and flour not only to their traditional market of Peru, but also to lands far away on the rim of the Pacific such as California and Australia. Gold booms at mid-century in these areas helped promote an incredibly rapid expansion of Chile's agricultural exports. Between the 1840s and 1860s, for example, wheat, flour, and barley exports quintupled in value.

As Chile entered this period of economic prosperity, the capital city of Santiago and its port of Valparaiso rose to even greater prominence in the nineteenth century. Valparaiso attracted a large community of foreigners—especially Englishmen—as it blossomed into an intermediary center of trade and commerce in the Pacific. Santiago, with a population of over fifty thousand at mid-century, emerged as an intellectual and cultural center in South America. The founding of the University of Chile in 1842 symbolized this role of Santiago. Many expatriates from all over South America found a home in a stable Chile, away from the feuding caudillos and the instabilities of their homelands in this first half of the century.

Peru and Bolivia

While Chile prospered economically and maintained political order, its two neighbors to the north, Peru and Bolivia, stumbled into independence with considerably less stability. An attempted union in the 1830s between the two nations failed, stagnation rather than growth marked their economies, and they both arrived at mid-century worse off—measured by most indicators—than they had been at the end of the eighteenth century.

Bolivia was hampered in its development during the nineteenth century by being basically a landlocked nation in the interior of South America. Its limited access to the sea—through the remote Pacific port of Cobija or down the long Paraná River to the Rio de la Plata estuary controlled by other nations on the Atlantic—placed it at the mercy of its stronger neighbors, especially Argentina, Chile, and Peru. Compounding the problem of geographic isolation was the stagnation of its mining economy. A lack of capital for the important silver mining industry proved to be "fatal for sustained growth in the national economy," in the words of one of Bolivia's most astute students.[5] Even with such enlightened early leaders as José

---

[5]Klein, p. 114.

Antonio de Sucre, its first president, and an equally able successor, Andrés Santa Cruz, who governed through the 1830s, Bolivia stagnated. Furthermore, immense expenditures on the army, sometimes amounting to 40 and 50 percent of the government budget, strangled efforts at internal improvements to better the economy. The result was not measured simply in economic terms.

Amerindian tributes survived from the colonial period and continued to constitute the principal source of government revenue—at least 40 percent—through mid-century. The result was the continued subservience of the great majority of Bolivia's Amerindian population to the small white and mestizo elite. In effect, a system of social and racial inequality survived the Wars of Independence, the constitutions, and the fine rhetoric of liberty, republicanism, and equality. More than 80 percent of the population spoke only Quechua or Aymara and possessed a profoundly agricultural and traditional culture far removed from the currents passing through the ports and capitals of Bolivia's neighbors. Of those neighbors, none was more intimately involved in Bolivia's internal affairs than Peru.

Bolívar withdrew from Peru in 1826, frustrated by what he considered to be Peruvian perfidy and disloyalty. The Liberator's armies had been victorious on the battlefields, but he could not seem to impose his will on the Peruvians, who plotted and schemed to get rid of him. Peru's politics subsequently dissolved into factions and then chaos. Between 1823 and 1850, for example, six constitutions were proclaimed, and at least thirty men occupied the executive office. Population declined between 1800 and 1850, and the presence of English merchants and capital shrank precipitously in the late 1820s due to glutted local markets and a moribund mining sector. Even the capital city of Lima, once the center of a resplendent viceroyalty that ruled over all Spanish South America, was reported by travelers as tarnished and inward-looking.

From these inauspicious beginnings, however, certain dreams of past glories mingled with visions of future glories. Among the most powerful of these was the reunification of Bolivia and Peru. Both General Andrés Santa Cruz of Bolivia and General Agustín Gamarra of Peru, who came to power in 1829, shared the desire for strength through unity. Both were mestizos born in the Andes Mountains common to Peru and Bolivia and, although rivals for power, they strove for the same end. Gamarra failed in a planned invasion of Bolivia, but Santa Cruz was more successful.

In 1836 Santa Cruz brought Peru and Bolivia together into a confederation and had himself declared its "grand protector." The Peru-Bolivia Confederation, however, proved most unacceptable to Chile. Chile viewed the confederation as a threat to the balance of power and international political equilibrium in South America. A strong Peru threatened Chile in two ways: as a rising commercial power in the Pacific and as an unstabilizing internal force.

Chile was extremely irritated that a favorable commercial treaty signed in 1835 between Peru and Chile was nullified in 1836 by the new Santa Cruz government. The treaty had been signed earlier when a rival of Santa Cruz, Felipe Salaverry, temporarily occupied the presidency in Peru. Santa Cruz's government also allowed an insurrectionary expedition led by a rival for power in Chile, Ramón Freire, to sail from Peruvian ports in 1836. This act provoked the Chileans to declare war on Peru and Bolivia. The war lasted three years.

Before it was over, Argentina also joined the fray against the Peru-Bolivia Confederation. Argentina, then under Rosas, wished to incorporate territories along the Argentine-Bolivian border (principally the province of Tarija) that had been disputed since the Wars of Independence. Furthermore, many of Rosas's enemies had fled into Bolivia, where they found sanctuary, and Rosas wished to bring down the Santa Cruz government that aided his enemies.

The Battle of Yungay in 1839 ended the war. A stunning military triumph for Chile, it broke the confederation, and Peru and Bolivia went their separate ways after Santa Cruz fled into exile.

After the passion for the confederation subsided, the combatants, especially Peruvians, were drawn to matters other than political intrigues and military maneuvers. A commercial revolution was beginning on some barren islands off the coast of Peru, and the promise of new wealth mesmerized the latent entrepreneurs in Peru, both native and foreign.

The basis of this commercial revolution was a rather prosaic commodity called *guano*—bird dung. For thousands of years sea birds had been visiting the islands off the coast of Peru after they fed on the teeming sea life in the cold Humboldt Current. Bird droppings had accumulated to depths of hundreds of feet on these islands. Although the ancient peoples of Peru had long realized and carefully exploited the fertilizing properties of guano, it was not until the 1840s that North American and European farmers discovered guano's rich agricultural benefits.

Guano was soon being hauled by hundreds of ships from the islands of Peru to the ports of England and North America to be sold to turnip and tobacco planters eager to replenish their exhausted soils with this remarkable fertilizer. The Age of Guano had dawned in Peru, and before it ended in the 1870s when the guano piles were depleted, guano netted over $600 million on the retail markets of the world.

The guano boom transformed Peru. The new wealth not only flowed from taxes into the government's coffers, but also it hastened the formation of a Peruvian commercial class that sought to modernize the country as rapidly as possible. For example, the Peruvian government abolished slavery in 1854 and compensated the slave-owners with the new revenues. More important, perhaps, was the abolition of the Indian tribute. Liberating the black slaves and removing the stigma of the Indian tribute did not radically alter Peru's economic and social structures, but they did *symbolize* the new mood of the modern age that stressed the individual and individual natural rights. They bore testimony to the conspicuous relationship between the application of classic liberal doctrines and Peru's great new wealth. This relationship underscored the links between the economic and social consequences of the Age of Guano in Peru.

Gran Colombia

Gran Colombia was created in 1821 from three former Spanish colonies—Ecuador, Colombia, and Venezuela. The new republic of Gran Colombia, though born with

Ships taking guano off the Chincha Islands, Peru. Beginning in the 1840s and lasting until the 1870s, bird droppings called guano were exported from Peru to Europe and North America for use as excellent fertilizers. This "guano boom" fueled the first modernization of Peru. In the background, behind the ships, one can see the guano "stacks" already depleted by the removal of millions of tons.

great optimism and forged by the Liberator, Simón Bolívar, himself, turned out to be short-lived. It ceased to exist in 1830 when Venezuela and Ecuador broke away to become independent states.

Ecuador

Ecuador, the smallest of the three new nations, was divided by the rivalry of two cities and the competition of two powerful men from 1830 to mid-century. The capital city of Quito, set in a high mountain valley in the Andes, and the Pacific port of

Guayaquil had been competing against each other since colonial times. Independence merely changed the players for these two rival cities.

Quito was the seat of government, aristocratic, cultured, proud, and a bit pompous in its attitudes toward the rest of the country. Guayaquil, in contrast, was afflicted with a hot and muggy climate, flooding, and periodic ravages of tropical diseases. Nonetheless, natives of the port city loved it fervently. Their commercial drive, mercantile spirit, and close contact with the world bred an independent spirit and a willingness to adapt to new ways and circumstances. In the post-1830 period, Guayaquil almost naturally emerged as a promoter of change and progress associated with the liberal ideology. Quito embraced conservatism with equal ardor.

The preeminent spokesman for liberalism in Ecuador in this period was Vicente Rocafuerte. Not surprisingly, he was a native of Guayaquil. After a long residence abroad, he returned to Guayaquil in 1833 and soon emerged as the principal challenger to the conservative rule that Quito wished to impose on Ecuador. Rocafuerte's opponent was President Juan José Flores, elected in 1830 as Ecuador's first president.

Flores was born in Venezuela and possessed a distinguished war record. Although darker skinned than most *quiteños* (natives of Quito) would have preferred, Flores had married into a prominent family and secured a position of prominence in the capital. Furthermore, the army's backing (with many Venezuelans still in it) guaranteed him a powerful base of support. Flores's instincts were to be tough and autocratic at a time when many centrifugal forces—some pro-Gran Colombia, some pro-Peru, and some pro-Spain—threatened the fragile new nation. Conservatives rallied around Flores, especially because Flores supported the Church and the landed aristocrats.

Liberal discontent with the Venezuelan-born dictator and with his foreign troops welled up in 1833 and erupted into a revolt in Guayaquil. Liberal intellectuals in Quito added their backing to the Guayaquil rebels led by Rocafuerte.

Flores defeated the liberals and captured Rocafuerte. But then he surprised his friends and foes alike in one of those about-faces that mystify students of the past. Flores freed Rocafuerte, and in 1835 Rocafuerte was elected president. Why? Flores was more of a pragmatist than an ideologue, and compromise with the strong liberal opposition was infinitely better than protracted warfare and division. Besides, recognizing that Ecuador was not yet ready for political democracy so dear to liberals, Rocafuerte proved to be as authoritarian as he was progressive in his four years as president. He introduced a new constitution brimming with such liberal principles as popular sovereignty, guaranteed individual freedoms, and anticlericalism, but he governed with a strong hand. During his term he expanded education, promoted road building, and established fiscal order.

In 1839 Flores was again elected president, but when his four-year term expired, the old dictator, now more conservative and unyielding, scrapped the Constitution and devised a new one enabling him to be reelected for an eight-year term. It was quickly dubbed the "Charter of Slavery" by liberals, who rose in revolt and drove Flores into exile in 1845. From exile in Europe Flores plotted his return to power and added a novel twist: He would restore monarchy to Ecuador by bringing a European prince to sit on the new throne. Furthermore, Flores was eager to restore what he considered Ecuador's rightful boundaries. These were based on sometimes vague territorial divisions inherited from the colonial period. The Ecuadorian claims included provinces now belonging to Peru and Colombia.

Peru, under President Ramón Castilla, acted decisively. Not only was the restoration of a monarchy repugnant to most Latin Americans, but also Flores's ambitions at the expense of Colombia and Peru threatened equilibrium throughout the continent. Castilla called for a congress of American nations to convene in Lima in 1847.

Castilla presided over this General American Congress, which brought together delegates from Colombia, Ecuador, Peru, Bolivia, and Chile. The Flores plot to establish a monarchy in Ecuador was not the sole order of business on their agenda. The delegates also wished to cooperate in making common policies to protect the future integrity and independence of Latin American nations. The backdrop to this congress, which met from December 1847 until March 1848, was the U.S. war with Mexico.

The delegates were of two minds concerning the war, reflecting the ambivalence that Latin Americans have felt toward the United States over the years. They viewed the war as a brazen example of Yankee manifest destiny and territorial aggrandizement and condemned it thoroughly. Yet, *because* the United States was involved in a war, the dependence of Latin America upon the United States to help prevent intrusions from Europe—such as the one being plotted by Flores—was sharply undermined, leaving Latin America more vulnerable and exposed. When the Peruvians sought to buy two steamers from the United States, for example, they were unsuccessful. The United States needed all of its resources to wage war on Mexico.

In the end, the delegates produced little more than some nonpolitical conventions regarding commerce, maritime rights of neutrals, duties and powers of diplomats, and postal matters. And the Flores expedition eventually stalled. Spain—where the Flores expeditionaries were recruited—and England—where they expected to sail from—blocked the Flores plans.

Flores's ambitions and intrigues kept the country off balance during the next fifteen years. Rocafuerte died in Lima in 1847—a great loss to a country that was plunged into internal strife until 1861. No fewer than eleven changes of government occurred during that period before another truly strong man, Gabriel García Moreno, imposed order.

Colombia

Colombia went its own way after Ecuador and Venezuela seceded from Gran Colombia in 1830. What happened to Bolívar's grand vision of a united state, founded on the former viceroyalty of New Granada? Basically, independence proved to be a two-edged sword for the leaders of Gran Colombia. Long campaigns fought to free their lands from Spanish rule bred an independence of mind and spirit. Venezuelan and Ecuadorian leaders were unwilling to acknowledge the superiority of a government located in Bogotá, a government perceived as too distant and too unresponsive to their regional needs. Besides, both Ecuador and Venezuela had been governed as separate provinces during the viceroyalty, and both had become accustomed to a measure of local rule under Spain. It was natural to complete the Wars of Independence by moving toward formal independence, as they did in 1830.

Colombia did not challenge the breakup of the short-lived Gran Colombia. It looked to one of its great Wars of Independence heroes, Francisco de Paula Santander, for leadership as it emerged in the 1830s.

Santander is generally credited with inspiring formation of the Liberal Party in Colombia. He was elected the first president of Colombia in 1832 and governed until 1837. Mildly anticlerical, Santander promoted education and economic reforms in the liberal fashion of the day. Yet, he was also a caudillo and hanged members of the opposition who conspired against his rule. This mixture of authoritarianism and liberalism, perhaps odd from the point of view of North American students of Latin America, was perfectly consistent with the temper of the times. Liberalism was a fashionable and persuasive set of ideals, but a strong hand was needed to fend off chaos and political anarchy. Santander, like Rocafuerte of Ecuador and Santa Cruz of Bolivia, fit the mold.

After Santander stepped down in 1837, political factionalism divided Colombia in the late 1830s and through the 1840s, leading to the formal establishment of the Liberal and Conservative parties before mid-century. In fact, no other nation in Latin America suffered more from this basic political division in the nineteenth century than did Colombia. Reinforcing the traditional differences between liberals and conservatives in Colombia (see Chapter Six for a more thorough discussion of this phenomenon in Latin America) was Colombia's strong regionalism. Its political and economic power was diffused among three or four regions—principally Santander, Antioquia, Cundinamarca, and the Caribbean provinces. Competition among these regions often led Colombians to feel a stronger sense of identification and affiliation with those regions than with their nation, especially with its capital at Bogotá. Liberals, given to federalism, tended to support this feeling; Conservatives, centralists in the main, naturally opposed it.

Venezuela

Like its neighbors both north and south, Venezuela rode into the first stages of its modern history as an independent nation on the strong back of a remarkably able and successful caudillo, José Antonio Páez. Born into a humble family, Páez developed into one of Bolívar's greatest cavalry leaders and, after Bolívar, Venezuela's preeminent military hero. He not only led Venezuela out of Gran Colombia in 1830 but also, in one fashion or another, dominated his nation until mid-century. Part of his success in imposing order and stability was due to his excellent qualities as a caudillo. A remarkable transition in agriculture in Venezuela also helped Páez in the reconstruction of his country after the turmoil of the Wars of Independence.

Although traditional exports such as cotton, cacao, tobacco, and cattle products expanded considerably after the wars, it was coffee that truly took off and set the pace. Between 1831 and 1841 coffee production tripled, and the subsequent economic prosperity facilitated the political tranquillity that Páez imposed.

As one student of Venezuela noted, coffee "planters engaged in an orgy of planting and expansion" to take advantage of the growing preference for coffee in North America.[6] Coffee matured faster than cacao, and planters found easy credit among European merchant houses established in Caracas. Thus Venezuela embarked on a strong export economy early in its national life as its bonds to the merchants, markets, and capitalists of Europe and North America developed in the 1830s and 1840s.

Páez in turn was able to keep the centrifugal factors of Venezuela at bay, these being largely regionally based caudillos who rose up periodically to challenge the commercial and bureaucratic elites of Caracas. Páez met these threats to his authority head on. In 1831, for example, Páez forced one of the most feared bandits and petty caudillos, Dionisio Cisneros, to submit to his will. Páez, the greatest of the *llanero* chieftains and now chief executive, defeated his rivals not by subtle arguments, appeals to constitutional authority, or other legal and oral arguments, but rather by the strength of his personality and will power.

Páez the Caudillo

All of this is not especially remarkable except that the bandit Cisneros did not submit to the authority of the state; he did not really acknowledge the supremacy of civil law, but instead subordinated himself to the greater personal power and charisma of Páez, the national caudillo. Thus the peace and civil order brought about by this submission came as a direct result of the caudillo's personal authority and not through the government's claim on its citizens' loyalty. To be sure, Páez was president of the Republic, but the significant element in the maintenance of public order came not from this anointment by civilian government but from the enforcer's personal authority. Páez made the government legitimate, not the other way around.

(John V. Lombardi, *Venezuela: The Search for Order, the Dream of Progress* (New York: Oxford University Press, 1982), pp. 165–166.

In the 1840s, however, Páez's rule began to fray as the Liberal Party, founded in 1840, challenged the caudillo's rule. A fall in coffee prices on the world market heightened discontent and led to the overthrow of Páez and his followers—now labeled "Conservatives"—in 1848. Páez went into exile in the United States. Venezuela plunged into two decades of political turmoil at mid-century, pitting Liberals against Conservatives, rival *caudillos* against each other, and Páez (who was in and out of exile) against his enemies.

Mexico

Mexico, after the overthrow of Emperor Agustín Iturbide the First (and the last, it turned out) in 1823, declared itself a republic and in 1824 drew up a constitution

---

[6]Lombardi, *Venezuela*, p. 174.

modeled on the one that its neighbor to the north, the United States, had enacted in 1789. It was a compromise between the conservatives and liberals who, as in the rest of Latin America, were lining up against each other in the politics of their nations. Other problems buffeted Mexico during these years between independence and mid-century, which one historian aptly characterized as teetering "between simple chaos and unmitigated anarchy."[7] In this period, it is difficult to follow the tortuous events of revolving-door politics and economic instability that snarled most attempts to bring prosperity and peace to the nation. Luckily for the student, but perhaps unluckily for Mexico, one man dominated the period. In his virtues—small—and in his flaws—magnified—we can trace much of Mexican history in this age.

Antonio López de Santa Anna was president of Mexico, elected or otherwise, eleven times between 1833 and mid-century, while the presidency itself changed hands thirty-six times. The country ran up an immense deficit, and the army continued to be a cancer that not only debilitated the treasury but also was constantly drawn into politics. Taxes, both new and old, went uncollected, graft and fraud became commonplace, and, in the most disastrous climax to this period, Mexico lost half of its national territory in a war with the United States in 1846–1848.

Mexico's problem was not the lack of a national vision, but rather the lack of a firm and widely based constituency to enforce such a vision. Conservatives and liberals divided on such traditional issues as the role of the Church, centralism versus federalism, the powers of the executive, and land policy for the Amerindians.

Guadalupe Victoria was elected the first president of Mexico in 1824 but was almost overthrown in a coup in 1827 led by his vice president! In the election of 1828, the actual winner was displaced by the rival candidate, Vicente Guerrero, who used a combination of force and intimidation to secure his victory. Guerrero was in turn overthrown by *his* vice president in 1830. Ex-President Guerrero was then executed in 1831. Ex-Emperor Iturbide suffered the same fate in 1824 when he returned to Mexico from European exile to offer his services in helping defend Mexico against a rumored Spanish invasion. Accused of treason, Iturbide died before a firing squad. And so it went. Santa Anna, a model caudillo, exploited this instability magnificently.

A Creole from the coastal state of Veracruz, Santa Anna fought for the royalist cause during most of the War of Independence. In 1821, like so many Creoles, he switched sides and worked for independence, while in 1823 he helped to overthrow Iturbide for the republican cause. In 1829 he led the Mexican army in repulsing a Spanish invasion at Tampico. By 1830 he was a national hero. In 1833 he was elected president for the first time. Bored with the tedium of government, he then retired to his estate, Manga de Clavo, in Veracruz, preferring to leave the reins of government with his vice president, Valentín Gómez Farías.

When Gómez Farías proved too liberal for the conservatives, who especially objected to the strong anticlerical measures imposed by the vice president, Santa Anna came storming back from Veracruz. He threw Gómez Farías and the liberals out, restored those rights of the Church that the liberals had trampled on, and even established a new centralist constitution more to his liking. By 1836, however, Santa

---

[7]Meyer and Sherman, *The Course of Mexican History*, p. 324.

General Antonio López de Santa Anna, Mexican caudillo who dominated his country's politics from the 1820s to mid-century. He fought in the disastrous 1846–48 Mexican American War, after which the United States took half of Mexico's territory. Santa Anna's militarism, authoritarianism, and disregard for administration threw Mexico into a period of post-independence political and economic instability.

Anna faced another challenge in the north. The province of Texas had revolted and declared its independence from Mexico.

Texas had been a Spanish colony since the early eighteenth century and naturally became part of Mexico after independence. In order to populate this vast land, which contained fewer than seven thousand inhabitants in the 1820s, the Mexican government allowed American immigrants to come and settle. This decision proved disastrous for Mexico. Those Americans who flooded into Texas in the 1820s and 1830s eventually threw off Mexican rule in 1836, and Mexico lost Texas. But hindsight is not available to contemporaries. In the 1820s more settlers meant more wealth and more taxes for the government.

The Americans who came in, led by empresarios such as Stephen F. Austin, also brought in an Anglo-American culture that conflicted with Mexican culture. They were largely Protestants, although nominally professing Catholicism to satisfy Mexican law. They carried with them their slaves, although slavery was abolished in 1829 throughout Mexico. And they came with a different language and vastly different political customs. They balked at their subservience to Mexican rule, especially as the American population of Texas swelled to more than thirty thousand by 1835.

Santa Anna again responded to the call to save his country in 1836. He led an army north to Texas and overwhelmed a small contingent of Texans holed up in the old Franciscan mission of the Alamo in San Antonio. The entire Texas contingent, including five prisoners, was killed or executed by Santa Anna's army—an unrepentant policy toward prisoners that was common during the Wars of Independence.

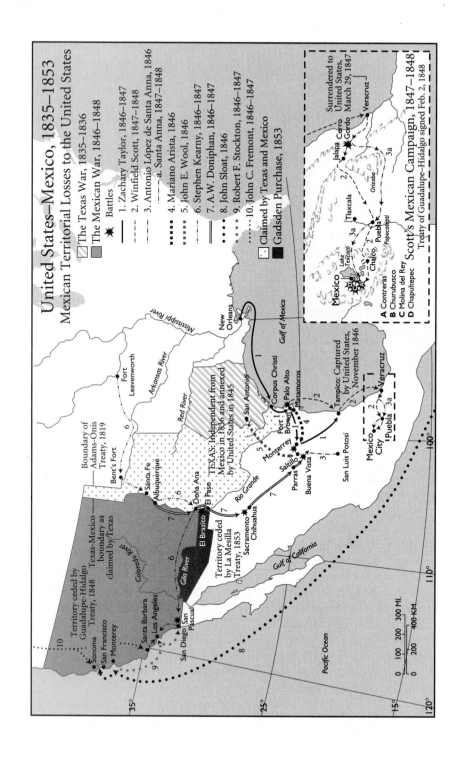

United States–Mexico, 1835–1853
Mexican Territorial Losses to the United States

The Texas War, 1835–1836
The Mexican War, 1846–1848

Battles

1. Zachary Taylor, 1846–1847
2. Winfield Scott, 1847–1848
3. Antonio López de Santa Anna, 1846
   a. Santa Anna, 1847–1848
4. Mariano Arista, 1846
5. John E. Wool, 1846
6. Stephen Kearny, 1846–1847
7. A.W. Doniphan, 1846–1847
8. John Sloat, 1846
9. Robert F. Stockton, 1846–1847
10. John C. Fremont, 1846–1847

Claimed by Texas and Mexico
Gadsden Purchase, 1853

Scott's Mexican Campaign, 1847–1848

Treaty of Guadalupe-Hidalgo signed Feb. 2, 1848

A Contreras
B Churubusco
C Molina del Rey
D Chapultepec

Surrendered to United States, March 29, 1847

Veracruz
Jalapa Cerro Gordo
Orizaba
Tlaxcala
Puebla
Popocatépetl
Lake Texcoco
Mexico
Chalco
Molino del Rey

Mississippi River
New Orleans
Gulf of Mexico
Corpus Christi
Palo Alto
Matamoros
Fort Brown
Tampico: Captured by United States, November 1846
Veracruz
Arkansas River
Fort Leavenworth
Red River
Bent's Fort
San Antonio
Boundary of Adams-Onis Treaty, 1819
TEXAS: independent from Mexico in 1836 and annexed by United States in 1845
Santa Fe
Albuquerque
Doña Ana
El Paso
Rio Grande
Monterrey
Saltillo
Parras
Buena Vista
San Luis Potosi
Mexico City
Puebla
Territory ceded by Guadalupe-Hidalgo Treaty, 1848
Texas-Mexico boundary as claimed by Texas
Colorado River
Gila River
El Brazito
Sacramento Chihuahua
Territory ceded by La Mesilla Treaty, 1853
Gulf of California
Pacific Ocean
San Francisco
Monterey
Santa Barbara
Los Angeles
San Diego
San Pascual
Sonoma

0 100 200 300 MI.
0 200 400 KM

120° 110° 100°
35°
25°
15°

The defense of the small mission of the Alamo in San Antonio by Texas in 1836, against the Mexican army led by General Santa Anna. Texans have sentimentalized the spirited defense of the Alamo and demonized the Mexican attackers into a metaphor for Texas nationalism and patriotism.

This slaughter, plus another mass execution of Texas prisoners at Goliad, hardened feelings on both sides and provoked an immense flow of sympathy, arms, and volunteers from the United States to Texas. On April 21, 1836, Sam Houston, commanding the Texas army, jumped Santa Anna's army encamped on the San Jacinto River and routed it. Santa Anna then conceded defeat.

He signed a peace treaty with Texas by which he promised to recognize Texans' independence. The Mexican caudillo was repatriated to his homeland. Humiliated by Santa Anna's concessions, Mexico refused to recognize Texas independence. The misadventures in 1836 were but a prelude to a greater Mexican disaster in 1848. Santa Anna, however, proved to be almost impervious to national disasters, especially those that he presided over.

Santa Anna's Texas disgrace was short-lived, and he was soon back in the saddle, this time in 1838 to rescue his nation from a French invasion. The origins of this "Pastry War," as it was dubbed, dated back to 1828 when some marauding Mexican soldiers plundered a Frenchman's bakery shop in Veracruz. The Frenchman sued for damages, but trying to collect from Mexico in a state of near political anarchy proved impossible. So the French government finally intervened, and its king, Louis Philippe, demanded an indemnity not only for the French cook, but also for other French claims against Mexico. When the Mexicans delayed, the French sent a fleet to Veracruz. The Mexicans agreed to pay, but then the French demanded more money, this time to cover the costs of their blockading fleet. The Mexicans balked, and the French fleet bombarded Veracruz on November 27, 1838. The Mexicans fell back. And then the indomitable Santa Anna offered his services once again to help the nation defend its honor. In the fighting that ensued between French expeditionary soldiers and the Mexican army, Santa Anna's horse was shot out from under him by a French cannon ball. Shortly thereafter surgeons amputated his left leg below the knee.

Santa Anna was in his glory. He expected to die and played the dying hero for all it was worth. The French army had been beaten back to its ships by his gallant soldiers, the Pastry War had been concluded on satisfying terms (the earlier indemnity, without the costs of the blockade, demanded by the French), and a thankful country was devoted to his service. He did not die, but he did continue to govern in an extravagant fashion. The army grew in size, new taxes were levied, bribery was practiced on a scale heretofore unknown in Mexican history, and, at the center, Santa Anna grew rich. He became the caricature of an Oriental despot, surrounding himself with personal guards called the "Lancers of the Supreme Power" and styling himself "His Most Serene Highness."

Santa Anna's Leg

In perhaps the most eccentric episode in the career of Santa Anna, he had his leg disinterred and reburied in 1842. Lesley Byrd Simpson captured the episode in his *Many Mexicos.* "The year 1842 marked the apogee of the glorious dictatorship. Mexico City enjoyed a continual fiesta: holidays to celebrate Santa Anna's birthday, Independence, and what not; parades of the guard; drums and bugles and salvos of artillery; solemn Masses at the cathedral. . . . On September 27, 1842, occurred the greatest and most solemn celebration of the year. The corpse of Santa Anna's leg was dug up at Manga de Clavo and brought to the city. His Serene Highness's bodyguard, the cavalry, the artillery, the infantry, and the cadets from the military academy at Chapultepec, all dressed for parade, escorted the urn containing the grisly relic across the city to the magnificent cenotaph that had been erected for it in the cemetery of Santa Paula. Ministers and the diplomatic corps attended, hat in hand. Speeches, poems, salvos. A graceful acknowledgment by the Liberator himself, who solemnized the occasion by wearing a new cork leg. . . ."

(Simpson, *Many Mexicos*, pp. 248–249)

In 1845 the United States annexed Texas in a wave of intense nationalism and expansionism known as "manifest destiny." Mexico rejected this aggression, which was made doubly insulting in 1846 when Texas and the United States claimed the Rio Grande as the true border with Mexico. Historically, the Nueces River had been considered the border. A quick look at the map shows that by claiming the more southerly and westerly trending Rio Grande, the Americans were asserting that Texas was twice the size that it truly was. When Mexican troops attempted to defend the region between the Nueces and the Rio Grande in May 1846, a skirmish ensued, some American troops under General Zachary Taylor were killed, and the United States declared war.

Five American armies invaded Mexico: One struck into New Mexico and quickly took that province; a second, marching overland from New Mexico, invaded California only to find that a combined American force under Commodore John D. Sloat and Colonel John C. Fremont had already secured that state; a third, also coming from New Mexico, took Chihuahua; a fourth, under Zachary Taylor, struck south from Texas toward Monterrey; and a fifth, commanded by General Winfield Scott, attacked Veracruz from the sea and then headed directly inland to Mexico City.

Taylor took Monterrey after a fierce three-day battle and then a few months later faced a large Mexican army assembled by none other than Santa Anna. The armies met near Buena Vista in February 1847. It resulted in a stalemate, with Taylor claiming victory. Santa Anna then withdrew to the south, carrying some captured battle pennants and also claiming victory. The claim proved false and short-lived. In March Scott assaulted Veracruz, took that city after a devastating forty-eight-hour bombardment from the American fleet, and proceeded inland toward Mexico City. The Mexicans defended themselves tenaciously and with courage, but ultimately they could not resist the better-trained and better-equipped American army as it inexorably approached the city. Furthermore, political divisions and rivalries among the Mexican defenders of their capital fatally undermined their efforts to oppose the advancing Americans. It was but one more example of the long-standing feud between liberals and conservatives that was so afflicting Mexico during this era.

The final battle occurred on the morning of September 13, 1847, when American soldiers and marines stormed Chapultepec Castle on a hill overlooking the city. Following a furious artillery barrage, the Americans scaled the precipitous walls and breached the defenses, some of which were manned by the young cadets of the Mexican military academy. Enough heroism was displayed and blood spilled by both sides to provide the myth makers and songwriters of both nations with tales of courage and sacrifice for generations. The war ended with the surrender of Chapultepec.

The Treaty of Guadalupe Hidalgo, signed on February 2, 1848, stripped Mexico not only of Texas but also of its immense territories of New Mexico and California. Mexico lost, in fact, half its national territory. The United States paid a little over $18 million for this bargain made possible by its victory at arms, while a legacy of distrust and suspicion between Mexico and the United States was sown by this war that so humbled and humiliated Mexico. Through it all Santa Anna fought, plotted, surrendered, and remained a major player, not being overthrown for the last time until 1855.

Central America

Although independence came easily to Central America in 1823, the unity and prosperity that the region sought in the following decades proved elusive. Central America, too, was wracked by many of the divisions afflicting other areas of Latin America. Conservatives vied with liberals over economic policy, Church-state relations, forms of government, and other issues, while Guatemala sought to impose political unity on the area.

The United Provinces of Central America was founded in 1824 and consisted of Guatemala, El Salvador, Honduras, Nicaragua, and Costa Rica—or modern Central America (Panama remained a province of Colombia until independence in 1903). As in Gran Colombia, however, the vision of union was soon ruined by the reality of politics, geography, new economic determinants such as the ascendancy of the English influence, and administrative configurations that persisted from the colonial period. Instead of emerging into independence strong and unified, by 1839 the United Provinces split apart, and each province went its separate way as a nation.[8]

Between 1823 and 1837 Central America probably was more deeply influenced by liberal reform programs than any other new nation in Latin America. Leaders such as Francisco Morazán, a Honduran liberal who became president of the Central American union in the late 1820s, pursued reforms in business, in Church-state relationships, in the judicial system, in educational opportunities, and across a wide spectrum of private and public life. These reforms challenged traditions and produced a widespread reaction in the late 1830s that not only split the union but also brought a classic caudillo into power.

The problem for the well-meaning liberals was twofold: One, many of their measures that were enacted to promote prosperity backfired; and, two, when conservatives criticized and opposed liberal measures, the liberals responded almost despotically with harshness and force.

What were some of the liberal measures? Land reform that was meant to entrust land to individual landowners tended instead to assist the wealthy to acquire larger properties at the expense of the Amerindians and *ladinos,* as the mestizo population of Central America was known. The Church was attacked on a broad front. Church property was seized, many Church holidays were abolished, and marriages and education were secularized by allowing for civil marriages and by establishing public schools. Clergymen who opposed the reforms were systematically removed, while those who defended the Church rallied parishioners to oppose the liberals.

A head tax and mandatory public service were reestablished to raise revenue and to provide a workforce for the new roads and ports that were contemplated. These two measures immediately provoked a public reaction, especially from the peasantry. Liberals, enchanted with the promise inherent in opening Central America to the world, promoted free trade, immigration, loans, and an increase in the production of indigo and cochineal, two dyes that fetched good prices in the English textile industry. Nonetheless, many felt that Central America was being sold out to foreigners whose profits, both in kind and cash, seemed to be gained at the expense of native Central Americans. Many merchants, for example, long accustomed to the protection enjoyed under the old Spanish monopoly, saw their businesses destroyed by free trade, which allowed large amounts of cheap English goods into Central America.

---

[8]Most of the preceding and following is from Ralph Lee Woodward, Jr., *Central America: A Nation Divided* (New York: Oxford University Press, 1976, 1984).

The English colony of Belize and English support of the "Mosquito Kingdom" stretching along the coastline of Nicaragua and Honduras promoted a wide open, commercial, Protestant way of life that many conservatives—still very much inclined to Hispanic, Catholic traditions—found galling. When a revolt began in Guatemala in the late 1830s, a young, ambitious *ladino* named José Rafael Carrera took its lead.

Carrera was reared in the army, fighting against the liberal forces of Morazán as early as fourteen years of age. He continued his military vocation and rose rapidly as a leader of peasant uprisings against the liberals. A fierce and courageous leader, he was a natural caudillo who eventually rode his talents and the wave of the times to the top in the 1840s, becoming the dictator of Guatemala and allying himself with the conservatives who proceeded to undo many of the liberal reforms in the 1840s and 1850s. By then the Central American union had ceased to exist, and Conservative regimes supplanted the Liberals who had presided over the union.

It would be tedious to list the means by which the Conservatives, especially in Guatemala, undid many Liberal reforms. These means ran the gamut from restoring the rights stripped from the Church to more symbolic acts such as incorporating the Spanish colors of red and gold into the Guatemalan national flag. Central authority and traditional order supplanted the Liberal devotion to experimentation and an open society. The Conservative reaction proved to be but a temporary dam, however, holding back dynamic forces pressuring Central America for change.

These forces were championed not only by Liberals but also by foreign entrepreneurs, especially Englishmen and Americans. These foreigners promoted new, lucrative markets for crops such as coffee that eventually transformed the Central American economy in the nineteenth century. They planned, argued, cajoled, and schemed for the rights and concessions to one of the western world's grandest dreams—cutting a canal through the Central American isthmus to connect the Atlantic and Pacific oceans. And, as we will see later, in 1855, an army of American filibusters even invaded Nicaragua and established a new rule with an ambitious dreamer from Nashville, Tennessee, as president.

Cuba and the Caribbean

The story of Cuba and the other Caribbean islands to mid-nineteenth century can best be understood by a consideration of two phenomena: the decline of slavery and a booming sugar economy, especially in Cuba. With one major exception, Hispaniola, the Caribbean islands continued as European colonies after the Wars of Independence. The largest of them all, Cuba, remained a Spanish colony until 1898, while independence did not come to the other islands until well into the twentieth century. Hispaniola, however, proved to be a large and important exception.

The Haitian Revolution of 1791 cast off French rule on the western side of Hispaniola, and the black republic of Haiti emerged in the early nineteenth century. The chaos of this revolution and its aftermath ruined the sugar culture of that French colony, and Cuba stepped in to become the principal supplier of sugar for European and North American consumption. Between 1810 and 1833, for example, sugar exports from Cuba doubled (from 33,708 to 72,635 tons),[9] while from 1833 to mid-century they *tripled* (to 208,599 tons). Cuba's remarkable rise to preeminence in sugar was paralleled by the decline of the sugar industry throughout the rest of the British and French Caribbean islands. The abolition of the slave trade and finally of slavery itself contributed to the decline of the sugar industry.

The momentum to abolish slavery welled up from many sources, some humanitarian, some political, some economic, but by the early nineteenth century international efforts, especially those of the British, were well underway. The slave trade was first abolished by the British in 1807, and by 1820 most other European nations had followed suit, with the enthusiastic prodding of the English who led the abolitionist movement.

Slavery itself was abolished throughout the British empire in 1833. On the other hand, in Cuba slavery survived until 1886. While the sugar economy of the British and French Caribbean islands declined and languished with the end of the slave trade and finally of slavery itself, Cuba's economy prospered, based precisely on slavery and sugar. Even the self-righteous and powerful British, supported by international treaties and the most formidable fleet in the world, failed to stem the illegal flow of slaves into Cuba. Over four thousand slaves per year arrived at Cuban ports until the 1860s.

Yet, it was not simply slavery that gave Cuba the edge. Cuba also was the first of the Caribbean colonies to begin modernizing its sugar industry. Although this trend would not become significant until the second half of the century, Cuban sugar planters were quicker to adapt to steam power for their mills, to centralize and make their operations more efficient, and to take full advantage of other technological improvements such as the railroads.

Cuba also moved closer to the North American economic and political orbit in this period. Feeling threatened by the powerful British abolitionist movement and unwilling to rely on a weakened Spain for their defense, many Cubans looked to the United States for assistance in maintaining the integrity of Cuba's social and economic system based on slavery and sugar. The American South, too, perceived its prosperity as flowing from slavery and a single crop, cotton, and annexationist sentiments ran high in the 1840s and 1850s among many Americans and Cubans.

Three American presidents attempted to buy Cuba from Spain in the 1840s and 1850s, but these, and other more violent, unofficial efforts, failed. Cuba's destiny, nonetheless, was to be more tightly woven, for better or for worse, into the fabric of American history in the second half of the century.

One other smaller Spanish colony in the Caribbean did follow a more traditional path during this period. The eastern half of the island of Hispaniola had remained a Spanish colony after Haitian independence, but in 1821 the Dominican Republic declared its independence from Spain. Haiti, however, squelched this effort, and the Dominican Republic freed itself of Haitian rule only in 1844.

---

[9]Eric E. Williams, *From Columbus to Castro: The History of the Caribbean, 1492–1969* (New York: Harper & Row, 1971, 1970), p. 361.

Puerto Rico remained a Spanish colony, as Cuba did, until the end of the century. It, too, was boosted economically by an expanding, modernizing sugar industry, but its increasing prosperity in the nineteenth century was fueled more by the growth of the coffee industry.

By the middle of the nineteenth century, in fact, one could discern new forces at work not only in the Caribbean—the expanding, modernizing sugar industry, for example, and the demise of an ancient evil, slavery—but also throughout Latin America. The key word in the air among Latin Americans was "progress." It meant many things to many people, as we will examine in the next chapter, ushering in a new era in Latin America's relationship to the world. As this relationship developed, it also transformed Latin America.

Conclusions and Issues

The search for political order was paramount among leaders in the first two or three decades of independence. The ideal of constitutional republicanism was belied by the political realities of the region. In Brazil, they did not even bother with a republican form of government but went directly from colony to independent empire. After a discordant start, Brazil took its native emperor, Pedro II, to heart and settled into a long period of political stability and economic progress. In other parts of Latin America, caudillos such as Santa Anna of Mexico presided over a bewitched brew of feuding liberals and conservatives. In Mexico they tore the country apart and left it open to Mexico's greatest national disaster, the war with the United States in 1848. Yet, the presence of caudillos was not necessarily a prescription for disaster.

In Chile, a strong centralized and conservative constitution provided for presidents who governed with authority and discipline, and Chile's political trajectory was immensely stable when compared with that of its neighbors Peru and Bolivia, for example. Chile, like Brazil, was nonetheless exceptional in an era of feuding liberals and conservatives, centralists and federalists, each with a claimed monopoly on political wisdom and moral truth. More often than not, the feuds, such as in Central America, Venezuela, Ecuador, Peru, and other countries, lessened the ability of their peoples to rise out of the economic stagnation bequeathed by the Wars of Independence.

Discussion Questions

1. Describe the principal characteristics of a caudillo. Other than Santa Anna of Mexico, select three caudillos and describe how some of these characteristics were reflected in their lives. Were some caudillos progressive and even liberal?

2. Why do you think Mexicans kept calling Santa Anna back to power even after some of the fiascoes that he presided over?

3. What is the relationship among Cuba, sugar, the other Caribbean islands, and abolition?

Bibliography for Part One

Anna, Timothy, *The Mexican Empire of Iturbide* (Lincoln: University of Nebraska Press, 1990).

Anna, Timothy E., *The Fall of Royal Government in Peru* (Lincoln: University of Nebraska Press, 1980).

Arrom, Silvia M., *The Women of Mexico City, 1790–1854* (Stanford: Stanford University Press, 1985).

Barman, Roderick J., *Brazil: The Forging of a Nation, 1798–1852* (Stanford: Stanford University Press, 1988).

Bushnell, David, *Reform and Reaction in the Platine Provinces, 1810–1852* (Gainesville: University Press of Florida, 1983).

Bushnell, David, and Neill Macaulay, *The Emergence of Latin America in the Nineteenth Century* (New York: Oxford University Press, 1988).

Butler, Kathleen Mary, *The Economics of Emancipation: Jamaica and Barbados, 1823–1843* (Chapel Hill: University of North Carolina Press, 1995).

Cavaliero, Roderick, *The Independence of Brazil* (New York: St. Martin's Press, 1994).

Costa, Emilia Viotti da, *The Brazilian Empire* (Chicago: Dorsey Press, 1985).

Costeloe, Michael P., *The Central Republic in Mexico, 1835–1846* (Cambridge: Cambridge University Press, 1993).

Di Tella, Torcuato, *National Popular Politics in Early Independent Mexico, 1820–1847* (Albuquerque: University of New Mexico Press, 1996).

Green, Stanley C., *The Mexican Republic: The First Decade, 1823–1832* (Pittsburgh: University of Pittsburgh Press, 1987).

Guardino, Peter F., *Peasants, Politics, and the Formation of Mexico's National State: Guerrero, 1800–1857* (Stanford: Stanford University Press, 1996).

Hamill, Hugh, ed., *Caudillos: Dictators in Spanish America* (Norman: University of Oklahoma Press, 1992).

Humphreys, R.A., ed., *The Origins of the Latin American Revolutions, 1808–1826* (New York, Knopf, 1965).

Hunefeldt, Christine, *Paying the Price of Freedom: Family and Labor among Lima's Slaves, 1800–1854* (Berkeley and Los Angeles: University of California Press, 1994).

Johnson, John J., *A Hemisphere Apart: The Foundations of United States Policy towards Latin America* (Baltimore: John Hopkins University Press, 1990).

Johnson, John J., with the collaboration of Doris M. Ladd, *Simon Bolivar and Spanish American Independence, 1783–1830* (Princeton, N.J., Van Nostrand, 1968).

Juan, Jorge and Antonio de Ulloa, *Noticias secretas de America* (Madrid, Editorial-America, 1918).

Kinsbruner, Jay, *Independence in Spanish America* (Albuquerque: University of New Mexico Press, 1994).

Lynch, John, *The Spanish-American Revolutions, 1808–1826* (London: Weidenfeld and Nicolson, 1973).

Lynch, John, *Argentine Dictator: Juan Manuel de Rosas, 1829–1852* (New York: Oxford University Press, 1981).

Lynch, John, *Caudillos in Spanish America, 1800–1850* (New York: Oxford University Press, 1992).

Macaulay, Neill, *Dom Pedro: The Struggle for Liberty in Brazil and Portugal, 1798–1834* (Durham: Duke University Press, 1986).

Paquette, Robert L., *Sugar Is Made with Blood: The Conspiracy of La Escalera and Conflict between Empires over Slavery in Cuba* (Middletown: Wesleyan University Press, 1989).

Russell-Wood, A. J. R., ed., *From Colony to Nation: Essays on the Independence of Brazil* (Baltimore: Johns Hopkins University Press, 1975).

Stevens, Donald F., *Origins of Instability in Early Republican Mexico* (Durham: Duke University Press, 1991).

Stolcke, Verena, *Marriage, Class, and Colour in Nineteenth-Century Cuba,* 2nd ed. (Ann Arbor: University of Michigan Press, 1989).

Stoner, K. Lynn, *From the House to the Streets: The Cuban Woman's Movement for Legal Reform, 1898–1940* (Durham: Duke University Press, 1991).

Whitaker, Arthur Preston, *The United States and the Independence of Latin America, 1800–1830* (New York, Russell & Russell, 1962).

White, Richard Alan, *Paraguay's Autonomous Revolution, 1810-1840* (Albuquerque: University of New Mexico Press, 1978).

Woodward, Ralph Lee, Jr., *Rafael Carrera and the Emergence of the Republic of Guatemala, 1821–1871* (Athens: University of Georgia Press, 1993).

Part 2

Nation Building

In Part One of this book we briefly reviewed the colonial background of modern Latin America and the Wars of Independence era. These wars brought on many changes, not the least of which was political and economic instability that lasted for several decades after the end of the wars. Nonetheless, the outlines of a more stable, prosperous region could be discerned by mid-century as several forces came to influence the historical evolution of these new nations.

Not the least of these forces was economic development. Throughout the region, the pace of integration into the European and North American economic orbit quickened in the second half of the century. Latin American exports to Europe—especially England—and, to a lesser extent, to the United States, increased dramatically. Coffee from Costa Rica, guano from Peru, copper from Chile, sugar from Cuba, meats from Uruguay and Argentina, and other products from fields and forests, mines and ranches produced a remarkable upturn in the economic prosperity of the region. These events, in turn, promoted political stability. And with political stability each country began more systematically to develop the characteristics of a true nation.

Coincidentally with economic development and political stability came a new devotion to liberal and modern ideals, described in the following chapter entitled "Progress." Very loosely, *progress* meant the desire and willingness to change and adopt new customs, new technologies, and new agendas that served to transform Latin America. The term *modernization* is often associated with this period, and, of course, modernization proceeded even more rapidly in the twentieth century. But the roots of the process lay in the nineteenth, and Part Two of this book is devoted to those changes that accompanied the beginnings of modernization.

Progress moves unevenly, as we all know. In Latin America, for example, it produced excesses of wealth and of poverty. These are especially explored in a chapter on the ways of life, a chapter that serves not only to describe the changes associated with modernization, but also to identify the vast diversity of experiences in the region. Life was transformed in the cities and countryside by the coming of the railroads, by the changes in how one made a living, by immigrants pouring in from Europe, by the emancipation of the slaves, and by many other destabilizing influences. Some people prospered, and a small but true middle class began to emerge, but the great majority of people in such nations as Mexico became even poorer and marginalized by these changes. From the disparities of power and influence that arose during this era, new phenomena—the revolutions of the twentieth century—were born. These will be dealt with directly in Part Three.

Furthermore, as nations began to define themselves more properly as national units, as they fixed their boundaries, developed state bureaucracies, and stabilized issues of authority and power, they also came more often into conflict with each other. The resulting wars and international disputes left deep and lasting scars on some of the new nations. The origins of the wars were sometimes legacies of old territorial disputes and border problems, but, even more important, the wars were produced by the process of modernization itself. The War of the Pacific (1879–1883) between Bolivia, Chile, and Peru, for example, was basically fought over natural resources—principally guano and nitrates—that had become important sources of income as demands in Europe and North America drove up their prices and value.

Throughout this era, and increasing in range and depth in the twentieth century, the United States played a role in the region. Beginning with the ambitious Monroe Doctrine declared in 1823, U.S. interests in Latin America slowly grew as the century proceeded. Having largely commercial interests in the beginning, the United States expanded its diplomatic and imperialist activities so that by the end of the century, when the last Spanish colonies—Cuba and Puerto Rico—fought *their* wars of independence from Spain, the United States was the principal actor.

Although the Wars of Independence certainly took Latin America down a radically different political road—the one of national liberation—they really did not significantly alter some of the basic social, ethnic, and cultural realities of the region. These, however, did begin to change under the impact of modernization, and Part Two takes us down that road.

Progress

Bao Lai, Wang Tuo, and Mr. Meiggs's Railroads of Peru

"It's damn cold," Bao Lai said to his companion, Wang Tuo, sleeping next to him in the drafty barracks erected for the laborers. They were at a pass nine thousand feet high in the Andes. The temperature outside had dropped to near freezing, although they were still in the tropical latitudes of central Peru.

"So what's new?" Wang Tuo answered, half asleep, irritated by Bao Lai's voice. They huddled closer, pulling the thin woolen blanket tightly around them. The whole room was filled with Chinese men, some snoring, some tossing and turning, others coughing quietly from diseases of the high altitudes.

"I can't take more of this," said Bao Lai.

"So what are you going to do, shit-for-brains?" Wang Tuo answered, now awake, even more aware of how cold he was. His feet and hands felt frozen. Perhaps they were.

"When can we get some more opium?" Bao Lai asked softly, trying not to wake his neighbors. They all were exhausted from ten to twelve hours of labor on the railroad as don Enrique Meiggs drove it from the coast into the mountains. They were Chinese coolies imported to work on the plantations of the Peruvian coast, the guano islands, and the railroads being laid into the mining regions of Peru. Other coolies labored in Chile, Costa Rica, Cuba, California—anywhere the railroads, the ever-demanding railroads, called for strong men to swing the hammers, manhandle the crossties, lay the rails of progress. To Bao Lai, the railroad was a nightmare, a diabolical fate for such a simple being. If only he could get a sufficient dose of opium. Then he could doze off into eternity, freed from the pain, the coughing, the cold, the misery, and humiliation of this damned world he had come to in search of work and a little silver to take back with him to China. Now he would never see his homeland again. He began to whimper softly.

"What's wrong with you, idiot?" Wang Tuo hissed, now thoroughly awake, cold, but not wishing to disturb his neighbors. "You could still be back at Cañete, struck dumb by the heat, eating dust, and working for that damned don Julio."

"This is better?" Bao Lai growled.

"We have plenty to eat, we only work six days a week, and no one has killed himself yet," Wang Tuo said.

It was true. Life on the railroads for the five hundred coolies working for Henry Meiggs as he drove the Lima to Oroya railroad from the coast into the mines of the Andes in 1872 was better than the miserable existence of the coolies on the cotton and sugar plantations of the coast.

Everywhere, it seemed, business was booming. Cotton and sugar loading for the ports of the United States and Europe, railroads penetrating to the silver and copper mines of Peru and Chile, new buildings in the cities, prosperity, and progress. But for Wang Tuo and Bao Lai it was work from dawn to dusk, although on don Enrique's gangs the dawn began with meat and rice, and the men were well fed and treated with some tolerance. Henry Meiggs was famous for treating his workers well, although Chinese names were awkward. They all were assigned numbers. Wang Tuo was 1450; Bao Lai was 1478.

Each had signed a contract, called an "indenture," to work for seven years. Then they would be free to return to their homeland with their silver upon completing their service. It was the price of progress.

All over Latin America the sounds and sights of progress marked the region. In a few months, numbers 1450 and 1478 would be gone, probably back down to the coast to labor on a cotton plantation, perhaps freed after seven years to set up a little shop in Lima or Callao, the nucleus of Chinese colonies that came to dot many parts of Latin America. For Bao Lai and Wang Tuo, the sounds of progress were hammers striking rails, the grunts and groans of the workingman.

For others listening to the sounds of progress, it was the steam whistle of the locomotive blasting the quiet valley as Enrique Meiggs pulled on the whistle cord that ran along the top of the engine cab. A wisp of steam from the whistle drifted back from the engine, now pressing higher and higher into the Andes, following the route where a few months ago the chants of Chinese swinging hammers echoed through the canyons. Again Meiggs tugged on the cord, and again the whistle cut through the valley. Children came scampering down from the high pasture where they were tending their sheep and llamas to wonder at the monstrous black locomotive, spewing smoke, steam, and fire. It was, indeed, a marvelous time to be alive, although for Bao Lai, Wang Tuo, and millions of other workers and peasants, progress was a double-edged sword that could cut silver and sweat in vastly different proportions for those who lived in Latin America.

Europe's and North America's influence in Latin America deepened and widened in the second half of the nineteenth century. After the disruptive period following the Wars of Independence, a measure of political stability ensued in most countries, and this in turn promoted economic growth and prosperity based on Latin America's exports.

Both the implicit and explicit foundations of this change in Latin America were a commitment to progress. Liberals were especially dedicated to progress, whereas conservatives considered the liberal obsession with progress and modernization both erroneous and immoral. Liberals wished to unshackle the creative energies of the individual to create new wealth that would ultimately benefit the entire nation. Conservatives were more cautious, unwilling to part so easily with traditional values and institutions that preserved social order and privilege. Yet, differences between liberals and conservatives, especially over volatile subjects such as the Church, were blurred in the second half of the century as a majority of Latin America's politically and economically active population embraced progress with gusto.

What did it mean for Latin America? We have already seen how the Age of Guano began to transform Peru at mid-century, how growing copper and nitrate exports from Chile fueled that country's growth, how the modernization of the sugar industry was propelling Cuba into an era of unprecedented wealth. Let us first examine the intellectual elements of this progressive mood that captivated Latin Americans.

Perhaps the underlying assumption was that change is inherently more desirable than continuity. If change were promoted, then the well-being of all individuals would be improved. This well-being was not only material but also political and social. The feeling was that people were advancing toward a better world, as if on a line moving from the past toward the future. The railroad was an apt symbol of this commitment to linear progress. As it penetrated the plains and mountains and valleys of Latin America in the second half of the century (the first tracks being laid in Cuba in 1838), the railroad opened new vistas and markets for Latin Americans.

One of the great obstacles to change was political disorder and the intransigence of some powerful conservative institutions. To overcome these obstacles and to clarify their philosophy, liberals borrowed freely from a persuasive philosophy then in fashion in Europe: positivism.

The Positivists

Positivism sprang from the writings of the French philosopher Auguste Comte, who was one of the pioneers of modern sociology. His long philosophical treatises published in the 1830s and 1840s essentially outlined three stages in human thought: theological, metaphysical, and the positive. In this last stage humans would base their thinking and actions on empirical, scientific observations.

Latin American intellectuals, especially in the last quarter of the nineteenth century, embraced positivism with enthusiasm as they sought to modernize their economies and societies and to break the old colonial patterns that still survived.

Positivism closely linked twin goals so often sought by humanity: social and political order with material progress. To achieve material progress, one needed social and political order. To establish a true and enduring order, one needed to make material progress. They complemented each other perfectly in the view of Latin American positivists. In Mexico, Brazil, Argentina, Chile, and throughout the hemisphere, the positivists, as the followers of the Comtean philosophy were called, ardently embraced Comte's teachings and adapted them to Latin America.

Positivism took many forms. In Argentina, for example, one of the highest priorities voiced by positivist leaders such as Juan Bautista Alberdi was to promote European immigration to his vast country, not only to populate the seemingly empty spaces and thereby increase the national prosperity, but also to revitalize the Argentine people with vital, dynamic European elements. Alberdi wrote that "to govern is to populate," and Argentina was spectacularly successful in promoting immigration in the second half of the nineteenth century.

Positivists in Chile such as José Victorino Lastarria and Valentín Letelier promoted modern, scientific development that found a ready following in that prosperous country. Chilean positivists remodeled and secularized the educational system. They promoted the restructuring of the government and the economy along scientific principles. Whether true or not, Chile's unprecedented prosperity in the second half of the nineteenth century was attributed by many positivists to their own actions.

In Brazil, positivists found many adherents who favored the abolition of slavery (certainly an institution hopelessly outmoded by the times and definitely not progressive), the separation of Church and state (an old liberal creed), and the establishment of a republic. A mathematics professor in the military academy, Benjamin Constant, was especially influential in the pro-republican movement that led to the overthrow of the monarchy in 1889. When the republicans created a flag for their new republic, they could think of no motto more appropriate than "Order and Progress," the battle cry of positivists throughout Latin America. To this day, the Brazilian flag carries this motto.

Mexican positivists, labeled *científicos,* flourished in the latter half of the century and profoundly influenced the course of Mexican history. In Mexican positivism, we find many of the elements common to the positivist movement throughout Latin America, with its emphasis on a practical, scientific approach to the organization of their world, repudiating the unchanging, conservative, almost mystical approach associated with Spanish ways and the Spanish heritage. In Mexico, curiously, the *científicos* in many instances looked to the United States (their conqueror in the Mexican-American War of 1846–1848) for inspiration because they saw in that practical and rational people a model for their own development: a way out from anarchy and chaos, and a way toward order and progress.

Mexican positivism, which found expression through the newspaper *La Libertad,* was ironically founded on the necessity of a dictatorship to promote order and thus to facilitate the material progress of the nation. One Mexican positivist,

Francisco G. Cosmes, called this dictatorship an "honest tyranny," to be distinguished from the chaos that tore Mexico apart in the first half of the century.[1] The dictator who fulfilled that role, Porfirio Díaz, governed Mexico with an iron hand from 1876 to 1911 and admirably imposed order.

Other Mexican positivists, such as the great educator Gabino Barreda, who first popularized positivism in Mexico, and Justo Sierra, one of its foremost promoters, freely adapted the theories of Charles Darwin, especially as reinterpreted by the English positivist Herbert Spencer, to the Mexican reality. Spencer claimed that Darwin's theories of evolution were perfectly applicable to society. Society, too, was an organism that was evolving slowly to a higher and better form. The mechanism for this evolution was the constant working of a law expressed by the phrase, "the survival of the fittest." In a free society, those people and institutions best adapted to making progress would naturally survive and prosper, thereby raising the level of all people with them. This seemed to be perfectly compatible with those Mexican positivists and their Latin American colleagues who wished to advance their people scientifically and practically. By applying the rule of order, they encouraged the establishment of strong, often dictatorial, governments. By embracing Spencerian principles as the means for achieving material progress, they encouraged competition, free enterprise, and, especially, the introduction of foreign capital, foreign ideas, and foreign initiative, all intimately associated with the practical application of positivist principles.

Positivists also adopted some of the most pernicious racism then prevailing in the western world. In Brazil and Mexico, for example, they viewed the blacks and Amerindians as racially inferior people who had degraded their countries' populations through the massive miscegenation, or mixing of the races, that had taken place over the centuries. So, European immigration was encouraged with immense enthusiasm by these positivists who desired to "whiten" their societies as a prelude to true scientific modernization. All sorts of "scientific" proofs were concocted—from measuring cranial capacities to associating substandard races with the tropical climates, for example—to support their racial policies.

The positivists of the second half of the nineteenth century claimed to have worked virtual revolutions in their homelands: They "claimed credit for reforming outmoded political institutions, for bringing about the industrial revolution, for beginning the process of mass popular education, for destroying the traditional power of the Church, for giving the military professional status, for reforming penal codes, for expanding national frontiers, for modernizing the cities, for introducing immigration of both men and ideas and, thus, for fomenting the material welfare of the continent."[2] If the intellectual framework provided by the positivists did not produce results as total and as good as they claimed, the economic transformation of Latin America—that "material progress" so dear to the positivists—was nonetheless spectacular in the second half of the century.

---

[1] From a quote in Leopoldo Zea, *The Latin-American Mind* (Norman: University of Oklahoma Press, 1963), p. 276.

[2] Ralph Lee Woodward, *Positivism in Latin America, 1850–1900: Are Order and Progress Reconcilable?* (Lexington, Mass., Heath, 1971), p. x of introduction.

Economic Transformation

In analyzing economic changes that Latin America underwent in the second half of the century, the statistical evidence is seductive and impressive. Argentina's exports between 1870 and 1900 increased 500 percent. Between 1833 and 1889 the value of Brazil's foreign trade increased at least sixfold. Between 1879 and 1900 the export of nitrates from Chile increased from 125,000 tons to almost 1,500,000 tons. Cuban sugar production rose from 322,000 tons to over a million tons between 1853 and 1894. During the heyday of the positivists in Mexico, from 1877 to 1910, Mexican exports increased in value eightfold and in volume sevenfold.

Exports fueled the growth of other Latin American nations with equally dramatic effects: coffee from Colombia and Costa Rica, guano from Peru, minerals (silver, gold, copper) from Chile, Peru, and Mexico, bananas from Central America, rubber from the countries sharing the Amazon basin, tin from Bolivia; the list is large and diverse. Taken as a whole, the effects were not only impressive but also controversial.

The growth of the export economies produced three broad changes: one, the creation of new wealth; two, a deepening relationship with Europe and North America; and three, a more unequal distribution of that new wealth and income. All three were evident in the second half of the century. Cities grew, banks were founded, railroads pushed into the interiors, industrialization commenced, telegraph and cable lines appeared, a middle class began to develop, education became more public and available, and, in some countries such as Argentina and Uruguay, the flood of foreign immigrants considerably altered the social scene.

The growth of the cities and of railroads was the most visible symbol of the material and cultural transformations taking place throughout the region. E. Bradford Burns, a historian of Latin America, observed that "by the beginning of the twentieth century, nearly all the capitals and many of the largest cities boasted of electricity, telephones, streetcar service, covered sewers, paved streets, ornamental parks, and new buildings reflecting French architectural influence."[3] In San José, the capital of Costa Rica, the crowning jewel in the transformation of that city was set in place in 1897 when the National Theater, modeled on the Paris Opera House, was inaugurated with a production of *Faust*.

The imitation of European architecture, fashions, and culture was a natural extension of the deepening ties between Latin America and the rest of the world. Latin Americans looked abroad not only for their markets and for sources of capital, but also for those trends, in politics (positivism) and in culture (from hat styles to the latest in horseless carriages), that marked "modern" society. And nothing was more modern or progressive to the Latin Americans than the railroad. It was both the preeminent agent and the symbol of progress and modernization.

Peru aptly illustrates the links between the growing export economies and the introduction of the railroads. The boom in guano exports produced a surplus of

---

[3]E. Bradford Burns, *Latin America: A Concise Interpretive History* (Englewood Cliffs, N.J.: Prentice-Hall, 1986), p. 141.

capital, and this capital was in turn invested in building railroads. The railroads invariably began on the coast and penetrated into the highland interior, with the twin goals of making potentially rich mines (silver and copper, for example) accessible and bringing progress to those remote parts of Peru largely untouched by the Industrial Revolution.

Manuel Pardo, a president of Peru in the 1870s, was a typical apostle of the railroads. His arguments are representative of the times. Not only would the railroads catalyze increases in production and commerce, but also they would be endowed with an even higher mission in Peru: "to create where nothing today exists, to spawn and stimulate the elements of wealth which today are found only in a latent and embryonic state."[4] In an effusive display of almost missionary-like optimism, Pardo went on about the impact of the railroads: "Who denies that the railroads are today the missionaries of civilization? Who denies that Peru urgently needs those same missionaries? Without railroads today there cannot be real material progress. And without material progress there can be no moral progress among the masses, because material progress increases the people's well-being, and this reduces their brutishness and misery. Without the railroads, civilization can proceed only very slowly."[5] Pardo was, in effect, a positivist to the core, committed to change and modernization. His counterparts flourished over the rest of Latin America.

In Mexico, a frenzy of railroad building occurred from the 1870s to the end of the century, most of these railroads penetrating Mexico on a north-south axis, making Mexico more accessible to the United States. Not only were old silver mines revitalized, but also new sources of zinc, lead, and copper came into production, made possible by linking the mining areas with the markets in North America. As early as 1880 it was possible to travel by rail from Chicago to Mexico City, and, perhaps just as important, North American and English capital dominated in the expansion of the railroads. The great names in U.S. capitalism, such as Guggenheim, appeared frequently in the roster of those agents of economic transformation in Mexico.

In the rest of Latin America, railroad fever ran just as high as in Peru and Mexico. Argentina's railroads, largely financed by British capital, promoted a different kind of economic development based on cattle and agricultural exports. The traditional exports of salted beef, hides, tallow, and wool were supplemented and then superseded by exports made possible by new factors: technological improvements, immigration, and, of course, the railroads. Refrigerated mutton and wheat came to dominate Argentine exports by the turn of the century and promoted a spectacular rise in the prosperity of the nation. A map of the railroads of Argentina at the end of the century looks like a plate of spaghetti strands strung out across the nation, all converging on Buenos Aires.

Along with the railroads came the telegraph, steamships, electricity, and a host of other technological improvements or breakthroughs that promoted the economic transformation of the region. In this era of invention and growth and prosperity, any-

---

[4]Lawrence A. Clayton, *Grace: W.R. Grace & Co., The Formative Years, 1850–1930* (Ottawa, Illinois: Jameson Books, 1985), p. 55, who cites the biography of Pardo by Jacinto Lopez, *Manuel Pardo* (Lima: Imprenta Gil, 1947).
[5]Ibid.

Railroad Fever

In 1853, the Argentine Juan Bautista Alberdi (1810–1884) wrote about the railroads in a typical fashion that extolled them as the primary agents of modernization and nation-building.

"The railroad and the electric telegraph, the conquerors of space, work this wonder better than all the potentates on earth. The railroad changes, reforms, and solves the most difficult problems without decrees or mob violence.

"It will forge the unity of the Argentine Republic better than all our congresses. The congresses may declare it 'one and indivisible,' but without the railroad to connect its most remote regions it will always remain divided and divisible. . . .

"Without the railroad you will not have political unity in lands where distance nullifies the action of the central government . . . political unity, then, should begin with territorial unity, and only the railroad can make a single region of two regions separated by five hundred leagues.

"Nor can you bring the interior of our lands within reach of Europe's immigrants, who today are regenerating our coasts, except with the powerful aid of the railroads. They are or will be to the life of our interior territories what the great arteries are to the inferior extremities of the human body: sources of life. . . ."

(Juan Bautista Alberdi, *Bases y puntos de partida para la organización política de la República Argentina* [Buenos Aires, 1951], pp. 62–63, 85–88, 90–92, 240–242), in Benjamin Keen, editor, *Latin American Civilization: History & Society, 1492 to the Present*, 6th ed. [Boulder, Colo.: Westview Press, 1991, 1996])

thing was thought possible, human endeavor being limited only by a failure of will or of imagination. Is it any surprise that perhaps the greatest engineering feat ever attempted in Latin America was launched in the second half of the nineteenth century?

The goal of linking the Atlantic and Pacific oceans by cutting a canal through the Central American isthmus had been envisioned ever since the sixteenth century. But the task seemed overwhelming. The various proposed routes were plagued by tropical diseases and blocked by mountains, earthquakes, and drenching downpours. Efforts to dig were quickly swept away in torrents of water that both impeded work and demoralized canal builders. Yet, commencing in the 1870s, Europeans and North Americans launched a series of canal-building endeavors, both in Panama and Nicaragua, that ultimately culminated after the turn of the century in an American commitment to complete the canal in Panama. Earlier, in the 1880s, the French undertook the task under the leadership of Ferdinand de Lesseps. But de Lesseps, the builder of the Suez Canal, and his project ultimately failed in Panama, broken by yellow fever and malaria, floods, and finally bankruptcy.

There were, of course, some catches to this unprecedented burst of prosperity and boundless optimism that propelled and captivated Latin Americans during the grand age of positivism and economic transformations. A price had to be paid, and in the case of Latin America, it was paid in two broad areas: One, the wealth was unequally distributed; and two, Latin America became even more dependent upon

Stock certificate sold to finance the French company that tried unsuccessfully to build a canal in Panama during the 1880s.

Europe and the United States. Each of these phenomena will be discussed in detail in subsequent chapters because they are highly controversial issues in Latin American history whose effects persist, in one form or another, even to today. One immediate outcome of this growing prosperity was a maturing sense of nationalism.

This nationalism was fueled by old feuds over undefined borders inherited from the Independence era and by new premiums put on the value of plains, mountains, jungles, and even deserts now yielding ever-increasing amounts of exports—nitrates, rubber, copper, sugar, coffee, wheat, and so forth—so keenly sought by the industrializing nations of Europe and North America. The result was an increasingly complex and competitive international politics marked by a number of wars in the nineteenth century. They served to further mark Latin America as a part of the world with distinct nations, each developing a sense of uniqueness that served to distinguish one from another.

The Issue of Dependency

The relationship between Latin America and the rest of the world—principally Europe and the United States in the nineteenth century—has been described as dependent. A dependent relationship is one in which an unequal partnership exists that benefits one partner more than the other. In the theory of dependency that has been developed to explain Latin America's relationship to the rest of the world,

Latin America has most often been analyzed as the junior partner whose growth and development were accomplished only by paying the price of becoming more dependent upon Europe and the United States.

In most analyses, this dependency is accorded a negative value. Furthermore, dependency cut across economic, political, and social categories. Not only did Latin America become dependent upon foreign markets for its exports, and upon those same foreign producers for much of its imports, but also economic clout carried with it political influence. Where the English merchant went, the English consul or minister and the English warship were not far behind. The same was true for the French and Americans, both of whom contributed heavily to the rise of dependency in the second half of the nineteenth century.

Another way of describing dependency—this time in a more historical framework—is to call it "neocolonialism." Formal colonialism existed from the sixteenth century until the Wars of Independence. That is to say, Latin America was a colony of Spain and Portugal, very clearly—legally, politically, economically, ecclesiastically, and so forth—tied to Spain and Portugal. When those bonds were broken by the wars, Latin America became independent politically, but it continued to be dependent upon Europe, especially Great Britain, for its economic growth and prosperity. This relationship deepened, and the United States's role in Latin America in the nineteenth century gradually grew at the expense of the British. Although not a formal colony of Europe, Latin America continued to be a neocolony of Europe and North America, increasingly dependent in an economic fashion—hence, "neocolonialism."

A third way to describe the dependent relationship has been to invoke the term "imperialism." Again, as in neocolonialism, Latin America in the nineteenth century did not form a legal or political part of the expanding British or American empires, but Latin America's subordination to British capital, British investments, American railroad builders, and so forth in effect spread the British and American empires over Latin America. Thus, imperialism becomes closely associated with a description of the relationship between Latin America and the rest of the world, especially, of course, Great Britain and the United States.

Finally, the dependency theory has a competing theory that must be considered by the student of Latin American history. This theory, labeled the "diffusionist" theory, maintains that the spread of European and North American capital, investments, values, technology, and immigrants to Latin America was positive rather than negative. The benefits of progress and modernization were slowly "diffused" to Latin America, spreading to Latin America like ripples on a pond. The center of the ripples, often labeled the "metropolis," was Europe and North America. Here invention and industrialization were proceeding rapidly. The effects of this phenomenon gradually spread out to the rest of the world, labeled the "periphery," promoting change and prosperity in a gradual manner.

The modern revolutions of Latin America, beginning with the massive Mexican Revolution of 1910, make it quite apparent that whichever theory one subscribes to—dependency or diffusion—modernization produced wildly uneven results in Latin America. Although cities were electrified and prosperous middle classes began to emerge, many of the people, the masses, continued to toil in hardship and privation that were often more severe than that of their immediate ancestors under the Spanish and Portuguese empires.

Conclusions and Issues

One of Isaac Newton's theories about the laws of nature is that a body at rest tends to remain at rest, whereas a body in motion continues in motion. Latin American political, social, and economic leaders in the second half of the nineteenth century sought to get their countries into the latter mode, to break the economic stagnation of the postindependence decades. They passionately embraced the notion of "progress" and took up the tools of "positivism" to realize their ambitions. They promoted change across the economic spectrum, invited foreign capital and ideas in with enthusiasm, successfully put a cap on racial and social aspirations for a more egalitarian and just world, and even managed to impose an unprecedented degree of political stability at the end of the century.

Latin American material progress did indeed take off in the era of the positivists. Exports expanded dramatically, railroads penetrated economically viable areas, and old and new products of fields and forests, mountains and deserts such as coffee, guano, and nitrates all powered a new prosperity. With it came increasing dependency upon the European and North American centers of technology, banking, and entrepreneurial and scientific skills. This dependent relationship possessed a number of facets, some considered positive and some negative in the process of nation building.

Discussion Questions

1. What did the word *progress* mean to nineteenth-century Latin Americans? What does it mean to you, in the context of your life today? How does knowing how others viewed progress influence the way that you see it?

2. Why was positivism such an attractive philosophy to Latin American intellectuals who helped influence political and economic directions in the second half of the nineteenth century?

3. What does *dependency* mean in the context of the increasingly modernizing Latin American nations of the second half of the nineteenth century?

The Ways of Life

Liberals and the Enduring Church

The priest Ernesto Gutiérrez hurried back to his quarters from evening prayers. Again, the scandalous new president of the republic, Tomás C. Mosquera, was attacking Ernesto's beloved Church. In Bogotá, where Gutiérrez lived in the monastery alongside his Dominican brothers, the rumors were flying. Since July 1861, when Mosquera's victorious liberal army vanquished the conservatives and took control of the capital, decrees and rumors of decrees had forced the Church to the wall.

The Dominicans would be disbanded and outlawed in Colombia.

The brothers—the few who remained—would be banished, exiled. Where would they go?

Along with a few others, the younger Father José de Calasanz Vela among them, Gutiérrez was determined to make his stand. But how? Where? Now, on the evening of November 5, all of the worst nightmares seemed to come true.

Gutiérrez opened the door leading into the chapter room and was greeted by a chorus of voices.

"Have you heard? What are you going to do, Ernesto? I, for one, am staying. They *will not* force me out."

"Bah," said another, "under the circumstances they offer, you will be little more than a prisoner."

What were the choices, wondered Gutiérrez. They soon became apparent. Either accept Mosquera's draconian measures to curtail the Church, making priests and nuns mere mendicants and supplicants of a hostile government that instead of protecting them assaulted them, or face imprisonment, or perhaps exile.

"I will stand with you, José," Gutiérrez heard himself saying to Calasanz Vela.

Calasanz Vela looked at his older colleague and asked gently, "Are you sure, Ernesto? It will be prison or exile if we resist. Are you sure?" Gutiérrez was in his fifties, an older man by the measure of the times. He was a slender and somewhat fragile, nervous individual, never still. Calasanz Vela was, on the other hand, barely twenty-one, strong as an ox and imbued with the fire of the faith that had brought him to Christ and the Dominican order. He was worried that the consequences could hurt his brother, Ernesto Gutiérrez.

"Yes," Gutiérrez answered almost too swiftly. "Yes, I go with you."

The soldiers arrived the next morning and arrested the monks for refusing to obey Mosquera's destructive decrees. Five days later, Calasanz Vela, Gutiérrez, the prior Antonio Acero, and three others were marched off into exile. Or, more properly, muled off. Their destination was the small frontier town of Villavicencio in the great tropical lowland plains, the *llanos,* of the interior.

"I don't know how much longer I can take this mule," Gutiérrez said to Calasanz Vela riding behind him along the narrow, serpentine trail wending its way down from the great *cordillera* (system of mountain ranges) behind them.

"Father Gutiérrez," Calasanz Vela said cheerily, "we could be walking!"

"God save us," Gutiérrez answered, shifting about constantly to find some comfort for his bony frame on this weaving, bobbing animal.

Gutiérrez was in agony. Calasanz Vela, on the other hand, was enraptured by the magnificence of the high mountain passes, the ravines, the canyons—all views of God's inspiring work. When they reached the final outcropping of the Andes and viewed the plains before them, Calasanz Vela inhaled a breath of wonder, awestruck by the beauty and majesty of the endless tropical world spreading out before them.

This tiny Dominican caravan was welcomed in Villavicencio by a small throng of well-wishers, eager for the ministrations of priests long absent from the region.

But not so Capitán Fulgencio Suárez. A defiant liberal and priest baiter, he immediately challenged the monks.

"Swear obedience to the law or die!" Suárez roared that afternoon.

"Satan!" Father Acero, the prior, answered. "You will reap what you sow!"

"Do you not swear?" Suárez asked again loudly, swaying from a full afternoon of drinking, his breath coming from the bottle, his bile rising.

"No oaths before the devil," Acero shot back.

"Shoot him," Suárez yelled to his soldiers, turning on his heel.

The sergeant in charge of the ragtag militia that represented the national authority in this vast and remote part of the nation wondered what to do.

"Ah, Capitán?" he queried Suárez. "Where?"

"Build a scaffold, you fool!" Suárez barked back.

By evening a crude scaffold, no more than a platform with some four-by-fours to stand a man before the public, had been nailed together. The soldiers were embarrassed, but they were frightened of Suárez. He was a crude, brutal *caudillo*, not to be brooked easily. Yet, to kill a priest was crazy! Suárez may be brutal, but to commit one's soul to eternal hell-fire—that was another matter.

Suárez personally gave the command.

"Fire!" The old muskets clicked as the firing pins, released by squeezing the triggers, hit the chambers loaded with powder. Then, the explosion of powder and, *blam,* the priest would be blown away. Good riddance.

Suárez looked stunned. Nothing happened. No explosion. The muskets all failed to fire. All failed to fire!

"You bastards!" Suárez shouted, drawing his sword from his scabbard. The soldiers had deliberately sabotaged the execution, failing to powder their muskets.

Now almost deranged, Suárez leaped at the priest, but the crowd surged forward and knocked him down. They freed Father Acero and dragged Captain Suárez off to jail.

Father Gutiérrez almost fainted from the tumult. He leaned on the younger Calasanz Vela, who helped his brother Dominican into the shade while the crowd moved down to the jail with Suárez, dust and noise dropping down like a shroud around the confused Gutiérrez.

Within a few weeks the tropics laid siege to Father Gutiérrez, and his fragile nature succumbed to the terrible, deathly fevers of malaria. He died, trembling and delirious, in the arms of Father Calasanz Vela, who gave his friend the final unction and blessed his soul.[1]

The Church and state were locked in combat in many parts of Latin America in the nineteenth century—an unsavory but terribly real chapter in the rough transition from colonialism to independence. Tradition and modernity clashed across many areas, sometimes spectacularly between a conservative Church and a liberal state, as in the preceding instance, and sometimes more subtly as the peoples of Latin America accommodated themselves to new forces, new ways of thinking in the land.

The Peoples of Latin America

The turbulence accompanying the Wars of Independence changed many things, most notably by rupturing the Spanish empire and fostering the rise of the new independent nations of Latin America. What did not change was the ethnic makeup of

---

[1]For those wishing to know more about the life and times of the remarkable Father José de Calasanz Vela, we recommend Jane M. Rausch, "José de Calasanz Vela: Frontier Priest," in Judith Ewell and William H. Beezley, editors, *The Human Tradition in Latin America: The Nineteenth Century* (Wilmington, Del.: Scholarly Resources, 1989), pp. 141–160.

the people. The region entered and emerged from the Wars of Independence with about the same mixture of Amerindians, blacks, Creoles, mestizos, mulattoes, and *pardos.* The percentages varied widely from country to country.

However, throughout the nineteenth century, due to better sanitation, medicine, urbanization, and other factors, the population of Latin America expanded dramatically. The proportion of the ethnic groups was altered substantially in some nations by the flow of immigrants from Europe—most noticeably in Brazil and the nations of the Southern Cone. In others, the mestizos, *pardos,* and mulattoes (sometimes collectively labeled the *castas*) expanded proportionally within the overall population at the expense of Amerindians and blacks. The end of the slave trade during the course of the century contributed to one aspect of this trend, slowing down the increase of African-descended people, for example. Nonetheless, well into the twentieth century, the Amerindian element remained in the majority or represented the most significant proportion of the population in the five nations of Mexico, Guatemala, Ecuador, Peru, and Bolivia.

In a population that increased from about four million to almost eighteen million in Brazil in the nineteenth century, for example, the free population of color constituted *more than half* (around 58 percent) of the total population by the 1870s. The black slave population declined from close to two million to a little more than a half-million by 1888, when the last were finally freed. Meanwhile the number of immigrants (largely European) swelled the percentage of foreign-born in the Brazilian population from about 4 percent to over 7 percent by the end of the century.

In Spanish America, at the end of the Wars of Independence era, the nine million Amerindians accounted for between one-half to two-thirds of the total population. Mixed-bloods, or the *castas,* accounted for at least one-quarter, while the remainder were of European extraction. The figures are imprecise because the data are scarce and incomplete, and we will never know the exact proportion of the races in the nineteenth century.

Mexico's Amerindian population, for example, at the beginning of the independence movements numbered close to four million, while the European, or white, population was a little over one million. Blacks and Afro-mestizos numbered over half a million, while mestizos numbered about three-quarters of a million. In other countries, such as Venezuela and Colombia, mestizos and the *castas* were in the majority.

Race Mixture in Latin America

"In the famous words of José Vasconcelos, the Mexican philosopher," wrote Magnus Mörner, "it is in Latin America that a new race will come into being, 'made of the treasury of all the previous races, the final race, the cosmic race.' It is true that Vasconcelos's words, in his book *Raza Cósmica* (1925), are abstract and cultural. Nevertheless, his vision of a new tropical race does reflect an existing situation. No part of the world has ever witnessed such a gigantic mixing of races as the one that has been taking place in Latin America and the Caribbean since 1492. In fact, it is impossible to determine the racial status of most Latin Americans without a genetic and anthropometric investigation. Toward the end of the eighteenth century, if we are to believe a very knowledgeable historian, miscegenation . . . , or *mestizaje*, in Spanish, was so advanced in Mexico 'that there were few individuals of pure race left in the country.' This observation probably could be applied to most parts of Latin America at the time. In that immense region every variation of crosses among the three main stocks, Mongoloids, Caucasoids, and Negroids can be found, and everybody there is aware that biological fusion is very real . . . In some countries mestizaje itself has been transformed . . . into a symbol of nationality. . . .

" . . . Visual observation and some basic knowledge enable us to discern the principal racial patterns of Latin America today. In the Caribbean (except for Puerto Rico) and the northeast of Brazil, the zones in which plantations are found, is an Afro-Latin America. A Euro-Latin America comprises most of Argentina, Uruguay, southernmost Chile, and the south of Brazil; that is, the zone that has received the great waves of European immigrants during the last hundred years. The rest of the region is a Mestizo America with scattered enclaves of indigenous population in Mexico, Guatemala, and the South American Andes, as well as in the Amazon basin."

(Magnus Mörner, *Race Mixture in the History of Latin America* [Boston: Little, Brown, 1967], pp. 1, 2)

From Simón Bolívar at the dawn of the century to Euclides da Cunha at its dusk, Latin Americans struggled to explain and benefit from their mixed racial heritage. Like so many Latin Americans, Bolívar waxed and waned on the subject. At one moment he expressed pride in people of mixed blood, at other moments he was weighed down with shame and contempt at carrying the stigma of mixed blood.

In 1819 he addressed the Congress of Angostura and spoke candidly and proudly of Latin America's heritage.

> We must bear in mind that our people are neither European nor North American; they are a mixture of Africa and America rather than an emanation of Europe. . . . It is impossible to determine with any degree of accuracy to which human family we belong. The greater portion of the native Indian has been annihilated. Europeans have mixed with Americans and Africans, and Africans with Indians and Europeans. While we have all been born of the same mother, our fathers, different in origin and in blood, are foreigners, and all differ visibly as to the color of their skin, a dissimilarity which places upon us an obligation of the greatest importance.[2]

That Bolívar was dark skinned and that his great-grandmother may have been a mulatta were sources of both pride and anxiety for the Liberator. Were these ennobling factors in his background? Was it good to be descended—no matter how little—from African peoples? The black, just as surely as the white and the Amerindian, made a deep imprint in the ethnic composition of many parts of Latin America. A part of Bolívar answered "yes."

Yet, toward the end of his life, Bolívar spoke more as a member of the ruling Creole elite, who felt guilt and fear toward the castes and the masses. In 1826 Bolívar

---

[2]Quoted in Mörner, *Race Mixture*, pp. 86–87.

expressed himself with anguish and doubt about people of mixed heritage whose origins arose from the conquest and rape of the New World.

> We are very far from the wonderful times of Athens and Rome, and we must not compare ourselves in any way to anything European. The origins of our existence are most impure. All that has preceded us is enveloped in the black cloak of crime. We are the abominable offspring of those raging beasts that came to America to waste her blood and to breed with their victims before sacrificing them. Later the fruits of their unions commingled with slaves uprooted from Africa. With such physical mixtures and such elements of morale, can we possibly place laws above heroes and principles above men?[3]

In his despair of ever getting his beloved nation, which to him included all of South America, to embrace republicanism, rationalism, and the other principles of the Enlightenment that had inspired him in his early life, Bolívar turned upon the races. A perceptive student of race in Latin America, the Swedish historian Magnus Mörner, observed: "In shocking contrast to his optimistic declaration of 1815 [Bolívar's "Letter from Jamaica," which was very pro-Indian], Bolívar now speaks of the 'natural enmity of the colors,' prophesying gloomily about the day 'when the people of color will rise and put an end to everything.' "[4] The remark was reminiscent of Bolívar's "plowing the seas" metaphor when, frustrated and brokenhearted near the end of his life, he summarized his efforts to transform Latin America into the vision of his youth. Like the wake of a ship, cresting, foaming, beautiful to watch but entirely ephemeral, Bolívar's efforts to bring political unity and order to Latin America had also appeared to be ephemeral and short-lived, "plowing the seas," in the memorable phrase of the Liberator.

The conflagration between the races did not occur as Bolívar had predicted. Occasional wars and insurrections with a racial basis did flare up in the nineteenth century in scattered areas from Brazil to Mexico (the Yucatan Caste War of the 1840s, for instance). None, however, was massive enough to destroy the prevailing caste system, itself a good deal more flexible and responsive than Bolívar realized. As Latin America steered unsteadily through the age of the caudillos and into the uncertain but sought-after promises of modernization, the very mixed racial nature of Latin American society tended to blur the sharp edges between the races. Mestizos, mulattoes, and *zambos* all found room to maneuver, to move up the military, economic, and political ladders. The least favored of all the various peoples in the nineteenth century were the Amerindians.

Amerindians and Mestizos

The Amerindians fell victim to a liberal political philosophy throughout Latin America. This philosophy, when enacted, deprived Amerindians of colonial protections and restraints, which were abolished during the Wars of Independence. This left them vulnerable to exploitation born of liberal political ideals and impersonal and often brutal economic forces.

---

[3]Ibid., pp. 87–88. From letter to Santander in 1826 upon being informed that Páez was in revolt.
[4]Ibid., p. 88.

These ideals and forces have been represented elsewhere in this text as both positive and negative. Well-meaning liberals freed Amerindians of ancient shackles, such as the tribute, and broke up the Amerindian communal lands, giving each family clear title to its own plot of land. Liberals hoped that these actions would remake Amerindians into independent landowners, endowed with their own resources, moving along the road to prosperity, learning the rudiments of self-sufficiency and democracy in the liberal, progressive, modern world then thought to be dawning. We know that it did not work that way.

Millions of Amerindians were cheated and despoiled of their lands in Mexico, Guatemala, Colombia, and on down the Andes through the great Amerindian nations of Ecuador, Peru, and Bolivia. It is a tribute to the enduring nature and tenacity of these Amerindian nations, however, that many communities—holding their lands together as ancient Amerindian communities that owned the land collectively, called *ejidos* in Mexico or *comunidades indígenas* or *ayllus* in Peru—survived the nineteenth century. As many as 40 or 50 percent retained their collective identities both in law and in practice.

The demands of a modernizing plantation and hacienda economy further undermined the quality of life for Amerindians. As industrial capitalism developed in Europe and North America, the ever-increasing demands of the industrializing world stimulated the agrarian systems of Latin America to produce more for new markets. New and more efficient ways developed to make money by growing and selling Latin American agricultural products, such as sugar, coffee, bananas, wheat, henequen (agave fiber), and the like. In essence, this meant transforming the paternalistic hacienda into a capitalist estate.

This transformation degraded Amerindians and mestizos laboring on these estates. Although the forms of labor varied widely across Latin America, from the henequen plantations of Yucatan to the great wheat-producing estates of Chile's central valley, the net result was depersonalization of labor. During the long colonial period, the relationship between hacendado (hacienda owner) and peon had often been close, dependent, and, in many instances, mutually supportive, based on a paternalistic system that lessened the distance between owner and worker. When labor became something other than the expression of a legal and social relationship between individuals, even if they were masters and peasants, the relationship suffered. As plantations and haciendas became larger, more efficient, and more tightly wedded to the necessities of an external market, labor became but one more element in the economic formula for boosting profits. In the crudest sense, individuals became mere figures in the equation of capital, resources, and markets that governed capitalist relations. Alienation rather than paternalism marked the growing modernization of the haciendas. The redress of these sad circumstances for most Amerindians would not begin until the twentieth century.

The End of Slavery

Ironically, whereas the lot of the Amerindian worsened in the nineteenth century, the black slave won emancipation. The institution of slavery retreated during the century throughout Latin America, although unevenly. First, the slave trade had to be eliminated. Then slavery itself was gradually abolished as humanitarian sentiments and practical political and economic considerations argued ever more persuasively for its end. More difficult to assess is how the black man, woman, or child, slave or free, fit into nineteenth-century society because implicit in that question is the nature of slavery in Latin America. Was it different than the form that slavery took in North America? Was it more harsh, or more benign?

What is indisputable is the progression that abolition took. First, the Wars of Independence dealt a body blow to the institution. Not only was human bondage incompatible with the high principles of equality written into the nascent Latin American constitutions, but also blacks, mulattoes, *zambos, pardos,* and other castes had fought, and fought well, in the wars. In Argentina, for example, thousands of Afro-Argentines, both free and slave, served in the patriot armies, sometimes in segregated units, sometimes well integrated into the mainstream battalions and regiments. They fought for the promise of advancement and freedom, and some rose to high levels in the military or later gained political office. Yet, progress to emancipation was not inevitable.

Afro-Mexicans in the Wars of Independence

New research has identified "AfroMexicans," or Mexicans with African backgrounds, as leading actors in Mexico's War of Independence (1810–1823). Based on the genealogical records of the Church of the Latter Day Saints (Mormons), for example, the scholar Theodore Vincent has found that Mexican revolutionary leadership became increasingly AfroMexican during the course of the movement. By 1818, most of the leaders were AfroMexicans or Afromestizos, Mexicans with both African and Indian backgrounds. José María Morelos and Vicente Guerrero were perhaps the most famous of these. Morelos succeeded Hidalgo as the leader in the wars, while Guerrero eventually became president in 1829. Leaders such as Morelos and Guerrero played down their mixed ethnic origins, preferring to emphasize the equality of all Mexicans and do away with the racial labels so common at the time—mestizo, *pardo,* mulatto, etc. This was a key to rallying the ordinary people of Mexico for a progressive, egalitarian agenda, notes Vincent. So black roots were played down. Vincent makes a compelling case that other AfroMexicans, such as the Flores Magón brothers who helped bring on the Mexican Revolution of 1910, remained in a high profile in Mexican history. He writes "I think the story of the rise of Mexico, and the vision of the mestizo people, especially the Afromestizos, is a feather in the cap of African achievement in the New World. . . ."

(Communication received via Internet from Ted Vincent [address: fslnted@uclink.berkeley.edu] to AFROLAT mailing list, January 12, 1996)

As in the American Constitution of 1789, slavery was not eliminated with one stroke of the pen simply because the principle that "all men are created equal" carried the day. Slavery continued to exist in the United States after 1789, and slavery continued to exist in most of Latin America after 1825. Bolívar and other Creoles

In Brazil and Cuba, African men and women continued to toil as slaves in sugar mills like this one until emancipation in the 1880s.

were troubled by this contradiction. Freedom *should* be the natural state of all people, but to free the black slaves massively and immediately might threaten the predominance of the white elite.

The Haitian Revolution of 1791 and its terrible aftermath haunted the Creoles of Latin America. There the white race had either been massacred or had fled, abandoning the island to its black and mulatto rulers. Nor were the implications of the Hidalgo revolt in Mexico in 1810 ever far from the consciousness of Creoles. The beginnings of the Mexican independence movement had rapidly spun out of the control of the Creoles, loosening hordes of Amerindians and mestizos to wreak vengeance on their white masters of more than three hundred years. For Bolívar and others to abolish black slavery was to fulfill the high resolutions that inspired the Wars of Independence. To free them also was to open the door to the spectacle of social revolution and anarchy, a state intolerable to Creoles long accustomed to governing their lands. While Creoles vacillated, another strong wind of freedom blew through Latin America, strengthening the abolitionist forces.

In 1833 Great Britain abolished slavery throughout its empire. The British also pressured the rest of the western world where slavery existed to conform. The British motivation was nurtured not simply by humanitarianism but also by a complex amalgam of political and economic motives. The result was increasing pressure on the new Latin American nations to join the British.

In their efforts to persuade Latin Americans, the British played many cards. One, the British were Latin America's principal trading and commercial partners in

The Weight of the Slave Trade

The British poet of the *fin de siècle* who proved the most effective abolitionist was Robert Southey.... His simple and poignant ballad, in 1798, "The Sailor who had served in the Slave Trade," dealt with a sailor found by a minister in Bristol, groaning and praying in a cowhouse [barn]. The sailor had been ordered by the captain of a slave ship to lash a female Negro slave who had refused to eat. The captain stood by, cursing whenever the sailor paused because of the woman's cries. When she was taken down, the woman groaned and moaned, her voice growing fainter and fainter until she died. No anti-slavery propaganda was quite so effective as the final stanza of Southey's ballad:

"They flung her overboard, poor wretch
She rested from her pain . . .
But when . . . O Christ! O Blessed *God!*
Shall I have rest again!"

(Eric Williams, *From Columbus to Castro: The History of the Caribbean, 1492–1969* [New York: Vintage Books, 1970, 1984], pp. 269–270)

the nineteenth century and could bring economic pressure to bear. The trump card, however, was the powerful British Navy, undisputed sovereign of the seas in the nineteenth century. The British chased and hounded slave traders from the African coast to the waters of the new American states, lobbying with their cannon as well as with their humanitarianism.

Poets and Slaves

Poets contributed significantly to the abolitionist cause. Two mulattoes, Gonçalves Dias and Castro Alves (1847–1871), wrote some of the most beautiful poetry produced in Brazil in the nineteenth century. Although Gonçalves Dias was chiefly concerned with the Indian, he also touched very eloquently on the theme of slavery. Castro Alves dedicated himself fervently to the cause of the slaves. He depicted the plight of the slave with such moving verses that he awoke the social conscience of his readers to the injustices inflicted on the slaves. One of his best known poems, "Navio Negreiro" (The Slave Ship), evoked the inhuman suffering of the captives during the crossing from Africa to Brazil. Life on the slave ship recalls some of the scenes of Dante's *Inferno.*

(E. Bradford Burns, *A History of Brazil* (New York: Columbia University Press, 1970), p. 267.

Genuine, internal Latin American motivations, combined with British pressures, produced the momentum finally to rid Latin America of slavery. By midcentury, the institution itself had been abolished everywhere in Latin America except Brazil and Cuba (still a colony of Spain), while the British had virtually

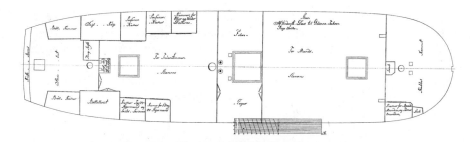

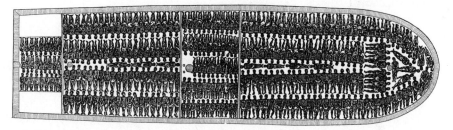

*"Tight" packing a slave ship engaged in the Atlantic slave trade from Africa to the Americas.
Such graphic displays and accounts, focusing on the inhumanity of the trade and the dangers
Africans faced, fueled the movement to suppress the trade.*

suppressed the slave trade. Slavery persisted longest in those two regions where it
continued to play an important role in their economies, and the ruling planter class
stalled as long as possible. Cuban slavery came to an end officially in 1886, followed
two years later by the Golden Law of Brazil.

One of the most powerful arguments made against slavery invoked simple economics: Free, wage labor was more efficient than slave labor. In the late eighteenth
century, the foremost thinker in England, Adam Smith, declared that slave labor was
the least productive of any in the world. His followers, among them the great English prime minister, William Pitt, reframed that argument as they sought—successfully—to destroy in the nineteenth century the slave trade and ultimately slavery
throughout the western world.

In Brazil, new immigrant labor and a dwindling slave population eroded the institution of slavery, so that even the planter class was willing to abandon it by 1888.
The planter class of Cuba, which had long championed slavery for economic and
political reasons, abandoned its commitment as new forces upended its universe.
One, the end of slavery in the United States after the Civil War broke the ties to the
American South. These ties had been sustained in the 1840s and 1850s by the possibility of Cuba's being annexed to the United States as a slave state. Many Cubans
from the 1860s to the end of the century were preoccupied with changing their island's political status in a different way. They wanted independence from Spain, and
as they moved toward this goal, they also argued for freedom for all of their people,
especially, of course, for blacks, who could be expected to be willing revolutionaries.

New economic forces also tipped the scales toward abolition in Cuba. Immigrant laborers from Mexico (Yucatecan Indians) and from China were brought in to

work in the sugar fields and on the railroads of Cuba. They tended to displace slave labor as the sugar plantations became larger and more efficient.

Less clear is how the recession of slavery throughout Latin America affected blacks. Had slavery tattooed a stigma onto black people, not easily erased by the act of abolition? Or was the opposite true? Did slavery take a milder form in the nations of the old Spanish empire, and did blacks emerge from slavery better off than their counterparts in the United States?

Slavery and Race Relations in Latin America

When attempting to interpret the meaning of a particular institution in the historical development of a nation, or a group of nations such as Latin America, one can profitably *compare* how that same institution evolved in other nations. The comparison itself sheds light on the institution by showing how other people in other lands and with other cultures dealt with that institution. Such is the case with slavery.

The basic question that all Americans (North, Central, and South Americans) have addressed is: What effect did slavery have on race relations between white and black people? In the Latin American experience, some have contended that certain mitigating factors lessened the vast social and racial distance between masters and slaves, between whites and blacks, after slavery was abolished. Among these factors were the influence of the Roman Catholic Church, the legal protection of slave rights provided for under Spanish colonial law, and the long association of Portuguese and Spanish people with darker peoples of north Africa. These factors, and others, were woven together in more detail and complexity to explain that the black experience in Latin America was less harsh than the comparable black experience in North America.

A North American historian, Frank Tannenbaum, best explained this point of view in the late 1940s, and the Tannenbaum thesis, elaborated and refined, still represents this sympathetic analysis of slavery and race relations in Latin America.

Over the years, the Tannenbaum thesis has been systematically attacked by others with equally powerful arguments. They contend that slavery was pretty much the same institution across the Americas, conditioned not by the vague factors that Tannenbaum described, but rather the result of other more precise determinants: economic and geographic being the most important. In other words, slaves working in a tropical or subtropical plantation in Cuba, Venezuela, Trinidad, or Brazil, for example, were subjected to pretty much the same system of exploitation and same degree of brutality as were their counterparts in the rice plantations of South Carolina or the cotton plantations of Louisiana.

This form of "economic determinism" is a very powerful and persuasive tool for explaining the role of certain institutions—such as slavery—in history.

In the 1930s the Brazilian social anthropologist Gilberto Freyre stressed that more subtle cultural and sexual factors bridged the gulf between masters and slaves. Living in close proximity to each other on the great plantations, sharing the same bed, worshiping the same saints, being reared by the same black and mulatto nannies—all of these cushioned the natural friction that might have poisoned relations between the ruling and slave races.

Later studies done in the 1960s and 1970s by such historians as Herbert Klein and Carl Degler comparing slavery in North America, Cuba, and Brazil furthered our understanding of the relationship between slavery and racism by drawing on new evidence and points of view.

In the end, one need not categorically embrace one point of view or the other. Each point of view has merit, and each contains much truth. The truth, in fact, lies only within each nation's history and perceptions of itself. If blacks in Cuba or Panama or Ecuador do not feel exploited or deprived or socially ostracized (as blacks in North America have legitimately claimed), then perhaps we can say with a bit more certainty that in the long course of Latin American history, blacks survived and emerged from slavery as fuller and happier people.

Women in the Nineteenth Century

Home was the sanctuary where women were regarded to be safe from the temptations of the world and where they could fulfill their natural destinies as mothers and wives. To move from family-oriented matters to issues of the outside world proved a slow and difficult process for women.[5]

The rise of feminism in the modern world has revolutionized the way that men and women relate to each other, from the bedroom to the workplace. Although this is largely a twentieth-century phenomenon, it has also sparked a vigorous and creative reinterpretation of history from a nontraditional point of view. Put another way, history is largely the result of what *questions* one asks in the search for historical reality. By the mid-twentieth century, the stage was set for this reinterpretation of history, or the application of a new set of research questions. As women sought their rights in the contemporary world, they also looked into the past to see how women fit into the historical patterns of humanity.

They found, for example and as expected, that during the colonial period and well into the nineteenth and twentieth centuries, the principal role for a woman was as wife and mother. But to be wife and mother was a complex business, best described by Evelyn Cherpak, a student of women in Latin America.

> Although women married early and were encouraged to produce large families, they did make contributions to certain areas of life both in and outside the home. Women engaged in trade and commerce; held large amounts of money and property; collected debts; controlled the female religious orders; sponsored, organized, and financed *colegios* for girls; sustained charitable activities; contributed to the religious literature of the day; managed and organized their homes; supervised the servants; gave the rudiments of education to their progeny; and moved to exert control over their husbands. The Latin American woman, although homebound much of the time, was not a docile, passive type invested with little responsibility, for she took on much and exerted herself on behalf of her family and society in general.[6]

---

[5]Asunción Lavrin, *Latin American Women: Historical Perspectives* (Westport, Conn.: Greenwood Press, 1978), p. 8.

[6]Evelyn Cherpak, "The Participation of Women in the Independence Movement in Gran Colombia, 1780–1830," in Lavrin, *Latin American Women*, pp. 219–220.

The formative nineteenth century affected the nature of women in society, although not as dramatically as the abolitionist movement changed the lives of blacks or as dramatically as misguided liberalism consigned the Amerindian even further down the social scale. The Wars of Independence opened new doors for women. Women fought alongside their men, spied for the patriots (in some instances paying for their heroism with their lives), and marched with the armies as camp followers doing the cooking, the mending, and the nursing for the men. On the island of Margarita off the coast of Venezuela, for example, women helped with the artillery during one defense of the island that repulsed a royalist attack, and their skill and dexterity in working the cannon were much praised. Bolívar pointed out the savagery that patriotic women had had to endure at the hands of the Spanish royalists.

> Even the fair sex, the delights of mankind, our amazons have fought against the tyrants of San Carlos with a valor divine, although without success. The monsters and tigers of Spain have shown the full extent of the cowardice of their nation. They have used their infamous arms against the innocent feminine breasts of our beauties; they have shed their blood. They have killed many of them and they loaded them with chains, because they conceived the sublime plan of liberating their beloved country.[7]

The Liberator himself was enraptured by an Ecuadorian beauty named Manuela Sáenz. Their passion and their affair lasted from the moment they met in 1822 until Bolívar died. Married at an early age to an Englishman, Manuela courted Bolívar instantly and, many think, outrageously. She defiantly left her husband and followed Bolívar to Lima, where she played a prominent role in social and political life. Known as "the liberator of the Liberator," she was more than a mistress. In 1828 she saved Bolívar from an assassination plot in Bogotá and attacked his enemies with vigor. She continued to defend him and his faction even after his death and in 1833 was exiled to the small fishing port of Paita in northern Peru, where she lived simply, selling sweets, until her death in 1856.

The Wars of Independence were nonetheless an unusual time. The pressures and demands of the wars loosened normal traditions and habits, allowing for excesses and unusual behavior, such as the women tending the cannon on the island of Margarita. Until near the end of the nineteenth century, women continued to be confined by the traditional roles of wife and mother. The man dominated the home in a patriarchal society.

The word that best captures this unequal relationship is *machismo,* a word that has by now passed into common English usage. It meant many things, among them virility, dominance, and power. Within Latin American society, over the centuries a countercult had developed to celebrate femininity, tolerance, love, docility, virginity, and other virtues associated with the Virgin Mary. The worship of the Virgin Mary, *marianismo,* did not detract from the centrality of Jesus Christ in women's faith, but it did celebrate the virtues of motherhood and resignation, thus reinforcing the traditional roles expected of women. The noble ideal was to be submissive

---

[7]Cherpak, p. 222, quoting from *Las fuerzas armadas de Venezuela en el siglo xix; textos para su estudio,* 12 vols. (Caracas, 1963), vol. I: 242.

and obedient, given to sacrifice and tolerance, submerging one's own feelings in nurturing the family, the cradle of values and morality. It was a role, in fact, that the great majority of Latin American women accepted as fulfilling and natural. Sexual submission and fidelity to husband were part and parcel of their society, even though husbands and lovers were free to philander, and the double standard was acceptable.

But times were slowly changing. Not only did modernization bring steam loco-motives puffing and blowing their way through the jungles and plains of Latin America in the nineteenth century, but also attitudes began to be altered subtly. In politics, positivism was in vogue. In economics it was laissez-faire liberalism. In race relations, it was abolition. And among some women, it was the stirring of something less definable, but no less important. It was the need to find something outside the home, outside the nunnery, to satisfy an urge to have more control over their lives. It was not full-fledged feminism as would flower in the mid-twentieth century, but rather a more subtle move to channel some of their energies beyond the home. They found or created a need in three basic areas: philanthropy, education, and some feminist activities. Of these three, none was more important than education.

Women in education were found earliest and with greatest influence in Argentina, a nation that modernized among the fastest. It is ironic, but not unusual, for a man to have been at the forefront of promoting education for women. Domingo F. Sarmiento was Argentina's foremost educator, a president (1868–1874), a writer, and one of the foremost apostles of modernization in his country and, indeed, throughout Latin America. Inspired by the progressive educa-tional reforms being made in the United States, where he spent several years in exile, he introduced them into his native Argentina. For Sarmiento, public secular educa-tion for citizens was the ultimate weapon for eradicating ignorance, reducing preju-dice, and transforming Argentina into a prosperous, civilized nation. A key element in Sarmiento's thinking—as well as that of Juan Bautista Alberdi, another reformer and leader—was to bring women fully into the educational system. The philosophy of Sarmiento and Alberdi was well captured by Cynthia Jeffress Little.

> Alberdi, who coined the motto "to govern is to populate," believed that Argentina would not advance until its women no longer lived under the yoke of Spanish law and customs that subjugated them first to their fathers' and then to their husbands' control. He main-tained that with scant opportunities to develop identities beyond wife and mother, most women were no more than mere children. Alberdi advocated that Argentine women should be educated to assume the full duties of citizenship and to contribute to the country's economic growth.[8]

Sarmiento was convinced that the educational models being developed by Horace Mann and others in North America were exemplary. And women played a central role, not simply as persons to be educated to fulfill their new roles of citizens, but as educators themselves, as teachers who could transmit values and knowledge

---

[8]Cynthia Jeffress Little, "Education, Philanthropy, and Feminism: Components of Argentine Womanhood, 1860–1926," in Lavrin, *Latin American Women*, p. 237.

in the new normal schools of Argentina. Sarmiento invited young North American teachers to come to Argentina to be leaders in this movement, and more than sixty came between 1869 and 1898, bringing with them the newest ways then being pioneered in the United States.

Although these ways were not particularly advanced or modern, they extolled the virtue of universality—little red schoolhouses that taught the three *r*s and ideally reached all children. They also stressed practical, vocational education.

Under Sarmiento's tutelage, these normal schools deemphasized the traditional method of rote learning, which did not promote education in the broadest sense. Self-discipline, physical fitness, technical training, and manual labor all were stressed in these new normal schools, while home economics became a linchpin of the curriculum. Old Church curricula were abandoned for a more secular, scientific study. Young women were challenged to learn new ways to improve their lives, the lives of their families, and, ultimately, the life of their nation.

In Brazil a small but active feminist press came into existence in the 1870s and 1880s, dedicated to women's issues such as improved education, respect for women, careers for women, and changes in women's legal rights. By the end of the century, even suffrage, the right of women to vote, was emerging as an issue in a society still traditionally oriented around men.

Countless other examples of women's breaking away from the traditional mold exist. In Peru, for example, Chlorinda Matto de Turner wrote *Aves sin nido* (*Birds without Nests*) in 1899, the first major Indianist novel describing the plight of the Amerindians in her country. A trailblazing book, it helped spark the Indianist movement that revolutionized Latin American society in the twentieth century. Equally important, it helped legitimize women as writers and social critics.

Life for women in nineteenth-century Latin America, nonetheless, still centered on the home, on cooking, on drawing water from the well, on courting, on early marriage, on children, and on watching the cycle repeat itself. It was a cycle marked often by love and embraced by security. If anything, the nineteenth century opened for women new horizons that supplemented, rather than competed with, the comfort and satisfaction of home and family. Fanny Calderón de la Barca, a Scotswoman married to a Spanish diplomat, lived in Mexico from 1839 to 1842, and her recollections of women in Mexico are revealing, taking into consideration that she was commenting in the following passages only on women of the upper class.

> Belonging to countries [Scotland, United States] where the lowest of the lower classes can generally write and read, we should naturally consider a country where the *highest of the higher* classes can do no more, as totally without education. But we must, in justice, compare the women of Mexico with those of the mother country [Spain]; and when we consider the acquirements of the fair [sex] in old Castile, we shall be apt to be less severe upon their . . . descendants. In the first place, the climate inclines everyone to indolence, both physical and morally. One cannot pore over a book when the blue sky is constantly smiling in at the open windows; then, out of doors, after ten o'clock, the sun gives us due warning of our tropical latitude and, even though the breeze is fresh and pleasant, one has no inclination to walk or ride far. Whatever the cause, I am convinced that it is impossible to take the same exercise with the mind or with the body in this country, as in Europe or in the northern states.

Generally speaking, then, the Mexican señoras and señoritas write, read, and play a little—sew, and take care of their houses and children. When I say they read, I mean they know how to read; when I say write, I do not mean they can always spell; and when I say they play [music], I do not assert that they have generally a knowledge of music. . . . In fact, if we compare the education of women in Mexico with that of girls in England or in the United States, we should be inclined to dismiss the subject as nonexistent. It is not a comparison, but a contrast.[9]

Clearly, Fanny Calderón's perspective was somewhat condescending. But, just as clearly, it was a world bound by the home and the cares of the home for the great majority of women.

And as in other aspects of Latin American society, a vast gulf divided the privileged Creole ladies surrounded by servants and protected by wealth from the poor Amerindian and black women subordinated by their gender and color. In other words, class divided women as well. Upper-class women found numerous avenues for the expression of their desires and skills, but lower-class women were bound largely by the simple demands of living. Their whole lives were devoted to tending the young, cooking, housekeeping, with perhaps a little entrepreneurial activity on the side, such as we saw in the action introduction to Chapter Two. A major determinant of not only women, but of all Latin American people, was where one lived, because the distinction between life in the city and life in the country became even more pronounced in the nineteenth century.

Country Life

"[In Mexico] the white is the proprietor; the Indian the worker. The white is rich; the Indian poor and miserable. The descendants of the Spaniards have within their reach all the knowledge of the century and all of the scientific discoveries; the Indian is completely unaware of it. The white dresses like a Parisian fashion plate and uses the richest of fabrics; the Indian runs around almost naked. The white lives in the cities in magnificent houses; the Indian is isolated in the country, his house a miserable hut. They are two different peoples in the same land; but worse, to a degree they are enemies."[10]

This grim observation of Mexican rural life at mid-century was not unusual. Rural life in nineteenth-century Latin America was, in fact, altered substantially by the introduction of new techniques, by the opening of new markets, by more efficient forms of organization, and by improved methods of production. The rural population declined in the second half of the nineteenth century, but it still represented about 80 to 85 percent of the total population, although the ratio of rural to urban population in countries varied tremendously. The social and economic

---

[9]Fanny Calderón de la Barca, *Life in Mexico*, edited and annotated by Howard T. Fisher and Marion Hall Fisher (Garden City: Doubleday, 1966), pp. 286–287, quoted in June E. Hahner, editor, *Women in Latin American History: Their Lives and Views* (Los Angeles, Calif.: UCLA Latin American Center Publications, 1976, 1980), p. 44.

[10]Quote is from Francisco Pimentel in 1865, quoted in Daniel Cosío Villegas, editor, *Historia moderna de Mexico*, vol. 3: *La república restaurada, la vida social*, by Luis González y González, et al. (Mexico, 1957), p. 151, in turn quoted in Meyer and Sherman, *The Course of Mexican History*, p. 416.

distance that divided the owners from the workers, the hacendados from the peons, and the masters from the slaves tended to widen.

Of the many forms of land tenure prevalent in Latin America, the most common ones devoted to commercial operations were the hacienda and the plantation. Both were large estates controlled or owned by the few and worked by the many. At the other end of the land-use spectrum were the small plots and minifarms that, along with sharecropping, probably predominated in Latin America. In much of Amerindian America—such as Mexico, Guatemala, Ecuador, Peru, and Bolivia—a significant proportion of land was still held and worked communally by Native Americans.

Haciendas and plantations were basically the same. They were not, however, simple institutions, because they fulfilled several different goals and were conditioned by regional differences. They evolved in the rapidly changing conditions of the nineteenth century and were quite dynamic rather than static institutions.

Economically, the haciendas and plantations were among the principal forms of livelihood in nineteenth-century Latin America. They were, in many instances, self-sufficient, producing foods, animals, and rudimentary goods for local consumption. Cash crops and animals—from sugar to cattle—also came off the plantations and haciendas to be sold for profit either in domestic markets or through export. Socially, haciendas and plantations were the basic source of wealth to maintain and increase the status of the elites who owned or controlled them. And politically, they nurtured the rulers who by and large shared a common background—commercial landholding—which was their source of power. One has simply to refer to the great and small caudillos of the nineteenth century to witness how closely they resembled each other in their sources of power. Santa Anna of Mexico and Rosas of Argentina, for example, were hacendados who drew strength from fellow hacendados.

The haciendas produced everything from beans for their peons to sugar for export to the emporiums of Europe. Life on the haciendas varied widely. It depended upon who one was. The historian James Scobie captured some of this variety in the following passage written about Argentina. *Estancias* was simply another term for ranches, in this instance haciendas geared more for livestock production.

The Estancias of Argentina

A few of the rural population—the wealthy landowner or cattleman—enjoyed the amenities of a civilized existence. By the end of the nineteenth century the *estancia* headquarters had changed from a bare frontier outpost into a Mediterranean villa, a French chateau, or a gabled English country house, surrounded by eucalyptus groves, cropped lawns, rose gardens, and tennis courts. But for these people, country residence was limited to summer or weekend visits, and they were far better acquainted with the streets of Buenos Aires or Paris and the beaches of Mar del Plata than with the land which provided their wealth. Those who actually lived on the pampas led quite another existence. . . .

(James R. Scobie, *Argentina: A City and a Nation* (New York: Oxford University Press, 1971), p. 126)

For Mexico, another historian, Michael Meyer, described the flip side of the coin: life on a hacienda for the peon.

The Haciendas of Mexico

Working conditions varied considerably from region to region and even from hacienda to hacienda, but they were generally poor. Peones often availed themselves of the talents of a scribe to spell out their gamut of complaints. While it was not uncommon for the peon to be allotted a couple of furrows to plant a little corn and chili and on occasion he might receive a small ration of food from the hacienda, he worked from sunrise to sunset, often seven days a week, raising crops or tending cattle. Sometimes he was allowed to cut firewood free; on other occasions he paid for the right. The scant wages he received most often were not paid in currency but in certificates or metal discs redeemable only at the local *tienda de raya,* an all-purpose company store located on the hacienda complex. Credit was extended liberally, but the prices, set by the hacendado or the mayordomo were invariably several times higher than those in a nearby village. For the hacendado the situation was perfect. The taxes on his land were negligible; his labor was, in effect, free, for all the wages that went out came back to him through the *tienda de raya* with a handsome profit. The peon found himself in a state of perpetual debt, and by law he was bound to remain on the hacienda so long as he owed a single centavo. Debts were not eradicated at the time of death but passed on to the children. Should an occasional obdurate peon escape, there was scarcely any place for him to go. Many states had laws making it illegal to hire an indebted peon.

(Meyer and Sherman, *The Course of Mexican History,* p. 461)

Stanley Stein described life for a slave on a sugar or coffee plantation in Brazil.

The Fazendas of Brazil

"Greater or lesser perfection . . . of discipline determines the greater or lesser degree of prosperity of agricultural establishments." Constant supervision and thorough control through discipline joined to swift, often brutal punishment were considered an absolute necessity on coffee plantations. Proper function of a fazenda [Portuguese for hacienda] varied directly with the steady application of the working force; in an epoch of little machinery, slave labor or what Brazilians termed "organized labor," had to be guided carefully and supervised closely. . . .

Most visible of the master's authority over the slave, the whip enjoyed several names: there was the literate term *chicote* which was usually a five-tailed and metal-tipped lash, colloquially known as the "codfish" or "armadillo." Probably because Portuguese drivers went armed with such cat-o'-nine-tails, slaves tagged it with the name of the favorite article of Portuguese diet—codfish. It was felt that sometimes it was used too much, sometimes too little, for often masters had the "very poor habit of failing to whip on the spot, and prefer to threaten the vexatious slave with 'Wait, you'll pay for this all at once' or 'The cup is brimming, wait 'til it pours over and *then* we'll see'—and at that time they grab and beat him unmercifully; why? because he paid for his misdeeds *all at once*!!!!" It was difficult to apply legal restraints to the planters' use of the lash. When one of the founding fathers of Vassouras [a Brazilian coffee-producing region], Ambrozio de Souza Coutinho, proposed, as one of the municipal regulations of 1829, that "Every master who mistreats his slaves with blows and lashes, with repeated and inhuman punishment proven by verbal testimony . . ." be fined, fellow-planters refused to accept it. Not sheer perversity but the desire to drive slaves to work longer and harder motivated liberal use of the lash. "Many inhuman fazendeiros [Portuguese for *hacendado*]," wrote Caetano da Fonseca, more than thirty years after Souza Coutinho, "force their slaves with the lash to work beyond physical endurance. These wretched slaves, using up their last drops of energy, end their days in a brief time."

(Stanley Stein, "Masters and Slaves in Southern Brazil," in Robert G. Keith, *Haciendas and Plantations in Latin American History* [New York: Holmes & Meier, 1977], pp. 94–95)

These three examples of life on haciendas and *fazendas* provide only a small glimpse into the diversity of the relationships that developed on these estates. Some research has suggested that life was not as rigidly regulated or as demeaning as these three passages suggest. For example, the system of debt peonage described so well in the passage on Mexico may not have so dominated the relationship between landlord and peon as was once thought. In Peru, Amerindians who were persuaded to come down from the highlands to work seasonally on the sugar and cotton plantations of the coast soon learned to bargain actively for their labor with the hacienda owners. In other countries, slaves could be brutalized by overseers intent on getting the most work out of the slaves' short life span. Or conversely, slaves might have been given relatively mild treatment, such as described by Gilberto Freyre, created by the intimacy of life within the great houses on the sugar estates of the Brazilian Northeast.

Not all land was owned by the hacendado class in Latin America. Perhaps 30 to 40 percent of the land in the great Amerindian nations (Mexico, Guatemala, Ecuador, Peru, and Bolivia, principally) was still preserved by the ancient communities that owned the land collectively.

In other parts of Latin America, workers on the haciendas might also have been small landowners, or tenants who were allowed to farm a portion of the hacienda's land for their own benefit. Such people were called *inquilinos* in Chile, *parceiros* in Brazil; again, other names were applied in other places. Their lot may or may not have been onerous, depending upon the conditions and the place.

Labor on the haciendas could be permanent or seasonal. Coffee plantations in the highlands of Guatemala or sugar plantations in Cuba or Peru necessitated large amounts of labor at selected times of the year, principally, of course, during harvest time. In these areas, especially as those crops developed larger markets abroad, migrant laborers tended to be treated more as components in the economic formula that produced capital. As wage laborers, they could be hired and fired at will. This gave the owners surer control over labor, and thus better control over their exports, whose market conditions also varied widely.

The haciendas and plantations themselves took on different complexions in the nineteenth century to meet the changing market conditions abroad. As they shifted to producing more and more for export, they became larger and more commercialized, necessitating greater amounts of labor and capital. If the labor was not available locally, they reached into other parts of the country for labor. As noted earlier,

Chinese "coolies" being auctioned off for labor on the railroads and in the sugar mills of Cuba. Beginning in the 1840s, tens of thousands of Chinese peasants boarded ships bound for the Americas. They worked as indentured servants all across Latin America where rapid economic growth put a premium on agricultural and industrial laborers.

coastal sugar plantations in Peru attracted Amerindians down from the highlands who came as seasonal, paid laborers.

When domestic sources of labor were insufficient, hacendados and other employers (such as the great railroad builders in the second half of the century) looked abroad. Chinese coolies were imported into Costa Rica, Peru, and Cuba not only to work on the railroads but also to plant and till and harvest on the expanding plantations. Emigrants from Italy swelled the rural population of Argentina and Brazil to allow for the rapid expansion of the wheat and coffee industries, for example. Although the experience of Italians in the coffee groves of Brazil might have been harsh, it was different from the experience of Yucatecan Indians, nearly enslaved by tradition and force on the sugar and henequen plantations of their native homeland.

Throughout the nineteenth century, land tended to be concentrated more and more into larger estates controlled by fewer people. The goal was to make haciendas and plantations more efficient, to produce more with lowered costs for the export market. In Cuba, great *centrales* (large, modern sugar plantations) replaced the smaller and less efficient sugar mills of the past. The same occurred in Peru, where concentration reached such an extreme that by the turn of the century, most of the sugar industry was controlled by a handful of people. The result, from Chile north to Mexico, from Cuba south to Argentina, was the impoverishment of the people who worked the land, whether they were tenants, seasonal laborers, immigrants, Amerindians, mestizos, blacks, or free men.

When one considers that Latin America in the nineteenth century was still overwhelmingly rural, this tendency certainly worked against the majority of the people. For every trend, however, there is usually one, under way or in the genesis, that contradicts the larger trend or that argues in the face of it for a different view. As life got tougher in the country, it improved in the cities.

Life in the Cities

The Hispanic and Portuguese legacy of Latin America emphasized the city as the center of culture and society. The tendencies set loose by the modernization and industrialization processes in the nineteenth century reinforced urbanization. Cities grew larger and more prosperous, becoming the diadems of progress, crisscrossed by the new trams and streetcars clanking along wide boulevards carved out from the narrow colonial alleys and streets.

Opera houses and salons catered to the wealthy, while business and politics hummed in the countinghouses and government palaces built to accommodate the new lifestyles. Although there were great differences in statistics between nations, the number of people living in cities increased dramatically in Latin America from the 1870s through the 1930s, so that by the early twentieth century from 10 to 20 percent of the population of Latin America was urban.

The influence of Europe was pervasive in the great, and even not-so-great, cities of Latin America. Paris fashions adorned the women, and English customs were affected by many. Jockey clubs, cricket clubs, and other trappings of European life popped up in Mexico City, Buenos Aires, and Santiago. If Europe was the center of

Downtown Buenos Aires, Argentina, at the turn of the twentieth century. The signs of modernization are easily recognizable: cars, wide boulevards, architecture inspired by European styles, a city and a nation on the move.

civilization, then its ways were to be imitated. Sons were sent packing off to the cities of Europe to be educated, artists escaped the suffocating provinciality of Latin America to breathe in the invigorating streams of innovation and experimentation, and even European political ideals and philosophies (positivism and racial determinism, for example) were imported wholesale into Latin America.

Buenos Aires, a Great City in the Making

This was the city that by 1910 even Parisians would claim as the Paris of South America after a Cinderella-like transformation from *gran aldea* [big town] into the beautiful and prosperous queen of the Rio de la Plata. Much of the change was physical.... Open sewers and dirt streets disappeared from downtown Buenos Aires during the 1880s ... and by the turn of the century porteño ladies were enjoying relatively comfortable carriage rides (aided by the first use of rubber tires) over a steadily expanding network of asphaltic streets and avenues.... By 1905 electricity had largely replaced the overworked horses of the city's trolley system.... How rapidly the city was changing was emphasized in 1911 when work began on the Avenida de Mayo subway. Three years later, the British-built line was opened to its present extension four miles west of the Plaza de Mayo—only a decade after New York City had opened the first major subway in the hemisphere.... Office buildings, hotels, and private palaces replaced many of the one- or two-story, patio-style houses in the center of Buenos Aires....

(Scobie, *Argentina*, pp. 164–167)

Valparaiso

I was struck by the very civilized look of the famous Chilean seaport. . . . In the dining-room of the hotel the electric light was used, as well as in very many of the stores. In the streets is a "Belgium" pavement, and the sidewalks are smoothly and neatly flagged. The architecture of some of the buildings is very fine, and there are several rich and elegant churches. The principal streets are threaded by tramways. The trams, or cars, are of two stories as in Paris and other European cities.

(Burns, *Latin America*, p. 141, quoting from Frank Vincent, a traveler in Valparaiso in 1885. No other citation.)

People flocked to the city from the countryside, and immigrants further swelled the populations. São Paulo's population jumped from 64,000 in 1890 to 240,000 barely a decade later. Santiago's population went from 160,000 in 1880 to 400,000 by 1910. Mexico City was swept along in the same trend, its population rising from 200,000 in 1874 to almost 500,000 in 1910.

Smaller cities sometimes recorded even more spectacular increases, their populations tripling, quadrupling, quintupling as railroads, mining, port improvements, and other incentives promoted growth.

Of the great cities of Latin America, Buenos Aires perhaps underwent one of the most spectacular transformations. Its population jumped fivefold from 300,000 in 1880 to 1,500,000 in 1914. James Scobie subtitled his classic study of Argentina "A City and a Nation" in recognition of the dominating position of the city within modern Argentina.

In Chile, Valparaiso, a beautiful port city rising from a bay into the hills that climb steeply from the water's edge, also was transformed, provoking a rave review from one observer in 1885.

The observations about other Latin American cities differed only in details from those about Buenos Aires and Valparaiso. Although madly modernizing their cities, Latin Americans were not insensitive to the need to beautify and humanize as they tore down the old and built the new. Parks and promenades, great trees and shaded walks all were planned into the new cities. Mexico City's great Alameda Park was a gathering place for young and old, rich and poor, while public activities such as bullfights also brought all the classes together in the city.

The Latin American city had a leveling effect on society that did not occur in the countryside. The principal beneficiaries of this effect were members of the expanding middle class, a rather vague group that we can begin to define as everybody who was not a member of the elite or of the lower classes, sometimes also called the "working class." In fact, there were no harder workers with no more powerful ambitions than the middle class. Who were they?

By profession and economic activity they were bank clerks, government bureaucrats, low-ranking army officers, teachers, clergymen, small businessmen, skilled artisans, journalists, neighborhood grocers, people on the way up. Ethnically, they could be mestizos, whites, European or Asian immigrants, mulattoes, blacks—all persons, in fact, whose economic activity was more important in defining them than was their color. They aspired to move up the economic and social ladder. This meant finding larger, more modern apartments or homes equipped with the best of the modern, city life: running water, sewerage, electricity. They dressed for prosperity and wished to give evidence of their prosperity. They often spent more than they made to keep up a good front and to give their children the best chances at a good education. They were subject to fluctuations in the economy, being pinched severely in times of inflation and recession. Perhaps most important, they did not have a clearly defined sense of class. They were glad to have risen above the lower classes, and they aspired to be like the upper classes. Their values thus tended to be adopted from the elites. They possessed little political cohesiveness and were scattered around the many political groupings in the nineteenth century. In numbers they represented about a tenth of the population, largely concentrated in the cities, where the industrialization and urbanization processes provided the opportunities for advancement.

The bulk of the population in the growing cities was the lower classes. Synonyms are colorful, but sometimes not very helpful, in describing the lower classes: the "working class," the "masses," the "proletariat" in the most dispassionate analysis; the "mobs," the "ignorant," the "brutes" in the eyes of many contemporaries at the turn of the century. They worked in the factories, as stevedores on the piers and wharves, as pick and shovel men in the vastly expanding public works sponsored by the governments. They were, in fact, everywhere where strong backs or nimble fingers were needed to dig ditches or work the looms of textile mills or labor in any other of the many enterprises associated with the growing economies.

And members of the lower classes, be they Amerindians recently arrived in the coastal cities of Peru, or Italians in the cities of southern Brazil, or mestizos migrating from country to city throughout Latin America, they received few immediate benefits from their work. They were, in fact, underfed, overworked, exploited, and in the main helpless to protect themselves in a political society where laissez faire was the reigning philosophy. Laws to protect men, women, or children in the workplace simply did not exist, whereas laws and traditions that forbade the formation of labor unions *did* exist and were often enforced with brutality by governments largely controlled by the elites. Illiteracy and poverty were associated with life among the lower classes. Infant mortality ran as high as 30 percent among Mexico's lower classes, a dismal statistic to contemplate when translated into the human suffering that dead and dying children meant to mothers and fathers. In Argentina, real wages among the urban poor climbed slightly during the booming 1880s and 1890s, then spiraled downward in succeeding downturns of the economy.

The temptation is strong to overdramatize the situation of the lower classes, or the "plight of the poor," as a more popular literary phrase puts it. But, in even the most dispassionate analysis of the quality of life of Latin America in the nineteenth century, one cannot ignore the gulf that separated the elites, the aspiring middle classes, and the great mass of people labeled the "lower class." Although the *promise* of a better life was inherent in the profound changes being induced by modernization—greater opportunities, new jobs, new industries, new hopes (being best realized by the small middle class)—the great majority of people still led humble lives, prevented from rising out of an existence that is difficult for us to imagine by their il-literacy, their poverty, and powerful traditions and institutions. Indeed, the great rev-olutions of the twentieth century in Latin America, covered in succeeding chapters, began when these contrasts in wealth and opportunity could no longer be tolerated.

Amidst all these changes, one of the principal institutions from the colonial pe-riod emerged intact from the Wars of Independence into the nineteenth century. It survived political assaults on its power, economic assaults on its property, and philo-sophical assaults on its significance, but it survived, as it still does today in Latin America, as one of the great sources of spiritual and physical solace and comfort for the great mass of Latin Americans. That institution is the Roman Catholic Church.

Religion and the Church

There was in the Church a social unity as well as a unity of belief. The Catholic religion was implanted not only on the coasts but also in the highlands, not only in the towns but also in the country, among peasants, miners, and artisans.

Religion in nineteenth-century Latin America was expressed in a wide variety of ways. Much of it remained what it had been during most of the colonial period—largely practiced through the Roman Catholic Church. Although the Church repre-sented the principal form of organized religion in Latin America, other religious

Religion of the People

It has been said of Peru: "From Spanish cities to the most primitive Indian communi-ties in the bleak *altiplano* [high plains] the same signs and symbols of the Christian faith were recognized and revered, pointing to a unity of religious belief that cut across steep economic, social and linguistic barriers. . . ." [The sacred landscape was] the local world of images and relics, patron saints, vows, shrines and miracles, and all the other spiritual aids which these urban and rural communities invoked against the scourge of plague, earthquake, drought and famine. The religion of the people was expressed in various ways, vows to Our Lady and the saints, relics and indulgences, and, above all, the shrines and sacred sites of local religious life. These were the scenes of cures, miracles and visions, the holy places where prayers were said and heard, the objects of processions and pilgrimages, part of the landscape of the peo-ple. Everyday life was pervaded by religion, which appeared to the people in meta-physical truths and physical forms; it answered their questions and satisfied their needs which nature itself could not. The great religious processions, Christ of the Miracles in Lima, Our Lady of Chapi in Arequipa, the Lord of Solitude in Huaraz, Our Lady of Copacabana in Bolivia, Our Lady of Luján in Argentina, Our Lady of Guadalupe in Mexico, these testify to the popular base of the Church and the strength of popular religiosity."

"The Catholic Church in Latin America, 1830–1930," Leslie Bethell, *The Cambridge History of Latin America*, vol. IV, c. 1870–1930 (Cambridge: Cambridge University Press) pp. 553–554.

Religious procession in Lima, Peru, circa 1935. Thousands of believers surrounded the statue of Christ, Cristo de los Milagros, as it was carried through the streets of the capital.

currents flowed through the spiritual life of the people. Many African Americans, for example, developed alternate religious institutions such as *candomblé* in Brazil, *vodon* (voodoo) in Haiti, and *santería* in Cuba. In the heavily populated Amerindian regions of Latin America, such as in Mexico, Guatemala, and along the Andes of the west coast of South America, many syncretized (or combined) forms of worship developed. Catholicism was accepted, but the worship of aboriginal gods and spirits, often associated with geographic locations and natural phenomena, also co-existed with formal Catholicism. Even Protestantism made some inroads into the region in the nineteenth century, largely through the missionary movements of main line denominations such as Presbyterian and Methodist. The main impact of

Protestantism, however, would come in the second half of the twentieth century with the dramatic expansion of the Evangelicals and Pentecostals.

The Roman Catholic Church underwent some drastic changes as it adapted to the conditions brought on by independence and modernization. The formal separation of Church and state came about as the new countries broke their ties with Spain. The Church also had to meet the challenges of a rising tide of secularism and positivism, which challenged its ancient monopoly on truth and morality. It had to adjust to a world where its word and its jurisdiction were not simply accepted on the basis of faith, law, and tradition. The transition for the Church was wrenching in many instances, and its struggle for survival began with the shock of independence.

When the ties between the colonies and the Spanish crown were severed by independence, the centuries-old bond between the Church and its principal benefactor, the crown, was also cut. The new national governments in turn quickly assumed the old powers of the crown to appoint Church officials, collect and distribute tithes, and, in effect, administer many aspects of Church life. Some new governments also moved to strip much of the Church's economic wealth by confiscating lands and property while eliminating or cutting back the religious orders, secularizing education, and attacking other rights and privileges of the Church.

For the rest of the nineteenth century, the Church essentially adjusted to the harsh conditions forced upon it by liberals, positivists, and nationalists who wanted to gain control over the Church and its many powers in such diverse areas as education and property holding, for example. Eventually cut loose from the support of the state (which became its antagonist when controlled by ardent liberals), the Church became more independent by the dawn of the twentieth century. Instead of looking to the crown or to the republic, it became more closely tied to the papacy in Rome. There, occupying the ancient seat of the apostle St. Peter, activist popes—especially Pius IX in the 1860s and 1870s and Leo XIII in the 1890s—reasserted control over the Church in Latin America and moved to revitalize it.

In the second half of the nineteenth century, reform and renewed evangelization became passwords of the changing Church. New priests emerged from the seminaries instilled with a strict morality and a deep commitment to their flocks. Becoming more orthodox, they also fought liberalism passionately, underscoring the tendency of the Church to associate with conservative factions in political battles. Pope Pius IX reaffirmed the Church's antagonism to liberalism with his *Syllabus of Errors,* an annex to an encyclical published in 1864.

The *Syllabus* condemned liberalism, freedom of thought, toleration, and secular education. The Church lashed out at its enemies who undermined its authority. Positivism especially drew the Church's fire because it seemed to represent an alternative religion, a faith in science rather than in tradition and revelation. Intellectual radicals such as the Peruvian Manuel González Prada (1848–1918) attacked the Church directly, calling for it to be eliminated from all public life and for science, as its substitute, to be raised as "'the only God of the future.'"[11]

---

[11]"The Catholic Church in Latin America, 1830–1930," in *The Cambridge History,* p. 560, and Jeffrey L. Klaiber, S. J., *Religion and Reform in Peru, 1824–1976* (Notre Dame, Ind.: University of Notre Dame Press, 1977).

As the Church sought to renew and protect itself, it also had to face a rapidly changing world, marked not only by hostile philosophies such as positivism, but also by modernization, urbanization, and industrialization. To meet the challenges of the new working classes in the cities, of immigrants, and of countless other phenomena associated with modernization, Pope Leo XIII in 1891 issued a critical encyclical entitled *Rerum Novarum* (*Of New Things*). In it he took the revolutionary position that the Church must protect the rights of workers and fight the injustices of the liberal system. Catholics had the duty to promote social justice and to ensure that the immense gaps between rich and poor would be closed by state intervention or by the application of justice. It denied the validity of socialism, which competed with the Church for the allegiance of the masses, but it also attacked unbridled capitalism as a source of inequality and injustice. *Rerum Novarum* was, in effect, a modern response by an ancient institution, the Church, to challenges to its worth and validity.

The Church before the Modern World

Yet the Church in Latin America had adjusted to change. At the beginning of the nineteenth century it was a colonial Church, dependent on a metropolis, Spain or Portugal. A century later it was truly independent, compatible with the nation state yet part of the universal Church. It still fulfilled a basic responsibility of the Church, to bring people to God, and it preserved intact Christian doctrine and religious observance for transmission to future generations . . . the compromising alliance of the altar and the throne, of the church and the state, was gone forever . . . [yet] this new independence . . . enabled the Church to speak more clearly to the poor and oppressed. It sharpened the division between religionists and secularists . . . at the same time the Church expanded materially, increasing its own revenues and strengthening its own institutions.

("The Catholic Church in Latin America, 1830–1930," p. 595)

As the Church adjusted to the demands of the modernizing world, the people of Latin America continued to practice and develop other forms of worship that reflected the immensely diverse ethnic and cultural population of the region. *Candomblé* in Brazil combined African spirits and liturgies into a Catholic context where African religious traits, folk Catholicism, and native Brazilian Indian folklore all commingled in novel forms. Haitian voodoo, based on the belief systems of Dahomeans, an African people enslaved and brought to the island in the eighteenth century, focused on spirit worship. It became a crucial focal point in the slave rebellions that eventually overthrew the French colonial authorities and established a free Haiti. And along the Andes and other parts of Amerindian America ancient gods and spirits continued to coexist with Christian saints, sometimes subsumed into Church ritual, sometimes simply practiced alongside Christian forms of worship. Mountains, streams, and lakes all could be the abode of spirits whose presence far predated the arrival of Christianity.

Religion in Latin America was the natural expression of a desire to understand and live in harmony with the supernatural world beyond people's immediate senses. As we probe the history of Latin America, it becomes evident that the reality is far deeper and richer than simple economic and political approaches, for example, can reveal. Running beneath the surface of political and social realities are rich cultures that open different windows into the human condition.

Conclusions and Issues

In this chapter we have considered broad areas of what is traditionally called "social" history. The multicolored ethnic makeup of large portions of the population and the nature of racism provide us with immense insight into the nature of a society that was often heterogeneous in the extreme. Within such societies extremes of wealth and privilege, poverty and subjugation exist, and Latin America was no different. Between these extremes of the white wealthy elite and the powerless and penniless black slaves, there existed a broad stratum of Amerindians, free blacks, poor whites, and powerful mestizos, mulattoes, and *pardos* who belied the stereotypical situation of a simple privileged white elite governing a mass of Amerindians, black slaves, and castes. The situation of women is one striking example of how our research questions often drive our answers, which, in turn, can alter our perception of history. Women were not simply passive actors on the stage, but rather actively sought their own goals and set their own agendas, even if limited within the prevailing norms of the culture to what are often perceived as domestic and family issues.

Likewise, we examined the abolition of slavery, some of the major ways in which people related to each other in urban and rural environments, and the role of religion in the region. Each of these topics gives us insight into how people lived, worked, played, and worshiped within complex societies. Extremes did indeed exist within Latin American societies, but there were immense "spaces" between the very rich and the very poor, spaces occupied by native and African religions, spaces occupied by small but emerging middle classes, spaces marked by the evolution of a people who possessed a rich and varied culture and society.

Discussion Questions

1. How was racism expressed in nineteenth-century Latin America?

2. How have feminist interpretations of gender history changed our view of women in nineteenth-century Latin America?

3. How were ideals and practical elements woven into the abolition of slavery in Latin America? Which was more important? Can we really determine?

The Development of Nations: Mexico and Central America

Mr. Mora's Cup of Coffee

"Well, Mr. Mora, we make sail in two weeks," Captain Le Lacheur said to Juan Rafael Mora.

They were sitting in the shade of Mora's backyard in Costa Rica's small capital city of San José. It was 1843.

"*Otro cafecito para el Capitán, por favor* ("Another coffee for the Captain, please")," Mora waved to one of his servants.

"I've got a half-empty ship, don José," Captain Le Lacheur continued his line of thought as he watched the servant girl disappear into the kitchen to fetch him another cup of the strong, dark roasted brew of the tropics that he had grown accustomed to in these past few weeks. "I need to fill the holds to make this trip pay," Le Lacheur said to Mora.

It was already warming in the early afternoon in this tiny capital city slung like a small village in a broad valley between the volcanoes and mountains. In the Pacific coast town of Puntarenas, where Captain Le Lacheur's ship, the *Monarch,* rode at anchor, he knew that it was hot and sultry, with only perhaps a late afternoon sea breeze to cool the brow. Up here, well over three thousand feet above sea level, the tropical heat was mellowed by the altitude. It was the rainy season, so Le Lacheur also expected a round of showers later in the afternoon. You could almost set your clock by the appearance of the dark clouds scudding over the mountains to bathe the town in rain. It poured for an hour or two, then, just as suddenly, the clouds rolled away, and the late afternoon sun dried the town and its people.

"Yes, we need to get the *Monarch* loaded," Mora said. Captain Le Lacheur had come to Mora based on a letter of recommendation that he had received many months ago, before pushing the small *Monarch's* prow into the stream of the Thames River to carry it down to the sea and thence around the world. Sometimes Le Lacheur thought he wasn't even on the same planet, as his senses filled with the sweet-smelling, luxuriant flowers and vines of the tropics in this small Spanish-speaking mountain hamlet seemingly untouched by the obnoxious engines of industrialization. London was shrouded in smog, pitched into a seemingly eternal—some say infernal—gray world of soot and smoke. San José was a siesta in a hammock with a pleasant breeze caressing your cheek, the sounds of farm animals not too distant, the smells of earth and flowers, the sights of awesome, inspiring volcanoes to fill your eyes and remind you of God's presence.

"What about coffee, Captain?" Mora spoke, breaking Le Lacheur's reverie.

"Uh, no, thanks, this is quite enough," Le Lacheur responded, wondering why Mora was offering him another cup just after the servant girl Manuela had placed a fresh cup by his side.

"No," Mora said with a smile. "Why not fill the rest of your hold with coffee?"

"Coffee?" Le Lacheur echoed Mora, looking down at his cup. Why not coffee? Why not indeed? There was already a market for it in England, that nation of hard-core tea drinkers who were not afraid of developing new tastes.

"We send coffee to England already, as you know," Mora said to Le Lacheur. "But it goes through Chile."

"Yes, I have met some of the masters back in London who shipped coffee from Valparaiso. That was Costa Rican coffee?" Le Lacheur asked, now more than simply curious.

"For ten years we have sent our bags of coffee to Valparaiso, Captain," Mora continued. "To the Chileans, who then raise the price and sell it to your compatriots, English merchants in Chile. Then to the shipmasters. Then to England."

"Why not ship it direct, eh, Mr. Mora?" Le Lacheur quickly followed the line of thought.

The patio where they sat seemed to shake ever so slightly, and Le Lacheur felt a slight dizziness. "Am I lightheaded from something?" Le Lacheur thought to himself. He looked quizzically at his coffee. It was shimmering in the cup.

"*Temblor*," Mora said just as two of the servant girls came tumbling out of the back door from the kitchen into the patio.

"*Terremoto! Terremoto!*" they both screamed.

"Ay, *chicas,* calm yourselves. It's only a tremor," Mora said as Le Lacheur watched his coffee, transfixed by how the liquid sloshed around the cup, moved by the minor earthquake. It was over in a few seconds. Le Lacheur remembered reading something by the great German naturalist, Alexander von Humboldt, about this part of the world. What did he call it? The rim of fire? Volcanoes and earthquakes were as much a part of the scene as the rains and winds of his homeland, far away facing the English

Channel. They could be nasty and fatal for an unwary shipmaster. But this business of earthquakes was another matter.

"Felt one before?" Mora asked, now standing and quickly hushing the girls and telling them to go back inside. It was over.

"No, can't say that I have," Le Lacheur answered.

"It is nothing to worry about, Captain. God's will is not for us to determine, no?" Mora asked rhetorically.

"Indeed, Mr. Mora. We sometimes forget who is in charge," Le Lacheur answered.

Within a few months Captain Le Lacheur was back in England with the first load of Costa Rican coffee to reach London, direct from the small Central American nation. When Le Lacheur returned to Costa Rica in 1845 with the money for the coffee growers, the cycle was complete. A new commerce had been established that would transform much of Central America and eventually make coffee the king of export crops there. The relatively backward, traditional, and even parochial little nation was being integrated into the growing world economy.

While Costa Rica was about to be transformed by a new commerce, Mexico, its larger, more complex neighbor to the north, was plunged into an equally transcending moment in its history. Except that in Mexico, the changes were ushered in by war, not by the quiet, profitable trade of a bean.

Mexico

The history of Mexico from the overthrow of Santa Anna in 1855 to the turn of the century is divided into two chronological parts: the triumph of the Liberal Party, called the Period of the Reform; and the *Porfiriato,* or the long rule (1876 to 1910) of the dictator Porfirio Díaz. The man most intimately associated with the first period is Benito Juárez, a revered figure in Mexican history, and justly so.

The War of the Reform

Benito Juárez, a Zapotec Indian, came from the state of Oaxaca. Born poor in 1806 and illiterate until the age of twelve, he nonetheless strove to improve himself, eventually finishing law school and rising in the ranks of the political order in his native state. His predispositions and training were mainstream liberal, and he naturally enough questioned and subsequently attacked the privileged society of Mexico dominated by wealthy landowners and a profoundly conservative Church. When Santa Anna was overthrown by a revolution in 1855, Juárez emerged as a leader and was appointed the secretary of justice in the new government dominated by Liberals.

No other figure in Mexican history is more beloved than Benito Juárez. He rose in Mexican life to become a hero, delivering his country from a foreign invader,

This portrait of Benito Juárez, the great liberal leader of his country in the 1850s and 1860s, shows the pronounced Indian features that helped him forge such a strong bond with Mexico's immense Amerindian population. Perhaps the most beloved of Mexican historic figures, he was an effective advocate of classic liberal doctrines.

becoming the quintessential activist for liberal causes. That he was an Amerindian endowed him with even more affection in a country where Amerindian blood ran through more than 90 percent of the population.

He was orphaned at the age of three and raised by an uncle in a small village, San Pablo Guelatao, where Spanish was spoken by very few in favor of their Zapotec dialect. An intrepid spirit governed the boy, and at the age of twelve he took off walking for the state capital of Oaxaca forty-one miles distant. There an older sister gave him refuge and found him a job working in the home of a Franciscan lay brother who did bookbinding in his spare time. In return for work, the Franciscan paid for Benito's first schooling, which eventually led him to study law. Benito received his certificate in 1831 at the age of twenty-five. Early on he was attracted to letters and to the law, and it was certainly not hard to develop the sense of injustice in Mexican society and of the need for reform that marked his career.

Even as he entered politics in Oaxaca, successively being elected to the city council, state legislature, and eventually the governorship (1848), he found time to defend poor people exploited by members of the clergy who demanded exorbitant fees for the sacraments, and to protest the actions of the local landholding elites against the poorer villagers and farmers, most of them Amerindians.

By the early 1850s Juárez's liberal credentials were well established, and when Santa Anna returned to power one last time, he had Juárez arrested and exiled. Juárez found other liberals in New Orleans, where he joined them in plotting the overthrow of this last Santa Anna dictatorship. The exiles drew up a statement of principles that evolved into another one of Mexico's famous plans, this one the Plan of Ayutla. It was, as usual, a call for insurrection, outlining grievances and offering solutions. For Santa Anna, it was the beginning of the end. He resigned and went into exile for the last time in 1855. For Juárez and his Liberals, it was the beginning of a prolonged internecine war that savaged Mexico from 1858 to 1860.

It was not long before the Liberals and Juárez, the secretary of justice, struck at some of their favorite Conservative targets. The Constitution of 1857 was a Liberal instrument, and it attacked the Church and the rights and privileges (*fueros*) of both the military and the clergy. The Conservative reaction was violent and led to civil war.

The Constitution incorporated two Liberal laws that had been passed the year before and that set the tone of the conflicts of La Reforma (the period of Liberal reforms). The *Ley Juárez* and the *Ley Lerdo* both directly attacked the corporate privileges of the military and the Church, but it was the reaction to the latter that produced the most acrimony. The *Ley Juárez* essentially stripped military and ecclesiastical tribunals of their right to try all cases—civil or criminal—involving soldiers and priests in their own private courts, while the *Ley Lerdo* forced the Church to sell off many of its properties. The Constitution of 1857 not only incorporated the *Ley Lerdo* and the *Ley Juárez* but also went further in implementing Liberal principles.

A wide-ranging bill of rights was created, including freedom of the press, of speech, of petition, of assembly, and of education. Slavery was abolished, and the right of *habeas corpus* guaranteed, but none of the provisions sparked more controversy than those attacking the Church. Conservatives viewed the entire Constitution as a monstrous violation of historical sense and religious order; even the pope, Pius IX, got into the fray, directly condemning the work of the constitutional assembly.

The War of the Reform

"The Chamber of Deputies," wrote the Pope, "among the many insults it has heaped upon our Most Holy religion and upon its ministers, as well as upon the Vicar of Christ on Earth [i.e., upon the pope himself], has proposed a new constitution containing many articles, not a few of which conflict with Divine Religion itself, its salutary doctrines, its most holy precepts, and with its rights. . . . For the purpose of more easily corrupting manners and propagating the detestable pest of indifferentism and tearing souls away from our Most Holy Religion, it allows the free exercise of all cults and admits the right of pronouncing in public every kind of thought and opinion. . . . We energetically reprove everything the Mexican government has done against the Catholic Religion, against its Church, its sacred ministers and pastors, and against its laws, rights, and properties. We raise our Pontifical voice in apostolic liberty . . . *to condemn, to reprove, and declare null and void everything the said decrees and everything else that the civil authority has done in scorn of ecclesiastical authority and of this Holy See. . . .*"

(Lesley Byrd Simpson, *Many Mexicos*, 4th ed. revised [Berkeley: University of California Press, (1941), 1971], pp. 274–275)

By 1858 the nation was at war with itself again, Liberals against Conservatives. The War of the Reform quickly turned into what one study of Mexican history labeled the "most passionate and horrifying civil war to date."[1] Excesses of violence were committed by both sides, cruelty practiced and murders perpetrated in the name of religion or of freedom and democratic government. When it was finally over in 1860, the Liberals under Juárez emerged triumphant, and the Church was even more constrained. In the heat of battle, Liberals radicalized their program against the Church, secularizing cemeteries, nationalizing Church properties, confiscating monasteries, and the like. Weakened by civil war, Mexico was a prime target for European countries—such as France—attempting to rebuild American empires. With the United States immersed in its own civil war between 1861 and 1865, the French occupied Mexico between 1862 and 1867 in the greatest challenge to Mexican independence.

The French pretext was that Mexico, torn and tattered by the War of the Reform, had defaulted on its foreign debts and that the European powers thus had the right to intervene and collect those debts. The issue of debt and the right to intervene to collect debts arose often in the nineteenth-century affairs of Latin America with both European powers and the United States. In the case of Mexico, it was true; Mexico could not service its debt and had declared a moratorium on debt payments. Yet, when English, Spanish, and French troops landed at Veracruz to seize the customs house (the principal public revenues at the time came from import and export taxes, or duties, charged at Veracruz), the French were fishing for more than money. Emperor Napoleon III dreamed of reestablishing the French empire in America, and the situation in Mexico seemed ripe.

When the English and Spanish withdrew, the French stayed and marched inland to consolidate their hold on Mexico. In 1864 they even installed a European prince, Ferdinand Maximilian, as emperor of Mexico, although Maximilian's place was secured only by the presence of French troops.

Resistance to Maximilian came from two quarters: from the Mexicans themselves led by Benito Juárez, the great Liberal leader who was pushed out of his presidency by the French invasion; and from the United States. In 1865 the United States, with almost a million soldiers in the most powerful war machine in the world, began to pressure Napoleon III to get out of Mexico. It was especially galling to the United States to witness the displacement of a native Mexican government by a foreign monarchy. Furthermore, Juárez's forces were daily growing in strength, isolating Maximilian and his French troops from their supporters in Mexico, largely Conservatives who had accepted Maximilian as a tool in their long struggle against Juárez and the Liberals.

Napoleon III got the message, even though Maximilian did not. The French troops pulled out in 1867, but Maximilian, an appealing if tragic figure, stayed, refusing to escape and run away like a culprit. He surrendered to Juárez and was executed on the outskirts of Querétaro by a firing squad on June 19, 1867. Following Maximilian's execution, Juárez was elected for a third term in 1868.

---

[1] Meyer and Sherman, *The Course of Mexican History*, p. 382.

Juárez, the Redeemer of His People

"Juárez was indeed a man ... [He] possessed the great virtue of the indigenous race, to which, without a single drop of admixture, he belonged, and this virtue is perseverance. His fellow believers in Reform had faith in its inevitable triumph. So did he, but success, to him, was a secondary matter. What came first was the performance of his duty, even if the consequence was to be disaster and death. *What he sought, far beyond the Constitution and the Reform, was the redemption of the indigenous people* [italics added]. In his pursuit of this ideal he never faltered: to free his people from clerical domination, from serfdom, from ignorance, from mute withdrawal—this was his secret, religious longing, the reason why he was a liberal and a reformist, the reason why he was great.... He towers, morally, above any other figure of our civil wars."

(Justo Sierra, *The Political Evolution of the Mexican People,* notes and introduction, Edmundo O'Gorman and Alfonso Reyes, translator, Charles Ramsdell [Austin: University of Texas Press, 1969], pp. 283–285, in John Charles Chasteen and Joseph S. Tulchin, editors, *Problems in Modern Latin American History: A Reader* [Wilmington, Del.: Scholarly Resources, 1994], pp. 49–50)

The execution of deposed Emperor Ferdinand Maximilian in 1867. Imposed by the French, he ultimately was captured and executed by Mexican patriots, led by Benito Juárez. Here Maximilian is depicted awaiting the final shots as a priest holds up a cross to comfort him.

Juárez moved to consolidate the Liberal victory by healing the nation. During his administration, Juárez initiated a wide variety of activities, especially in education and the economy, to help modernize Mexico. For example, in 1872 he inaugurated the first major railroad, running between Mexico City and Veracruz, the principal port of entry on the coast. To reduce banditry and to promote security in a country plagued by disorder, Juárez established a rural police force called the *Rurales*. Later, under Porfirio Díaz, the *Rurales* would bring a peace and quiet heretofore unknown in nineteenth-century Mexico. The Mexican Abraham Lincoln, as many styled Juárez, died in office in 1872 of a coronary seizure. Juárez's successor to the presidency in 1872, Sebastián Lerdo de Tejada, proceeded along the same lines as Juárez, laying the foundations for Díaz.

The Porfiriato

Porfirio Díaz came to power through a revolution that overthrew Lerdo de Tejada in 1876. Díaz's Plan de Tuxtepec called for effective suffrage and no reelection. Ironically, Díaz remained in power until 1911, occupying the presidency for the entire period except for the 1880–1884 term. His tenure as Mexico's dictator over this long period bears his imprint, the *Porfiriato*, and it altered the course of Mexican history dramatically.

The key to understanding Mexico during the *Porfiriato* is the word "contradiction." Under Díaz Mexico reached a material prosperity, based on railroading, mining, industrialization, and commerce, of unprecedented proportions, although the great mass of its people, especially its rural laborers, the peons, were ground deeper into poverty.

All of the economic indicators took off, producing a boom in prosperity that Mexico had never known before. Under a financier named José Ives Limantour, a balanced budget was achieved, the immense national debt was paid off, and Mexico's reputation abroad—critical if investors were to be attracted—did an about-face. Previously known as a country of violence, banditry, and political chaos, Mexico became a paragon of tranquillity, fiscal stability, and political order. Foreign investors, principally British, French, and American, sank their capital deeply into building Mexico's new railroads, opening new mines, and either modernizing old industries or pioneering new ones such as petroleum.

Mexico: The Mother of Foreigners and the Stepmother of Mexicans

"If the dictatorship of Don Porfirio meant the return of the Silver Age for the Creoles and the clergy," wrote Lesley Byrd Simpson, "for the foreigner it was the Golden Age. Mexico became 'the mother of foreigners and the stepmother of Mexicans.' The foreigner soon learned that he could buy justice and favors from the swollen and underpaid bureaucracy, which grew to include a large percentage of the literate population of the country. *Empleomanía*, the government-job mania, infected the whole middle class of Mexico. But the foreigner was king, for he knew paradise was made possible by his money and industry, and the sweat of Mexican workmen. His factories and mines were rarely disturbed by strikes and similar un-pleasantnesses, and, when they were, the Rurales [rural police], the army, and the judiciary saw to it that the malcontents gave no more trouble. Strikers were slaugh-tered by the score and by the hundred at the Cananea mines and the textile mills of Río Blanco. 'You can't make an omelet without breaking eggs.' Díaz made Mexico a colony of foreign capitalism, principally American. . . . "

(Lesley Byrd Simpson, *Many Mexicos* [Berkeley: University of California Press, (1941), 1971], pp. 290–291)

With balanced budgets, surpluses in the treasury, and an expanding economy, Mexico was transformed by prosperity. Mexico City doubled in population, and its reputation as a civilized and cultured capital was enhanced by electricity, streetcars, hotels, weekly newspapers, and broad boulevards. The same progress—although not as spectacular as that achieved in the capital—could be measured in Mexico's lesser cities, now tied together by railroads (fifteen thousand miles in 1911 compared to four hundred miles in 1876) that were responsible for the movement not only of materials, but also of men and ideas crisscrossing the country.

To accomplish all this, Díaz forged one of the most efficient dictatorships ever to govern in modern Latin America. Peace and stability in city and countryside were achieved by a combination of rewards and intimidation, the latter enforced through fear, threats, and brutality if necessary. To the Mexican of the time, the system was known as *pan y palo* ("bread and clout"). By adroitly manipulating his political and military officials, Díaz kept potential opponents off balance. The press was effec-tively muzzled, elections were rigged, and the *Rurales* kept the peace in the country, earning a reputation (well deserved in the main) for cruelty that tyrannized Mexi-cans. Workers might strike, bandits might rob, and political opponents might cry out against censorship and tyranny, but they did so at the peril of being beaten, pummeled, and killed by the *Rurales*. In such a society, it was best to keep one's mouth shut and suffer silently. That, indeed, was the lot of the Mexican peon under the *Porfiriato*.

The Roman Catholic Church became a tacit ally of Díaz's government by the 1880s, helping to forge a broader consensus among Mexico's elite. Although Díaz remained a Liberal and did not formalize relations with the Vatican, he did deal qui-etly with Church leaders and assuaged their concerns about anticlericalism. Díaz's wife, doña Carmen, played a major role in this rapprochement, carrying out a back door diplomacy that softened her husband's harsh methods when it came to reli-gious matters. Improved relations with the Church brought Liberals and Conserva-tives into closer proximity and also removed one of the major causes of unrest among the masses of peasants and Amerindians.

Classically, the peons, be they Amerindian or mestizo, lived on the land, usually on a hacienda. The lot of the peons during the *Porfiriato* was dismal, marked by ab-ject poverty and increasing deprivation. The hacendados were thoroughly imbued with the prevailing racism among the Mexican positivists, who considered the peons

Possibly the most successful dictator in modern Mexican history, Porfirio Díaz governed his country from 1876 until 1910 when he was ousted by a revolution that changed the course of Mexican history. Díaz imposed order and stability that led to an unprecedented prosperity in turn-of-the-century Mexico, but at the tremendous cost of massive social and economic inequities.

biologically inferior. This simply reinforced the hacendados' tendency to view themselves as the natural lords of the land, born to govern. Hacendado haughtiness and positivist racism combined to make life miserable for Mexico's peons.

The proof, as the old adage goes, was in the pudding. The peons' average daily wage—thirty-five cents—did not rise during the nineteenth century, while the cost of their staple food—beans, corn, and chili—increased between 200 and 600 percent. In terms of diet, peons were worse off in 1910 than in 1810 when still under the rule of Spain. They were bound to the hacienda by the pernicious system of debt peonage. Kept perpetually in debt by the hacendado, who controlled access to stores and food, peons were effectively bound to the land and to the service of the hacendado forever. Debts were inherited by children in the Mexico of the *Porfiriato*.

The hacendados, on the other hand, ruled the land and reached mind-boggling extremes of wealth during the *Porfiriato*. Porfirian policies directly contributed to the expansion of the hacienda system in the late nineteenth century. New land laws, such as that of 1883 designed to encourage foreign immigration, awarded huge tracts—both public lands and communal lands stripped from Amerindians—to land companies that in turn sold to the hacendados. The results were spectacular concentrations of land in the hands of the few, with the many going begging.

One family, the Terrazas-Creel clan of the northern state of Chihuahua, amassed over seven million acres by 1900! It directed much of its wealth into diversified investments, such as banking, railroads, telephone companies, sugar mills, and the like; controlled local and gubernatorial politics; and sat astride a mountain of

Coffee pickers in Costa Rica picking the "grano de oro," or the little "golden grains" that coffee represented for many Latin American countries, from Guatemala to Brazil. This profitable crop was labor intensive and fostered small-to middle-sized land holdings in some countries such as Costa Rica and Colombia.

privilege and wealth as Mexico passed into the twentieth century. The great gulf between the "haves" and the "have-nots" would finally rupture the *Porfiriato* in 1910.

Central America

Central America's history, from the 1850s to the turn of the century, was deeply influenced by priorities set beyond its borders. The coffee brokers of London, the canal builders of France, the banana barons of New Orleans and Boston—they and many other foreigners were encouraged by the resurgence of outward-looking, positivist, and progressive Liberal parties of Central America to invest in and develop Central America. The broad goal—shared by Central Americans and foreigners—was to integrate the region into the western world's quickening international economy in the second half of the nineteenth century. It was an age of mutual admiration. Central Americans looked to the brokerage and investment houses of London, Paris, and New York for markets and monies, while foreigners made handsome profits in booming new activities, such as the coffee and banana industries. At mid-century, however, Central America faced another priority: the preservation of its sovereignty.

The Walker Invasion

In 1855 Liberals in Nicaragua contracted with some North American mercenaries led by a Nashville-born adventurer named William Walker to help them in their battle against Conservatives. Walker arrived in Nicaragua in June 1855 with fifty-seven Americans recruited in California. In the space of a few months, the Liberals, with the assistance of Walker's small army, soundly defeated the Conservatives. What Nicaraguans and other Central Americans did not expect was Walker's vision: to carve out an American empire in Central America.

In 1856 Walker took over Nicaragua. He legalized slavery, made English the official language, and offered large land grants. Consequently, hundreds of American adventurers flocked to his standard. Central American patriots, on the other hand, prepared to oust the invaders.

Patriots, led by President Juan Rafael Mora of Costa Rica, challenged and finally defeated Walker's mercenaries in a series of pitched battles that ranged over northern Costa Rica and Nicaragua, causing widespread destruction. Walker was finally defeated in 1857 and, saved by the intervention of the United States, went into exile. Twice he tried to return to Central America and reconstitute his putative empire. On his second return in 1860, Walker was captured by British marines and turned over to the Hondurans. They executed the "gray-eyed man of destiny" with dispatch.

The struggle against Walker united Central Americans and endowed them with a sense of pride and nationalism based on this war of liberation. Meanwhile, remarkable changes were occurring in the economies of these small countries.

Canals and Coffee

In 1833 a few sacks of coffee beans were shipped to England from Costa Rica's port on the Pacific, Puntarenas. It was a long trip, ships having to sail far south to round Cape Horn, where cold, tempestuous seas challenged vessels and crews alike. Then ships had to sail up the Atlantic Ocean for thousands of miles before arriving in England. But it was a highly profitable trip. The English, it turned out, liked good coffee and were willing to pay the price. And Costa Rica, as well as most of its Central American neighbors, possessed excellent highlands for growing the highest quality beans.

Coffee growing soon outstripped all other commercial activities in Central America. By the 1880s it represented 70 to 80 percent of all exports, and its profits had increased the overall wealth of Central America by thousands of percent. Foreigners, especially in Guatemala and Nicaragua, moved into the growing industry in large numbers. A new oligarchy prospered from the growing and marketing of the coffee bean, which was called, appropriately enough, the *grano de oro,* or "grain of gold," in Costa Rica.

Coffee profits were in turn plowed into two areas: one, extravagant expenditures by the emerging coffee elites (ornate estates, trips to Europe, expensive imports); and two, the modernization of the countries under a series of Liberal presidents, such as Justo Rufino Barrios of Guatemala, José Zelaya of Nicaragua, and Tomás Guardia of Costa Rica. These leaders were, somewhat paradoxically, liberal in their economic policies but dictators in their politics. They were, in fact, apostles of the positivist principle that to achieve economic progress, one needs political order. These presidents, some governing for a decade or more, provided political stability, while the new income from coffee was plowed into those sectors—railroads, telegraphs, ports, for example—that were associated almost viscerally with progress.

Much as computers symbolize the cutting edge of technology at the approach of the twenty-first century, railroads seized the imagination of Central Americans just as they did the imagination of other Latin Americans from Mexico to Argentina in the last third of the nineteenth century. In Central America, the first railroads were begun in the 1870s to bring the coffee-producing regions of the interior into better communication with the ports on both the Atlantic and Pacific coasts.

Representative of this effort was Costa Rica's contract with a family of North American entrepreneurs, the Meiggses, to build a railroad from the highland central valley to the Atlantic Ocean terminus of Puerto Limón. The task fell to a younger member of the family, Minor Cooper Keith, who completed the task only in 1890. His persistence overcame obstacles created by both people and nature, from bankruptcy in the international marketplace to the torrential rains of the tropics.

As Keith lay track slowly through the difficult Atlantic coastal jungle, he constantly experimented with ways to make the railroad pay before it was finished and could transport coffee from the interior to Puerto Limón. Among his experiments was importing some banana trees (they are actually bushes, but such big ones that we have grown accustomed to calling them trees) from Panama and planting them along the railroad. He began to export bananas in small numbers to New Orleans in the late 1870s. Another American entrepreneur, a ship captain from Boston named Lorenzo Baker, had already experimented as early as 1870 with bringing bananas from Jamaica to Boston.

Keith and Baker in effect pioneered a new industry—bananas from the Caribbean and Central America exported to the United States—whose growth and profitability still startle us. In Costa Rica and Honduras, bananas challenged coffee for the lead in exports by the beginning of the First World War, accounting in some years for more than 50 percent of exports. The foreign banana growers in turn merged in 1899 and created the United Fruit Company, an institution that came to symbolize the widespread penetration and dominance of foreigners by Central America.

While coffee and then bananas powered the Central American economies to the turn of the century, the canal-building momentum built to a climax in the same period. North Americans tended to favor a route across Nicaragua, employing the San Juan River and Lake Nicaragua, whereas Frenchmen were persuaded that Panama offered the best conditions. In the 1880s Ferdinand de Lesseps, the French entrepreneur who built the Suez Canal, launched a massively publicized effort to cut the canal across the isthmus of Panama. It failed, brought down by torrential tropical rains, almost nightmarish engineering problems, diseases, and, finally, bankruptcy. The North Americans clucked their tongues at the French and prepared to dig in Nicaragua.

A privately sponsored company, the Maritime Canal Company, elicited a charter from the U.S. Congress in 1887, and in 1890 it began operations in Nicaragua. In

1893 it, too, went bankrupt, and the canal between the oceans seemed no nearer to completion in Nicaragua than in Panama. But it was an age of high optimism and rapidly increasing technological and medical breakthroughs. At the end of the century, a coincidence of circumstances related to the Spanish-American War of 1898 once again provoked canal fever.

The war was waged on two oceans, making Americans extremely conscious of their need for a canal to transfer warships and their supply vessels between the Atlantic and the Pacific. That an isthmian canal would be a boon to maritime commerce as well by eliminating the long voyage around South America was almost taken for granted.

The question became where to build the canal: Panama or Nicaragua. The Panama lobby, led by a bold French engineer named Phillipe Bunau Varilla, argued hard that 30 percent of the canal had already been constructed by the French, and the North Americans had only to buy out the French interests and concessions and complete the work. The Nicaraguans and their supporters in the United States, led by the tenacious senator from Alabama, John Tyler Morgan, pushed for the route across Nicaragua. This route was thought to pose fewer engineering problems and to be healthier, and, furthermore, it was located nearer to the United States. In the end, Panama won the "battle of the routes." In 1902 the U.S. Senate voted to support the Panama route, persuaded in part by a dramatic lowering of the price that Bunau Varilla and his backers were asking for the French investment in Panama.

For Nicaraguans, and most Central Americans, it was a great disappointment, a promise unfulfilled. Yet, as the liberal dictators and their supporters turned the century, they viewed the last half of the nineteenth century as one of unprecedented progress, marked by the building of railroads and ports, the modernization of their capitals, and the increase of the material wealth of Central America, especially based on coffee and banana exports.

This positivist age in Central America also witnessed failures, however. One, the prosperity was not shared by the great body of Central Americans. Although a new class of Liberal oligarchs replaced the Conservatives, wealth did not trickle down to the masses, to the Maya of Guatemala or to the *ladinos* of Nicaragua. Two, much of the new economic infrastructure of Central America was dependent upon foreigners, from German coffee growers in Guatemala to North American banana barons in Honduras. This trend would make Central America especially vulnerable to foreign meddling in the twentieth century. Three, with the exception of Costa Rica, which continued to invest in education and to lay the foundations of a modern political democracy, public order and tranquillity were maintained largely by a series of dictators and caudillos who looked to the military more than to the ballot box for their legitimacy.

Conclusions and Issues

Mexico at mid-century suffered through a period of devastating turmoil marked by the War of the Reform and the French occupation. Internal divisions and weaknesses in Mexican politics and society contributed to this internecine warfare as Mexicans sought to define a number of immensely controversial issues in society, such as the place of the Amerindian and the proper relationship between Church and state. A stronger Mexico emerged in the 1870s and 1880s under the leadership of Porfirio Díaz, who established a dictatorship that endured until 1910. His emphasis on order and stability encouraged foreign investors, merchants, miners, and railroad builders—all of whom helped produce an unprecedented material prosperity in the Mexico of the *Porfiriato*. However, it was a radically unbalanced prosperity that divided Mexico more deeply between the haves and have-nots. A small percentage of Mexicans and the foreigners took the bulk of the newly developed wealth, alienating the great majority of Mexicans who viewed the growing disparity as a monstrous injustice. The result would be the monumental Mexican Revolution of 1910.

In Central America, the invasion of an American filibuster, William Walker, at mid-century symbolized the growing interest of the United States in Central America. Walker's defeat helped define Central American nationalism and also symbolized the beginning of a new era in Central American life. In the second half of the nineteenth century, the increasing production of coffee and, later, bananas began the rapid integration of Central America into the world economy and produced a quickening of the modernization process in these small countries. The desire for a transisthmian canal by the great maritime and naval powers of the world—especially Great Britain, France, and the United States—focused increasing attention on Central America toward the turn of the century.

Discussion Questions

1. How did the *Porfiriato* satisfy those who wished to stabilize Mexican political life and to modernize the nation?

2. How did coffee serve to begin the modernization of Central America?

3. How did William Walker and the transisthmian canal represent different interests of the United States in Latin America?

The Development of Nations: South America

Peru and Chile at War

From one deck above his crew, Captain Miguel Grau, grasping a handrail and leaning slightly forward, addressed his men.

"Men of the *Huascar!* The hour to punish the enemies of our homeland has arrived! *Viva* Peru!" Grau shouted.

Grau's warship, the *Huascar,* was armed with two Armstrong ten-inch-guns, each capable of firing a three-hundred-pound projectile, and driven through the seas by a powerful twelve-hundred-horsepower engine. The smaller, lighter-armed, and armored Chilean ships, *Esmeralda* and *Covadonga,* blockading the roadsteads (anchorages) before the Peruvian city of Iquique were no match for *Huascar.* Her six-foot ram attached to its prow was guarded by a watertight bulkhead immediately behind the ram to protect it from the shock of collisions.

Below decks, the *Huascar's* engineers secured everything possible as the word filtered down into their oily, gloomy world of pounding pistons and rackety steam fittings: Prepare for action. Stokers, stripped to the waist, complained and cursed faithfully about the bad air and heat, all the while working themselves up for the moment of combat. Grau ordered battle pennants hoisted and sounded general quarters for his small squadron of *Huascar* and *Independencia.*

Aboard the Chilean frigate *Esmeralda,* assigned to maintain the blockade across Iquique's bay, its young captain, Arturo Prat, had been up for hours. Now to prepare for battle. Prat's small ship swarmed with sailors making ready. Bulkheads were knocked down, guns run out, the decks cleared for action. Far down in the bowels of the ship the surgeon and his assistants prepared for the grisly work of tending the wounded and dying.

Naval battle historically was short and intense. What did one wag once observe, Prat thought, as he watched the *Covadonga* draw nearer?

"A sailor's life is marked by long hours, days, weeks, and even months of tedium, and a short flash of terror and thunder and death."

As Grau closed with *Esmeralda* and *Covadonga,* he could see beyond them to the shoreline at Iquique. He squinted through his glasses. Now he saw them: hundreds of its citizens teeming on the bluffs and beaches, waving and apparently in an uproarious mood. What Grau could not hear, but what he could easily guess from the situation, were hundreds of voices not only echoing his harangue to the crew, "¡Viva Peru! ¡Viva Peru!" but also crying, "¡Ahora si! ¡Ahora si!" ("Now! Now! Now!"). What sweet revenge was to fall on the hated Chileans! Iquique was still Peru's, and its citizens had been chafing under the Chilean blockade.

Huascar launched a grenade that splashed in between the Chilean ships and exploded, sending a spectacular but harmless geyser of foam and water into the air. The battle was joined.

Prat issued his last orders to his crew.

"Boys, the fight is unequal. Our flag has never been struck before the enemy. And I don't expect us to be the first! As long as I live, this flag will wave, and I assure you, if I die, my officers will know how to do their duty! *Viva* Chile!"

"*Viva* Chile!" his crew responded, throwing hats into the air as *Huascar's* first grenade exploded.

The battle was indeed uneven. It lasted until just past noon, Grau and *Huascar* focusing their tremendous firepower on *Esmeralda,* while *Covadonga* and *Independencia* steamed off to the south in their own duel.

The pounding of *Esmeralda* by *Huascar's* ten-inch Armstrongs devastated the smaller Chilean frigate, although Prat managed to keep his fire up until almost the end. It came around noon, when *Huascar* rammed its smaller foe three times, finally puncturing *Esmeralda's* hull fatally and sending it down, its pennants and flags tattered but still flying. Prat and three-quarters of his crew perished in the battle. Grau lost one of his officers.

Prat was martyred, and Grau was promoted to admiral, but the Chileans caught up with Grau and *Huascar* later that year with their more heavily armed and more powerful *Cochrane* and *Blanca Encalada.*

The battle between *Huascar* and *Esmeralda* was fought early in the War of the Pacific, which erupted in 1879 between Chile on the one hand, and Peru and Bolivia on the other. Economic developments—especially the rapid growth of profitable exports—in the nineteenth century contributed to border disputes and commercial rivalries that sometimes broke out in major conflicts such as the War of the Pacific. This war, like several others, notably the Paraguayan War (1865–1870) between Paraguay and a coalition of its neighbors consisting of Argentina, Brazil, and Uruguay, left deep scars not only on the losing nations, but also promoted the growth of nationalistic sentiments that gave these countries a stronger sense of identity and national unity.

Yet, political instability continued to plague the national life of many South American nations in the second half of the nineteenth century. Some of this instability was manifested in bloody civil wars such as those that ravaged Venezuela at mid-century.

Venezuela and Its Caudillos

Following the ouster of José Antonio Páez at mid-century, Venezuela plunged into a period of intense political instability. More than 350,000 people perished during these Federal Wars, which lasted until 1863, as caudillos warred against each other for power. A new caudillo, Antonio Guzmán Blanco, emerged out of this civil tumult, and he dominated the country for over a decade.

Guzmán Blanco, the son of a Liberal leader, was born to politics and *caudillo* warfare. He earned his spurs and became a general during the Federal Wars, and then emerged in the late 1860s as the supreme caudillo. Under the dictatorial and vain Gúzman Blanco, who styled himself the "Illustrious American," Venezuela, at the very least, passed into a period of civil order and peace. Having established this most basic of all positivist prerequisites—order—Guzmán Blanco then moved to promote the modernization of the nation.

Caracas—the capital and acknowledged metropolis of the nation—was rebuilt with wide boulevards, while sewers, electricity, water, and public transportation were added and reinforced the modernization and dominant role of the city in national life. The coffee trade was revitalized, centered now more in the Andean states of Táchira, Trujillo, and Mérida. With new foreign loans and credits generated from the export not only of coffee, but also of cacao and cattle, Guzmán Blanco pursued his policies of encouraging public education, building railroads and telegraphs, and initiating an ambitious public works program, which included statues of the Illustrious American as often as roads and telegraphs. Yet, his ruthless persecution of the Catholic church and of Conservatives in general—along with the hero worship that he required to gratify his ego—mark his regime as one of mixed blessings.

Were the changes in Venezuela during this period as broad and profound as they seemed to be? The population, about two and a half million at the turn of the century, remained profoundly rural, traditional, and illiterate, having suffered generally from the wasting effects of countless caudillo wars after mid-century. Although *caraqueños* (the residents of Caracas) might show off the newest French clothes imported from Paris in the 1890s, the great mass of rural Venezuelans, *campesinos* (rural folk) on the plantations or *llaneros* roaming the great, open plains of the interior, still ate and lived and danced in simple, basic folkways tuned to the ancient rhythms of the land.

In 1888 Guzmán Blanco left his native country for Paris, drawn irresistibly by the attractions of a city and a nation that many considered the center of the civilized universe. Venezuela drifted politically for a decade before another strong caudillo, Cipriano Castro, imposed himself into power in 1899. During this interlude, Venezuela was drawn tighter into the orbit of European and North American economic and political interests. These, as noted in an earlier chapter, were expanding rapidly in Latin America on many fronts.

In 1894–1895 a dispute flared up between Venezuela and Great Britain over the boundary they shared between British Guiana (modern Guyana) and Venezuela. Unable to stand up to Great Britain alone, Venezuela appealed to the United States for arbitration, and the United States obliged, with a roar. Richard Olney, U.S. secretary of state, crowed after Great Britain accepted arbitration that "the United States was practically sovereign in this hemisphere." When the final decision was announced in 1899, Venezuela retained control of the vital Orinoco River delta but had to give up an immense chunk—sixty thousand square miles—of Venezuelan territory to British Guiana. Venezuelans were discovering at the turn of the century that appealing to the United States in their disputes with the great powers of Europe could produce mixed results.

Cipriano Castro fought his way into power in 1899 through a revolution and governed Venezuela with a flair until his overthrow in 1908. Don Cipriano possessed a temperamental, *bon vivant* personality, characterized as much by philandering and dancing as by tending to matters of state. His intense nationalism and Venezuela's foreign debts combined to produce another international crisis in 1902 and 1903, that again brought the United States into the picture.

Irritated by Venezuela's inability to pay off debts contracted largely during the Guzmán Blanco era, Great Britain, Germany, and Italy took matters into their own hands. They blockaded Venezuelan ports in 1902 and 1903 to force Venezuela to pay. The United States once more stepped in and arranged for lifting the blockade and resuming debt service; but the intervention of the United States came with a price: the Roosevelt Corollary to the Monroe Doctrine (see Ch. 13). President Theodore Roosevelt adamantly rejected *any* form of European intervention in American affairs, preferring in all instances that the United States step in to settle disputes.

During Cipriano Castro's regime, and especially so under his successor, Juan Vicente Gómez, a pattern in modern Venezuela emerged. Political power issued from Andean leaders such as Cipriano Castro and Gómez, who had the instincts and skills to forge a more unified modern nation. They relied on the skills and knowledge of the more sophisticated *caraqueño* elite for the economic and commercial integration of Venezuela into international markets, especially as oil rose in importance. The Andean dictators and the *caraqueño* elites—working together— forged the makings of the modern state in Venezuela. Beneath these trends, others also were apparent, especially the formation of a new semi-industrialized work force with its own priorities and agendas that would later challenge the prevailing order.

Colombia

Colombia, in the second half of the nineteenth century, was beset by more political tumult than perhaps any other Latin American nation in that same period. From the 1860s to the turn of the century, civil war between Liberals and Conservatives interrupted national life more than ten times, in some instances (1860–1863, 1899–1902, for example) lasting in excess of two or three years and costing thousands of lives. The causes of such internal stress still spark lively debate among historians.

Historical Debates

Very often historians themselves cannot agree on how to interpret events in particular nations or periods of time. They all agree on the basic facts, the "names and dates" that so often plague students who are first learning history, but then go their separate ways in *interpreting* those facts. Indeed, this aspect of history is the one that so often makes the past glow with intellectual excitement. A good case is interpreting Colombian historiography (the study of history) in the late nineteenth century.

One school of historians contends that the tumultuous politics of the period, marked by nearly incessant civil war between Liberals and Conservatives, was caused by the internal differences between the partisans of these two political groups. Deep differences over the role of the Church, over whether the country should be federal or centralized, over free trade or protectionism, and other issues—some particular to Colombia and others shared in general by other Latin Americans of the same generation—proved irresolvable and led to civil war. The War of the Thousand Days at the end of the century was the saddest and most disruptive of these civil wars, laying waste to the land and the people.

Other historians view this period of intense conflict through a different lens. They maintain that the fortunes of the Liberal and Conservative parties were closely linked to events *outside* of Colombia, especially to the rise and fall of Colombia's principal exports in the period, tobacco and coffee. The parties and their leaders were more apt to respond to these external pressures than to internal, ideological differences. For example, if Liberal fortunes were tied to a prospering export—as tobacco was in the 1860s—they were able to lord it over the Conservatives and maintain power. When the export economy faltered, so did the power of the Liberals, and Conservatives ascended, blaming the Liberals, of course, for depression and bad fortune.

Even the nature of Liberal and Conservative parties challenges the historian. One wrote that "by mid-century the Liberal and Conservative parties had achieved clear definition," whereas another said that "in the realm of ideology, it is vain to seek perfect consistency among nineteenth century Liberals."[1] Each of these views can be explained and sustained, but they reflect an exciting dimension of history: its dynamic rather than static nature as we take those names and dates and facts and debate their meaning and significance.

[1]Park, *Rafael Núñez*, p. 2, and Delpar, *Red against Blue*, p. 190.

The basic alignment between Liberals and Conservatives achieved by mid-century provided the framework for events as they unfolded from the 1860s onward. In 1863 the Liberals triumphed in a civil war over the Conservatives and wrote a new constitution for the country. By promoting free trade, they encouraged the expansion of the tobacco economy, and a boom in that crop's export helped sustain the Liberals in power. When the prices of tobacco began to drop in the 1870s, so did Liberal unity.

Not only did Liberal leaders quarrel over personal rivalries, but also their feuding represented much of the continuing competition for power between the regions of Colombia. For example, the dominant personality of the period, Rafael Núñez, divided Liberals by frankly promoting his native region, the Atlantic coast, in the forums of power. Núñez was not unique. It was a fact of political life in Colombia that each region competed hotly for power at the national level.

In 1885, Conservatives, allied with independent Liberals led by Núñez, recaptured power from the Liberals. Núñez, a prolific writer and accomplished statesman, had already served two terms as a Liberal president in the early 1880s before he switched allegiances and led the Conservatives to power. In 1886 he oversaw the creation of a new constitution that lasted more than a century.

As coffee exports rose dramatically in Colombia, so did the strength of Núñez and the Conservatives. By 1896 coffee constituted 70 percent of Colombia's total exports. The new wealth from coffee pumped revenue into the government and fostered the beginnings of modernization in the nation. A fall in international prices after 1896, however, triggered a depression in the coffee industry, and Liberals blamed Conservatives.

Furthermore, Núñez and his successors had thoroughly antagonized the Liberals, especially by systematically excluding them from power. The festering feud between the parties came to a head when the activist Liberal leader, Rafael Uribe, pushed for a resolution of the power struggle. The result was the War of the Thousand Days (1899–1902), one of the bloodiest in Colombia's history.

When the combatants finally called a truce in 1902, the country was nearly prostrate. At least eighty thousand Colombians perished from the fighting, disease, and turmoil brought on by the conflict. Plantations were devastated, families torn from their lands, and business paralyzed. The peso was terribly debased during the war, and Colombia emerged exhausted and weak, the Conservatives still in power but unable to withstand another threat, this time from the United States.

In 1903 the United States supported a revolution in the Colombian state of Panama by which Panama became independent and a protectorate of the United States. Colombians were shocked and outraged but could not prevent the loss of Panama, soon to be the site of the transisthmian canal. It was a rude introduction to the twentieth century for Colombians, but as the price of coffee slowly recovered on world markets after 1900, so did Colombian prosperity.

Ecuador

In 1861 Gabriel García Moreno seized power after a decade and a half of political chaos in Ecuador. Born in 1821 into a prominent family of Guayaquil, he had studied theology and law in Quito and then married into a well-to-do Quito family. García Moreno was thus eminently well equipped to govern Ecuador because his roots sprang from both Guayaquil and Quito, the twin poles of power in Ecuador. García Moreno began his political career as a liberal disciple of his fellow *guayaquileño* (native of Guayaquil), Vicente Rocafuerte.

García Moreno's behavior while governing Ecuador until 1875 proved quixotic, but not out of keeping with an age in transition. Men such as García Moreno championed liberal principles and often acted as liberals economically, but they were just as naturally committed to profoundly conservative political, cultural, and religious causes.

Wild as a youth, García Moreno embraced Catholicism as he matured. When he came to power, he, in fact, recommitted Ecuador to a brand of Catholicism that had not been seen since the colonial period. He invited the Jesuit order to return, he normalized relations with the Vatican, and he regenerated and enlarged the educational establishment by bringing in members of French teaching orders. Ecuadorian Liberals, inspired by the brilliant Juan Montalvo, raged against this intensely Catholic, conservative *caudillo* who seemed to have sold the soul of Ecuador to foreign priests and the pope.

But there was another side to García Moreno. He was also committed to modernization. He built the first railroad, encouraged the expansion of exports, and backed native industries, all the while acting decisively in promoting education as the key to progress. He left a decidedly mixed legacy, very positive and progressive in many respects, dictatorial and repressive in others. He died at the hands of an assassin in 1875, chopped up by a fanatical, machete-wielding Liberal.

After García Moreno's assassination, Ecuador's Conservatives and Liberals fought for control of the national stage until 1895. Then Eloy Alfaro, known as the "Old Battler," emerged as the strong leader of a surging Liberal movement. Alfaro dominated the country until his barbaric assassination in 1912, and he left a deep imprint on the country. His regime was characterized by progressive, pro-United States acts of modernization, all consistent with Liberal principles of the time.

A growing export economy paved the way for Alfaro and the Liberals to consolidate power at the turn of the century. Cacao, the basic ingredient in chocolate, had been exported since the colonial period, but only after 1870 did the industry really take off. By 1894 Ecuador was producing more cacao than any other country in the world. The general prosperity caused by the cacao industry contributed to the political equilibrium that the Liberals achieved after 1895, and it provided much of the revenues for projects that Alfaro felt were essential to the progress of the nation. The commercial and mercantile classes of the coastal region were especially committed to looking abroad not only for markets but also for inspiration in modernizing the economy and the nation in general.

The old problem of uniting the diverse regions of Ecuador was partially solved under Alfaro by the completion of the Guayaquil-to-Quito railroad in 1908. Regionalism and limited natural resources, however, continued to plague Ecuador even as it moved into the twentieth century on the wave of prosperity induced by the cacao boom.

While the division between the coast—Guayaquil—and the mountains—Quito—was most evident and the cause of continuing rivalry, the highlands themselves were broken up into regions isolated from each other by the high Andes. Each region, whether coastal or mountain, sought to better its situation at the expense of those individuals who wished to give the national government more powers to centralize and rationalize the nation's economy. Taxes, which were largely derived from duties on imports and exports, tended to be siphoned off by the regions rather than invested in national improvements. The long struggle between Guayaquil and Quito, between Liberals and Conservatives in general, reflected the intensity of this regionalism in Ecuador.

Nonetheless, Ecuador under Alfaro and the Liberals changed. The completion of the Guayaquil-to-Quito railroad, itself the symbol of progress to all Latin American modernizers, was accompanied by public works programs that began to modernize the cities with better sanitation, modern communications systems, and, in the case of Guayaquil, the gradual eradication of tropical diseases that had so long plagued its people. When the railroad was completed, the switchback climb into the Andes proved to be one of the engineering marvels of the world.

Peru

Peru's history in the second half of the nineteenth century resembled a roller coaster ride. First it rode up to dizzying heights of success on the guano boom, then it was driven down to despair and defeat by the War of the Pacific (1879–1883). From that war until the turn of the century, Peru strove to overcome the legacy of an economic boom that had turned sour and of a war that had left it prostrate, embittered, and in debt.

Henry Meiggs, the "Messiah of the Railroads"

"Henry Meiggs was perhaps the most remarkable railroad builder who ever appeared on the Latin-American scene," wrote J. Fred Rippy, describing the life of this remarkable North American entrepreneur. "Landing in Chile early in 1855, a stranger and 'like a thief in the night,' he obtained the first railway contract three years later, and by the end of 1867 had managed the construction of nearly 200 miles, a good part of it across the Chilean coastal range. In 1868 he went to Peru, where the railway era was at its dawn, with less than 60 miles in operation. At his death in Lima on September 30, 1877, Peru had approximately 1,200 miles of track, more than 700 miles of which had been built under Meiggs's direction. . . .

"Meiggs knew how to win Latin-American sympathies. He was a great dramatist and a great orator. His banquets, celebrations, and charities were long remembered both in Chile and Peru. . . . He distributed thousands of pesos and soles (Peruvian currency) among the poor and the victims of earthquakes. He spent tens of thousands on ceremonies and entertainments. . . .

"One of the banquets Meiggs gave in Lima during the celebration that marked the beginning of work on the Oroya Railway was attended by 800 of the double creme of society. On that occasion he promised eternal fame to the top-flight officials who were soon to collaborate in unlocking the treasure vaults of the nation and expanding its role in history:

'This happy event proclaims ... a great social revolution whose triumph and whose benefits are entrusted to the locomotive, that irresistible battering ram of modern civilization. At its pressure will fall those granite masses which physical nature until today has opposed to the ... aggrandizement of the Peruvian nation. Its whistle will awaken the native race from ... [its] lethargy. ...

'Peru, ever noble and generous, will ... inscribe in the book of its glorious history, at the head of its lofty benefactors, the names of all the illustrious citizens to whose indefatigable exertions and patriotism [are] due the establishment of this iron road.'

"The Bolivian minister [to Peru at the inauguration of the Mollendo-to-Arequipa railroad] called Meiggs a 'colossus of fortune and credit,' a 'contractor without fear,' a wizard who had come to Latin America to erase the word 'impossible' from all the dictionaries, a miracle-man who had joined Valparaíso and Santiago and brought Arequipa down to the sea.... After the banquet was over the guests began to dance.... In Arequipa ... Almighty God, President José Balta, and Henry Meiggs were praised and thanked. Handing Balta the hammer and the last spike, Meiggs declared:

'Be certain, most excellent sir, that as you place the last rail ... the civilized nations will look upon you as the collaborator of Newton, Fulton, and Humboldt in science, and that the history of the fatherland will open to you its pages alongside those of Bolívar and San Martín, because the steam and iron with which you are endowing your country affirm also the liberty and independence of nations.' "

(J. Fred Rippy, *Latin America and the Industrial Age* [New York: G. P. Putnam & Sons, 1944], in Lewis Hanke and Jane M. Rausch, editors and contributors, *People and Issues in Latin American History: From Independence to the Present, Sources and Interpretations* [New York: Marcus Wiener, 1990, 1992], pp. 110–116.)

Part of Peru's problems resulted from massive debt incurred in the 1860s and 1870s, as it turned guano profits into railroads. When the guano piles were depleted, Peru turned to mining its nitrate fields in the South, but both sources of income proved incapable of servicing the debt incurred in the European bond market. These loans, in the tens of millions of dollars, not only were directed toward paying for the railroads but also were swallowed up by an expanding, and bloated, bureaucracy and military. Peru's economic problems were exacerbated by a growing dispute with Chile over borders—a dispute that led to war.

On the simplest level, the War of the Pacific (1879–1883) was caused by competition among Chile, Bolivia, and Peru for the guano and nitrate riches discovered along the rugged coastal desert shared by all three countries. The value of this wealth was not evident until the middle of the nineteenth century, when Europe and North America, with rapidly expanding populations and increasing agricultural production, stimulated the export of guano and nitrates. Even before then, however, old border disputes and rivalries had produced friction among the countries that shared the near-barren, rainless Atacama Desert.

After Chile defeated the Peru-Bolivia Confederation in 1839, Chile advanced its claims on the Atacama northwards into the Bolivian coastal province of Antofagasta. Bolivia and Chile continued to spar over this province, reaching agreements in 1857 and 1866 that gave Chile wide-ranging commercial and mining rights in the

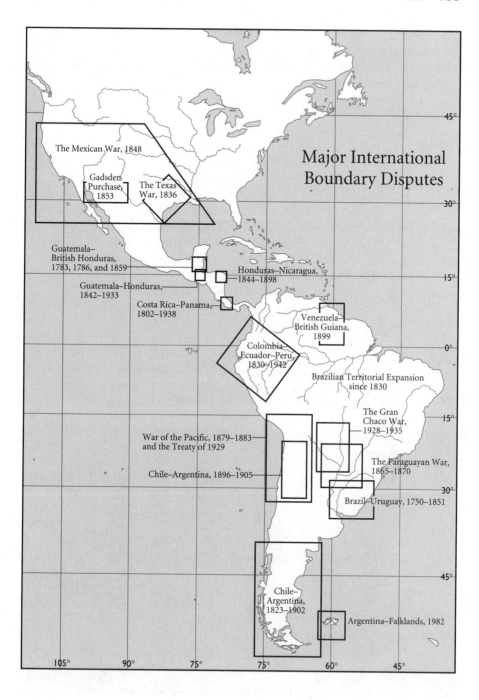

The Mexican War, 1848

Gadsden Purchase 1853

The Texas War, 1836

Major International Boundary Disputes

Guatemala–
British Honduras,
1783, 1786, and 1859

Honduras–Nicaragua,
1844–1898

Guatemala–Honduras,
1842–1933

Costa Rica–Panama,
1802–1938

Venezuela–
British Guiana,
1899

Colombia–
Ecuador–Peru,
1830–1942

Brazilian Territorial Expansion
since 1830

The Gran
Chaco War,
1928–1935

War of the Pacific, 1879–1883
and the Treaty of 1929

The Paraguayan War,
1865–1870

Chile–Argentina, 1896–1905

Brazil–Uruguay, 1750–1851

Chile–
Argentina,
1823–1902

Argentina–Falklands, 1982

region but that preserved Bolivian sovereignty over the province. The production of guano and nitrates was increasing the wealth of this desert coast, and it was Chilean capital and miners in the main who developed it. The Bolivian presence was tenuous at best, and conflict developed naturally between those who were working and developing the mines—the Chileans—and those who nominally exercised sovereignty over the province—the Bolivians. Sovereignty, of course, implied the right to tax, and it was this specific issue that triggered the war.

Yet, in the Pacific, a further complicating factor existed—Peru. Chile and Peru had been commercial rivals in the Pacific since the colonial period, and this rivalry intensified in the nineteenth century. Both nations feared that the other was attempting to dominate the region, especially by manipulating the weaker Bolivia. By the 1860s a naval arms race developed between Chile and Peru. When the Bolivian government imposed a new tax on Chilean business in Antofagasta in 1879, the conflict erupted. Chile and Peru set out to gain naval dominance of the theater of war, deemed imperative given the nature of the long barren coastline shared by the three combatants. If armies were to be moved effectively, the challenges at sea had to be met. To this end, the first, critical stage of the war was fought at sea.

Both countries had been modernizing their fleets in the years before the war, and now the ironclads and battle cruisers were put to the test. In a series of sea battles between April and October 1879, naval officers and men of both countries fought and died as heroes. Ultimately, the more powerful, heavily armed Chilean warships prevailed. At the Battle of Angamos, the Chileans captured the best Peruvian ship, *Huascar*, and killed its commander, Miguel Grau. With superiority established at sea, Chile launched a devastating series of military campaigns.

In a deadly duel in late 1879, the Peruvian warship Huascar *is brought to bay and captured by more powerful Chilean ships in the Battle of Angamos during the War of the Pacific. The defeat of the* Huascar, *and the death of her brilliant commander Miguel Grau, gave Chile command of the sea and led to her ultimate victory in the war.*

First, Chile gained control of the disputed nitrate provinces and effectively eliminated Bolivia from the war. Then, in a series of seaborne raids commanded by General Patricio Lynch, Chile ravaged the Peruvian coastline. As war fever rose in Chile, demanding that the battle be carried to Lima, the Chilean commanders did precisely that. In 1881, they attacked the Peruvian capital in strength and overwhelmed its defenses. Although some sporadic resistance continued in the interior for the next two years, the capture of Lima effectively broke the main Peruvian armies. The Treaty of Ancón, signed in October, 1883, brought the war to an end.

Chile ultimately took the province of Antofagasta from Bolivia, and, as a result, Bolivia lost the last of its Pacific coast and became a landlocked nation. Peru ceded Tarapacá to Chile, and the territory of Tacna-Arica was left in Chilean control, its future to be decided by a plebiscite. The plebiscite was never held, however, and it took until 1929 for a final disposition of the territory to be made. Tacna went to Peru, and Arica to Chile.

The War of the Pacific left Peru, and to a lesser extent Bolivia, bankrupt and bitter from the defeat and the loss of both pride and territory to the Chileans. The Chileans, in turn, savored the triumph with relish and emerged as a power broker on the continent of South America.

As bitter as defeat was, Peru still faced the old bogeyman of debt, now increased by the costs of defeat at war. Peru's valuable nitrate-producing province of Tarapacá was stripped away by the Chileans, and as Peru emerged from the Treaty of Ancón in 1883, it faced $260 million in debt.

The careers of many of Peru's national leaders, members of the Civilista Party, had been severely tarnished by the war. The Civilista movement, Peru's first true political party, had emerged in the 1870s in the attempt to rationalize and modernize Peru's government, and especially in the attempt to wrest control from military-style caudillos. But the War of the Pacific discredited the Civilistas, who had led Peru into that conflict, and they were unable to return to power until the 1890s. The major issue through the 1880s and 1890s remained how to deal with the legacy of the war.

The war not only exacerbated Peru's financial plight but also strained the social order. Peru's society was extremely fragmented along ethnic lines, and the tensions of conflict opened many avenues for the redress of old grievances, not only by the Amerindians of the highlands, but also by blacks, mulattoes, and mestizos along the coast. As the war broke up into guerrilla actions in 1881 and 1882, many of these dispossessed groups took advantage of the chaos and disorder to press for their own rights. Amerindians, for example, sought to regain many of their indigenous communities that had been taken from them during the past four centuries. They murdered whites, collaborated with the Chilean armies, and threatened to overturn the established social order that oppressed them.

From 1881 to 1883, a crusty old general named Andrés Cáceres earned the trust of his countrymen by keeping the war alive against the hated Chileans with courage, honor, and some success. After the Treaty of Ancón was signed in 1883, Peru renegotiated its foreign debt under Cáceres and laid the foundation for finishing its railroads into the ore-rich highlands. At the center of settling the debt was a remarkable Irishman named Michael Grace.

Basically Michael Grace negotiated between the Peruvian government and the English bondholders who held the largest portion of the debt. He persuaded the Peruvians to turn over to the English bondholders various assets of the nation, principal among them the railroads, both finished and unfinished. This Grace Contract was ratified in 1890. The debt was forgiven in return for the concessions made to the bondholders, now called the Peruvian Corporation. Peru's credit abroad, so vital to any economic recovery of the nation, was reestablished. In 1893 the railroad from Lima into the interior was completed to La Oroya, the center of one of the wealthiest areas of silver and copper deposits in the world, and the economic recovery of Peru was truly under way.

Then, in 1895, the politicians of Peru did one of those remarkable about-faces that makes politics such an interesting spectator sport. The Civilistas buried the hatchet with one of their old antagonists, Nicolás de Piérola, and sponsored a revolution that brought them back to power in 1895 with Piérola as president. This Civilista oligarchy presided over a spectacular growth of the Peruvian economy into the twentieth century, fueled not only by the growing exports of minerals but also by sugar and cotton produced by modernized plantations along the coast.

Bolivia

Bolivia—like several of its neighbors—was plagued by particularly venal caudillos from mid-century to the 1880s. The most notorious of them all was Mariano Melgarejo. His sexual excesses, alcoholic rampages, and cruelty to his enemies were so beyond the norm that they led to the coining of a new word in Bolivian Spanish—*melgarejismo.*

Good material though he may be for an engrossing history of scandal, despotism, and madness, Melgarejo unfortunately also dragged down Bolivia's fortunes with his own demented existence. He negotiated the transfer of disputed lands to Brazil and thus refocused Bolivia's aspirations on its Pacific coast. There, major concessions to Chilean entrepreneurs developing the nitrate business became the basis of a protracted dispute between Bolivia and Chile that led to Bolivia's disastrous defeat in the War of the Pacific.

Melgarejo also attacked the ancient patterns of Amerindian communal land-holding. He broke up the lands and sold them to the highest bidders, further impoverishing an already poor people. He was overthrown and fled to Lima in 1871. There he was assassinated by the brother of his favorite mistress, perhaps an apt end for the debauched life of a despot.

After the War of the Pacific, Chile deprived Bolivia of its only province on the Pacific coast, Antofagasta, and left Bolivia landlocked. Although Bolivia seemed to face a bleak future in the wake of this war, several developments boded well for the country. They were based on Bolivian exports of silver, rubber, and tin, each one in turn stimulating the economy and producing social and political changes within the country itself.

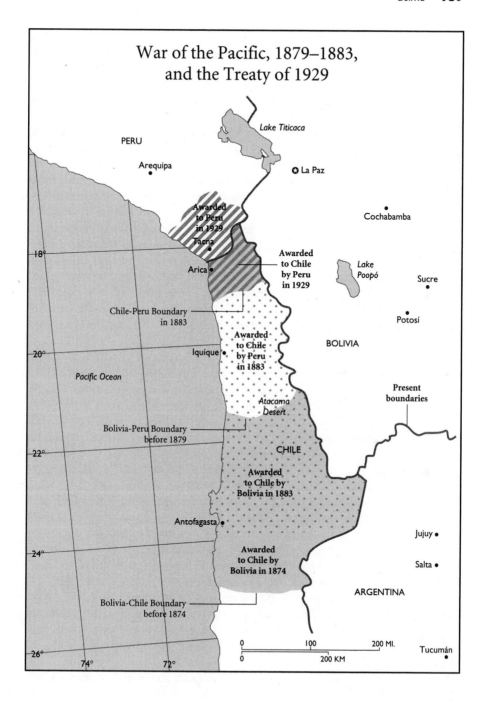

War of the Pacific, 1879–1883, and the Treaty of 1929

PERU

Lake Titicaca

Arequipa

⊛ La Paz

Cochabamba

Awarded to Peru in 1929

Tacna

Lake Poopó

18°

Awarded to Chile by Peru in 1929

Arica

Sucre

Chile-Peru Boundary in 1883

Potosí

BOLIVIA

Awarded to Chile by Peru in 1883

Iquique

20°

Pacific Ocean

Present boundaries

Atacama Desert

Bolivia-Peru Boundary before 1879

22°

CHILE

Awarded to Chile by Bolivia in 1883

Antofagasta

Jujuy

24°

Awarded to Chile by Bolivia in 1874

Salta

ARGENTINA

Bolivia-Chile Boundary before 1874

0   100   200 MI.

0   200 KM

Tucumán

26°

74°   72°

Silver enjoyed a resurgence in the 1860s and 1870s as the industry was modernized, especially through advances made in electrification and transportation. Equally important was the discrediting of the military after the war and a return to civilian government from 1880 to the turn of the century. With relatively peaceful transitions of government, energies were directed into developing Bolivia's resources so sought after in Europe and North America.

When the silver boom began to taper off in the 1890s, due to depressed prices on the world market, Bolivia was able to take advantage of growing demand for another of its abundant natural resources: rubber.

Rubber put the world on soft tires, first as the bicycle craze spread in the 1880s and 1890s and later as the horseless carriage (predecessor of the modern automobile) began to revolutionize transportation at the turn of the century. This product was also important as an insulating material in the burgeoning electric appliance industry. Rubber trees occurred naturally in the Amazon rain forest, with especially dense stands in Bolivia's Acre province on the eastern slopes of the Andes. Brazilians dominated the early decades of the rubber boom, and by the 1890s tappers had penetrated far into the Acre province. The Bolivian government saw the boom as a potential windfall, because it could tax the export of rubber down the Amazon River. Most of the tappers, however, were Brazilians.

The Bolivian government decided that its presence was too weak to enforce tax collection, so it gave a contract to a group of New York-based bankers and industrialists, the Bolivian Syndicate. Presumably, its capital resources, combined with the diplomatic support of the U.S. government, could keep Acre under Bolivian jurisdiction.

Brazilian tappers objected to the arrangement and revolted, upon which Brazil's foreign minister offered to purchase Acre for ten million dollars plus perpetual Amazon navigation rights. By the 1903 Treaty of Petropolis, Bolivia ceded the province to its much larger and more powerful neighbor.

Yet, a rise in demand in the industrialized countries for another of Bolivia's products, tin, triggered a more lasting boom. Tin had long been a by-product of the silver mining industry, and when the demand abroad rose, Bolivia was able to respond efficiently. By the 1920s Bolivia was supplying more than a fifth of the world's tin, and exports of the commodity, which quintupled between 1900 and 1915, accounted for more than half of all Bolivian exports.

The tin boom was accompanied by a series of factors similar to those in other export booms in Latin America. Each was characterized by modernization of the industry with capital and expertise from abroad, the construction of railroads connecting key producing areas with ports for export, a growing demand from abroad, and an ambitious and often brilliant group of entrepreneurs who were able to take advantage of all these factors. In the case of Bolivia's tin boom, one name stands out, that of Simón Patiño.

A *cholo* (as mestizos were known in Bolivia and Peru) of humble birth, Patiño rose in the industry due to hard work, a willingness to gamble, and, of course, luck.

A Bolivian Amerindian girl works the tailings from a tin mine. Bowler hat in place, ruddy faced, and swaddled in multiple petticoats, this Bolivian woman, as many throughout Latin America, performed hard manual labor for her livelihood.

He acquired his first mine, La Salvadora, in the 1890s and within a few years struck an immensely rich vein of tin. He was especially adept in drawing in both foreign capital and the best of foreign technicians to help him play out his hunches. In 1905, La Salvadora (located near Oruro) emerged as the largest tin mine in Bolivia, and Patiño's wealth soared.

Despite these changes in the nation, Bolivia remained, as one of its most able students wrote, "predominantly a rural and Indian peasant nation well into the twentieth century."[2] Furthermore, the attacks on Amerindian communal land-holdings begun by Melgarejo were continued by the white and *cholo* elites who controlled the government as Conservatives or Liberals at the end of the century. The ancient patterns of communal landholding were broken, and the Amerindians were given individual titles to their land. With their solidarity broken, they became easy prey for whites and *cholos* who bought, or simply stole, the land from them. Old haciendas were enlarged, new haciendas formed, and Amerindians were even more humbled as they now toiled not on the land they owned, but for another master.

---

[2]Klein, *Bolivia*, p. 153.

Chile

Contradictions marked Chile's history in the second half of the century. Its victory in the War of the Pacific confirmed it as a rising military power in South America. Its economic booms, through the exports of silver, copper, nitrates, and wheat, bespoke a prosperous nation. The evidence was everywhere. Santiago and Valparaiso became modern cities, where the affluence of the nation was demonstrated by streetcars and museums, mansions, and great public buildings: all of the artifacts that we have come to associate with modernization and affluence. Railroads and steamships and telegraphs linked its mines, its cities, and its ports with England, Germany, Australia, the United States. Politically, Chile was a model of stability in a part of the world where instability was the rule. Presidents and congresses were elected on schedule, dissent was tolerated, exiles from across Latin America arrived to live and work in freedom. The wealth and freedom, however, were enjoyed only by a minority of the elite. Underneath Chilean prosperity a great mass of agricultural and mining workers lived beyond the reach of electricity, a decent wage, and political liberty. Even the oligarchy—those few who governed the many—were divided rather bitterly along the traditional lines of conservatives and liberals, free enterprisers and state interventionists, centralizers and federalists, democrats and authoritarians. The upshot was a violent revolution in 1891 that took the lives of ten thousand Chileans, including that of the president, José Manuel Balmaceda, who committed suicide.

Balmaceda was opposed most vocally and effectively by the Chilean Congress. It objected to Balmaceda's increasingly high-handed, almost dictatorial style, which coincided fatally with other factors between 1889 and 1891 to produce the dramatic and tragic end of Balmaceda. A series of differences between Congress and the president over constitutional powers gradually grew more embittered and poisoned the atmosphere. Instead of searching for consensus and compromise over a host of matters—control of municipal politics, control of the president's cabinet, control over the national budget—the two sides grew more intransigent. A strike among the nitrate workers in the North spread to other sectors of industrialized labor, and Balmaceda antagonized the workers by angrily dispatching the army to restore order by force. When Balmaceda refused to submit the new budget to Congress for approval as required by law, congressmen bolted. They packed their bags, boarded naval vessels in Valparaiso, and set up their revolutionary headquarters in northern Chile. The battle was joined.

With the support of the navy and the rich nitrate mining sector, the congressmen waged an effective and ultimately successful war against the president. When it was over, the traditional power of the strong executive in Chile was broken, and the country entered a period of parliamentary control that lasted until the 1920s.

Chile's evolution into a modern nation progressed along many fronts. Intellectually, people, such as José Victorino Lastarria in the middle and second half of the nineteenth century, promoted a more liberal and secular society. The historian Diego Barros Arana argued successfully for ridding education of any religious control or affiliation. In Chile the *estado docente,* or "teaching state," emerged and effectively secularized public education. It established Chilean higher education as one of the most progressive and advanced in all of Latin America. It became, in effect, a model of excellence.

The boom in the nitrate industry continued through the turn of the century, and its prosperity rippled out through other sectors of the Chilean economy. When the copper industry recovered after 1900 with the infusion of large amounts of foreign capital, it, too, added to the rippling effect. The industrial base of Chile continued to expand and diversify. Chilean factories and foundries produced cement, paper, sugar, beer, iron, glass, bottles, and chemicals, while the coal fields of southern Chile expanded their production. Increasingly, European immigrants, although never reaching more than 5 percent of the total population, came to control important segments of the economy. And the lifestyle of the Chilean elite—the rich and the famous—was heady, marked by the good life of café society, balls, aristocratic social clubs, theater, opera, and the imitation of the latest fashions from London and Paris, a demonstration of pretentiousness in keeping with the new prosperity.

On the other hand, the increase in the laboring force, the maintenance of a semi-feudal system on the great landed estates of Chile, and the pressure of population on the growing cities all contributed to another side of Chile. One student of Chile described it all as having "occurred in a country where more than half of all deaths recorded in 1913 were of infants and children under five years of age, and where the infant mortality rate more than tripled that of the United States or the United Kingdom, and significantly exceeded the rates in Egypt, Mauritius, Japan, Argentina, and even Mexico."[3] This was the "social question" that began to concern Chileans with increasing passion after 1900. How could a celebrated prosperity and political stability be reconciled with a population where large and growing segments of the people suffered from deprivation, poverty, and political alienation?

Argentina

"During the three colonial centuries the territory that is now Argentina was one of the least important of Spain's far-flung dominions in America. By 1910, however, it had become a world leader as a source of foodstuffs, as a field for capital investment, and in railway trackage. Among the twenty Latin American nations it had taken first place in almost every respect: politics, economics, and culture. Most of this remarkable change had come about in the last fifty of the nearly four hundred years since Spanish settlement began, and it was on so large a scale and due to such an extraordinary coincidence of domestic and foreign factors as *to seem almost a miracle* [italics added]."[4]

The change in Argentina from mid-century, when the dictator Rosas was overthrown, to the turn of the century was indeed miraculous. Another observer

---

[3]Loveman, *Chile,* p. 232.

[4]From Whitaker, *The United States and the Southern Cone,* p. 27.

identified the sources of this change: "Economic growth . . . resulted from a simple trinity: foreign investment, foreign trade, and immigration."[5] Some of these changes were economic, others were political.

The political struggle between Buenos Aires—the city and the province—and the rest of Argentina continued to plague Argentina after Rosas fell. Nonetheless, a new constitution drawn up in 1853 was eventually ratified by all the provinces, including Buenos Aires, and in 1862 Bartolomé Mitre was voted the first president of the whole Argentine republic. In 1880 the city of Buenos Aires was detached from the province and became the federal capital of Argentina.

European immigrants swelled the Argentine population in the late nineteenth century. They came first by the hundreds, then by the thousands, and finally by the millions: 5.9 million between 1871 and 1914, in fact. The city of Buenos Aires grew from about 300,000 in the 1880s to over 1,500,000 by 1914, the result of immigration from all across Europe, mostly from the Mediterranean countries of Italy, France, and Spain, with the majority coming from Italy. Why did they come? In a word, opportunity, the chance to get ahead in a new world where the restraints of the old country did not prevail. Many did realize their immediate dreams of becoming small landholders. The majority, however, found employment as wage earners in the cities or as shepherds in the booming wool business or as tenants and sharecroppers. Their importance was to be measured in many ways, but the most significant in the period 1870–1910 was in providing a labor force that underlay Argentina's miraculous economic growth. It began with a wool boom in the 1860s.

While immigrants swelled the human population, sheep did the same in the animal population, increasing from 7 million in 1852 to 88 million in 1888! Wool remained the largest export until after 1900. The sheep industry opened up new lands and transformed other segments of the littoral (coastal region) from immense cattle ranches into small- and middle-sized ranches more intensively worked by sheep farmers. In the same period, wheat farming increased at an equally astounding rate, exports jumping from seventy-seven tons per annum in the 1870s to more than a million tons annually in the 1890s, prompting observers in the United States to take note of this growing rival.[6] Although the system of *latifundia,* or large (immense, in some instances) landholdings producing beef, continued to exist, small- and middle-sized farms, especially in the interior provinces of Entre Ríos, Córdoba, and Santa Fe, grew rapidly.

The cattle business itself underwent some major changes. Where salted beef, tallow, and hides traditionally formed the bulk of the exports, by the turn of the century new markets and innovations were transforming the industry. When slavery came to an end in Cuba and Brazil (1886 and 1888, respectively), so did the old market for salted beef. Meanwhile, a rapidly expanding European population (and thus a market for beef) and new technologies in seaborne transportation and refrigeration began to open up the possibilities of selling vast quantities of meat in Eu-

---

[5]From Rock, *Argentina,* p. 131.

[6]Scobie, *Argentina,* "Concern began to be voiced in the United States where *Harpers Weekly* forecast: The Argentine Republic promises to become the greatest wheat-producing country in the world." p. 119.

rope. At first, in the 1870s, packing plants sent frozen sheep carcasses to England and the continent in recently invented refrigerated ships. By the end of the century, they began selling frozen beef slaughtered in Buenos Aires fattening yards. The best arrangement, however, proved to be shipments of chilled beef, which aged during the crossing and found eager clients throughout Europe.

The railroad catalyzed the agricultural revolution on the pampas. A railroad-building boom in the 1870s and 1880s increased mileage from 470 in 1870 to over 10,000 by 1900. As in the United States, railroads not only opened new lands for settlement and farming but also triggered an orgy of land speculation, inflation, and feverish expansion that ultimately contributed to a financial crisis in 1890.

Not all people shared in the booming times. As the ranching and farming frontier pushed west and south into the vast, flat, prairie-like land of Patagonia, the advance of western-styled "civilization" met the Argentine Amerindian. Much like the white North Americans as they rolled westward, whites in Argentina made war on the native Americans to determine who would rule on the great prairie. In 1879 General Julio A. Roca led a major expedition into the southern frontier, and in this one final campaign, the "conquest of the wilderness," Roca finally and definitively broke the resistance of Amerindians, drove them into reservations, and secured the south of Argentina for its pioneer white settlers. He also succeeded in making Argentina's claims to Patagonia and its far southern frontier more secure against claims by Chile. Still, the two countries continued to spar over these territories well into the twentieth century.

The booming Argentine free enterprise economy crashed with a loud thud in 1890. Banks closed, credit dried up, inflation devastated the middle class, and an armed revolt against the government flared for three days in the streets of Buenos Aires. Corruption and speculation among public servants further fueled discontent among many Argentines. Rather than a country cynically manipulated by an old oligarchy, they wanted a republic in which suffrage was meaningful and in which democratic institutions could prosper.

In one fashion, the crash of 1890 and the subsequent economic recession were but symptom of laissez-faire capitalism across the world. Triggered by rejection of Buenos Aires-issued bonds underwritten by Baring Brothers Bank in London, the crash forced the Bank of England to bail out Baring and soured the market for all South American bonds. This in turn dashed investor confidence more generally and led to a global depression. Latin America had definitely joined the international economy.

Argentina rebounded sooner than the rest of the Atlantic economies, and by the end of the century it was soaring again with increasing exports of wheat, the continued infusion of immigrants, and a renewal of railroad building, public works, and, ultimately, the restoration of trust. Similarly, in 1893 the U.S. economy also stumbled mightily, and it, too, recovered, not to crash again until 1929.

In Argentina, a new political group, the Radical Party, emerged from the crisis of 1890, and with it, a new leader, Hipólito Yrigoyen. He struggled for the next four decades with the most intriguing question of modern Argentina: its failure to develop a viable political establishment to mirror its spectacular economic development in the late nineteenth and early twentieth centuries.

There is another, equally challenging, aspect of Argentine life that became quite apparent at the end of the century. There were "two" Argentinas for the nation makers to contend with: one rural and one urban. No one has better described this dichotomy than James Scobie, a historian of Argentina:

What Is Argentina?

The nation which emerged from the late nineteenth century was, nevertheless, a divided and uncertain people. On the one hand the ports, immigrants, and agricultural products provided Argentina with the trappings of a prosperous and expanding economy. Yet to step from cosmopolitian Buenos Aires into remote Salta or Jujuy was to move backward a hundred years. What was Argentina? Was it the educated, progressive elite who administered the nation, as their patrimony, from the floor of congress or the stock exchange or over an after-dinner brandy at the Jockey Club, the Club del Progreso, or the Círculo de Armas? Or was it the burgeoning middle class so evident as grocers, clerks, office managers, and foremen in the coastal cities? Or was it the Indian working in the cane fields of Tucumán or the quebracho forests of the Chaco, the Italian sharecropper in his hovel on the pampas, the Irish shepherd in Patagonia, or the native peon in the province of Buenos Aires? Or was it the rapidly expanding urban proletariat in the ports—the mestizo cook from Santiago del Estero, the Basque laborer in the slaughter house or packing plant, the porter from Galicia, or the Italian peddler? Little wonder was it that, after a century of independence, Argentines were still searching for identity and that the nation presented simultaneously all shades of prosperity and poverty, progress and reaction, learning and illiteracy.

(Scobie, *Argentina*, p. 135)

Uruguay and Paraguay

Uruguay and Paraguay in the second half of the nineteenth century followed rather different paths in their national histories, although they shared certain unchanging elements, most noticeably, common borders with Argentina and Brazil. These two larger nations injected themselves with maddening regularity into the internal affairs of smaller Uruguay and Paraguay, and, in fact, during the Paraguayan War of 1865–1870, they nearly destroyed Paraguay. Furthermore, the destinies of both small nations were tied—again by geographic reasons—to the mighty Rio de la Plata, which gave them access to the sea and the world through a river and estuary system dominated by Argentina.

Of the two smaller nations, destiny favored Uruguay much more than Paraguay in the second half of the century. Whereas Paraguay suffered a terrible blow delivered by the Paraguayan War, Uruguay prospered and emerged at the end of the century much like Argentina, lifted up by economic forces and, in many ways, transformed by waves of immigrants and modernizing tendencies.

Although the two were similar, Uruguay's prosperity was narrower than Argentina's. Uruguay is smaller and more limited in natural resources and geology. Livestock raising, principally cattle and sheep, continued to prevail as the chief economic activity, although wheat exports added to the country's income. As in Argentina, a burgeoning population added to the prosperity equation. Between 1852 and 1908, the population increased by over 700 percent. Many of those people were immigrants from the Mediterranean countries of Italy, France, and Spain. Improvements in the production of wool and meat (better genetic strains, refrigeration, etc.), a relatively stable monetary system that benefited the middle classes, and an intense urbanization centered around the capital of Montevideo all contributed to a golden age. A well-merited optimism buoyed the population and added to the feeling of well-being.

It was a period, as one of its native sons phrased it, of "optimism, expansion, accomplishments, and facility. It was a belle epoque characterized by full employment, high salaries, social mobility (especially among first generation immigrants), confidence in equality of opportunity, strengthening of the middle classes and, last but not least, the progressive resolution of social and political tensions through institutional means."[7] By the first decade of the twentieth century, democratically elected regimes were replacing caudillos and military rule. But there were problems. A high foreign debt (the highest in South America in 1900), contracted largely by the warring caudillos of the nineteenth century, soaked up much of the revenue produced by the prosperous export sector. And in 1900 one of Uruguay's most celebrated intellectuals, José Enrique Rodó, published a long essay lamenting the march of materialism and positivism through his country and the Western Hemisphere in general. In *Ariel* he expressed a profound hope and faith that matters of the spirit might balance the rampant secularism and materialism of the times (see also Ch. 10). (Rodó pictured the United States as perhaps the worst example of the trend that he criticized.) Whereas Uruguayans possessed the luxury of commenting on the sources and consequences of their wealth and prosperity, the lot of Paraguay was dismal.

In 1864 Paraguay went to war against its powerful neighbors, setting off a tragedy of epic proportions for that landlocked nation so carefully nurtured by the dictator Dr. Francia in the 1820s and 1830s.

The War of the Triple Alliance that pitted Paraguay against an alliance of Argentina, Brazil, and Uruguay nearly destroyed Paraguay as a people and a nation. The war was born of a complicated amalgam of international politics and human ambitions. Before it was over, nearly half of Paraguay's population (about 450,000 in 1865) perished, and Paraguay survived as an independent nation only because its suspicious larger neighbors—Brazil and Argentina—were unwilling to allow each other a preponderant influence in this Platine country.

At the vortex of the Paraguayan tragedy was Francisco Solano López. In 1862 he succeeded his father, Carlos Antonio López, to the Paraguayan presidency, and his

---

[7]Benvenuto, *Breve historia del Uruguay*, pp. 80–81. Interesting that the phrase "last but not least" is in English in the original text.

actions drew Paraguay into the near-fatal confrontation with its neighbors in 1864. Solano López was a complex man, modern and even progressive in some ways, the more traditional caudillo of large appetites and ambitions in others. Said to be a sexual profligate, he took women and the daughters of the best families of Paraguay with the callous abandon of a man who recognized few boundaries to his power. He dealt with his enemies, real and imagined, cruelly, employing torture and execution to consolidate his position.

While in Europe as his father's representative in 1853–1854, he met Eliza Alicia Lynch. Smitten by this beautiful Irish courtesan, whom he met in Paris, he brought her to Paraguay and set her up as his mistress, flaunting her before his friends and relatives. She not only bore him five sons but also proved to be his most loyal supporter during the war. She urged Solano López to think in terms of grandness, hoping herself to become an empress of the New World. Solano López was a willing believer in himself, especially puffed up by the ambitious Eliza.

His European experiences also turned Solano López into a more cosmopolitan person. In Paraguay he sought to raise Asunción from a provincial town to a more European-like city, with theater performances and fashionable events. He encouraged railroad expansion and telegraph construction, and fostered the increase of doctors, teachers, and engineers and a more modern economy. In the meantime, Eliza and Solano López accumulated vast amounts of personal wealth.

In the international arena, he fancied himself a power broker in the complicated politics of the Rio de la Plata region shared by Paraguay, Uruguay, Brazil, and Argentina. He built up the Paraguayan military, established fortifications on the rivers that served as key highways into the interiors of Brazil, Argentina, and Paraguay, and in 1864 warned Brazil to cease meddling in the internal affairs of Uruguay. That was a mistake.

Brazil, under the Emperor Pedro II, ignored Solano López's warnings. Solano López then seized Brazilian ships going up Paraguay's rivers en route to Brazilian towns in the interior of that vast country. Soon thereafter, Solano López provoked Argentina into the war when he violated Argentine territory that he needed to cross in order to attack a part of Brazil. Brazil and Argentina then joined to declare war on Paraguay, taking Uruguay into the alliance with them.

The ebb and flow of battle need not concern us here. The war lasted five years, until 1870, when the Paraguayan people were finally exhausted and prostrated by the exertions of a hopeless struggle against a much more powerful enemy. Curiously, Solano López,—in spite of his multiple and flagrant transgressions against social conventions and his paranoidal behavior towards the end of the war when he tortured and executed hundreds of Paraguayans suspected of treason—tapped a deep patriotism among the tens of thousands of Paraguayans who went to war and death for him and the *patria* (the fatherland). By the end of the war, his ragtag army was made up of as many children and women as men, and they fought valiantly in a cause doomed to failure. Solano López himself struggled to the end and was killed by a Brazilian lancer in 1870 just after his capture, refusing the unconditional terms of surrender demanded by the allies. Eliza witnessed his death and was captured and deported by the Brazilians at the end of the war. She returned to Asunción to try to claim her property after a few years, but, failing that, she sailed to Paris, where she died destitute in 1886. Paraguay survived as a nation but was crushed by the defeat and knocked out of international politics for at least a generation.

Argentina emerged more powerful and confident than ever, now truly beginning to consolidate its strength and to project itself beyond its borders. By contrast, one student referred to the Paraguayan War of 1865–1870 as "The Immolation of Paraguay."[8] In fact, Paraguay—having lost half its population and having been devastated by the war—simply marked time for a generation. Although Brazil and Argentina occupied Paraquay for six years after the war, neither was prepared to take advantage of their neighbor's prostration. In a sense, it continued to exist *because* both of the larger powers were wary of each other's intentions toward Paraguay, and neither would tolerate Paraguay being dominated by the other. Attempts to promote immigration failed dismally, the politicians of the new Colorado Party ruled arbitrarily, and by 1904, when Liberals took power, Paraguay was very little changed from fifty years before.

Although a generation was devastated by the war, the sturdy Guaraní Indians recovered on the land quickly. And in 1936, Paraguay won a war against Bolivia, testifying to the recovery of a nation from its "immolation" in 1870. By contrast, Brazil in the second half of the nineteenth century boomed to the rhythm and cacophony of progress as its empire surged forward.

Brazil

Brazilian history passed through a watershed in 1850. Regional rebellions ended, and Brazilians began to move together as one nation. Furthermore, with the end of the slave trade, which prefigured the ultimate abolition of slavery itself in 1888, new forces were released in the nation. Capital, imagination, and energy were poured both into new enterprises and into old industries being revitalized by the inventions and technologies of a century imbued with progress.

The emperor, Pedro II, emerged as a modern, enlightened monarch who governed with tolerance and the approval of most Brazilians. Certain export crops, such as coffee, cacao, and rubber, boomed in value and provided capital that was transformed into railroads, ports, banks, and other elements key to the beginnings of a modern economic infrastructure. In foreign affairs, a string of successes on the battlefields and in diplomatic forums ensured Brazil's emergence as one of the great powers in Latin America.

Of all the changes noted earlier, perhaps none was so dramatic in human terms as the abolitionist movement that finally destroyed slavery in Brazil. No other Latin American nation was wedded more closely than Brazil to slavery as an economic and social system, and no other nation included so many slaves within its population. Indeed, at the beginning of the nineteenth century, slaves constituted a majority of the population, although by mid-century the free black population was

---

[8]Chapter 13 of John Hoyt Williams, *The Rise and Fall of the Paraguayan Republic, 1800–1870* (Austin, Texas: Institute of Latin American Studies, 1979).

Pedro II ruled Brazil from 1841 until he was overthrown by the army in 1889. He presided over major developments, such as the expansion of coffee, the encouragement of immigration and foreign investment, and a more active role in South American affairs.

gaining on the slaves. The trend to abolish slavery gradually gained momentum in the second half of the century.

The emperor himself believed in the emancipation of all slaves. He personally had freed his own slaves in 1840. He moved cautiously as the leader of his nation in this regard, however, always conscious of the tremendous economic, political, and social power wielded by members of the sugar and coffee planter class, who continued to defend slavery as essential to their prosperity and way of life.

Pedro II

Historians praise the honesty, integrity, and moderation of Pedro II. His rule probably benefited Brazil.... Pedro tried to rely on national opinion, which he distinguished from public opinion, as his guide. He seemed to equate national opinion with national well-being and thus divorced it in his mind from public opinion, which was, according to his thought, often misguided, erroneous, and emotional and therefore not always in accord with the best interests of the realm.... He pointed out to his daughter, Princess Isabel (1846–1921), who on occasion served as regent, that the surest way to ascertain national opinion was to "hear honest and intelligent men of all political views, to read fully everything the press throughout Brazil has to say, and to listen to what is said in the legislative chambers both on the national and provincial levels." More often than not, the emperor sought his advice in the Council of State, in theory—and probably in practice as well—an august body of wise men.

(Burns, *Brazil*, pp. 215–216)

The Paraguayan War (1864–1870) knocked some cracks into the slave system that gradually evolved into deep splits. Slaves who volunteered to serve in the Brazilian army were promised their freedom, and over six thousand were liberated in this fashion. Such men, often decorated and honored by the nation for their courage and bravery in battle, helped push for the destruction of an oppressive system whose very existence insulted their patriotism and service to their country.

The officer class also emerged from the war with a new consciousness, a new sense of mission and power gained from its victories in the battlefield. Many of these officers rose from the middle class and did not share the sentiments of the old, landed oligarchs who defended slavery. A proud and militant army restlessly argued for a greater role in politics and in determining the course of Brazil's destiny. Many of these officers became ardent abolitionists and republicans. Embracing positivism and imbued with egalitarian sentiments fostered by the shared experience of war, they condemned slavery as an antiquated and irrational remnant of an earlier world.

They were joined in their efforts to abolish slavery by an increasing number of Brazilians who shared their sentiments. In 1871, under the leadership of the emperor and Viscount Rio Branco, the Law of the Free Womb was enacted to free all children born of slave mothers after the date of the passage of that law. Children were to remain with their mothers' owners until age eight, at which time the owners had the option of paying six hundred dollars, or accepting the children's labor until the age of twenty-one. In any event, the Law of the Free Womb, coupled with the end of the slave trade in 1850, effectively doomed slavery.

For the abolitionists, however, even the end of the slave trade and the Law of the Free Womb were too slow. Led by such men as Joaquim Nabuco (1849–1910), who founded the Brazilian Anti-Slavery Society, these abolitionists waged a relentless war on slavery based on moral and religious grounds. As in the United States, a number of blacks and mulattoes took part in the campaign, writing, lecturing, raising money, and counseling slaves on their rights and opportunities for freedom.

Although the philosophical repugnance of slavery was perhaps the clinching argument within the movement, other factors in the push for total emancipation also drove the abolitionists. The most persuasive of these was the antiquated nature of an institution in a nation so committed to progress. Slavery reminded the abolitionists of a stagnant, elitist way of life that had to be swept away to make room for the railroad, for industrialization, for the sinews of modernization.

The rapid expansion of the coffee industry represented one facet of this new, liberal Brazil. The export of coffee began in the eighteenth century, and by the era of independence coffee exports accounted for 20 percent of Brazil's foreign earnings. Spurred on by British traders and entrepreneurs, the coffee culture expanded rapidly in the Paraíba Valley of the state of Rio de Janeiro and spread into the states of São Paulo and Minas Gerais in the second half of the century. By the 1890s, coffee came to dominate Brazil's export trade, accounting for over 50 percent of total exports, producing high profits, and fueling the growth of the economy. Although coffee plantations initially were worked wholly by slave labor, they hired increasing numbers of European immigrants. Half of all coffee exports were going to the United States by the end of the century, reinforcing the ties slowly growing between the two largest countries in the Western Hemisphere.

Coffee stimulated the railroad boom in Brazil as well. The first railroads were strung from the coastal cities of Rio de Janeiro and São Paulo (connected to its port of Santos by a railroad) into the interior coffee-growing regions. The very first railroad began operating in Rio de Janeiro in 1854. By 1889, over six thousand miles of track were in use. In the forefront of this swelling movement was the viscount of Mauá, a pioneer entrepreneur and industrialist. Mauá has been likened to the heroes of American industry—the Goulds, Vanderbilts, and Rockefellers—and could well have fit the Horatio Alger mold. Alger, whose readers were in the millions, wrote stories of poor boys made rich by dint of their hard work, good luck, and fantastic opportunities created by the industrialization of the land and its people.

Baron Mauá, a Brazilian Modernizer

Mauá was widely recognized as the leading industrial capitalist before the Paraguayan War. At the age of thirteen he had begun working for Richard Carruthers, head of a large English importing firm. This was the turning point in his life: seven years later he became a partner in the firm. And the next year Carruthers retired to England, leaving the future *visconde* de Mauá, aged twenty-four, as manager of the Brazilian house, a position through which he amassed a large fortune. He became involved in a wide variety of enterprises, most important of which were a foundry-shipyard, railways, and banks. The initial impetus that led him to broaden his interests and eventually break away from the importing business altogether was a visit to England in 1840. The industrial might of Great Britain greatly excited him and he dreamed of creating a similarly powerful and industrialized Brazil. Of particular importance was Mauá's visit to an iron foundry in Bristol. He later wrote that 'I was deeply impressed by what I saw and observed, and right there the idea of founding in my country an identical establishment was born in my spirit.' . . . He bought a small iron foundry and shipyard in 1846. It prospered from the first. . . . During its days of prosperity, this establishment was the basis of a business empire. The firm built 72 ships, most of them steam. . . . He also made the pipes and lamps to be employed in the Mauá-owned gas company in Rio de Janeiro. . . . Railroads were one of Mauá's greatest enthusiasms. The very first railroad in Brazil was his creation. . . . Mauá visualized banks as the partners of railways in pushing the country toward economic development. . . . Mauá created, in 1851, the Banco Mauá e Companhia, which was merged into a semi-governmental bank two years later. He then organized the banking house Mauá, MacGregor & Cia. with branches in Buenos Aires, Montevideo, Rio Grande do Sul, Pelotas, Pôrto Alegre, Santos, São Paulo, Campinas, and Belém.

(Graham, *Britain and the Onset of Modernization in Brazil, 1850–1914*, pp. 187–190)

Other exports, such as rubber, fueled the modernization of Brazil. Charles Goodyear's invention of the vulcanization process in 1839 opened the way to the wide use of rubber in industry. It was used in a variety of processes, from railway mechanics and general engineering to insulation in the new electrical businesses. As these industries grew rapidly, they, in turn, stimulated the increasing production of rubber. Exports from the Amazon rose from fifteen hundred tons in 1850 to three thousand tons by 1867, and by 1880 over eight thousand tons were being exported annually. Production again doubled between 1880 and 1890 as demand increased in the electrical and engineering industries. By the turn of the century, the rubber boom was in full swing, catalyzed by the bicycle craze and the growing automobile industry, both dependent on pneumatic tires.

The Amazon was transformed by the process. The cities of Belém and Manaus exploded with an influx of immigrants, entrepreneurs, and merchants. Manaus, located nearly a thousand miles up the Amazon, became the richest and most modern city in all Brazil, sporting an opera house, Paris fashions, electric lighting, and trams. In 1901, rubber accounted for 28 percent of Brazil's total exports, second only to coffee, and constituted one of those fuels for the engines of change that were transforming Brazil.

British, American, and native Brazilian entrepreneurs such as the Baron Mauá pushed the vanguard of modernization along other fronts as well. Flour mills, modern sugar mills, and a dynamic textile industry all were established in this period, testifying to the faith in capitalism, risk-taking, and, ultimately, industrialization as the key to a progressive, modern Brazil. Rather than subscribing to the static and stable life of old Brazil—characterized by slavery, a plantation economy, and an unwillingness to change or experiment—the Baron Mauá, the abolitionists, the republicans, and the military challenged the existing order. In the end, the old empire fell, itself an anachronism that, to most Brazilians, had to be swept away along with slavery. The end of slavery came in 1888, and the empire itself fell in 1889, to be replaced by the republic of Brazil.

The empire was undermined by a number of factors. Intellectually, the positivists paved the way, arguing that slavery and monarchy were outdated institutions in a modern, scientific society. Republicans, furthermore, were on the ascendant in the 1870s and 1880s. Men such as Benjamin Constant, veteran of the Paraguayan War, instructor in mathematics at the military school, and tutor of Emperor Dom Pedro's grandchildren, promoted with candor and persuasiveness the end of slavery and the establishment of a republic, which he considered to be absolutely necessary reforms.

Religious controversy further added to the stew of discontent in the 1870s and 1880s. The emperor alienated many conservative Catholics by his apparent highhanded regalism that held that, in Brazil at least, the state continued to govern the Church in spite of Vatican efforts to the contrary. In a complicated controversy over Masonry and ultramontanism (the theory that the Church in all nations must be more responsible to the Vatican and the pope than to any secular authority), the emperor offended both conservatives and republicans.

In this charged atmosphere, the abolitionists were the first to triumph. On May 13, 1888, Isabel, Dom Pedro's daughter ruling as regent while he traveled in Europe, formally abolished slavery in Brazil. She signed the Golden Law, which freed all slaves with no conditions and no compensation to the owners. Slavery came to an end quite abruptly in Brazil, but it had been preceeded by a consistent and determined campaign by abolitionists to eradicate the institution. A number of factors

Princess Isabel, Pedro II's oldest daughter, twice served as head of state in her father's absence. During the second time, in 1888, she decreed the end of slavery. Had the army not deposed Pedro II, she would have succeeded to his throne.

worked toward this end. The ending of the slave trade at mid-century, the growing antagonism of the urban professional sectors towards an institution that supported the old planter class, the gradual increase in European immigrants to take the place of slaves, and the initiative of the slaves themselves who fled the plantations in ever-increasing numbers all undermined the institution, now considered an anachronism in a progressive, modernizing Brazil. The news of emancipation was greeted joyfully in Rio de Janeiro with fireworks, bands, speeches, and hosannas. Within eighteen months, the empire was toppled as well, and a republic proclaimed. The events were inexorably linked, because abolitionists, positivists, and republicans all were rolled into the same movement.

The army led the way. On November 15, 1889, Marshall Deodoro da Fonseca, the army's ranking general, ordered troops out of the barracks in Rio de Janeiro. They surrounded the Royal Palace and secured other public buildings, and Deodoro announced the end of the monarchy. Very few people objected. Two days later the royal family went into exile. Dom Pedro lived two more years before dying in Paris in 1891.

In a sense, an unlikely combination of factions brought the empire to its end. The army felt insulted and ignored by the politicians of the empire. Officers wished to restore credit and prestige to their institution, now also thoroughly imbued with the doctrines of republicanism and positivism cultivated by teachers such as Benjamin Constant. Church leaders, still very conservative, were put off by Dom Pedro's attitude, which seemed to threaten their autonomy and growing ultramontanism. The growing middle classes, the new industrialists, the pioneers of progress and industrialization all found the monarchy too unresponsive, too anachronistic. Even the planter class, the most powerful conservative supporters of the monarchy, lost faith in that institution when it failed to prevent abolition.

Ironically, Dom Pedro himself did more to prepare his nation for the transition to a free society and republicanism than any other single factor. The emperor was a remarkably enlightened man who encouraged republicanism, tolerated dissent, fomented the sciences, and, in a sense, paved the way for the end of his own regime.[9] That the transition from empire to republic was virtually bloodless testifies to the disposition of politically active Brazilians to make this dramatic change in their form of government, although the vast majority of the population stood by inert.

A new republican constitution was approved in 1891, and Deodoro was elected the first president. He resigned in 1892 amidst bitter feuding, and much skirmishing followed before a new president, Prudente de Morais, was elected in 1894, the first of a long line of Paulista (from the state of São Paulo) presidents. They would alternate in the presidency with Mineiros (natives of the state of Minais Gerais) until 1930, when this republic was toppled by a revolution.

Although a sharp recession caught Brazil short in the mid-1890s, its economic momentum recovered quickly. By the early years of the twentieth century, Brazil was recognized as a growing and prosperous nation.

Coffee exports continued to increase, the rubber boom reached its peak in the first decade of the twentieth century, and Brazil flexed its muscles as a major power on the South American continent. Boundary settlements were made with its neighbors, under the leadership of the Baron Rio Branco. Immense Brazil shared boundaries with *all* of the nations in South America except for Chile. These settlements were always peaceful, but several of Brazil's smaller neighbors, such as Bolivia and Peru, were forced to accept Brazilian interpretations in the end.

With the publication of Euclides da Cunha's *Rebellion in the Backlands* (*Os Sertões*) in 1902, a milestone was reached in Brazilian life. This classic explored the themes of barbarism and civilization that grappled for control of the Brazilian backlands, and it probed deeply into the very nature of Brazilian society, made up of a mixture of three peoples—Amerindian, white, and black. This mixture sometimes confounded and at other times edified those who sought to explain the heart and soul of their country.

In the next chapter, we explore some of those themes, and others, that fascinated men and women such as Euclides da Cunha as they explained the ways of life in their land and among their people.

Conclusions and Issues

South American countries, like Mexico and Central America to the north, were gradually transformed in the second half of the nineteenth century by forces that continued to change them well into the twentieth century. These forces are generally subsumed under the term "modernization," a process that involved the progressive transformation of economic and social structures. This process sometimes simply

---

[9]Worcester, *Brazil.*

emphasized well-established economic activities—such as relying on export crops and products for income—but the economic activities vastly increased their production and level of activity. Such was the case of nitrates in Chile and silver in Bolivia, for example.

Another important phase in modernization was the development of relatively new crops and products. Some, such as coffee in Colombia, cacao in Ecuador, or beef products from the Platine countries (especially Argentina and Uruguay), had been in limited production for decades, but the demands from Europe and North America propelled their production to new heights.

And then there were the "new" products, such as rubber from the Amazon, nitrates from Chile, tin from Bolivia, and petroleum from Venezuela. The rapidly industrializing nations of Europe and the United States required these products in ever-increasing quantities, leading to booms in the economies of those countries that produced them.

Concomitantly, the increasing exports drove internal improvements and changes from Colombia to Chile. Railroads and new urban developments were but two examples. Cities were transformed by gas lights, then electric streetlights, then trams, and in numerous other ways became more "modernized," often being physically refashioned with new boulevards, plazas, and monumental buildings to copy the styles of the great European cities.

And, as witnessed in Brazil, new fashions and modern ways also swept out old traditions and social structures. Slavery was finally abolished in Brazil because it was an institution made obsolete and anachronistic by the modernizing world. That slavery held on for so long in Brazil is testimony, however, to the enduring patterns of traditional life that did not yield easily to change.

Discussion Questions

1. What were the basic differences between Liberals and Conservatives in the context of late nineteenth-century Latin America? How were they alike? Which would you have been?

2. Why have some labeled the War of the Pacific a "modern" war? What was its legacy for Peru? Bolivia? Chile?

3. Why were European immigrants so avidly sought by many South American countries in the late nineteenth century? How did these immigrants participate in the transformation of these countries?

The Cultural Milieu

Martí in Exile

They were on a ferry going out to the Statue of Liberty, a recent gift from the French people to the American people. The statue was to be inaugurated soon. Mayor William R. Grace had invited a few journalists, including José Martí, to join him. Martí, Cuban patriot, pamphleteer, journalist, and poet, resided in New York, exiled from his homeland. He wrote much on life in the United States in the 1880s, most of it published in Latin American newspapers. One of the ways to keep life and limb together was to sell his articles about the great republic to the north to newspapers in Argentina, Venezuela, anywhere he could find a buyer and an audience.

The two men ducked into the main cabin of the ferry, protected from the cold wind whipping up the bay.

"You've traveled much in your life, Mr. Mayor," Martí asked as much as stated as the two sat down. Grace, Irish-born, had already established a profitable career as a trader in Latin America. Martí shared coffee with the Irishman. The two had moved often in their lives, one seeking commercial fortune, the other the political liberation of his homeland. Now, ironically, Grace was the mayor of the greatest city in America, with much political power at his disposal.

"You, too, I've heard, Señor Martí?" Grace responded with a question. He, too, knew how to query and probe, and enjoyed the give-and-take of not only politics, but also of wits with such men as Martí.

"Yes," Martí reflected momentarily, taken off guard.

"Tough life being a revolutionary, Mr. Martí?" Grace asked, curiously, not without sympathy. He knew that Martí was involved in the movement to free Cuba from Spain.

"Yes, but it is a noble cause, Mr. Mayor," Martí said. "After all, isn't the freedom of one's people from old oppressors the noblest of goals?" Asking an Irish person about oppression invariably could be expected to produce a response about the long English domination of the island.

"But the Spanish have endowed you with so much, Mr. Martí," Grace said, dodging the bait. He continued, "Your faith, your language, your very being is Spanish."

"So is their political tyranny, Mr. Grace. Rather like English rule in Ireland. It has been that way for so long. Why change it now?"

Grace looked directly at Martí and then off through the windows into the harbor waters, perhaps past the coastline, across the wide Atlantic, seeing Ireland before his misty view, rather than the choppy waters of Upper Bay. Yes, the Irish, too, wished to be free of oppressors, as did the Cubans.

"*Touché,* Mr. Martí. Perhaps Cuba should be free. Then its destiny will be truly free. And what a wonderful relationship could then spring up between these United States and your Cuba. Trade, prosperity, commerce, the sinews that serve to bind peoples!" Grace said, his voice rising, as if addressing a crowd at Cooper Union on the immense value of promoting inter-American trade, one of Grace's visions for a better, more prosperous, and peaceful world.

"Yes, Mr. Grace, but," Martí continued, "after the United States is in Cuba, who will drive *it* out? To change masters is not to be free."

"You have nothing to fear from the United States, Mr. Martí. This country wants trade, not empire. We are not the British," Grace said, echoing another Irish-like sentiment that still formed part of the mayor's being.

"Perhaps Mexicans might disagree with you, sir," Martí said.

"That was then, Martí, this is now," Grace threw off the reference to the immense territorial acquisition that the United States had made at the expense of Mexico in 1848. "Cuba, like Peru, like Brazil, like all of Latin America," Grace continued, "needs more of what this country stands for—industry, enterprise, trade, progress."

"Yes, Mr. Mayor, but our hearts resonate to different strains, our poems celebrate different values, we yearn for a freedom that will not fall prey to much of the greed and materialism that so disfigures this beautiful country."

"Nonsense," Grace harumphed. "All people want food and shelter, a decent wage, a decent living. That comes through trade and industry. Everything flows from material prosperity, sir. Provide an honest living, and you will have an honest people, devoted to those principles—truth, liberty, freedom, dignity—that you hold so dear. Set it all within the eternal teachings of the Church, and you have the makings of a people who will triumph over all evil."

"Perhaps, Mr. Mayor, perhaps," Martí answered, hearing echoes of Walt Whitman, a poet who exalted the vital, churning energies of his native land.

Some reporters drew nearer to Mayor Grace, and he turned to them, excusing himself from Martí, who wandered out onto the deck to catch the breeze, warmed a bit by the late morning sun, as they neared the statue. On days such as this, he missed his native Cuba, caressed and bathed in tropical airs. The longing could sometimes be painful, an emptiness welling up deep inside that displaced one's joy. How could Cuba be free? And after it was free, how could it stay free? It was not like the United States, no matter what the mayor and others like him claimed. Its soul was different. It could, *should,* not be subordinated to the reigning values of the United States.

Martí wrestled with the concept of culture, the only true definition of a people's soul. It was a question that many faced in nineteenth-century Latin America.

The cultural milieu of a people is basically that network of ideas, of literature, of art, of customs, and more, all of which taken together are expressions of their reality. We all are familiar with culture in one form or another, be it high culture (the opera, classical drama) or popular culture (rock and roll, cinema, MTV). They are insights into how a people think and feel, about themselves, their land, their ancestors. Culture includes a people's daily worries, their intellectual searches, their aesthetic expressions. Culture is about both the spiritual and the natural worlds, sometimes apart, sometimes intersecting.

Culture is a somewhat diaphanous term in the context of nineteenth-century Latin America, largely for three reasons. One, Latin America is such a large area with so many different "cultures," from the slaves of Bahía in tropical Brazil to the privileged Creole elites of Santiago in temperate Chile. Two, Latin America was a region changing rapidly, a region where impermanence and political instability made cultural inventiveness and creativity difficult. And three, Latin America tended to look abroad for intellectual and cultural values, especially, of course, to Europe. This tendency often suffocated the earnest attempts of Latin Americans to explore and define their own native culture, to establish their own national identities.

In spite of all the preceding reservations, expressions of culture pushed up like weeds and flowers after a heavy rainfall in a lush garden during and after the Wars of Independence. The wars themselves released new energies and promoted new thinking, as Latin Americans examined themselves to determine who they were and where they were going as a distinct civilization.

The first important novel in Latin American literature was produced precisely during the wars. Written by José Joaquín Fernández de Lizardi, *The Itching Parrot* (*El periquillo sarniento*) appeared in 1816 in Mexico, condemning many social wrongs of the day through the picaresque adventures of its hero. Lizardi's life transcended the epoch, because he began his writing career during the viceroyalty and lived to 1827. Not an ardent revolutionary, he nonetheless was an ardent reformer and satirist. Lizardi condemned the excessive powers of the Church, defended freedom of the press, and was often in trouble with the Spanish authorities.

Lizardi's strength was satire, and he wrote in a somewhat old-fashioned style, imitating the great Spanish masters of the picaresque novel. Others were to search more deeply for the Latin American heritage soon after the wars were concluded. If things Spanish—the monarchy, the Inquisition, despotism—were to be rejected, then an alternative culture had to be discovered or invented. That became one of the principal goals of Latin American intellectuals for the rest of the century.

Mental Emancipation

We shall be Argentines when we feel in ourselves the attachment to the soil that the Indian had, making it the source of his art and myths; when we feel the urge to create civilization which the Spanish founders of cities possessed; when we feel the plasticity of the gaucho on the limitless pampas and his inspiration to rise above his environment and to tell of it in song; when we have the capacity for disciplined work, like the gringo; when we are neither Indians, nor gauchos, nor Spaniards, nor gringos, but Argentines.[1]

So wrote Domingo Faustín Sarmiento as he sought to give form to the new nation of Argentina. Sarmiento's concerns were echoed by contemporaries across the Latin American scene as they faced the task of essentially defining—and forging, if necessary—a new national consciousness, a national culture, to accompany the political emancipation that had been achieved by the wars themselves.

In moving toward this goal, many Latin Americans repudiated their Hispanic heritage with scorn. Catholicism and feudalism were vilified as twin evils inherited from Spain. One of the champions of this anti-Hispanic view drew blood and created a tremendous stir in 1844, when he delivered an address before the University of Chile entitled "Investigations of the Social Influence of the Conquest and the Colonial System of the Spanish in Chile." José Victorino Lastarria minced few words in this famous polemic:

"The Spaniards conquered America, soaking its soil in blood, not to colonize it, but rather to take possession of the precious metals that it produced so abundantly." America was just a booty of war. . . . When Spain attempted to colonize it, she transplanted into Hispanic America "all the vices of her absurd system of government, vices that multiplied as a result of causes that had their origin in the system itself."[2]

Lastarria's thinking was echoed by fellow Hispanophobes, such as Sarmiento himself in Argentina and José María Luis Mora in Mexico. Mora hotly criticized the clergy and the military of Mexico for prolonging the crisis that followed Mexico's independence, and he labeled both institutions as hopelessly archaic. Furthermore, in an early analysis of the corporate nature of the Hispanic world, he faulted the tendency to sacrifice the true national interests to those of corporations (such as the military, the Church, the merchants, etc.) whose structure was inherited from Spain. A corporate view and structure of the world simply meant that individuals were not as important as the corporate entity to which they belonged or identified with.

Sarmiento raged with venom, and not a little humor, against the Spanish legacy. Citing the physiological fact that little-used organs tend to wither and grow weak, Sarmiento said that the Spanish brain had not advanced since the fourteenth century, when the Inquisition began, and that the ability of the nineteenth-century Latin American to deal with the concepts of liberty and freedom was almost dead from lack of practice.

---

[1] Crawford, *A Century of Latin American Thought*, p. 38, quoting from Comisión Nacional de Homenaje a Sarmiento, *Sarmiento: cincuentenario de su muerte.* 5 vols. (Buenos Aires, 1939), I, 140.

[2] Zea, *The Latin American Mind*, p. 57, quoting from Lastarria, but not citing him in this instance.

Other potshots were leveled at things Hispanic across the Americas. In Mexico, poets, composers, and writers creatively condemned the inheritance of Spain, which was typified as being made up of equal parts of avarice, inhumanity, and bigotry. The Mexican composer José Mariano Elízaga dropped the title "don" from his name because it was an ancient Spanish practice that denoted a gentleman. Others argued successfully to change the spelling of "Méjico" to "México," figuring that the letter x was more truly Mexican and Amerindian than was the Spanish "*j*."

A Scathing Indictment of Spain and Hispanicism

Javier Prado y Ugarteche (1871–1921), a Peruvian educator and politician, condemned Spain for much of Peru's backwardness. In the following passage, Alejandro O. Deustua reviewed the new (1941) edition of Prado's book, which originally appeared under the title *Estado social del Perú durante la dominación española: estudio histórico-sociológico* (Lima, 1894).

"Politically, it [the colonial period] bequeathed to us the vices of totalitarianism, the enemy of all social liberty.... We have received traditions of incorrigible bureaucratic abuses in public administration; bribery nourished by avarice and impunity that extended even to the highest officials; and, as Prado puts it, 'a sick obsession with wealth, no matter how acquired, that became an all-pervasive and incurable disease....'

"What has been our inheritance in the economic order? As Prado explains it, "'The immediate exploitation of our sources of wealth without long-term planning and with only immediate results in mind.' In short, we have inherited a most pernicious system that in Peru has produced abominable and destructive habits persisting even to the present day because of the immutable law of psychological inheritance.

"The colonial ecclesiastical heritage has left in our church officials an unbridled ambition to govern, even in the temporal order; an instransigent fanaticism, developed to the most refined point of cruelty by the Holy Office of the Inquisition . . . clergy, whose individual morals are weakened by the abundance of pleasures attaching to their positions.... All they did during three hundred years was to abuse their power. As teachers, they suffocated the spirit of scientific investigation. As models of perfect men, they served only to weaken the ties of social morality. They poisoned the atmosphere with superstition, pride, wrath, impurity, and their terrible train of consequences. Cloaked in a primitive doctrine of charity and chastity, they proceeded actually to institute a policy of hatred, extermination and profligacy...

"Under colonial influences, intelligence atrophied and the practical spirit of work and economy disappeared, along with concern for political rights. All that remained were absurd ideals, aggressiveness, hallucinatory fanaticism, and a reverential form of homage to the king and his government. Such was the spirit of the race to which the conquerors belonged. Such was the spirit that they imparted to the blood of our creoles."

(Fredrick B. Pike, editor. and contributor, *Latin American History: Select Problems, Identity, Integration, and Nationhood* [New York: Harcourt, Brace & World, 1969], pp. 199–200)

Not everyone was so quick to condemn everything Spanish. In the search to find, or attempt to forge, the new Latin American civilization, one simply could not ignore three hundred years of history. The blood and language and faith of Spain coursed through Latin America, a fact that the intellectual Andrés Bello recognized quite well.[3] Bello, a Venezuelan by birth who spent many years in Chile, was revered by many as an educator, philosopher, poet, and statesman.

To Bello, the evidence of the positive Hispanic heritage was perfectly clear. One had but to consider the sacrifices, the nobility, the courage, the steadfastness shown by the patriots during the Wars of Independence to witness the strength and virtues that the Latin Americans had inherited from Spain. The very ability of Latin Americans to rise up and overthrow Spain was an ability born within the Hispanic bosom. The vices attributed to the Spaniards—injustice, treachery in war, atrocity—were vices common to humanity, and certainly not uniquely Spanish.

Bello, Sarmiento, and others such as the great Mexican conservative historian Lucas Alamán were not content with a simple-minded condemnation of things Spanish. They were creators—a much more difficult job than being destroyers. After political emancipation had been achieved through the Wars of Independence, they sought what the modern Mexican philosopher, Leopoldo Zea, called "mental emancipation." It proved to be a difficult task, because one is never truly freed of one's past. But for the student of Latin America, the search for a new identity was infinitely more satisfying because the creative process edifies rather than denigrates the human condition.

Literature

Two basic literary currents flowed in Latin America during the nineteenth century: romanticism in the first half and modernism in the second half. Scholars of literature also identify subcurrents such as naturalism, realism, and positivism as running concurrently through the century, sometimes complementing, sometimes contradicting the basic currents.

What is most important to recognize, however, is that the truly significant literature of the period was concerned ultimately with American themes. Thus, although the Argentine poet and writer Esteban Echeverría sought during his life to be a good romantic, he is best remembered for a work that appeared posthumously, a quickly written piece of prose fiction with a political message.

Echeverría's *El matadero* (*The Slaughterhouse*), probably composed about 1840, was a thinly disguised attack on the Rosas regime. The story is best synopsized by Jean Franco.

> It relates an incident at the abattoir [slaughterhouse] in Buenos Aires where, during the slaughtering of the animals, a bull escapes, killing a boy as he does so. The bull is recap-

---

[3]See Rafael Caldera, *Andrés Bello: Philosopher, Poet, Philologist, Educator, Legislator, Statesman* (London: George Allen & Unwin, 1977), translated by John Street, for an impassioned and loving account of the many faces of Bello, written by a fellow Venezuelan.

tured and the butchers, excited by the thrill of the pursuit and capture, make a blood-thirsty ritual of the killing. As they finish off the animal, a refined-looking young man passes on horseback. They turn against him, drag him down from his horse and torment him. The youth struggles valiantly against the attackers but has a hemorrhage and is left for dead. The reason for the attack on him is that he is "'unitarian'" (that is, in opposition to Rosas and the federalist party). The butchers know this because their victim carries no outward sign of support for the Rosas regime and also because he rides with a foreign saddle. He is thus identified with an "un-American" way of life. Echeverría's own sympathies are not left in doubt. He is unmistakably on the side of refinement and civilization, against the native "butchers."[4]

The second major work of the period attacking Rosas was written by Domingo Sarmiento, the great Argentine man of letters, educator, and political leader of his generation. In his *Facundo* (1845), subtitled *Civilization and Barbarism,* Sarmiento told the story of the rise and fall of an Argentine gaucho caudillo named Juan Facundo Quiroga. Facundo represented all that was rough and wild and untamed in Argentina. Opposed to Facundo were the forces of civility, education, and progress represented by Buenos Aires and the civilization from abroad that inspired it. *Facundo* the novel is in fact Sarmiento's statement of the classic battle between civilization (the city, European influences) and barbarism (the gauchos, unbridled passions) that Argentina, and indeed much of Latin America, was fighting. To Sarmiento, who later became president and worked to implement his vision of a progressive, modern society, Rosas, Facundo, and other caudillos had to be destroyed or, at the least, reined in, if Latin America ever was to rise above the political anarchy that tore it apart in the first part of the nineteenth century.

In *Facundo* and other works, we see the power of creation at work. Although *Facundo* and *The Slaughterhouse,* for example, borrowed from the romantic style, they were essentially American works, inspired by the strengths and failures of their traditions, describing the sweep of plains and mountains and forests and their inhabitants in a vital, American prose. *Facundo* went through several editions, and was translated into English by Mrs. Horace Mann in 1868, and its impact in nineteenth-century Latin America was long-lasting.

Not all Argentines were so quick to condemn their past and the gauchos and their simple, although often brutal, life in the pampas. In response to the denigration of the gaucho and his way of life, José Hernández wrote *Martín Fierro* (1872), the greatest epic poem in Argentine history. It depicted the gaucho as a victim of the new, modern world that was gradually stripping him of his freedom, his way of life. Fences, railroads, unscrupulous politicians, and greedy ranch owners drove gauchos such as the hero of the poem, Martín Fierro, to become an outlaw. In the poem Hernández especially protested the sending of gaucho conscripts to fight on the Amerindian frontier, depriving them of their rights, denying them of their traditional livelihoods, which sprang from being born on the wide expanses of the pampas.

---

[4]Jean Franco, *The Modern Culture of Latin America: Society and the Artist* (New York: Frederick A. Praeger, 1967), p. 7.

Hernández wrote *Martín Fierro* as the *gaucho* himself might have spun his story, in a language familiar to most Argentines, interlaced with idioms, proverbs, and folk imagery. It became immensely popular, being read by wide sections of the public, being recited in remote farmhouses. It reached across the country as no other work had before it.

Other writers, such as Ricardo Palma of Peru, found equal inspiration in the rich past of his homeland. He wrote his *Tradiciones peruanas* (*Peruvian Traditions*) over the course of forty years, from the 1870s to 1910. They were stories based on his intense curiosity about the human condition in the colonial period. Still the most widely read of his country's writers, Palma ransacked libraries and archives for the manuscripts that illuminated the viceroyalty's past, filled with stories of glory, intrigue, debaucheries, loves, and murders, all drawn from true life and rewritten by Palma for his readers. Palma is, in fact, credited with creating this new genre of literature, called the "traditions," although it was a genre not unknown both in Spain and Latin America before Palma. Yet, perhaps even more important, it was an "American" theme, and an "American" form that Palma dealt with and created, respectively. He provided for his people a continuity with the past, looking to the viceroyalty not as an iniquitous period of Spanish occupation, but rather as the cradle of Peruvian traditions. Many of these traditions include miracles and incredible acts that contradicted the laws of nature. In some ways then, they prefigured the literature of magical realism of the mid-twentieth century that earned Latin American authors praises and prizes from around the literary world for creativity and genius.

A Story of Old Peru

Once upon a time there was a lay brother who lived . . . in Lima, in the convent of the Franciscans, where he performed the duties of refectorian in the nursing home or hospital of the devout friars. The people called him Fray Gómez, Fray Gómez he is called in the conventual records, and tradition knows him as Fray Gómez. I believe that in the petition for his beatification and canonization that was sent to Rome, this is the only name he is given. . . .

Fray Gómez was in his cell one morning, given over to meditation, when a couple of timid knocks sounded on his door, and a plaintive-toned voice said "*Deo gratias.* . . . Praise be the Lord."

"Forever, amen. Come in, brother," answered Fray Gómez.

"And the door of the humble cell opened to admit a ragged individual, a *vera efigies* of a man crushed by poverty, but whose face revealed the proverbial forthrightness and honesty of the Old Castilian.

The entire furnishings of the cell comprised four rawhide chairs, a table that had seen better days, a cot without mattress, sheets, or blankets and with a stone for a pillow.

"Sit down, brother, and tell me frankly what brings you here," said Fray Gómez.

"Well, father, I want to tell you that I am an honest and decent man. . . ."

"That is plain, and I hope you will continue that way, for it will give you peace of heart in this life, and bliss in the next."

"You see, I am a peddler, and I have a big family, and my business does not prosper because I am short of capital, not because of laziness or lack of effort on my part."

"I am glad, brother, for God helps a man who works as he should."

"But the fact of the matter is, father, that so far God hasn't heard me, and he is slow in coming to my help. . . ."

"Don't lose heart, brother, don't lose heart."

"But the fact of the matter is that I have knocked on many doors asking for a loan of five hundred *duros* and I have found them all locked and bolted. And last night, turning things over in my mind, I said to myself, Come, Jerónimo, cheer up and go ask Fray Gómez for the money, for if he wants to, a mendicant friar and poor as he is, he'll find a way to give you a hand. And so here I am because I have come, and I beg and request you, father, to lend me the trifling sum for six months, and you can be sure that it will never be said of me:

"The world is full of folks

"who reverence certain saints,

"But whose gratitude ends

"When they've answered their plaints."

"What made you think, son, that you would find such a sum in this poor cell?"

"Well, father, the fact is that I wouldn't know how to answer that; but I have faith that you will not let me leave empty-handed."

"Your faith will save you, brother. Wait a minute."

And running his eyes over the bare, whitewashed walls of the cell, he saw a scorpion that was crawling calmly along the window frame. Fray Gómez tore a page out of an old book, walked over to the window, carefully picked up the insect, wrapped it in the paper, and turning to his visitor, said "Take this jewel, good man, and pawn it; but don't forget that you are to return it to me in six months."

The peddler could hardly find words to express his gratitude; he took his leave of Fray Gómez and like a flash was on his way to a pawnbroker's shop.

The jewel was magnificent, worthy of a Moorish queen, to say the least. It was a brooch in the shape of a scorpion. A magnificent emerald set in gold formed the body, and the head was a sparkling diamond, with rubies for eyes.

The pawnbroker, who understood his business, greedily examined the jewel and offered the peddler two thousand *duros* on it; but the Spaniard insisted that he would accept only five hundred *duros* for six months, at a [high] rate of interest, of course. The papers or tickets were made out and signed, and the moneylender comforted himself with the hope that after a time the owner of the jewel would come back for more money, and that with the compound interest that would pile up, he would be unable to redeem it, and he would become the owner of a jewel so valuable in itself and because of its artistic merit.

"With this little capital the peddler's affairs went so well that, when the time was up, he was able to redeem the jewel, and wrapping it in the same paper in which he had received it, he returned to Fray Gómez.

"The latter took the scorpion, set it upon the windowsill, blessed it, and said, "Little creature of God, go your way!"

"And the scorpion began to crawl happily about the walls of the cell."

The rest of the story came from an oil painting over a cell in a small cloister that was still used as a hospital in the nineteenth century.

"The Venerable Fray Gómez. Born in Extremadura [Spain] in 1560. Took the habit in Chuquisaca in 1580. Came to Lima in 1587. Was a nurse for forty years, displaying all the virtues, and was endowed with celestial gifts and favors. His life was a continuous miracle. He died on May 2, 1631, and was held to be a saint. The following year his body was laid in the chapel of Aranzazú, and on October 13, 1810, was placed beneath the high altar in the same vault where the remains of the priors of the convent are interrred."

[(Emir Rodríguez Monegal, editor, with the assistance of Thomas Colchie, *The Borzoi Anthology of Latin American Literature*, vol. I, *From the Time of Columbus to the Twentieth Century* [New York: Alfred A. Knopf, 1984 (1977)], pp. 267–270, from *The Golden Land*, pp. 138–140, and *The Knights of the Cape*, translated by Harriet de Onis [New York: Knopf, 1945], pp. 224–229 and 165–169)

If the plight of the *gauchos* attracted Argentine poets such as Hernández, Peruvians and other Latin Americans were no less attracted to the deplorable condition of the Amerindians in their homelands. The ennoblement of the Amerindian as a major and positive contributor to Latin American civilization would not reach full-blown proportions until the twentieth century, especially spurred on by the Mexican Revolution of 1910, but already in the late nineteenth century writers were being drawn to the subject. The most acerbic and polemical of these was the Peruvian Manuel González Prada.

After a sojourn in Europe, González Prada returned to his native Peru a confirmed anarchist and atheist. Unlike Ricardo Palma, González Prada attacked the colonial heritage and became a radical defender of the Amerindian. He advocated a thorough purge of Peru by destroying the old system of social order and economic privilege, and he championed the Amerindian as the truly dynamic and potentially redeeming force in Peruvian society. Untouched by the greed of capitalism and made virtuous by a collective lifestyle that emphasized sharing and the well-being of the community rather than the individual, the Amerindian seemed the ideal to González Prada.

As González Prada was extolling the virtues of the Amerindian, a compatriot, Chlorinda Matto de Turner, published *Aves sin nido* (*Birds without Nests*) in 1899. It was the first Indianist, or *indigenista*, novel. With its forthright description of the plight of the Amerindian, Turner's book earned her the contempt of both the Catholic church and the Peruvian elites, both of whom were held to account for the oppression of the Amerindians. But the novel became a landmark in the Indianist movement.

A short novel published in Colombia in 1896, *El alma de Pablo Suesca* (*Pablo Suesca's Soul*), belonged to the same genre. Its author, Enrique Cortés Holguín, shared the sentiments of the better-known Peruvian Indianists.

Chlorinda Matto de Turner was the author of
Los aves sin nido, *the first great Indianist novel
of Peru that presaged the rise of indigenismo
across Latin America in the twentieth century.
This movement, given power by the Mexican
Revolution (1910-1917), elevated Indian culture
as equal to the reigning Hispanic values
inherited from Spain.*

Modernism

Modernism was an intense movement of the late nineteenth and early twentieth centuries that was closely identified with the beginnings of a true Latin American literature. A complicated movement, it had as its goal basically to revolutionize the form and content of both prose and poetry, to raise art to a level in Latin America where it could be practiced for its own sake. Its guru was a Nicaraguan poet named Rubén Darío, who not only coined the term *modernismo* but also inspired a generation across the wide spectrum of Latin America. Although most modernists such as Darío traveled to Europe and North America and borrowed art forms from abroad, especially from France, most found their themes and their inspiration at home, in the *pampas* of Argentina, in the islands of the Caribbean, in the backlands of Brazil, wherever their ideal views of art and life clashed with the reality of their homelands.

The Cuban poet and revolutionary José Martí best personified the combination of artist and activist in the late nineteenth century. His poems inspired modernism; his polemics fomented revolution. Martí was born in Havana in 1853 of Spanish parents. An eager learner, he was writing and publishing poems and essays as a teenager and was soon involved in anti-Spanish activities, espousing the liberation of his homeland from Spain. He dedicated his life to this cause, for which he would eventually die.

In 1871 he was arrested for revolutionary activities, among them founding a political newspaper, *The Free Fatherland.* He was imprisoned for six months and exiled to Spain. There he continued his education, receiving a degree in law and philosophy from the University of Zaragoza, but also keeping up his revolutionary polemics by publishing a pamphlet on the political prisons in Cuba. He left Spain in 1874, traveled through Europe, and met the elderly Victor Hugo, who was considered the apostle of French letters in the nineteenth century. Back in the Americas, he landed in Guatemala where he wrote his first book, *Guatemala,* dedicated to a girl he secretly loved. In 1878 he returned to Cuba but was soon forced into exile again. In 1881 he arrived in New York, passionately recommitting his life to Cuban independence. He traveled widely from his base in New York and wrote for prestigious Latin American newspapers, such as *La Nación* of Buenos Aires.

During his years in exile, Martí produced some of his most memorable poems, especially *Ismaelillo* (*Little Ishmael,* 1882), dedicated to his young son, and *Versos sencillos* (*Simple Verses,* 1891), which dealt with themes such as friendship, love, sincerity, justice, and freedom. His poetry was not convoluted or abstract, but rather drawn out in simple lines, low-keyed, popular, simple, and elegant. He did not hate Spaniards; he hated the tyranny that they practiced in Cuba. In his poems, he expressed not only a love for things Cuban and American, but also for things Spanish. The following excerpt attested to this love.

> For Aragon, in Spain,
> I have in my heart
> a place all Aragon, frank, fierce, faithful, without cruelty.
> If a fool wants to know
> why I have such a place, I tell him
> that there I had a good friend,
> that there I loved a woman.
> There, in the flowering plain,
> > plain of heroic defense,
> > to defend what they think
> > people gamble their lives.
>
> > And if a mayor besets him,
> or a sullen king annoys him,
> the peasant puts on his cloak
> and goes with his gun to die.
>
> > I love the yellow earth
> that the muddy Ebro bathes,
> I love bluish Pillar
> of Lanuza and Padilla.
>
> > I honor him who with a blow
> casts a tyrant to the ground;

I honor him if he is Cuban;
I honor him if he is Aragonese.

I love the dark courtyards
with embroidered staircases;
I love the silent naves
and the empty convents.

I love the flowering earth,
Muslim or Spanish,
where the scanty flower of my life
burst its corolla.[5]

Martí was also an essayist, revolutionary, political commentator, and social observer, and, after his beloved island, the United States most attracted his attention. Most fundamentally, Martí was ambivalent toward the United States. An ardent ad-

José Martí, a Cuban writer who inspired his fellow countrymen with his patriotism and poetry to fight for independence from Spain. He was killed in 1895 while participating in the movement that eventually led to the Spanish-American War of 1898 and Cuban independence.

[5]From *Versos sencillos,* translated by Donald Walsh, in Emir Rodríguez Monegal, editor, with the assistance of Thomas Colchie, *The Borzoi Anthology of Latin American Literature: Vol. I., From the Time of Columbus to the Twentieth Century* (New York: Knopf, 1984), pp. 345–346.

mirer of its political democracy, he nonetheless was appalled by its system of economic monopoly and big business. On the one hand, he saw political freedoms and individual rights guaranteed under a constitution that worked. On the other hand, he was disgusted by the economic exploitation of the poor, especially the masses of immigrants whom he saw arriving daily in New York. He wrote that "'The Cubans admire this nation, the greatest ever built by freedom, but they distrust the evil conditions that, like worms in the blood, have begun their work of destruction in this mighty Republic. . . . They cannot honestly believe that excessive individualism and reverence for wealth are preparing the United States to be the typical nation of liberty.'"[6]

Other Currents

The modernists did not monopolize literature in the late nineteenth century. Others turned away from the excessive sentimentality of romanticism of earlier years and began to write in a more realistic vein. Using both a barer realism and a style now called naturalism, they delved deeply into their own personal and national experiences for themes peculiarly Latin American. Brazilian writers were especially prominent in this movements. Two in particular stand out: Joaquim Maria Machado de Assis and Euclides da Cunha.

Machado de Assis was born humbly to a mulatto housepainter and a Portuguese mother in Rio de Janeiro in 1839. He was an avid reader and educated himself by reading at the library. He became an apprentice typographer early in life and rose through the government bureaucracy to eventually become the first president of the Brazilian Academy of Letters in 1897. He married a refined Portuguese woman and lived a modest middle-class life, superficially humdrum and perhaps even boring. Yet his liabilities—having been born a mulatto in a racialist society, being a physically ugly person, and being subject to epileptic seizures—affected his literature profoundly.

He began writing poems when he was sixteen, and by the end of his life, his works filled thirty-one volumes. An ironic and cynical mind pointed out the follies and foibles of his world with wit and sarcasm. A near-total disillusionment with humankind produced few "good" characters in his books, most of them tormented by their own doubts and demons, caught in a web of their fears and dreams. His finest work is considered to be *Dom Casmurro* (1900). It is the classic story of the husband who suspects adultery and of his obsession with revenge: on his wife, her lover, and his son, who may or may not have been the son of the lover. The novel is told by the tortured narrator himself, and its involved and ironic style of writing presaged the brilliant flowering of the Latin American novel in the twentieth century.

While Machado de Assis worked out his demons in his literature, another Brazilian, Euclides da Cunha, produced *Os Sertões* (*Rebellion in the Backlands*, 1902), considered to be a classic in Brazilian letters. It is the story of government

---

[6]Jaime Suchlicki, *Cuba: From Columbus to Castro*, 2nd. ed. Washington: Pergamon-Brassey's International Defense Publishers, 1986, p. 77.

suppression of a commune in the backlands (the rough, interior regions of north-east Brazil called the *sertão*) at the end of the century. Like Sarmiento's *Facundo,* it is a story of the epic conflict between civilization and barbarism.

Like Machado de Assis, da Cunha was born in Rio de Janeiro. He was trained in the army as an engineer but in 1896 mustered out and took up journalism. As a correspondent for the prestigious newspaper *O Estado de São Paulo,* he was assigned to cover the last stages of a remarkable conflict between peasants, led by their messiah, Antônio Conselheiro, and the federal government, represented by the army. From this conflict da Cunha spun out the story that emerged as *Rebellion in the Backlands.*

Conselheiro was born into a middle-class family who had fallen onto hard times. After running afoul of local authorities and losing his wife, he began to wander the Brazilian backlands. He lived off charity and learned to preach folk religious sermons to anyone who would listen. Because most villages in the interior had no priest, Conselheiro (a pseudonym meaning "the Counselor") became a religious messenger. By the early 1890s he had gathered a small following, so he settled on an abandoned ranch called Canudos. Gradually his fame as a healer and provider spread, and peasants by the hundreds flocked to join his informal congregation. A description of Conselheiro in 1876 was included in *Rebellion.*

> In 1876 the Counselor, as he was known, appeared in the town of Itapicuru de Cima. His fame had become widespread. A document published that year in the capital of the Empire bears witness to this:
>
> There has appeared in the *sertão* of the north a man who calls himself Antônio the Counselor and who exerts a great influence on the lower classes, utilizing for this end his mysterious aspect and his ascetic habits, which make a great impression on the ignorance of these simple-minded people. He has let his hair and beard grow long, he wears a cotton tunic and eats very little, looking almost like a mummy. He goes about in the company of two women converts, and he spends his life praying and preaching and giving advice to the multitudes that gather to hear him wherever the priests permit it. By playing on their religious sentiments he attracts the people and does what he likes with them. He shows himself to be a man of intelligence, though devoid of culture.
>
> These remarks, which were the exact truth, published in a journal hundreds of miles away, are eloquent testimony to the fame he was acquiring.[7]

Da Cunha's own powerful and evocative description of Conselheiro highlights not only the mystical power of Conselheiro but also the brilliance of da Cunha. He draws upon contemporary scientific theories and his own native insight to portray the ways of Conselheiro, and especially the willingness of peasants to be duped and led by such a person.

> He went on his way leaving the superstitious countryfolk awed and apprehensive. He acquired an ascendancy over them without making any effort to do so. In a primitive society in which, by reason of its racial composition and the influence of the nefarious "holy missions," life rested on a basis of miracles they could not fathom, his mysterious mode of life began to create an atmosphere of supernatural prestige about him which, perhaps,

---

[7]Euclides da Cunha, *Rebellion in the Backlands,* translated by Samuel Putnam (Chicago: University of Chicago Press, 1944), in Emir Rodríguez Monegal, *The Borzoi Anthology,* p. 326.

aggravated his deranged temperament. Little by little all this domination which he unintentionally exercised on others seemed to have taken hold on him. All the conjectures and legends by which he was soon surrounded stimulated the growth of his aberration. His madness acquired outward form. He saw it reflected in the intense admiration and unquestioning respect that in a short time made his word law in all disputes and quarrels and converted him into the supreme authority in all decisions. This attitude on the part of the multitude spared him the ordeal of trying to understand his own mental state, the painful effort of self-analysis and that obsessive introspection which drives an unhinged mind to madness. The multitude recast him in its own image, created him, enlarged him beyond all human proportions, and launched him upon a sea of errors two thousand years old. It needed someone who should translate its own vague idealism and guide it along the mysterious paths that lead to heaven. The evangelist emerged, but inhuman, an automaton. This agitator was a puppet. He acted passively, like a sleepwalker. But in his behavior he reflected the obscure, formless aspirations of the three races.[8]

The rebellion that Conselheiro led was essentially one of resistance by peasants and backlanders to conformity to a "civilized" standard. Organized in small communities, they practiced free love, raided neighboring landowners, evaded taxes, and refused to conform to the traditional structures of the Church. Four expeditions were sent by the government in the 1890s, and only the fourth succeeded in quashing the rebels in their stronghold of Canudos. It was with this fourth expedition that da Cunha arrived to observe the final defeat of the rebels.

Rebellion in the Backlands is above all else a first-rate narrative that draws the reader into the world of the *sertão*, a story told with full attention to the geographic and political setting before it focuses with clarity, and not without sympathy, on the protagonist Conselheiro. The book quite obviously champions the forces of light and civilization over the ignorance and brutality that the rebellion represented. Da Cunha is quite clear on this.

> This entire campaign [to destroy Canudos and the rebels] would be a crime, a futile and a barbarous one, if we were not to take advantage of the paths opened by our artillery, by following up our cannon with a constant, stubborn, and persistent campaign of education, with the object of drawing these rude and backward fellow countrymen of ours into the current of our times and of our national life. . . . Our biological evolution demands the guarantee of social evolution. We are condemned to civilization. Either we shall progress or we shall perish. So much is certain and our choice is clear.[9]

Da Cunha does not spare the barbarity shown by the army in its extermination of the Canudos rebels, nor does he fail to point out the grandeur of Conselheiro, a man whose life both attracted and repelled him.

Da Cunha's ambivalence crops up in other great literary interpreters of national developments in the nineteenth century. Although a commitment to progress and change is quite evident, there is also an unwillingness to forego the bittersweet, powerful, and sensual life of *gauchos* and peasants, of Amerindians and mulattoes. The

---

[8]Ibid., p. 325.

[9]Da Cunha, *Rebellion*, pp. 54, 408; excerpt drawn from Samuel Putnam, *Marvelous Journey: A Survey of Four Centuries of Brazilian Writing* (New York: Knopf, 1948), p. 204.

vastness and wildness of the land profoundly stamped people with its own nature. These elements were not so easily dismissed by writers who not only wished to send a message of culture and civilization but also to represent life for what it was: still wild and primitive in many parts of Latin America.

Ariel and Caliban

In 1900 the Uruguayan José Enrique Rodó published an essay, entitled *Ariel,* that became extraordinarily popular throughout Latin America. Borrowing from the symbolism employed by Shakespeare in *The Tempest,* Rodó represents Latin America as Ariel and the United States as Caliban in his story. Ariel is the "'noble and winged part of the spirit,'" whereas Caliban represents materialism and grossness.[10] At the simplest level, Rodó pictures Latin America as a land where spiritual harmony, ethics, and aesthetics still prevail, whereas the United States not only is given to materialism but also governed by the mundane priorities of the present, with little or no sense of the past or future.

In *Ariel,* which essentially is written in the form of a revered master distilling for his young disciples the essence of his wisdom, humanity is constantly being tugged apart by the opposite forces of spirituality and sensuality. Ariel, through which Rodó counsels the youth of Latin America, calls upon young people to live by a morality and for a beauty that transcends the moment. Art, science, religion, and other matters of the spirit should always be governed by a morality founded firmly in eternal principles. Contrasted with this view are those people who follow the utilitarian way of life, who put a premium on the present, on the accumulation of material goods, on the satisfaction of carnal and ephemeral needs.

Basically, Rodó called upon Latin Americans to pursue non-personal ends, to cultivate an ideal that transcended material goals. Otherwise, they were condemned to embrace vulgar materialism just as had occurred in North America, and the spiritual needs of people would go begging.

Rodó left a mixed legacy.

His views, as interpreted and perpetuated by others, encouraged the myth that Latin Americans possessed a spiritual superiority over North Americans. The lack of culture and the greedy materialism of these northerners crippled their civilization, in spite of all its extraordinary economic and political accomplishments. In a more positive vein, Rodó encouraged a whole generation of Latin American intellectuals to embrace the notion that ideas and ideals *can* shape and reform societies. This notion gave rise in the twentieth century to important movements in education, movements to use education as a transforming element in uplifting the masses and changing the political and social life of Latin America.

Rodó had a vision of a unified Latin American culture, not one divided by nationalities and regions, each one distinct from the other. He, in effect, encouraged

---

[10]Franco, *The Modern Culture of Latin America,* p. 50.

Latin Americans to think of themselves as being culturally unified. Although the pan-American movement was as old as Simón Bolívar, it was given a new impetus by Rodó and others. And it came at a time when Latin America's great neighbor to the north, the United States, was on the move once again at the end of the century. The intermingled destinies of these parts of the Western Hemisphere are considered in the next chapter.

Conclusions and Issues

Culture is a multifaceted window into the life of a people. In this chapter we reviewed some of the most insightful of these windows. Literature certainly represents one of the most powerful prisms through which to view culture. Through this prism Latin Americans, such as Rodó in *Ariel*, Hernández in *Martín Fierro*, and Martí in his poems and essays, examined their reality and explained it with passion. Sarmiento's great work, *Facundo*, delved deeply, for example, into the very nature of Latin American civilization, which, according to Sarmiento, was a warring ground between the raw forces of nature and civilization.

The making of a Latin American civilization was also entrusted in part to the intellectuals and writers of the region. What was Latin America? It was derived from a remarkable combination of several different civilizations, including the host Amerindian, the invading European, and the uprooted African, but it fell to the writers, to the essayists, to the poets, and to artists of all stripes, from painters to folk musicians, to define it, to explain its special sense, to render through their talents and creativities the rich panorama that was Latin America.

Discussion Questions

1. What is your definition of "culture"? How does it provide insights into Latin American history?

2. How does *Rebellion in the Backlands* reflect the struggle between the traditional and the modern in Brazil?

3. What is meant by "mental emancipation" in the context of creating a new Latin American culture in the nineteenth-century wake of the Wars of Independence?

Changing Worlds
and New Empires

Mr. Zelaya and the Gringos

"They're all gringos, don José. What difference does it make if some are gringos from New York and others gringos from Gran Bretaña?" Felipe Aguirre asked as much as stated.

José Zelaya, the provisional administrator of the port of San Juan del Norte, located on the Atlantic coast of Nicaragua, looked at Aguirre and responded as a tutor might to his pupil.

"Gringos from Britain, and France, and from all over Europe, are not Americans, Felipe."

"Well, yes," Aguirre had to admit. Gringos from New York and New Orleans and other places up north called themselves "Americans," whereas the other gringos certainly didn't. But they all seemed to be large, English-speaking, rather impressive types, regardless of where they came from.

"And we'd rather work with gringos who are Americans," Zelaya continued.

"Why?" Aguirre asked. The day was warming, and the breeze off the ocean was dying back. It would be a hot day. It was December, 1887, and out to sea a smudge of smoke appeared on the horizon. It was the ship they were waiting for.

"Why?" Zelaya repeated. "Because the gringos from England want our land, they take our fine trees, they don't care to respect us." Zelaya, too, looked out to sea. A ship carrying American engineers and surveyors was expected to drop anchor in this small, tropical port—the British called it Greytown—in a few hours. "The gringos from New York," Zelaya continued, still looking out to sea but addressing Aguirre, "want to build a canal right here, Felipe, right through our Nicaragua. It will bring prosperity and progress."

"I thought Monsieur de Lesseps and the French were doing that in Panama," Aguirre said.

"Yes, they are trying," Zelaya answered. He, too, had been reading in the old newspapers that reached them—from New York, London, Paris—days, weeks, sometimes months late in San Juan del Norte, about the great French canal builder, Ferdinand de Lesseps. The conqueror of the Suez. He was now engaged in Panama. But from what the gringos said—the North American gringos, that is—the Panama effort was turning into a disaster. De Lesseps was mired in landslides triggered by tropical deluges. Or his men were dying like flies of yellow jack (yellow fever). Or his money was failing. What a pity. Zelaya admired the French immensely. But they were failing in Panama.

The first canal would be built right here in Nicaragua. And, Zelaya thought, it would begin right here in San Juan del Norte, which he administered temporarily.

The Americans—those from the United States—would indeed begin to dig a transisthmian canal in the early 1890s, expecting to complete the great engineering project across Nicaragua, in contrast to the dismal French failure in Panama. Through the canal and through other ways, the destinies of the United States and Latin America became even more woven together as the nineteenth century gave way to the twentieth.

The Emerging Colossus to the North

Today the United States is practically sovereign on this continent, and its fiat is law upon the subjects to which it confines its interposition. Why? It is not because of the pure friendship or good will felt for it. It is not simply by reason of its high character as a civilized state, nor because wisdom and justice and equity are the invariable characteristics of the dealings of the United States. It is because, in addition to all other grounds, its infinite resources combined with its isolated position render it master of the situation and practically invulnerable as against any or all other powers.[1]

Secretary of State Richard Olney's imperious proclamation in 1895 confirmed the worst suspicions that people such as Martí and Rodó held about the United States. It was an empire on the make in the late nineteenth century, and its principal target appeared to be Latin America. What had begun as a hemisphere of equal states during the heyday of Simón Bolívar and the period of independence had turned into a hemisphere of unequal nations where one—the United States—was determined to realize its destiny in spite of or at the expense of Latin America, if necessary.

---

[1]Secretary of State Richard Olney's message to Great Britain, July 20, 1895, quoted in Thomas G. Paterson, editor, *Major Problems in American Foreign Policy: Documents and Essays, Vol. I: To 1914* (Lexington, Mass.: D. C. Health, 1978), p. 246.

Many points of contact were made between the United States and Latin America during the nineteenth century. They began even before the Wars of Independence; Yankee traders and whalers penetrated the old Spanish empire as they sought markets and friendly ports. During the wars the United States consistently supported the patriots in their revolution against Spain. Americans such as John Quincy Adams were motivated as much by the threads of a common ideology and political inheritance as by commercial motives, although the latter were never subordinated to the former.

In the broad sweep of Latin America's international history after independence, scholars have tended to divide the period into two halves: one, roughly to the 1860s; and two, from about the 1860s to the turn of the century. During the first half, the new nations were particularly susceptible to interventions by European nations—principally Spain, England, and France. The United States also took advantage of the weakness of the new nations, such as Mexico, then in a state of political and economic chaos. During the second half, the growing stability and strength of the Latin American nations diminished the ability of the foreign powers to intervene so blatantly in Latin American affairs.

Two other factors also have to be considered. One, rivalry among European powers tended to restrain their ambitions in Latin America, none wishing to see the others gain advantages in Latin America. Instead, they turned their imperial ambitions on Africa and Asia. And two, the United States itself tended to check European ambitions in Latin America because it was committed, according to the Monroe Doctrine of 1823, to preserving the territorial integrity and political independence of Latin America.

Gradually a new sense of mission, which Americans called "manifest destiny," had gained the ascendancy in the relations between the United States and Latin America as the nineteenth century progressed. The Mexican War of 1846–1848, the many suggestions to annex Cuba, the William Walker invasion of Nicaragua in 1856, and other acts reflected the ambitions of Americans to extend the fruits of democracy and the advantages of a free people not only across the North American continent, but also south into Latin America. Naturally enough, those neighbors closest to the United States—principally Mexico, Central America, and the Caribbean—bore the brunt of American expansionism.

A Latin American's View of Manifest Destiny

In 1856, the Chilean Francisco Bilbao expressed sentiments shared by many fellow Latin Americans.

". . . the United States daily extends its claws in the hunting expedition that it has begun against the South. Already we see fragments of America falling into the jaws of the Saxon boa that hypnotizes its foes as it unfolds its tortuous coils. First it was Texas, then it was Northern Mexico and the Pacific that hailed a new master.

"Today the skirmishers of the North are awakening the Isthmus with their shots and we see Panama, that future Constantinople of America, doubtfully suspended over the abyss and asking itself: Shall I belong to the South or to the North? . . .

"Is there so little self-awareness among us, so little confidence in the intelligence of the Latin American race, that we must wait for an alien will and an alien intellect to organize us and decide our fate? Are we so poorly endowed with the gifts of personality that we must surrender our own initiative and believe only in the foreign, hostile, and even overbearing initiative of individualism?"

In his essay, Bilbao then calls for Latin American unity, and he identifies and even extols the virtues of North America, challenging his fellow Hispanics to emulate the best and most noble of North American virtues, while not neglecting the growing imperial power of both the United States and Russia. In a passage remarkable for its prescience, Bilbao concluded that:

"United [writing of Latin American unity], Panama shall be the symbol of our strength, the sentinel of our future. Disunited, it will be the Gordian knot cut by the Yankee axe, and will give [it] the possession of empire, the dominion of the second focus of the ellipses described by Russia and the United States in the geography of the globe."

(Francisco Bilbao, *La América en peligro* (Santiago de Chile: Ediciones Encilla, 1941), pp. 144–154, in Benjamin Keen, editor and contributor, *Latin American Civilization: History and Society, 1492 to the Present*, 6th ed. revised and updated [Boulder, Colo.: Westview Press, 1991, 1996], passage translated by the editor)

Two factors impeded the uninterrupted flow of American power and influence into Latin America. One was the American Civil War, which temporarily turned Americans inward, consumed by the passionate necessity of determining once and for all the great questions of national power and slavery. The other factor was the strength of England in Latin America. Throughout the nineteenth century, and up to the First World War (1914–1918), England was Latin America's principal trading partner, and English diplomats consistently opposed American encroachments. The Clayton-Bulwer Treaty of 1850, for example, was the result of British efforts to keep the Americans from dominating the site of a possible transisthmian canal across Central America. If a canal were to be built, in Nicaragua or Panama, then the British wanted to guarantee that it would be a joint undertaking. In the short term, however, it was the U.S. Civil War that opened the door to European meddling in Latin American affairs in the 1860s.

While France sought to reestablish its American empire through its Mexican venture with Emperor Maximilian, Spain also was adventuring in quest of lost empires. In 1861 it reannexed the Dominican Republic, and in 1866 it seized the guano-rich Chincha Islands off the Peruvian coast, provoking a war not only with Peru, but also with Chile and Ecuador. Spain's efforts at remaking its empire proved as futile as France's.

The Spanish reoccupation of the Dominican Republic, which lasted only to 1865, was born of basically the same reasons as the French intervention in Mexico: instability in Latin America and the inability of the United States to invoke the Monroe Doctrine with force during the American Civil War. In the case of the Dominican Republic, its independence from Spain *and* Haiti (the first gained in 1821 and the second in 1844) was weakened by its inability to prevent constant foreign meddling in its affairs. Spain promised to restore security and prosperity to its former possession, its first major colony in the New World established long ago during the age of Christopher Columbus. The new relationship did not work, and the Dominicans threw out the Spanish in 1865, warmly supported by the United States.

The Spanish were no less active in the Pacific in trying to remake their lost empire. In 1864–1865 a Spanish fleet under the command of a rather hyperpatriotic admiral named José Manuel Pareja provoked both Peru and Chile into war by seizing the Peruvian Chincha Islands and bombarding the Chilean port of Valparaiso. Ecuador and Bolivia joined their neighbors in this war against their former mother country.

Spain had many pretexts for returning to the Pacific: Peru was not yet formally recognized by Spain as an independent nation; Spanish nationals employed on a Peruvian plantation had been mistreated, and Spain was forced to take action to obtain proper indemnification; the Chileans "insulted" Spanish honor and therefore had to be punished; and so forth. What Spain ultimately hoped to accomplish with this small fleet of eight warships is questionable. In the end, Spain was forced to concede that its empire could never really be remade. The United States helped mediate the peace.

By 1870 the chapter on new or restored European empires in the Americas was closed. The French failed in Mexico, and the Spanish in the Dominican Republic and the Pacific, and the United States made it clear that further European efforts to remake empires were intolerable intrusions into American affairs. The Monroe Doctrine was producing more than rhetoric, especially in the light of the massive military and naval power that the Civil War left in its wake. The threat to act against Maximillian's French troops is but one example.

From the 1880s onward, the United States moved with even greater ambition in Latin America, manifest destiny by then having been folded into a newer, more potent and nearly universal instinct: the one for empire. *Imperialism* is today a word that has a negative meaning because the domination of one nation by another undermines the right of each nation and every people to determine their own destiny. In the late nineteenth century, as we will shortly explore in more detail, Americans were swept up by the notion that they possessed a God-given right to empire. In its simplest terms, that meant both acquiring new territories and expanding American influence, whether it be commercial, political, military, or combinations of all the above.

Many expressed themselves on the need and justification for this new American empire, none perhaps so forcefully as the Reverend Josiah Strong in his 1885 book *Our Country.* An avowed social Darwinist, he felt that the Anglo-Saxon race was destined to rule the world of lesser races. His rhetoric pounds home the theme of superiority and destiny.

> This race of unequaled energy, with all the majesty of numbers and the might of wealth behind it—the representative, let us hope, of the largest liberty, the purest Christianity, the highest civilization—having developed peculiarly aggressive traits calculated to

impress its institutions upon mankind, will spread itself over the earth. *If I read not amiss, this powerful race will move down upon Mexico, down upon Central and South America*, out upon the islands of the sea, over upon Africa and beyond [italics added].[2]

Not all Americans agreed with the Reverend Strong or Secretary of State Olney. Serious reservations, to be manifested in an anti-imperialist movement at the end of the century, were held by those who felt that democracy is incompatible with empire. But they were in the minority for the time being.

Commerce and Pan-Americanism

U.S. interest in Latin America issued from many diverse motives: Political, military, religious, economic, and commercial motives all figured in the equation. Because both the United States and Latin America laid so much stress on the beneficial processes of industrialization and modernization in the latter half of the nineteenth century, their points of view often coincided. Both North Americans and Latin Americans agreed that increasing trade not only promoted economic prosperity but also increased understanding and harmony within the Western Hemisphere.

U.S. interest in Latin America was growing as early as the 1870s. In 1870, for example, the U.S. minister in Colombia signed a treaty for the construction of a canal across the isthmus of Panama (still a province of Colombia); the Dominican Republic was almost annexed to the United States; and the Ten Years' War (1868–1878) by Cuban insurgents against Spanish rule stirred nationwide sentiments to recognize the rebels as legitimate belligerents.

In this same spirit the U.S. Senate passed a resolution in July, 1870, asking the State Department for information on the state of commercial relations between the United States and Latin America. The resolution also requested recommendations on how to compete more effectively with Great Britain, which commanded the lion's share of Latin American trade. Secretary of State Hamilton Fish dispatched a circular letter to all ministers and consuls of the United States in Latin America asking them to report on trade and relations in their areas.

The replies soon began crossing the secretary's desk. In a general category, inattention or misjudgment by American manufacturers and merchants was cited as a distinct disadvantage. American prices tended to be higher at the point of shipping than those of their English counterparts. Insurance and commissions were apt to be higher as well; for example, they could be as high as 2.5 percent in New York versus 0.5 percent in European ports. Heavy American textiles lost out to English ones, because most Latin American nations charged tariffs computed by weight. Europeans granted Latin American merchants longer credit terms than did Americans. English interest rates were frequently half of what Americans charged. Other suggestions by American consuls and ministers on how to best, or at least match, the English, included: learning the language and customs of their customers better, subsidizing

---

[2]Quoting from Josiah Strong's *Our Country* in ibid., pp. 244–245.

American steamship companies, sponsoring an interoceanic canal, and encouraging reciprocity treaties to lower tariff barriers.

The firm of W. R. Grace & Co. was representative of U. S. commercial interests in Latin America. As early as 1870, the company was trading over much of South America out of its headquarters in New York, a city evolving rapidly into the premier center of commerce and trade along the Atlantic coast of the United States.

The Grace brothers and their partners were good merchants, attuned to the different worlds of the United States and Latin America. They learned to speak Spanish well. They eventually established the first U.S. steamship service to the west coast of South America (1894), sponsored an interoceanic canal (through Nicaragua) at the end of the century, and actively sought in the 1880s and 1890s to improve hemispheric relations both politically and economically.

W. R. Grace & Co. developed rapidly in the last three decades of the nineteenth century, becoming the first American multinational company operating in Latin America. Founded in Peru in 1854 by an enterprising Irish immigrant, William Russell Grace, it grew rapidly as a commercial enterprise based primarily on trade, yet willing to expand in any direction that business took it. By the 1870s the company was not only operating ships between the Americas, but also was selling everything from locomotives to threading needles in South America. It imported new machinery for those interested in modernizing industries, acted as a banker by floating mortgages to local entrepreneurs, and constantly sought new opportunities. The company became actively involved in railroad building from Peru to Costa Rica, and in the 1880s expanded into the growing rubber industry in Brazil and promoted the first telegraph cable networks between the United States and Latin America. The Grace company moved swiftly at the front of the tide of industrialization and modernization that swept both Latin Americans and North Americans along the road to progress.

The Grace enterprises grew at a time when the United States actively promoted greater involvement in Latin American commercial affairs. President Chester A. Arthur declared in 1884:

> The countries of the American continent and the adjacent islands are for the United States the natural marts of supply and demand. It is from them that we should obtain what we do not produce or do not produce in sufficiency, and it is to them that the surplus productions of our fields, our mills, and our workshops should flow, under conditions that will equalize or favor them in comparison with foreign competition.[3]

The facts that the British still dominated trade and commerce with Latin America and that in the mid-1880s the United States possessed less than 20 percent of total Latin American trade spurred Americans even more in their determination to expand vigorously U.S. enterprises. American diplomats were especially aware of the relationship between close commercial ties and political and diplomatic

---

[3] James D. Richardson, editor, *A Compilation of the Messages and Papers of the Presidents, 1890–1897*, 10 vols. (Washington, D.C.: Government Printing Office, 1896–1899), 9:251, cited in Jospeh Smith, *Illusions of Conflict: Anglo-American Diplomacy toward Latin America, 1865–1896* (Pittsburgh: University of Pittsburgh Press, 1979), p. 120.

*From the 1860s on, rubber tappers like these extracted
millions of tons of latex for use by the industrial countries of
Europe and by the United States.*

influence. Secretary of State Frederick Frelinghuysen promoted this point of view
before the Senate in 1884.

> I am thoroughly convinced of the advisability of knitting closely our relations with the
> states of this continent, and no effort on my part shall be wanting to accomplish a result
> so consonant with the constant policy of this country, and in the spirit of the Monroe
> Doctrine, which, in excluding foreign political interference, recognizes the common in-
> terest of the states of North and South America. It is the history of all diplomacy that
> close political relations and friendships spring from unity of commercial interests. The
> merchant or trader is the forerunner and aid to diplomatic intimacy and international
> harmony.[4]

Throughout Latin America in the 1880s and 1890s, American entrepreneurs
spread their influence not only through trade but also through direct investments,
through the railroads and mines of Mexico and Central America, and through the
sugar industry of Cuba, for example. The banana industry that grew to huge pro-

---

[4]Frelinghuysen to John F. Miller, March 26, 1884, cited in West to Granville, no. 116, April 16, 1884, in Public Records
Office, *The Records of the Foreign Office, 1782–1939* (London: Her Majesty's Stationary Office, 1969), 5/1869, cited in
Smith, *Illusions of Conflict*, p. 121.

portions in the twentieth century was established precisely in this period by ambitious American entrepreneurs.

While Minor Keith was building the railroads in Costa Rica in the 1870s and 1880s to connect the rich coffee-growing regions of the highlands with the Atlantic terminus of Puerto Limón, he found himself constantly facing financial crises. To create some momentum and to generate cash, Keith initiated a variety of businesses, such as exporting precious tropical woods. He also brought in a few banana plants from Panama and planted them along parts of the railroad that were already completed near the warm and wet Atlantic coast of Costa Rica. He began shipping bananas to the Boston market, which had developed a taste for the nutritious and delicious fruit a few years earlier when an enterprising Boston merchant imported a few from Jamaica. The market expanded rapidly, and by the late 1890s, Keith had plenty of competition as bananas were moving with speed and profit from the newly cleared jungles of Costa Rica, Honduras, and Guatemala through the ports of Boston and New Orleans into the homes of North Americans. In 1899 Keith and his competitors came together and formed the United Fruit Company, which came to dominate the industry for the next half century.

The story of penetrating and creative American enterprise was replicated throughout Latin America at the end of the century. The Guggenheim family developed one of the most prosperous mining empires in Mexico. American syndicates channeled large amounts of capital and technical expertise into the silver mines of Peru, the tin mines of Bolivia, the copper mines of Chile, and into hundreds of other enterprises, from brewing beer in Peru to building canals in Nicaragua.

While the American penetration, development, and exploitation of resources and opportunities in Latin America were largely the result of private enterprise, the governments of the North and South American states recognized the need to reach some sort of general accord in the promotion and encouragement of trade, industry, and diplomacy across the hemisphere. In 1889 an historic meeting convened in Washington to discuss hemispheric problems and opportunities.

The meeting, called the First International American Congress, was largely the inspiration of Secretary of State James G. Blaine, a long-time promoter of the pan-American movement. The goal of the Congress, popularly called the Washington Conference, was to promote trade between the Americas and to provide mechanisms for solving inter-American disputes such as the War of the Pacific. Delegates from all of the Latin American nations convened in Washington in October, 1889.[5] The delegates were promptly sent on a six-week train tour of the United States to impress them with the vastness and magnificence of the country. Instead, it left most of them exhausted and irritable with this flexing of muscle and pride by the Americans.

The conference met through the spring of 1890; however, in the end nothing of substance was accomplished. No reciprocal trade treaties were approved; no tariff or customs barriers were lowered; no agreement was reached on a mechanism for compulsory arbitration of international disputes. Many Latin Americans, especially

---

[5]The Dominican Republic was the only exception, claiming that it already had a reciprocal treaty of trade and commerce with the United States and that attendance at the conference was thus redundant.

the Argentinians and Uruguayans, were too committed to British and European interests to consider seriously altering significantly those relationships in favor of the United States. Bickering political factions within the United States itself prevented a unified American position.

When the conference adjourned, it left only one sure accomplishment: the establishment of a commercial information bureau in Washington. But that bureau was the seed of the Pan American Union, which in turn was the seed of the Organization of American States founded in 1948. Pan-Americanism embodied the concept that the nations of the Western Hemisphere have a great deal in common. Disciples of pan-Americanism stressed shared political ideals, a geographic unity, and membership within the mainstream of western civilization. The ideal was as old as the expressions of it made by such great thinkers as Thomas Jefferson and Simón Bolívar. The ideal took more definite form in the twentieth century, although it was most certainly born and nurtured in the nineteenth.

Cuba, Voluptuous Cuba

No other Latin American regions were subject to such intense American interest as were the Caribbean and Central America in the last half of the nineteenth century. It was natural for American imperialists to look southward to the Caribbean basin, and, as we have seen, the acquisition of huge portions of Mexico's territory after the Mexican-American War of 1848 certainly signaled a willingness to make manifest destiny a reality. The lure of building a canal through Nicaragua or Panama also focused American interests on those lands washed by the Caribbean Sea.

Within this region, however, Cuba dominated the American interest and imagination. Not only was it the closest Latin American land, apart from Mexico, but also as Cuba moved haltingly towards independence from Spain, Americans were drawn into the Cuban struggle for freedom. Cuba's various wars for independence lasted thirty years (1868–1898) and became bloodier and more tormented after 1896 when the Spanish poured in armies to try to suppress the rebels.

H. Wayne Morgan captured the essence of what fired the American imagination during this period. The following passage tends to ignore the commercial and strategic values of Cuba to the United States, and overplays the emotional and altruistic sentiments of Americans. But many genuinely felt this way at the time.

Cuba's agony inevitably and understandably aroused humanitarian sympathy in the United States. This American is generously and honestly endowed with the desire to relieve suffering and to extend to others what he considers the blessings of his way of life. Believing that his country is history's chosen child, he deems it not merely a right but a duty to give the best part of his heritage to the less fortunate. Some men fight for their country's boundaries or to add a province to their nation's domains. The American is more easily moved to liberate the provinces of the heart and mind. He is seldom repaid in gratitude, rarest of all human currencies. And such actions are often erroneous, rash, or averse to his own country's immediate interests. But these feelings, so deeply and honestly a part of the nation's history and thought, have been the greatest single force in American foreign policy. Cuba in 1898 was a classic example of their operation.[6]

What brought Cuba to this juncture in 1898? Basically, Cuba's desire for independence was twofold: political and economic. Politically, Cubans desired an end to what they considered to be a despotic and inconsistent Spanish rule. Their liberties were suppressed, their leaders, such as Martí, jailed or exiled. Cuban sentiments of nationality and independence were crushed. Economically, Cuban sugar planters, increasingly prosperous and growing more powerful within the island, desired to overturn—by radical reform or revolution if necessary—the protectionist, monopolistic tendencies of the Spanish. Cubans, in effect, felt increasingly suffocated by a mother country that did not understand their needs, persecuted them, and denied them their destiny. The Ten Years' War (1868–1878) was but one manifestation of their determination to chart their own destiny.

Although a peace pact ended the war in 1878, Cuban sentiments and passions for independence did not subside. Spanish promises of reform and/or more autonomy for the island were not kept, and by 1895 the embers of revolution once more flared up into war. When the Spanish, especially under a particularly harsh general named Valeriano Weyler, in 1896 initiated a policy of concentrating the population in defensible towns and cities, the suffering of the general population increased, and so did the outcries of Americans watching the war.

The intensity of the war effort between 1896 and 1898 produced dislocation and suffering in Cuba. Not only did the economy go into a tailspin, exports of sugar falling almost 75 percent between 1893 and 1898, but also the concentration camps created by Weyler compounded the misery of living in a war zone by adding the specters of hunger and disease. American reporters, especially from the competing newspaper empires of William Randolph Hearst and Joseph Pulitzer, combed through Cuba looking for good stories to help sell the popular tabloids of their bosses. Americans in the streets of New York, St. Louis, and San Francisco eagerly soaked up the news of Cuba, depicted as being in near extremis because of the actions of cruel Spanish soldiers. The United States was, in fact, primed to intervene in Cuban affairs.

The U.S. Press and the Spanish-American War

The intense rivalry between two North American press moguls—William Randolph Hearst and Joseph Pulitzer—in the 1890s for circulation prompted them to focus intensely on Cuba and the alleged atrocities committed by Spanish authorities on the Cuban population. It made great copy and sold newspapers, but much of the reporting was gross exaggeration and patently false. Some excerpts, read with fascination by the U.S. public, follow:

[Spanish General] Weyler was a "fiendish despot . . . a brute, the devastator of haciendas . . . pitiless, cold, an exterminator of men . . . there is nothing to prevent

---

[6]H. Wayne Morgan, *America's Road to Empire: The War with Spain and Overseas Expansion* (New York: Alfred A. Knopf, 1965), pp. 8, 9.

his carnal, animal brain from running riot with itself in inventing tortures and infamies of bloody debauchery," opined the February 23, 1896, issue of the *New York Journal*.

(Hugh Thomas, *Cuba: The Pursuit of Freedom* (New York: Harper & Row, 1971), p. 331)

On May 17, 1896, a *New York World* correspondent in Havana wrote: "Blood on the roadsides, blood in the fields, blood on the doorsteps, blood, blood, blood. The old, the young, the weak, the crippled, all are butchered without mercy."

(Thomas, *Cuba*, p. 336)

Perhaps the most famous of all the acts perpetrated by the inventors of "yellow press," as Hearst and Pulitzer's tactics were labeled because of their flamboyant, colorful headlines, occurred in early 1897. One of Hearst's premier cartoonists, Frederick Remington, was holed up in the Hotel Inglaterra in Havana, barred from accompanying Spanish troops in the field. Remington cabled his boss, "Everything is quiet. . . . There will be no war. I wish to return." Hearst fired back: "Please remain. You furnish the pictures and I'll furnish the war."

Thomas, *Cuba*, p. 340; James Creelman, *On the Great Highway: The Wanderings and Adventures of a Special Correspondent* (Boston: Lothrop, 1901)

U.S. investors in Cuba, in fact, did not want an invasion. But their reservations were drowned out by the sentiments sweeping across the United States. The Cuban patriots seeking independence were portrayed in much the same light as the American Founding Fathers over a hundred years earlier. The attempts of the Spanish government to compromise, to provide Cuba with autonomy, and to end the war honorably were drowned out in the impassioned mood gripping the American public.

When the U.S. battleship *Maine* blew up in the harbor of Havana in February, 1898, Americans clamored for war. The *Maine* was visiting Havana to represent American interests and to "show the flag." An explosion on the evening of February 15 tore through its underwater hull. Most of its crew were killed. Who set off the explosion? Was it internal (the result of a boiler accident?) or external, set by the Spaniards? The truth didn't make any difference because nine out of ten Americans believed that the explosion was caused by the cowardly Spaniards. The cry of "Remember the *Maine*" became wildly popular among those jingoes (the popular name for boastful patriots with an aggressive foreign policy agenda) and war hawks determined to fight the Spanish. Fresh reports in Pulitzer's and Hearst's yellow press came from the concentration camps, describing emaciated and dying children, and quickened the adrenaline in a Congress pushing a reluctant President William McKinley to take action.

On April 11, 1898, the United States declared war on Spain. The war lasted a little more than four months and resulted in total victory for the United States and ignoble defeat for Spain. Spain lost Cuba, Puerto Rico, Guam, and the Philippines, all of which the United States acquired except for Cuba, which became semi-independent.

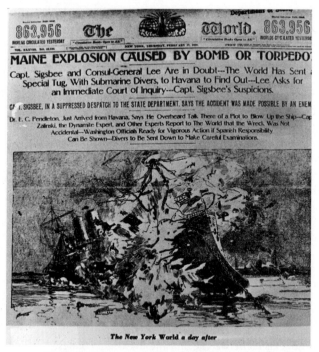

Headlines from the New York newspaper The World *recounted the explosion and sinking of the U.S. battleship* Maine *in Havana Harbor, Cuba. "Remember the* Maine*" became a battle cry of Americans determined to punish Spain and free Cuba.*

"Cuba, voluptuous Cuba"—so described by a Kentuckian writing to President Ulysses S. Grant in 1872—did not fall ripely into the new American empire largely due to the determination of the United States to honor its commitment to Cuban independence. But Puerto Rico, Guam, and the Philippines did become colonies of the United States, which strode into the twentieth century standing tall, a triumphant new power, complete with empire and festooned with the banners of victorious battles.

Conclusions and Issues

U.S. interests in Latin America were composed of many different elements. They included an altruistic or noble sentiment, a baser desire to spread U.S. political and strategic influence over Latin America, and a commercial motive that viewed Latin America as a great marketplace where U.S. economic power should eventually prevail over European competitors such as the English. The experience of the Grace brothers as extraordinarily active and successful merchants and businessmen in Latin America is an example of the latter.

From the Latin American perspective, the United States was courted as a political friend, trading partner, and important agent for modernizing and developing Latin America. But the United States was also eyed with suspicion as a dominating and imperious neighbor whose might could easily turn friend into foe. The trajectory of Mexico's history with the United States in the nineteenth century certainly was one example of this ambivalent relationship. So was the experience of Cuba.

As the twentieth century approached, new events, such as building a transisthmian canal and waging the Spanish-American War of 1898, drew the United States and Latin America even closer together. The commercial relationship also deepened, U.S. entrepreneurs drawn to Latin America to develop a host of industries and activities, from building railroads to exporting bananas. The Washington Conference of 1889 was the first major inter-American conference, and it gave official expression to the rapid development of relations between the American nations at the end of the nineteenth century.

Discussion Questions

1. Identify and analyze some of the salient features of "manifest destiny" and "imperialism" as expressions of the U.S. interest in Latin America.

2. What special relationship existed between Cuba and the United States?

3. How did W. R. Grace & Co. represent U.S. commercial and economic interests in Latin America in the second half of the nineteenth century?

Bibliography for Part Two

Andrews, George Reid, *The Afro-Argentines of Buenos Aires, 1800–1900* (Madison: University of Wisconsin Press, 1980).

Bauer, K. Jack, *The Mexican War, 1846–1848* (Lincoln: University of Nebraska Press, 1992).

Blakemore, Harold, *British Nitrates and Chilean Politics, 1886–1896* (London: University of London, 1974).

Blanchard, Peter, *The Origins of the Peruvian Labor Movement, 1883–1919* (Pittsburgh: University of Pittsburgh Press, 1982).

Blanchard, Peter, *Slavery and Abolition in Early Republican Peru* (Wilmington: SR Books, 1992).

Calderón de la Barca, Frances, *Life in Mexico*, reprint ed. (Berkeley and Los Angeles: University of California Press, 1982).

Clayton, Lawrence A., *Grace, W.R. Grace & Co., the Formative Years, 1850-1930* (Ottawa, Illinois: Jameson Books, 1985).

Clegern, Wayne M., *Origins of Liberal Dictatorship in Central America* (Niwot: University Press of Colorado, 1994).

Conrad, Robert E., *The Destruction of Brazilian Slavery 1850–1888*, 2nd ed. (Melbourne: Krieger, 1993).

Dean, Warren, *Rio Claro: A Brazilian Plantation System, 1820–1920* (Stanford: Stanford University Press, 1978).

Dias, Maria Odila Silva, *Power and Everyday Life: The Lives of Working Women in Nineteenth Century Brazil* (New Brunswick: Rutgers University Press, 1995).

Dias, Maria Odila Silva, *Power and Everyday Life: The Lives of Working Women in Nineteenth-Century Brazil,* trans. by Ann Frost (New Brunswick: Rutgers University Press, 1995).

Dumond, Don E., *The Machete and the Cross: Campesino Rebellion in Yucatan* (Lincoln: University of Nebraska Press, 1997).

Ewell, Judith and William H. Beezley, *The Human Tradition in Latin America: The Nineteenth Century* (Wilmington, Del.: SR Books, 1989).

Gilmore, Robert L., *Caudillism and Militarism in Venezuela, 1810–1910* (Athens, Ohio University Press, 1964).

Graham, Richard, *Britain and the Onset of Modernization in Brazil, 1850–1914* (Cambridge: Cambridge University Press, 1968).

Graham, Richard, *Patronage and Politics in Nineteenth-Century Brazil* (Stanford: Stanford University Press, 1989).

Graham, Sandra Lauderdale, *House and Street: The Domestic World of Servants and Masters in Nineteenth Century Rio de Janeiro* (Austin: University of Texas Press, 1992).

Gudmundson, Lowell, and Hector Lindo-Fuentes, *Central America, 1821–1871* (Tuscaloosa: University of Alabama Press, 1995).

Hale, Charles A., *The Transformation of Liberalism in Late Nineteenth Century Mexico* (Princeton: Princeton University Press, 1991).

Holloway, Thomas, *Immigrants on the Land: Coffee and Society in São Paulo, 1886–1934* (Chapel Hill: University of North Carolina Press, 1980).

Holt, Thomas C., *The Problem of Freedom: Race, Labor, and Politics in Jamaica and Britain, 1832–1938* (Baltimore: Johns Hopkins University Press, 1991).

James, Marquis, with an introduction by Lawrence A. Clayton, *Merchant Adventurer: The Story of W.R. Grace* (Wilmington, Delaware: SR Books, 1993). P2

Olga Jiménez de Wagenheim, *Puerto Rico: An Interpretive History from Pre-Columbian Times to 1900* (Princeton, NJ: Markus Wiener Publishers, 1997).

Orlove, Benjamin, ed., *The Allure of the Foreign: Imported Goods in Postcolonial Latin America* (Ann Arbor: University of Michigan Press, 1997).

Levi, Darrell, *The Prados of São Paulo, Brazil* (Tuscaloosa: University of Alabama Press, 1987).

Levine, Robert M., *Vale of Tears: Revisiting the Canudos Massacre in Northeastern Brazil* (Berkeley and Los Angeles: University of California Press, 1992).

Levy, Claude, *Emancipation, Sugar, and Federalism: Barbados and the West Indies, 1833–1876* (Gainesville: University Press of Florida, 1980).

Lewis, Paul H., *Political Parties and Generations in Paraguay's Liberal Era, 1869–1940* (Chapel Hill: University of North Carolina Press, 1993).

Martinez-Alier, Verena, *Marriage, Class and Colour in Nineteenth-Century Cuba* (Ann Arbor: University of Michigan Press, 1989).

Offner, John L., *An Unwanted War: The Diplomacy of the United States and Spain over Cuba, 1895–1898* (Chapel Hill: University of North Carolina Press, 1992).

Pang, Eul-Soo, *In Pursuit of Honor and Power: Noblemen of the Southern Cross in Nineteenth-Century Brazil* (Tuscaloosa: University of Alabama Press, 1988).

Sater, William F., *Chile and the War of the Pacific* (Lincoln: University of Nebraska Press, 1986).

Schoonover, Thomas D., *The United States in Central America, 1860–1911* (Durham: Duke University Press, 1991).

Scobie, James R., *Revolution on the Pampas: A Social History of Argentine Wheat, 1860–1910* (Austin: University of Texas Press, 1964).

Scott, Rebecca J., *Slave Emancipation in Cuba* (Princeton: Princeton University Press, 1986).

Slatta, Richard W., *Gauchos and the Vanishing Frontier* (Lincoln: University of Nebraska Press, 1983).

Slatta, Richard W., *Cowboys of the Americas* (New Haven: Yale University Press, 1990).

Szuchman, Mark D., *Order, Family and Community in Buenos Aires, 1810–1860* (Stanford: Stanford University Press, 1988).

Tenenbaum, Barbara, *The Politics of Penury: Debts and Taxes in Mexico, 1821–1856* (Albuquerque: University of New Mexico Press, 1986).

Vallens, Vivian J., *Working Women in Mexico during the Porfiriato, 1880–1910* (Palo Alto: R & E Research, 1978).

Vanderwood, Paul J., *Disorder and Progress: Bandits, Police, and Mexican Development* (Wilmington: SR Books, 1992).

Voss, Stuart F., *On the Periphery of Nineteenth-Century Mexico: Sonora and Sinaloa, 1810–1877* (Tucson: University of Arizona Press, 1982).

Weinstein, Barbara, *The Amazon Rubber Boom, 1850–1920* (Stanford: Stanford University Press, 1983).

Whigham, Thomas, *The Politics of River Trade: Tradition and Development in the Upper Plata, 1780–1870* (Albuquerque: University of New Mexico Press, 1994).

Woodward, Ralph Lee, ed., *Positivism in Latin America, 1850-1900: Are Order and Progress Reconcilable?* (Lexington, Mass., Heath, 1971).

Part 3

The Early Twentieth Century

Latin America in Global Perspective

During the first three decades of the twentieth century, Latin America became more and more engaged in world affairs. Europeans, caught up in fren-
zied imperial expansion, swept into Asia, Polynesia, and Africa. The United
States avoided full-scale imperialist ventures but did extend its investments
and control over the Caribbean basin and build an inter-oceanic canal in
Panama. No place in the world remained entirely isolated, and Latin Americans often engaged in developments that had global implications. The hemisphere became more tightly knitted into the fabric of world affairs.

Compared with the subjugation of Asia and Africa under European imperialism, Latin America enjoyed considerable freedom of action. Except for the
Caribbean colonies, most of its peoples were politically sovereign and reasonably independent in world affairs. Economically, too, Latin Americans enjoyed
better standards of living and greater self-determination than did Asians and
Africans. Their cultures drew on European, Amerindian, and African sources,
and their arts enjoyed some recognition abroad. By most measures, Latin
America occupied an intermediate status between the imperial powers and
their colonies.

Nevertheless, most Caribbean islands still belonged to one or another
European nation or, in the case of Puerto Rico and Cuba, lived under U.S.
control. U.S. influence would grow during the First World War (1914–1918),
as a function of U.S. security interests. Even fairly mature countries like Mexico, Argentina, Brazil, and Chile sometimes found themselves fending off foreign pressures and even military incursions. Their leaders recognized that nation-building did not happen all at once—it was an ongoing, difficult struggle.
Hence, many began to advocate the kind of nationalism that had galvanized
Europeans during the preceding century.

In general, the larger nations of Latin America charted their own destinies. In most, these destinies included continued expansion of exports of
minerals and agricultural goods. Prices mostly rose, so investors and workers
kept on producing. Factories sprang up on the outskirts of major cities. New
ports and rail lines stitched cities to far-off regions and foreign markets.
Slowly but surely, political systems opened up to accommodate more voters
and special interests, even those previously disenfranchised. Latin America's
first populist movements, described in Chapter Twelve, arose out of this
growing participation.

The first decade of the new century, 1900–1910, saw generalized peace
in Latin America. Dictators promoted exports and industrial growth and dis-
couraged labor action. Foreigners poured money into new plants and

The Countries
of Modern Latin America

⊙ Capitals

infrastructure. The expanding economies achieved promising levels of profits and employment, although not everyone benefited equally. Few political upheavals shook the region, especially after the 1902 treaty that ended the Thousand Days' War in Colombia.

The second decade, the 1910s, witnessed major disruptions and violence in the region. Foremost was the Mexican Revolution, which occupied the entire period. The First World War also brought submarine conflict, U.S. protective occupations, and substantial labor strikes. Many South American countries, cut off from imports, began to industrialize during this era. The success of guerrilla actions in Mexico encouraged others to take up these new military tactics. And anarchist labor movements reached their peak in 1917–1919, producing a wave of general strikes and labor violence that would linger in people's memories for years to come.

The 1920s saw the return of peace and business as usual to most of Latin America. In some countries, populists or revolutionaries managed to introduce more democratic procedures. In others, autocratic regimes went through the motions of governing by constitutional law. U.S. bankers and businessmen, meanwhile, elbowed out most German, French, Belgian, and even British investors, taking leading roles in the capital markets. A number of countries joined the League of Nations, in hope of furthering international norms and conduct. The U.S. Senate's refusal to join the League, however, meant that most substantial inter-American problems had to be addressed bilaterally or in the framework of the Pan American Union (see Chapter Eleven).

The hopeful mood of peace and growing economies was shattered in late 1929, when the New York stock market collapsed and ushered in the Great Depression.

Hemispheric Visions in 1900

When the year 1900 dawned in Latin America, observers found much to be optimistic about. Pundits foresaw that during the next century the hemisphere would achieve the highest levels of prosperity and happiness of the entire second millennium A.D. Most commentators were certain that the Latin nations, fast becoming modern and attractive, were catching up with Europe and the United States. Celebrations marking the arrival of the new century emphasized material progress, economic expansion, urban growth, and public order.

Mexico topped the list of modernizing countries, followed by Argentina, Brazil, and Chile. Europeans would soon call these the ABC Countries, a shorthand way of saying "the more advanced nations" of the region. Underlying that judgment were the Euro-centric perceptions that Latin America was becoming racially whiter and more civilized. Neither assumption was entirely true nor even welcome to all the people of the region.

Urban development provided a visual index of the so-called progress—virtually all the major cities had grown and been redesigned according to European models. Buenos Aires, whose facelift in the 1890s led it to be nicknamed "the Paris of South America," boasted nearly a million people by the turn of the century. Rio de Janeiro, soon to be extensively remodeled as well, had about two-thirds of a million people in 1900. Mexico City was somewhat smaller, at 344,000, in part because the nearby cities of Guadalajara, Puebla, and Monterrey captured urban-bound migrants. Santiago, Chile, had about 300,000 inhabitants by 1900, some of whom lived respectably in Parisian-style apartments and flats. Well-to-do residents in these and most other capitals enjoyed such amenities as running water, sewage systems, electricity, telephone, and gas. Moreover, they had railroads, streetcar systems, street lighting, telegraphy, and international cable connections. In fact, automobiles made their Latin American debut almost immediately after their invention. So at least the wealthy few in the region lived as well as the middle classes of Europe and the United States.

The elites of these countries, and people below them on the social ladder as well, had mixed feelings about Europeanizing. Their education had evoked admiration and emulation of the Old World, yet their location in the New World suggested that they should be different. But how? Some argued that the Americas had a common heritage distinctive from other world regions. This argument stressed newness (only four hundred years since Columbus), openness to outsiders (they were nations of immigrants), aversion to imperialism and its wars, and an affinity for democracy. This view, which undergirded the pan-American system discussed earlier, lumped together Latin America and the United States as the American republics or the Western Hemisphere nations.

Another line of elite thinking, however, distinguished between U.S. and Latin American realities. Anyone traveling to the United States (and many well-off Latins did) clearly saw a nation devoted to achieving industrial wealth and military power far beyond the reach of its Latin neighbors. Indeed, the U.S. seizure of Cuba and Puerto Rico during the Spanish-American War suggested that the United States was an imperial power in the making. Latins also saw in the United States widespread poverty, racism, class antagonism, monopoly capitalism, and urban disorder worse than anything they had encountered in Europe. Rather than emphasize similarities north and south of the border, some intellectuals highlighted the contrasts. Out of this analysis arose a distinctively Latin American self-conception or ideal.

Latin Americans' new philosophy in the early years of this century drew on diverse sources. One was nineteenth-century liberalism and positivism. These views suggested that humankind is perfectible, that evolution depends upon individual initiative by persons endowed with superior intelligence, and that scientific progress will eventually satisfy material needs and banish suffering. This view of the world often contained a social Darwinist component that recommended doing nothing for the poor and disadvantaged, in the spirit of survival of the fittest. These ideas convinced leaders in government and business that they were destined to rule over the hapless masses. They also believed that foreign investment would spur progress. Finally, they doubted that anything that they could do would really help the masses. Only continued immigration of Europeans, with the prospect of "whitening" their populations, would improve their genetic stock.

A second source of Latin American thinking in these years was Spanish liberalism, sometimes called Hispanismo. This in turn drew heavily on the writings of the German philosopher Karl Christian Freidrich Krause (1781–1832). Krausismo, as reinterpreted by Ibero-Americans, offered an antidote to positivism, arguing in favor of social unity and solidarity. It embraced Judeo-Christian values, including the need for uplifting the less fortunate. It also stressed education at all levels, women's rights, labor unions, international law as the basis for peace, and correct living and personal virtues. According to Krausismo, social hierarchy was natural and necessary, sorting people into strata according to their abilities and intelligence. But everyone was part of the same whole, a concept called "social organicism." Finally, *Krausismo* valued ethical behavior and appreciation of culture over material success—the ideal was to live by moral and spiritual values, not merely ostentation and wealth.

Just as European liberalism prevailed among persons in the business and financial worlds, Krausismo took root among teachers, intellectuals, and artists. Liberals approved of importing the latest technology and fashions from Europe, bringing progress at any cost. Krausists feared that foreign influences would erode the positive qualities that they wished to promote. They denounced the materialism and vulgarity of foreigners, especially Americans. Rodó's 1900 essay, *Ariel,* introduced in Chapter Ten, gave literary expression to these sentiments.

A new Latin American nationalism emerged by the time of World War I, drawing on the second line of elite thinking in the region. This nationalism mixed progressive ideas like universal education, women's rights, labor unionism, democracy, and social welfare, with traditional moral values. This nationalism favored solidarity, care for the downtrodden, and obligations to society. It evoked a spirit of harmony among citizens in the pursuit of good government and social justice.

Those people promoting the nationalist program of the early 1900s had their work cut out for them. Nowhere had education achieved any degree of quality or extension—few countries could boast even a 10 percent literacy rate. Universities, often run by religious orders, followed medieval curricula and avoided contact with the contemporary world. Women lived in the shadows of their menfolk with few legal rights and scant access to education. Labor relations were desultory at best, punctuated by periodic uprisings of oppressed men and women against their employers, who called on police or army contingents to quell them with force.

No Latin American country conducted fair elections, even by the minuscule proportion of citizens qualified to vote. Instead, autocratic or dictatorial regimes ruled on behalf of monied interests, old families, the Church, and foreign investors. So, from a sociopolitical standpoint, the progressiveness of Latin America, even in the advanced ABC countries and Mexico, was a sham. Much needed to be done, yet the elites had no intention of carrying out reforms that would reduce their own wealth and power.

Out of this tension between appearance and reality, the ideal and the practical, arose different movements and kinds of leaders in the Latin American countries. In some, modernizing autocrats like those of the nineteenth century continued to treat the masses as cattle needing to be herded. In others, revolutionary currents erupted and challenged entire systems of government and society. In some cases, leadership reverted to dictators in the mold of nineteenth-century caudillos. One of the most remarkable developments in the region, however, was the rise of the populists, in many ways unique to Latin America.

Early Populism in South America

Yrigoyen Selected as President by Argentine Congress, 1916

Tens of thousands of delirious supporters jammed the plaza in front of the Argentine Congress. It was a warm spring day in October 1916. The electoral college had ratified the recent elections, and the new president, Hipólito Yrigoyen, had just been sworn into office. For years—decades, in fact—Yrigoyen had led a quiet but extremely effective campaign to discredit the established government and take over power. Now he had succeeded, to the overwhelming delight of his followers. When he emerged onto the marble steps in front of Congress, a tidal wave of cheers rose from the crowd. He was its hero, its savior, its god.

Yrigoyen raised his hand in salute and then walked slowly down the steps toward the presidential touring car. His appearance was regal—he strode slowly, rigidly upright, wearing a black tuxedo and a shiny black top hat. He seemed oblivious to the clamor and adulation that washed around him. When he arrived at his car, onlookers opened the doors and ushered him in. Then soldiers in his escort began pushing it down the street toward the Casa Rosada, Argentina's presidential palace. His driver didn't even start the engine.

When his enormous entourage reached the Casa Rosada, Yrigoyen stepped from the car, waved again, and disappeared through the doors. His worshipping throngs waited hour after hour for Yrigoyen to emerge onto the balcony to give an impromptu acceptance speech. But he never appeared, and by sundown most of the crowd had drifted away.

A few stalwarts stood together in a corner of the plaza, looking disappointedly at the palace.

"He must not be well," said one person. "All that fighting in Congress to get confirmed must have sickened him—he is such a good man. Otherwise he would have come out to speak to his people."

"I don't know," said another. "Perhaps the God-damned ranchers and gringo businessmen grabbed him and bought him off! That's what they always do. Who could refuse millions of pesos in bribes? He's only human."

The first person responded, "No, you are wrong! Dr. Hipólito would never do that! He is as honest as the day is long, even more honest. How many years did he refuse any government job or privilege, even when his friend the president offered it to him personally? No, he would never accept a bribe, never!"

Another said, "He's probably preparing a list of people from the last administration to fire. You know, those thieves and ass-kissing bastards who acted like they owned the government. We called it 'El Régimen,' it was so bad. You had to be totally dishonest just to get a job. Good riddance to all of them! I hope they end up in jail!"

A woman standing with the others said, "You know, I think he is going to clean up the factories and make the supervisors respect us workers. Every day in the mills we get pinched and fondled by those sons-of-bitches. And for what pay? We get half of what the men get on the looms. We got a group of women who are going to talk to Dr. Hipólito as soon as we can, so that we get some respect. The men in the union say he's on our side."

"Don't hold your breath, sister," said a colleague. "The Socialists think he's bad as the rest, that he doesn't know Lenin from Bakunin when it comes to labor. Still, I voted for him just to see if he can make a change. The Socialists haven't done anything for us so far, even if they know all that stuff about classes and the workers' struggle. And they've had a majority in the city council for years!"

The first person spoke again: "I don't know—life's hard, and we never get any hope, except with Dr. Hipólito. He's clever and wise, and he seems to know exactly what Argentina needs. I'm glad he'll get a chance to clean up this country."

The woman spoke again, "Let's go and celebrate with some wine."

The others agreed and left.

Yrigoyen the enigmatic, mysterious, careful conspirator. Now sixty-four years of age, he had spent virtually his whole life in politics, but almost none of it in public office. He dominated Argentine politics for the next fourteen years, displaying the same bizarre and secretive behavior he had in the past. He had mobilized the masses for the elections, and now that he was in power he did not know how to act.

Despite his erratic behavior and failed programs, Yrigoyen retained his mass popularity until the end. A political innovator, he had unwittingly created a style of leadership that observers later termed "populism."

In addition to his style, Yrigoyen had the stamina and courage to stay in politics for the long haul. Analysts regard him as one of the country's great leaders. He joined a small group who actually changed the course of national history. Only Rosas in the 1830s and 1840s, and Juan Perón in the 1940s and 1950s, wielded similar influence.

The Populists

Beginning in the early twentieth century, principally in the Southern Cone, a new form of leadership appeared that was later dubbed "populism." Gradually it spread to other large and small countries. After World War II, populism seemed to be the predominant form of politics in South America. By the 1960s, however, it had run its course, and a series of military coups brought an end to the populist era.

We can distinguish two phases of populism: one that prevailed before the Great Depression of the 1930s and another that appeared afterward. The first has been called the "reformist phase" of populism. Leaders generally addressed such issues as voter rights and elections, nationalism, and labor relations. They found broad agreement on these issues and built their movements around them. Members of most social classes voted for the populists, whose strategy was to reform society in order to protect it from the onslaughts of radicals.

The second phase of populism began in the late 1930s, when issues of political economy dominated the agenda. Urbanization and industrialization swelled the cities, creating a need for more planning. Working-class voters, who now outnumbered rural voters, were approachable through their unions, retirement institutes, and associations. Populist leaders appealed to these new voters by offering larger shares of the national income and more factory jobs. Their programs were nationalistic as well, pledging to end the economic dependency that had prevailed since the last century. This type of leadership can be called "national developmentalist."

All of the populists shared certain characteristics. First, they used election campaigns to get into office, worked to improve voting systems, and expanded suffrage and participation. They were driven by both altruistic and opportunistic motives. They decried the oligarchical regimes inherited from the nineteenth century. Constitutions provided for democratic procedures, but citizens had little say, and elections were controlled by bosses. Second, populists believed that material progress driven by exports could not be shared widely without enfranchisement of the masses. Of course, electoral reform would also permit the populists, who were not machine politicians, to win high office without the support of the traditional parties. So populism as a strategy required expanding the suffrage and cleaning up voting procedures.

Third, the populists advocated other reforms as well, especially in education and labor relations. The populists argued that these areas, left to private action by the previous generation, were too important to be ignored by the state. Such issues had broad appeal to the electorate. Improved education, for example, would give children of immigrants and workers the opportunity to move up the social ladder. It would also create more jobs for the middle class. And even members of the elite could see the benefits of a literate, better-off citizenry.

Regulation of labor relations also had wide popularity because it promised to eliminate some of the worst abuses by employers and to ameliorate conflict in the workplace. Akin to labor reforms were proposals to extend educational opportunities and equal rights to women, including the vote.

In a general way, the populists favored increasing the role of the state in social and economic affairs, and some had mildly socialistic ideas. Still, they preferred evolutionary change over radical change. The specific reforms depended upon time, place, and opportunity—their significance lay in the promise to improve the general welfare. Recent research has traced the origins of these reforms to Krausismo imported from Spain in the late 1800s.

The populists attracted followers from many walks of life, so we refer to their parties as "multiclass." The older, traditional parties, run by a small number of wealthy men, employed lots of political hacks who herded obedient rural voters to the polls on election day. They were small and ineffectual. Populist parties, in contrast, appealed to such disparate groups as the urban poor, organized labor, students, artists, businessmen, white-collar employees, professionals, feminists, and intellectuals. Moreover, these voters behaved in an independent fashion and displayed genuine loyalty to their candidates. The populist campaigns were more broadly representative, then, but they required fast footwork by the leaders.

Populists possessed that elusive quality called "charisma," that is, they were believed to have attributes that elevated them above the common people and warranted awe and reverence from their followers. These attributes might be superior communication skills, integrity, honesty, concern for the downtrodden, political prowess, energy, or dedication to a cause. Charismatic leadership made the populists more dynamic and attractive to the voters, accounting in part for their success and persistence.

The populists validated folk culture, insisting that native songs, dances, crafts, literature, and poetry were as legitimate as foreign imports. In this they broke ranks with the traditional elites, who looked down upon non-European art. By embracing popular culture, these leaders were able to reach out to poor persons, children of immigrants, and others who wished to take pride in their lives. The populists revered the essential national spirit, called *lo mexicano, lo argentino,* or *lo peruano.* Largely for this reason they were known as nationalists.

Dozens of politicians adopted at least some of these new electoral strategies in the first three decades of this century, and these were genuine populists. The style took hold first in the Southern Cone countries, probably due to their large cities, higher levels of literacy, intense contact with the outside world, and relative prosperity because of the export booms. Then it spread northward by emulation.

The Reform Populists

The most prominent reform populists were José Batlle y Ordóñez of Uruguay, Hipólito Yrigoyen of Argentina, and Arturo Alessandri of Chile. Born after the middle of the nineteenth century, they had relatively long apprenticeships before gaining the presidencies of their countries. Batlle and Alessandri were born into prominent families, whereas Yrigoyen's origins were middle class. Highly educated for the times, they were products of urban Latin America and were intensely aware of the contradictions between constitutional ideals and political realities. They had strong wills and personalities and avoided the usual paths to power. In particular they avoided military service and alliances. Their foreign experiences were limited to European visits and

Table 12-1 Early Populists

Country	Name	Years in Power	Born	Class	Urban Rural	Race	Ed	Mil?	Party	Foreign Influence	Died
Argentina	Yrigoyen	1916–22 1928–30	1852	middle	urban	wh	law	no	UCR	indirect	1933
Uruguay	Batlle	1903–7 1911–15	1856	upper	urban	wh	law	no	Colorado	yes	1929
Chile	Alessandri	1920–25 1932–38	1868	upper	urban	wh	law	no	Liberal	yes	1950

ideas—they resided abroad only after attaining prominence. They set in motion changes that would affect the conduct of politics for the next half-century.

José Batlle y Ordóñez

Batlle, or don Pepe as he was known to the masses, was born in Montevideo in 1856. His father, an army general and a prominent politician, served as president from 1868 to 1872. By the end of the 1870s Uruguay's political life had stabilized around a two-party system (Colorados and Blancos), and Batlle was able to grow up in a peaceful if not opulent environment. He studied in the British School and later read law at the university in Montevideo. In 1880 he went to Paris for a year to round out his education.

Batlle seemed born to lead. Tall, burly, and gruff, he stood out in crowds. His exceptional intelligence pulled him into politics, usually on the side of civilian control and democratic procedures. In 1887 he founded *El Día,* a pioneer mass-circulation daily that became the conscience of his party, the Colorados. Urbane, reform-minded, self-assured, Batlle fashioned a high moral position for himself and his wing of the party. He stood for open, competitive politics that addressed issues, not old-style backroom dealings.

Ironically, Batlle managed to win the 1903 election in Congress by the very backroom dealings that he denounced. Once in office, though, he immediately set out to open up and modernize the system. When his arch-rival declared civil war in 1904, Batlle was forced to defend his office militarily, which he did successfully. From then until his death, Batlle became the foremost figure in Uruguayan politics. His remarkable career boosted Uruguay into the forefront of progress in the entire region, making it a country envied and imitated by others. Batlle's Uruguay became known as the Switzerland of South America, a socialist utopia, and the "model country," because of his extensive reforms. Even today his name is revered.

Batlle's initiatives spanned a wide range of areas: education, governance, labor, women's rights, industry, technology, Church-state relations, social welfare, and transportation. Because Uruguay was a compact country whose population lay within easy reach of Montevideo, Batlle's reforms could spread quickly. Moreover, with easy access to maritime shipping, he could finance them with taxes from the booming export trade in cereals and livestock products. Most people approved of these changes and hailed them as progressive. Even foreign corporations appreciated his orderly government, if not necessarily his scrutiny of their profits.

Tens of thousands of voters registered during Batlle's first term (1903–1907), and they took part enthusiastically in the new direct elections. The Colorado Party reaped their loyalty and votes, and Batlle won renewed mandates in successive elections. Indeed, the terms *Colorado* and *Batllista* became almost synonymous. In his second term (1911–1915) Batlle pressed ahead with his reforms and laid the groundwork for eventual approval of a new constitution in 1919. By the 1920s Uruguay was unquestionably the best-governed, most prosperous, and most admired country in Latin America. It was also among the most ethnically homogeneous, with few persons of African or Amerindian descent.

Of all of Batlle's legacies, one needs emphasis here: his populism. He pioneered an approach to politics that others would imitate, consciously or otherwise. His devotion to Krausismo, his faith in popular sovereignty, his campaigns to expand electoral participation, and his efforts to create a modern nation mark him as the first genuine reform populist. That heritage belongs to Latin America, not just to Uruguay.

An Early Feminist Leader in Uruguay, Abella de Ramírez

Women in the Southern Cone led the drive to gain broader rights and equality before the law. Asuncion Lavrin's book, *Women, Feminism, and Social Change in Argentinea, Chile, and Uruguay, 1890–1940* (Lincoln: University of Nebraska Press, 1995), provides a detailed account of these efforts and their eventual accomplishments.

Suffrage was one of the foremost goals of the women's movement in Latin America. These women, on the cover of the popular magazine Fon, Fon *marched in 1914 in support of the vote.*

María Abella de Ramírez, an Uruguayan feminist and leader of the cause of equal rights, figures prominently in Lavrin's book. Born in 1863 on a cattle *estancia,* Abella gained an excellent education in local schools. She later moved to La Plata, Argentina, but returned to Montevideo, where she married into a politically active family. As an adult, Abella came to regard the Catholic church as women's greatest enemy. She advocated separation of Church and state, public education, and secular social services. Above all, however, she believed that Uruguayan women needed the divorce. By networking with leaders in neighboring countries, she developed a "minimum program" for women's rights, consisting of seventeen reforms. Her activism led to forming of the Pan American Feminine Federation, by which she maintained ties with leaders abroad. The minimum program covered full educational opportunities, equal access to and salaries in all professions, paternity laws, economic equality in marriage, suppression of the husband's legal tutelage over his wife's affairs, absolute divorce, decriminalization of adultery, equality for all children, an end to government licensing and exploitation of prostitutes, political and citizenship rights, and criminal prosecution of wife-batterers. These and other reforms would end the "enslavement of women" represented by marriage under existing laws.

Even though Abella died in 1926 before achieving the vote for women, suffrage was approved in 1932, and her minimum program was eventually enacted in the Women's Civil Rights Law of 1946.

Hipólito Yrigoyen

Only twenty miles from Montevideo, across the La Plata estuary, Hipólito Yrigoyen began his career in Argentine politics about the same time that Batlle rose to influence in Uruguay. The two men shared many similarities. They embraced the Krausismo popular in the late nineteenth century and thus focused on many of the same reform programs when they gained power. They fought for honest, competitive, issue-driven elections and worked hard to expand the franchise. They both remained down-to-earth in their personal lives yet were worshipped like saints by their followers. They strengthened the power of government, demanded respect from other countries, and fostered a spirit of nationalism among their citizens. And they both are considered innovators for creating an early form of populism.

Yrigoyen grew up in Buenos Aires and apprenticed in politics under the tutelage of his uncle, Leandro Alem. After a promising start, he dropped out in the 1880s, only to re-enter politics advocating revolutionary action against Argentina's corrupt oligarchy. After several unsuccessful revolts, their party, the Unión Cívica, largely disbanded, and the despairing Alem committed suicide in 1896. Yrigoyen then inherited leadership of the group. He changed its name to Unión Cívica Radical (UCR but generally known as the Radical Party) and shifted its strategy to nonviolent resistance. Called *intransigencia,* the new strategy required abstention from voting and diligent assembly of a network of neighborhood and employee groups to keep alive the spirit of defiance. Yrigoyen proved brilliant in this conspiratorial activity, inspiring tens of thousands to work for eventual triumph of the Radical program.

Yrigoyen, unlike Batlle, was not an effective, outgoing speaker who could rally outdoor crowds. Instead, he invited small numbers of collaborators into his parlor

The military often intervened in political affairs in Latin America. This photo captured a full dress parade of Argentine regiments passing in review beneath the stands of the race track in turn-of-the-century Buenos Aires.

and inspired them with a mystical sense of their righteous crusade against evil and corruption. He vaguely promised a better world when they governed Argentina, and he called on all citizens to abstain from voting until they could win honest elections. This brilliant tactic allowed the Radicals to claim as theirs all those disenchanted voters who stayed away from the polls or cast unmarked ballots. Each successive election became a further indictment of the regime.

By not making explicit his program, Yrigoyen became all things to all people. Ward heelers, neighborhood agents, regional bosses, and party whips all made promises as if they were sacred pledges from Yrigoyen himself. Meanwhile, his semi-conspiratorial party distributed food, jobs, and favors that further cemented followers' loyalties.

Yrigoyen's breakthrough came in 1912 when the president of Argentina, Roque Sáenz Peña, decided to extend the vote to all males over the age of eighteen. Sáenz Peña, who considered himself a friend of Yrigoyen and a liberal, hoped that this measure would ward off growing public cynicism and absenteeism. It did, but it also allowed the Radical Party to sweep the next congressional elections and to expand its following in the major cities of Argentina. Yrigoyen stood poised to win the presidency in 1916.

The Radicals drafted and elected Yrigoyen, who after an entire career in the opposition could hardly believe that he had finally won. He stumbled many times in his first term (1916–1922), failed miserably in his second (1928–1930), and was ousted by a military coup. Yet, his impact on Argentine politics cannot be exaggerated. He oversaw the incorporation of hundreds of thousands of new voters and local representatives into the system. He carried out a university reform in Córdoba in 1918 that served as a model throughout Latin America. He sponsored legislation to extend recognition to more labor unions and to require decent working conditions, especially for women. (These efforts came to little, however, because his term coincided with a surge of anarchist activism that was met with brutal repression.) He established national monopolies over new railroad, shipping, and petroleum concessions. And he launched Argentine diplomacy into a trajectory of neutrality and international law that counteracted and rivalled U.S. imperialism of the era.

In some ways, Yrigoyen left a larger legacy than that of Batlle. Some see him as the model for Juan Perón, who in the 1940s would take the populist strategy to its limits. And many more Latin American politicians read about, witnessed, and emulated politics in Argentina, the unquestioned spiritual leader of the Spanish-American world. For example, in the mid-twentieth century populists like Velasco Ibarra of Ecuador and Arnulfo Arias of Panama (see Chapter Nineteen) spent considerable time in exile in Buenos Aires. So Yrigoyen's innovations spread outward in space and forward in time.

Arturo Alessandri

The third early reform populist in Latin America was Arturo Alessandri of Chile. The son of an Italian diplomat who decided to stay in Chile, Alessandri grew up in upper-middle-class style and received a good education. Alert to the new ideas circulating in Europe, Alessandri surprised his college professors in 1892 by choosing a social law topic for his dissertation: urban tenements. He attempted to find the causes of the alcoholism, moral degradation, and short life spans of workers in Santiago and Valparaiso. He concluded that overcrowding in those cities' slums, called *conventillos,* was a major contributing factor.

> In Santiago, the majority of the rooms are low, dark, humid, unventilated, even when cooking is carried on . . . [this crowding] is greatly detrimental to health and moral well-being. In Valparaiso there are 543 conventillos with 6426 dwellings which house over 17,000 persons, which gives an average of three persons per room. Of the 543 conventillos, 203 are in reasonable repair; the rest are completely inadequate for occupation and lack the most basic conditions required for habitation.

> (Julio César Jobet, *Temas históricos chilenos* [Santiago: 1973], p. 220)

Alessandri proposed a series of incentives to encourage private builders to improve low-cost housing.

Alessandri moved into the world of politics and easily advanced up the ranks because of his talents and physical attributes. He was tall and handsome and had a robust voice that carried well in outdoor rallies. He emerged as a leading figure in the Liberal splinter groups that had formed under Chile's parliamentary democracy, and he managed to forge a Liberal Alliance coalition for the congressional elections of 1916. Having done that placed Alessandri in position to run for president in 1920.

Arturo Alessandri (second from the right, front row), a pioneer populist in South America, barnstormed Chile's countryside to win votes in the 1920 election. A strong-willed, reform-minded leader, he helped to reestablish a presidential system through a broad set of constitutional reforms in 1925.

Alessandri had done a number of things to groom himself for the presidency. After launching his career in the central-south province of Concepción—an important shipping, coal-mining, and agricultural zone—he moved to the northern desert nitrate districts and ran for election there. Tarapacá, the main nitrate processing and shipping city, was home to tens of thousands of Chile's rugged miners and dockworkers. Alessandri appealed to these laborers with a program calling for recognition of unions, protection against work accidents, limitations on work hours, and government neutrality in industrial disputes. He gained the nickname "Lion of Tarapacá" because of his billowing mane of hair and his forceful image while campaigning among the miners. By all accounts, he became committed to social reforms that would ameliorate the suffering of the working class and improve the representative character of the political system.

The year 1920 began catastrophically for Chile. The nitrate market plummeted due to the end of wartime purchases and the spread of air-reduction nitrogen technology. Tens of thousands of miners were thrown out of work, and strikes erupted up and down the country. The rest of the economy went through post-war adjustments that exacerbated unemployment. The political elite, however, stood by idly waiting for the invisible hand of laissez-faire capitalism to sort things out. All of the social tensions of poverty, disease, alcoholism, and dislocation surfaced again, and the crisis deepened. The masses no longer believed in the benevolent leadership of the elite and seemed ready to take matters into their own hands.

Arturo Alessandri rose to the occasion, conducting Chile's first genuine presidential election campaign in history. He traveled up and down the country making speeches and meeting with local leaders. He appealed especially to workers who had suffered the brunt of the depression. He argued that the country was on the verge of breaking up and needed serious reforms to mend class divisions. He advocated constitutional changes to allow government to intervene in social and economic matters. He would separate Church and state, legislate rights for labor, allow the government to take over lands needed for public purposes, extend the vote to all men and women, create an income tax, and increase the power of the president vis-à-vis Congress. These changes would give the president the ability to pass social legislation that Congress would have difficulty vetoing. In reality, he advocated a presidential system to replace the quasi-parliamentary system in force since the 1890s.

Conservative leaders banded together in 1920 behind the candidacy of one of their own, and they managed to get enough rural sharecroppers (*inquilinos*) to the polls to win the election by a tiny margin. Alessandri carried the mining and industrial regions, using traditional techniques shrewdly and energetically. This election marked the transition from elite parliamentarism to mass politics, a harbinger of populism. Because the vote totals were so close, Congress had to decide the outcome. The house was deeply split, and for several weeks it delayed. Finally pro-Alessandri demonstrations and public outcry overcame the resistance of the elite, and they decided in favor of Alessandri. He took office in late 1920.

For the next two years Alessandri worked on his reform program and tried to help the unemployed miners who had voted for him. Tens of thousands were transferred to other parts of the country to lesser jobs, but the economy could not absorb all of them. Meanwhile, Alessandri could not get his bills passed by Congress, whose members refused to give up any of their elite privileges. Congress stymied him with its right of ministerial censure, whereby a simple vote of no confidence would force the resignation of a cabinet member. By 1924 Alessandri had dealt with eighteen cabinets turnovers. That year he decided to campaign in the by-elections to gain majorities in both houses of Congress, in order to pass his program. He succeeded, furthering the transition to mass politics.

Even after the new, Liberal-dominated Congress was seated, it would not pass Alessandri's reforms, because even Liberal members wanted to protect their vested interests. Public outcry arose at the lack of progress, and in late 1924 agitation reached alarming levels. At this point, the Chilean army, long a model of the nonpolitical military, intervened. Army officers, enraged that their pay increases were sidetracked while legislators debated paying themselves salaries, marched to Congress to demand action. Intimidated, the legislators complied, and soon Alessandri signed his entire reform package into law. Then he resigned to protest the military violation of the Constitution!

Chile's early experiment with populism proved fateful in many ways. Alessandri resumed the presidency in 1925 and oversaw the constitutional revision that he had campaigned for five years earlier. Yet, he soon resigned again in a confrontation with his minister of war, Colonel Carlos Ibáñez, who aspired to the presidency himself. So Chilean affairs developed into a tense rivalry between reform electoral politics and military authoritarianism. Populism did not return to any degree, because party loyalty, class antagonism, and even military intervention prevented the kind of cohesive mass movements that characterized populism elsewhere.

The Shift from Nitrate to Copper Exports in Chile

At the turn of the century, Chile supplied most of the world's demand for nitrates, used for fertilizer and explosive powder. Production took place in the Atacama Desert in northern Chile, one of the driest regions in the world. Great salt flats in the coastal mountains contained high-grade potassium nitrate, which miners broke

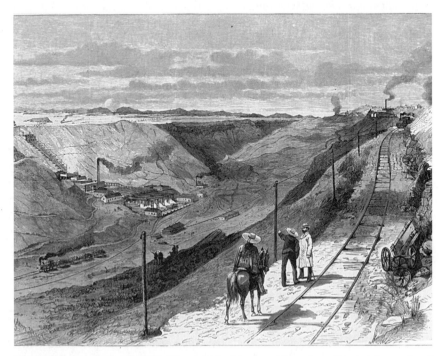

Nitrate mine, or oficina, *in Chile. Nitrates mined in the arid, northern desert region produced much foreign income for Chile and were used for both fertilizers and the manufacture of gunpowder in Europe and North America.*

up and delivered to the coast using narrow-gauge railroads. Huge refining plants ground up and purified the mineral, which was then bagged and shipped all over the world by freighter. During the First World War, German scientists developed an industrial process for extracting nitrogen from the air and combining it with other elements. After the war, demand for mineral nitrates fell precipitously, throwing the Chilean economy into a depression.

Copper, which Chileans had long mined and shipped, made a dramatic comeback in the early twentieth century and replaced nitrates as the leading export in the 1920s. El Teniente, the first industrial plant installed, was about 155 kilometers south of Santiago. It was financed and built by an American mining engineer, William Braden, who shortly afterward sold his interest to the Guggenheim Copper Company, which then sold it to the Kennecott Company in 1915. El Teniente hauled coal from Concepción to smelt the ores, gaining efficiency from mass production. During and after World War I, in response to demand for copper, U.S. firms invested in two huge open-pit mines, Chuquicamata and Potrerillos. These mines used the new Jackling process for smelting and easily surpassed El Teniente in production. The three mines, known as the Gran Minería (Big Mining), accounted for 80 percent of Chilean copper exports by the late 1920s. It was a classic enclave sector, highly automated and completely controlled by foreign management, with few links to the rest of the economy.

Conclusions and Issues

The early experiments in populism in Latin America ended about 1930 when the Great Depression struck the region and brought autocratic regimes to power virtually everywhere. The 1930s were not favorable for expansive electoral politics. Even Alessandri, who returned to office in 1932, abandoned his earlier style and ran an administration unresponsive to labor and the masses. Despite the disappearance of full-blown populist movements in the 1930s, certain broad trends favored their reappearance after World War II. Latin American industrialization spread due to wartime shortages. Meanwhile, agricultural and mining enterprises that had previously flourished due to lucrative export markets stagnated. Many laid-off workers decided to look for jobs and better lives in the cities. In most places urban migration grew, and it grew even faster after the war. Finally, new means of transportation and communication made it easier for politicians to create the kind of bonds that fostered mass electoral movements. So the 1930s marked merely a hiatus, not a demise, for populism.

Discussion Questions:

1. What conditions favored the rise of populism in the Southern Cone countries in the early twentieth century? Could it have risen in Central America or Mexico at this time?

2. To what extent did populism introduce new political agendas in South America? What constituted these agendas? Were they ever enacted?

3. What lasting impact did early or reform populism have on the political systems of South America? Did the populists leave successors? Who lost out to populist up-starts?

Dictators of the Caribbean

The Genesis of Nicaragua's National Guard in 1927

General Moncada arrived in the capital city of Managua, escorted by diplomat-soldier Henry Stimson, a personal emissary of U.S. President Calvin Coolidge. Moncada's car was mobbed by happy Nicaraguans, who shouted "*Viva la Revolución*" and "*Viva* Moncada." Many well-wishers wore red bandannas and waved red flags—the colors of Moncada's Liberal Party. One old lady thrust red roses into the car window. Moncada leaned over to his passenger and said, "Colonel Stimson, you see how my people love me and want my party to take power? This is democracy!"

"Yes, they love you," Stimson replied. "But, unfortunately, my instructions are to restore Dr. Adolfo Díaz to the presidency and then supervise clean elections. You understand our position, I hope?"

"Oh, yes, Mister Stimson, I do. We can tolerate Dr. Díaz for a while longer, if you keep the marines here to make sure he can't use his army to attack us secretly. I don't trust Díaz."

"General, my country called the marines home two years ago, in 1925, and we sent them back last year only reluctantly," Stimson said, looking at the crowd. "We don't want to fight a war here. If you win the election—and you obviously are very popular—we'll pull the marines out, this time for good. Can your army take over when we leave?"

"Yes, of course we can keep peace here, when I win a democratic election. When will it be?" Moncada asked curiously.

"Next year," Stimson said. "As soon as we can get it organized. Meanwhile, you need to convert your army into a national guard, like the ones our states have back home. They have light arms and trucks, maybe a few recon planes, nothing heavy like tanks and artillery. A national guard here could maintain the peace without encouraging army officers to take power themselves. You could control a guard much more easily than an army—or three armies, like you have now."

"Good idea," said Moncada. "I'll need advisors and ammunition from you. Then I assure you, the marines can leave."

"I can promise you, General Moncada, that our boys will stay long enough to give you full control over the country," Stimson said. "After that, it will be up to you."

When the car reached the presidential palace, Moncada and Stimson got out and spoke with local reporters. In Spanish, Moncada said that even though his Liberal armies were winning and could have seized power, they were convinced by this fine representative of the U.S. president to hold back. They would accept the administration of Dr. Adolfo Díaz until elections were held next year. He himself would be a candidate, and he promised to abide by the results of the election.

A reporter stepped forward and blurted out to Moncada, "But, General, are all of your officers in agreement with this truce? Aren't some of them still fighting in the mountains? How can you keep your Liberal Party together if some leaders don't accept the peace?"

"Ah, you are probably referring to my friend, Colonel Sandino, who refuses to put down his weapons," Moncada responded. "Sandino is a good officer but is too passionate for politics. He thinks we must kill all the Conservatives and drive the 'gringo devils' out of our country before peace can come. He's afraid the yankees will turn our country into a colony if we don't fight back.

"Well, Sandino's a bit touched," Moncada said, tapping his head, "and on this issue. He's wrong," Moncada continued, "because here is an American friend of Nicaragua, Colonel Henry Stimson, by my side. He came here from Washington to help us build our democracy. Mister Stimson is not a gringo devil, as you can see. He has no *cachos* [horns] under his hat. He'll help us to have elections and train our soldiers to be men of peace, not makers of war. The Liberal Party regards the great nation of North America to be a true friend of Nicaragua."

"Mister," another reporter addressed Stimson, "are we going to have your marines here forever and ever? Why can't Nicaragua protect itself without your soldiers? Do you think we are like Haiti or Panama, that we cannot take care of ourselves?"

"Yes, of course we know you can take care of your own affairs," Stimson said. "Since 1912 we simply stationed a contingent in our diplomatic offices, a small company of marines, I think it was, to protect the premises and lend support to the constitutional government. It was just a legation guard, nothing more. In the last few years we landed more marines, at the request of your government, to try to stop the bloodshed of civil war. But our job is to promote peace and then go home."

"When will you go home, Mister Stimson?" the reporter asked.

"We can't say for sure, but it will probably take a few more years before your army can handle the job alone. Meanwhile, General Moncada and I were just talking about transforming your army into a national guard, which will be less likely to cause trouble. We'll be pleased to help with training and light weapons."

"Can you catch Colonel Sandino," the reporter persisted, "if he refuses to cooperate? He says you'll never find him in the jungle. It will be like your General Pershing trying to capture Pancho Villa in Mexico. You never did!"

Stimson smiled "Well, that was a different case, there in Mexico. Besides, Sandino would be a Nicaraguan problem, not ours. We are here just to advise and train, not to carry out actual combat operations. I am confident that, should Colonel Sandino refuse to go along with the general truce, then General Moncada here will deal with him quickly."

Stimson then waved and told Moncada that he declined to speak any more. The two men, escorted by U.S. Marine guards, entered the presidential palace and closed the great wooden doors. Several reporters ran back to their offices to file stories about the interview.

General Moncada won the elections of 1927, held under U.S. Marine supervision, and soon he organized the Nicaraguan National Guard. As expected, Liberal chieftain Augusto Sandino balked at Moncada's deal with Stimson and launched a guerrilla campaign in the mountains, which will be described in Chapter Fifteen. Meanwhile, Moncada brought stability and U.S. investments into Nicaragua, paving the way for one of the longest-lived dictatorships in the hemisphere, that of the Somoza family (see Chapter Sixteen).

The Dictators

During the 1910s and 1920s, while populism was expanding the electorates in South America and promoting more open politics, an opposite trend occurred in the Caribbean basin (the region embracing the West Indies and Central America). This ominous trend was brought on by a new generation of leaders—the Caribbean dictators. As a group, they were power-hungry, ruthless, despotic, and vain. They were among the strongest-willed of Latin America's leaders, and they fed many negative stereotypes in the minds of U.S. and European observers.

One of the more common epithets used to describe the countries of the Caribbean basin was "banana republics." The depth of negative attitudes toward Latin Americans was probed in two fine studies: John Johnson's *Latin America in Caricature,* and Frederick Pike's, *The United States and Latin America.* The first shows that Americans stereotyped Latins as racially inferior, childlike, violence-prone, and untrustworthy. The second concludes that Americans projected onto Latins images of primitivism, anarchy, passion, and degeneracy, which in turn were the product of European myths about nature and civilization. Without doubt, such negative imagery reached its height in the early twentieth century, the age of the Caribbean dictators.

Dictators chose to assume command of their countries for simple, uncomplicated reasons. First, the core legacy of the previous century had been *caudillismo* and arbitrary seizure of power. No tradition of democracy, shared power, constitutional-ism, or governmental restraint limited potential dictators. Second, the economic re-wards of becoming a dictator rose dramatically after 1900. Sugar, coffee, tobacco, cotton, petroleum, minerals, and other commodities earned lucrative prices in U.S. markets, and after profit margins were known, U.S. banks were willing to lend large amounts of money for development projects. Export prosperity, in turn, meant huge profits for the person in control, usually a dictator. Protecting U.S. property headed the list of the dictators' priorities. Third, the U.S. government sent naval and army contingents to occupy and govern several countries, including Nicaragua. Re-lationships between U.S. and local commanders tended to awaken ambitions of power in the latter. It became quite natural for heads of national guard forces to as-sume political control when U.S. troops withdrew.

U.S. policies were ambiguous. On the one hand, reform-minded, moralistic U.S. officials frequently committed their efforts to modernizing and democratizing their southern neighbors, as if that were a simple chore. The American ambassador to England during the period of the Mexican Revolution, for example, told his British counterpart that his country's aim was to:

> "Make 'em vote and live by their decisions."
> "But suppose [the Briton asked] they will not so live?"
> "We'll go in again and make 'em vote again."
> "And keep this up 200 years?" asked the Briton.
> "Yes. The United States will be here two hundred years and it can continue to shoot men for that little space until they learn to vote and to rule themselves."
>
> (Burton J. Hendrick, editor, *The Life and Letters of Walter H. Page* [Garden City, NY: Doubleday, Page, & Co., 1925], p. 188.)

On the other hand, U.S. authorities often felt more confident leaving Latin American affairs in the hands of strong leaders. As Franklin Roosevelt once said of a Central American dictator, "He may be a son of a bitch, but he's *our* son of a bitch!" So whereas the rise of populism in South America is complex to explain, the appear-ance of dictatorship in the Caribbean basin was quite natural.

Evolving U.S. Influence

U.S. policy evolved significantly during the period known as the imperialist era (1898–1933). Interventionist actions characterized the early years, especially after Theodore Roosevelt's enunciation of his "corollary" to the Monroe Doctrine. This statement asserted that the United States would police the region to supervise irre-sponsible regimes. The United States regularly intervened politically, economically, and militarily in the circum-Caribbean countries. Cuba, Panama, the Dominican Republic, Nicaragua, and Haiti were occupied by U.S. forces for extended periods and kept under control by naval intimidation, often called "gunboat diplomacy." Even Mexico did not escape such demeaning treatment. The years 1901–1928 saw a total of fifty U.S. armed interventions in the region. Only the South American coun-tries remained free of armed interference.

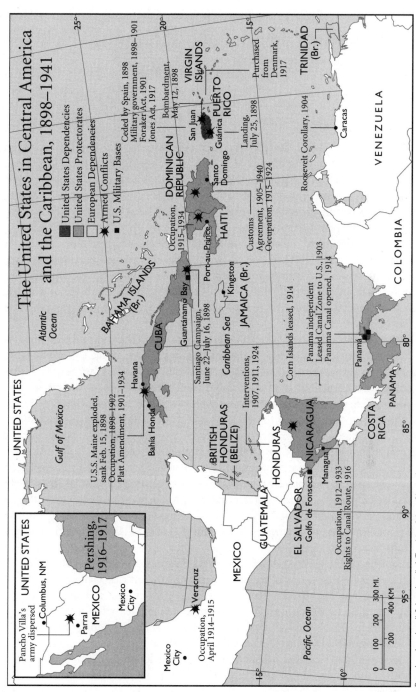

The United States in Central America and the Caribbean, 1898–1941

Legend:
- United States Dependencies
- United States Protectorates
- European Dependencies
- ✶ Armed Conflicts
- ■ U.S. Military Bases

UNITED STATES

Gulf of Mexico

Atlantic Ocean

BAHAMA ISLANDS (Br.)

CUBA
- Havana
- Bahía Honda
- U.S.S. Maine exploded, sank Feb. 15, 1898
- Occupation, 1898–1902
- Platt Amendment, 1901–1934
- Santiago Campaign, June 22–July 16, 1898
- Guantánamo Bay

Caribbean Sea

JAMAICA (Br.)
- Kingston

Ceded by Spain, 1898
Military government, 1898–1901
Foraker Act, 1901
Jones Act, 1917

VIRGIN ISLANDS
Purchased from Denmark, 1917

PUERTO RICO
- San Juan
- Guánica
- Bombardment, May 12, 1898
- Landing, July 25, 1898

DOMINICAN REPUBLIC
- Santo Domingo
- Occupation, 1915–1934
- Customs Agreement, 1905–1940
- Occupation, 1915–1924

HAITI
- Port-au-Prince

Roosevelt Corollary, 1904

VENEZUELA
- Caracas

TRINIDAD (Br.)

BRITISH HONDURAS (BELIZE)

GUATEMALA

HONDURAS

EL SALVADOR
- Golfo de Fonseca
- Managua

NICARAGUA
- Interventions, 1907, 1911, 1924
- Corn Islands leased, 1914
- Occupation, 1912–1933
- Rights to Canal Route, 1916

COSTA RICA

PANAMA
- Panamá
- Panama independent
- Leased Canal Zone to U.S., 1903
- Panama Canal opened, 1914

COLOMBIA

Pacific Ocean

0 100 200 300 MI.
0 200 400 KM

Inset: Pershing, 1916–1917

UNITED STATES
- Columbus, NM
- Pancho Villa's army dispersed
- Parral
- Mexico City

MEXICO
- Veracruz
- Mexico City
- Occupation, April 1914–1915

25°
20°
15°
90°
85°
80°
95°
15°
10°

Based on Lombardi & Lombardi, *A Teaching Atlas of Latin America.*

Roosevelt's "corollary" to the Monroe Doctrine, included in his December 1904 address to Congress, stated that:

> Chronic wrongdoing [may] ultimately require intervention by some civilized nation, and in the Western Hemisphere the adherence of the United States to the Monroe Doctrine may force [us], however reluctantly, in flagrant cases of such wrongdoing or impotence, to the exercise of an international police power.
>
> (*Congressional Record*, 58th Congress, 8th session, p. 19.)

U.S. occupation often played into the hands of those who aspired to become dictators. The commanding officers of these U.S. occupying forces were little versed in diplomacy or Latin American politics, so their actions were often quite disruptive. Traditional politicians found it increasingly difficult to retain control over their countries. U.S. commanders, meanwhile, in order to preserve law and order (their first priority), helped disarm existing armies and turn them into national guards. This further undermined the ability of the traditional elites to regain power, because the older armies had previously served their interests and often put them in power. Finally, the disruption and bungling that usually accompanied U.S. occupation fired up anti-American sentiment, which often was used to inflame crowds and to start riots. In the end, gunboat diplomacy actually led to greater instability and helped the dictators come to power.

The Caribbean dictators received a great deal of attention in the U.S. press because their countries lay near the United States, they guarded huge U.S. investments, and they operated within a major security zone during World War I. Some of these dictators became well known to the ordinary U.S. citizen. Occasionally public opinion swayed U.S. policy, usually toward some form of intervention. That was the case of Cuba during the 1890s in the events leading to the Spanish American War of 1898. In most cases, however, neither the public nor the decision-makers really understood the workings of the countries they attempted to control.

The dictators of the early twentieth century were born after the mid-1800s and hence were mature, even elderly men when they took office. They usually belonged to old families that claimed descent from the conquistadors and monopolized the best lands and positions in society. Most dictators had served as officers in their countries' armies until mid-career, when they felt a calling to assert their leadership in government. In fact, the armies of these Caribbean countries were really just police forces for internal security, existing largely to protect the interests of the wealthy elites. The dictators usually had advanced education from their countries' civilian schools, and some studied military science elsewhere. Those who were not military officers had usually completed college. Most had some personal contact with the outside world, either through travel, study, work, or business dealings abroad. Spanish was, of course, the principal language of these men, but several spoke English well.

Once in office the dictators held onto power for a long time, using fraudulent re-elections or other subterfuges. Their opponents were usually rival members of the Hispanic elites or occasionally mestizos trying to win a following among the Amerindian or black majorities. Typically the dictators favored their friends with lavish treatment and punished their enemies mercilessly. Some cultivated reputations of ruthless cruelty

Table 13–1 Selected Caribbean Dictators

Country	Name	Years in Power	Born	Class	Urban Rural	Race	Ed	Age @ first off	Mil?	Foreign Influence	Died	@ Age
Nicaragua	Santos Zelaya	1893–1909	1853			wh	univ.		n		1919	65
Guatemala	Estrada Cabrera	1898–1920	1857	lower		wh	univ.	35	n	n	1924	66
Venezuela	Gómez	1908–35	1857	middle		wh	n/a	42	y	n	1935	78
Cuba	Menocal	1913–21	1866	upper		wh	military	38	y	n	1941	71
Cuba	Machado	1925–33	1871	lower		wh	univ.	53	n	y	1939	67

to discourage challenges to their power. Non-elite rivals were dealt with especially harshly, because they threatened the social preeminence of Europeans over Amerindians and blacks. Most dictators ended up being overthrown by other dictators, usually at a ripe old age. Their families could live comfortably for a long time off their accumulated wealth. Indeed, the dictators tried to create the bases for family dynasties, in which children and other relatives continued to enjoy the spoils of power.

Estrada Cabrera in Guatemala

Manuel Estrada Cabrera is a good example of the early twentieth-century dictator. Estrada ruled Guatemala for nearly a quarter of a century—the longest one-man rule in the region. During that time he preserved the archaic social system through

President Estrada Cabrera posed for a formal portrait late in his career. Such presentations emphasized their subjects' European features and dress.

The history of a people is more than a chronological listing and analysis of political, economic, and military events. It is a richly textured insight in the way people think, act, and see the world around them. It is expressed in many ways, none perhaps more visually than through their art. The following pieces were selected not only for their artistic merit, but as representations of themes and places in Latin American life, some peculiar to the region, some transcending Latin America and reflecting universal themes.

Pedro Figari, Uruguay, 1861-1938, *Idilio Campero (Country Idyll)*, (n/d).
Oil on board, 13 1/4 x 19 1/4".
Collection of the Inter-American Development Bank, Washington, D.C.

Carlos Salazar Herrera, 1906-1980, *Paisaje campestre (Country Scene),* 1935.
Oil on canvas, 42.5 x 58.5 cm. Property of the Banco Central of Costa Rica.

Emilio Span, 1869-1944, *Paisaje de Turrialba (Turrialba Countryside),* 1912.
Oil on cardboard, 34 x 47 cm. Property of the Banco Central of Costa Rica.

Pedro Figari, *Dance in the Courtyard*. Private Collections. Art Resource, N.Y.

Benito Quinquela Martín, Argentina, 1890-1977, *Entrando en la Boca
(Entering La Boca, Buenos Aires Harbor)*, 1965. Oil on canvas, 31 x 35".
Collection of the Inter-American Development Bank, Washington, D.C.

Wilfredo Lam, IBAYA, 1950. Oil on canvas, 104.5 x 87.6 cm.
Tate Gallery, London/Art Resource, N.Y.

José Clemente Orozco, México, 1883-1956, *Zapatistas*
(Mexican Revolutionaries), 1935. Lithograph (20/130), 13 x 16".
Collection of the Inter-American Development Bank, Washington, D. C.

Frida Kahlo (Mexican, 1907-1954), *Self-Portrait Dedicated to Leon Trotsky*, 1937.
Oil on masonite, 30 x 24". The National Museum of Women in the Arts.
Gift of Clare Booth Luce.

José Sabogal, Perú, 1888-1956, *El Señor de la Fortaleza*
(The Lord of the Fort), 1919. Oil on canvas 22 x 26".
Collection of the Inter-American Development Bank, Washington, D. C.

brutal repression and violence. Still, as a man of his times, he also carried out a classically liberal program of economic change. In this he continued the tradition of Justo Rufino Barrios of the 1870s and 1880s. Estrada in turn was followed by a dictator of legendary proportions, Jorge Ubico (1931–1944).

At the turn of the century Guatemala was very much a divided land. Over 80 percent of the population belonged to Amerindian communities whose cultures and activities had little connection with the outside world. They spoke nearly two dozen Maya-derived languages, cultivated New World crops with pre-industrial methods, and had minimal contact with the European segment of the population. The Amerindians owned lands and maintained towns, but they also worked for planters and agricultural corporations when required to do so.

The other 20 percent of Guatemala's population, sometimes called modern by outsiders, was genetically and culturally descended from Spain. A few families claimed direct descent, but the majority were mestizos and *ladinos* claiming to be white. They governed the country, ran the money economy, controlled trade and production, made the laws, and supported a European-style culture. The lives of Amerindians and *ladinos* rarely intersected.

The two Guatemalas had one major point of contact: labor. As had been the case since the Conquest, the Europeans needed the Amerindians' labor to make their businesses profitable and their lives satisfying. Amerindians had traditionally worked their fields and plantations and had served in their homes as servants. They were harnessed to transport goods to markets. Older forms of labor exploitation had evolved into the standard debt peonage by the early years of the twentieth century. Under this system, the Amerindians had to pay a tribute tax and religious tithes in cash, which was very scarce in their communities. Those who failed to pay could be jailed until they promised to work off their debts.

Alternatively, those who lived as peasants on lands owned by Europeans often found their debts to the hacienda stores impossible to pay off. They were literally trapped in debt servitude attempting to pay off their bills. The ultimate goal of these systems was exploitation of Amerindian labor, without which the *ladinos* could not maintain the European standards that they aspired to.

The antagonism of the two Guatemalas—Amerindian and *ladino*—created deep tensions and hatreds. For this reason, Guatemalan presidents usually devoted much of their time to suppressing violence and enforcing the labor and debt laws.

Manuel Estrada Cabrera, who became president in 1898, was no different. Estrada used his relations with military colleagues to preserve himself and his friends in power and to fend off rivals. He employed such brutal measures that other politicians labeled him a psychopath and attempted to impeach him. They failed. In the end he was overthrown by his own army.

Estrada also carried out a program of economic modernization that brought wealth to some, but misery to the masses. This was the era when European and U.S. companies looked abroad for sources of raw materials, tropical commodities, and markets for their manufactures. The arrival of foreign investors in Latin America was generally hailed as progress because they brought capital, technology, skilled laborers, and permanent contacts with the outside world. Their advent in the Caribbean basin—they had long since arrived in Mexico and South America—had

Late in the 19th century, bananas—shown loaded on a mule cart—became a lucrative export crop from around the Caribbean basin.

been delayed by political turmoil and colonial restrictions. Now, it seemed, the smaller countries of the region could partake of progress and modernity.

For the most part, foreign companies did what they promised. They installed railroads, streetcar systems, port facilities, processing plants, electric and gas utilities, telephones, and banks. They developed plantations, mines, ranches, and factories, mostly oriented toward foreign markets. They supplied capital and technology that was nonexistent in these poor countries. And their managers, who circulated in the highest spheres of society, served as models for the progressive Latin American citizens. In compensation, foreign companies reaped great earnings, often recovering their investments in a year or two and then enjoying clear, steady, secure profit flows afterward.

Estrada and his counterparts welcomed these developers with open arms and lavish incentives—after all, these developers would allow the region to catch up with the rest of the world. Guatemala, because of its size, diverse resources, and huge labor supply, succeeded especially well in attracting investors. The United Fruit Company (UFCO), chartered in Boston in 1899, had already begun purchases of bananas along the Caribbean coasts, and Guatemala became a prime supplier. UFCO received generous land concessions to grow bananas, as well as subsidies to build a modern harbor at Puerto Barrios, on the Caribbean coast. In time it became the leading exporter of bananas to the United States.

Along with plantations and the port, bananas brought a railroad, because the fruit had to be transported quickly to market. Estrada's government subsidized the construction of the rail line between the capital and Puerto Barrios, and then authorized linkages with other Central American lines. By the 1920s this expanded system, known as the International Railways of Central America, transported 90 percent of the freight in Guatemala.

Coffee, whose price had remained amazingly high over decades, was another crop that Estrada encouraged. The rich volcanic soils of Guatemala's mountain regions were perfectly suited to coffee. Planting, cultivating, harvesting, and processing were complex tasks, however, that the Amerindian majority had no interest in learning. In order to set up the coffee industry, Estrada subsidized the immigration of thousands of German families and settled them on large tracts of choice land. The strategy paid off in terms of international earnings, because by the 1920s Guatemala was the third-largest coffee exporter in the world.

By the usual measures, Guatemala had made great progress during the Estrada reign. Capital investments, exports, railroad freight, urban growth, per capita income, and consumption all rose rapidly. Yet, only the small portion of Hispanic Guatemalans and the immigrants benefited from the prosperity. The Amerindians were forced to work more and harder under modern labor regimes. Many lands that had belonged to their communities were taken over for coffee and other crops. Taxes levied on their wages and purchases wiped out any chance that they might save money. The government, meanwhile, did not spend money on such things as education, housing, health, or literacy. The Amerindian majority remained largely outside the system of rewards (but not of punishments), alienated from the so-called modern sector in the cities and ports.

Estrada kept up a fiction of democratic procedures. He had himself "re-elected" several times. He also insisted on defending his nation's sovereignty by opposing U.S. pressure to declare war on Germany in the First World War. Eventually, though, he did so and then expropriated German-owned property, including the electric power system and dozens of major coffee plantations.

Estrada was finally overthrown in 1920 by his army, backed by an alliance of neighboring countries with the approval of the United States. U.S. displeasure with the excesses of Estrada's dictatorship certainly proved influential in his removal. Many features of today's Guatemala may be traced back to the Estrada era: transport grids, cities, plantations, and wealthy families. Likewise, many of Guatemala's problems also date back to the Estrada era: hostility and disaffection of the Amerindian masses, inadequate government services, a polarized society, illiteracy, and a highly unequal distribution of income. Yet, Estrada was not alone in following what he believed to be the path to progress. Most other dictators did virtually the same thing.

García Menocal of Cuba

Cuba offers variations on the theme of the Caribbean dictators. Mario García Menocal (1913–1921) and Gerardo Machado (1925–1933) both resembled Estrada Cabrera in many ways, yet they governed a country more heavily penetrated by

President García Menocal was photographed on the deck of one of the many cruise ships that visited Havana harbor.

foreign capital and very closely monitored by the U.S. government. Some background on Cuban independence is necessary before exploring their regimes.

Chapter Nine described how the United States declared war on Spain in order to end the Cuban civil strife and free the island from colonial oppression. Other Spanish islands—the Philippines, Guam, and Puerto Rico—were taken as spoils of war and became part of the emerging U.S. empire. Cuba, however, presented a dilemma to U.S. policy-makers. They had intervened in Cuba in the name of freedom, yet they doubted that the Cubans could immediately become self-governing. Moreover, some U.S. leaders had long coveted Cuba as a territory for economic, strategic, and political benefits. Now that they had it, some reasoned, why give it up?

For two years the U.S. Army administered Cuba as occupied territory; it managed to clean up corruption, restore economic activity, and initiate the first successful campaign against yellow fever and malaria. Meanwhile, Cuban representatives debated a constitution and elected officials in expectation of becoming a sovereign country. Yet, self-government would not come that easily.

Eventually the U.S. Congress reached a compromise that was embodied in the infamous Platt Amendment, which was a rider to the military appropriations bill of 1901. This amendment determined that the following year Cuba would become independent, but would remain under the tutelage of the United States. The latter retained certain rights, including:

- intervention to preserve law and order and to guarantee Cuban independence;
- free use of naval bases that the United States might choose (Guantánamo was the choice);
- veto of any treaties or foreign loans that might compromise Cuban sovereignty or U.S. security.

The Platt Amendment, rescinded in 1934, limited Cuban independence and reminded observers of the ultimate U.S. authority in the region. It also served as a model for U.S. rights in Panama under the 1903 treaty, as will be discussed in Chapter Fourteen.

Cuba, then, emerged from Spanish colonial rule only to fall under the supposedly benign supervision of the United States. The arrangement proved awkward and unpopular in both the United States and Cuba. Not only did it prevent full exercise of sovereign powers by Cuba's leaders, but also it made it possible to blame the United States for Cuba's failure to achieve stable government. Governments rose and fell, and marines landed and departed, in a desultory parade of humiliation. The dictatorship of Mario García Menocal seemed at first to break this pattern.

Menocal had fought heroically as a commander in the independence war and later served as police chief of Havana. He had also earned a fortune and valuable business experience by managing several U.S. firms. A Conservative, he favored strong government, restricted suffrage, balanced budgets, and pro-business policies. He won election fairly in 1912, and when inaugurated the following year, he set about trying to restore the economy and the administration.

Menocal attempted to enact his campaign promises, but corruption in his party and government soon overwhelmed his good intentions. Money flowed into Cuba, especially after the First World War broke out in Europe, and greed and personal ambition gripped his associates and relatives in office. Many former supporters (but not the U.S. government) gradually withdrew their approval, and it appeared that his party would lose the 1916 election. Menocal decided to run again, however, and he used the considerable powers at his disposal to rig the results in his favor. His opponents protested and eventually revolted, but Menocal carried the day, in part because the United States did not wish further instability as it prepared to enter the war in 1917. Menocal won his second term with fraud and force of arms.

The usual suppression of protest following the fraud was unnecessary, because most people were distracted by a stupendous economic boom—called the "Dance of the Millions"—caused by immensely profitable sugar sales to the Allied countries during the final years of the war. More sugar lands were planted, mills installed, railroads built, ships commissioned, and workers imported than during any time in the past. The corruption and inefficiency of the government did not seem to matter.

Gradually Cuba developed an addiction to sugar earnings that could be satisfied only by even greater exports to the industrial countries. In the 1920s Cuba's relations with its richer customers epitomized the condition of dependency, or heavy reliance on wealthy countries to supply technology, machinery, capital, marketing services, and consumer goods. Cubans did only a few things on their own: cut and mill cane, refine the sugar, and load the ships. And, of course, spend the profits. Dependency robbed Cuba of its sovereignty just as surely as did the foreign troops stationed on its shores.

Dependency brought ever-greater concentration of mill ownership and operations in foreign hands. Small- and medium-sized plantations were gobbled up by huge mill complexes, called *centrales,* mostly owned by U.S. corporations. Workers and even former operators found themselves permanently separated from capital ownership and forced to labor for others. One writer argued that the entire island had become proletarianized, citing Karl Marx's analysis of the conversion of craftsmen and tradesmen into a proletariat when they lost ownership of their tools.

Politics in the 1920s drifted because most major decisions were dictated by the sugar barons and managers. Menocal did not run for a third term in 1920, perhaps so that he could enjoy the $40 million that he was rumored to have accumulated. Instead, he sponsored a former rival and rigged elections so that he won. In return, Menocal's successor did nothing to disturb his golden retirement.

U.S. supervision of Cuban politics relaxed in the 1920s, as part of a general retreat from imperial ventures in the Caribbean. The last marines stationed in Cuba withdrew to the Guantánamo base in 1922. The Cuban government, meanwhile, became even more corrupt and tyrannical. Menocal decided to run again in 1924 on the Conservative ticket, but he was defeated in a genuine public rebuke of his previous record.

Suppression of the *Partido Independiente de Color* in 1912

In 1908 Afro-Cubans, including many veterans of the struggle for independence, organized the *Partido Independiente de Color* (Independent Party of Color) to defend their interests, gain jobs and pensions from the government, and combat racism. They came from many walks of life but were mostly employed and owned property. Among other demands, they petitioned for clean government, better working conditions, and free higher education. Below the surface, however, they fought against discriminatory treatment by government officials.

The government tolerated the party for a time, but in 1911 the president passed a law barring racially based parties, aimed at outlawing the Independent Party.

In mid-1912 leaders of the banned party organized a revolt in the eastern end of the island, where most lived. They hoped to force the government to compromise. Instead, the president ordered the army to attack without mercy. Over the next several months, thousands of Afro-Cubans were killed in the fighting, a stark message to non-whites.

Gerardo Machado

Cuba's next president, Gerardo Machado, at first seemed to defy categorization as a Caribbean dictator. He came from a modest family in the provinces and had worked his way up with little formal education or foreign experience. Though a military officer, he had won his commission fighting for independence. Later, Machado proved to be an effective administrator in several high public offices. He won the 1924 election fairly and promised a good, honest, efficient administration. And indeed the solid, reliable, efficient Machado prevailed during his first administration (1925–1929).

Machado not only constructed new railroads but also made them run on time. An indefatigable builder, he laid out highways, parks, utilities, public buildings, ports, and other public works. Most of them were financed with easy bond money from Wall Street, authorized by an approving U.S. State Department. Progress also required training, so Machado expended much effort on schools, from elementary to university levels. He resisted challenges to his authority, however, and dealt harshly with unrest among laborers, students, and the opposition. In these respects, he resembled a number of other widely admired political leaders of the 1920s: Benito Mussolini of Italy, Carlos Ibáñez of Chile, and Augusto Leguía of Peru, for example.

As for Machado's economic policies, they departed little from the past. American capital continued to flow in, further displacing Cuban businesses and assembling ever-larger corporations for profit. Sugar was king, as it had been throughout the nineteenth century.

Signs of the typical dictator were present in Machado's career, however, and would be revealed more fully after his unopposed reelection in 1929. Machado had amassed considerable wealth throughout his career, and he easily used force to deal with the opposition. He had learned that any successful president of Cuba must get along with Washington and Wall Street. So he spoke passable English and conducted himself with dignity and charm when around the gringos. And most important, when seriously challenged, Machado would lash out at opponents with the powerful army he had assembled. Well-armed and loyal, the army was his ultimate guarantor of power.

The year 1929 proved fateful for Cuba, as it did for so many other countries. Machado was reelected virtually unopposed, and an amended constitution gave him a six-year term with more power than ever. As chief of both the major parties, he monopolized politics and grew even less tolerant of criticism. He began to imagine himself a benevolent and perpetual ruler of Cuba. Most Americans thought that would be best for Cuba, although the U.S. ambassador deplored Machado's autocratic tendencies.

In October 1929, however, the stock market crash sent sugar prices plunging to only a tenth of their previous levels, halved tax revenues, dried up bond money, and ended the prosperity that Cuba had enjoyed. When 1930 and 1931 proved even harder financially, Machado faced emboldened dissenters and dealt with them harshly. He invoked emergency powers to justify censorship, riot control, propaganda, school closures, exiles, and murders. The despot ceased to be benevolent.

Yet, the more violence he unleashed, the less control Machado had over politics. The heightened suppression led to conspiracies against Machado, including a network of secret cells called the "ABC movement." As the Depression worsened, Cuba drifted toward civil war.

Non-intervention Policy in the 1920s

Cuban politicians and intellectuals were not the only ones concerned about the perilous developments in Havana. The U.S. ambassador and the business community believed that the island could go up in flames if the violence escalated. By then, however, a subtle but profound change had taken place in U.S. policy toward the Caribbean region and its dictators. They would no longer enjoy unquestioned support from Washington merely because they protected U.S. property. The new approach—eventually called the "Good Neighbor" or non-intervention policy—had in fact been evolving for several years in the State Department and White House. Among other things, it meant that the United States would abandon Machado and broker a transition to a new government.

The instability that erupted in Cuba in the early 1930s had already become widespread in other Caribbean nations during the 1920s. Dictator challenged dictator, and the ensuing bloodshed affected all persons, including U.S. residents. The usual gunboat patrols in the region did not always intimidate revolutionists. On numerous occasions U.S. Marines had to be landed to settle disputes and keep the peace. Such measures were only temporary, however, and often led to deep anti-American sentiments. By the same token, permanent mechanisms to solve these problems without U.S. intervention, such as the World Court in the Hague and the Central American Court of Justice, failed utterly.

The mid-1920s shift in U.S. policy came about largely due to the influence of Henry L. Stimson, secretary of state under President Herbert Hoover (1929–1933). In 1927 Stimson had served as mediator in Nicaragua. A large contingent of marines had been sent to the country the year before, and Stimson hoped to find a way to remove it without becoming mired in a Nicaraguan civil war. Continual deployment of U.S. forces in Central America and the Caribbean seemed to do more harm than good. Nicaragua, it turned out, was the test case that was soon replicated in the Dominican Republic, Haiti, Panama, and Cuba.

The basic scenario for withdrawal from Nicaragua was simple. A marine contingent was landed to protect a cooperative government. Meanwhile, the local army, often politicized, demoralized, and poorly armed, would be fashioned into a professional police force or national guard that could keep the peace and allow the marines to withdraw. The marines, then, trained their own replacements. The level of armament and training that the marines had in mind was that of a U.S. National Guard unit as deployed during World War I. Thus, the Central American constabulary force was usually called the *guardia nacional,* and its leader a *comandante.* After the *guardia* demonstrated the capacity to keep order, the marines departed.

An important enunciation of the evolving new policy came in 1928, when the State Department circulated a brief written by its legal counsel, Reuben Clarke. Known as the Clarke Memorandum, the brief argued that the United States should

American public sentiment against U.S. imperialism in Nicaragua—reflected in this 1928 photo—helped bring a shift to non-intervention policies.

not automatically send troops into civil conflicts in Latin America, even when U.S. citizens and property were endangered. The tendency to do so, under the authority of the 1904 Roosevelt Corollary, actually violated a much older policy toward Latin America—the 1823 Monroe Doctrine. Monroe had promised U.S. opposition to foreign interference only. U.S. intervention following the Roosevelt Corollary was entirely new and counterproductive because it often destabilized the republics and invited further intervention. Clarke's message was clear: The United States should refrain from landing forces in the region unless a real extra-hemispheric threat arose, as was Monroe's original intent.

The full meaning and ramifications of the new policy emerged in the years following the Great Depression, but events in Central America and Cuba certainly convinced U.S. decision-makers that new approaches were called for.

Conclusions and Issues

Caribbean dictators and U.S. political supervision seemed to go together in the early years of this century. Strong-willed and crude, yet effective, the dictators governed their new nations like despots. They took advantage of high prices for their countries' exports and amassed personal fortunes. Their cronies, often relatives and fellow military officers, likewise profited greatly from the bounty of the new economic ventures. The dictators demanded obedience, adulation, and loyalty from their citizens. Those who refused could expect persecution at the hands of government officials and the dictators' thugs. The Mexican dictator Porfirio Díaz once enunciated a policy that his Caribbean basin successors certainly followed: *pan y palo* ("bread for my friends and the stick for my enemies."). Díaz put it differently another time: "for my friends, everything; for my enemies, justice [i.e., criminal persecution]." These men used crude but effective means to keep their people in line.

U.S. officials sometimes decried brutality in neighboring countries, yet they seldom took action against abusive dictators. Instead, compelling U.S. interests—security, profitable investment climate, and international cooperation—actually seemed better served by stable, friendly autocrats. If these regimes could appear law-abiding and democratic, all the better. Many U.S. observers condescendingly believed that Latins were incapable of orderly republican government anyway. They hoped, however, that U.S. guidance and example might someday help to overcome this basic incompetence.

Theodore Roosevelt put things even more bluntly in his 1904 corollary to the Monroe Doctrine: If the Latin Americans could not abide by his rules of conduct, they could expect a reprimanding visit and perhaps a military occupation to boot. Only during the 1920s did Washington policy-makers recognize that they could not enforce, teach, or otherwise induce behaviors that they wished to encourage. Rather, the frequent U.S. invasions and disciplinary operations often backfired, creating more instability and undermining the very interests that drove U.S. diplomacy. Stimson and Reuben Clarke pointed toward a new acceptance of governments as they existed in the region. Events in Mexico, Brazil, Panama, and other places eventually vindicated analyses by the proponents of non-intervention.

Discussion Questions:

1. How did the leaders of the Central American and Caribbean nations react to U.S. imposition during the imperialist era? Were their reactions effective?

2. What did the dictators have in common, in terms of background and style of rule? Compare and contrast them with the nineteenth-century caudillos.

3. Did the non-intervention policy arise out of a better understanding of Latin America by U.S. authorities, or simply from disinterest? What changes in Central American and Caribbean politics might have reinforced the new policy?

Panama, Brazil, and Peru

West Indian Workers on the Panama Canal Project

The Jamaican train engineer eased his locomotive back to hitch onto a string of sixteen dump cars. The sides of the cars bore the letters "ICC"— for "Inter-oceanic Canal Commission." President William H. Taft, who succeeded Theodore Roosevelt, had appointed members of the ICC to oversee the construction work in Panama. But by the middle of his administration he relied increasingly on the chief engineer, George W. Goethals, a colonel in the U.S. Army Corps of Engineers, to make policy decisions.

A deafening crash rang out, as the dump car couplers closed onto one another and locked. The Jamaican set the brake, jumped down, and walked over to the water barrel, where a half-dozen pick-and-shovel men, mostly Barbadians, were resting and drinking from tin cups.

The Jamaican took a long swallow of water, rinsed his mouth, and spat onto the ground. Over the men's heads, huge cranes swung buckets of wet cement that was being poured into frames for the canal lock walls. The Panama Canal had been under construction for six years, and the men now concentrated on the massive works needed to dam the Chagres River and create the three tiers of concrete ship locks at each entrance to the canal.

"Hey, mon," the Jamaican said to the Barbadians, "You heah wha'de boss-man, Higgins, say? He say de white man's union gon' kick us offa dese train jobs, you believe dat?"

"Yeah, a heah dat dey movin' all de skill men down t'ree grades and takin' 'em offa dat machin'ry," answered one of the Barbadians. "S'posed to be due to de labor rules dem AFL guys come down heah wifd. But a's think is to keep us black mans on low pay so the white 'Mericans can have de jobs wifd big dollah."

"For sure dis job don' pay big money, it jus' pay wha' it do drivin' train back home fo' de sugah mill," said the Jamaican.

"Yeah, but all a dat be changin' when we finish dis canal—dey bringin' in all 'Mericans for de good jobs and sen' us back home, to de islans."

"It ain' jus' dey treat we colored man dey treat like southern niggers! You see what dey doin' to de Panama president?" said another Barbadian. "He too dark for de 'Mericans so dey boot him outa dere. He name Mendoza, and Colonel Goethals, he jus' up and fire he ass. Mon, dese 'Mericans don' like us colored folk!"

A whistle blew on one of the trestles spanning the work, and the men picked up their tools and turned toward their excavation site. Just then an explosion rocked the ground, and dynamite blew hundreds of tons of rock and dirt off a nearby hillside. Dust filled the air, and gravel fell near the men.

An American supervisor, James Bradley from Pittsburgh, came up to the workmen and asked gruffly why they weren't working.

A Barbadian answered, "We jus' tek a minute, boss, to get a drink-a watah. We goin' to hit dem rocks again, yess! Hard." The others nodded in agreement and then picked up their tools.

"Well, I better not see you lazy bastards resting again, or I'll dock your pay an hour," said Bradley. "We''ve got a damn canal to build here, and it ain't gonna dig itself! I knew we shoulda brought in Chinese coolies—they work a lot harder'n you niggers, and they eat less."

The West Indians walked off to the slope where they were cutting a terrace to relocate the dump-train tracks. They spoke in low voices and looked over their shoulders at Bradley.

The Jamaican, meanwhile, climbed into his locomotive. He released the brake and gave it forward throttle, easing the train toward the Gatun Dam fill track, where he would dump his load. Little by little the dam was filling the gap left by diverting the Chagres River, and soon they would have it finished. When it was, the Jamaican knew, all the little towns and farms in the Chagres valley would be flooded to make way for the eighty-five-foot-high lake that would allow ships to pass from one ocean to another. It was a clever plan, the Jamaican thought, something that only canal builders from the United States might dream up.

The 1914 completion of the Panama Canal, one of the great engineering feats of the twentieth century, required over a hundred thousand men laboring for a decade. Most workers came from the British colonies in the West Indies, especially Barbados and Jamaica. Tens of thousands more came from the French, Dutch, and U.S. islands. The islanders made up a human tidal wave that swept over Central America, first in Panama and later in neighboring countries.

The canal construction left a legacy of hatred among Panamanians, who resented not being able to profit from the canal's operation. It also left an underemployed workforce in Panama, made up largely of black, English-speaking, Protestant West Indians. Long ostracized but eventually accepted, the West Indians in Panama formed a tight-knit local community and fought for secure lives. Still, they suffered the same kind of discrimination as did blacks throughout the Americas.

After three generations, one of the West Indian descendants managed to run in the presidential election of 1994. Singer and actor Ruben Blades, who spent most of his career in the United States, founded his own party, Papa Egoró, and ran a creditable campaign. He came in third, but his candidacy marked a breakthrough for Panamanians of West Indian descent.

Panama, Brazil, and Peru

While most of southern South America developed under a new style of mass politics, and most Caribbean basin countries modernized under dictatorships, Panama, Brazil, and Peru faced special challenges. These dramatic episodes warrant closer attention as critical moments in national consolidation.

The antecedents of one of these episodes—the Panama Canal construction—saw a French company formed by Ferdinand de Lesseps fail in its attempt to build a canal during the 1880s. The French company managed to sell its canal rights to the United States in 1903 at the same time that Panamanians revolted and declared their independence from Colombia. Deeply implicated in this revolt, the United States quickly signed a treaty giving it quasi-sovereign rights to build and operate a ship canal. Within months, the United States exercised dominion over the Isthmus and built a canal that even today serves as a major maritime facility.

Panamanian leaders responded to U.S. impositions by demanding larger shares of the jobs, revenues, and business generated by the canal. The United States refused to share the spoils for many decades. Thus, Panama's history for much of the twentieth century revolved around diplomatic struggles with the Colossus of the North. Eventually, however, the two countries negotiated and signed a treaty that stipulated that Panama would receive the canal and all of its accouterments by the end of 1999.

Brazil marched to another drummer in the first quarter of the twentieth century, a period known as the Old Republic. Not dictatorial, nor populistic, nor nationalistic, Brazil's political system was a peculiar mix of patriarchal control at the regional level and a detached, ineffectual federal government based in Rio de Janeiro. Although the Old Republic is often portrayed as a hiatus during which little of importance occurred, in fact much of modern Brazil was forged during these years.

Finally, in the early twentieth century Peru managed to shrug off the defeatism and failure of the previous century and moved toward a more national form of governance. Peru's segmented population, fragmented geography, and divided elite could not form a genuine nation-state. Yet, the foundations were laid, especially during the eleven-year rule (*oncenio*) of President Augusto Leguía in the 1920s. The central government made full economic use of high world prices for Peru's resources but failed to address the poverty and oppression of the masses. Instead, popular protests and discontent drew an extraordinary young leader, Víctor Raúl Haya de la Torre, into the limelight. Haya introduced mass campaigning and a progressive social agenda into politics. Although he would never become president, his long career permanently changed the conduct of politics in Peru.

Panama and the Canal

Events in the early 1900s ruptured the usually good relations between Colombia and the United States. For one thing, Colombia's War of a Thousand Days disrupted rail traffic across Panama and forced several U.S. troop landings to keep the peace. The U.S. Navy kept part of its fleet in the vicinity to prevent depredations against the Panama Railroad. That railroad firm was operated by the New York corporation that had built it in 1850–1855, but it was owned by the New French Canal Company, which emerged from receivership in 1894. The Colombian civil war finally ended in 1902, when the last Liberal general gave in to U.S. pressure and signed an armistice aboard the U.S.S. *Wisconsin.* Although Liberals believed that they had been robbed of victory by a partisan United States, both Liberals and Conservatives were exhausted by three years of warfare.

Rights to a canal crossing in Panama also bedeviled relations between Colombia and the United States. By 1900 the U.S. Congress had decided to build a transisthmian canal, favoring a route across Nicaragua. But the accession of Teddy Roosevelt to the presidency in 1901 changed that. He and his party favored the Panama route chosen by the French, as long as rights could be secured for a reasonable fee. His secretary of state negotiated a treaty to that effect with the Colombian minister in Washington. But there was little sentiment in Bogotá to accept the rather miserly terms offered by the Americans.

When the Colombian Senate rejected the draft treaty in early 1903, Panamanian leaders and Roosevelt alike decided on an alternative path. If Panamanians declared independence, they could write and approve a treaty without Colombia. The Panamanians conspired to revolt, helped by the railroad and French canal managers, and Roosevelt dispatched warships to both coasts to protect the fledgling nation. Independence came virtually as planned, on November 3, 1903, and within days the United States and other powers recognized Panama as sovereign. No one doubted that Panamanian aspirations and U.S. canal designs had coincided deliberately. Meanwhile, Colombians bitterly accepted the loss of their wayward province and future revenues that the canal would have provided.

In the thick of the plotting, Panamanians named a French engineer, Philippe Bunau-Varilla, as minister plenipotentiary in Washington. Bunau-Varilla had given Panama money, intelligence, and supplies on the condition that he be named Panama's representative to the United States. In the first weeks following independence, Bunau-Varilla huddled with U.S. Secretary of State John Hay and signed a new treaty even more advantageous to the United States than the one rejected by Colombia. The Panamanians were furious and attempted to renege, but they relented when warned that the U.S. warships might turn over Panama to Colombian forces. The 1903 canal treaty was ratified, but it became the original sin in Panama-U.S. relations. It was signed by a Frenchman who felt no loyalty at all to Panama's future, and it gave away virtually all canal rights and revenues to the United States.

After Panama's separation became a fact, two projects went on simultaneously: Panamanians worked to build a nation out of their colonial and provincial heritages, and Americans labored to construct a canal that would move ships between

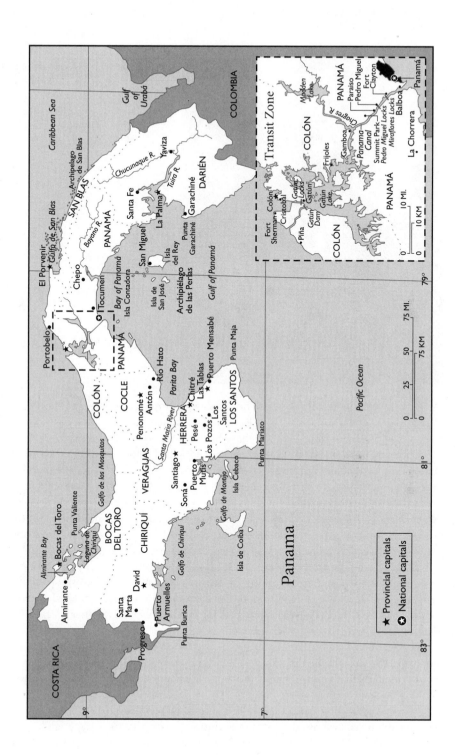

Panama

Provincial capitals ★
National capitals ⊛

COSTA RICA

COLOMBIA

Caribbean Sea

Gulf of Urabá

Pacific Ocean

Transit Zone

Gulf of Panama

Bay of Panamá

Archipiélago de las Perlas

BOCAS DEL TORO

CHIRIQUÍ

VERAGUAS

COCLÉ

COLÓN

PANAMÁ

HERRERA

LOS SANTOS

DARIÉN

SAN BLAS

Almirante Bay

Golfo de los Mosquitos

Golfo de Chiriquí

Golfo de Montijo

Parita Bay

Archipelago de San Blas

Gulf of San Blas

Almirante ★
Bocas del Toro ★
Santa Marta •
David ★
Puerto Armuelles •
Progreso •
Punta Burica
Punta Valiente
Laguna de Chiriquí
Isla de Coiba
Isla Cébaco
Soná •
Santiago ★
Puerto Mutis •
Pesé •
Los Pozos •
Santos •
Los Santos •
Penonomé ★
Antón ★
Río Hato
Chitré ★
Las Tablas ★
Puerto Mensabé
Punta Maja
Punta Mariato
Santa María River
Portobelo ★
El Porvenir ★
Chepo •
Tocumen ⊛
San Miguel •
Isla Contadora
Isla del Rey
Isla de San José
Santa Fe •
La Palma ★
Punta Garachiné
Garachiné •
Taviza
Tuira R.
Chucunaque R.
Bayano R.

Transit Zone inset

Fort Sherman
Piña
Gatún Dam
Gatún Locks
Gatún Lake
Cristóbal
Colón
Frijoles
Gamboa
Chagres R.
Madden Lake
Paraíso
Pedro Miguel
Fort Clayton
Panamá
Summit Park
Panama Canal
Pedro Miguel Locks
Miraflores Locks
Balboa
La Chorrera

COLÓN
PANAMÁ

0   10 KM
0   10 MI.

0   25   50   75 KM
0   75 MI.

9°   81°   79°
7°
83°

President Theodore Roosevelt took great pride in having started work on the Panama Canal. This photo captured him at the controls of a giant Bucyrus steam shovel used to dig the canal.

the Atlantic and the Pacific oceans. The canal was completed in 1914, and has been in continuous operation since 1919. Panamanians managed to create a genuine nation by the 1950s, but since then they have had to refashion it several times.

The canal was a marvel of American engineering and helped to project the United States into global affairs on the eve of World War I. Three sets of locks at either end raised ships to an eighty-five-foot-high artificial lake that, when connected to a dredged canal, made it possible for ships to steam from one ocean to the other. Water power operated the locks by gravity flow, so that little energy was needed to run the canal. Ships using it saved thousands of miles and weeks at sea. It was the largest and costliest construction project ever undertaken by a government up to that time.

After the canal began operating in 1914, the U.S. government set up an efficient community in the Canal Zone (a fifty-by-ten-mile enclave) to administer it. Panamanians were largely excluded and received few of the canal's benefits. In fact, Panama had two parallel governments: one for the republic and another for the U.S. zone. No one doubted which was more powerful.

For the next twenty years or so the United States meddled in Panamanian affairs regularly, usually in the name of building and running the canal efficiently. Among the most damaging affronts to Panamanian sovereignty was the 1904 dissolution of its small army, which was replaced by a national police. Some years later, U.S. Marines even confiscated high-caliber rifles used by the police.

Panamanians swallowed their disappointment with the 1903 treaty and organized their affairs as quickly as possible. They wrote a constitution in 1904 and held elections in alternate years. They adopted a very controversial article, Number 136, giving the United States virtually the same rights that the Platt Amendment gave it in Cuba. Because the rights were already implied or spelled out in the 1903 treaty, it was largely redundant.

The United States exercised treaty authority to build, operate, maintain, and protect the canal and to import any people or machinery necessary for those tasks. The United States could take over any lands or waters deemed necessary for the canal, in addition to the five hundred-square-mile zone. The United States could police and administer sanitation in the terminal cities of Panama and Colón. And the right of military intervention meant that Panama could not adopt any policies deemed threatening to U.S. interests. Panama was not exactly a colony, but neither was it entirely independent. Perhaps "protectorate" is the best term.

Meanwhile, Conservatives, who had spearheaded the independence movement, managed to win the first elections, using government favors and police interference. In 1908 and 1910 the U.S. government stepped in and supervised elections, giving the Liberals a chance to win but also creating a dependence on outside arbitration. The shortcomings of U.S. mediation became clear in 1910, when the incumbent president died, and U.S. authorities objected to the succession of the vice president. The latter, though an able and popular figure, was dark-skinned and

Workmen took their breaks on the massive locks of the Panama Canal.

independent-minded. The American minister convinced him to step down. From then on, the Panamanian elite usually nominated only white candidates from well-to-do families. Candidates for presidents usually spoke English and had studied in the United States. Indeed, one president claimed that Washington was the stage upon which future presidents of Panama rehearsed.

U.S. Canal Chief in Panama Barred Panamanian from Presidency Because of his Color in 1910

Long-time British Minister in Panama, Claude Mallet, reported to the Foreign Office that the U.S. government had blocked the succession of second Vice President Carlos Alberto Mendoza to the presidency:

"It is really farcical to talk of Panama as an independent state. It is really simply an annex of the Canal Zone. . . . I am in a position to state positively that the attitude in Washington [against Mendoza's becoming president] was taken entirely on the initiative and recommendation of [Canal Chief] Colonel Goethals, who is prejudiced against Señor Mendoza on account of his color."

National consolidation began in earnest in the early 1910s. A Liberal, Belisario Porras, won the 1912 election and gave the country stability and a constructive administration. Porras had apprenticed in politics at an early age and gained much experience—for example, he studied law in Paris, worked for the French canal company, and commanded a Liberal army during the War of a Thousand Days.

In exile when the independence movement broke out, Porras criticized the leaders for being subservient to the United States and especially for approving the 1903 treaty. In retaliation, the new government revoked his citizenship to block him from high political office. The measure did not last for long because Porras's strengths and the Liberals' numerical superiority endowed him with power. The Liberals remained in control for nearly twenty years, ten of them under Porras's leadership.

Porras made his peace with the American canal authorities and hosted an international exposition in 1915 to celebrate the completion of the canal. Panama, after all, depended heavily on employment and business generated by the canal's operation. Hordes of laborers and clerks flowed into the zone each morning to work on the canal. Porras also set out to equip the country with institutions and infrastructure that had been neglected by the Colombians. He constructed or authorized the construction of hospitals, schools, roads, government offices, railroads, plantations, factories, and ports. Business prospered in the two cities that paralleled the Canal Zone: Panama City and Colón.

Immigrants flocked in from all over the world looking for work and opportunities to get rich. By the end of World War I Panama had become a far more urban, cosmopolitan, trade-oriented nation than ever before. West Indian blacks from Jamaica, Barbados, and other Caribbean islands were the most numerous. Although they suffered much discrimination, they stayed and forged a cohesive subculture in

Panama. The small Jewish community there swelled during the construction years and continued to receive newcomers in subsequent decades. Large numbers of Europeans, Asians, Middle Easterners, South and Central Americans, and, of course, gringos made their homes in Panama. They built their churches, schools, businesses, lodges, and other organizations, creating a kaleidoscopic society in the tropical isthmus. For the most part, they got along well, especially when business was good.

World War I led U.S. authorities to expand their military presence in Panama. They argued that submarine activity in the Caribbean and political instability in Central America made military bases in Panama necessary. They interpreted the 1903 treaty as authorizing conversion of the Canal Zone into a military fortress. The U.S. Army Corps of Engineers, which had taken responsibility during construction, continued to manage the canal itself, but the War Department set up a separate command in Panama that gradually eclipsed the canal itself in importance. Then, during and after World War II, the U.S. Navy and Air Force set up more bases in the Canal Zone, joined by the several intelligence agencies. Panamanians as well as other Latin Americans had little choice in the matter.

Porras was a strong-willed autocrat who managed the country efficiently. He did not, however, integrate many nonelite figures into his circle of power. In the 1920s, many other groups emerged to seek their fortunes in the political arena. Occasionally Porras had to call in U.S. troops to keep order, because his own police were too weak. Ethnic tensions also broke out, often sparked by natives resentful of the many outsiders flooding the country.

Unable to succeed himself in the presidency in 1924, Porras selected Rodolfo Chiari, a sugar baron and grandson of an immigrant, to take over the government. A quiet man, Chiari was thought to be weak and manipulable. He turned out to be his own man, however, and quickly gained control over the Liberal Party. The balanced approach of the Porras years ended, and an even more pro-business atmosphere prevailed in Panama's presidential palace.

Of the many dissident groups that arose in the 1920s, one would prove fateful: the secret society called "Common Action." Made up of middle-class professionals, students, writers, and aspiring politicians, this group sought to strengthen nationalistic feeling in the country and to lessen the influence of the United States. It denounced concessions of new lands, questioned U.S. treaty rights, clamored for immigration controls, and advocated a more forceful administration of the country. It claimed that Panama was merely a self-governing protectorate of the United States. Among other victories, the group claimed to have blocked congressional ratification of a new commercial treaty with the United States in 1926. The accession to power of Common Action leaders in the early 1930s decisively affected Panama's quest for national status.

Brazil's Old Republic

Brazil's 1890s elite (minus the aristocratic crowd that fell from power when the empire was overthrown) attempted to give the country a modern system of government that would also allow maximum freedom for individuals and businessmen.

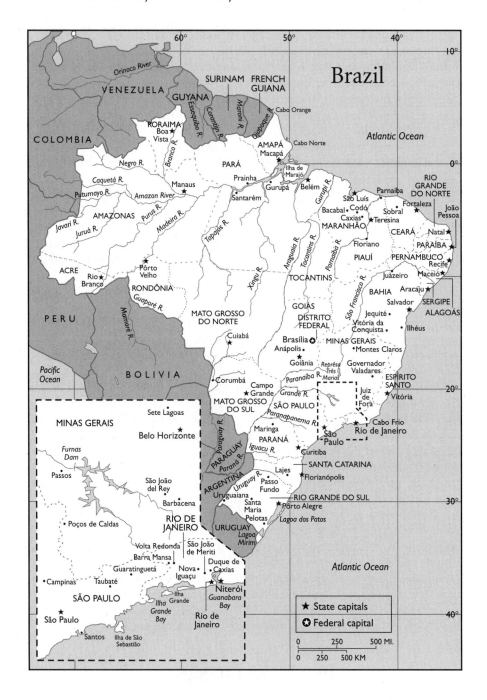

The 1891 Constitution looked very much like that of the United States, with a four-year presidential term, a bicameral legislature, states' rights, and a federal judiciary. However, the Constitution weakened central government in Rio de Janeiro in several ways when compared to Washington. The president could not be reelected; states could levy export and interstate taxes and organize military forces; and states conducted all elections. On paper, Brazil adopted an advanced and efficient federal model, but it was never fully implemented.

In a short time, this ideal system was replaced with a home-grown arrangement called the "politics of the governors." Because the governors of the largest and wealthiest states were not restricted in their terms, revenues, and police powers, they became veritable dictators in their states. São Paulo state led the way, followed by Minas Gerais, Rio Grande do Sul, Rio de Janeiro, and Bahia. Other state governors played along with the powerful first team. The governors chose presidential successors and elected them through manipulation of state voting. If they disagreed the governors sent troops out to skirmish until a decision was reached. Even the federal Congress came under the sway of the powerful governors. Thus, Brazil's government was hyper-federalist during the Old Republic (1889–1930).

São Paulo and Minas Gerais states, in particular, derived enough money from coffee export taxes to rival the federal government. For a time they actually agreed to alternate native sons in the presidency, an arrangement called *café com leite,* (coffee and milk), symbolic of the two states' economic strengths. So, despite the democratic and federal character of the Constitution, the reality of politics rested firmly on money and military clout manipulated by the states.

At the regional and local levels, landowners and political bosses ruled like Oriental despots. Influential leaders were called *Coronéis,* or (colonels), after a system of national guard commissions held over from the nineteenth century. In fact, local family rule was too deep-seated to be changed by mere constitutional provisions. *Coronéis* used a great deal of violence, abuse, and intimidation to preserve their power, leading to frequent outbreaks of fighting in rural areas. Banditry and gun fighting were endemic throughout Brazil until the 1940s.

The central government was led by weak presidents whose authority extended little beyond the capital city itself. Occasionally they gave subsidies to the states for railroads, immigrant labor recruitment, and economic development, but the states themselves raised money from overseas banks. One remarkable subsidy, however, was begun by the states and later assumed by the federal government to support commodities prices: coffee valorization.

In 1906 a bumper crop of coffee threatened to drive down prices to ruinous levels. The states of São Paulo, Minas Gerais, and Rio de Janeiro vowed to buy up excess stocks to prevent a disastrous glut on the international market, but they could not convince the president to finance the stockpiling scheme. Ultimately, São Paulo, with the help of a shrewd broker in New York, managed to buy nearly half the 1906–1907 crop and withhold it, thereby averting a major drop in prices. In later years the coffee was gradually released in world markets without distorting prices. The federal government soon saw the benefit of the deal and assumed responsibility for buying up occasional surpluses. To this day, a federal agency buys and markets coffee in order to maximize foreign earnings.

The reluctant intervention of the government into the coffee industry reflected a retreat from the ideal of laissez-faire economics that had inspired the founders of the Old Republic. Little by little, Congress voted more money for transportation, communications, and banking. Because of this, the country's economy grew rapidly, and some cities displayed signs of industrial progress. Factories, modern docks, sky-scrapers, streetcars, utility systems, and public buildings sprang up in the early twentieth century. Behind the façade of commodities export prosperity, a solid foundation of industry was laid. By the early 1930s a half-dozen Brazilian cities were highly industrialized and provided for most domestic consumption.

Urban renewal and beautification transformed Rio de Janeiro, São Paulo, and other capitals into attractive places to live. Brazil's culture, an exotic blend of African, Amerindian, and Portuguese elements, became more widely known. Movies shot in Rio glamorized its beaches, and the samba invaded dance halls throughout the western world. Rio's pre-Lenten Carnival, in particular, became a symbol of revelry that rivaled New Orleans's Mardis Gras. Tourism further publi-cized Brazil's positive aspects.

The nagging perception of Brazil's's racial and cultural backwardness (as evinced in da Cunha's *Rebellion in the Backlands,* discussed in Chapter Eight) seemed to evaporate with signs of urban progress. Universities opened, and a num-ber of states upgraded their education systems. European immigrants flooded the cities of the Southeast, tending to "whiten" Brazil's multiracial population. The army justified universal military service as a way to raise levels of literacy, hygiene, physical fitness, and nutrition among the masses. Brazil seemed on the way to be-coming Europeanized and modern, like the United States.

Little was done, however, to uplift the nearly one million former slaves or their dependents, who increasingly clustered in the shantytowns and tenement districts of regional and state capitals. And Brazil's huge population of African descent—the largest outside of Africa—suffered systematic disadvantages that constituted an un-spoken form of racial discrimination. Whereas immigrants moved swiftly upward in income and status, Afro-Brazilians remained at the bottom of the socioeconomic ladder. Most also were excluded from higher education, political offices, artistic ca-reers, and business opportunities.

Brazil's native population and tropical forests likewise felt the impact of Euro-pean-style modernization. Coffee planters had already denuded vast regions of the Southeast, and cattle ranches had replaced native forests in central Brazil. The Ama-zon had not suffered major depredations from rubber production only because its gathering depended on native stands of trees. Rubber tappers living in jungle huts daily drained off buckets of latex, which they sent on to Manaus or Belem for pro-cessing and export.

Native peoples of Amazonia were not so fortunate, however, because their labor was required to produce latex. European and American factories, producing electri-cal goods, tires, and rubber articles of all sorts, consumed latex voraciously. Travel-ing merchants and brokers in the Amazon, called *aviadores* (lenders), created a

Brazil's Carnival celebrations, which date back to the eighteenth century, were suppressed as vulgar and dangerous until the 1930s. Since then, however, Rio de Janeiro's samba schools (like the one pictured here) have become a symbol of national culture.

system of exploitation similar to debt peonage in Mexico and Guatemala. In addition, diseases from the outside world caused mini-epidemics among native villagers. And in some regions, such as the Putumayo, outright slavery was reintroduced as a way to gather rubber. Population losses would certainly have been greater except that after 1910 cheaper rubber from Asian plantations drove Amazon rubber almost completely off the market. Manaus's sumptuous opera house, a symbol of the region's once-extravagant wealth, fell into disrepair.

In many ways Brazil's hyper-federal political system failed to govern a country that was undergoing rapid social and economic change. With an impractical constitution and archaic institutions, the government could barely keep pace with the nation's progress, let alone solve its burgeoning problems. By the 1920s the tensions caused by government ineffectiveness erupted into major challenges to the state.

Far and away the biggest challenge was a series of military rebellions called the Tenente Revolts (*tenente* means lieutenant in Portuguese). Civil-military relations had not been smooth since the early days of the Old Republic, and in 1922 several hundred officer cadets seized army installations to demand reforms. Their revolt was put down brutally, and those who survived were jailed or fled into exile. In 1924 the cadets captured the capital of São Paulo and held it for nearly a month to protest their mistreatment and blocked aspirations. When dislodged, they embarked on the Great March through the Brazilian backlands, which eventually covered twenty-four thousand kilometers and lasted over two years. The rebels disbanded in early 1927, but their cry for reforms left a potent impression on educated Brazilians (see Chapter Fifteen).

Other sectors began to organize to change or overthrow the Brazilian government. A small Communist Party, founded in 1922, managed to win some converts among intellectuals and labor leaders in Rio and São Paulo, and elected several representatives to city councils in 1928. Catholic leaders, dismayed at the general decline of religiosity since the separation of Church and state in 1889, sought to resuscitate their moral and civil leadership through political means. And other groups promoted nationalism, improved education, stronger military defense, and better public health. Building a stronger nation preoccupied informed citizens.

A vigorous artistic revival, called *Modernismo,* also arose in the 1920s. Its proponents rejected the romantic and naturalistic aesthetics of Europe and tried to give expression to authentic Brazilian styles in painting, literature, music, sculpture, and even architecture. They chose the unlikely metaphor of cannibalism to convey their desire to eat and digest, not merely to copy, foreign artistic models. Their leading journal, *Antropofagia,* conveyed to readers the latest developments and experiments in modernist art.

The defining moment of the movement came in 1922, when aesthetic rebels convoked the Modern Art Week in São Paulo. There, for several days practitioners of the new styles showed off their paintings, read their writings, and held debates over the future of Brazil's artistic life. It was an artistic declaration of independence. By the 1950s, São Paulo's periodic exhibitions became institutionalized in the *bienal,* a regular event in even-numbered years that alternated with the Venice Biennale.

Visual artists in São Paulo made by far the most striking impressions. Paintings by Anita Malfatti, Vitor Brecheret, and Di Cavalcanti blended European Expressionism and Cubism with scenes from Brazil and nativist themes. Later Cândido Portinari reflected Rio-based visions of the modernist aesthetic, with striking paintings of the *cidade maravilhosa* (the marvelous city), as Rio inhabitants referred to their city. Meanwhile, sculptors wrought work that Brazilianized the latest styles from abroad.

Novels, poems, plays, and musical performances enriched the offerings at São Paulo. Mario de Andrade emerged as something of a poet laureate of the decade. His famous *Macunaíma* became a best-seller when it appeared in 1928. This rambling allegory of the Brazilian Everyman traced the history of the country through the experiences of its anti-hero, Macunaíma. Spiced with irony, wit, folklore, sex, and social criticism, this work strove to define a genuinely national genre. Meanwhile, Heitor Villa-Lobos composed and conducted orchestral pieces that were based on folk music and that used native instruments along with traditional ones. He sought to portray musically the lives of farmers, Amerindians, cowhands, and city dwellers. His lush arrangements evoked the sense of great jungles and savannas stretching across the continent. He remains Brazil's best-known composer of all times.

Accompanying these currents of artistic, intellectual, and political renewal came more forceful expressions of labor and peasant dissent. Unions, often under the leadership of anarchists and syndicalists, formed federations and called numerous general strikes between 1917 and 1919. Although these failed for the most part, and strike activity diminished in the 1920s, workers had taken important steps by asserting their rights. Politicians increasingly sought to address labor rights and to win workers' votes. By the late 1920s a kind of proto-populism arose in Rio de Janeiro to push for action. By then many citizens believed that the government needed to address workers' rights and union representation, the so-called social question.

Brazil's peasants, on the other hand, had no clear means of organizing to improve their miserable lives. *Coronéis* and their henchmen rode close herd over the rural masses, and they could always call in state and federal troops to back them up. Periodically the rural poor would erupt into violent confrontations with local authorities, only to be massacred by troops from the outside. Some of the most famous uprisings were Canudos, the subject of da Cunha's social interpretation; the Contestado, a bloody land and labor dispute in Santa Catarina; and the Muckers, a rebellious quasi-religious community in Rio Grande do Sul.

In addition, some regions fell under the grip of bandit gangs, like those of Lampião and Antônio Silvino. These two gang leaders operated in arid northeastern Brazil, away from population centers and beyond the reach of justice. For years they lived off the poor people and towns of the interior. Originally gunmen recruited by the great landowners, these two became freelance criminals. They were finally hunted down and eliminated in the 1930s.

In the end, the Old Republic was brought down not by the *tenentes* or the laborers or the peasants or the communists or any other disgruntled sector of Brazilian society. Instead, it was brought down by a military revolt in the states of Rio Grande do Sul and Minas Gerais, which rose up against the federal government and the state of São Paulo.

According to the *café com leite* alternation agreement, the governor of Minas Gerais should have been the sole candidate in 1930. The president reneged, however, and put his hand-picked successor, the governor of São Paulo, up for election. The governor of Minas Gerais, in turn, nominated his counterpart from Rio Grande do Sul, a little-known lawyer named Getúlio Vargas. He hoped to intimidate the president and force a compromise. The president stood firm and rigged the election in his candidate's favor. In mid-1930 the losers decided to mount a revolt to overthrow the government. They acted in October, and after several weeks the army high command stepped in. Fearing a bloodbath, the generals decided to remove the sitting president and usher in a rebel government, headed by Vargas. The rebels took over in October 1930, promptly labeling their victory the Revolution of 1930.

The rebels soundly denounced the Old Republican elites for having done too little for the country. Few of the presidents, mostly of European descent, had been memorable. Little social legislation had been written, let alone enacted. The educational system remained in the hands of state and local authorities who, like their counterparts in the empire, did not wish to tax themselves to educate the masses. The coffee protection programs largely defended the profits of planters and exporters in the state of São Paulo. Industry gradually replaced imported goods, but the consumer now paid more for inferior goods.

The Old Republic elite could certainly boast some accomplishments. Theirs had been a time of relative peace and plenty. No foreign wars touched Brazil; the territory had been enlarged by 350,000 square miles without conflict; foreign investments had soared while the public debt remained modest; and they had won new respect for Brazil from foreigners impressed with its cities, resources, and energetic people.

Perhaps the strongest indictment of the Old Republic was that it did not pay attention to electoral politics. Only a tiny fraction of the public voted, and their efforts were usually invalidated by fraud. No loyalty had been generated between an active and supportive electorate and an effective government. As in 1889, the masses stood by idly in 1930 when soldiers overthrew the government. Brazil would not be the same afterward.

The "Social Question" in Getúlio Vargas's 1929 Platform Speech in Rio de Janeiro

We cannot ignore the social question in Brazil, one of the problems that must be taken up seriously by the authorities. The scant social legislation on the books is rarely applied, or is enforced only sporadically. This despite our obligations as signatories to the Versailles Treaty and as a member of the International Labor Organization, whose standards we do not uphold.

If our government's protective tariffs give great profits to industrialists, then we should also give some protection to the workers, providing them with a comfortable and stable existence and help with sickness and old-age benefits.

Women and children working in factories and stores receive special protection in civilized countries, yet such rules are unknown here.

The federal and state governments must coordinate their efforts in order to produce a unified Labor Code. Urban as well as rural workers require legislation covering their labor rights, depending upon local circumstances. The Code should cover education, hygiene, nutrition, housing; protection of women, children, the infirm and the aged; and credit, salaries, and even recreation, such as sports and popular arts.

We should create agrarian and vocational schools, inspect conditions in our factories and mills, clean up swamps, build workers' housing, and enforce laws on vacations, minimum wages, and consumer cooperatives.

In the cities, where a large industrial proletariat exists, the situation can easily be improved. Workers should have access to telephones, electricity, and paved streets.

(*A Revolução Nacional,* 1930)

Peru in the 1920s

Peru's history since independence has been more tumultuous, yet also more fascinating, than that of many other Latin American countries. The nation's trajectory rose and fell abruptly, shaken by heroes and scoundrels, earthquakes, booms and busts, and world events seemingly beyond the Peruvians' control. During the 1920s, however, Peru looked as though it would break out of the pattern and achieve stability and progress. The reasons why it did not are both gripping and suggestive of the causes for long-term volatility in Peru.

One man, Augusto Leguía, gave Peru its facade of solidity and affluence in the 1920s. In most ways an unremarkable politician, Leguía was swept in and out of office in the early twentieth century without making many waves. A leader in the

Civilist Party, he had won election and served most of the 1908–1912 presidential term. Although his party stood for reducing the role of military force in politics, it was often the cause of such force. Leguía was also the beneficiary of a climate of unrest and renovation sweeping the country in the early twentieth century. A middle class had arisen in major cities and worked to modernize the society and gain access to political power. This meant, among other things, recognizing Peru's most downtrodden peoples: the Amerindians and the workers. It also meant adopting new institutional forms, such as the separation of Church and state, which was achieved in the Constitution of 1919. The spirit of the times combined hopeful expectation with a desire for secure leadership. Leguía successfully satisfied both during more than a decade between 1919 and 1930.

As a civilian, Leguía provided stable government punctuated with periodic elections (he himself was reelected twice). A well-traveled and educated man, he realized the need to cultivate public opinion. He dubbed his administration the Patria Nueva (New Fatherland), charged with implementing the new constitutional order. He devoted much attention to mingling with crowds while posing as a citizen-president and to convincing newspapers to treat him favorably in their pages. In fact, Leguía was an urbane dictator, along the lines of Benito Mussolini in Italy and Primo de Rivera in Spain during those years. He also recognized the importance of controlling coercive force, so he kept the army and navy loyal to him by providing them pay increases and expensive new armaments. Given favorable circumstances, it was not difficult to keep most Peruvians happy, and his elections were at least honest.

Leguía took in more state revenues than had any other president before him and many since. The 1920s brought great prosperity to Peru, based upon the export of minerals and agricultural products. Some of Peru's exports were traditional—for example, sugar, silver, cotton—whereas others responded to twentieth-century demands—for example, petroleum, rubber, and copper. In any event, jobs were plentiful, businesses profited, and most Peruvians lived adequately. Leguía also managed to borrow enormous sums of money from the New York and London bond markets. He courted U.S. businesses and investments and initiated an ambitious program of public works. Construction of roads, railroads, ports, and public buildings went on throughout the 1920s. Thus, the modest social and economic reforms that he undertook met with public approval.

The changes that Leguía introduced in Peru had limited impact, both structurally and spatially. He gave in to worker and student protests and created a department to provide workers with disability insurance and to oversee industrial relations. But most Peruvians did not belong to unions and hence were ineligible for these benefits. He recognized Amerindian rights in some parts of the Andes but revived the hated *mita* work system, under which Amerindians were obliged to provide free labor for public works. He guaranteed citizens basic civil rights yet routinely violated them when he felt threatened by criticism.

Many Peruvians, especially those whose precarious middle-class lives depended upon government jobs or contracts, believed that the country needed Leguía's firm, steady hand on the helm of state. They were definitely in the minority, however, because vast numbers of citizens had no say in government and did not feel represented by Leguía and his people. The highlands Amerindians, for example, had long avoided contact with government in Lima, which intruded into their lives only to extract labor, taxes, military service, votes, or all of the above. They were content to sell their potatoes and hand-woven textiles to urban merchants. The rural workers along the coastal valleys, who toiled on estates producing sugar, cotton, vegetables, brandy, and fruit, labored under systems of exploitation little better than the days of slavery. Even the urban poor benefited little from the business affluence of the 1920s. So the stability of the Leguía era was only a lull in the traditionally conflictive politics of Peru.

Another Peruvian leader, Víctor Raúl Haya de la Torre (1895–1979), had his finger on the pulse of his people. He emerged as a leader in the 1920s and played a prominent role in public affairs until his death. Haya, as he was known to his followers, grew up in the provincial capital of Trujillo in northern Peru. His father had been a school principal and intellectual, so as a youth Haya had been exposed to a great variety of writers, including Peruvian radicals such as Manuel González Prada and José Carlos Mariátegui, the founder of the Peruvian Communist Party. Haya was more realistic about the ethnic, class, and regional differences dividing Peru, and he was also more passionate about reconciling his fellow Peruvians and leading them into a promised land. He became, in fact, one of the great messianic populists of Latin America.

In his early twenties Haya moved to Lima to study at the university, and he soon became active in student politics. He vaulted into national affairs by helping to mediate the 1919 general strike in Lima. From there he founded a workers' university, such as had sprung up in Mexico and Russia after their revolutions. He was clearly a politician on the make, and he became known throughout Lima. He seemed equally at home in intellectual salons, union halls, and student gatherings. In 1923, however, he played such a leading role opposing a Leguía policy that he was jailed and deported. While he wandered through the Americas or Europe for seven years, the government back home shut down the schools and unions that he had helped to found. In the long run, however, Haya converted this exile into martyrdom and a pilgrimage. Haya brilliantly turned adversity to his advantage.

He first visited Central America and Mexico. In Mexico City he founded a hemispheric movement called APRA—the Alianza Popular Revolucionaria Americana—a leftist but not communist-inspired organization. His followers became known as Apristas. In point of fact, APRA never developed an international following, and most of its support came from Peruvians. In Central America Haya conferred with Panamanians who opposed U.S. canal policies and with the revolutionary Augusto Sandino, who fought U.S. imperialism in Nicaragua. (See Chapter Fifteen.) He traveled in Europe for several years, where he observed and studied a variety of new doctrines and leadership styles. He felt anointed from his travels, ready to return to his homeland to fashion its destiny.

Haya was unable to put his ideas into effect until the overthrow of Leguía in 1930. In the eyes of many Peruvians, the president had become a dictator, subservient to the business elite and foreigners and unable to sustain the economy after the 1929 Depression hit. The dictator had to go; yet, it was just as wrong to blame him for the 1930s collapse as to credit him for the 1920s opulence—both were

Haya de la Torre's sixty-year career helped pull Peru out of colonial-era practices and to modernize the country. Still, despite his abiding popularity, Haya never won a presidential election.

driven by outside forces. An ambitious army colonel, Luis Sánchez Cerro, nevertheless led a revolt in the South that soon toppled and imprisoned Leguía. An old man, Leguía perished in jail the following year.

The Sánchez Cerro junta promised a return to democracy and allowed exiles—including Haya—to return and participate in elections the following year. Haya's reputation had grown during his absence, and his party naturally nominated its leader for president. Sánchez Cerro also ran for president in 1931, setting the stage for one of the great populist contests of modern Latin America.

The 1931 Peruvian elections represented a sharp break with the past, promising democracy instead of dictatorship, youth instead of age. The APRA program that emerged during the months of Haya's campaigning combined remarkable vision with vague goals. Like many other men of his time, Haya tried to wrap his considerable intellect around too many philosophies and doctrines at once. He embraced mysticism, nationalism, and socialism. He claimed kinship with the Inca dynasty. He championed the worker and the peasant farmer. And he conveyed his half-baked ideas with such passion and sincerity that the masses of Peruvians were drawn to him spiritually. His political instincts led him to run for president in 1931, a critical time in modern Peruvian history.

Luis Sánchez Cerro also ran for president, however, and he, too, cut a flamboyant figure. A *cholo* (part white, part Amerindian), he reveled in being a man of the people. He won the election by appealing to the same voters as Haya—the young, undereducated, poor, and mestizo population—and promptly jailed his rival Haya, accusing APRA of plotting to annul the election. His administration tried to aid the workers with more jobs and benefits, and it also attempted to transfer lands into the hands of peasants. But his meteoric career was cut short by an Aprista assassin's bullet in 1933, and the reform efforts languished.

For the next half-century, Haya flitted in and out of the political limelight like a moth. The army never forgave him for a massacre of soldiers and government officials by APRA followers during a 1932 aborted uprising in Trujillo. The army effectively vetoed his ever serving as president. The elite also feared that Haya would make good on his vague promises to restore the rights of Amerindians and to provide decent wages for workers. Finally, the U.S. government found his nationalism too strident. So Haya never became president, even though he enjoyed massive popularity, and his party usually held a share of seats in the Congress.

Despite the fact that Haya never served as president, his program and popularity forever altered Peruvian affairs. Never again would a man like Augusto Leguía be able to govern the country while neglecting the interests of the masses.

Conclusions and Issues

A few common threads tie together the experiences of Panama, Brazil, and Peru in the first three decades of the twentieth century. Their economies grew in terms of technology, productivity, and size, and their engagement with world markets deepened. More and more citizens worked for salaries and belonged to the money economy. And increasing numbers of persons took part in political campaigns, even though the suffrage remained very restricted. The oligarchies that dominated governments in these countries were forced, however grudgingly, to take the interests of workers and peasant farmers into account. Legislatures passed the first measures to protect the rights of laborers and peasants.

These countries exhibited the outward appearances of the nation-state—they possessed stable governments, a monopoly on coercion, and territorial integrity—yet, their societies remained segmented and fragile. Large Amerindian and immigrant groups, in some regions a majority, did not fully identify with their nations' leaders. Rural and urban lifestyles were so different as to be almost irreconcilable. There were no easy ways for leaders to imbue their people with a sense of nationalism, and indeed during the tense era of the Great Depression and World War II, many societies grew more polarized.

Discussion Questions

1. Was Panama really a sovereign nation after independence in 1903? How did Panama benefit from having the canal built in its territory? Was U.S. policy imperialistic in Panama?

2. Did Brazilians have a special knack for solving problems by letting them drift? Was the Old Republic "politics of the governors" democratic? Why did the system break down in 1930?

3. Was the image of Leguía's Peru as a modern, unified nation in the 1920s an illusion? Which peoples were left out of politics and denied economic rewards? Would APRA have created a fairer society had it won the 1931 election?

Early Revolutionaries: Mexico, Brazil, and Nicaragua

Pancho Villa Eludes General Pershing in 1916

Pancho Villa leaned forward in his saddle and looked west into the afternoon sun that beat down on his native Durango mountains. He turned to his aide.

"Oye, Chico, I think I see the gringos coming up that valley."

"Could be them, don Pancho."

"I wonder if that fool Pershing is with them," Villa continued, squinting to focus better on the distant dust being kicked up by Pershing's army. "I'd love to use my *pistola* to make him do the dance of the Mexican sombrero!"

Chico laughed, and the other horsemen chuckled.

A dry, stuttering sound rattled up the canyon. Villa pointed towards a hilltop to the north. "Look, they send the airplanes to look for us." Indeed, a tiny speck could be seen just above the horizon for a few seconds, one of Pershing's reconnaissance aircraft.

Villa turned and ordered his men to move their horses deeper into the shadows of some nearby boulders.

"They'll never find us here."

"Our German friends tell me that the gringo army is ordering more cannon and tanks, weapons of all sorts, in case they have to fight in the European war," Villa's trusted publicist, a university graduate, said. "Little chance the gringos will have of making a difference," he snorted. "The Germans will win."

"And so will we," observed Villa.

"Their president is a *maricón*," one of Villa's lieutenants chimed in. "We killed those gringo railroad engineers, and what did he do? Nothing. We rob that bank in New Mexico, and what did he do? Nothing, except send this *chingue* Pershing to catch us. I tell you, Wilson's a coward, and Germany is going to win the war."

"I hope so," Villa said. "But that damned Carranza in Mexico City is playing along with the gringos. He lets Pershing bring that army into our country! He stops selling oil to the Germans. Now he ordered the police to arrest German spies. Crazy Carranza just about declared war on Germany," Villa steamed. "We could do a lot better helping the Germans."

"Well, the Germans are sure happy we've got Pershing tied down here," the publicist said. "They know the gringos can't do anything in Europe when their top general is here."

The little plane buzzed closer to the group. It flew a pattern resembling lazy eights, slowly crisscrossing the sky. But Villa knew the fragile aircraft also carried sharp eyes.

"Deeper into the shadows, boys," Villa said, throwing his head back into the shadows of the canyon.

A few minutes later the plane turned away and disappeared.

"Mi general," an aide piped up, "let's ride down and shoot at the gringos a little, so they follow us up the valley. We can escape down Devil's Canyon."

"Good idea, Chico. Then we ride to Chihuahua City and pick up the money the Germans said they left for us. Maybe we'll hire some more soldiers and buy enough horses to really scare the gringos. We'll make them remember the Alamo, all right!"

Several miles below Villa's camp, a column of fifteen hundred American soldiers on mules struggled to move its artillery pieces across the valley floor. The soldiers had abandoned their armored vehicles two days earlier because they had gotten stuck in a sandy river bed. The Chihuahua Desert could swallow up anything mechanical and not leave a trace.

General Pershing himself knew that the desert was a far worse enemy than Pancho Villa. But he had orders to harry Villa and to capture him if possible, so his men pressed farther south into Mexico. He cursed President Woodrow Wilson for sending him on this wild-goose chase, when the army ought to be getting ready to fight in Europe. "One day," he thought, "someone is going to give Villa what he deserves—a helping of hot lead in the stomach. I hope I'm there to see it!"

Pershing never did engage Villa's guerrilla forces. Following some desultory skirmishes with local Mexicans, Pershing was ordered to retreat back across the border. President Carranza could no longer tolerate this breach of sovereignty, even though he hoped fervently that Villa would be shot and killed.

The following year, the United States declared war on Germany and entered the conflict on the Allied side. A few years later, Villa's automobile was run off the road and riddled with machine gun fire. His head was removed and never has been recovered.

Revolution

Revolutions have occurred throughout history, yet only in recent decades have scholars developed general theories of revolution. The concept is easily misused—for example, to speak of a Roosevelt or a Reagan revolution in the United States is inaccurate—so we should begin with a working definition.

> Revolutions are outbursts of intense and sustained violence, involving major segments of a country's population, that destroy existing institutions and fundamentally alter the country's political, social, and economic systems.

By this definition, true revolutions are rare and cataclysmic events. Some of the best-known political revolutions in world history have been those in France (1789), Russia (1917), and China (1949).

In describing the general patterns of revolution, Crane Brinton (*Anatomy of Revolution,* 3rd ed. [New York: Vintage, 1965], pp. 198–202) notes that after several years they lapse into a "reign of terror." He enumerates the causes of terror in this way:

> First, there is what we may call the habit of violence, the paradoxical situation of a people conditioned to expect the unexpected. The more violent and terroristic periods of our revolutions come only after a series of troubles have prepared the way.
>
> . . . a second and more important variable is the pressure of a foreign and civil war. War necessities help explain the rapid centralization of the government of the Terror. . . .
>
> Third, there is the newness of the machinery of this centralized government. The extremists are certainly not . . . altogether without experience in handling men, though they have dealt with revolutionists, not with all men.
>
> Fourth, this is also a time of acute economic crisis—not merely what we now call a depression, but a definite shortage of the necessities of life.
>
> . . . fifth variable, class struggles, clearly appears in the crisis . . .
>
> our sixth variable is . . . based on observation of the behavior of the relatively small group of leaders formed during the revolution and now in control of the government of the Terror.
>
> Finally, there is . . . the element of religious faith . . . heroic attempts to close once and for all the gap between human nature and human aspirations.

The revolutionaries who led such dramatic upheavals are even less understood than the upheavals themselves. Over the centuries, they have been denounced as bandits, madmen, demons, and villains. Yet, they were often revered and idolized by the poor and destitute who followed them, sometimes rising into the hallowed pantheon of national heroes. Later we will present several composite profiles of the early revolutionaries of Latin America.

Latin America has experienced three genuine revolutions: those that began in Haiti in 1791, Mexico in 1910, and Cuba in 1959. Each continues to influence the course of its country's history to some degree. Latin America has also witnessed a large number of revolutionary movements, some of which succeeded partially, like

that of Peru between 1968 and 1975 and that of the Sandinistas in Nicaragua between 1979 and 1990. We will discuss them because their impact was often large.
We do not, however, include mere coups or revolts in our treatment of revolutions.

A number of factors predisposed Latin American countries to revolution. The
presence of the United States seemed to be important because two of the biggest revolutions occurred in the neighboring countries of Mexico and Cuba. Long before the
twentieth century, in fact, the United States had played major roles in the independence
movements, serving as inspiration and as supplier of arms. More recently, U.S. influence has been more complicated: On one hand, the United States stood for the ideals
that many revolutionaries evoked, like equality, justice, and democracy. On the other
hand, the United States represented capitalist exploitation and imperialism. As we will
see, the U.S. response to revolution in Latin America has usually been ambivalent.

Certainly the rise of communism as a rival model of state organization was another important catalyst for revolutionary forces in Latin America, helping to account for their antagonism toward the United States. The first true communist state,
the Union of Soviet Socialist Republics (USSR), was consolidated out of the ruins of
imperial Russia in 1917. The United States and the USSR viewed each other as constant threats during the entire seventy-five years of their rivalry. Any Latin American
nation that pursued major reforms or revolutionary changes that resembled the
communism of the USSR automatically faced U.S. opposition.

The Revolutionary Process

The revolutionary process in these countries [Mexico (1910–1940), Bolivia
(1943–1964), Guatemala (1944–1954), and Cuba (1956–1961)] can be divided
into three stages. In the first stage, rebel movements organized and overthrew the
old regime, usually dominated by military dictators. In the second stage, the rebels
gained control of the governmental apparatus and, instead of revolutionizing society,
established reformist governments; some of these governments were overthrown
by force. After an interval, the revolutionaries returned to power and established
revolutionary governments. At this point, the third stage and revolutionary change
itself began: the revolutionaries gained control of and revolutionized the political
and governmental systems, seized land and other properties, and introduced
changes in foreign relations.

(Cole Blasier, Hovering Giant [Pittsburgh: University of Pittsburgh Press, 1976], p. 4)

Another precondition for revolution was extreme disparity in levels of living—
societies that consisted of a conspicuously wealthy elite amid masses of very poor
people. In addition, revolutions occurred when times were getting better for most
people, a time of "rising expectations," but when continued improvement was then
threatened by a government or some other actor.

Yet another reason for revolution in Latin America was the cultural gap sepa-
rating the elites and the masses. The former tended to glorify European lifestyles,

languages, and aesthetic norms, whereas the latter identified with Amerindian and African cultures. These conflicting identities led to social antagonism and fueled conflict, thereby exacerbating revolutionary tendencies.

The Mexican Revolutionaries

Mexico, deemed to be one of the most stable and advanced of the Latin countries at the turn of the twentieth century, plunged into a devastating civil war in 1910 that has since been accepted as a genuine revolution. Some of the most colorful—and ruthless—men in history played leading roles in that revolution, and the history of the hemisphere was permanently altered. Relations with the United States figured prominently in the revolution, and anti-American sentiment characterized the period. Among the many issues that clouded relations were U.S. land and mineral investments, rights of Mexican laborers, migration, and Church-state relations. Ultimately, however, internal factors proved decisive in the Mexican Revolution.

The long dictatorship of don Porfirio Díaz (the *Porfiriato*), already covered in Chapter Eight, came to an unexpected and humiliating end in 1911. A vicious recession in 1907–1908 had bankrupted many businesses and left over a million workers unemployed. Foreign owners, however, weathered the crisis and emerged with even more control over the economy. Declining standards of living provoked huge workers' strikes, most of which were put down brutally by rural police or occasionally by security forces from across the border. Class struggle reached alarming levels by 1910, but Díaz did not heed the warnings of anarchists, socialists, labor leaders, intellectuals, and even some government figures.

One of Díaz' severest critics, Ricardo Flores Magón, founded the virulent oppositionist paper, *Regeneración,* in 1900. The following year he helped organize a movement that later became the Liberal Party of Mexico. Harassed and jailed on numerous occasions, Ricardo and his brothers eventually fled to the United States and Canada, where they continued to publish their opposition paper. In 1907 they changed its name to *Revolución.* In 1906 and 1908 they issued calls for revolt, but in both cases they were thwarted by U.S. agents. Ricardo Flores Magón, after his conversion to anarchism, became vehemently anticapitalist and anti-American, calling the United States a "nation of pigs." The Flores Magón brothers kept the radical wing of the opposition movement against Díaz alive and dangerous.

Díaz, meanwhile, had grown old and careless, unmindful of the maneuvers by his ambitious associates to replace him. For a time he considered retiring and passing the mantle to a younger man. When he saw the dissension that this notion caused, he decided to run again and perhaps arrange a succession in mid-term, after which he would retire in Europe. The 1910 election would definitely be his last, so he did not give it much attention. He expected it to be like the seven others he had rigged before: a mere formality. Instead, he walked into a political firefight.

Francisco I. Madero, the young scion of an extremely wealthy family from the northern state of Coahuila, had decided to challenge Díaz for the presidency in 1910. He announced his candidacy and developed a reformist platform, which he touted in several regional campaign trips. Something of a mystic, Madero believed he had a calling to rid the country of dictatorship, to provide honest democratic government, and to modernize the economy through education and better administration. Hardly in touch with the Amerindian masses, Madero nonetheless addressed some issues that mattered to millions of Mexicans. In short, he offered hope for a better future. His candidacy snowballed as 1910 wore on.

Díaz decided to eliminate this unexpected threat by the usual methods, having Madero jailed and rigging the vote count in his own favor. Election officials announced a Díaz landslide, acknowledged a few opposition ballots, and then declared Díaz the winner. It looked like business as usual for the 1910–1915 term. Díaz celebrated his eightieth birthday and even presided over a lavish celebration of the centennial of the Hidalgo revolt of 1810. He seemed not to recognize the peril of his own situation and the irony of the commemoration.

Madero made his way to Texas before unleashing a protest, in the form of a "letter from jail." He called it his Plan de San Luis Potosí. Its main slogan called for "free suffrage and no reelection." He declared the need to end political bossism. He made vague reference to restoring despoiled lands to the Amerindians. He decried the lack of schools, widespread illiteracy, and the enslavement and shipment of Yaqui Indians to labor in the henequen fields of Yucatan.

The Plan de San Luis Potosí was not a major blueprint for radical socioeconomic reform because it did not endanger private property nor even disrupt the evolutionary progress that Madero believed Mexico was making. Still, it offered hope of some change to millions of downtrodden Mexicans. Perhaps its most important clause was a call to military arms, rallying all Mexicans to overthrow the Díaz dictatorship on November 20, 1910.

To everyone's surprise, in late 1910 a number of revolutionary movements sprang up throughout the country in answer to Madero's call. The mule driver-merchant Pascual Orozco led a powerful military contingent in the North, in league with the rebel governor Abraham González. Orozco was not particularly committed to Madero, but he used the plan to launch his movement. By January 1911 he had taken Mexicali and Chihuahua City. His early successes attracted other local military bands, notably that of former bandit Pancho Villa.

In the South, Emiliano Zapata also raised his revolutionary banner. Zapata inherited lands that his family had owned in the village of Anenecuilco, in the state of Morelos. For generations the Zapatas had supplied political leaders. Therefore, it was natural for Zapata to be elected mayor and to take up the villagers' land claims against the encroachments of large sugar plantations. Unable to get satisfaction, Zapata then recruited a band of armed followers to take back their land, by force if necessary. He declared against Díaz in early 1911 and then spent the next eight years fighting to get land reform onto the revolutionary agenda.

The breakthrough for Madero came in May, 1911, ironically in spite of his own actions. That month Orozco and Villa wanted to take Ciudad Juárez, a large and strategic city on the Rio Grande, bordering El Paso, Texas. Madero feared a bloodbath and at the last minute attempted to call off the attack. Orozco defied him, however, and managed to take the city after several days of intense fighting. This victory turned the tide and persuaded Díaz to step down from the presidency. He left for Paris, where he died several years later.

Madero, heir apparent to the presidency, organized a triumphal train journey to the capital. Most of the revolutionaries were pleased and expected Madero to reward them handsomely, but they remained watchful. Zapata's peasants had started seizing lands and had taken over many towns and garrisons. Villa and others in the North had stolen cattle and provisions, and they now controlled factories and towns. And as yet, Madero had not proven himself as a revolutionary.

Great celebrations erupted upon Madero's arrival in Mexico City, but very quickly the popularity of his regime shrank. He refused to be sworn in as president until a new election could be held late in 1911, so he appeared weak and lost the opportunity to make rapid changes. He insisted on governing with the consent of an unpopular Congress, elected during the Díaz period. He appointed conciliatory politicians from the upper class who would not accept the more radical measures pushed by Zapata's Amerindians and Villa's *rancheros*. Finally, Madero lacked a strong sense of survival in politics. Raised in a wealthy family and educated at the Sorbonne and Berkeley, he was an idealist who trusted that good intentions and smart ideas would carry the day. That was a naive, and ultimately fatal, mistake.

Madero soon faced enemies and conspirators on all sides. Congress refused to pass even the mildest reform legislation that he proposed. Conservatives who had worked with the Díaz regime could not accept this newcomer and so started conspiring for a military coup. And the revolutionaries grew impatient with his lack of accomplishments and took matters into their own hands. When Madero sent envoys to coax them into line, they balked and prepared to fight once more. The false peace of 1911 quickly dissolved into hostilities and new fighting.

Zapata left the fold first. Madero had insisted that lands could not be taken without legislation; thus, the seizures by Zapata's men were illegal. Because Zapata's sole aims were to take back lands seized by the big sugar concerns and to regain control over village politics, he could not comply. Madero dispatched General Victoriano Huerta to assert federal authority in the South, thereby forcing Zapata back into rebel status. Soon Orozco and others also parted ways with Madero. Mexico drifted deeper into conflict.

The regular army, meanwhile, virtually collapsed from incompetence, graft, and unwillingness to fight. Within a year, five regional skirmishes were under way, and Madero was incapable of controlling any of them. In office only sixteen months, Madero was unable to satisfy the many demands made upon him, to reward followers, to distribute land, or even to appoint loyal military officers.

Madero's end was even more humiliating than Díaz's. General Huerta, whom Madero had sent north to quell the revolts, returned from the front in early 1913. Then, allied with a nephew of don Porfirio, Huerta conspired to overthrow Madero. Worse, after the coup, they assassinated him and his vice president during a staged escape attempt. The effect on the country was shattering. Still, Madero's reputation soared. Having failed as a reformer, he could now serve as a martyr to the revolutionary cause.

After Madero's death, the crisis deepened, and fighting spread further afield. The United States, meanwhile, refused to recognize Huerta's government, throwing international relations into limbo. Opposition to Huerta soon coalesced around a clever and ambitious man, Venustiano Carranza, an elderly rancher and politician from Coahuila. Carranza mobilized opposition to Huerta and won the secret approval of the United States. Calling his forces the Constitutionalists, he seemed to have the support of Villa and Zapata, who were fighting Huerta, too. These politico-military positions created a giant north-south pincer movement against the Mexico City regime. The country sank into generalized civil war.

The United States intervened directly in the spring of 1914 to aid Carranza by seizing the port of Veracruz and thereby halting the flow of arms and revenues to Huerta. After some months Huerta resigned and fled the country, pitching it even deeper into chaos.

Villa and Zapata both aspired to push the revolution forward, but leadership proved elusive. They chose a weak compromise figure who took over the presidential palace in Mexico City but remained isolated and vulnerable. Carranza, meanwhile, wisely occupied Veracruz after it had been evacuated by U.S. forces. He unleashed his best general, Alvaro Obregón, against Villa, and in several spectacular battles Obregón defeated Villa and neutralized him militarily. Obregón lost an arm during one battle but fought on, becoming a legend among his men. Zapata, sensing the turning tide, retreated to his stronghold in Morelos. From mid-1915 on, the conflict waned in intensity.

Pancho Villa and Emiliano Zapata (seated second and third from the right) met in 1914 to create a constitutional government, but the situation was too chaotic for conciliation at that time.

Gral. Obregón   Francisco Villa   Gral. Pershing.

Rival generals Alvaro Obregón, Pancho Villa, and John Pershing posed for a photo in 1915. Later they resumed their deadly contests.

Villa, however, could still inflict serious damage in the northern deserts of Chihuahua and Durango. He chose the desperate measure of provoking the United States in the hope that U.S. intervention would weaken the Carranza administration. He was goaded on by German agents, who desired to stir up trouble between Mexico and the United States, thereby keeping the latter from declaring war on Germany. The first atrocity occurred when Villa's troops ambushed and murdered over a dozen U.S. mining engineers. Then Villa crossed the border and raided the town of Columbus, New Mexico, to seize cash supposedly left there by German agents. In early 1916 President Wilson, under increasing pressure to do something about lawlessness in Mexico, sent General John "Black Jack" Pershing with ten thousand troops (the so-called Punitive Expedition) into Mexico to capture Villa. Pershing was unable to find Villa and instead fought with local residents, provoking a protest from Mexico City. After nearly a year Pershing was called back, and subsequently he assumed command of the U.S. expeditionary army sent to fight in Europe when the United States entered World War I.

Revolutionary leaders who were committed to change forced President Carranza to convoke a constitutional convention in 1916. Early in 1917 that body concluded its work, producing a remarkably advanced constitution that, although still in force, has yet to be completely fulfilled. It was the first socialist constitution of the twentieth century, predating the Bolshevik victory in Russia.

Young Mexican soldiers of the Revolution and their female companions, the famous soldaderas, *or camp followers.*

The 1917 Constitution followed strongly nationalistic and socially progressive lines. It declared that the state would confiscate landholdings in excess of certain limits and distribute them to peasants. It restored the *ejido* (ancient system of lands in which villages managed production communally). It also nationalized all subsoil mineral, water, and hydrocarbon rights. Henceforth, mines and wells could be worked only under concessions from the government. It subjugated the Church to the state by nationalizing all religious property and prohibiting public displays of faith, including the wearing of clerical garb. It decreed universal free education. And it contained a full bill of rights for labor. The 1917 Constitution helped qualify the Mexican upheaval as a genuine revolution.

One more episode of 1917 warrants mention: the Zimmerman telegram. The German government, desperately hoping to keep the United States out of World War I, proposed in a secret telegram that Carranza invade the United States to forestall U.S. intervention in the war. In exchange, after Germany won the war, Mexico would receive the southwestern territories that it had lost in the Treaty of Guadalupe Hidalgo (1848). Carranza wisely turned down this offer. British agents, however, intercepted the telegram and made public its contents, provoking an indignant response in the United States that helped push Congress into joining the war.

The last few years of the revolution were relatively quiet. General Obregón became disenchanted with Carranza's unwillingness to carry out the reforms and quit. Villa and Zapata were marginalized and then several years later were murdered by government agents. The United States, preoccupied with ending the war in Europe and negotiating a peace, paid little attention to Mexico. In 1920 Carranza tried to install a puppet in the presidency, and, failing that, tried to flee with the national treasury. He was captured and executed. The ranking generals of the revolution chose Alvaro Obregón for president and oversaw his election in 1920. That marked the close of the revolution, though hardly the cessation of revolutionary change.

The Revolutionaries

The biographical information in Table 15–1 helps explain the origins, motivations, and personalities of these extraordinary figures, the Mexican revolutionaries. The first observation one can make is that the old guard—epitomized by Huerta and Carranza—were not revolutionaries in the usual sense. They were mature men in their fifties by the time they took part and did not fit the profile of angry young men. In some ways, they were opportunists, moving in on the heels of other events and seizing the initiative. They did embrace some reforms and courted the radicals, but they never intended to carry out a total overhaul of Mexico's society and economy. Both Huerta and Carranza died shortly after being forced out of power, Huerta of natural causes and Carranza of murder.

The true revolutionaries, on the other hand, followed dangerous paths and perished young. They were born within a few years of one another—between 1872 and 1880—and mostly came from northern Mexico. Zapata and Flores Magón, by contrast, were from the South. With the exception of Madero, they came from poor or modest origins. Several were mestizos. Most were businessmen, but their chances of prospering evaporated when the revolution broke out. Rather than lose everything, they joined the war. They were ambitious and anxious to get ahead, so they enlisted while in their thirties.

None of the young revolutionaries had formal military training. Instead, they learned to fight on the job. They possessed combat cunning and excellent tactical skills, and they intuitively practiced guerrilla warfare before it became standard procedure in mid-twentieth-century revolutions. The revolutionaries who succeeded all became generals, and they always maintained some capacity for military action, even after the fighting ended. They understood, as a later revolutionary would say, that "power comes from the barrel of a gun."

The revolutionaries were smart, reasonably well-educated (except Villa and Zapata), and appreciated professional expertise. They surrounded themselves with university-trained aides, usually lawyers, who could transform their wishes into decrees, press releases, and laws. These lawyers, for example, dominated the proceedings of the 1917 constitutional convention. Without these aides, many of the measures that the revolutionaries advocated would not have been formulated.

Few of the revolutionaries traveled abroad before entering politics, yet foreign contacts and examples seem to have been important in shaping their ideas and careers. Madero certainly nurtured his visionary ideals while studying abroad. Flores Magón derived his socialist philosophy from European writings and honed it against the stone of U.S. capitalism. The other *norteños* (Villa, Orozco, González, and Carranza) had acquired a healthy awareness of U.S. economic and ideological penetration across the border. Most were suspicious of U.S. impositions and tried to uphold Mexican national sovereignty. They saw U.S. intervention as a national humiliation.

Table 15-1 Early Revolutionaries

Country	Name	Years in Power	Born	Class	Urban Rural	Race	Ed	Age @ first off	Mil?	Party	Foreign Influence	Died	@ Age
					Mexican Old Guard								
Mexico	Huerta	1913–14	1845	middle		mest	mil	60	y		n	1916	70
	Carranza	1915–20	1860	upper		wh	med	27	n		n	1920	60
					Mexican Young Turks								
	Madero	1911–13	1873	upper		wh	univ	36	n		y	1913	39
	Flores Magón	n/a	1873	middle		wh	law	31*	n	Lib	n	1922	48
	Villa	n/a	1878	lower		mest	n/a	31*	n		y	1923	45
	Zapata	n/a	1879	lower		ind	n/a	31*	n		n	1919	39
	Obregon	1920–24	1880	middle		wh	2nd	40	n		n	1928	48
					Prestes and Sandino								
Braz	Prestes	n/a	1898	middle		wh	mil		y	Comm	y	1990	92
Nica	Sandino	n/a	1895	middle									

*Began revolutionary activity and became military leaders

Most of the revolutionaries sympathized with socialism without being doctrinaire socialists. Theirs might be called a "spiritual socialism," but it derived from empathy with poor people, shared suffering, and a vague desire to help the downtrodden. They were too busy with politics and warfare, however, to devote much time to reflective analysis of ideology.

Uneasy Twenties

After the burst of revolutionary activity in Mexico in the 1910s, Latin American politics seemed to calm down in the 1920s. Economic recovery and modern weapons purchased after World War I helped this process. Throughout the region, strong regimes kept the peace and managed to defuse labor and political radicalism. In Mexico, Presidents Alvaro Obregón and Plutarco Calles stabilized affairs. Calles even created an official party in 1929, after his predecessor was assassinated. Elsewhere, too, enforced stability and growth seemed the order of the day, provided by such people as Leguía in Peru, Yrigoyen and Alvear in Argentina, the Conservatives in Colombia, Gómez in Venezuela, and Alessandri and Ibáñez in Chile.

The Mexican elite still had major problems to contend with. A Catholic rebellion in the highlands, called the "Cristero Revolt," mobilized Conservatives, the faithful in major cities, and thousands of devout peasants in the countryside. It smoldered for years and left a bloody legacy of Church-state antagonism. Because it was motivated by anticlerical measures in the 1917 Constitution, it was a major aftershock of the revolution itself.

Two other exceptions to the general stability occurred: the Prestes Column march in Brazil (1924–1927) and the civil war in Nicaragua led by Augusto Sandino (1927–1933). Prestes and Sandino were revolutionaries whose actions cast shadows far into the future.

Luís Carlos Prestes

Luís Carlos Prestes enjoyed a long and varied career in Brazilian politics. Cast as heroic *comandante* of a revolutionary march in the 1920s, he later became the undisputed leader of the Brazilian Communist Party for nearly fifty years. Until the advent of Fidel Castro, Prestes was Latin America's most famous communist leader, and he was certainly the most ideological of the early revolutionaries.

Prestes was born in Porto Alegre, Brazil, an only son with four sisters. His family moved to Rio de Janeiro when his father, an army officer, was transferred there in the early 1900s. His father died when Prestes was only ten, so in his teen years he drew close to his mother and sisters.

Because of his father's commission, Luís Carlos gained admission to the military academy, from which he graduated in 1919 with degrees in physical science and math. The next year he was commissioned to a post in a railroad engineering company. A quiet, serious man, he had trouble with both superiors and private contractors, whom he regarded as corrupt and unpatriotic.

Prestes apparently sympathized with colleagues who carried out the first *tenente* revolt of 1922, but he was bedridden with typhoid and did not take part. That revolt occurred in Rio and mobilized young officers and cadets who protested the policies of the federal government. (See Chapter Fourteen.) The several hundred participants objected to President-elect Artur Bernardes's alleged statements about the army's senior officer, which the *tenentes* regarded as an affront to the army. Loyal units crushed the revolt and jailed hundreds of rebels and stripped them of their ranks. The Rio government prosecuted the men with a severity unusual in Brazilian politics.

Two years later, some of the original rebels and hundreds of sympathetic young soldiers took part in a second *tenente* revolt, this time in the capital of São Paulo. They captured and held the city for a month, showing that not even the main industrial center was safe from military attack. Their aims remained vague: justice for workers, honesty in elections, reinstatement at rank for the 1922 revolutionaries, and respect for the armed services.

General Miguel Costa, a charismatic officer who commanded the São Paulo state police, led the 1924 revolt. After the city was surrounded by federal troops, he took his men north by railroad, and after several days they met up with Luís Carlos Prestes. The latter had convinced about a hundred of his men to join the revolt, after which they commandeered a train and made their way to the rendezvous with Costa's forces. Together they continued their trek to the northeast, abandoning the train at its last station.

During the next two and a half years, the rebel forces made one of the most extraordinary marches in military history. They covered twenty-four thousand kilometers through some of the most forbidding terrain in the world. They were harassed by government forces, by state police, and even by bandit gangs. They had to drag their artillery and provision wagons, often by mule, over mountains and deserts. They forded rivers even in periods of flood. All the while the *tenente* column lived off the land, buying or confiscating supplies as it needed them.

The very survival and continuation of the column depended to a great degree on the leadership of Luís Carlos Prestes. He took upon himself the tasks of preserving morale, discipline, hope, and forward movement. He proved a genius at tactical maneuvers to evade large pursuing forces and then ambush them with lightning attacks. He intuitively developed a form of guerrilla warfare that was perfectly suited to his troops and the terrain. Within a few months the revolutionaries were called the "Miguel Costa/Luís Carlos Prestes Column." Within a year they were known simply as the Prestes Column.

In the course of their marches, the revolutionaries developed a rationale and simple philosophy that became known as *tenentismo*. It began with the original grievances of 1922 about political corruption, misuse of public office, and indifference toward the military. Expressed in hurried press encounters and sketched out in rural backwoods, *tenentismo* gradually expanded into a broad call for social, economic, and political reform. *Tenente* spokesmen demanded that the government address rural poverty, illiteracy, malnutrition, bossism, and violence. Many of the *tenentes* saw rural suffering for the first time in their lives during the march. And, of course, they demanded reinstatement in the army.

After his arrest in 1936, Luís Carlos Prestes (shown here) faced treason charges in court. His conviction and 10-year imprisonment did not, however, prevent him from participating in underground activities nor dissuade him from a later political career as head of the Brazilian Communist Party.

The government paid little heed to the revolutionaries and continued to hound their dwindling ranks. Yet, in the cities middle-class Brazilians regarded the *tenentes* as young idealists who cared enough for their country to risk death. Their prescriptions struck many educated Brazilians as reasonable and indeed overdue. Some of the *tenentes* became quite famous for their exploits and for their articulate calls for reforms.

In early 1927 the column abandoned its march, its ranks having thinned to several hundred men. Its members crossed into eastern Bolivia, then dispersed to several countries in the region. Some *tenentes* sneaked back into Brazil and formed an underground revolutionary movement. Prestes found employment as a mining engineer for a time, then made his way to Buenos Aires.

The *tenente* movement eventually had its greatest impact during the early years of the Getulio Vargas regime and then quickly waned (see Chapter Sixteen). Prestes, however, continued to develop his ideas, and his prestige rose throughout Brazil. While in Argentina he became convinced that communism was the best form of government for Brazil, and he traveled to Moscow for further training.

Prestes became more famous in the 1930s due in part to Brazil's most famous modern novelist, Jorge Amado. Amado's sympathetic biography of Prestes, entitled *The Cavalier of Hope*, represented the handsome Prestes as both an idealistic revolutionary and an example of the finest elements of the Brazilian character. Amado contended that if Prestes ever came to power he would solve the problems of the poor. Meanwhile, intellectuals called Prestes the savior of the country. They were not put off even by his disastrous leadership of a communist *putsch* (coup) in 1935, which led to his arrest and imprisonment for ten years. His new image as martyr merely complemented that of revolutionary.

After World War II Prestes got out of prison and began his long career as head of the Brazilian Communist Party. He refused to take part in day-to-day politics after his party was outlawed in 1948, yet he enjoyed great prestige among subsequent generations of young people. Not until the early 1980s did a rival group oust him as general secretary of the party, by which time he was an octogenarian.

Unlike most other revolutionaries, Prestes lived to a ripe old age. Apart from his time in prison, Prestes lived for many years in Moscow and spoke fluent Russian. In the 1930s he had one daughter with a German agent, Olga Benaro, who was sent to help him. Olga later perished in a Nazi prison camp. Prestes remarried in the 1940s and raised a large family of daughters.

Augusto Sandino

Nicaragua's most famous revolutionary, Augusto Sandino, was born in a rural province a few years before Prestes. Sandino's father, the teenage son of a wealthy hacienda owner, had an affair with an Amerindian servant, and she bore him the child they named Augusto. The family recognized the baby and raised him on the hacienda, together with its other children. Augusto grew up steeped in Liberal politics, which basically meant hating the Church for meddling in politics and hating the rival Conservatives. Augusto also read extensively in the family library and developed a superficial yet convincing grasp of general philosophy.

In 1920 Augusto fought and killed another youth. He fled the province and made his way north to the Caribbean coast. There he got odd jobs with banana farmers and mining firms operating in the rain forests. Hounded by the police, he escaped to Honduras and continued on to Guatemala, Mexico, and even Texas. He learned some English and supported himself working as a mechanic and general laborer. While in Mexico, he gained respect for the revolutionary ideals of the 1917 Constitution and for Mexican defiance of the Yanquis. He pledged that he himself would some day bring about the same kind of national renovation in Nicaragua.

In 1926 Sandino returned to Nicaragua and found a job as supervisor in a gold mine. At nights, though, he met with the workers and taught them the rudiments of revolutionary ideology as he had learned it in Mexico. Soon most workers had pledged their loyalty to Sandino. The following year he and his twenty-nine followers joined the cause of General José María Moncada, who had declared war against the Conservative president. Sandino's band took to the hills, where it learned the basics of soldiering and guerrilla warfare. It balked, however, when General Moncada agreed to turn over his arms to a large U.S. Marine occupational force in exchange for guarantees of a supervised election (which he won). Sandino declared himself in rebellion, and his force became a guerrilla army. Many disgruntled soldiers from the Liberal army also joined him. *Sandinismo,* as his credo became mythologized, was forged by these events.

For several years Sandino's forces controlled thousands of square miles in northwestern Nicaragua. He perfected the techniques of guerrilla warfare, which he

Augusto Sandino (center) led an impressive struggle against U.S. intervention in Nicaragua in the early 1930s. He helped develop guerrilla warfare techniques that spread throughout the region in the 1950s.

used against the U.S. Marines and the new national guard that the marines were training for peacekeeping duty. Sandino became a master of feint and subterfuge. His success astonished many because the thousands of U.S. Marines looking for Sandino represented the largest force that the United States deployed abroad between the two world wars. Moreover, the marines used the latest weaponry, including airplanes. The echoes of Pershing's failed expedition to Mexico resonated in the volcanic valleys and rain forests of Nicaragua.

Sandino had superb political abilities and a capacity to convince his own men and peasants that they would triumph and bring about a better form of government. He was able to articulate a spiritual vision—described by biographer Neill Macauley as a "vague messianic mysticism"— that defied analysis yet appealed to poor peasants and farmers. Passionate in his love of Nicaragua, he hated the Americans for invading and imposing their will. His struggle was a crusade for national sovereignty.

Like any successful guerrilla campaign, Sandino's drew support from urban groups such as students, intellectuals, labor leaders, and Liberal politicians. Recruits from the cities took money, supplies, and intelligence to El Chipote, Sandino's mountain refuge.

An officer who served under Sandino in the 1927 campaign provided this description:

> Sandino is of medium height, very slender, weighs about 115 pounds; education limited to primary grades; an extreme optimist and possesses unusual ability in convincing others of the feasibility of his most fantastic schemes; extremely energetic; explains his plans in great

detail to his lowest subordinates but often keeps his officers in doubt; is far from being coldblooded and was never known to commit an act of cruelty himself; very religious and believes that for every wrong committed adequate punishment will be meted out . . . little interest in acquiring money for personal use and rarely has a penny in his pocket; is very vain and sophisticated, fully believing that his wisdom is infallible . . . his one slogan is "The Welfare of Our Fatherland," always stressing an interest in the peasant class.

(Neill Macauley, *The Sandino Affair*, 2nd ed. (Durham: Duke University Press, 1985), p. 57)

Sandino's resistance became famous throughout the hemisphere, a David and Goliath story that fascinated readers from New York to Buenos Aires. The young Haya de la Torre from Peru stopped and spoke with him, as did journalist Carlton Beals from the United States. News of his feats reached as far as China. Liberals in most places saw Sandino as a well-meaning nationalist who wished only to end the U.S. occupation of his country.

Sandino's fortunes waxed and waned, and from 1929 to 1931 he lived in Mexico, earning money and recruiting men. Mexican President Portes Gil promised moral and diplomatic support and perhaps even aided Sandino materially.

When Sandino returned to Nicaragua, he found the climate much less amenable for revolution. Election preparations were already under way for 1932, with security for the balloting provided by the new national guard. This time, Liberal Juan Bautista Sacasa seemed destined to win. U.S. authorities, meanwhile, favored a convivial, outgoing fellow named Anastasio Somoza to head the national guard. Somoza spoke good English, got along with gringos, managed politics well, and seemed content to be the leader of the guard. Somoza's troops gradually replaced the U.S. Marines, as they withdrew from safeguarding cities, towns, and transport facilities. Sandino's operations, meanwhile, were effectively limited to the north coast banana regions.

After the election the U.S. Marines completed their withdrawal, and the country seemed calm under the benign rule of President Sacasa. Sandino decided that he had no more reason to fight, so he sued for peace. He sent his pregnant wife to Managua to work out an agreement. Under it, he and his men would retire to an agricultural colony in the North and still retain some of their weapons for self-defense.

After about a year at the colony, Sandino began to run into trouble with local authorities, so he flew to Managua to demand that Sacasa comply with their agreement. He had dinner with the president, and the two settled their problems. On the way out, however, Sandino and his aides were seized by Somoza agents, taken to the edge of town, and murdered. Shortly afterward the national guard invaded the agricultural colony and seized all of its weapons. *Sandinismo* came to an abrupt end.

The story of Anastasio Somoza's rise to power and his long dictatorship is told in the next chapter. Sandino's legacy, however, proved remarkably long. In the 1950s one of the old Nicaraguan revolutionaries spent considerable time being interviewed by some Cuban exiles about the methods that Sandino used to defy the gringos in the late 1920s. The Cubans included Fidel and Raúl Castro, who would become famous for leading their own revolution.

Later, in the 1960s, young Nicaraguan patriots fighting against Somoza's son, the dictator Anastasio Somoza Bayle, named their clandestine guerrilla group the Frente Sandinista de Liberación Nacional (FSLN) after their hero from the 1930s. Throughout the 1980s *Sandinismo* offered hope for a social-democratic alternative to both capitalism and communism in Central America.

Conclusions and Issues

Luís Carlos Prestes and Augusto Sandino are two more examples of early revolutionaries in Latin America who would become heroes for later generations. They were born a few years later than their Mexican counterparts, whom they emulated to some extent. They came from respectable rural middle-class families who did not have roots in the urban societies. They were outsiders who felt a strong obligation to correct things that they perceived as wrong.

Moreover, they had certain advantages—family support, white or near-white parentage, and good educations for the period in which they lived—that carried them through the difficult years of warfare. Neither man was religious, but both had strong commitments to spiritual and moral values. Sandino traveled abroad and developed a revolutionary ethos while in Mexico. Prestes did not go abroad until after his participation in the column, and then his travels definitely radicalized his philosophy. Both men took up revolutionary activities while still very young. Sandino, like most of the other early revolutionaries, died after a short career; Prestes defied the odds and died of old age in the 1980s.

Revolutions probably are more common in Latin America than in other world regions because more talented young men and women are drawn to lives that defy authority and use violent means to correct ills and injustices in society. From the evidence presented in this chapter, it can be seen that the revolutionaries were from decent families, some of European and others of mixed background, who raised their children to lead moral lives. As youths, the future revolutionaries acquired good educations that later served them well in their struggles against the establishment. Societies regarded these revolutionaries as visionaries, idealists, and eventually martyrs, so that younger generations came to revere their memories. As we will see, revolution continues to be an option in the political life of the region.

Discussion Questions

I. Was there a single Mexican Revolution or many revolutions? Should the events of the 1910s be called a "great rebellion" instead of a revolution? What led men and women to drop everything and join the fighting?

2. Does personal background and experience predispose a person like Luís Carlos Prestes to take up arms against the government? How does such a leader establish his authority over other revolutionaries?

3. The United States has been ambivalent about revolutions, opposing most but supporting some. When and why did U.S. leaders decide that their nation's interests coincided with revolution? What outcomes did these exceptional decisions have?

Bibliography for Part Three

Albert, Bill, *South America and the First World War: The Impact of the War on Brazil, Argentina, Peru, and Chile* (Cambridge: Cambridge University Press, 1988).

Bergquist, Charles, *Labor in Latin America* (Stanford: Stanford University Press, 1986).

Brown, Jonathan C., *Oil and Revolution in Mexico* (Berkeley and Los Angeles: University of California Press, 1993).

Brunk, Samuel, *Emiliano Zapata: Revolution and Betrayal in Mexico* (Albuquerque: University of New Mexico Press, 1995).

Bulmer-Thomas, Victor, *The Political Economy of Central America since 1920* (Cambridge: Cambridge University Press, 1987).

Dosal, Paul J., *Doing Business with the Dictators: A Political History of United Fruit in Guatemala, 1899–1944* (Wilmington: SR Books, 1993).

Haber, Stephen H., *Industry and Underdevelopment: The Industrialization of Mexico, 1890–1940* (Stanford: Stanford University Press, 1989).

Hart, John Mason, *Revolutionary Mexico* (Berkeley and Los Angeles: University of California Press, 1987).

Helg, Aline, *Our Rightful Share: The Afro-Cuban Struggle for Equality, 1886–1912* (Chapel Hill: University of North Carolina Press, 1990).

Hernandez, Jose M., *Cuba and the United States: Intervention and Militarism, 1868–1933* (Austin: University of Texas Press, 1993).

Katz, Friedrich, *The Secret War in Mexico* (Chicago: University of Chicago Press, 1981).

Knight, Alan, *The Mexican Revolution,* 2 vols. (Lincoln: University of Nebraska Press, 1986).

McCreery, David, *Rural Guatemala, 1760–1940* (Stanford: Stanford University Press, 1994).

Monteon, Michael, *Chile in the Nitrate Era* (Madison: University of Wisconsin Press, 1982).

Nunn, Frederick M., *Yesterday's Soldiers: European Military Professionalism in South America* (Lincoln: University of Nebraska Press, 1983).

Ortiz, Fernando, *Cuban Counterpoint,* 2nd ed. (Durham: Duke University Press, 1995).

Salas, Elizabeth, *Soldaderas in the Mexican Military* (Austin: University of Texas Press, 1990).

Salisbury, Richard V., *Anti-Imperialism and International Competition in Central America, 1920–1929* (Wilmington: SR Books, 1989).

Topik, Steven, *The Political Economy of the Brazilian States: 1889–1930* (Austin: University of Texas Press, 1987).

Walter, Richard J., *Politics and Urban Growth in Buenos Aires, 1910–1942* (Cambridge: Cambridge University Press, 1993).

Wolfe, Joel, *Working Women, Working Men* (Durham: Duke University Press, 1993).

Part Four

Confronting Global Challenges

From the 1930s to the 1960s, Latin America underwent abrupt and sometimes painful transitions of modernization. Global events impinged more forcefully than ever, especially in the form of the Great Depression (1929–1939), World War II (1939–1945), and the Cold War (1947–1989). The larger nations found themselves unable to sell all their traditional exports and hence to continue importing basic necessities. This provoked an increase in domestic manufacturing and eventually led to a new economic nationalism throughout the region. Together with these stressful adaptations came heightened ideological conflict, partly as the ripple effect of international struggles and partly as responses to internal dislocations. Hundreds of thousands of unemployed rural folk moved into towns and then cities in search of jobs and opportunities for better lives. The Depression decade became a watershed in most countries of the hemisphere.

Dictatorship seemed the *régime du jour* in the 1930s, probably as a response to these tumultuous events and adjustments. One by one, governments fell to military or strongman regimes in 1930 and the years following. Some leaders, influenced by communism, fascism, and Nazism, began to experiment with radical forms of leadership. Even the U.S. government, long a proponent of democratic procedures, swore off intervention and often gave its blessings to dictators who could maintain the peace and protect U.S. investors. Where the military did not rule outright, it wielded great influence from behind the scenes.

World order deteriorated in the late 1930s and collapsed into all-out war. From Asia to Europe, from Africa to America, conflict swept the world into a vortex of destruction and death. Most of Latin America experienced shortages, security breaches, political challenges, and even armed clashes. The Caribbean Sea for a short time became a cemetery of Allied shipping because of German submarine attacks. After the United States declared war on the Axis powers, Brazil attempted to lead Latin America into solidarity with the Allies. Mexico became a strong supporter of its northern neighbor. The record in other countries was mixed. No country, however, avoided some impact from the war.

After the 1945 peace was signed and the world moved into a new era, Latin America seemed to bloom in a number of ways. For those countries that had supported the Allies, a glow of pride in victory shone through. In most places democratic forces arose and restored constitutional government. The urban economies that burgeoned with migrants and industrial growth now burst forth as world-class cities. Mexico City, Rio, Buenos Aires, Lima,

Santiago, São Paulo, and Caracas joined the ranks of world metropolises. Their governments reached out to the masses of citizens with modern election techniques and communications systems. The arts, literature, and university life all blossomed in the postwar environment.

The greatest change in postwar Latin America was the return of populism as the foremost expression of mass politics. The populists took up where their predecessors of the 1910s and 1920s left off, emboldened by huge new urban populations, radio, mass-circulation dailies, and modern transportation. Brazil experienced such a surge in populist leadership that the period 1945–1964 is often called the Populist Republic. Juan Perón and his wife, Evita, the quintessential populists, captured the hearts and minds of most Argentines after 1945. Elsewhere, too, charismatic, forceful, and dynamic figures rode waves of adulation into the presidential palaces of their nations. These were optimistic times, when citizens believed that their political influence and chances for attaining middle-class status and standards of living were never better.

By the mid-1960s, however, the optimism was gone, and more and more governments fell under military control. In large part, the populists had fallen prey to Cold War pressures from within and without. In a few cases, though, they also had failed because of sheer incompetence. Populism seemed to disappear almost as quickly as it had emerged after World War II.

The 1930s: Years of Depression and Upheaval

The 1938 Nazi Party Putsch *in Chile*

Hundreds of goose-stepping Chilean youths, dressed in soldiers' uniforms, paraded out of the morning mist that cloaked the streets of downtown Santiago. The sound of their boot heels striking the ground echoed off buildings empty of people. They marched resolutely toward La Moneda, the eighteenth-century Spanish mint that now served as Chile's presidential palace.

"Column halt!" barked the colonel. They stopped in unison and clicked their heels. "Port, arms," he shouted, and they thrust out the assorted weapons they had managed to gather in preceding weeks. In the eerie silence, not a few of the youths glanced sideways into the dark alleys on either side of them.

"Long live the Nazi Party," the colonel shouted, "and down with the scum Alessandri!" "Heil!" the youths chorused as they clicked their boots.

It was the fifth of September. Chile was just emerging from an unusually cold winter, and the 1938 elections would occur shortly. Members of the Nazi Party leadership had decided that their candidate, former President and army General Carlos Ibáñez, was unable to secure enough votes to win and must be installed by force. Without Ibáñez's knowledge, they organized a *putsch* to be executed by the paramilitary Nazi Youth Brigades.

Earlier that morning the Nazis had already captured the university and the Social Welfare ministry. Their coup would be completed in a few more hours now that they were only two blocks from La Moneda.

The colonel split the force into three groups and sent them along different streets to surround the palace. At the stroke of seven o'clock they would disarm the presidential guard, invade the palace itself, and assassinate President Alessandri in his private quarters. Other presidential contenders would also be killed, and the Nazis would cancel the elections and install Ibáñez.

At precisely seven o'clock, shots rang out, screams pierced the cold air, and bullets ricocheted down the streets. It was a fiasco. The crack *carabineros* guarding the presidential palace were waiting for the Nazis. The *carabineros* were skilled marksmen and disciplined soldiers. When the first shooting erupted, they counterattacked with lethal effectiveness. Dozens of the young Nazis fell wounded; more broke and ran, some throwing down their pistols and shotguns. Acting quickly, the *carabineros* trapped nearly a hundred in a dead-end street, where they surrendered.

One of the captives turned and tried to escape. A *carabinero* captain raised his rifle quickly and shot him. The other *carabineros* thought it was a general attack and fired into the group of captives. Tragically, sixty-two of the young Nazis died in a few minutes. They were no match for the *carabineros* and had not gotten even close to the president.

Stunned and embarrassed by this bloody episode, Ibáñez withdrew from the election and gave his support to the opposition candidate. The Nazi Party disbanded, although some German agents and sympathizers continued to work underground. Chile was not ready, it would seem, for a Nazi government. Would the next generation be ready for a Marxist government, when it elected Salvador Allende president? Apparently not, because on September 11, 1973, almost exactly thirty-five years later, the army (with the collaboration of the *carabineros*) invaded La Moneda, resulting in the death of President Salvador Allende.

The *putsch* in Chile was only one of many coups and attempted coups in Latin America during the 1930s. At first they were largely provoked by the economic crisis of 1929 that triggered the Great Depression. Within the year six civilian governments were overthrown by the military. Soon more fell or simply collapsed from exhaustion. The achievements of the populists and democrats during the first decades of the century seemed to evaporate like so much smoke in the air. The Depression created a sense of crisis, peril, and doom. Emergency measures were required to save the countries from anarchy and collapse. Those who had not lost their faith in liberal republicanism during World War I certainly lost it during the 1930s. European hegemony, especially the Pax Britannica, had ended.

Yet, the crisis of the Great Depression gave many Latin Americans a new sense of nationalism, a spirit of defensiveness, and the determination to protect what they had. In country after country, writers and politicians harped on the need to create strength within their borders. They pledged to develop stronger governments, more effective militaries, more robust economies, and more loyal citizens.

Economic Nationalism and Social Reform

Along with the new nationalism came new economic theories designed to foster independence or better insulate Latin America from the shock waves of international turmoil. In the larger countries especially, bureaucrats and intellectuals began to favor long-term industrialization as a solution to the cyclical battering that their economies received in the global arena. Coffee faced prolonged market crises and had to be subsidized; world grain supplies often exceeded demand; beef prices were notoriously unstable, and exports were subject to restrictions by importing countries; mining income fluctuated wildly with changing demand by refiners; and the sugar trade was discriminated by importing countries. Each downturn in economic fortunes caused widespread unemployment and suffering in Latin America. Moreover, the loss of export earnings caused grave shortages of imports that crippled domestic life.

The solution, according to many, was to diversify and strengthen the economies by fostering domestic manufacturing. Argentina, Brazil, Chile, and Mexico were especially interested in this possibility. They, along with many other countries around the world, joined in the general debt moratorium of 1932 and considered the possibilities of bowing out of the international market altogether. This strategy, called "autarky," was a more elaborate form of protectionism that had always been present in one form or another in international trade. New international deals not requiring hard currency could revive traditional lines of trade. In addition, high tariffs would be linked to a general plan for developing basic industries and broadening domestic markets. Multiyear plans would set targets and change investment patterns. In addition, they would be accompanied by campaigns that promoted nationalist feelings of pride. The words "Hecho en México," "Indústria Brasileira," and "Producto Argentino" began to appear on goods and in advertising. Economic nationalism became a major feature of Latin America after the 1930s. (See the miniessay on economics in Chapter Twenty-Five.)

The 1930s was also a decade in which governments actively undertook programs to promote the general well-being of their citizens. All of a sudden, leading citizens and politicians began to speak of the "social question." The phrase had been coined in Europe in the 1890s to refer to working-class demands and actions to achieve decent standards of living for working people. Pope Leo XIII gave weight to these concerns in his 1891 encyclical *Rerum Novarum*. In general, the social question called for government and private initiatives on behalf of the poorest sectors of society, including the retired, disabled, infirm, handicapped, and chronically unemployed.

Until the widespread suffering of the Great Depression struck, labor-management relations had been left to the marketplace, with very little involvement by government. This contributed to a variety of glaring social problems: strikes, proliferation of slums, periodic crises of unemployment, abandonment of persons injured on the job or too old to work, child labor, and hostility toward the elites.

To be sure, the social question had been addressed by some constitutions, notably those of 1917 in Mexico, 1919 in Uruguay, and 1925 in Chile. Yet, actual programs and compliance were rare. The 1930s saw far more actual legislation passed and real institutions created to deal with labor and social problems. Labor codes became common, governments stepped in to mediate industrial conflict, social security systems were set up, and new programs began to provide food and medicine to the destitute. The social question was transformed from a charitable concern for the poor into a major commitment of progressive governments.

Argentina and Brazil

In Argentina and Brazil, military coups toppled two governments within weeks of one another. On September 6, 1930, a contingent of army cadets marched on the Casa Rosada and deposed President Yrigoyen, whose senility had left him unfit to govern. On October 3 rebel forces in two of Brazil's most powerful states, Rio Grande do Sul and Minas Gerais, declared war and began maneuvers that led to the overthrow of President Washington Luís three weeks later. Although the underlying causes of these two movements were complex, the outcomes were relatively simple: Strong regimes took power and imposed order in the face of growing instability brought on by the Great Depression.

In Argentina, coup leader General José F. Uriburu purged the government of top Yrigoyen collaborators and reined in public spending. He outlawed strikes, banned meetings, censored newspapers, and attempted to create a dictatorship. Within a short time, however, a more conservative coalition of landowners, businessmen, and political leaders formed behind the candidacy of General Juan P. Justo. The latter won an election and took office in 1932, inaugurating a term of limited and controlled response to the Depression.

The centerpiece of the Justo years was a treaty with Great Britain extending the favorable terms of trade that both had enjoyed since the previous century. Argentine meat and cereals would continue to be sold in England virtually duty free, while British goods would enter Argentina with low tariffs. The effect was to postpone the harsh choices forced on other governments in the region, and Argentina suffered fewer effects of the Depression as a result. Justo was succeeded by a civilian president in 1938. Labor bosses and leftists exercised little influence under these autocratic regimes.

It is clear, however, that nationalistic sentiments and demands for better labor rights were growing during the 1930s. Justo's regime, which strictly controlled politics for the benefit of the elite, failed to make any concessions to the middle and working classes. Historians later called the 1930s the "infamous decade."

To the north of Argentina, the Brazilian coup, pretentiously named the Revolution of 1930, ushered in the long regime of Getúlio Vargas, former governor of Rio Grande do Sul. Vargas and his aides had to deal with far more serious problems than Uriburu had to deal with in Argentina. Coffee prices plunged, loan payments depleted hard currency reserves, the number of unemployed swelled in the cities, and all over the country discontented politicians clamored for jobs and favors. Vargas responded by imposing a dictatorship, provoking a revolt in the state of São Paulo in 1932. After this was quashed, he moved to restore democracy by holding elections and sponsoring a constitutional assembly. The resultant Constitution of 1934 enfranchised women and eighteen-year-olds, recognized the rights of labor, and mandated a system of balances between the executive and legislative branches. The assembly chose Vargas as president for the 1934–1938 term.

Brazilians, like other Latin American citizens, began to consider different ideologies rising to prominence in Europe—notably fascism, Nazism, and communism—as replacements for the liberal capitalist models earlier in vogue. Movements arose to promote each of these, yet most politicians stuck close to Vargas because he controlled jobs and patronage. Clashes between the left and right became more vicious in 1935, culminating in a major communist-led revolt in November. Vargas used the failed revolution as an excuse to impose a dictatorship, and within two years he formalized it with a constitution (1937) and the name Estado Novo (New State), borrowed from Antônio Oliveira Salazar's Portugal.

Vargas ruled as an old-fashioned dictator, ignoring the Constitution and the fascistic preferences of some collaborators. Wags dubbed his regime a *dictablanda* (weak dictatorship). Vargas centralized power in Rio de Janeiro, signaling the end of loose federalism. To emphasize the change, he had state flags burned in a ceremony marking the beginning of the Estado Novo. Finally, he strengthened the army and used it to secure his regime.

Just as important, Vargas carried out policies of economic nationalism and social reform that transformed Brazil by the end of World War II. He regulated mining and hydroelectric power, supervised foreign trade, intervened in export dealings, and further nationalized transport companies. In 1942 he struck a deal with the United States by which Brazil gave a naval base in its Northeast in exchange for a steel mill. When operational in 1946, this mill—named Volta Redonda—formed the core of an integrated steel industry. Slowly government tutelage spread to many areas of the economy. Vargas's progressive social policies, meanwhile, culminated in the Labor Code of 1943 as well as fostered a system of social security that covered most urban workers and employees.

Chile

Chileans, who had experienced military coups in 1924 and 1925, were disinclined to resort to revolution in 1930, despite the virtual collapse of their economy. Nitrate sales nearly stopped, and copper prices fell to only 15 percent of their former levels. President Ibáñez set up a public nitrates company, COSACH, to try to shore up prices, but it had little effect. Agricultural goods, meanwhile, rotted on docks and in warehouses for lack of customers. Perhaps half the employed lost their jobs. The government of General Ibáñez became so discredited by 1931 that student protests and a white-collar strike were all that it took to persuade the president to resign.

For nearly a year Chile had no real government as the vice president and Congress fruitlessly attempted to solve the crisis. In one bizarre twist, a popular figure from the 1920s, Colonel Marmaduke Grove, seized control and decreed a socialist government, but it proved utterly ineffectual. Grove gave up after two weeks, and his successor resigned three months later. Eventually a conservative coalition emerged to support former President Arturo Alessandri and duly elected him in late 1932. By then the economy had bottomed out, and most Chileans had found ways to survive.

In the presidency again, Alessandri was not inclined to undertake any reforms—as he had in the 1920s—because the treasury was empty and his government's survival was precarious at best. Besides, he had spent some time in Italy during the early years of Benito Mussolini and had come to believe in the benefits of autocratic government. He backed emergency industrialization efforts and kept a lid on labor agitation in the interest of productivity. In 1936 he employed the army to intervene in a national rail strike and soon thereafter closed Congress. Toward the end of his term, he relented and expanded social security benefits (which included medical care) to a larger number of workers. Using such methods, he managed to hold on until his term ended in 1938.

Ideological conflict whipsawed the Chilean citizenry, however, and both Nazi and leftist movements became quite influential. The former backed Carlos Ibáñez in the 1938 presidential election, whereas several parties on the left formed the Popular Front, which nominated a wealthy businessman and former cabinet minister, Carlos Aguirre Cerda, for president. The election was disrupted by the Nazis' failed *putsch* (depicted at the beginning of this chapter), which discredited the party and helped to elect Aguirre Cerda.

Immediately Aguirre Cerda implemented some of the nationalistic economic policies that had appealed to leaders elsewhere in Latin America. For planning purposes, he created the National Development Corporation (CORFO), which received a large credit from the U.S. government. Soon this agency stimulated production in a wide range of industries: textiles, mining, fishing, ranching, and timber. Of particular importance was its sponsorship of Chile's first large-scale steel mill, built in Concepción in 1941. All across the board, Chile experienced a remarkable economic recovery because of judicious government planning and rising demand caused by the onset of World War II.

Aguirre Cerda paid special attention to social needs overlooked by earlier administrations. He appointed Salvador Allende, a visionary physician, as minister of public health to oversee the social programs that he had promised in his election campaign. Allende, a committed socialist, expanded the hospital and clinic networks in poor communities to the point that Chile could boast of having the healthiest people in the hemisphere. Meanwhile, the social security system expanded to embrace nearly the entire employed population. Finally, Aguirre Cerda invested heavily in schools and teachers' salaries, giving rise to his slogan, "to govern is to educate."

In 1941 Aguirre Cerda died and was succeeded by a member of his party, Juan Antonio Ríos, also a businessman committed to economic expansion. For the remainder of the war Chilean industry grew rapidly and drew more and more people to manufacturing jobs in the cities. Ríos did not cultivate the support or cooperation of the Socialist and Communist parties, however, and instead used special wartime powers to secure his government.

Mexico

Events in Mexico during the 1930s proved even more remarkable than those in South America. Tranquillity had returned when General Alvaro Obregón gained power in 1920, created a stable government, and four years later stepped down for his successor, Plutarco Elías Calles. Like Obregón, Calles cleverly kept the generals in line through bribes and physical intimidation. Calles also managed to settle some lingering diplomatic problems with the United States.

Mexico's orderly train of events derailed during the 1928 election campaign. An assassin murdered Obregón, the leading candidate. Calles called off the election and resumed his reign. He convinced himself that he was indispensable for the well-being of the country. He adopted the title of Jefe Máximo de la Revolución. By extension his new reign came to be known as the Maximato. Calles established his control to such an extent that he could withstand military revolts and eventually exercise control over labor unions and peasant organizations (*agrarios*).

In order to broaden his support and manage elections, Calles created a party in December 1928. First named the National Revolutionary Party (PNR), it comprised three major sectors of the nation: the *agrarios,* labor unions, and the army. On paper this structure was designed to formalize these sectors' political activities and convey their wishes to the president. In fact, however, Calles gradually imposed his will on the sectors and manipulated the party to control their behavior. This left the party firmly in the hands of Calles.

Beginning in 1929, the party cloaked the nomination and election processes with a façade of legitimacy while also coordinating the efforts in various bureaucracies to get out the vote. The PNR became a regimented, top-down party answerable only to a few men at the top. Government employees above a certain rank had to belong to the party and contribute seven days' pay per year to its coffers. The party could also flush out potential contenders for the presidency and force them to declare their intentions. It moved Mexico slowly toward institutionalized presidential succession, though not toward democracy. Paradoxically, however, its very success in controlling the process allowed the president to postpone agrarian and labor reform efforts promised in the Constitution.

Calles could not succeed himself in 1929, so he appointed men to occupy the presidency. They served as puppets, beholden to him and obliged to consult with him and his cronies on major decisions. After a few years, though, Calles's power began to slip a little because of his declining health and extended absences from the capital. Simultaneously, civilian groups became more assertive, especially as they became desperate in the Depression-struck economy.

Behind the scenes, one of Calles's top men, Lázaro Cárdenas, former head of the PNR and now war minister, cultivated the support of unions and agrarian groups, carefully preparing the way for the presidential succession of 1934. A critical opportunity came in 1933, when a labor activist whom Cárdenas favored, Vicente Lombardo Toledano, put together the Mexican Workers' Confederation (CTM), which became a main source of Cárdenas's support.

Calles, who intended to install another puppet president to extend the Maximato, was unaware of Cárdenas's activities until too late. Cárdenas befriended junior military officers in the capital and won popularity among the enlisted men as well. Because no general had bothered to do that since 1920, a great chasm had arisen between the officers and the enlisted men. By the time the PNR convened in 1934, Cárdenas had sewn up the nomination. Calles bowed to the inevitable, confident that he could control Cárdenas in the way that he had the previous three

Lázaro Cárdenas, who served as president from 1934 to 1940, came to know Mexico better than almost anyone else. His military career, 1934 presidential campaign, and widespread travels took him to the most remote corners of the country. His patient, receptive manner led many poor people to call him Tata Lázaro, or Father Lázaro.

presidents. He was deeply mistaken about this, however. Cárdenas not only gained full power but also began to implement the revolutionary program that was charted by the 1917 Constitution but that was still largely unfulfilled.

Lázaro Cárdenas, perhaps the greatest president of Mexico since the revolution, was born in a small town in Michoacán in 1895. His family was middle class and of mestizo racial stock. Cárdenas was a smallish man with an active, versatile mind. After finishing primary school he worked at a number of odd jobs: as an artisan, pool-hall operator, and even editor of a pro-Madero paper in 1910–1911. He was both honest and savvy—critical attributes for a career in the army and politics.

Cárdenas had joined the revolution in 1913 at the age of eighteen, when he enlisted in Zapata's army. Later he switched to Obregón, to Villa, and finally to Calles. He served with unwavering loyalty to the latter throughout the 1920s. Then, as a progressive governor of his native state of Michoacán between 1928 and 1932 and simultaneously president of the PNR from 1930 to 1933, he began to aim at the presidency. In 1933 he became war minister—the second-most powerful post in government. He was clearly a rising power: a good general but a civilian at heart. Ideologically, he was inclined toward the left, whereas Calles and the rest were drifting in a conservative direction.

Cárdenas handled the succession expertly, without any serious challenges to his nomination. He had cultivated the support of the *agrarios* and labor (led by the CTM). He pushed for educational advances, nearly always a popular cause. He won the backing of junior officers and troops.

The party convened in early 1934 to work up a platform for the next six-year term. Dubbed the Plan Sexenio, the platform stressed labor, land, and educational advances for the masses. The tenor of the program was quite radical for Calles, but he accepted it as necessary for propaganda purposes. At that point Cárdenas felt secure enough to resign from his post as minister of war.

Cárdenas then decided to make a real campaign out of the election, even though he was assured the support of the official party. He traveled 26,500 kilometers and visited all the states. His revolutionary slogan preceded him: "Workers of Mexico, unite!" On the road, he was careful to meet with local *caciques* and army garrison chiefs, but he also held audiences with common people. He often sat for hours in town plazas listening to peasants and workers who had come to town to speak with him. They gave him the nickname Tata Lázaro (Father Lázaro) because he listened like a priest. His election in 1934 was one of the smoothest in years. Even after his election, he continued to tour the country meeting with people. He was a very popular man when inaugurated in December 1934.

Cárdenas accepted Calles's suggestions for cabinet members and PNR president so that the Jefe Máximo would think he was in charge. By mid-1935, however, Cárdenas was ready to make his move. While Calles was in Los Angeles for medical treatment, Cárdenas announced new and radical land and labor programs. He made it clear that he would lend official backing to agrarian and leftist union groups, and he even issued light arms to them. Cárdenas openly associated with such well-known leftists as Francisco Mújica (a principal architect of the 1917 Constitution) and the CTM's Lombardo Toledano. Political tension reached a fever pitch, with right-wing fascist groups, the Gold Shirts, often clashing in the streets with their leftist counterparts.

Calles returned to Mexico in May 1935 and denounced Cárdenas's initiatives as a "marathon of radicalism." But it soon became clear that Cárdenas could count on the backing of some generals, about half the politicians, most junior officers and troops, plus the recently armed *agrarios* and organized labor groups. Calles realized that he had been beaten and returned to Los Angeles. Over the next year, Calles and his followers sparred with the government until April 1936, when Cárdenas exiled them and asserted his full authority. The Maximato was over.

Cárdenas then proceeded to make good his promises. During the rest of his term he distributed fifty million acres of land through the land reform agency—more than all of his predecessors combined had done. Most of Mexico's arable land changed hands. This signaled the virtual demise of the traditional hacienda and the influence of the hacendado class. An unfortunate side effect of the land redistribution, however, was a decline in productivity. The new owners were not as efficient as the old, and peasant farmers tended to consume most of their profits rather than to reinvest them.

In the North, Cárdenas created one very large *ejido*, or community farm, meant to be a model for hundreds of others. It was the former Terrazas estate on the Coahuila-Durango border. Authorities renamed it Laguna and gave title to the thirty thousand families who resided there. The families ran cattle and raised cotton and cereals as a collective. Laguna was a good example of land reform limitations: It was never a commercial success. But land reform raised the level of pride and sense of well-being among the millions of previously landless peasants. Mexican land reform had to be justified as a program with political and social goals rather than on strictly economic grounds.

Meanwhile, the CTM labor federation quickly grew to a million members, and it worked so closely with the Ministry of Labor that it was virtually an official agency. Lombardo Toledano, a strong-willed socialist as well as a pragmatic politician, became a major ally of Cárdenas. He did not indulge in graft the way others had, and he always kept the workers' interests foremost in mind. He knew that he could count on Cárdenas to help his unions win better contracts.

Cárdenas also promoted educational expansion and reform, giving education even more prominence than Obregón or Calles had. He embraced the concept of a "socialist education" that valued the general welfare over individualism and capitalism. He even passed a law including this brand of socialism in the official curriculum. Cárdenas was willing to put his money where his mouth was: Education's share of the federal budget rose substantially, and he was able to build three thousand schools and train one hundred thousand new teachers, mostly recruited from the cities. Cárdenas challenged his teachers to be agents of change in their communities, spreading the word about the Constitution and mobilizing adults to assert their rights under it. Despite such advances that put more children than ever in the classroom, the number of illiterates actually rose because of extremely high birth rates in rural areas.

Table 16-1	Public School Enrollment
1907	0.8 million
1925	1.0 million
1935	1.7 million
1940	2.2 million

Because his socialist program evoked open opposition from conservatives and the Church, Cárdenas attempted to reach an agreement with the Catholic archbishop. He urged the latter to concern himself more with social problems and issues, in the spirit of the progressive 1931 papal encyclical known as *Quadragesimo Ano*. The prelate agreed, and Church-state relations have remained tranquil since then.

One of the most remarkable episodes of Cárdenas's presidency, the petroleum nationalization, came to a head in 1938. The episode began two years earlier, when petroleum workers' unions formed a federation and affiliated with Lombardo Toledano's CTM. These workers earned more than most laborers in Mexico, yet they had special hardships connected with living in oil field camps, buying in company stores, and being away from families for long periods. The oil companies, led by major British and American firms, refused to recognize the unions. The CTM backed the federation's call for a strike, which then brought on a mandatory six-month cooling-off period and eventual government mediation.

The labor ministry mediators ruled in favor of the laborers, thanks to Lombardo Toledano's influence with Cárdenas, but the companies still refused a settlement. Instead, they appealed the case to the Supreme Court. Cárdenas and other high officials were already irritated with the oil companies because they had shifted their purchases away from Mexico in the 1920s and 1930s, largely to Venezuela. Exports had fallen from 193 million barrels in 1921 to 41 million in 1936.

When the Supreme Court also ruled in favor of the laborers in early 1938, seventeen of the biggest companies sent a joint message to Cárdenas refusing to comply with the judicial ruling. Cárdenas took this as defiance of Mexican sovereignty and immediately nationalized the companies. He put them under a government corporation, Petróleos Mexicanos (Pemex), created to administer public oil lands and contracts.

The foreign companies expected the U.S. State Department and White House to give them full backing, so they submitted huge claims to the Mexican government: $200 million for the U.S. properties and $250 million for the British. Cárdenas countered with an offer of $10 million, saying that he would pay only for actual capital investment, not untapped oil reserves. Besides, he stated, most oil firms had long since paid off their capital and equipment in the form of excessive profits.

In the next two years the companies waged a vicious campaign to force Mexico to return their assets or pay their claims. President Franklin D. Roosevelt refused to intervene, however, because Ambassador Josephus Daniels convinced him that the companies had erred in defying the Supreme Court decision and that they got what they deserved. The two governments eventually set up an arbitration commission that awarded the U.S. companies $24 million in 1941.

Late in 1938 Cárdenas decided to restructure the official party. Renamed the Party of the Mexican Revolution (PRM), it was to represent four sectors: the existing ones of labor, *agrarios,* and the army, plus a new one, the *populares.* These latter were in fact mostly public servants, who could be manipulated by the bureaucracy and the president. By the late 1930s the CTM claimed 1.25 million members, the National Farmers' Confederation (CNC) 2.5 million, the military its highest authorized strength at 55,000, and the *populares* 55,000. Significantly, in 1938 soldiers were given the right to vote, which enhanced the influence of junior officers who could broker the votes of their troops.

The four PRM sectors were conceived as hierarchical pillars of the party, ostensibly to channel information and aspirations up. In fact, they passed orders only down from the top, collected money for the campaigns, and sent down instructions about who would be elected. PRM's successor, the PRI, would operate the same way after 1946.

By 1937 the top army generals were the only wild cards in the political deck capable of challenging Cárdenas's authority. One unsuccessful conspiracy and a failed revolt, however, helped strengthen the president's hold on power. By 1938 those who remained in the army were loyal to Cárdenas. He had succeeded in pacifying the army and reducing its share of the federal budget from 25 to 19 percent. Younger academy-trained officers who had not fought in the revolution were by then reaching command positions.

In 1939 Cárdenas passed a military reorganization bill that attempted to eradicate the spirit of caste that had previously bound together officers against civil society. He hoped instead to implant a desire to be of service to the nation. Meanwhile, the 1939 Obligatory Service Law helped diminish the gap between officers, troops, and the civilian population. A final measure to subdue the army was authorization of civilian armed forces, especially the CNC and CTM militias, to serve as deterrents to ambitious generals. The peasants, always armed and ready to intervene in civil wars, proclaimed their loyalty to Cárdenas. In 1938 Lombardo Toledano paraded one hundred thousand men in Mexico City for Labor Day and bragged that he had thirty thousand arms. Tension became palpable between the army and the militias, but the maneuvers averted open violence.

The succession crisis of 1940 proved that Cárdenas had tamed his rivals. The atmosphere of crisis and ideological confrontation that year brought out radical candidates for the presidency. Yet ultimately, Cárdenas was able to name and elect a moderate as his successor: General Avila Camacho. The latter was relatively unknown, a desk officer who had not fought in the revolution. His main advantage was having few enemies. He was the only candidate not opposed by at least two PRM sectors.

The resultant landslide election was predictable. Furthermore, Avila Camacho was the last general ever elected president. Cárdenas's pacification of the army became complete in 1943 when the army was dropped from the PRM.

Cárdenas won a place of honor among Mexican revolutionary leaders due to his successful reforms in the 1930s. His administration was the last to pursue the 1917 constitutional mandates vigorously. Most authors agree that the revolution died around 1940, after which it was kept alive only rhetorically by party hacks. Cárdenas continued to play a role in politics, though never in an official capacity, through the 1960s. He became an unofficial "conscience of the revolution," a reminder of what the original revolution had been fought for.

Colombia and Venezuela to World War II

The two countries that span the northern edge of South America could hardly have had more unlike experiences during the Depression decade. Venezuela endured the classic dictatorship of Juan Vicente Gómez until his death in 1935 and then continued under military presidents until 1945. Colombia, on the other hand, not only held a peaceful election in 1930 but actually transferred the executive branch from the Conservative Party to the Liberal Party without incident. Oddly, these experiences reversed the nineteenth-century traditions of these two countries.

Venezuela gained some respite from petty caudillos and intermittent civil wars through the imposition of a dictatorship by army General Cipriano Castro (1899–1908), who was replaced by his vice president, Juan Vicente Gómez, in 1908. The latter wielded power as an autocratic modernizer, much like Mexico's Díaz and Argentina's Roca. He provided maximum administration with a minimum of democratic procedure. He also became famous as one of the most ruthless dictators in the region.

A sailing vessel passing an oil derrick in Lake Maracaibo, Venezuela. During the 1920s oil exports from this region surpassed those from the Mexican gulf coast, the leading producer before World War I. Throughout this century the Venezuelan economy has depended heavily on oil revenues.

Gómez, a native of the western Andes state of Táchira, continued the tradition of government by army officers and strong-willed rulers. Rural in outlook and accustomed to obedience from underlings, the dictators from Táchira had a lock on the presidency, which they exercised through military domination.

Gómez's extraordinary twenty-seven-year rule coincided with the rise of Venezuelan oil production for export. This development, made possible by Gómez's guarantee of order and progress, deeply altered the future of the country. It set in motion developments that few could have predicted.

Earthy and unconcerned with appearances, Gómez ran Venezuela as his personal realm. He tolerated a Congress as long as it did what it was told and obediently reelected him president. He supported a bureaucracy in Caracas, though he preferred to live on his cattle ranch sixty miles away. He had an unerring sense for holding and exercising power and cared little about the formalities of office. He promulgated four constitutions, none of which infringed on his absolute powers. He differed from his nineteenth-century predecessors mostly in the effectiveness of his administration, one that did not tolerate the kinds of revolts and strife that had plagued the country previously.

The oil deposits of Venezuela, centered around Lake Maracaibo on the northwestern coast, had long been known to exist. World War I spurred huge growth in war industries in Europe and North America, thereby awakening interest in the Venezuelan oil deposits. Furthermore, the shaky reliability of the Mexican oil fields led the big international oil companies (called the "majors" and later the Seven

Sisters) to invest in development around Maracaibo. The first well came in after the outbreak of the war, and by 1918 Venezuela began exporting crude. Gómez had Congress pass legislation favorable to the majors but also protective of the rights of the workers.

Soon European and U.S. companies built huge refineries offshore, on the Dutch islands of Curaçao and Aruba, where they would be safe from depredations. The companies did not want to repeat their experiences in Mexico, where revolutionaries routinely threatened to blow up refineries. These installations converted crude into bunker, heating, and fuel oil for export throughout the Atlantic basin. As the world economy shifted from coal to oil, demand for crude burgeoned. In the course of the 1920s Venezuela become the world's largest petroleum exporter and enjoyed an economic bonanza.

Gómez's success was due to several initiatives. First, he professionalized the army by providing it with trained officers and modern weapons. He made absolutely certain that it remained loyal to him, sending to the firing squad anyone who challenged his authority.

Second, Gómez created a secret police branch that spied on civilians and reported dissent. Anyone overheard criticizing the government ended up in jail, exile, or the grave. Press censorship was the accepted practice, softened by government subsidies to publishers. When students at the Central University protested his policies in 1912, he closed it indefinitely; it did not reopen until 1923.

Third, he gave the country unprecedented income from petroleum, spreading around the benefits. This depended upon keeping the majors happy, which he achieved by giving them unusually favorable terms. The companies responded by shifting their purchases to Venezuela.

Although most Venezuelans were content to go about their business during the Gómez regime, a few nationalists became critical of the concessions given to the oil companies. In 1928 a group of student activists almost seized power with a rapid coup. The group was subdued, however, and 220 ended up in jail. Afterward, most were released on the condition that they leave the country. Later these exiles reemerged as an important force in politics, calling themselves the Generation of 1928.

The Depression barely affected Venezuela, so efficient was Gómez's rule. Even when he died in 1935, at the age of seventy-eight, the regime continued without much change. The next two presidents, both generals who had served as ministers of war, did relax censorship and sentences of exile, so that by the late 1930s limited political activity had resumed. Moreover, the labor unions—led by the oil field workers—began to exert more influence in the political arena. Still, the military dictatorship remained in place until 1945.

In Colombia, a miraculous transformation had occurred in the early twentieth century, leading to the end of the vicious, bloody struggles for power of previous generations. This was attributed largely to the firm control of General Rafael Reyes (1904–1914), an autocratic modernizer in the mold of Porfirio Díaz or Guzmán Blanco. Reyes created an ingenious bipartisan system called the National Union. Basically, the Liberals and Conservatives each received half the appointive positions in the entire government, including cabinet posts, satisfying their parties' need for patronage. In exchange, the Liberals accepted the seemingly permanent occupation of the presidency by the Conservatives. This calmed partisan rancor and prevented the appearance of rival parties for at least a generation.

The Colombian economy began to recover in the early years of the century, in part buoyed by Brazil's coffee price support program, which sustained the world price of coffee. Mild Colombian beans became prized for their flavor and were used to improve blends sold in the United States and Europe. Bananas also made their debut along the north coast, and by the late 1920s Colombia was the world's second-largest producer. Other crops also found lucrative export markets. The expanding economy complemented Reyes's successes in quelling political fighting.

In the 1920s the Colombian government signed two important treaties. In the first, with the United States, Colombia forgave the U.S. role in the 1903 secession of Panama and received an indemnity of $25 million. This normalized relations and allowed U.S. companies to begin exploring for petroleum, recently discovered on the north coast. Shortly afterward oil exports began out of the port of Barranquilla. The second treaty, with Peru, provided Colombia with a corridor stretching down to the town of Leticia on the Amazon River. More generally, settling outstanding foreign problems opened the way for foreign investment and bond sales, which expanded rapidly in the late 1920s.

Colombia's alpine geography, dominated by three mountain chains and divided by major rivers, had long hampered regional transportation. A major step toward overcoming this problem was taken in 1920, however, with the formation of the first South American airline, SCADTA. In addition, new rail lines and roads began to integrate the country economically.

The long Conservative reign, however, had allowed many social problems to fester, and discontent surfaced in manufacturing cities and plantation towns. One labor action became infamous—the Santa Marta banana strike. The U.S.-owned United Fruit Company called in Colombian troops, who opened fire on the strikers, killing hundreds. This scene, which dramatized the injustices committed by foreign companies, became immortalized in Gabriel García Márquez's novel, *One Hundred Years of Solitude.* In many other parts of the country, moreover, poor people became upset over the lack of roads, schools, hospitals, and welfare programs. The Depression exacerbated these shortcomings.

Novelistic Account of Santa Marta Banana Strike of 1928

The great strike broke out. Cultivation stopped halfway, the fruit rotted on the trees and the hundred-twenty-car trains remained on the sidings. The idle workers overflowed the towns . . . it was announced that the army had been assigned to reestablish public order. . . . There were three regiments, whose march in time to a galley drum made the earth tremble. Their snorting of a many-headed dragon filled the glow of noon with a pestilential vapor. They were short, stocky, and brutelike. They perspired with the sweat of a horse and had a smell of suntanned hide and the taciturn and impenetrable perseverance of men from the uplands. . . . Martial law enabled the army to assume the functions of arbitrator in the controversy, but no effort at conciliation was made. As soon as they appeared in Macondo, the soldiers put aside their rifles and cut and loaded the bananas and started the trains running. The workers, who had been content to wait until then, went into the woods with no other weapons but their working machetes and they began to sabotage the sabotage. They burned plantations and commissaries, tore up tracks to impede the passage of the trains that began to open their path with machine-gun fire, and they cut telegraph and telephone wires ... the authorities called upon the workers to gather in Macondo. ... Around twelve o'clock, waiting for a train that was not arriving, more than three thousand people, workers, women, and children, had spilled out of the open space in front of the station. ... The captain gave the order to fire and fourteen machine guns answered at once. It was as if the machine guns had been loaded with caps, because their panting rattle could be heard and their incandescent spitting could be seen, but not the slightest reaction was perceived. ... They were penned in, swirling about in a gigantic whirlwind that little by little was being reduced to its epicenter as the edges were systematically being cut off all around like an onion being peeled by the insatiable and methodical shears of the machine guns. ... [Later] an extraordinary proclamation to the nation ... said that the workers left the station and had returned home in peaceful groups. The proclamation also stated that the union leaders, with great patriotic spirit, had reduced their demands to two points: a reform of medical services and the building of latrines in the living quarters.

(Gabriel García Marquez, *One Hundred Years of Solitude*, translator Gregory Rabassa [New York: Harper & Row, 1970], pp. 307–315)

The presidential election of 1930 not only went ahead peacefully, but also the Liberal candidate, Alfonso López, defeated his Conservative opponent, which had not happened for fifty years. López's success was owed partly to the Colombian electorate's sense that a change was overdue and partly to López's appealing platform, called the Revolution on the March. Arguing that the federal government had to address pressing social problems, he proposed far-reaching reforms that ultimately required constitutional amendments. He suggested that without these reforms, Colombia might drift toward a violent revolution.

It took several years for the Liberals to assemble their reform program, which was largely carried out in 1936. That year a package of constitutional amendments was adopted that separated Church and state, created universal male suffrage, gave labor the right to collective bargaining and strikes, and authorized government economic planning. In addition, Congress passed much larger budgets for education and social security. Finally, Congress passed a land reform bill committed to the principle of giving property to those who work it. In many ways, these Liberal reforms paralleled those of Lázaro Cárdenas in Mexico.

The Liberal era that lasted until 1946 also expanded democratic processes. The individual's civil rights were complemented by full freedom of the press, freedom of assembly, and honest elections. In these years Colombians bragged that their democracy had withstood all threats, and they called Bogotá the Athens of South America, referring to the birthplace of democracy.

Peru

The populist era launched by the election of 1931 was destroyed a year and a half later by an assassin's bullet that took President Sánchez Cerro's life. The country plunged into a dictatorship organized by the army and the oligarchy. Congress installed one of Peru's top generals, Oscar Benavides, in the presidency, where he remained until 1939. Even after passing the office on to a civilian successor, the army remained powerful behind the scenes. APRA, meanwhile, grew more popular despite the fact that its activities were severely proscribed by the government.

The Benavides regime weathered several years of economic depression and then began to enjoy expanding production and employment in the mid-1930s. In keeping with the times, Benavides introduced legislation creating new welfare and educational agencies to deal with the social question. These agencies included a ministry of health, labor, and welfare—which expanded public services to the working class—and a social security system. In addressing the social question, Peru was merely following the lead of many other governments in the hemisphere, and its reforms were milder than most. The benefits of these programs remained largely in the cities, thereby attracting a steady stream of migrants from the countryside. By the 1950s the influx of rural people would create huge shantytowns, called *barriadas,* in major cities.

Toward the end of the 1930s, the army felt secure enough to hold elections. APRA was disqualified from nominating candidates, however, because of its revolutionary past. The official candidate for president predictably won. Manuel Prado Ugarteche served for a six-year term (1939–1945), guiding the country through the Second World War. He at first flirted with right-wing movements and Axis sympathizers, but after the United States joined the war, he threw his country behind the Allied effort. Peruvians did not fight in the war but instead supplied strategic materials to U.S. arms factories.

Evolving U.S. Policy in the Caribbean Basin

During the 1920s the U.S. State Department began to view military occupation and intervention in the region as counterproductive. Marine and army landings cost money, squandered goodwill, and often stirred up more trouble than they suppressed. The Clarke Memorandum, made public in 1930, set out the new policy, which became known as *noninterventionism* (see Chapter Thirteen).

Franklin Roosevelt most fully enunciated the new Good Neighbor Policy regarding Latin America during his first year in office. The United States would no longer intervene militarily in the internal affairs of neighboring nations, regardless of whose interests were at stake. U.S. citizens had to obey the laws of the country in which they resided. U.S. investors with complaints were to exhaust local courts and other means to redress their grievances. The United States would no longer answer calls to support one or another side or even to supervise elections in the region. The U.S. foreign policy community achieved such a broad consensus on nonintervention policy that it held remarkably steady until the mid-1950s.

FDR's Good Neighbor Policy

In the field of world policy, I would dedicate this nation to the policy of the good neighbor—the neighbor who resolutely respects himself and . . . respects the rights of others.

(Franklin Roosevelt, inaugural address, March 4, 1933)

The essential qualities of a true Pan Americanism must be the same as those which constitute a good neighbor, namely, mutual understanding, and through such understanding, a sympathetic appreciation of the other's point of view.

(Franklin Roosevelt, Pan American Day address, April 14, 1933)

That is a new approach that I am talking about to these South American things. Give them a share. They think they are just as good as we are, and many of them are.

(Franklin Roosevelt, speech, January 1940)

The pledge not to intervene militarily by no means meant that the United States would stop pursuing its national interests in the region. On the contrary, during the 1930s, as in other eras of U.S. isolationism, the hemisphere was watched even more closely. The U.S. government employed a more active diplomacy, spying, a judicious military presence, political intrigue, and economic persuasion to further its interests. In the case of several troublesome Caribbean nations, this meant working with dictators who promised to defend U.S. interests in exchange for providing various kinds of support. Thus the Good Neighbor Policy consisted of shifting from military intervention to more subtle kinds of intervention in Latin American affairs.

The Roosevelt administration made the most use of several innovative kinds of diplomatic persuasion in the 1930s. First, it created an economic aid program, administered by the Export-Import Bank and later by other agencies. Cuba and several other Latin American countries were among the first to receive such aid. Second, U.S. military presence continued to be projected throughout the region from several bases in the Caribbean and the Panama Canal Zone and by means of naval and air patrols. These were reinforced in the late 1930s by multilateral meetings and treaties to defend against possible European aggression in the hemisphere. Third, the president himself visited Latin America several times and made concerted efforts to win friends through a more responsive diplomacy. These measures, essentially public relations gestures, paid off handsomely in goodwill and a spirit of cooperation. And finally, presidential emissaries and friends serving in the region used their authority to help install governments that were willing to work with the United States. Backroom deals, clandestine financing, shared intelligence, and subterfuge became standard operating procedures. It is fair to say that the U.S. presence was stronger despite the military restraint exercised.

The Classic Dictators

Partly as a result of U.S. policy, a new generation of dictators took over Latin America during the 1930s. Most of them were military officers who had police organizations to take over when U.S. forces withdrew. They were, for the most part, chosen by U.S. officials to safeguard U.S. interests, and they received special treatment from the U.S. State Department. They exercised absolute authority and wielded it arbitrarily, yet they always cooperated with the Yankees. Roosevelt acknowledged this kind of arrangement once when he said of Nicaraguan dictator Anastasio Somoza: "He may be a son of a bitch, but he's *our* son of a bitch!" With people like Somoza protecting U.S. interests, it was unnecessary to keep marines stationed in the region.

Who were these classic dictators? They were born in the 1890s and early 1900s, usually into poor or lower-middle-class families. They came from rural areas, with little access to the amenities of the capital cities. They lost contact with their fathers at an early age, through abandonment, death, or other causes. They were usually nonwhites in countries where the elites prided themselves on European lineage. Finally, they had only primary or secondary schooling, in countries where aspirants for power usually had university training, often abroad. For all these reasons, a few years earlier it would have been impossible to predict that they would become heads of state in their respective countries.

If the United States bore some responsibility for the rise of the dictators, local politics and society determined the kind of men who would prevail. Each local army or police force typically had a small number of elite officers who enjoyed a privileged status and political power because of their upper-class family connections. Noncommissioned officers and soldiers, in contrast, were held in contempt by the well-to-do, tolerated only because someone had to keep the lower classes in line, through violence if necessary. And occasionally these forces had to fight the armies of neighboring countries. These forces were not true armies in the modern sense: Their officers meddled in politics, fought among themselves, stole money and supplies, and cared little about the effectiveness or discipline of their troops.

The noncommissioned officers, on the other hand, usually came from the rural middle or lower classes, where loyalty to the white landowning elite was traditional. They held effective control over the rank and file and were only tenuously supervised by the elite officers. Thus a social gap opened up between the noncoms and the elite that would allow the former to assume command of troops in moments of crisis. Once in command, such officers could then transform their positions into political leadership by appealing to the masses, assuming populist stances, or by eliminating rivals. This, in a general way, describes the rise of the dictators in the 1930s and 1940s.

These men had other, more personal characteristics, that warrant description. They were quite intelligent despite their lack of regular schooling. They were politically astute and possessed the will power to take advantage of opportunities that came their way. They displayed innate understanding of military tactics that, despite meager formal training, allowed them to prevail in actual combat. They distrusted colleagues, suspecting them of wishing to take power, so they never cultivated protégés who might become rivals. Instead, they groomed their sons for power in the hope of creating family dynasties. In many cases this succeeded: Somoza's sons Luis

Table 16-2 Classic Dictators

Country	Name	Years in Power	Born	Class	Urban Rural	Race	Ed	Age @ first off	Mil?	Foreign Influence	Died	@ Age
Dominican Republic	Trujillo	1930–61	1891	middle	R	mul	1st	33	y	y	1961	69
Nicaragua	Somoza	1936–56	1896	middle	R	wh	univ	31	y	y	1956	60
Cuba	Batista	1940–58	1901	lower	R	mul	2nd	32	y	y	1973	72
Panama	Ramón	1952–55	1908	middle	R	mest	mil	47	y	y	1955	47
Paraguay	Stroessner	1954–89	1912	middle	R	mest	mil	40	y	y		

Source: *Encyclopedia of Latin American History and Culture* and author's compilation.

and Anastasio Jr. (Tachito) both wielded power in Nicaragua after their father's death. François Chevalier, Haiti's infamous Papa Doc, was succeeded by his son Claude, nicknamed Baby Doc. In the Dominican Republic, however, Rafael Trujillo failed in his efforts to shape his son Ramfis into an iron-fisted successor.

Most of the classic dictators managed to rise to the top as army officers, having been born into modest circumstances. They cleverly blended the skills of military command with political savvy. All were ruthless in getting power and holding onto it. They thought nothing of ordering the murder of a rival. They often enjoyed considerable popularity among the nonwhite lower classes, who admired their cunning and empathized with their successes. They recruited middle- and upper-class collaborators using nationalistic rhetoric and appeals to Hispanic tradition. Finally, the dictators served as "cultural brokers" by mediating between and sometimes even translating for the U.S. military occupational forces. Then during the transitions from armed forces under U.S. tutelage to national guards, they naturally emerged as future commanders.

The remainder of this chapter is devoted to two classic dictators who were representative of the entire generation.

Batista and Trujillo

Perhaps the most complex and long lived of the dictators, Fulgencio Batista, ruled Cuba off and on from the mid-1930s until 1959. His background, talents, style, achievements, and failures make him almost a prototype of the Caribbean dictator.

Batista's parents both were poor mulattoes. His father, Belisario, a sugar cane cutter in the Northeast, was said to have fought with Antonio Maceo during the independence struggle. Shortly before Fulgencio's birth, the family migrated to the sugar port of Veguita in Oriente province. Fulgencio was dark-skinned like his parents, but some features (straight black hair and a sharp nose) suggested some Amerindian heritage as well.

As a child Fulgencio cut sugar cane, but he also learned to read and write in a public school and a Quaker night school. His mother died when he was fourteen, and he wandered from town to town, doing odd jobs that he got by his good looks, charm, and speaking ability. At one point he worked as stable boy in an army barracks, where he earned the nickname *el mulato lindo* (pretty brown boy).

In 1921 he enlisted in the army, where he was assigned to the legal affairs office because of his ability to read, write, and speak well. His work as a law clerk taught him to type and take stenography. Later he taught these skills in the staff school. Another assignment required guarding President Zelaya's estate, for which he was given temporary army leave. In 1924 he married Elisa Godínez and transferred back to regular service. There he became a trusted aide to his battalion commander, who promoted him to corporal and eventually first sergeant. Batista thus had a wide range of experiences and enjoyed an insider's view of the internal politics of the Cuban Army.

In 1933, during the depths of the Machado dictatorship, Batista served as stenographer in kangaroo courts impaneled to punish the dictator's enemies. His disgust led him to join a subversive organization, the ABC. In that same year Machado was deposed amid terrible rioting, and a stand-in was installed as president. In September, however, Batista helped lead a sergeants' revolt against the commissioned officers, which toppled the government again.

Batista's success in 1933 derived in part from the degeneration of command in the army. The commissioned officers were mostly from the traditional elite and were white, unlike the noncoms and soldiers, who were mulattoes and blacks. The officers spent most of their time in leisure and political activities, centering on the aristocratic officers' club, far from the barracks. They had gradually lost the loyalty of the rank and file because of their isolation. This allowed Batista and his fellow conspirators to preempt command and overthrow the government.

The provisional government installed in September 1933 came under the leadership of Ramón Grau San Martín, a university professor of economics who had been prominent in anti-Machado activities. However, Sumner Welles, the U.S. State Department emissary in Havana, refused to accept San Martín because of his socialist ideas and inability to impose order. So in January 1934 Batista, by now a colonel and the most powerful man in Cuba, removed San Martín, with the blessing of Welles. During the coming months the U.S. government supported Batista's de facto regime by extending to Cuba a $4 million Export-Import Bank loan, awarding Cuba the largest sugar quota of any Latin American country, and nullifying the Platt Amendment.

Batista exercised power from behind the throne because of his connection with the U.S. embassy. He moved to stage center in 1936, however, when he became chief of staff of the army. From then on he ruled Cuba more openly, using an informal alliance with labor, the Communist Party (legalized in 1938), and the army. Taking cues from the Roosevelt administration, Batista pushed for social and economic reforms, such as university autonomy, labor organization, women's suffrage, expanded primary and secondary education, and industrialization.

Eventually Batista called a constituent assembly that wrote the progressive 1940 Constitution. After its enactment he ran for president and won, partly due to his popular reforms and restraint as ruler. His four-year term saw great prosperity in Cuba, due to wartime spending by the United States.

Rafael Trujillo was born in San Cristóbal in the Dominican Republic in 1891. He belonged to the small-town middle class of his region. He had eight brothers and two sisters. His scanty education, Haitian lineage, and Negroid features barred him from the white, aristocratic society. He was shrewd and intelligent, nonetheless, and used his charm to move around in the regional society. He gained a reputation for womanizing and rowdiness as a youth. At one point he worked as security officer on a sugar plantation.

Trujillo's political career began during the U.S. military occupation of his country (1916–1924). In 1918 he signed on as an officer in the police force organized by the U.S. Marines and won rapid promotion. When the United States pulled out, Trujillo became commander of the unit, which had been strengthened into an army. Although powerful now, Trujillo did not enjoy acceptance by the elite, which looked down on military officers.

Trujillo had married a woman of the lower class in 1917, but he divorced her in 1924, partly because she held back his political career. Three years later he remarried, this time to a high society woman of good family. This marriage proved unhappy, too, because Trujillo consorted with a string of mistresses for the rest of his life. In 1927, for example, one of these women bore him his son Ramfis, whom he unsuccessfully tried to groom as successor.

Trujillo seized power in 1930, aided by the disorder caused by economic depression and a devastating hurricane. From then until his assassination in 1961 he ruled the country like an Oriental despot. Until the late 1950s he was never seriously opposed by the United States, which indeed helped him remain in power by awarding the country a generous sugar quota in 1935.

Trujillo's personality defies easy description. Preoccupied with sex, he pursued women with all the means at his disposal and treated women with a jealous possessiveness. He was exceedingly vain and preened himself with hair grease, perfume, makeup, and powder. Later in life he used talcum to whiten his complexion. He always dressed formally and obliged his aides to do likewise. An indicator of his vanity was his renaming the capital city after himself: Santo Domingo became Ciudad Trujillo.

Trujillo dominated the country and all its institutions. No one was beyond his influence. He used terror, secret police, spies, torture, propaganda, intrigue, graft, and subterfuge to manipulate others.

Massacre of 25,000 Haitians in the Dominican Republic in 1937

For a century and a half Haiti and the Dominican Republic have shared the island of Hispaniola, between Cuba and Puerto Rico. The arrangement has always been awkward, for the two peoples differ sharply in language, ethnic tradition, skin color, religion, government, and family makeup. The border between the two nations had not been fully delineated until the 1930s, and even then tens of thousands of Haitians remained on the Dominican side. The interpenetration of the two peoples grew during the annual sugar harvest, when thousands more Haitians crossed the border to cut cane.

The Dominican dictator Rafael Trujillo, who inspected the border region in October 1937, expressed great irritation at the large number of Haitians living in his territory. He instructed the army to issue an ultimatum obliging Haitians to leave the country in four days; after that they would begin executing those who remained. One eyewitness report stated that:

"The guards picked up a lot of people to help them with the raids on the Haitians and the killings . . . guards and the people who were helping them out dug big holes, then they brought the Haitians they had captured. They were tied one to another in groups, and they brought them to the edges of the holes. One by one they untied them before killing them. They were beaten to death. They were told to bend down and then they gave them a blow to the neck. They fell into the holes dead. Some of them were still alive when they fell, and still suffering. My cousin told me. He became sick when he saw what was happening and they threw him out of that place. . . .

Practically without stopping, day and night, they spent many days killing Haitians. They used bonfires fueled with wood so they could see in the night."

A U.S.-supervised investigation of the incident concluded that Trujillo should issue an apology and pay Haiti an indemnization of $750,000. This was done in 1938, on the eve of World War II. The case was never formally reopened.

(Miguel Aquino, *Holocaust in the Caribbean* [Waterbury, Conn.: Emancipation Press, 1997], pp. 130, 140)

Conclusions and Issues

The 1930s proved to be a complex, troubled, and dangerous era in Latin America. The Great Depression created severe hardships and suffering for the masses, and it bankrupted most governments. Partly as a result, rival parties and groups sought power, provoking a spate of revolts and coups in the region. The laissez-faire economic policies that had prevailed before 1929 had left governments open to indebtedness and financial shocks, and many wealthy families faced ruin. Disenchantment with the old order led Latin American leaders and intellectuals to turn inward in search of national preservation. They sought strength in their own people and traditions, and they offered protection for native industry.

At the same time, some of the radical experiments of the era, like communism in the USSR, fascism in Italy, and Nazism in Germany, appealed to young people. Radical movements arose and competed with the traditional parties, sometimes leading to violent clashes.

In most cases, the wealthy families managed to retain control over their countries' governments. Many governments sought to soften the harsh effects of the Depression with enlightened social policies, like retirement benefits and free health care. Their response to labor assertiveness tended to be more stern: They used police to beat down strikes and created official union movements that could be controlled from the top down. Most countries abandoned democratic procedures, if they existed, and relied on autocratic regimes to maintain stability.

In some areas, outright dictatorships emerged in the 1930s, usually with the blessing of the U.S. government, which had decided no longer to station military forces in the region. The leaders of these regimes became the classic dictators, portrayed in movies and novels about Latin America. Although not representative of the region as a whole, they do form a coherent group of leaders who can be portrayed collectively.

Discussion Questions

1. How did the 1930s Depression differ from those of the 1890s and 1830s in terms of its impact on Latin America? Did politics drive economics, or vice versa?

Account for the varying outcomes of economic hardship in the major nations of the region.

2. Is it possible for a revolutionary party to become institutionalized, as the Mexican leaders claimed? Why is Lázaro Cárdenas still regarded as the greatest figure in the revolution?

3. How would you describe the relationships between the Roosevelt White House and the strongman regimes that emerged in the 1930s throughout the Caribbean basin? Were these relationships based more on principle or on expediency?

Race, Culture, and Gender

Students at Venezuela's Central University Plan Demonstration in 1936

Luiza looked down the boulevard, past the trees. She carried a placard and along with hundreds of other students was waving it wildly in the late Caracas afternoon, shouting slogans, having a great time.

"What's that down there?" she shouted to her friend Raquel. They looked down the broad avenue, built by the dictator Gómez, now dead in his grave.

"I don't know. Don't worry about it pal! Long live the revolution! The son of a bitch is dead!" Raquel shouted, carried away by the sound of her own voice, and those of hundreds of others. Courage sometimes builds its own momentum in numbers.

"Looks like horses to me," Paco shouted toward Luiza. Indeed, far down the boulevard, but advancing inexorably toward the demonstators, trotted a phalanx of mounted troopers.

"Don't worry, don't worry, *compañeros*," Raquel exhorted. "We've got right on our side!" She hoisted her placard, "DEMOCRACY NOW! DOWN WITH TYRANNY!" with more enthusiasm, pumping it up and down.

Gómez is dead, Raquel," Paco responded, "but the army still rules the country." His placard drooped a bit as he looked at the cavalry advancing. What would they do? A dust cloud formed as the horses kicked up the debris in the street. The army already had jailed one of their comrades earlier in the week, Olga Luzardo, in Zulia, for her strong views in the newspaper.

Last night as they hammered and nailed their placards, carefully stenciling their messages, they wondered what would happpen as they stepped outside the university environs. Traditionally, universities were sanctuaries of sorts for political freedom and expression, but they had to go beyond the students, lawyers and teachers.

"We have to reach the people."

"Sure we do, but how? Join the Communists?"

Someone spat in a corner in disgust. "They're Soviet puppets. We're Venezuelans."

"Form our own party?"

"Why not? I heard that's what Rómulo said to do."

"Betancourt said that?"

"Sure, form a party, keep it legitimate, but the secret agenda is revolution."

"Strengthen our ties with the petroleum workers. Man, their union is stronger and stronger with the expansion of production on Lake Maracaibo."

"And richer!"

"And the peasants?"

Silence followed. They all, Raquel, Luiza, Paco and the others, knew that the most oppressed people in Venezuela, all across Latin America, were the peasants, the *campesinos* and *peones*. These were middle-class children. It still was somewhat of an abstraction for them. But they knew their revolutions.

"The great revolutions, remember, have always brought the peasants forward. Look at Russia, Mexico, heck, even France."

"Students, Workers and Peasants to the Barricades!"

Someone snickered. "What barricades, silly?"

Revolutionaries and barricades are synonymous! You can't have one without the other!"

They all laughed, breaking the tension. Tomorrow they would march and demonstrate. What would happen? A few years earlier, in 1928, Rómulo Betancourt, later elected president of his country, had been jailed and exiled for demonstrating and writing against the dictator Gómez. Betancourt and fellow exiles wandered over Latin America and Europe. Betancourt himself took up residence in Costa Rica where he rubbed shoulders with fellow exiles, communists and socialists, democrats and fascists, picking up many strands that he would later form into a successful party in his home country.

"Solidarity. That's the name of the game," someone said, standing, looking at his placard with evident self-satisfaction.

"The movement is worldwide, *compañeros*. We must stand with revolutionaries everywhere. Juan Perejil came back from Paris a while back. Said he met a fellow named Ho Chi Minh who wants to overthrow the colonialists and imperialists in his home of Indochina."

"Right," someone added reflectively. "And movement we form needs international connections, and not just with those straitjacketed communists from Moscow!"

Now they were out on the street. Paco stopped chanting and moving as he saw the mounted troops near. Luiza and Raquel, and all the other students, also quieted. The horses, at a walk, broke into a canter at the bark of an order from one of the officers. At a block's distance between the cavalry and the students, another order could be heard and the troopers drew their swords, turning them so the flat of the blades would rain down on the insolent lawbreakers before them.

The students broke and dashed for cover just as the horses hit them, in a melee of screams and curses. The blows fell equally on men and women, the boys and girls of the night before.

In Venezuela and elsewhere in the 1930s, many women found their voices in the struggles against dictatorship and economic injustice. Female activists, even when they could not vote, took part in university organizations, party formation, and labor actions. They usually came from well-to-do families hurt by the Depression and denied influence by oppressive regimes. Columns written by women began to appear in newspapers, and some women became professors in the better schools and universities. Most of the activists had lived abroad for a time, in Belgium, France, England, or the United States. The feminist vanguard, though largely forgotten today, paved the way for equal rights and participation by women after World War II.

Theories of Race

In the late nineteenth century, most writings by Latin American intellectuals applied frankly racist ideas borrowed from Europe and the United States. Social theorists, biologists, anthropologists, and philosophers believed that humanity could be divided into three races—Caucasoid, Negroid, and Mongoloid—and that these could be typed scientifically. This pseudo science asserted that Caucasians, based on what is today recognized as false evidence, are superior to the others. A corollary held that racial mixing leads to degradation and "mongrelization."

In the 1920s equally questionable theories known as *eugenics* held that selective mating and breeding could also improve the racial characteristics of a given population. These theories, too, enjoyed a small vogue in Latin America.

As a result of such spurious science, Latin American writers believed that they faced serious handicaps when it came to economic development and cultural achievement. To remedy this situation, many urged that their leaders encourage European immigration and other means to whiten or Europeanize their populations.

Several Latin American writers in the 1920s counterattacked scientific racism and eugenics with their own myths of racial hierarchy. Although no more valid than the theories that they refuted, these ideas encouraged Latin Americans to stop worrying about their supposed inferiority and also helped to diminish racism in their societies. These ideas had a profound impact on later generations and are still widely held today.

Vasconcelos, Freyre, Haya de la Torre, and *Indigenismo*

The extraordinary activist and intellectual José de Vasconcelos carried out the reinvention of Mexico's racial character in the years following World War I.

After the revolution, President Obregón appointed Vasconcelos as both minister of education and rector of the Autonomous University of Mexico (UNAM) in 1920. From these two positions and with his towering intellect, Vasconcelos led a renewal of philosophy in his country. The first order of business was to create an ideology that would justify the revolution. This required rehabilitating the Amerindians, mestizos, and workers who had fought to overthrow the Díaz regime. He did so in the introduction to *The Cosmic Race,* an account of his travels through South America in 1922.

Vasconcelos argued that human life probably originated on the legendary continent of Atlantis, which disappeared or perhaps reappeared as part of the American continent. Early humans migrated outward and formed four genetic trunks of our family tree: Negroes, Caucasians, Asians, and Amerindians. Vasconcelos believed that Amerindians may be the most direct descendants of the Atlantis ancestors. The four peoples evolved separately in Africa, Asia, Europe, and the Americas, with little contact among them.

Columbus changed all that, however, by setting off great waves of European migrations to the New World. The Europeans also brought millions of Africans to labor in their plantations and mines. In the late nineteenth century, even Asians flocked to the Americas, as indentured workers and immigrants. So the Americas became the site of a racial reunification of the earth's peoples. This was more true in Latin America than in the northern colonies of Britain and France because of the accommodating nature of the Catholic church.

Whites temporarily dominated the other races because of their technological superiority, but that would soon change. In fact, the great racial and cultural experiment taking place in Latin America had produced a fifth race, *la raza cósmica* (the cosmic race). Spanish and Portuguese settlers had intermarried with Amerindians and Africans, fulfilling "a mission to melt together ethnically and spiritually all peoples." They also absorbed the best elements of their respective cultures. The new race, made up of mestizos and mulattoes, was counteracting the earlier dispersion of humankind and effecting a "racial synthesis of the world."

In addition, Vasconcelos refuted two other sources of the Latin inferiority complex. First, he debunked the idea that miscegenation, or racial mixing, leads to genetic deterioration. In fact, he argued, it actually brings gradual improvement in characteristics, similar to hybridization of plants and selective breeding of animals. Second, he stated that the tropical climates of much of Latin America represent no obstacle to the emergence of advanced civilizations. Most of the ancient world developed in the tropics, including the Maya, Aztec, and Inca empires. History simply did not uphold the notion that the tropics stifle humans' creative energies. The cosmic race had not developed its full potential, Vasconcelos said, merely because it

Gilberto Freyre synthesized Brazil's history using the lore of his plantation society upbringing and his advanced social science studies in the United States.

was still emerging. In time the mixed races of Latin America would realize their full potential.

This remarkable, optimistic, and ethnocentric theory helped Mexican intellectuals and artists re-create their nation's past in a better light. Aided by Vasconcelos and other government officials, mural artists painted vast depictions of Mexico's history, idealizing the pre-Columbian era. In these paintings, the Amerindians, mestizos, and mulattoes were strong, productive, peaceful, and down to earth. Europeans, on the other hand, were either partners of the Amerindians or were portrayed as corrupt and degenerate.

In Brazil, Gilberto Freyre invented a new racial past for his people, similar to Vasconcelos's. Having grown up in the decadent sugar region of Pernambuco, Freyre sensed that his people had inherited a unique society, one that their ancestors had forged in the tropical plantations. They had fallen on hard times, but current conditions were not due to the supposed racial inferiority of Brazil's mixed population.

Freyre's college studies in Texas (Baylor) and New York (Columbia) provided him with an opportunity to read broadly in history and anthropology. From his studies he devised an account of Brazil's past, which he published as *Casa grande e senzala* (1933), later translated as *The Masters and the Slaves. Casa grande* became an immediate best-seller and was followed by sequels in the 1940s and 1950s. In the overall work, Freyre single-handedly rewrote his nation's past and constructed a new self-image for Brazil. His most innovative ideas had to do with racial mixing.

Freyre stated that three racial groups had come together in lowland Brazil during the colonial era: the Portuguese, Amerindians, and Africans. Each people brought physical and cultural characteristics especially suited for life on the plantations.

Africans and Amerindians, of course, were already of the tropics and hence needed no special adaptation to the climate. The Portuguese brought a genius for organization and enterprise and founded cities. Brazil became, then, a crucible for blending these populations and cultures into a new people especially fit for life in tropical America.

The blending, both physical and cultural, took place largely in the plantation big house, where members of all three races commingled. Masters sired many illegitimate children with the slave girls. Slaves and Amerindians joined together at night. Children of the masters, the slaves, and the Amerindians played in the big house and learned from their African nannies. Food recipes, children's games and stories, home medicine, folklore, hygiene, and all other aspects of daily life became fused into a peculiarly Brazilian synthesis. Meanwhile, the harsh aspects of slavery and plantation production were ameliorated by familial relations among all. The upshot was the racially mixed and culturally blended Brazilians, who were especially adapted to life in the tropics.

Freyre sidestepped issues of genetic change and merely stressed that Brazilians had proven themselves successful in their homeland. With distinctions of race blurred, people behaved as if they were members of one big family, and life took on a sensuous flavor derived from the rich flora and fauna of Brazil. Freyre wrote that Brazil's political culture, inherited from the days of masters and slaves, also obeyed the rules of patriarchalism. This included avoidance of confrontation and deference to officeholders. In all, Brazilian society worked well.

Educated Brazilians applauded Freyre's theories and disseminated them in school books, magazine articles, poetry, and newspapers. His views on race relations, in particular, became a virtual consensus by the 1950s. Today we call this the "myth of racial democracy" because, contrary to Freyre's romantic ideas of the past, racism still exists in all facets of life.

Freyre's unique vision of Brazil found resonance among artists of the 1930s as well. The Modernist movement (see Chapter Fourteen), which continued to thrive, increasingly portrayed blacks and mulattoes as the body and soul of the nation. Cândido Portinari and Di Cavalcanti, in particular, chose to paint scenes of poor nonwhites in their work.

Candomblé in Brazil

In 1938 and 1939, ethnographer Ruth Landes traveled to Bahia and Rio de Janeiro to study race relations and Afro-Brazilian culture. Her account of this trip, *The City of Women* (2nd ed., Albuquerque: University of New Mexico Press, 1994), provides a wonderful portrait of the country under the *dictablanda* (weak dictatorship) of Getúlio Vargas. It also contains strikingly modern descriptions of the Afro-Brazilian religion of Candomblé, illegal at the time and virtually unknown in the United States. In this excerpt, she asks a Brazilian colleague, Edison Carneiro, if Candomblé is:

"An 'opiate for the masses'?" I half jested.

"Call it that. But the real opiate is their ignorance and illiteracy—for which they are hardly to blame!" he protested impatiently. "Blame the landowners for that, and our whole inefficient economy. In my opinion, candomblé is a creative force. It gives the people courage and confidence, and they concentrate on solving the problems of this life, rather than on peace in the hereafter. I wonder, now, where the blacks would be without candomblé!"

"I notice that the priestesses are very close to the people."

"Very," he agreed. "The fathers and mothers are supposed to know all the answers, and also the few remaining diviners like Martiano. The daughters know certain answers, depending upon the length of their training and experience, and all the people have a general idea of what's to be done or of who can do it for them, because they all are related to somebody connected with candomblé.

"As in the popular Catholic belief, everything that happens has some mystery combined with it. I suppose nobody is believed to die a natural death, nobody gets married happily just as a matter of course, nobody is successful merely through luck or talent, nobody gets sick for natural reasons—but always there is some saint or god involved who is revenging himself or blessing his protégé, or some black magic is being practiced. The Catholic priests teach the people about the same thing as the mothers do—which is to rely on the saints and on obedience to commands rather than upon their own reason. God is a familiar idea here in this cathedral city. . . ."

(pp. 88–89)

In Peru, the young political activist Víctor Raúl Haya de la Torre also revised ideas about the racial origins of his people as part of his larger intellectual explorations. Although not as carefully formulated as the other theories, Haya's vision emerged in articles that he wrote in magazines and newspapers during his long years in exile and in hiding. (See Chapters Fourteen and Nineteen for Haya's career.)

Until the early twentieth century, Amerindians were thought to possess the same inferior attributes as Africans and Asians when compared with Europeans. Upper-class Peruvians looked down upon Amerindians and often treated them as little better than animals. The word *indio* had strong pejorative connotations. Scientific racism there, as elsewhere, held that in order to progress, Peru would have to diminish the proportion and influence of natives in its society. Raised in a well-to-do family, Haya was certainly exposed to such racist views as a youth.

Haya's spiritual awakening to native Peruvians came in 1918, when he went to live in Cuzco, the city built on the foundations of the former Inca capital. He became aware of and a convert to *indigenismo*—an appreciation for the character and culture of the Amerindian descendants. To Haya, this experience opened his eyes not only to his disadvantaged countrymen but also to his own soul, which he believed to be profoundly influenced by the native heritage of Peru. He began to call the continent Indo-America to reflect the huge debt owed to pre-Columbian civilizations. From then on, he became an advocate of recognizing the natives and of elevating them to their rightful positions in society.

Ready to discover some cosmic harmony among Peru's Amerindians, Haya imagined that he and all Peruvians could experience oneness with the Inca spirit world if they tuned to its frequencies. Even though he did not have an Amerindian phenotype, he began to refer to his Inca ancestors. He imagined that all Amerindians had access to this universe, which could be a tremendous psychic resource for unity in the Americas. To achieve this unity, he proclaimed his party to represent both North and South America.

Haya also believed that humanity would undergo a rebirth, as it had several times in the past, and that the rebirth would begin in Indo-America this time. With it would come a return to the social justice of the Inca world. This would mean, among other things, controlling the harsh exploitation of capitalism and the abuses by Catholic leaders.

Throughout his career, Haya's rhetoric referred to the great Inca traditions of Peru and the need to honor its peoples, the Amerindians. These appeals to national unity, ancient heritage, respect for each citizen, and basic justice were powerful themes in all of Haya's speeches and writings. Consciously or not, most political leaders after the 1930s adopted some of the language and goals of Haya's movement.

Racism was manifested in different forms in each region and period. The predominance of multihued, ethnically blended people, however, made any single racist doctrine difficult to sustain. Still, light-skinned and well-off people usually looked down upon those who were darker and less well off than themselves.

In addition to the remedies for racism offered by Freyre, Vasconcelos, and Haya, a generalized defense of native people surfaced in the early twentieth century, led by writers, intellectuals, and social activists. This defense came to be known as *indigenismo.*

In some ways, *indigenismo* went back to the earliest defenders of the Amerindians against European depredations. Over the centuries, a few intellectuals and clergy had always sympathized with and defended the Amerindians, perpetually at a disadvantage vis-à-vis the white establishment. (See Chapter Ten on earlier pro-Amerindian writers.) In the twentieth century such novels as Alcides Argüedas's *Raza de bronce* (1919), Jorge Icaza's *Huasipungo* (1934), and Ciro Alegría's *El mundo es ancho y ajeno* (1941) presented the strong qualities of indigenous peoples and cultures. Artists, especially those in Mexico, depicted the Amerindian past in positive, even heroic terms. Although little of this revisionism drew on hard research, it did begin to weaken prejudices among the educated.

The Mexican Revolution went far toward redeeming the native culture—indeed, the new official history claimed that the movement was devoted almost entirely to the Amerindians and workers. Still, more rhetoric than action flowed from government agencies. From Mexico *indigenismo* spread southward into Guatemala, where Miguel Angel Asturias wrote the wonderful *Hombres de maíz* (1949) about the modern Maya peoples.

In Brazil *indigenismo* did not take root as firmly as in Spanish America, perhaps because most of the native peoples along the coast had died out or fled inland. Still, the remarkable explorer/soldier/ethnographer Cândido Rondon, himself half native Bororó, established the Brazilian Indian Protection Service in 1910. Gradually its responsibilities expanded to management of vast reservations in the Amazon and far West.

Since the 1960s *indigenismo* has lost prominence, and other issues have captured the attention of policymakers. Internal divisions have also weakened the movement as leaders have debated its proper course and content. Even the powerful literary voice of *indigenismo* has been diluted by the hugely popular Magical Realism that came into vogue in the 1960s. Perhaps the strongest remnant of the movement today lives on in Guatemala, where Mayan peoples still struggle for their rights.

Gender in Modern Latin America

The roles of women in the region have always been active, dynamic, and, in some fields, decisive. Moreover, in the last hundred years, women have exercised far greater and broader influence across the board: in economics, academics, politics, and society. Various feminist movements, in addition, interlaced their actions with these changes. Not all modification in roles has been positive, but generally women have gained more civic rights, authority over their own lives, and economic independence than ever before. Women have become more mobile, in all senses, and participate more fully in major decisions facing their lives and nations. In many ways, women have achieved three different liberations: in the workplace, in schools, and in public life.

Women's economic liberation, at best a mixed blessing, came from the growth of service and industrial activity in major cities of the region. Urban life broke down the isolation of families because households gradually opened to local commerce, neighborhood groups, and social agents of all sorts. Children, moreover, needed more education than their mothers could provide, so schools came to assume importance to the family. With the end of slavery and hacienda peonage, it became necessary for affluent families to take maids and domestic help on a paid basis. And finally, the cities themselves required more diverse jobs and skills than small towns did. Women filled many of these new positions.

Women increasingly passed from the informal, domestic economy to the formal wage force after the beginning of the twentieth century. Labor had become chronically scarce during the export booms, and men took the better-paying jobs, leaving residual work to women. Also, poor women remained on the fringes of the elite cultural system and hence were free of traditional taboos against women's work. In Brazil, for example, such women were former slaves, immigrants, and rural migrants. For most of the century, women predominated in cityward migration. Soon migrants' daughters joined them in the labor market as well. They were "different" from well-to-do women and also easier to exploit. Only lower-class women could perform menial and service jobs—middle-class families barred their daughters from such work.

Family survival in cities was precarious and usually depended on women—they could no longer raise their own food, and in hard times they had to find extra work. Moreover, many poor households were headed by women. So the first liberation that women achieved was formal work outside the home.

By the 1920s working women constituted 10 to 15 percent of the economically active population, and they clustered around the bottom rungs of the occupational ladder. The greatest numbers provided domestic and personal services, working as maids, laundresses, retail workers, and prostitutes. These workers supplemented the household economy and at the same time gained skills necessary for moving up the occupational ladder. Women in such service jobs, however, could not easily organize for protection and advancement. Still, their experiences opened the labor market for later generations.

The second-largest group of women worked in industry. Factory work was abysmal in those years, paying miserly wages with few benefits and little stability. Even men could barely support families on factory wages, so they often sent their wives and children to earn supplemental income. Factory owners believed that machine work was more suited to women and children anyway. Skilled male employees usually moved up into supervisory positions, whereas women found it almost impossible to escape the production line.

Women's working conditions in the textile industry in Medellin, Colombia, in the first half of the century resembled those throughout the region. There factories employed only young, single women from nearby small towns. Many of the women had left the coffee-producing zone because their families could not support them. Their wages were so low that they often lived in dorms built by the managers and supervised by nuns.

Because industry employed so many "lesser beings," owners were not usually disturbed by collective bargaining disputes. Women seemed to be the ideal passive labor force. In fact, however, many working women did form groups to press for better treatment and wages, but they worked behind the scenes and rarely went on strike.

The economic liberation was a mixed blessing in that it presented women with a dilemma. On the one hand, opportunities for gaining money and skills outside the home exposed women to exploitation, male chauvinism, and the double standard in the workplace. On the other hand, working-class women—poor whites and mestizas as well as blacks and Amerindians—didn't have many other choices for earning money and seeking mobility. That growing numbers did work outside the home suggested that a mixed blessing was better than none.

Maquiladoras

Women workers predominate in the so-called *maquiladoras*—factories located along the Mexican side of the border with the United States. These are sometimes referred to as "in bond" or "twin plants" because they import duty-free raw materials and components and then reexport finished products exclusively to the U.S. economy. Mexican workers, mostly female, provide virtually all the assembly and packaging labor. Begun in the 1960s, *maquiladoras* became a major source of jobs in northern Mexico and an important part of the country's industrial economy. About a half-million people work in over two thousand plants making electronic goods, apparel, furniture, automobile parts, and other consumer products. Nicknamed *maquilas*, they have been criticized for low pay, exploitative labor practices (especially of women), pollution, and failure to contribute to Mexico's development. Defenders point out that they create jobs and transfer technology into Mexico. The 1994 North American Free Trade Agreement (NAFTA) has begun the process of extending the duty-free zone farther into Mexico and opening domestic markets to *maquiladora* goods. Eventually they should become integrated into the global market.

Working women had to manage households as well as jobs, so they called on their children and elderly relatives to help out. For many young women, working at a job was merely a temporary phase prior to getting married and staying home. In fact, their high turnover prevented them from gaining better benefits. In addition, those in better-paying jobs could hire domestic help.

Women's participation in the labor force gradually expanded, but women's wages remained below those of men. A study conducted in the 1970s revealed that women made up 26 percent of the workforce in Argentina, 24 percent in Colombia, 23 percent in Venezuela, 21 percent in Brazil, and a low of 14 percent in Bolivia. In cities, women made up even larger percentages. Most were premarital, between fifteen and twenty-four years of age. The rest largely were widowed or divorced. The study found that only a small minority were married.

Women's occupations had changed little since early in the century. Domestic and personal services still accounted for nearly one-half of women's jobs. Industry constituted the next-largest category, followed closely by commerce. These sectors paid the lowest wages, had the highest turnover, and carried the lowest status of all urban occupations.

For much of the century, women did enjoy one special work benefit: broad and generous social security coverage. From the 1920s on, inspired by similar legislation in Europe, governments set up contributory programs for retirement, health, and accident compensation. Women received additional protection, such as maternity leave and regulation of hours.

Women's second liberation, that of education, actually began in the nineteenth century. Politicians interested in increasing literacy founded secondary or normal schools to train women as teachers. After the turn of the century, women gradually replaced men as teachers in elementary schools. Today, teaching is the most common middle-class female profession in the region.

Primary education for poor women came next. When women took jobs in stores and shops and petty commerce—often family-owned businesses—they needed to read and write and perform basic arithmetic. These women learned on the job or attended school for several years. Immigrant families, in particular, placed high value on education, and second-generation immigrants swelled the school population. Although women stayed only a few years in school, they nonetheless acquired skills for nonmanual and clerical work. From there they could gradually take jobs as clerks, secretaries, shopkeepers, nurses, and so forth.

After receiving elementary training, many women began staying in school longer and even graduating in larger numbers. By the 1960s women had an average of 4.5 years of school, compared to men's 5 years. The 1960s saw especially rapid advances for women in secondary and even university education. Costa Rica had the highest enrollments, 42 percent, followed by Uruguay, Argentina, Chile, and Colombia. In some countries, by the 1990s little education gender gap remained, and women even enjoyed full representation on the teaching staffs of public universities.

By discipline, however, women seemed concentrated in less lucrative fields than men. They made up high percentages among teachers, humanists, social workers, civil servants, and social scientists. Men, on the other hand, predominated in law,

| Table 17-1 | Years that Women Gained and Exercised Suffrage in Latin America | | | | |

Country	Law Passed	First Voted Federal	Country	Law Passed	First Voted Federal
Ecuador	1929	1932	Chile	1949	1949
Brazil	1932	1933	Costa Rica	1949	1953
Uruguay	1932	1938	Haiti	1950	n/a
Puerto Rico	1920	1932	Bolivia	1952	1952
Cuba	1934	n/a	Mexico	1954	1955
El Salvador	1939	n/a	Colombia	1954	1957
Dominican Republic	1942	n/a	Honduras	1955	n/a
Guatemala	1945	1945	Nicaragua	1955	n/a
Panama	1945	1946	Peru	1955	1956
Argentina	1947	1948	Paraguay	1961	n/a
Venezuela	1947	1947			

Based on Elsa Chaney, *Supermadre: Women in Politics in Latin America* (Austin: University of Texas Press, 1979), and author's compilation from several sources.

medicine, engineering, and business. Some gender stereotyping and discrimination lingered from the past.

The third liberation of women was political, and it came just behind economics and education. For the most part, women gained the vote only after World War II, and effective suffrage came even later. Ecuadorian woman were the first to gain the right to vote in national elections (1929), followed by women in Brazil (1932), Uruguay (1932), and Cuba (1934). In other countries, women won the vote after 1947. Paraguay was the last country to recognize women's franchise, in 1961, a dubious right in a country that did not hold elections.

In Brazil and Cuba, leaders in revolutionary settings believed that women voters could help to stabilize their politics and lend support to the regimes. Women were thought to be fairly conservative in their preferences.

Where the franchise came only after World War II, historians have debated the causes of the late enfranchisement. The timing does not correlate closely with socioeconomic advancement nor political development. Rather, enfranchisement may have been delayed by cultural factors, such as the notion that politics is a man's game played by male values.

Another reason for men's reluctance to allow women to play larger roles in politics was fear of their conservative impact on public life. Women were considered more devout and cautious than men and likelier to let the Church influence their decisions. Women seemed to focus more on family and social issues than, say, economics, defense, or foreign affairs. Radical critics pointed to the tendency of women's magazines in Latin America to portray women exclusively as wives and mothers preoccupied with bourgeois trivia. A leading U.S. analyst, Jane Jacquette, disagreed, however, saying that the evidence supports only the conclusion that women do oppose radical structural change (such as revolution), not more evolutionary change.

For whatever reason, women have been grossly underrepresented in national politics. By the 1980s, only about 2 percent of the national legislators were female. Women made up only 5 percent of the Brazilian constituent assembly in 1987–1988.

A few women became very prominent in politics, however, and ranked among the best-known politicians in the world. Eva Perón has become the most famous woman in Latin American history. María Estela Perón, Lydia Guyler, and Violeta Chamorro served as heads of state in Argentina, Bolivia, and Nicaragua, respectively. María Eugenia Rojas achieved considerable power in Colombia before her untimely death. In most cases, the accession of these women to power came through their fathers or husbands and can be regarded as dynastic rather than competitive.

At the local level, however, more women have chosen to run for office and serve than at the national level. This was particularly true in Cuba, where the Communist Party encouraged female involvement in community governance. In Lima and Santiago in the late 1960s, according to Elsa Chaney's classic study, *Supermadre,* women made up 5 and 8 percent of the city councils. They came from the upper middle or upper class, had university education, and grew up in the capital cities. They tended to be older and to have smaller families than women in professional careers. Finally, these leaders chose to work on legislation affecting domestic and social welfare, such as health, education, and children, typically "women's issues."

Moving into the twenty-first century, Latin American women can look back on a century marked by several liberations that have led to much greater involvement in society, economy, government, and academics. They have taken leading roles even in the Protestant revolution that is sweeping the region—something that is still denied them in the Catholic church. Still, on the last frontier—politics—they remain far from equal.

Bertha Lutz, Early Feminist Leader in Brazil Who Helped Win the Vote in 1932

Bertha Lutz was born into a well-to-do Swiss-English immigrant family who had settled in São Paulo in the nineteenth century. Her father, a public health specialist, had carried out a sanitation program in the port of Santos in the 1890s. After the turn of the century, the family moved to Rio de Janeiro, where the father joined the staff at the Oswaldo Cruz Institute of Tropical Medicine. Bertha trained as a botanist and zoologist, following her father's interest in science. She later confessed that she found the usual women's careers, such as charity and education, boring. In addition, she became a proponent of women's suffrage in the 1920s.

In 1922 her colleagues chose her to attend the first Pan-American Women's Meeting in Washington, an event that changed her life. When she returned, she founded the Brazilian Confederation for the Advancement of Women. For the next several years she and her well-to-do associates wrote articles on feminine advances elsewhere. Their goals included making the elite Dom Pedro II Academy co-educational, putting women on the national councils on children and labor policy, and reducing the workday for employed women.

In 1924, this time sponsored by the U.S. embassy, Lutz attended another inter-American women's meeting. There she won election as president of the Inter-American Union of Women.

By the late 1920s, women decided to push for the vote in Brazil. Because the Constitution did not expressly forbid women from voting, they decided to push for a test case in the impoverished state of Rio Grande do Norte. Women helped elect a sympathetic governor, who in 1928 sponsored a law allowing women to vote in that state's election. When the Supreme Court upheld their suffrage, other northern states followed suit.

Brazil's revolution of 1930, led by Getúlio Vargas, erased those gains, so the feminist leaders decided to convoke a second National Congress of Women in 1932 to lobby for the vote. As president, Bertha Lutz took their petition to the new president. Vargas, desperate for support, promised to back their request but counseled them to get into the mainstream to help him. He urged them to join parties, run for office, and write newspaper articles.

True to his word, Vargas signed an electoral reform bill in 1932 that among other things gave women the vote. Four women ran for seats in the constitutional assembly the following year, but only Bertha Lutz got enough votes to win. She served on the São Paulo delegation for two years, then won reelection representing Rio de Janeiro.

In 1937 Vargas canceled all political activity and ushered in the dictatorial Estado Novo, during which no elections were held. When the political system was restored after World War II, however, no one questioned women's right to vote.

Conclusions and Issues

The 1930s proved the beginning of a new era in Latin America, one in which formerly denigrated peoples began to be recognized as citizens and equals, at least in speeches, books, and artistic works. An ethic of equality and racial oneness became unofficial creed in many societies. In addition to Brazil's myth of racial democracy and Mexico's "cosmic race," Venezuelans claimed that they all were *café con leche* (light brown). In the end, however, racial prejudices and discriminatory behavior persisted through the rest of the century. They simply became harder to see and combat.

Women, too, broke out of nineteenth-century restrictions to join men in the workplace, school, and voting booth. As in the rest of the world, Latin American women trailed in wages and rights, yet by the end of the twentieth century the gender gap appeared to be closing. Most countries provided full legal equality to women; customary and informal discrimination continued, however, despite the laws.

Discussion Questions

1. How did the new racial blending theories of Freyre and Vasconcelos differ from *indigenismo?* What impact did these theories have on nationalist thinking in these countries?

2. How significant was it that women first emerged into the labor market and only later gained political rights? What impeded them from gaining full equality before the law?

3. What differences exist between discrimination based on race or ethnicity and that based on gender? Which will likely last longer, and why?

Latin America in World War II

Mexicans in the "Arsenal of Democracy"

"Juan, *pásame el* screwdriver Phillips, *pues el chingue regulador está flojo!*" Pedro Valdez shouted over the din of factory machinery. Juan passed his co-worker the tool, then looked at the clock on the wall. It was almost midnight. When Pedro finished adjusting the equipment, they put away their work clothes and punched out on the timeclock. They washed and walked out the front gates.

At this time of night the air in El Paso, Texas, was cool and dry, a refreshing change from the heat, foul smell, and humidity inside the tire factory. They talked as they walked. "Pedro," Juan said, "did you hear that Rogelio joined the army and is going to Italy next month? They put him in a construction brigade."

"*No diga!* I hope he don' get shot," chuckled Pedro.

After a short walk along a tree-lined street, they turned and went into the Cantina Juárez, a ramshackle saloon in the Mexican district of El Paso, near the railroad tracks. The radio boomed *ranchera* music broadcast from a station across the border in Ciudad Juárez. The two cities, separated by the Rio Grande, shared just about everything these days because of the war effort.

Pedro and Juan crossed the room and sat at the bar. They ordered Tecate beers, trucked in from Mexico's industrial city of Monterrey. The border inspectors didn't charge duty on liquor, so Tecate was cheaper than U.S. beer. The clientele of the bar was made up of Mexican workers from the industrial district outside of El Paso. They had come across the border in a huge labor migration made possible by the Bracero (laborer) Program instituted by the U.S. and Mexican governments. Immigrants filled the jobs vacated when American workers were drafted for military service. Eventually, a large number of Mexicans also volunteered for army duty.

"That was too bad that Gonzalo got killed by the stamping machine," Juan said, taking a swig from his bottle. "Ay, Chihuahua, what a way to go!

I want to die in my bed when I'm old, *carajo!* An¹ back in México, too. I hope they give him a good funeral. You think they takin' him home to Michoacán to bury him?"

"I don' know," Pedro answered, "maybe. It cost a lot to get there— five dollars on the bus. Maybe they charge less for a casket, you think? Maybe the factory pay the family something down there and bury him here. You never know what these gringos will do."

"You know, Pedro, maybe we should sign up for the army. It's not no more dangerous than this *chingue* factory work, and they let you be a U.S. citizen when you get back. I don't mind living in San Antonio or Tucson or Los Angeles. They got a lot of Mexicans there already. And the life is good."

"Yeah, maybe," Pedro said, "and you can bring your family after a while. My wife says she wants to come here and bring the *muchachos.* They get a good school, plenty of food, learn English, and go to high school. *Caray,* back home they don' have no chance to finish school."

"I don' know, Pedro. The gringos hate us, and the Tejanos are worse than the others. Hell, they treat us like sheet—a supervisor called me a nigger the other day. They must think Spain is in Africa!"

Pedro looked up at the clock on the wall, "*Compadre,* I gotta go to sleep—the *cabrón* Mr. Smith gave me the morning shift. *Hasta manaña, cuate—cuídate bien.*"

Pedro got off his stool and headed for the door. On the way he waved and said goodnight to some of the other men drinking at tables.

Juan called the bartender and asked him to turn up the radio—it was playing a song he liked. It reminded him of his home in Durango, far to the south. He missed home and didn't know when he could visit his family there.

During World War II, Juan, Pedro, and perhaps a million other Mexicans continued the long process of integrating the U.S. and Mexican economies. Even after the war was over, border crossings and trade remained heavy, reflecting the growing assimilation of the peoples along both banks of the Rio Grande. Throughout the border region, millions of business transactions and workers went back and forth every day. The frontier became merely a transition zone between the two countries.

Fifty years later, in 1994, the North American Free Trade Agreement (NAFTA) would take that process another step forward, integrating the two economies, as well as Canada's. It was never true that Latin America stopped at the Rio Grande. From the seventeenth century on, Mexico had encompassed most of the U.S. Southwest. After the 1848 peace, the United States only partially succeeded in Americanizing the region. Moreover, from the time of the Mexican Revolution on, intensifying trade and migration have turned the tide back toward Latin Americanization of the Southwest. World War II accelerated the process. Soon after the year 2000, people of Hispanic descent will be the largest minority population in the United States. A scholar wisely named these expanding border regions *MexAmerica,* an apt term.

Mexican braceros worked in myriad jobs during World War II, replacing U.S. military labor drafted by the army. The men in this photo were employed in railroad maintenance in Pennsylvania.

Inter-American Defense

As the 1930s wore on, European diplomacy grew more tense and threatened to plunge the world into war again. Germany's chancellor, Adolph Hitler, flexed his nation's considerable muscle and promised to spread German influence throughout Europe and perhaps the world. Italy under Benito Mussolini grew aggressive, invading Libya and Ethiopia in northern Africa. The German and Italian regimes, Nazi and fascist, respectively, resembled each other in authoritarian structure, censorship, propaganda, militarism, and intolerance of minority populations. Meanwhile, Japan also began a decade of military expansion into China and Southeast Asia that would ally it militarily with the Nazi and fascist governments (forming the Axis) when war broke out in September 1939. These events reverberated with threatening tones in the Americas.

The nations of the hemisphere participated in a series of inter-American meetings convoked to deal with security concerns in the late 1930s. Because the level of threat increased with each year that passed, the meetings themselves took on increasingly more foreboding business, and U.S. activism increased. In 1936 the foreign ministers of the hemisphere convened in Buenos Aires and signed a treaty promising to submit conflicts to mediation. Two years later, responding to Axis aggression in Europe, inter-American delegates in Lima, Peru, passed a more forceful declaration that the hemisphere would unite to defend itself against internal or external attacks.

When war actually broke out, the foreign ministers of the Americas hurriedly met in Panama in September 1939 to discuss ways to keep the war from spreading across the Atlantic. They declared a neutrality zone around the continents, extending three hundred miles out to sea. They also set up committees to coordinate economic responses to the war. Yet these measures also proved inadequate.

The fall of France to Nazi armies in June 1940 brought the war to the Americas. French, Danish, and Dutch colonies in the Caribbean basin became a strategic concern because they could be used as platforms for aggression inside the neutrality zone. Martinique, in particular, could endanger oil tanker sea lanes, Panama Canal approaches, and air routes. The United States called a meeting of foreign ministers in Havana that immediately put those territories under an inter-American protectorate. In effect, they were administered by the United States for defense purposes. The foreign ministers also beefed up counterespionage programs. The United States followed up by persuading Latin American governments to nationalize German and Italian airlines operating in their countries. In a short time that was accomplished, and a network for inter-American defense planning began to take shape.

Between the Havana meeting and the December 1941 Japanese attack on Pearl Harbor that plunged the United States into war, the U.S. government took a number of initiatives to improve its defense posture in the Americas. Financial aid was offered to a number of countries in exchange for cooperation, and military aid (under the Lend-Lease Act and military training programs) began to flow south. By the same token, Latin American countries gave the United States the right to operate bases and observation stations in their territories. A cultural exchange program got under way to improve people-to-people relations. And the level of economic coordination increased markedly to avoid shortages due to the war. The Roosevelt administration, whose first priority was to support Great Britain, the principal enemy of the Axis nations, simultaneously strengthened the defense posture of its neighbors for the possibility of war.

Several sites were especially critical to hemispheric defense. Panama was regarded as most critical because of the canal's ability to move ships and supplies between the two oceans. A huge construction project on the canal brought prosperity to the Panamanians, and a friendly government after 1941 conceded lands for more defense bases.

Brazil's northeastern hump was also strategic because it extended into the south Atlantic and lay only nineteen hundred miles west of the African coast. With German General Erwin Rommel's rapid conquests across north Africa in 1941, it appeared that the German air force might be able to ferry planes to South America. From there they could reach Panama and even North America. To prevent that, the United States acquired a base in Natal, Brazil, used for moving aircraft, men, and supplies eastward to the European theater. Finally, U.S. security was vulnerable along the unguarded border and coastal waters shared with Mexico. The two governments negotiated a series of agreements that made Mexico a major ally during the war. By the eve of the U.S. declaration of war, most of the major vulnerable spots in the hemisphere had been protected.

Brazil in World War II

The most cooperative wartime ally in the hemisphere, Brazil, strengthened what was already an unwritten alliance with the United States. After some haggling, President Getúlio Vargas concluded a deal with the Roosevelt administration for the U.S. Army Air Corp to build and operate the base at Natal, where Brazil bulges out into the south Atlantic.

The U.S. base at Natal not only preempted a German air bridge but also made it possible to create a major Allied supply route to the European theater. In early 1944 Natal was the busiest U.S. air base in the world, the jumping-off point for tens of thousands of fighters, bombers, and cargo planes headed to Europe. Many of these planes were flown by female pilots, freeing male aviators for combat duty.

The Natal base was also the site of a historic meeting between Presidents Vargas and Roosevelt in 1943, while the latter was en route to the Casablanca summit meeting in north Africa. Later, celebrities like Charles Lindbergh, Jack Benny, and Eleanor Roosevelt visited the base.

In exchange for the Natal base, Brazil received financing for an entire steel factory to be transplanted from Pennsylvania to a site near Rio de Janeiro. This plant, called Volta Redonda, formed the nucleus of what would become the largest steel industry in South America. In addition, the United States supplied the Brazilian military with a wide array of weapons.

When German submarines sank several Brazilian freighters in November 1941, Vargas broke diplomatic relations with the Axis and forged even closer links with the United States. After the Japanese attacked Pearl Harbor, Brazil agreed to host an inter-American meeting of foreign ministers to seek a united front against the Axis. Most countries pledged their solidarity with the United States, severed ties with the Axis, signed the Declaration of the United Nations, and eventually declared war. The January 1942 Rio de Janeiro meeting presented a largely united front against the Axis. Brazil went beyond even that in the coming years.

The Amazon basin contained virtually all of the native rubber trees in existence in the 1930s, and U.S. defense planners looked to them as a source for latex, a raw material critical for war industries. The other major sources of rubber—Dutch, French, and British plantations in Southeast Asia—had already been occupied by Japanese forces. Therefore, the U.S. and Brazilian governments established a joint program designed to increase rubber production in the Amazon and earmark it for U.S. factories. Called the "Battle for Rubber," the program cost millions of dollars and led to massive migration into the rubber districts of the Amazon. In addition, scientists in Belem, near the mouth of the river, stepped up their research into better species and cultivation methods.

Although they never achieved plantation cultivation, they made outsiders aware of the rich natural resources hidden in the rain forest. Not coincidentally, U.S. citizens in remote locations served as spotters of aircraft that might belong to the enemy.

After the Rio meeting, President Vargas and his military advisors decided to send an infantry division to fight in Europe and began planning for it with U.S. military authorities. Two joint military commissions (one in Washington and one in Rio) worked out the myriad details of training, equipment, transport, maneuvers, command, and location. The division that eventually went to Italy was called the Brazilian Expeditionary Force (FEB). It numbered over twenty-five thousand men and women. The army also insisted on keeping up its strength at home, especially in the Northeast around Natal and along the southern border with Argentina. By the end of the war, the effort had a positive effect on the military and on nationalist sentiment in the country as a whole.

The FEB represented a level of training, logistics, coordination, and field combat far beyond the Brazilian military's previous experience. The troops were transported in Brazilian-made ships and equipped with supplies that were mostly manufactured at home. Even though the troops came under U.S. command, they operated as an independent division in the battlefield. It was an important experience in international operations for both nations.

President Franklin Roosevelt (center) visited the Natal air base in Brazil in 1944, en route to a meeting in Casablanca. President Getúlio Vargas (seated behind him) had struck a good bargain in exchange for leasing the base.

Some of the 25,000 Brazilian troops sent to Italy in 1944 to help drive out the German army.

From its arrival in Italy in mid-1944 until its return to Brazil in mid-1945, the FEB performed very well as part of Lt. General Mark Clark's Fifth Army. It participated in the capture of a key mountain redoubt, Monte Castello, took the surrender of a large German contingent, and helped clear the way for a spring offensive into northern Italy. U.S. Army planners tried to convince the Brazilians to remain in Europe after the war, as part of an international force, but they were called home and demobilized. Of all the Latin American countries, Brazil made the largest contribution to the Allied victory.

Almost as soon as the troop ships entered international waters, critics of Vargas began turning the FEB's participation in Europe into an appeal to end the dictatorship at home. How, they asked, could Brazil fight against dictatorship abroad while sustaining one at home? This and other attacks on Vargas had an effect, and many army officers returning home felt the need to help restore democracy. In August 1945, in fact, the army overthrew Vargas and ushered in a civilian government.

In the long run, the FEB had important impacts on domestic and hemispheric affairs. After the war, the Brazilian army renewed its commitment to joint planning and training with the United States, so the unwritten alliance continued. In 1949 Brazil created a high-level army officer academy with U.S. participation, the graduates of which later became prominent in the military takeover of 1964 and in the subsequent regime. Finally, much of what would later be called the "national security doctrine" among Latin American military thinkers was based on the writings of their Brazilian colleagues. And most of their ideas had been generated in consultation with American officers.

Rubber Supplies from Iquitos, Peru

Japanese occupation of virtually all Southeast Asian rubber plantations in 1939–1941 threatened U.S. supplies of this strategic material. Increased production of armaments, for shipment to England and for U.S. arsenals, added urgency to the search for new sources. The U.S. government created the Rubber Development Corporation (RDC) for buying Amazon rubber. To complement production in Brazil, the RDC encouraged shipments from Peru. The U.S. vice consul in Iquitos wrote about the effort in his memoir:

"I can remember the flurry of excitement . . . when, in May, 1943, the first token shipments of rubber, totaling about ten tons, were flown from Iquitos to Belem do Pará, at the mouth of the Amazon.

"The turning point came in 1944. The jungle monarch did not leap to his feet, but at least he began to stir. The pungent, smoke-stained balls gradually piled up in the RDC warehouse, a block from the Vice Consulate. In February, a record shipment of seventy-five gross tons of rubber slipped downstream aboard the RDC barge Manhattan. . . . When we read about the amount of natural rubber it took to manufacture one tire for a B-29, we hoped that the RDC Brazil was having more luck reviving the industry than was RDC Peru."

(Hank and Dot Kelly, *Dancing Diplomats* [Albuquerque: University of New Mexico Press, 1950], pp. 212–213)

Mexico in World War II

When President Cárdenas chose his official presidential candidate for the 1940 election, he made one of the most important decisions in modern Mexican history. The choices that he faced offered three divergent paths. On the right was the course offered by Juan Almazán and the National Action Party (PAN), a conservative group identified with business and the Church. They would roll back the revolutionary reforms to something like what had existed during the *Porfiriato*.

On the left lay increased socialization under either Francisco Múgica, the intellectual author of the 1917 Constitution, or Vicente Lombardo Toledano, undisputed leader of the workers' movement. Either of these men, as president, would have moved toward a workers' republic or perhaps even a communist state.

Finally, in the center lay a moderate path of stability, under the guidance of War Minister Avila Camacho. This path would lead to the virtual end of the revolution and to the abandonment of constitutional directives for change. Cárdenas sympathized with the leftist leaders but in the end chose the middle path. The onset of World War II, his recent confrontation with the Great Powers (United States and

Great Britain) over oil nationalization, the German-Soviet pact, and the likelihood of U.S. hostility to a radical government in Mexico probably influenced his decision to follow the middle path.

Cárdenas expected the revolution to cool off naturally after he stepped down. Avila Camacho echoed this sentiment in his inaugural address, which spoke of the normalization and consolidation of existing social and economic advances. Since 1940 social progress has been gradual, evolutionary instead of revolutionary.

Avila Camacho was a very different sort of leader than his predecessor. He had served in Obregón's forces during the revolution but had not seen combat since 1920. As a desk officer and administrator in the 1920s and 1930s, he gained recognition as a negotiator and conciliator. Still, he was jokingly referred to as the "unknown soldier" because he had so little public recognition. He owed his appointment as minister of war partly to the fact that his brother was one of the "big five" military chieftains in 1939.

Even during the now-obligatory election campaign it was clear that a change was under way. Avila Camacho stated at one point that he was a *creyente* (believer), meaning that he was a Catholic and not anticlerical. This signaled his desire to bury the religious hatchet and to seek a friendly relationship with the Church.

The pace of social and economic reforms slowed markedly under Avila Camacho. He distributed only about twelve million acres of land, and most of the land was awarded to individuals, not to *ejidos*. Private enterprise, hard work, and individual initiative replaced socialist doctrine in public school curricula. Rather than train more teachers to carry the revolution into the countryside, Avila Camacho and his minister of education devised a voluntary literacy campaign called "Each One Teach One." This avoided the tense confrontations between urban reformers and local village leaders that had arisen during earlier efforts. Yet, the success of this campaign was rather limited.

Leadership of the Mexican Workers' Confederation (CTM) shifted, too, at the new president's insistence. Fidel Velásquez, a moderate, replaced Lombardo Toledano. Wartime economic disruption gave rise to stiff inflation—283 percent between 1939 and 1946. Only in the latter year was the minimum wage increased, by 14 percent. Therefore, wages fell far behind cost-of-living hikes, and the CTM was correspondingly weakened.

Partly to compensate for dwindling real wages, the Avila Camacho administration created a social security system in 1942. Named the Mexican Social Security Institute (IMSS), it selected a few well-organized sectors in Mexico City for early inclusion. In 1946 the coverage remained small—only 287,000 in a nation of 25 million. It took another five years for its members to number one million. To this day, the Mexican social security system is one of the least effective in the hemisphere for coverage and quality. For example, only in the 1980s did it attempt to introduce some coverage of rural populations.

The Avila Camacho administration definitely promoted business prosperity. In 1940 the president expanded the role of the Nacional Financiera (created in 1934) into that of a national development bank. It was given a monopoly on incoming loans and investment capital, largely from the United States. All major projects had to be approved by the agency. Moreover, domestic businessmen could apply to it for venture capital, and during the war it became the equivalent of an industrial development agency. The new investments, wartime sales to the United States and Europe, and government encouragement gave a tremendous push to industrialization. Manufacturing grew at a fast clip during the war, and per capita income also rose rapidly.

The U.S. government made loans to the Nacional Financiera so that Mexico could continue to produce goods essential to American war industries. Eventually a generous financial package was worked out whereby the United States bought Mexico's entire production of silver at fixed prices. Tariffs and trade barriers virtually disappeared. The United States also made considerable loans to Mexico through the Export-Import Bank. Finally, a U.S. technical team went to Mexico to recommend improvements for the decrepit rail system.

U.S. businessmen were encouraged to invest in Mexico and to stimulate exports. In 1942 Avila Camacho recognized the newly formed National Chamber of Industry, which brought together foreign and national manufacturers. All of the trade that these programs generated turned Mexico into the "raw materials arsenal" of the United States, and by extension, of the Allied nations.

Finally, in order to counteract claims that foreign businessmen were becoming too powerful, the government passed a law in 1944 to require 51 percent Mexican ownership of any business corporation. Still, Avila Camacho doubtless ran a probusiness and pro-American administration.

World War II brought greater cooperation between the United States and Mexico than ever before. Desires for a common defense posture had led to successful arbitration in 1941 of the old oil and land claims against Mexico. In addition, the U.S. government supplied Mexico with coast guard cutters for patrol purposes. When German subs sank two Mexican tankers in the Gulf of Mexico in May 1942, Mexico declared war on the Axis. Several months later six former presidents of Mexico issued a joint communiqué endorsing the declaration of war.

Mexico had always been a haven for spies because of lax surveillance and easy access to the United States. This had been especially true in the late 1930s, when German spies operated quite openly. After Mexico declared war, however, the government cracked down on their activities, cooperating with the FBI. Minister of Interior Miguel Alemán was given counterespionage duties. A visible symbol of the new policy of cooperation with the United States came in 1943 when Presidents Avila Camacho and Roosevelt met in Monterrey and later toured the United States. From that time on all U.S. and Mexican presidents have exchanged visits at least once.

Eventually Mexico sent an air squadron to the Philippines in late 1944, which allowed Mexico to qualify for Lend-Lease war matériel and gave the country a strong sense of national pride. The decision to send combat forces came in early 1944 when the U.S. and Mexican presidents agreed that Mexican aviators would participate in the occupation of Manila. That spring the Mexican air force conducted maneuvers and carefully selected the participants of the group, known as Escuadrón 201. The final group, which included 38 pilots and 254 ground and support personnel, traveled to the United States for several months of training and indoctrination. They checked out in P-47s, which were among the largest fighter planes used in the war.

Escuadrón 201 arrived in the Philippines in May 1945 and was assigned to the U.S. Fifth Army Air Corps. In the following months the squadron flew fifty-nine missions in support of U.S. ground forces and acquitted itself well. When the war ended, members of the squadron returned to heroes' welcome in Mexico, and almost immediately their service became mythologized. The veterans of Manila monopolized the command of the Mexican Air Force for the next thirty years.

A final major cooperation program concerned manpower. The two neighbors agreed to allow three hundred thousand Mexican laborers, called *braceros,* to enter the United States to work in factories to help take the place of Americans who had joined the armed forces. The largest number employed at any one time was about seventy-five thousand, but several times that number streamed into the United States illegally. An additional agreement allowed Mexicans and Americans to serve in the armed forces of the other country without jeopardizing their citizenship. Under this agreement, 250,000 Mexicans enlisted in the United States, and about 14,000 saw combat duty.

Recognizing the important roles that Mexico had played in the war effort, hemispheric leaders decided to meet there in early 1945 to plan for the first United Nations (UN) conference, scheduled for San Francisco in April. Dubbed the "Chapultepec Conference" after the historic palace where it was held, the inter-American summit dealt with such issues as representation on the future UN security council, continuation of the Pan American Union, and the UN membership of Argentina, which had not severed relations with the Axis countries during the war.

The Chapultepec Conference delegates agreed to lobby for two permanent seats for Latin America on the security council and to authorize the Pan American Union to continue under UN aegis. In order to accommodate Argentina, they resolved that if Buenos Aires broke ties with the Axis, Argentina would be allowed to join the UN.

By the end of the war, Mexican society and politics had changed significantly. A middle class had emerged in larger Mexican cities—a class supported by employment in industry, government, banking, and commerce. This middle class increasingly voiced its desires through the official party, especially its *populares* section made up largely of public employees.

The official party likewise changed, dropping the army as an institutional member and drawing its rank and file increasingly from government employees. Technicians, bureaucrats, economists, and engineers replaced the labor and peasant leaders. It became a middle-class party whose revolutionary rhetoric was the principal reminder of its rural and violent origins.

Avila Camacho completed the transition from military to civilian rule begun by Cárdenas. At the end of the war, with prosperity returning and Mexico beginning to exercise a role in world affairs again, he reached out to the newest constituency in the party, government bureaucrats, for his successor. The presidential candidate, Miguel Alemán, came from within the party itself, having served as finance manager for Avila Camacho's election and as a government bureaucrat since.

Other Countries during the War

Throughout the Americas, countries responded differently to the war. From the U.S. point of view, the most important responses were those of Brazil and Mexico, which proved highly cooperative. Panama's response was deemed critical also because of possible German attacks on the canal or on ships that used it. The canal itself was highly vulnerable to sabotage. Moreover, merchant vessels carrying strategic supplies and even U.S. warships might become sitting ducks while approaching or leaving the canal. So early defense planning focused on the canal and its surroundings.

When U.S. authorities presented a long list of security measures for Panama to take, the new president, Arnulfo Arias Madrid, demurred, saying he would keep his country strictly neutral in the war. Arias's nationalism played well among Panama's masses but angered the elite, who usually identified with the United States. When Arias left the country secretly in mid-1941, U.S. observers alerted government officials, who promptly overthrew him. Arias's successor cooperated fully with U.S. defense planners, and the canal was not endangered for the remainder of the war.

While officials in Brazil, Mexico, and Panama worked most closely with their U.S. counterparts, leaders in the Caribbean archipelago, running from Cuba southeast to Aruba, cooperated to improve U.S. security. Early in the war German submarines scouted the waters of the Caribbean and the Gulf of Mexico and found U.S. coastal defenses virtually nonexistent. After the fall of France in June 1940, a far

Hundreds of Japanese citizens living in Peru were arrested and sent to internment camps in California. There they waited out the war in the company of Japanese-Americans from U.S. western states and other countries.

more dangerous situation arose for inter-American security. French and Belgian territories in the Western Hemisphere that came under German control could be used for submarine bases and even to mount air attacks. Therefore, at a special diplomatic gathering in Havana the governments of the hemisphere assumed jurisdiction over these territories until the end of the war.

The French island of Martinique and the Dutch islands of Aruba and Curaçao proved to be especially troublesome. The former had formidable naval defenses under the command of a pro-German officer. The large proportion of north-south shipping that passed close by could fall victim to torpedo or air attacks. Allied officials worked hard to neutralize the ships stationed there and to prevent Martinique from becoming a center for Axis espionage. Aruba and Curaçao, meanwhile, contained the Dutch Shell Oil Company refineries, which supplied much of the East Coast of the United States with heating fuel. An early submarine attack at Aruba nearly blew up the refineries and prompted Allied planners to station U.S. forces there permanently.

A Dominican Admiral Recalls 1942 Sub Threat

On the morning of the 18 of February, Kapitan Leutnant Achilles took [submarine] U-161 into Trinidad's Port-of-Spain harbor, which he knew well as a merchant ship officer, to sink two ships. A month later he replicated the operation at Port Castries, St. Lucia.

Little was known of the many exploits and actions of the German submarine service in the Caribbean and the West Indies during World War II. . . . Ships travelled unescorted, with their navigational marks and lights displayed. . . . In February 1942 as a result of Operation Neuland, 28 ships totaling 160,000 tons, were sunk in the Caribbean. . . . The most important oil supply bases in the Caribbean were the target of this mission. . . . Each of the U-boats operating there sank 6 to 10 ships. . . . During the first six months of 1942, Axis submarines sank 585 ships in the Atlantic. . . . Between February 1942 and December 1943 they sank 400 ships in the Caribbean Sea . . . U-516 made the most sensational raid on the isthmus of Panama since the days of Drake.

(Rear Admiral Cesar de Windt Lavandier, Dominican Republic Navy, retired, unpublished manuscript)

Argentina was the major exception to general hemispheric cooperation with the Allies during World War II. Just as the Buenos Aires government was about to declare its solidarity with Great Britain in 1943, a group of pro-Germany army officers seized power and declared absolute neutrality. They continued to sell beef and cereal to England but refused to break ties with Germany. Juan Perón, a leader of the coup who would come to dominate Argentine politics for a generation, believed as late as 1944 that Hitler might at least fight the Allies to a draw and remain powerful in world affairs. As a result of this belief, Argentina severed ties with the Axis only in March 1945, when German defeat was imminent, in order to join the United Nations.

Even so, thousands of German veterans and officials managed to escape to Argentina during 1945 and to establish new identities for themselves. Perón also employed German scientists to start a nuclear research agency. Remarkably, Perón's actions during 1944 and 1945 did not prevent him from winning the presidential election in 1946. U.S. opposition to him backfired, and by 1947 the U.S. State Department was obliged to mend fences with him.

Conclusions and Issues

The cataclysmic events of 1939–1945 left the world, including Latin America, deeply altered. Brazil's cooperation with the Allies gave it a huge boost in prestige and international projection. Brazil came close to gaining a permanent seat on the UN Security Council, and it definitely surpassed its rival, Argentina, in military and economic power. Ties with the United States remained close for decades afterward, especially linking the two countries' armed forces.

Mexico also forged a new and positive relationship with its neighbor to the north, ending the tension and antagonism of the previous generation. The economic and migratory flows caused by the war gradually erased the frontier as a barrier and created an intermediate land sometimes called *MexAmerica*. The war economy unquestionably improved the lives of people on both sides of the border and bound them closely together.

Meanwhile, the U.S. occupation of bases and territories in the Caribbean basin returned many of those areas to the status of protectorates, as they had been early in the century. Panama would have to live with the highly unequal 1903 canal treaty for another generation, and military bases in the region bristled with armaments. Regardless of the flags that flew over the Caribbean islands, no one doubted that the United States could exercise any de facto powers it wished there.

As a direct outcome of the war and the Chapultepec Conference, the governments of the hemisphere agreed to overhaul the diplomatic arrangements that had evolved since the late nineteenth century, today known as "inter-American law." First, they approved a multilateral agreement (the 1947 Rio Treaty) that created elaborate procedures for mutual defense. It was the most advanced agreement of its kind and served as a model for the later western European and Asian treaties of the North Atlantic Treaty Organization (NATO) and Southeast Asia Treaty Organization (SEATO). Second, they converted the Pan American Union (established in 1890) into the Organization of American States (OAS) in 1948. This organization fit within the larger framework of the United Nations and exercised prior jurisdiction over regional disputes.

The Latin American republics emerged from the war without major losses, except for the greater power that the United States now wielded in the world as a result of its victory over the Axis. In the postwar era the hemisphere leaders very soon found that world affairs continued to impinge on their lives.

Discussion Questions

1. Why did most leaders of the Latin American nations decide to cooperate with U.S. defense planners and then break relations with the Axis powers after December 1941?

2. How did aviation lead Brazil to play an important role in World War II? Mexico?

3. Why did the Southern Cone nations lag behind the other countries in joining the Allied war effort? Did this lag have historical roots?

The Classic Populists

Evita and Juan Perón Speak to the Masses

"*Compañeros,* I bring you hope and the power to change our nation," shouted Evita Perón, addressing thousands of supporters crowded in the Plaza de Mayo.

"General Perón has given Argentina a new future," she continued, "one with dreams and patriotism. I, who have had the honor of sharing with the general his concerns, feel proud to have followed the path pointed out to us by General Perón." Evita paused, and the crowd exploded with cheering. As the noise abated, the crowd settled into a chant: "*Viva* Perón, *viva* Perón, *viva* Perón."

When it was quiet, Evita continued, this time adopting the persona of the *descamisado* (coatless or shirt-sleeved one), the poor, working-class Argentine who had recently come to Buenos Aires looking for a job and a better life. She appeared to speak for the masses in addressing Perón:

"Mi General," she said, "we fight for economic independence. We fight for social justice. We fight for sovereignty and for the honor of our flag. We fight for the happiness of our children and for the humanization of a capitalism that has brought us only sterile struggles among brothers. We fight for the consolidation of our Fatherland under the extraordinary doctrine of Perón, our celebrated *líder!*"

A deafening roar rose from the crowd again, and Evita lowered her head dramatically. When the shouting had subsided, she looked up and spoke quietly, causing a hush to spread over the plaza. She now returned to her own role, that of humble companion and wife of Perón: "I thank you comrade workers for the honor bestowed upon this woman who only works trying to interpret the patriotic dreams of General Perón. . . . This spurs me to continue. It is the most honorable decoration on the breast of a woman who comes from the people, who is proud to belong to the people, and whose work is to listen to the heartbeats of the working people."

She paused, then concluded, "I am only the bridge of love between Perón and the people, helping to carry out our common revolution."

The crowd again erupted in cheering as Evita turned and looked at Perón, seated beside her on the balcony. She stepped demurely to him and kneeled. He held her hands and lifted her up as he himself rose. The crowd became hysterical upon seeing its two heroes standing together, basking in the glory of Argentine history.

Perón himself then spoke. "Compatriots, friends, Argentinos! Today we begin a new conquest. During the past few years we rescued our national dignity and declared economic independence from the old imperial powers of Europe. We nationalized the railroads and ports and took control over electric power and streetcar service. You all know how much better these industries run now that they are in our hands!"

A roar of approval burst forth from the crowd, along with new shouts of "*Viva* Perón!"

"Now," he continued, "we must restore our national finances by working harder and producing more. The unpatriotic ranchers have not helped us because they refuse to send cattle to the slaughterhouses. The droughts of last summer ruined the grain harvest. But we will prevail over economic hardships because we know how to labor together. We must forgo wage increases this year because we need the money to build new factories."

After a pause, he continued in a grave tone: "We must also increase our program of strengthening national security. Our army and navy need new weapons. Many of our warships and other weapons were purchased after the First World War, and they should be retired and replaced. The world is fraught with danger, and Argentina needs to be strong, reflecting the resolve of her people to secure a glorious place in history!"

Applause followed the last remarks.

"Today, fellow citizens, I meet with representatives of industry to see if they can manufacture many of our new arms here in Argentina. Only a nation capable of supplying its own defense needs is truly independent!" This statement, too, evoked applause.

"So I enjoin you to return to your homes and prepare to go to work tomorrow, determined to continue building a strong Argentina. You workers and teachers and farmers are the heart and soul of the nation. United, we will be a great nation!"

Perón turned and kissed Evita on the cheek, indicating the end of his speech. Shouting and clapping filled the plaza, and the couple turned and raised their hands to acknowledge the masses. Below the balcony, the army marching band struck up the national anthem, and Perón bent his arm in a formal salute. Then he and Evita stepped inside the Casa Rosada, leaving the doors open in order to hear the crowds outside.

Evita and Juan Perón both were quintessential populists, joined by charisma and bonds of leadership and marriage. Their extraordinary reign from 1946 to 1955 guided Argentine history for decades afterward. The Perón era marked the high-water mark of populism in Latin America.

Classic Populism

From the late 1930s until the late 1960s, the populist style of voter recruitment and leadership swept Latin America, affecting the region far more than did similar movements in the United States. Elections proliferated, and voter rolls burgeoned. For the first time ever, Latin Americans had the opportunity to choose freely their next leaders. Radio, television, mass-circulation dailies, and huge outdoor rallies became common ways to win voters' loyalties. The leaders themselves became known all over the world for their flamboyant images and bold initiatives. It seemed that Latin American politics had finally escaped from the grip of dictatorship and was coming of age. An American journalist entitled his book on this era *Twilight of the Tyrants.*

The populist era was an optimistic yet unsettling time because no one knew how the entrenched power structures—the Church, the army, the landed elite, the bankers, the foreign investors, and the traditional parties—would respond to this

Eva and Juan Perón in an outdoor meeting. This extraordinary couple shared charisma, or qualities that led followers to adore and idolize them.

challenge. For a time the populists and the establishment managed to cooperate. Most populists, to be sure, welcomed the support of any and all sponsors, and many power brokers believed that they could benefit by allying with popular leaders. These broad populist coalitions drew from all classes and walks of life, and their appeal reached into neighborhoods, small towns, cafes, and factories. They were the first nonviolent mass movements in the region's history. As long as the populists did not threaten existing power holders, they prospered and gave Latin American politics a more modern face.

By the mid-1950s, however, populist leaders began to upset the older elites, and confrontations became frequent. Sometimes the army reacted to mass mobilization, the Church opposed liberalizing laws, and industrialists prevented recruitment of their workers. For their part, the populists could do without elite supporters by then and appealed more openly to the masses. This heightened political tensions.

Eventually the horizon for populists clouded up and turned stormy. In Argentina, Brazil, and Peru, military coups removed leading populists on the grounds that they endangered the peace. Populists were accused of subverting the military, attacking the public order, breaking the law, overspending their budgets, and encouraging communism. Unspoken was the fact that the populists were successful enough at the ballot box to ignore the interests of the rich and powerful.

Classic populism had its roots in the 1930s. No full-blown populist movements arose then, due to hard economic times. Yet, a new mix of economic and social factors began to favor this innovative style of leadership. Virtually all the classic populist figures of the 1950s and 1960s got their start in the 1930s.

As was seen in Chapter Sixteen, the Great Depression struck the countries of Latin America with crippling force, destroying businesses and throwing hundreds of thousands of people out of work. Trade fell sharply, and prices for the region's products plummeted. Hundreds of thousands of rural workers and poor farmers made their way to the cities, hoping to find jobs and homes. They were desperate and ready to follow leaders who could promise them a better life. These leaders became the classic populists, who gained power and exercised it boldly—willful men determined to guide their countries through the hard times ahead.

Born in the 1880s and 1890s, the later populists were much younger than the reformers portrayed in Chapter Twelve. Three of them—Víctor Raúl Haya de la Torre, Lázaro Cárdenas, and Juan Perón—were born the same year, 1895. Some had spent time in the military before switching to politics, a fact that may account for their occasional autocratic tendencies. They pushed voter recruitment and built more modern parties with which to mobilize their followers. They learned to use the newly available medium of radio, and a few experimented with public relations techniques.

These classic populists were born into provincial families whose status ranged from lower middle to upper class. Although raised in relative comfort and security, they were forced to leave their homes in order to get ahead. Their origins outside the national capitals meant that they had to learn the ways of the national elite. This gave them an edge over traditional leaders because they could manipulate elite values and symbols better than could those socialized to wealth and power from birth.

Table 19-1 Classic Populists

Country	Name	Years in Power	Born	Class	Urban Rural	Race	Ed	Age @ 1st/off	Mil?	Party	Foreign Influence	Died
Chile	Ibáñez	1952–58	1877	lower	U	wh	mil	41	y		y	1960
Brazil	Vargas	1930–45 1951–54	1883	middle	R	wh	law	33	n		n	1954
Ecuador	Velasco	1934–35 1944–47 1952–56 1960–61 1968–72	1893	middle		wh	law	39	n		n	1979
Peru	Haya de la Torre		1895	middle	U	wh	univ		n	APRA	y	1979
Argentina	Perón	1946–55 1973–74	1895	middle	R	wh	mil	48	y		y	1974
Colombia	Gaitán	n/a	1898	middle	U	mes	law		n	Lib	y	1948
Bolivia	Paz Estenssoro	1952–56 1960–64 1985–89	1907	up/mid	R	wh	econ	22	y	MNR	y	
Panama	Arias	1940–41 1949–51 1968	1901	lower	R	wh	med	39	n	Pan.	y	1988
Brazil	Kubitschek	1955–60	1902	lower	U	wh	med	32	n	PSD	y	1976
Venezuela	Betancourt	1945–48 1958–62	1908	middle	R	wh	univ	37	n	AD	y	1979

Little interested in foreign travel, the later populists studied in their national universities or officer academies and often got their start in politics as student leaders. A few ventured abroad and brought back fresh ideas, especially from Europe. Loners as a rule, with few exceptions they had neither mentors nor protégés.

The populists who gained power after 1930 were dedicated politicians whose personalities drove them to run for public office. And they were extremely good at politics. They spoke well, projected appealing images, balanced diverse coalitions expertly, maintained composure in crises, and accomplished much of what they set out to do. Because the later populists evoked controversy as well as hero worship, historians have had a difficult time taking their measure. They do, however, deserve a prominent position in twentieth-century history.

Getúlio Vargas

Getúlio Vargas was born in the little town of São Borja, in the southern province of Rio Grande do Sul, Brazil. His father was an army general and a prominent politician in a region where those professions often went together. The family cattle business produced a comfortable income, but life in the pampas was often harsh and fraught with danger. From an early age, Getúlio aspired to be a soldier like his father, and he enlisted in the army when only eleven. He was probably not cut out for a military career, however, because he was physically unimpressive, bookish, guarded with others, and a loner.

After several discouraging incidents in officer training school, Getúlio soured on the military and enrolled in law school. He finished up in 1907 and began practice in Porto Alegre. He also began to dabble in politics, a common sideline for lawyers in Latin America.

Once engaged in politics, Vargas steadily climbed the ladder, becoming governor of his state for the 1928–1932 term. From that office he led a revolution in 1930 and seized the presidency for what turned out to be a fifteen-year stint, discussed in Chapter Sixteen. In these years, Vargas metamorphosed from a traditional leader to a dictator to a populist. Called a chameleon because of these alterations, he probably changed style to keep pace with world events—the Depression, the appearance of fascism, the world war, and the return of democracy after 1945.

Even before he became a full-fledged populist in the late 1940s, Vargas pursued policies that would enhance his success later. He issued decrees that protected Brazilian industry, jobs, resources, and trade in its relations with the outside world. This gave him a reputation as a nationalist. He centralized authority in federal agencies, curbing the traditional powers of state governments. In particular, he built up the army at the expense of state militias. He extended government control over labor relations, offering job protection and fringe benefits for workers while making strikes illegal. He extended the suffrage to women and eighteen-year-olds, though he later canceled all elections. Finally, he experimented with new communications media, using radio and the press far more effectively than had any of his predecessors.

Vargas's reputation for leadership grew during the dictatorial Estado Novo period (1937–1945). He instituted a civil service system that made government more effective.

Getúlio Vargas, far and away Brazil's dominant figure in twentieth century politics, governed the country from 1930–1945 and from 1950 until his death in 1954. He is shown here meeting supporters during his 1950 presidential campaign.

He skillfully bargained with the United States for an integrated steel mill, called Volta Redonda, which the United States donated in exchange for military bases during World War II. The mill later became the centerpiece of a bold industrialization program. And he decided to send troops to fight with the Allies in 1944–1945 to enhance Brazil's international standing. This infantry division, named the Brazilian Expeditionary Force, performed impressively in the Italian campaign. (See Chapter Eighteen.)

When the war was over, however, Vargas became the target of many protests due to his autocratic methods. He tried to transform himself into a democrat by promising elections and founding two new groups, the Social Democratic Party (PSD) and the Brazilian Labor Party (PTB). He was unable to carry out the transformation smoothly enough, however, and he was overthrown by the army in August 1945. Already sixty-two years old, he might have withdrawn from politics and enjoyed a quiet retirement.

After attempting for several years to defend his record, Vargas moved to his family ranch in Rio Grande and withdrew from the Rio political scene. When the 1950 election approached, however, he was urged by numerous collaborators to run again. The country and political system had changed profoundly since his last campaign—in 1930—so he relied on his daughter Alzira do Amaral Peixoto in Rio to manage his candidacy. It was largely on the basis of this election that Vargas gained renown as a populist.

Vargas's supporters worked around the clock in 1950 to give their leader a pleasing image and to get out the vote for him. They built his reputation as the "father of the poor," won earlier by his sponsorship of the 1943 Labor Code. They also portrayed him as a nationalist who would protect and expand the country's industry, providing jobs and infrastructure for the urban masses. His image, that of a grandfather figure smiling and smoking a cigar, familiar to everyone, was plastered all over the country. Toward the end of the campaign, Alzira organized a grueling airplane tour of the country that touched down in eighty-four towns. At each stop, Vargas gave a tailor-made speech drafted by staff members and revised by himself. His 48 percent victory in a three-way race was a veritable landslide, and he took office amid great popular acclaim.

Vargas tried very hard to carry out his promises to the masses, especially regarding protection of natural resources, economic planning, and a fair distribution of wealth. He created a national development bank to channel public loans to basic and critical industries. He proposed nationalizing all petroleum development and refining—a sector notorious for high profits and excessive remittances abroad. This proposal passed in 1953 and gave rise to Petrobras, today one of the world's major publicly held companies. Vargas also submitted to Congress a bill that would have nationalized electric utilities so that they could push service into poor and rural areas. This bill failed due to heavy lobbying from the industry. Finally, Vargas continued to give special attention to labor laws, social security, unemployment, and welfare services.

In all, Vargas's second administration produced some major social progress, yet it did so in a climate of heightened political and economic conflict. Vargas's PSD-PTB coalition in Congress began to unravel. The military became restive over advances made by labor unions. The economy plunged into a recession after 1952. And Vargas had lost some of the deft touch that he had shown in earlier times. His administration began to founder in early 1954.

Faced with multiple crises and likely removal by the military in mid-1954, Vargas decided to take his life rather than surrender. His suicide heightened people's sympathy for him and turned him into a martyr. His suicide note became a testament to his populist legacy.

> Once more the forces and interests against the people are newly coordinated and raised against me. . . . I follow the destiny that is imposed on me. After years of domination and looting by international economic and financial groups, I made myself chief of an unconquerable revolution. I began the work of liberation and I instituted a regime of social liberty. . . . I returned to govern on the arms of the people. A subterranean campaign of international groups joined with national groups revolting against the regime of workers' guarantees. . . . I have fought month to month, day to day, hour to hour, resisting a constant aggression. . . . I cannot give you more than my blood. . . . I gave you my life. Now I offer my death. Nothing remains. Serenely I take the first step on the road to eternity and leave life to enter history.

(Burns, *History of Brazil,* 2nd ed., [New York: Columbia University Press, 1980], p. 447)

After Vargas's death, virtually all other politicians tried to don his mantle, even some who had opposed him. By the same token, the methods that he had used to forge a majority in 1950 were widely adopted by others. In effect, Brazil in the 1950s became a populist republic, with at least eight major figures vying for national power.

Juscelino Kubitschek

One of Vargas's imitators attempted to outperform his mentor. Juscelino Kubitschek was born into a modest family, and his father died when Juscelino was one year old. He had only his mother to push him forward in life. He strove to overcome these handicaps, and after earning a degree in medicine he entered politics in his native state of Minas Gerais. He prospered in the tumultuous scene of urban politics and joined Vargas's PSD in 1945. By 1954, the year of Vargas's suicide, he had his sights set on the presidency.

Juscelino, as his followers called him, played a double game with all the expertise he could muster. On the one hand, he had to move deftly among the parties, factions, and other candidates in order to avoid being eliminated in backroom dealings. On the other hand, he hit the campaign trail in early 1955, emulating Vargas's historic 1950 campaign. He posed as a modernizer and promised to achieve "fifty years' progress" in his five-year term. He broke the sound barrier in a jet fighter. He barnstormed tens of thousands of miles in a leased DC-3 to visit hundreds of cities and towns. He used the radio with skill and recorded television spots for that new medium. He seemed to be everywhere at once. Even though he won just a plurality of the votes (two other candidates ran), he completed the process, begun by Vargas, of modernizing Brazil's electoral system. As president, he even signed into law a bill creating the secret, uniform ballot for national elections.

Kubitschek accomplished an amazing amount during his five years as president. Many observers believe that if he had been allowed to run for a second term he might have surpassed Vargas's record. He invited foreign manufacturers, especially automakers, to build plants in Brazil. By the end of his term, Volkswagen, Ford, and General Motors had begun production, and within a few years Brazilian cars were manufactured with 99 percent domestic components. Automobiles, in turn, spurred expansion in other areas, like petroleum and rubber products, highways, and repair shops. Soon cars became status symbols for the middle class and provided markets for a wide spectrum of goods and services.

Under Kubitschek, electric power projects, capital goods, mining, steel, and petrochemicals also received strong support from the government. Kubitschek skillfully blended selective foreign investment with nationalist protective policies. Industrialists, in particular, enjoyed huge profits during his term.

A new capital city at Brasília became the centerpiece of Kubitschek's administration. Conceived as a whim, the project grew into an obsession for him, and with customary energy he made sure that enough of the city was finished so that he could inaugurate it before his term ended. In January 1961 he handed over power to his successor, Jânio Quadros, in Brasília.

Kubitschek's Brasília

Kubitschek held a national competition to find the best team to design the new capital. Three outstanding planners, Lúcio Costa, Oscar Neimeyer, and Burle Marx, won the competition. Their plan laid out the city in the shape of a jet airplane. At the tip, where the cockpit would be, they located the president's office, Congress, and the Supreme Court. Behind them, in the "navigators' seats," were arrayed the twenty ministry buildings that headed up the executive branch. The two wings stretching north and south contained housing compounds, called "super-quadras," each with its own school, shopping center, playground, and church. The symbolism carried through to the city's orientation: It lies facing east so that it flies into the sunrise and the future.

Kubitschek was infected with *grandeza,* an enthusiasm for Brazil's future that bordered on the grandiose. He believed that by sheer will power and astute planning, he would be able to accomplish everything he dreamed. He and many others expected Brazil to join the First World and to become a major power within a short time.

Meanwhile, other populists came forward after Vargas's death in 1954 to vie for his following. One, longtime populist Adhemar de Barros, squared off against newcomer Jânio Quadros for the state governorship of São Paulo, a stepping-stone to the presidency. Surprising most observers, Jânio defeated Adhemar and went on to

Leonel Brizola, a tempestuous yet extremely effective vote-getter, rose from humble origins in Rio Grande do Sul and won more elections than any other national figure.

Jânio Quadros's meteoric career began and ended in his native São Paulo. For eight months he served a quixotic term as president.

President Juscelino Kubitschek and his vice president, João Goulart, representing different parties (PSD and PTB) and philosophies (mainstream and leftist), served between 1956 and 1961.

win the presidency in 1960, a stunning display of prowess and audacity. Ironically, his fall was just as fast because he resigned after just eight months in office, blaming conspiracies and opposition to his programs. Two years later he even lost a gubernatorial election to his archrival, Adhemar de Barros.

Two of Vargas's closest heirs arose from state politics in Rio Grande: João Goulart and Leonel Brizola. Goulart had been a friend and collaborator of Vargas and became labor minister and Labor Party chief in the 1950s. He served as vice president from 1955 to 1961 and then succeeded to the presidency when Jânio Quadros resigned. Brizola worked his way up in Vargas's Labor Party, married Goulart's sister, and became part of the inner circle after Vargas's death. Both used populist methods to win over voters and to build large followings. In other regions of the country, too, politicians stepped forward to claim the leadership that Vargas had pioneered. It seemed that Brazilian politics had become permanently infused with populism.

Juan and Eva Perón

In 1943, as Vargas began his shift toward electoral politics and his metamorphosis into a populist, the extraordinary Juan Perón led a coup against the Castillo administration in Argentina. Although the coup had trappings of a fascist *putsch,* Perón deftly steered it toward a populist government in 1944 and 1945. By then he had managed to become front-runner in the campaign for the presidency, which he won the following February. His phenomenal rise was just the beginning of a marked change in Argentine public life.

Perón was born in a small town on the pampas of Argentina into a family with only modest chances of advancement. Perón entered military school as a teen and virtually lost contact with his origins. After his commissioning, he rose slowly through the ranks, with few opportunities for advancement. He took part in the bloodless coup of 1930 that overthrew Hipólito Yrigoyen, but he did not take any civilian post afterward. In the late 1930s, in recognition of his growing stature as a leader among mid-ranking officers, he won a tour in Europe and witnessed Italy's preparations for war and the rearmament of Germany.

On his return to Argentina, Perón organized a secret officers' lodge, called the United Officers' Group (GOU). Its role was to strengthen the nation's military readiness, block communist advances, oppose an alliance with England, and promote its members' careers. In June 1943 the GOU took over the government in order to carry out its agenda. Perón expanded the circle of members and improved their positions, thereby winning their loyalty. As ringleader of the coup, he reserved key positions for himself: minister of war and vice president. Surprisingly, he also took over the Department of Labor, which for years had languished in neglect.

As labor chief, Perón called in union officials and convinced many to work with him. He offered them contract enforcement, higher wages, benefits, and relief from antiunion actions by employers in exchange for their following his lead. Under his direction, unions grew in membership and power, even though their leaders did not fully trust Perón. The labor movement did, however, provide a future base of support for his presidential bid.

Perón's physical appearance and his liaison with a well-known female radio personality boosted his growing recognition among voters. He was tall, handsome, and martial in his bearing. His demeanor exuded leadership qualities. Meanwhile, Perón (a widower) had formed a politico-romantic relationship with Eva Duarte, a star of radio and stage. She handled public announcements for him, and they began living together. Beautiful, willful, and outspoken in her support for Perón, she became his most effective spokesperson. Their romance scandalized some, but it also kept the couple in the public eye.

Perón's meteoric rise faltered in October 1945, when the army high command stripped him of his offices and jailed him to derail his presidential bid. At that point, major Buenos Aires unions mobilized their members in a huge protest in the downtown Plaza de Mayo to protest the arrest of *el líder,* Juan Perón. Although ambivalent about Perón's loyalty to labor, the union leaders had no doubt that his opponents would end the privileges that Perón had given them. Their protest, the largest in decades, convinced the generals to release Perón and allow him to run for president.

Perón and Eva quickly married and went on the campaign trail. It was an uphill battle, against the traditional parties, the U.S. embassy, and the government itself, but they pushed ahead, touting the gains that labor had made and his plans to nationalize basic utilities and services. Eva Duarte Perón, now known as Evita to her admirers, developed very effective speeches to persuade voters to support her husband. She helped turn the October rally into a creation myth for *Peronismo,* as his movement was called. When the election was held in February, Perón won an impressive majority of the nearly three million votes cast.

Once in office, Perón launched an energetic program to take control of transportation infrastructure and to promote industrialization. Because prices for Argentina's main exports, cereal grains and beef, were high, he created an agency, the IAPI, to market them abroad. By controlling exchange rates, Perón was able to skim off nearly half the export revenues for reinvestment in manufacturing. For a time, industrialists profited enormously from his subsidies and tariff protection.

Meanwhile, Perón also boosted wages to the highest levels in decades to create domestic markets for manufactures. Migrants streamed into Buenos Aires and other cities in search of the good life. Most were rewarded with union-protected jobs and low-cost government services. Evita was especially effective in addressing these migrants from the pampas, whom, along with the urban workers, she endearingly called the *descamisados.*

Perón's opportunistic economic program, sometimes labeled "import substitution industrialization" (ISI), fared well for several years without causing financial difficulties. Ranchers and farmers, to be sure, protested their forced contributions to government coffers, but everyone else seemed to benefit, especially the masses. Wages as a share of national income rose from 46 to 57 percent, helping to drive factory expansion. Only in 1949 did the boom falter, due to a number of factors. A drought cut Argentine production about the same time that European grain harvests began to satisfy domestic demand. Wartime foreign currency reserves finally gave out, forcing Perón to pay for imports with cash. And rural producers refused to send cattle to slaughter and left farmland fallow to protest the IAPI's confiscatory policies. For the first time since Perón won election, Argentina experienced food shortages.

Evita played a critical part in buoying Perón's popularity. She became his personal representative in the Labor Department (renamed a secretariat) and managed liaison with union officials. She also presided over a sprawling welfare organization called the Eva Perón Foundation, which operated as a charitable slush fund. During regular hours the ill and destitute could meet with Evita and receive favors, jobs, money, or simply attention. As time went by, her compassion and generosity became legendary among the masses. Much of Perón's appeal among the poor was due to Evita's work in the Foundation and the Labor Secretariat.

Evita targeted women as voters by organizing feminine branches of the Peronist Party after women won the right to vote in 1947. Women voted in 1948 congressional elections and then in the 1951 presidential race. In the latter, they overwhelmingly supported Perón, whom they credited with the franchise and other feminist measures.

Perón also undertook some remarkable foreign policy initiatives. Seeing that the United States and the USSR were drifting into the Cold War, he proposed that countries without a strong interest in the nuclear standoff and partition of Europe remain neutral. He termed this the Third Way, equidistant between capitalism and communism. He sent crack diplomats abroad to represent Argentina's case, and a number of Third World leaders gave their support. This stance gave Perón considerable flexibility and influence among the nonaligned nations. In addition, he created an inter-American confederation of labor, called ATLAS, which also remained apart from the U.S.- and Soviet-aligned confederations. In the early 1950s, a half-dozen national federations affiliated with ATLAS, increasing Perón's prestige.

Perón pressed to have Evita run as his vice presidential candidate in 1951, but the army high command vetoed her. Never happy with a first lady of dubious social background, the generals balked at the possibility of Evita succeeding to the presidency and assuming command of the armed forces in the event of Perón's death. Perón backed down, but conspiracies began to surface within the officer corps from that time on, and he could no longer count on the total loyalty of his comrades-in-arms.

In public, Evita played the firebrand to Perón's moderate, stable presence. Speaking as one from humble origins, she could condemn the wealthy and the powerful in colorful, vivid terms. She demanded lower prices, controlled rents, more charity, jobs, and respect for the downtrodden. Paradoxically, when she wore expensive furs, gowns, and jewelry, often purchased with Foundation money, the public loved it, vicariously participating in the elite baiting. She and Juan spoke to opposite ends of the social spectrum. She would stand up for the poor and oppressed almost literally while Perón hobnobbed with industrialists and bankers. Theirs was a unique case among the populists of shared charisma, when two leaders enjoyed separate yet related adoration by their followers.

Perón won reelection in 1951 by a landslide, but soon afterward the Peróns' success began to fade. The economy continued to shrink, in part due to government reallocation of capital. Inflation started to eat into the gains that workers had made in preceding years. Agricultural production and hence exports dropped far below their 1940s peaks. In his zeal to turn the economy around, Perón began to oppose labor strikes and wage increases, arguing instead for belt-tightening by workers. He invited large foreign firms to exploit natural resources and start up heavy industry, thus betraying in the eyes of workers his earlier nationalist stance.

The blow from which Perón never fully recovered was the death of Evita, a victim of cancer at the age of thirty-three. Inoperable, the disease quickly took away her life in 1952. She attempted to transfer her charisma to Perón with appeals to the masses and a biography, *The Causes in My Life,* but it did not succeed. Her passing left a painful gap in Argentine leadership.

By 1953 the burdens of governing without Evita were evident. Perón grew testy and combative. He took over the leading newspaper, *La Nación,* because of its criticism of him. He picked a fight with the formerly supportive Catholic church over refusal to declare Evita a saint. He quarreled with labor over contracts with foreign oil and auto companies. Regime supporters, calling themselves *mazorcas* (harking back to Rosas's thugs in the 1830s), beat up opponents and brawled in the streets. The steady, calm leadership that he had provided earlier had dissolved.

The end came in July and August 1955, amid signs of rapid deterioration in public order. *Mazorcas* attacked priests and damaged churches. Perón distributed arms to those unions that still supported him in order to counteract the threat of a military coup. He threw down the gauntlet to elite groups that had deserted him, threatening to kill one elite for every *Peronista* killed. His desperation was obvious.

The army finally acted by arresting and sending Perón into exile in Paraguay. A junta of generals chose one of its own to preside over the dismantling of the entire Peronist movement. It seemed that Perón and populism were about to be eradicated from Argentine politics.

Andean Populists

After World War II, the countries along the Andes experienced intense recruitment of the masses into politics, and a number of populist leaders rose to power. The distinctive peoples, history, and geography of the Andean republics gave populism characteristics different from those of Brazil and the Southern Cone. In particular, the strong native American traditions of Ecuador, Peru, and Bolivia gave rise to appeals to the Amerindian civilizations and their great conflicts with Spaniards. In societies divided by race and ethnicity, Andean populists stressed cooperation and consensus while promising to raise depressed standards of living.

In Colombia and Venezuela, greater Spanish immigration and mixing with the native peoples had produced mestizo majorities who constituted an ethnic as well as social middle class. There issues of equity, development, and nationalism proved more forceful. There, too, however, incorporation of lower-class persons into politics became the driving force of populism.

Chile was exceptional in this regard because its well-organized parties, constitutional tradition, and advanced social legislation prevented an upsurge in populism. Only one more president (after Alessandri) emerged as a populist: Carlos Ibáñez during his 1952–1958 term, and when he stepped down, politics resumed its impressive march toward socialism.

Haya de la Torre

Peru's leading populist was Víctor Raúl Haya de la Torre, whose active career spanned six decades, from 1920 until his death in 1979. Haya, as he was known to followers, grew up in Trujillo, a city on the north coast of Peru. His father was a schoolmaster, so Haya received a comfortable upbringing and strong academic formation from his family. (See the section on his early career in Chapter Fourteen.)

After graduating from high school, Haya attended the venerable University of San Marcos in Lima, where, someone joked, he majored in student politics. His initiation and first success occurred in 1919, when he joined a general strike among Lima workers and became their spokesman. From then on, he served as go-between for university students and Lima's fledgling labor movement.

In 1921 Haya founded the Popular University, inspired by comparable socialist schools in Europe. San Marcos students taught basic skills and life classes while gaining an acquaintance with how the other half lived and worked. He deepened his commitment to student activism in 1922 when he visited the University of Córdoba, Argentina, site of momentous reforms in governance in 1917.

Haya's biggest campaign came in 1923 when he led street protests against President Leguía's proposal to ally Peru formally with the Vatican. The protests turned violent, and the government shut down the Popular University and sent Haya into exile.

Haya spent the next seven years traveling, meeting distinguished figures and preparing for his eventual reentry into politics. He drank deeply of European culture and politics in the 1920s, connected with other dissident leaders in Latin America, and shaped the ideas that he would disseminate for the rest of his career. The most symbolic moment of his exile occurred in Mexico in 1924, when he founded his APRA Party (American Popular Revolutionary Alliance). The party continued to bear this name even though it never spread much beyond Peru.

The philosophy of APRA and Haya has received a great deal of attention for its mystical and inspirational qualities. It sought to harmonize Inca civilization with Hispanic traditions and ultimately to forge a nationalist synthesis of the two in contemporary Peru. (See Chapter Seventeen for Haya's racial theories.) In fact, Haya's success owed much more to his emotional speaking abilities and mesmerizing rhetoric than to a coherent doctrine. Followers believed in him because of his charismatic authority, which he exuded in all settings. U.S. writer John Gunther wrote of him in 1941, "I saw Haya three times, and each time I felt that I was meeting one of the greatest personages of America."

After the dictator Leguía was overthrown in 1930, Haya returned to Peru and won great acclaim from his followers, who had remained active in his absence. His party now blossomed, and he toured the country campaigning for the presidency. His opponent was Colonel Sánchez Cerro, the army officer who had led the coup against Leguía. Sánchez Cerro was himself something of a populist, a man of the people with mixed racial heritage and the ability to make credible promises to many constituencies.

Sánchez Cerro won the election of 1931 and assumed the presidency, only to be stymied by the Depression. Then in 1933 an APRA zealot assassinated him. This ended Peru's brief flirtation with democracy and populism. The army and representatives of Peru's wealthy classes assumed power again and instituted a dictatorship, banning all electoral politics.

In 1932 APRA had staged a revolt in Trujillo, and in the thick of the fighting it executed some sixty captive army officers and public officials. The army retaliated. Hundreds, perhaps as many as two thousand Apristas taken prisoner when Trujillo was recaptured, were executed near the ancient ruins of Chan Chan. The bitterness and distrust engendered by these events poisoned relations between APRA and the army for many decades. Haya and his lieutenants were jailed and the movement outlawed for many years. For the next three decades, the army and oligarchy barred Haya as a presidential candidate. He spent much of his time abroad or under house arrest, and he never did occupy the presidency. Yet, APRA continued to grow and became the country's largest and most successful mass-based party. There was never any doubt that Haya could have won the presidency had he been allowed to run.

APRA owed its success to many factors. Haya's charisma grew over the years, enhanced by his political persecution. In exile, censored, barred from elections, he symbolized the struggle against the elitist policies that kept most Peruvians from exercising their democratic rights. He also had the freedom to make opportunistic deals. In 1956, for example, he supported Conservative candidate Manuel Odría in exchange for special considerations in Congress. For long periods of time APRA managed to elect a large congressional delegation, one that kept its program and promises before the public.

In fact, APRA became a loyal opposition, able to criticize and denounce government misconduct while never having to shoulder much responsibility itself. Its message was simple: The oligarchy monopolized government positions and exploited the workers and peasants while mortgaging the country to foreign capitalists. Haya and APRA promised to restore national control over resources, to raise the standard of living, and to protect the interests of the downtrodden. The oligarchy, however, stole some of APRA's thunder by enacting the very reforms that it advocated, bringing a gradual modernization of government structures.

In the 1962 presidential election, the elite divided over whom to support and did not ban Haya from running. Haya, as candidate of the largest party, seemed destined to win. In fact, he received a plurality yet not the requisite one-third of the votes cast. According to the Constitution, Congress had to decide the election outcome. Recognizing that he could never get enough votes in Congress, he struck a deal for the Conservative candidate, Odría, to assume the presidency if APRA could control the cabinet, that is to say, the executive branch of government.

The military became incensed at this crass deal and stepped in to annul the election. It held a new election in 1963, in which Haya was not allowed to run. This time a Christian Democrat, Fernando Belaúnde Terry, won with promises to carry out social and economic reforms to benefit the masses. The United States backed Belaúnde, as did the moderate middle class, and he took office with a mandate for change.

Haya remained sidelined for the next twenty years. Just before his death, he presided over the 1978–1979 constitutional convention that restored civilian rule in Peru.

José María Velasco Ibarra

José María Velasco Ibarra, a middle-class law professor from Ecuador's Sierra (highlands) region, first occupied the presidency in 1934 as a result of Depression-era instability. He held office for only a year before being overthrown. At the time he did not display signs of his later populist qualities.

During several years in exile, however, he began to cultivate a personal following by posing as a defender of the laws and popular interest. In fact, he used his absences to build his popularity, claiming that the oligarchy banned him to keep the people from electing their true representative, *el gran ausente* (the great absent one).

In 1944 Velasco forced the resignation of the incumbent president, using his growing organization to mobilize huge protests and strikes. While serving as provisional president he oversaw a constitutional convention and then won election as president. He had no party or ideological platform, instead appealing to the masses of poor people, whom he called the *chusma* (rabble). He had superb speaking skills and was at his best when addressing crowds of his followers. He was a great critic of others' shortcomings, which he was able to exploit to advantage. A tempestuous and changeable leader, he began to lose support as soon as he was elected, and he came to rely increasingly on the Conservatives. By 1947 he had alienated many powerful collaborators and was overthrown by the military.

José María Velasco Ibarra (wearing a suit and tie) was elected president five times, lending credence to his boast, "Give me a balcony and I will be president."

In 1952 Velasco returned from his exile in Argentina to run again for president, and this time he won a huge victory, drawing most of his votes from the lowland provinces along the coast. In 1952 358,000 persons voted, or just over 10 percent of the total population. Campaign managers had now adopted public address systems, radio, mass leafleting, and other modern election techniques. Velasco was quite astute in making promises that the masses wanted to hear while assuring his wealthy backers that nothing would change.

Velasco was both cause and effect of the growing electoral participation. Velasco's style had become famous by the 1950s, conveyed most often by his boast, "Give me a balcony, and I will be president!" Velasco perfected a populist style and attracted massive numbers of loyal voters. Meanwhile, he had the knack of choosing issues that elicited widespread support. He denounced a 1942 treaty by which Peru had gained a huge tract of the Amazon basin belonging to Ecuador, and he convinced the people to back a campaign to reclaim it. Occasional border skirmishes with Peru punctuated his terms in office. He also claimed two hundred miles of territorial waters to protect Ecuador's rich fishing grounds. When he returned to power in the 1960s he actually impounded U.S. tuna trawlers that did not pay a special license. This became known as the "Tuna Wars."

Velasco was elected again in 1960 and 1968. Both times he was deposed by the military, even though in 1970 he had created a dictatorship with the backing of the army. He was nothing if not unpredictable.

Meanwhile, in the 1950s another populist movement, called the Concentration of Popular Forces (CFP), arose in the coastal city of Guayaquil. Its two main leaders, Carlos Guevara Moreno and Assad Bucarám, became the populist archrivals of Velasco. CFP was created by Guevara Moreno, a skilled speaker and charismatic figure. Guevara enjoyed a strong following and was expected to run for the presidency. In 1959, however, he surprised observers by withdrawing from politics.

In the early 1960s Assad Bucarám, the self-educated and energetic son of Lebanese immigrants, managed to take over the CFP and expanded its following among the multitudes of rural migrants streaming into Guayaquil's *barriadas* (slums). An imposing figure with a booming voice, Bucarám soon became the boss of Guayaquil politics. In the course of the 1960s his popularity spread throughout the lowland provinces, reflecting the basic coast-highland division in Ecuador's political geography. Traditional families viewed him with extreme displeasure, incensed at the idea of a rude and boisterous figure like Bucarám becoming president.

The elite eventually found a way to block the presidential ambitions of don Buca, as he was nicknamed, using his parents' immigrant status as an excuse. The old master managed to skirt the veto in two ways. First, he helped his close aide and relative, Jaime Roldós, win the presidency in 1979, giving Bucarám access to the highest level. Then he himself won election to Congress and muscled his way into the presidency of that body. Ironically, though, don Buca and Roldós began fighting almost immediately, and the latter asserted his independence by pulling out of the CFP. The military, meanwhile, seemed disinclined to get involved.

In 1981, however, Ecuadorian populism ended. Roldós perished in a plane crash, and Bucarám died a few months later. Since then, conservative figures have held the presidency. The only serious populist rebirth, the 1996 election of Bucarám's nephew, Abdalá (nicknamed El Loco), ended in his impeachment less than a year later.

Rómulo Betancourt

Like so many other populists, Rómulo Betancourt got his political start in a university. Born into a well-to-do family near Caracas, Betancourt showed great aptitude for school and moved to the capital for preparatory study. At the Central University in Caracas, he fell in with student activists and studied law on the side. In 1928 he and his colleagues staged protests and strikes against the seemingly perpetual dictatorship of Juan Vicente Gómez. In response, the government shut down the school and jailed the protesters. Many, including Betancourt, managed to escape from the country and live in exile. This group, later known as the Generation of 1928, became the legendary founders of the Democratic Action (AD) Party. Years later Betancourt would usher this generation into the government.

During his exile Betancourt traveled in the Caribbean and settled for a time in Costa Rica, where he associated with leftist intellectuals and edited a newspaper. There his ideas began to take shape, forming a vision for Venezuela to become a democratic, quasisocialist country. He imagined that the workers and campesino farmers would have to be mobilized for this to take place and that his generation would guide them. After a few ill-fated attempts at armed invasions, the exiles gave up trying to organize guerrilla movements and stuck to propaganda.

Gómez died in 1935, and his successor allowed the exiles to return and form political parties. Betancourt and others of the Generation of 1928 recruited teachers, rural leaders, and workers' union officials. Their most important coalition, Movement for Venezuelan Organization (ORVE), was the antecedent of AD. They paid special attention to the petroleum unions because during the 1930s Venezuela had become the world's largest oil exporter.

The two generals who governed Venezuela after Gómez both attempted to liberalize politics gradually, but only for groups willing to recognize their legitimacy. Betancourt kept his party separate and underground to avoid too close an association with the military regime. Finally, however, the party emerged formally in 1941 as AD, and it immediately began national recruitment.

For several years AD built its following and prestige as an independent party, Betancourt serving as its coordinator and ideological inspiration. He moved gradually away from his socialist beginnings and came to advocate a strong central government that would regulate but not take over the nation's businesses. In particular, he planned to overhaul the contracts enjoyed by the biggest international oil companies so that Venezuelans would benefit more from their profits.

In 1945 the incumbent government attempted to steer elections toward a hand-picked successor, while AD and other groups fought against such a move. After a great deal of maneuvering, AD joined with some middle-ranking army officers to overthrow the regime and install a provisional government, in which Betancourt was the chief authority. The military collaborators quickly melted back into the barracks, leaving AD in charge of reforming the entire system of government.

Betancourt and the AD enjoyed three years of relative freedom to enact a program to modernize their country. Betancourt's reputation largely stems from these halcyon years. First they overhauled the electoral system, giving the vote to women and eighteen-year-olds while also providing for secret ballots and widespread voter enlistment. AD went out of its way to create committees in rural towns and villages to complement its original urban constituency. Venezuela held its first modern elections ever under the AD, in 1946 and 1947, each of which drew over a million voters and established a model for future elections.

Betancourt then renegotiated the law covering oil production, providing for a fifty-fifty split of net profits from petroleum exports and refining. The leading companies, called "the majors," agreed to this in exchange for guarantees of labor cooperation and no expropriation. Betancourt spoke of using the oil profits to build basic industry and diversify the economy, so that one day the country would not have to depend on hydrocarbon exports. One of his supporters, novelist Uslar Pietri, called this policy *sembrando petróleo* ("sowing the oil"). AD also invested in schools, clinics, rural roads, light manufacturing, and electrification.

Finally, AD announced an agrarian reform program that not only made land available to the landless but also provided credit, training, access to markets, and extension services. This, too, won much support from both urban and rural citizens, who feared the instability brought on by a landless campesino class.

Betancourt had served as provisional president in the early years and so declined to run in 1947. Instead, the famous novelist Rómulo Gallegos, author of the classic novel *Doña Bárbara*, ran and won with 74 percent of the votes. AD seemed to be a juggernaut in these years. Expectations ran high that Gallegos would continue to implement the program that Betancourt had initiated.

Military commanders, however, urged on by wealthy businessmen and landowners, became uneasy with AD's rapid reforms. The AD leadership failed to take other party bosses into their planning, and within months after the election, plotting began against Gallegos. Confident with its massive election victory, AD did not take precautions, and it was easily overthrown by a military coup in December 1948. Betancourt and his colleagues again went into exile, and the populist experiment ended temporarily.

For the next decade Venezuela was ruled by General Marcos Pérez Jiménez, the last in a long line of dictators from the ranching state of Táchira. Pérez Jiménez rolled back many of the reforms, installed politicians who supported the army, and reassured foreign and domestic businessmen that their interests would be protected. The military diverted the oil revenues from education and health to major construction projects, like a superhighway from the inland capital of Caracas to the coast and a steel-producing center on the Orinoco River.

In 1958 disgruntled army officers, egged on by civilian forces, overthrew Pérez Jiménez and brought back constitutional government. The following year Betancourt won election as president, and he restored the policies of the late 1940s. Somewhat chastened now, Betancourt followed a more moderate course and worked closely with rival party leaders. He also took a strong stand against the guerrilla groups that had sprung up around the Caribbean basin following the Cuban revolution.

In 1959 Venezuela took the lead in creating an oil cartel that would later become quite powerful—the Organization of Petroleum Exporting Countries (OPEC).

After 1960 Betancourt and the AD alternated in office with a more conservative party, the COPEI, which had been organized in the 1940s. Representing a Christian Democratic philosophy, COPEI stressed honesty in office, protection of the family, and probusiness economic policies.

By the 1970s Venezuela had consolidated a strong democratic tradition and avoided the military takeovers that swept most of the region. Analysts credited the populist era forged by Betancourt's AD for this transition to democracy.

Jorge Eliécer Gaitán

Colombia instituted democratic traditions much earlier than most countries in Latin America. Conservative Party presidents had dominated elections from the 1880s on with few interruptions. The country earned reasonable returns on its exports and enjoyed a good reputation among foreign investors. The Liberal Party leaders seemed content in the role of loyal opposition. Virtually every citizen and civic organization was strongly committed to one party or the other.

In 1930 the Liberals managed to win the presidential election when the Conservatives split and ran two candidates. The Liberals took advantage to pioneer social and labor legislation that would soon turn them into the majority party. They not only guided the country peacefully through the Great Depression, but also initiated what would become a sixteen-year Liberal era. (See Chapter Sixteen.)

After a stabilizing term by President Enrique Oyala Herrera, Alfonso López Pumarejo won the presidency in 1934. Calling his administration the "Revolution on the March," he carried out social and economic reforms that were remarkably innovative for Colombia. He separated Church and state, created universal male suffrage, legalized labor unions and collective bargaining, and gave the government the power to regulate and even to expropriate private property in the public interest. Successors went even further with social and economic change, instituting land reform, expanding social security, and increasing federal funds for education.

Following World War II, however, social tensions erupted in Colombia, causing critics to charge that the Liberal reforms either had gone too far or had come too late. Only a small proportion of the eligible population voted, and voters always elected representatives of the traditional parties. Politicians were trapped in debates over philosophies from the last century, while masses of poor and unemployed people streamed into the cities in search of better lives. The time was ripe for a bold leader capable of grappling with modern problems.

That leader was Jorge Eliécer Gaitán, a young and ambitious lawyer from Bogotá. Gaitán and his dissident Liberals decried the old-fashioned ways of the party wing dominated by Alfonso López (elected to a second term in 1942) and called for a thorough renewal of its ranks and policies. Gaitán insisted on running for president in 1946, thereby splitting the party vote and allowing the Conservative candidate to win.

Colombia's most promising young politician in the 1940s, Jorge Gaitán, was assassinated on the eve of the presidential election, throwing the nation into social and political turmoil.

Gaitán was not only a rebel within Liberal ranks but also within the elite who traditionally governed Colombia. Born in Bogotá into a lower-middle-class family, he was of mestizo mixed racial heritage. He had to work his way through law school, and then he made a name for himself as a criminal lawyer. Outspoken and articulate in public settings, he gravitated toward politics and his father's party, the Liberals. In 1928 he leaped to national attention by denouncing a massacre of banana workers by the army, which was called in to break a strike against the United Fruit Company near Santa Marta. His investigation and speeches in Congress (to which he had won election in 1928) became a *cause célèbre*. He was clearly a young man on the rise.

During the Liberal republic Gaitán served in a wide range of public jobs. He finished out a term as congressman and was reelected. He served as a city councilman in Bogotá. In these jobs he represented well the people who elected him, and he gained notice as time went on. The Liberal bosses decided to test his mettle by appointing him mayor of Bogotá in 1936. He served only a year before alienating important people, who had him removed. Later, party chiefs tested him in the positions of minister of education and of labor. Faced with major policy choices that went against the Liberal grain, he invariably went with his instincts and had to step down before long. Still, these national positions gave him the opportunity to display his considerable administrative talents and to travel throughout the country. Combative, eloquent, ambitious, and devoted to attending to the needs of the rural and urban masses, Gaitán was clearly headed toward the top.

In 1945 the Liberal Party split badly, and Gaitán decided that he would make a run for president in the 1946 elections. No longer even nominally tied to Liberal

Party rules, he mounted a modern political campaign, complete with a convention, radio coverage, newspapers, and a punishing travel schedule. He remained the boss, however, as all populists did, and seemed to have limitless energy for every last detail of the campaign. This personal touch was translated into the name of his organization, simply *Gaitanismo*. Even persons who opposed his candidacy admitted that he possessed charisma and the power to arouse the masses.

As expected, the Liberals split their votes in the 1946 election, and Gaitán came in third. Analysis of the returns, however, indicated that he would be the man to beat in 1950. Even without major party backing or deep pockets, he took virtually all the major cities, plus the coastal provinces. His Liberal rival, Gabriel Turbay, bowed out of politics and died a short time later in Europe. So many people expressed their preferences for Gaitán in the 1946 election that the Liberal Party would have to nominate him in 1950.

Gaitán possessed a complex mixture of progressive ideas, a visceral drive to lead, and an innate ability to connect with the masses of poor people. Taken in isolation, his slogans sounded arrogant and overwrought, yet in the heat of a speech, on the radio, and in meetings with aides, they inspired faith and elevated him above the ranks of ordinary politicians. Perhaps his most famous statement best sums up his complexity: "I am not a man! I am a people!" Already he was compared with Juan Perón, whose inexorable drive to the presidency paralleled Gaitán's.

In 1947 and 1948 Gaitán recovered from the recent grueling campaign, built up his law practice, and got ready to run for the presidency. He kept his name and picture in the press and attended party meetings, but he did not have a particularly high profile. He managed to forge an alliance between *Gaitanismo* and the Liberal Party, though not without a great deal of argument and opposition.

Meanwhile, the general mood of the country grew more harsh, with rising rates of crime and violence, an uncompromising attitude on the part of the government, and increasing antagonism between Liberals and Conservatives. Thus began what would later be known as *La Violencia,* the decades-long conflict that claimed 350,000 lives. In all likelihood, Gaitán himself fell victim to this trend toward brutality and killing.

In April 1948, with diplomatic delegations from around the Americas present for the founding of the Organization of American States, Gaitán was fatally shot by a lone assailant. Gaitán had just emerged from his office, accompanied by several colleagues, when a deranged, shoddily dressed man stepped in front of the group and shot him dead.

Gaitán's death caused an immediate outpouring of grief and anger from Bogotá's poor, who rioted and looted for days. Their last, best hope of electing someone who cared about them had now vanished. The *Bogotazo,* as it became known, in turn fanned the violence in the countryside, so that by the 1950s Colombia descended into endemic civil war.

Other Colombian leaders attempted to reach out to the masses the way Gaitán had, but they failed. After a five-year military dictatorship in the 1950s, Colombia returned to the two-party system of before, power alternating between the Conservatives and the Liberals. Populism in Colombia died along with Gaitán.

Paz Estenssoro

The last Andean leader to be considered, Víctor Paz Estenssoro of Bolivia, enjoyed a double reputation as a populist and a revolutionary. As the events of his rise to power in 1952 fade into history, his party (the Nationalist Revolutionary Movement, or MNR) increasingly looks like many others in the populist mainstream.

Paz grew up in the southern district of Tarija, where he completed high school. He then attended the National University, graduating in economics. In 1932 he volunteered for duty in the Chaco War against Paraguay. After Bolivia lost, Paz joined a "young Turks" group of disillusioned officers and participated in the 1936 coup led by David Toro and Germán Busch. Paz served in several capacities, making economic policy and helping fashion a more modern constitution.

The reformers lost power in 1939, so in 1941 they decided to found a party, the MNR, to pursue their goals. The following year they seized power again and held it until 1946. Paz served as finance minister in this government.

Conservative military forces removed the reformers again, so Paz went into exile in nearby Argentina, staying for the next six years. He kept the party alive through clandestine networks, and he broadcast opposition radio messages to Bolivia. Paz was able to forge an alliance between his group, derived from veteran officers, and organized labor.

In 1951 Paz ran for president in absentia and won 53 percent of the votes. Before he could return, however, reactionary forces induced the military to take power again. At this point, the MNR carried out a coup, in which the powerful tin miners' union played a crucial role. Paz returned to take charge of a revolution.

One writer described the MNR government that emerged as a "many-headed monster" because of the disparate and competing forces it contained, from the miners to the urban middle class to the communists. Paz gave three cabinet posts to the tin miners and quickly carried out his campaign promises. He nationalized the tin mines on the grounds that they had not contributed to national development. In fact, the union controlled the mines. He then raised wages across the board and subsidized basic necessities to stimulate the economy. He also extended social security to virtually all urban workers. Finally, he carried out the most complete agrarian reform since the Mexican program of the 1930s.

Paz enacted several other reforms in order to bolster his political position. He extended the vote to all adults, regardless of literacy, hoping to reap support from the poorest strata of society. He also weeded out enemies from the army officer corps and kept the troop strength low in order to discourage army involvement in politics. He also allowed the miners and peasant leagues to keep weapons that they had obtained during and after the revolution. The government could use these irregular militias as a counterbalance against the military.

Because the MNR did not carry out widespread dismantlement of the socioeconomic structures, some writers refer to it as "populist." Paz certainly fits the definition: charismatic, chosen by election, reformist, and devoted to improving the lives of the poor. His later career—a productive term in the early 1960s and a spectacularly successful administration in the late 1980s—also fits the populist definition.

Central American Populists

Few populist leaders arose in Central America, due in large part to the oligarchical nature of these nations' governments. When challengers seemed capable of capturing power, they were simply suppressed by the military. The exceptional cases of Costa Rica and Panama confirm the general rule.

Costa Rica did not have an army capable of defeating an insurgency, so when a clever and popular landowner, José "Pepe" Figueres, organized a revolt, the army resisted and then fell to Figueres's "revolution" in 1948. A mix of a revolutionary and populist, Figueres quickly held elections, convoked a constitutional convention to restore democracy, and then ran successfully for president. Costa Rica returned to its democratic traditions, an exception in the troubled lands of Central America. (See the section on Figueres's movement in Chapter Twenty-two.)

Arnulfo Arias

Panama also lacked an army due to the presence of the U.S. canal administration and several military bases in the Canal Zone. Until 1930 U.S. authorities there monitored politics and stepped in to maintain law and order so that the canal could function efficiently. In 1931, however, the United States decided to stand on the sidelines while a group of middle-class reformers, who called their movement Common Action, took power and deposed a corrupt and ineffectual president.

Common Action was led by an extraordinarily gifted forty-five-year-old lawyer, Harmodio Arias, who arose from modest beginnings to become one of the country's best leaders. Though not a populist himself, Harmodio paved the way for the appearance of populism in his country. After the group's seizure of power in 1931, he went to Washington to serve as ambassador and to win the acquiescence of the U.S. government. Then he ran for president in 1932 and won in Panama's first free and honest election. He served as president for a four-year term, then wielded great influence during the early years of his hand-picked successor's administration.

Harmodio accomplished a great deal while in public life, much of it intended to turn his country into a genuine nation-state rather than a mere client of the United States. He oversaw negotiations with the United States that in 1936 resulted in a treaty that gave Panama more benefits from the canal. He founded the University of Panama, the country's first postsecondary institution. He strengthened the police force so that it could play a larger role in maintaining law and order. He established the Popular Savings Bank and attempted to deal with the lack of housing in Panama City and Colón. Most of all, Harmodio guided the country through the hardships of the Depression and served notice to the United States that Panama wished to be treated with greater respect.

Harmodio's brother, Arnulfo Arias, groomed himself for the presidency during the 1930s, and in 1939 he launched his campaign with the full backing of the government and the police. Overzealous and tempestuous, Arnulfo hounded his opponent into resigning and then won the 1940 election unopposed. Panamanian politics would never be the same again.

Born into a poor rural family in 1901, Arnulfo Arias managed to get a good education in Panama and eventually graduated from Harvard Medical School. Following in his brother Harmodio's footsteps, he entered politics in the late 1920s and did not abandon it until his death in 1988. An American observer said of him, "Politics is in his blood." He ran for president five times, was elected three times, and was deposed by the military three times. He served two and a half years as president, spent two years in jail, and lived fifteen years in exile.

The most successful vote-getter ever to arise in Panama, Arnulfo was a populist in the mold of Perón, Haya de la Torre, and Velasco Ibarra. His party, called the Panameñistas, was little more than a personal vehicle for its leader's career. Yet, his credo of *Panameñismo* (Panamanianism) struck sympathetic chords in the hearts and minds of a majority of the citizens.

Arnulfo Arias's accession to the presidency in October 1940 began a short and tumultuous term in which he was branded a Creole *fuhrer,* a petty tyrant, a megalomaniac, a gringo baiter, and worse. He lasted barely a year before being ousted by his own minister of justice, with the blessing of U.S. authorities.

Arnulfo returned to office in 1949 and presided over an administration characterized as one of "irresponsibility, pillage, and privilege." Many citizens were happy to see him overthrown in less than two years. For the next decade he instructed his followers not to vote at all, like Yrigoyen's campaign of *intransigencia* earlier in the century. In 1968 Arnulfo won the election with ample margin and was installed, only to be overthrown by a military coup after only eleven days. Finally, he is widely believed to have won the 1984 election, but the official vote count gave the election to his opponent, Nicolás Ardito Barletta.

Conclusions and Issues

In the two decades following World War II, Latin America saw the rise of an expansive, quasidemocratic politics known as populism. This style of politics consisted of electioneering by dark horse candidates, often with scant party backing, who mobilized masses of voters. These candidates were charismatic, spellbinding, ambitious, and colorful. They did not always prove to be effective as presidents, but they won and held the loyalty of huge numbers of people, sometimes even after their deaths. A few movements identified with these populists—even using their names—are still powerful in the region today.

Political scientists note that the populists did not foster town hall-style democracy nor empower their followers by consulting them on major decisions. Many of the populists were autocratic and willful egotists uninterested in what the masses thought. But they did promote the use of elections and expanded the suffrage into rural areas and into the ranks of the poor, female, and disenfranchised—a process that was irreversible.

The populists also managed—through a kind of mystical union with the people—to follow policies acknowledged to be the "will of the people." Whether they really perceived popular will or used their powers to create the illusion that they did, we may never know. The populists were, however, extraordinarily successful in generating mass enthusiasm, framing broad national issues, taking bold stands, and mobilizing people to achieve their ends.

For better or worse, Latin American politics has never been the same after the classical populists.

Discussion Questions

1. What traits and styles, if any, linked the classic populists with their earlier counterparts (Chapter Twelve)? How had changing domestic and global circumstances affected the opportunities for ambitious politicians? What role did new technology play?

2. Why did Brazil experience such a strong showing of populist leaders in the 1945–1964 era? How did populists interact with one another? To what extent did populists groom successors?

3. Did the populists bring on their own demise, or did overzealous elites and generals overreact to their mass mobilizations?

Bibliography for Part Four

Andreas, Carol, *When Women Rebel: The Rise of Popular Feminism in Peru* (Westport: Greenwood, 1985).

Andrews, George Reid, *Blacks and Whites in São Paulo, Brazil* (Madison: University of Wisconsin Press, 1991).

Becker, Marjorie, *Setting the Virgin on Fire: Lázaro Cárdenas, Michoacán Peasants, and the Redemption of the Mexican Revolution* (Berkeley and Los Angeles: University of California Press, 1996).

Besse, Susan K., *Restructuring Patriarchy: The Modernization of Gender Inequality in Brazil, 1914–1940* (Chapel Hill: University of North Carolina Press, 1996).

Brown, Jonathan C., ed., *Workers' Control in Latin America, 1930–1979* (Chapel Hill: University of North Carolina Press, 1997).

Conniff, Michael L., *Urban Politics in Brazil: The Rise of Populism, 1925–1945* (Pittsburgh: University of Pittsburgh Press, 1982).

———, ed., *Populism in Latin America* (Tuscaloosa: University of Alabama Press, 1999).

Delpar, Helen, *The Enormous Vogue of Things Mexican: Cultural Relations between the United States and Mexico, 1920–1935* (Tuscaloosa: University of Alabama Press, 1992).

French, John D., *The Brazilian Workers' ABC: Class Conflict and Alliances in Modern São Paulo* (Chapel Hill: University of North Carolina Press, 1992).

Hahner, June E., *Emancipating the Female Sex: The Struggle for Women's Rights in Brazil, 1850–1940* (Durham: Duke University Press, 1990).

Horowitz, Joel, *Argentine Unions, the State, and the Rise of Perón, 1930–1945* (Berkeley: Institute of International Studies, 1990).

Lavrín, Asunción, *Women, Feminism, and Social Change in Argentina, Chile, and Uruguay, 1890–1940* (Lincoln: University of Nebraska Press, 1995).

Longley, Kyle, *The Sparrow and the Hawk: Costa Rica and the United States during the Rise of José Figueres* (Tuscaloosa: University of Alabama Press, 1997).

Macias, Anna, *Against All Odds: The Feminist Movement in Mexico to 1940* (Westport: Greenwood, 1982).

Newton, Ronald C., *The "Nazi Menace" in Argentina, 1931–1947* (Stanford: Stanford University Press, 1992).

Pike, Frederick B., *FDR's Good Neighbor Policy* (Austin: University of Texas Press, 1995).

Potash, Robert A., *The Army and Politics in Argentina, 1928–1945* (Stanford: Stanford University Press, 1969).

Schaefer, Claudia, *Women, Art, and Representation in Modern Mexico* (Tucson: University of Arizona Press, 1992).

Schmidt, Hans, *The United States Occupation of Haiti, 1915–1934,* 2nd ed. (New Brunswick: Rutgers University Press, 1995).

Senior, Olive, *Working Miracles: Women's Lives in the English-Speaking Caribbean* (Bloomington: Indiana University Press, 1992).

Sharpless, Richard E., *Gaitán of Colombia* (Pittsburgh: University of Pittsburgh Press, 1977).

Stoner, K. Lynn, *From the House to the Streets: The Cuban Women's Movement for Legal Reform, 1898–1940* (Durham: Duke University Press, 1991).

Tamarin, David, *Argentine Labor in an Age of Transition, 1930–1945* (Albuquerque: University of New Mexico Press, 1985).

Traba, Marta, *Art of Latin America, 1900–1980* (Baltimore: Johns Hopkins University Press, 1994).

Vaughan, Mary Kay, *Cultural Politics in Revolution: Teachers, Peasants, and Schools in Mexico, 1930–1940* (Tucson: University of Arizona Press, 1997).

Walter, Knut, *The Regime of Anastasio Somoza, 1936–1956* (Chapel Hill: University of North Carolina Press, 1993).

Weinstein, Barbara, *For Social Peace in Brazil: Industrialists and the Remaking of the Working Class in São Paulo, 1920–1964* (Chapel Hill: University of North Carolina Press, 1996).

Part 5

The Contemporary Era

Most of the second half of the twentieth century has been dominated by the global conflict known as the Cold War (1947–1989). That conflict pitted the U.S.-led Western Bloc against the USSR-led Eastern Bloc. Latin Americans took sides reluctantly, viewing the conflict as peripheral to their interests. Many, in fact, remained neutral or followed Juan Perón's Third Way of independence from the Cold War struggles. A few, impressed with Fidel Castro's 1959 revolution in Cuba, actually defied the Colossus of the North and instituted socialist governments. Yet, no nation escaped the pressures brought to bear by the superpowers.

The geopolitical riptides created by the Cold War brought dramatic and even tragic outcomes in the hemisphere. Part Five deals with some of the coups, assassinations, espionage operations, secret atomic weapons programs, guerrilla conflict, counterinsurgency campaigns, and economic warfare that resulted from the U.S.-USSR confrontation. Even after its end, the Cold War casts long shadows throughout the region.

The economic experience of the Latin America region proved mixed. After World War II a boom in global markets for Latin America's exports raised hopes that the gap between rich countries and poor countries might gradually close. Then suddenly commodities prices collapsed in the early 1950s, to the detriment of Latin America. Most leaders reverted to the policies of import substitution industrialization (ISI) and protectionism designed in the 1930s. As a result, light industry increased, traditional exports were deemphasized, and foreign trade diminished as a source of national income. Heavy reliance on imported capital goods, however, soon undermined the ISI strategy. A few countries managed to build up their heavy industry sectors—Brazil and Mexico in particular—but the rest turned to common market schemes, directed economies, international loans, and other measures to keep their production expanding in pace with population growth. Nowhere were they fully successful.

In the 1970s two sharp hikes in oil prices caused widespread disruption in regional economies, even in Mexico and Venezuela, which exported oil. Most countries had to curb imports to maintain balance in their foreign payments. In the late 1970s inflation-driven global recycling of oil profits caused hundreds of billions of dollars to flow back into Latin America in the form of direct and indirect loans. This volatile situation could not last, and the Latin American economies nearly collapsed during the global recession of 1981–1982. Several countries defaulted on foreign loans and took drastic measures to survive. The so-called Lost Decade in Latin America ravaged labor relations, infrastructure, financial institutions, and even governments.

As these disruptions occurred, a radical shift in economic thinking took place in the industrialized countries and international banks. During the 1980s economic managers embraced neoliberal theories harking back to Adam Smith's classic work of the eighteenth century. These new theories gradually displaced the Keynesian economics that had prevailed since the 1930s. The new theories required privatizing government enterprises, reducing public spending, ending regulation, and promoting freer international trade. Huge and painful adjustments affecting hundreds of millions of people accompanied the shift to neoliberal policies in the 1980s and 1990s. Latin America reluctantly embraced these policies.

Politically, the Cold War brought heavy pressure to bear on hemisphere leaders to ally with either the United States or the Eastern Bloc. After the governments of Cuba, Chile, and Nicaragua became communist or socialist, with support from guerrilla forces, the United States toughened its stance and supported military dictatorships in Latin America. Virtually all of South America fell under such regimes, which differed from the traditional dictatorships in important ways. Chapter Twenty-Four relates how this occurred.

The smaller countries of the Caribbean basin responded to global events in quite distinctive ways. The Cuban Revolution, covered in Chapter Twenty-Three, led some leaders to veer to the left, especially in places still under imperialist control or influence. Revolution seemed a viable option for societies trapped in colonial-era backwardness and repression. Where dictators could resist, they became even more entrenched, usually with help from the United States. The region had not seen such intense turmoil since the era of emancipation and independence in the previous century.

Perhaps the brightest facet of Latin America's recent history has been the recognition of its cultural achievements. Long dismissed as derivative or underdeveloped, the arts in Latin America thrived and won global recognition after mid-century. Painters whose careers peaked in the 1930s—David Siquieros, Frida Kahlo, José Clemente Orozco, and Diego Rivera in Mexico, joined by Cândido Portinari, Anita Malfatti, and Di Cavalcanti in Brazil—became internationally famous. Soon Latin American artists representing many styles were featured in European and North American galleries. Caribbean music, Brazilian *bossa nova,* Andean waltzes, and Mexican *rancheras* enjoyed international fads. Films from Latin America began to win awards at festivals. A growing number of Latin American actors, writers, composers, and directors made fortunes in Hollywood. International critics came to recognize that Latin American arts drew upon an incredibly rich and diverse culture that combined elements of Amerindian, African, and European traditions.

The popularity of Latin American culture was most evident, however, in literature. Works of fiction dated back to the early nineteenth century, but none had won much attention until the following century. All of a sudden, in the 1960s the world discovered Jorge Amado, Gabriel García Márquez, Mario Vargas Llosa, Julio Cortázar, Alejo Carpentier, and Carlos Fuentes. Their styles, often called "Magical Realism" because of the fanciful events narrated, became a sensation in the United States and Europe. Later Clarice Lispector, Isabel Allende, and Elena Poniatowska won international acclaim for their novels, which emphasized feminist themes. Moreover, translated editions of these authors' books sold by the millions, generating a publishing boom. Latin America gained renown for world-class writers in the realm of fiction.

Poetry and essays from the region also gained recognition. Octavio Paz, Pablo Neruda, and Jorge Luis Borges captivated readers everywhere. They often traveled abroad to lecture or teach. By 1997 Latin American writers had won five Nobel Prizes for literature. The so-called Latin American boom in fiction led publishers to resurrect writers of the nineteenth and early twentieth centuries, and many of them also rode the wave of popularity.

During the last half-century, two Latin American countries followed paths substantially different from those of their neighbors. Mexico came out of World War II economically strengthened and stable under the one-party regime that Calles and Cárdenas had built in the 1930s. The official party, or PRI, has won all presidential elections since then and continuously held onto majorities in Congress until 1997. This steady political leadership, however, did not spare Mexico from considerable upheaval over economic and social issues. Chapter Twenty traces these events down to the present.

Colombia also pursued developments quite distinct from those of its neighbors, although it was subject to the same global forces as was the rest of the hemisphere. The populist option, prevalent in South America, disappeared with the death of Jorge Gaitán in 1948. The two-party Liberal and Conservative system then dissolved into a dictatorship in the mid-1950s, accompanied by the horrific warfare called *La Violencia*. In 1957 party leaders managed to restore their legitimacy with an agreement to share government between them. From then to the present, elected civilian presidents, more often from the Liberal Party, have governed Colombia. The violence abated in the 1960s, and the economy recovered, but still the government faced severe challenges from guerrillas and the drug cartels, as seen in Chapter Twenty-one.

As the 1990s drew to a close, the prospects for Latin America looked quite positive. Politically, most nations had democracies guided by constitutions. Socially, most indices of well-being had crept up from their low points in the 1980s: income, literacy, life expectancy, school enrollment, access to water and electricity, and housing. Economically, most had adjusted to neoliberalism and seemed to be improving their performances and ability to compete globally. Finally, the end of the Cold War brought respite from the battles and intrigues of previous generations. If not free of ideological biases, most leaders and movements at least were able to formulate positions and programs that addressed the needs of their constituents rather than global politics. Communism nearly disappeared and was replaced by social democratic movements inspired by European parties. Chapter Twenty-five summarizes the 1990s along these lines.

Mexico since World War II

The Zapatista Revolt of 1994

Panchita and Dolores turned away from the sobbing man and looked at each other. Their eyes filled with sadness and recognition. The soldier would probably die. Wordlessly Panchita took an ampule of painkiller from the medicine shelf, picked up a syringe, and walked over to the man's bed.

"This will help with the pain, señor," she said, as she filled the syringe. "We're only a little clinic, and we don't have doctors. But we'll do everything we can to save you. For now you should rest." She administered the dose in his hip, then covered him with a sheet. His crying quieted as the medicine took effect.

"Tell the sentry to use his radio to call Xinacateco," Panchita said, turning to Dolores. "Tell the *comandante* of the Zapatistas that one of his soldiers is badly wounded and needs a doctor." Dolores nodded and went outside the small dwelling.

The soldier, calmer now, asked Panchita, "How are the rest of the men? We were ambushed by government soldiers, and a shell exploded next to me. I blacked out. I, I don't know how I got here or how my group is." His voice trailed off as the sedative dragged him down toward semiconsciousness.

"Don't worry. Your guerrilla troops are safe, and the men have retreated into the mountains," Panchita lied. "You can join them in a few days, when you are recovered." She wiped his brow with gauze dipped in alcohol to cool his fever. Then she closed her eyes and crossed herself. She knew that the soldier had lost too much blood and that unless help and supplies arrived soon, he would die of his wounds before the night was over.

Panchita went outside, to where Dolores stood next to the sentry. The sentry had a sad, apologetic look on his face. "He talked to the *comandante*'s aide," Dolores said. "He said they could do nothing for this soldier. They have hundreds of casualties in all the towns of Chiapas. He asked me about the rest of the men in his unit. Do you know?"

Panchita shook her head. "This man is the only one who survived," she said. "The rest were all killed in the ambush." The sentry clicked on his radio and reported the information to the aide in Xinacateco.

"They want to know where the Mexican soldiers went after the ambush," the sentry said.

"When our market women brought this soldier here this morning, they didn't know exactly where they went," Panchita answered. "We have vendors in every town market who learn what is going on in the war. They report to one another, and we tell the Zapatistas. The rebels are our brothers and sons. But now we know only that the Mexicans took off west along the highway, in their trucks and jeeps. By morning we'll know where they are."

"I'll come back tomorrow to find out what you've learned," the sentry said.

Even though he barely knew the women, they were allies in the struggle against the Mexican Army. "We've got to keep up the fight against the government until we are all dead or we win," the young soldier said.

"They took our lands and cattle, and they're killing us with taxes. And now the damn NAFTA will suck us dry. That Salinas is evil and just wants our land and our children. The gringos are helping him, too." The nurses nodded solemnly.

"They say that we are just *indios* and that we don't know how to make money or run businesses. But we have plenty of businesses, and our farms and *milpas* (corn fields) are productive. All they want to do is conscript our children, take our money, and get rid of all us *indios*."

"It has always been this way," said Dolores. "Last year the big ranchers, they took my family's land, and when my father went to protest, they shot him. But the Mexican police didn't do anything!" she spat out, "not even give him a decent funeral. We had to ask the Belgian priests to come to our village to bury him."

"Then the Zapatistas came to our homes," said Panchita. "They are *indios* like us, and they know lots of important people. They have spoken with Señor Cuauhtémoc, son of General Cárdenas. My father voted for the general, many years ago. The Zapatistas also met with the bishop of Chiapas, who wants to help us. They think we can get rid of the corrupt governor and all his thieves."

An older woman, dressed in native clothing and carrying vegetables in a filthy shawl tied around her neck, came up quietly to the group and looked at Panchita and Dolores. The sentry understood and excused himself, walking toward a little *tienda* down the road.

"Lupita, did you find out anything about where the army went when it left here?" Dolores asked.

"*Sí, señora,*" whispered the Amerindian woman. "We found out they went to Ciénaga Grande and took the train south. They are going to guard the border so that no Zapatistas can escape into Guatemala. They will have three companies of soldiers and one motorized unit there in Tapachula."

"What else?" asked Panchita.

"They think Presidente Salinas will visit the troops soon, to show his appreciation. Will you tell this to the *comandante*?"

"We'll tell the sentry to radio this information to the *comandante* right away, Lupita. Don't let the *policía* see you talking to us. They know we are helping the Zapatistas, and they will report you to the government. Thank you and God bless you!" The old woman left noiselessly. Panchita went into the building to make note of the information in a secret journal. Then she looked at the injured soldier and froze—he had stopped breathing. She went to him and felt his neck for his pulse. After a moment she crossed herself, then pulled the sheet over his face.

Dolores walked down the road to get the sentry. They had much work to do that night. First, they would radio the new information to Xinacateco. Then they would join a new group of rebels from a nearby town. One of them knew explosives, and they would blow up a microwave tower on a hillside ten kilometers east of their village. That would make it harder for the forces in Tapachula to communicate with their headquarters in San Cristóbal de las Casas. A shudder went through her body, a mixture of fear and excitement. Perhaps now they would regain control over their lands and towns and lives.

The revolt that broke out on January 1, 1994, in the state of Chiapas was part of a broader protest against abusive government and deteriorating economic conditions in the south of Mexico. Long a region of poverty and unrest because of ethnic tensions and unstable livelihoods, Chiapas quickly became a symbol to observers all over the world of the failings of Mexico's most recent development programs. Neoliberal economics had won the endorsement of the international banking community, to be sure, but Mexican labor leaders, priests, intellectuals, and grass-roots activists decried the policies' impact on peasants and poor people. Once again, they argued, the interests of the masses were being sacrificed to benefit the super-rich of Mexico. The time had come, they said, to put an end to the crushing poverty of the working and farming people of Mexico.

Mexican history in the twentieth century has been exceptional in several ways. Mexico was the only country in the hemisphere to undergo a thorough revolution early in the century. It has endured almost constant meddling and powerful influences of all sorts from the United States, its colossal neighbor to the north. As the largest Spanish-speaking nation in the world, Mexico is a trend-setter for other countries in the Caribbean basin. And, except for the era of Cárdenas in the 1930s, Mexico has not been governed by a genuine populist.

In addition, compared with its own past and with other Latin American experience, Mexico has been politically stable and economically prosperous for most of the period since 1940. The official party, reorganized by Cárdenas in 1938 and

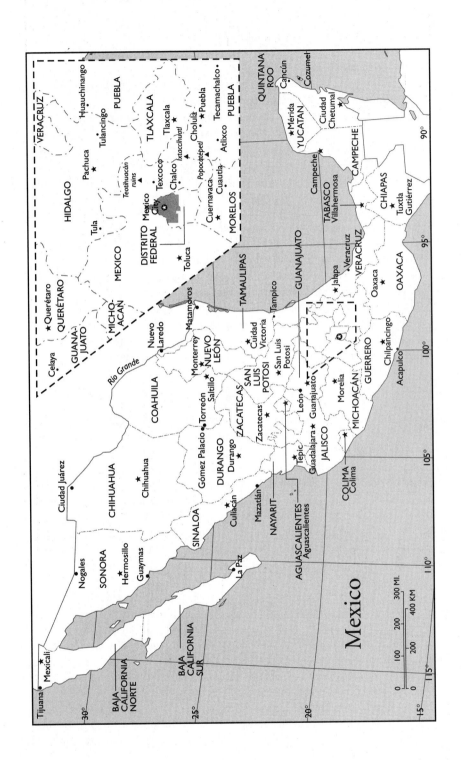

Mexico

renamed the Institutional Revolutionary Party (PRI) in 1946, has elected every president since that time, and all have served out their six-year terms. About 90 percent of the PRI candidates for state governorships and Congress have also been successful. This figure began to drop recently because of increased party competition and more honest elections. Still, Mexico has been exceptional in its political steadiness over several generations.

The Mexican economy received massive injections of capital and technology from abroad right after World War II, and it performed above average for the half-century since then. Some analysts even spoke of a "Mexican miracle." Mexico's economic integration with the United States and Canada in 1994, as part of the North American Free Trade Agreement (NAFTA), seemed to confirm its destiny to join the ranks of developed nations. In the last fifteen years, however, the economy has undergone major structural reforms that have shaken it to its roots and raised doubts about its long-term prospects.

Mexico's early revolution, political stability, and economic success do not mean, however, that it is somehow divorced from Latin America nor that it is immune to the problems faced by all countries pursuing development in the late twentieth century. Especially in the 1990s, the PRI has experienced serious defections and faced losing the presidency on the eve of the next century. Mexico was rocked in 1994 by a peasant rebellion in the southern state of Chiapas, one that brought back memories of the great revolution of 1910–1920. And Mexico is very much the heart of "northern Latin America," playing the role of big brother for Central America, trade partner in the Caribbean, and regional spokesperson in international organizations. In fact, nationalists emphasize that their independence from the United States and leadership in the Hispanic world form the core of Mexican identity.

Miguel Alemán, 1946–1952

The 1946 presidential succession raised a basic question about the future of Mexican government: Would the new president return to the revolutionary program of the 1917 Constitution and thereby complete Cárdenas's task? Or would he follow the moderate path taken by Avila Camacho, essentially cooling the revolution down to little more than rhetoric? The leading political figures of the day (known as the Revolutionary Family) decided that the latter would be the course. In May 1945 they secretly chose Miguel Alemán, minister of interior (*gobernación*), as the official nominee and almost certain victor in the election.

Alemán was a civilian, a bureaucrat, and a nonrevolutionary. He had been a mere eighteen years old when the fighting ended in 1920. The choice of Alemán proved decisive. From his election onward, all presidents have been civilian, all have come up through the ranks of the party, and all have shown little interest in revolutionary socialism. Miguel Alemán was the first of a long line of presidents whose style may be described as managerial.

Government and financial planners shifted their priorities after World War II. They deemphasized social goals (higher wages, education, welfare, health, nutrition,

Table 20-1 Mexican Presidents since 1934

Country	Name	Years in Power	Born	Class	Urban Rural	Race	Ed	Age @ 1st/off	Mil?	Party	Foreign Influence	Died
	Cárdenas	1934–40	1895	lower	R	mest	1st	33	y	PRN	n	1970
	Avila Camacho	1940–46	1896	lower	R	wh	2nd	37	y	PRN	n	1955
	Alemán	1946–52	1900	middle	R	wh	law	34	n	PRN	n	1983
	Ruiz Cortines	1952–58	1890	middle	U	wh	2nd	45	n	PRI	n	1973
	López Mateos	1958–64	1910	middle	U	wh	law	30	n	PRI	n	1969
	Díaz Ordaz	1964–70	1911	middle	R	wh	law	27	n	PRI	n	1979
	Echeverría	1970–76	1922	middle	U	wh	law	32	n	PRI	n	
	López Portillo	1976–82	1920	middle	U	wh	law	40	n	PRI	n	
	De la Madrid	1982–88	1934	middle	U	wh	econ	45	n	PRI	y	
	Salinas	1988–94	1948	middle	U	wh	econ	34	n	PRI	y	
	Zedillo	1994–	1951	middle	U	wh	econ	36	n	PRI	y	

etc.) and did everything they could to promote economic growth. Along with this shift came a concentration of ownership and wealth in the hands of a business elite (with its foreign partners) and of the state. Since 1945 the Mexican rich have gotten much richer, the government has penetrated every aspect of the economy, and the poor have benefited somewhat. Rural populations gained the protection of government crop supports, while urban residents enrolled in welfare and food subsidy programs. The choice of Miguel Alemán confirmed this shift in policy and marked the end of the revolution.

Alemán was born into a well-to-do family in Sayula, Veracruz, in 1902. In college he chose a career in law and showed much talent in his early days. During the 1930s he rose through the political ranks in his state to become governor in 1936. He remained steadfastly loyal to the official party, and in 1940 he became treasurer of Avila Camacho's campaign, a sensitive position. As a reward, he was appointed minister of interior, with powers roughly equivalent to those of the U.S. president's chief of staff and attorney general combined. A close personal friend of Avila Camacho, Alemán handled such delicate jobs as strike prevention, surveillance of Axis agents, and repression of the fascist *Sinarquista* movement. Essentially, Alemán managed the executive branch of government.

The 1945 party nomination came at Avila Camacho's request, made to the powerful inner circle of party bosses. Alemán's principal rival was General Miguel Guzmán, a radical in the tradition of the 1910s. Ex-president Cárdenas preferred Guzmán but bowed to Avila Camacho's wishes.

Futurismo

A persistent political phenomenon in Mexico is *futurismo*. It is open speculation about presidential timber in the public press and the premature booming of prospective candidates long before presidential elections are held. Every Mexican president dreads *futurismo*; after it is under way, even the routine acts of his officials and possible successors become clothed with future and undue political significance. The premature politicking hampers his personal manipulation of men and measures, which is the essence of Mexican politics. It is not surprising, therefore, that Mexican presidents try to defer *futurismo* as long as possible. But at some point each must take cognizance of it and indicate an heir apparent.

(Howard Cline, *The United States and Mexico*, rev. and enl. ed. [New York: Atheneum, 1969], p. 307)

Alemán's nomination also established a model for all successions. Invariably the top party leaders gathered fourteen months ahead of the election and secretly decided on the president-designate. Ex-presidents were called the "great electors" because of the influence they wielded. In most cases, they chose the minister of interior because he had been in charge of political coordination for the previous administration and knew the country inside and out. The man chosen was called the *tapado* (hidden one) because he was known to only a few powerful men.

Knowing the identity of the *tapado* was like money in the bank because it allowed access to the future president before other favor seekers. Persons in the know could negotiate deals, appointments, contracts, and the like without public scrutiny. Insiders typically got appointed to the official campaign staff. Once the nominee became widely known, he became the candidate and began to campaign.

The election campaign, obligatory since Cárdenas's 1934 candidacy, was an essential part of establishing the nominee's authority. It was an educational exercise to let the country know something about the man and his ideas. It also allowed the nominee to develop contacts throughout the country. Perhaps most important, the campaign exposed the nominee personally to millions of people and allowed them to form an image of him. This mass perception of his persona allowed him to assume full authority as a caudillo, albeit in constitutional clothing.

Miguel Alemán promised to continue Avila Camacho's programs, and he largely lived up to that promise. His was a businessman's administration that emphasized economic growth and stability. Indeed, government officials spoke of a planning strategy called the Stabilizing Development. This was nothing more than Avila Camacho's deemphasis of social goals in favor of private enterprise. Alemán's approach also contained the seeds of authoritarianism because the government became less responsive to popular protests that might endanger economic growth.

Stabilizing Development delivered what it promised: strong economic expansion. The Mexican gross national product (GNP) grew at an average annual rate of 6 percent from 1946 until the late 1970s, a truly remarkable record that doubled the size of the economy every dozen years. By the same token, the high population growth rate (3.5 percent per year) doubled the number of mouths to feed every twenty years. So real growth did occur.

Political leadership style changed markedly after 1940. Presidents became managers and party bosses, not revolutionaries. They avoided ideological discussions and pursued material growth at all costs. This strategy also required the government to participate in the economy as owner, manager, and regulator, producing what is commonly called "state capitalism" or a "directed economy." The state, through the development bank Nacional Financiera, became Mexico's leading investor.

In foreign policy, the presidents aligned Mexico with the United States because it was the best source of trade, tourism, technology, and investment capital. Even Daniel Cosío Villegas, the dean of Mexico's historians and a critic of the United States, admitted that because it was Mexico's destiny to be a U.S. neighbor, Mexico should make the most of any opportunities that geography presented.

One of Alemán's first acts upon taking office in 1946 was to call an official party convention. He devised a moderate program for adoption and changed the party's name to the Institutional Revolutionary Party, an obvious contradiction in terms. He completed the removal of the army from politics, begun by Cárdenas, when he dropped the military from formal party representation. The party's symbolic circle changed from four sections (workers, peasants, *populares*, and military) to three. This change reflected both the aging of the revolutionary generation and the rise of university-trained professionals to leadership roles.

From Alemán's administration onward, the revolution became a great myth to which government officials paid lip service but that had scant policy impact. In addition, the party became virtually identical with the government because all public jobs required party membership and contributions to its coffers. Public employees, in turn, used their positions to make money on the side through graft.

Miguel Alemán may also be credited with beginning the Green Revolution in Mexico. He almost completely eliminated land distribution and instead promoted commercial agriculture on a large scale. He began three major river valley projects that provided irrigation water for lowlands growers: the Rio Fuerte north of Mazatlán, the Tepalcatepec in Chiapas, and the Papaloapan in Veracruz and surrounding states. He also financed irrigation works on the Colorado River in Baja California that made the desert flower along the border. These huge projects not only encouraged commercial-scale agriculture but also provided cheap hydroelectric energy for industry. With these innovations came others that aided agriculture. Scientists introduced hybrid corn varieties adapted to the semiarid highlands, and in the course of the 1950s corn yields soared.

The most remarkable growth in agriculture came in the North, however. From Nuevo León to Baja California, agribusiness for export flourished. Many of the crops were the same as had been grown during the *Porfiriato*—cotton, cereals, sugar, and winter vegetables—but some new ones, like rice and sorghum, were introduced. Much of the prosperity of the North derived from this activity. In addition, commercial farms located near major cities profited by selling food to local markets.

Abundant farm production and the price support system encouraged rural families to have many children, thus Mexico's population grew faster than almost any other nation's in the hemisphere. This put severe strains on the education, health, and welfare agencies and required sustained economic expansion to absorb young people.

On the debit side of the Green Revolution ledger, the *ejidos* received scant support from the government and so tended to turn inward. *Ejidos* became almost anachronisms from a long-ago fight for land and equality.

Infrastructure projects helped private enterprise immeasurably during Alemán's term. His administration completed the Pan-American Highway, built an all-weather road across the isthmus of Tehuantepec, and quadrupled the number of miles of paved highway in the country. He also completed the reorganization of the National Railway Company. After negotiating a deal to restore Petróleos Mexicanos (Pemex) to private ownership, he met withering nationalistic opposition and desisted. Instead, he carried out a thorough restructuring of the oil company, managing to double its production and turn a profit besides. These and other projects made Mexican industry better able to keep up with foreign competitors.

Nacional Financiera attracted more and more foreign capital, which it channeled into industrialization. Foreign firms that produced automobiles, tires, electrical appliances, and other consumer durables moved into Mexico, usually finding ways to evade the 51 percent ownership law. Sears Roebuck de México was a major innovator, encouraging sales of Mexican-made goods in its stores. This import substitution industrialization (ISI) evoked a degree of national pride in the slogan,

Hecho en México, but it also created a trade dependence on the United States and Europe. This was because Mexican manufacturers had to import their machinery, capital, technical employees, and sometimes even raw materials from abroad. So ISI ironically increased rather than decreased dependence on foreign trade.

The growth model adopted by the Alemán administration did not provide for increased wages or benefits. Labor no longer had the ear of the president, and real wages declined throughout the years following World War II. Indeed, the government stated openly that it would continue to hold down wages in order to promote economic growth. When that growth was threatened by strikes, Alemán cracked down. In the case involving Pemex workers, for example, he actually sent in federal troops to break up their strike.

Finally, Alemán cultivated that old friend of the Mexican politician: graft. During his last year and a half as president, and continuing into the next administration, Alemán amassed a fortune, as did his close associates, known affectionately as "the gang." He also institutionalized electoral fraud, intervening in state elections so that the PRI would win close races. The blatant manner in which he did this alienated the middle class, which had otherwise benefited considerably during his term. Indeed, Alemán's years saw the middle class grow large and prosperous at the expense of the working class.

Corruption remained endemic in the Mexican political system, a fuel for elections and bait for winning converts. In fact, vast amounts of graft flowed up and down the governmental hierarchy, constituting a system of finance parallel to the public treasury. It began with the president, who received tens of millions of dollars for approving deals for his powerful associates. Ministers, heads of agencies, bureau chiefs, supervisors, and inspectors took in hundreds of thousands of pesos on the side and typically retired as wealthy men. Many lucrative jobs—for example, in the federal police, customs administration, bureau of taxation, and contracting authorities—were bought and sold for large sums of money. Virtually all public servants, all the way down to the street cleaners and traffic cops, took payoffs to supplement their wages.

Like everywhere else, payoffs greased the wheels of government, albeit often at the expense of real accomplishments, regulations, and the public interest. Yet, bribes and kickbacks sometimes went sour, leading to personal feuds, party divisions, assassinations, gang warfare, and regional disorder. Presidents paid lip service to eliminating graft, yet they proved to be the worst offenders. Graft could not be eliminated because every new administration was beholden to its predecessor and hence could not attack graft effectively.

Alemán's probusiness bias did not please all Mexican leaders in the late 1940s. Lombardo Toledano, for one, denounced the end of traditional worker and peasant policies after World War II. He and other leftists founded the Popular Socialist Party (PPS) in 1947 to revive the spirit of the revolution. By that time he had become one of the most influential leftists in the hemisphere and founder and president of the Latin American Workers' Confederation (CTAL).

Foreign policy under Alemán kept to the course charted by Avila Camacho. He maintained unusually close relations with the United States. Alemán and U.S. President Harry S Truman exchanged formal state visits in 1947. The two made agreements for foreign aid, loans, technical assistance, investment, and freer trade to flow across the borders, and in many ways the frontiers began to fade away as a barrier to the movement of goods, people, and capital.

Alemán also founded the National Autonomous University of Mexico (UNAM) to train future technocrats and professionals. By the 1970s UNAM had become the largest university in the hemisphere, with a quarter of a million students.

The army found itself increasingly marginalized from politics and national affairs in general. Its share of the federal budget had been cut to 8 percent by the end of Alemán's term and has averaged 7 percent ever since. The military establishment still has authority in its area and holds veto power over military alliances. For example, in 1947 the military accepted the U.S.-sponsored Rio Treaty for mutual defense, but the following year it vetoed a military role for the newly organized OAS and even prevented Mexico from signing a military assistance agreement with the United States in 1952.

For its size, Mexico is one of the least armed nations in the world. Since 1945 it has relied essentially on the United States for its global security. This made it unnecessary to have military officers become involved in high-level policy and tended to keep them out of politics. As for public office, military men occasionally serve as congressmen, but then they represent their constituencies, not the military as an institution.

So the Alemán presidency achieved solid economic accomplishments, virtually no social advances, and rather lackluster leadership qualities.

Adolfo Ruíz Cortines, 1952–1958

The next administration, that of Adolfo Ruíz Cortines, has been called "old wine in a new bottle." The new president continued the policies and administrative style of his predecessor. Ruíz Cortines was a sixty-two-year-old bureaucrat from Veracruz when elected. Born poor and orphaned at an early age, he had sought his fortune in politics. At the age of twenty-two he moved to Mexico City and did odd jobs for various revolutionary leaders. In these years he earned a reputation as a solid administrator. He became a close friend and associate of Miguel Alemán and served with him as treasurer in Avila Camacho's 1940 campaign. Later he was appointed minister of interior by Alemán, which almost assured him of the official nomination. Even Cárdenas backed Ruíz Cortines's nomination.

Ruíz Cortines managed to slow the growth of graft in government agencies, but only by allowing Alemán and his gang to steal shamelessly. One specialist suggested that "Morality in the public service probably reached a [low] level seldom achieved in Mexico" (Howard Cline, p. 161). According to José Silva Herzog, minister of finance in the 1980s, "Politics is the easiest and most profitable profession in Mexico."

Ruíz Cortines continued to stress that the main responsibility of government is to promote business growth. His slogan was "hard work, harmony, unity." Ruíz

Cortines was not a very inspiring leader, however, and his accomplishments were mediocre at best. In 1953 he devalued the peso to 12.5 per dollar, allegedly to reduce the real value of loans contracted with the U.S. government in the last days of the Alemán administration.

Under Ruíz Cortines the economy achieved the structure that it would retain for the next four decades. It contained nearly equal parts of private and public assets, with massive infusions of capital provided by investors in the United States and Europe. Between 1940 and 1958, foreign investment increased by seventy-two times. U.S. investment alone doubled from 1950 to 1958, and in the latter year made up some 65 percent of the foreign total. Most U.S. capital was invested in manufacturing.

Tourism became a major component of the economy, contributing on average 5 percent to GNP between the 1950s and the 1970s. The pattern of low wages and concentration of income continued virtually unchanged. Due to the high level of foreign involvement, Mexico's economy remained sensitive to fluctuations in the U.S. and world economies. For example, in the mid-1970s Jewish organizations in the United States and Europe boycotted travel to Mexico to protest its recognition of Colonel Muammar Qaddafi's Libyan government. As a result, Mexico lost tens of millions of dollars in revenues and experienced a sharp recession.

Ruíz Cortines did manage to increase the social security system somewhat, expanding its coverage in the isolated northern states and in rural areas. Still, the system mostly served employed persons in major cities. The government's welfare strategy was to allow the high rate of urbanization to bring clients to the social agencies, rather than to reach out to them in rural areas.

Ruíz Cortines pushed Congress to extend suffrage to women, which was done in 1954. Four years later women voted for the first time in federal elections.

The Alemán and Ruíz Cortines administrations confirmed the analyses of critics who claimed that the revolution was dead. These two presidents did, however, set important precedents for the future: the method of presidential selection, identification of progress with private enterprise, close association with the United States, and institutionalization of graft and fraud.

Adolfo López Mateos, 1958–1964

Adolfo López Mateos was born in 1911 in the central highlands state of Mexico. The son of a small-town dentist, he received a good education. While in college he became a student political leader and activist in the Socialist Labor Party. In the early 1930s he switched to the official party, drawn by Cárdenas's bold leftist policies. He eventually earned his law degree at UNAM, after which he became a professional administrator.

López Mateos served as minister of labor under Ruíz Cortines, and he earned a reputation as being sympathetic to labor yet also a strong party man. He proved especially good at averting strikes through official mediation. He won the presidential nomination in 1957 with the solid backing of Cárdenas, Alemán, and Ruíz Cortines. U.S. political scientist Philip B. Taylor described him as ". . . reasonably honest and efficient, personally attractive, intellectually superior to most . . . and ideologically moderate . . . clearly devoted to Cárdenas, and the regard is reciprocated."

López Mateos gave more attention than his predecessors to foreign affairs, in which he guided Mexico into the group of nonaligned developing nations. Not unfriendly toward the United States, López Mateos nonetheless felt obliged to keep his distance from the colossus. His major decision was to befriend Cuba after the 1961 Bay of Pigs invasion. López Mateos maintained good relations and trade with Cuba when the rest of the nations in the hemisphere broke relations with Fidel Castro. (See Chapter Twenty-Three.) The philosophical source of his position was the belief that other countries, in order to achieve national respect and sovereignty, may need to undergo a nationalist revolution like Mexico did in the 1910s. For example, in the 1980s Mexico upheld the rights of Central Americans to determine their own forms of government, even if communistic, and refused to endorse the U.S. Contra war there. The official Mexican position held that "Mexico neither imports nor exports revolutions" but respects its neighbors' right to self-determination.

López Mateos claimed credit for settling the Chamizal dispute with the United States. This dispute dated back to 1864, when the Rio Grande shifted its course and gave El Paso, Texas, six hundred acres of land formerly in Ciudad Juárez, Chihuahua. Negotiations begun by U.S. Presidents Kennedy and Johnson restored the land to Mexico. López Mateos also reached an agreement that obliged Arizona agribusiness to stop dumping highly contaminated water into the Colorado River before it entered Mexico.

In an attempt to redress rural problems that had become glaring during the 1950s, López Mateos instructed government agents to award thirty million acres to small farmers. By the end of his term they had transferred less than a third of that, mostly as colonization grants in the South.

López Mateos also paid more attention to social welfare than did his predecessors. Although he was not a practicing Catholic, he sympathized with the new policies contained in the Vatican II message and encouraged Mexicans to support social programs undertaken by their Church. He expanded the social security system markedly and pushed a public health program that included pest control. He also created a special social security institute for government employees, called ISSTE. It soon became the best in the nation, providing excellent benefits, including old age pensions, disability, health care, maternity, life insurance, funeral, layoff indemnization, vacation spas, housing, low-interest loans, sports complexes, day-care centers, scholarships, and discount stores.

López Mateos reformed the party system because the leading opposition parties, PAN and PPS, were becoming frustrated with electoral defeats every two years. PAN, dating back to 1939, represented urban, middle-class, largely Catholic voters. It consistently polled about 10 percent of the votes, with stronger followings in its core states of Guadalajara and Michoacán and among women voters. Lombardo Toledano's PPS suffered from endemic fighting among its leftist constituents and rarely elected more than a few candidates.

To put a better face on what was obviously one-party autocracy, López Mateos asked Congress to create a minority representation system to help small parties.

The system provided five congressional seats for every 2.5 percent of the national vote received and additional seats for every 0.5 percent above that. PAN and the PPS thus won several dozen seats between them and began to act more like a loyal opposition.

López Mateos pushed education with new, prefabricated schools that could be built with self-help techniques. He also funded teachers' quarters to make rural schools more attractive to urbanites. Nevertheless, new textbooks distributed during his term seemed leftist and aroused opposition in some local communities.

López Mateos tried to keep labor unions reined in, and in 1959 he decided to use federal troops to break up a national railroad strike. Soon afterward, to compensate for this harsh treatment, he devised a profit-sharing arrangement, mandated by the 1917 Constitution but never instituted. This benefit, eventually paid by all large enterprises, was the first such program in the Americas.

Mexico moved further toward state capitalism under López Mateos. Previously the government had merely directed the economy with various kinds of levers and with targeted investments made by Nacional Financiera. López Mateos decided to make the state an active participant in economic decisions. He used government funds to buy majority ownership in a number of industries, even foreign ones, and then used public proxy votes to assure that socially desirable goals were pursued in addition to profits. For example, he took over the motion picture distribution system, owned by an American expatriate, and used it for public education and entertainment. He also nationalized the foreign-owned electrical power industry so that rates could be subsidized.

López Mateos's final accomplishment was to distance ex-presidents from major policy decisions. Although Cárdenas had broken Calles's stranglehold on the presidency, many ex-presidents continued to throw their weight around and to criticize the incumbent in public. Alemán and Cárdenas, in particular, pressured López Mateos to support their ideological positions or pet projects. The president called in all of his predecessors and gave each of them specific responsibilities. As informal or kitchen cabinet advisors, they would have to limit advice giving to their own areas. This system had the desired effect of limiting high-level influence peddling.

Díaz Ordaz, 1964–1970

The next president, Gustavo Díaz Ordaz, was very much out of step with the leftist tendencies of his predecessor. He came from the conservative and heavily Catholic state of Puebla. While serving as minister of government under López Mateos, Díaz Ordaz had proven to be very much of an autocrat. As a signal that his administration would not tolerate liberal ideas, he fired the president of the PRI for advocating modernization of the party—including the institution of primary elections—to make it responsive to popular sentiment. Díaz Ordaz strengthened PRI's hegemony.

Student protests and strikes erupted all over the world during the late 1960s, including in Mexico. Under Díaz Ordaz, the government applied especially heavy repression to control them.

UNAM's library, decorated with Amerindian designs in mosaic tile, towers over the sprawling campus on the southern edge of Mexico City.

The most famous protest flared up in Mexico City in 1968, the so-called Tlaltelolco Massacre. The government had won the bidding to host the summer Olympic games—the first time that they were held in a developing country. Hoping to use the games to win greater prestige for Mexico, Díaz Ordaz spent $200 million in preparations. UNAM students decided to use the games as a forum to embarrass the government, arguing that the money should have been spent to alleviate poverty. Riot police, called the *granaderos,* skirmished frequently with student protesters who threatened to disrupt the games. Students issued an ultimatum, which the government rejected. Minister of Interior Luis Echeverría decided to crack down on the protesters to assure Olympic officials that Mexico City security would be tight. The army even occupied UNAM, breaking the school's long-standing autonomy.

On the eve of the Olympic games, some five thousand students and others gathered to demonstrate in the Plaza de las Tres Culturas, also known as Tlaltelolco Plaza. Sniper fire from unknown sources broke out, and police opened fire on the crowds. Official figures show that three hundred to four hundred persons were killed in the melee that ensued, but some observers claimed that thousands were killed. Army units, meanwhile, raked the Colegio de México, a prestigious and independent graduate school in downtown Mexico City. Although no one was hurt there, the attack appeared to be a warning to Colegio professors not to criticize the government.

Mexican soldiers rounded up and arrested thousands of protesters in the infamous Tlaltelolco Massacre of 1968.

The games went on largely as planned, but the massacre sent a chill throughout the population, and the government never recovered the prestige that it lost in Tlaltelolco. The intellectual and artistic communities, in particular, rarely lent their support to the state.

Díaz Ordaz's term ended in 1970, and with it ended the stable period of economic expansion that previous administrations had presided over. He had managed to maintain high growth rates only at the expense of overvaluing the peso, increasing foreign debt, and giving protection and costly subsidies to inefficient industries. As one critic noted, the state and the industrialists had joined together in an "alliance for profits," a pun on the name of the U.S. aid program Alliance for Progress. The economic model kept alive by Díaz Ordaz could not continue indefinitely, and external shocks would end it sooner than expected.

Luis Echeverría, 1970–1976

As minister of government in 1968, Luis Echeverría had authorized the attack on the Tlaltelolco protesters. When he was nominated to be the next president, then, he had a major public relations deficit to overcome. Perhaps because of this, Echeverría went out of his way to pose as a leftist and a reformer. In the words of one analyst, he tried to become a populist and outreform Lázaro Cárdenas (1934–1940), whose administration was still considered the high point of revolutionary change. He shifted uneasily from centrist to leftist positions during the campaign, hoping to re-build the labor-campesino-party coalition of the 1930s. Like Cárdenas, he cam-paigned at the grass roots, meeting thousands of constituents face-to-face in an at-tempt to fabricate charisma. Most observers believe that he failed.

The year after he took office, to atone for the Tlaltelolco Massacre Echeverría released the students imprisoned in 1968. He also lowered the voting age to eighteen to win support from young people. He used media and public relations consultants more than had any of his predecessors, projecting an image of himself as the restorer of the revolution. Echeverría's attempts to gain public support only slowed the grad-ual erosion of regime acceptance by the masses. He may also have won some respite from the criticism of intellectuals and newspapers. In the long run, however, the government paid a price for the years of autocracy and abuse of power. Public ap-proval in polls among voters plummeted. The loyal opposition party, PAN, began to win more elections.

Echeverría shifted the focus of economic policy toward the countryside. He funded rural highway and electrification programs and spoke of reviving the *ejidos* with massive new transfers of land. He completed the improvement and consolida-tion of the national railroad system, which opened to great fanfare. While supervising these projects, Echeverría traveled more than any other president since Cárdenas.

In addition to winning political support from campesinos, he hoped that his rural development program would prevent the spread of guerrilla warfare and ter-rorism, then on the rise throughout Latin America. Despite his efforts, however, several organizations became very powerful in the south of Mexico, and urban kid-nappings occurred with frequency.

In order to improve his image as a populist reformer among middle-class vot-ers, Echeverría closed some tax loopholes that benefited the rich while imposing price controls to help the rest of the population deal with inflation. He nationalized the tobacco industry and telegraph systems in order to supply these products to the masses at reduced prices. In 1972 he lifted Mexico's long-standing ban on birth con-trol programs and launched a family planning campaign to bring down the birth rate. He did so with the acquiescence of the Catholic Bishops' Council. This policy was popular with the middle class and won acclaim abroad, especially when the population growth rate fell from 3.4 percent in the 1960s to 3.2 percent in the 1970s. Mexico's program became a model for other developing nations.

The Burgeoning Population of Mexico City

In the last thirty years, Mexico City has grown into the largest city in the world, with over twenty million people living in the greater metropolitan area. The sheer size of the city challenges its leaders every day. Even minor problems—like traffic jams, power failures, and subway accidents—turn the city into a jungle.

Worse problems arise from long-term neglect. About a quarter of the popula-tion lives in shantytowns that are located in a dry lake bed north of the city and that have only electricity and water. Nearby factories recruit there for cheap labor but do not provide basic residential services. In addition, the bowl-shaped Valley of

Mexico, where the city is located, traps pollution and turns the air toxic during at least half of the year.

The terrible earthquake of 1985 leveled huge sections of the city and left thousands dead and millions homeless. Every fifty years or so, the great fault lines under Mexico City turn it into a killing field. In addition, depletion of underground water reserves has caused sections of the city to sink steadily into the ground—a total of twenty-two feet in the past sixty years! The very survival of the city depends upon finding a different source of water.

On the other hand, Mexico City is the promised land for most Mexicans, the cultural and financial center of their world. Great universities, publishing houses, museums, theaters, and research institutes sustain one of Latin America's most vibrant cultural atmospheres.

The economy began to falter during Echeverría's term because of a number of factors. His piecemeal, politically motivated actions exacerbated the socioeconomic imbalances inherited from Díaz Ordaz. Meanwhile, the oil crisis of 1973 had an equivocal impact on Mexico. Even though Mexico did not join OPEC, as an exporter nation it received greater revenues from rising prices. Yet, the general inflation and higher interest rates that accompanied the oil shock hurt Mexico, too. The general euphoria of increased oil revenues led the government to increase expenditures on a variety of social programs while selling petroleum-derived products at below cost in domestic markets. Poor planning, however, led to imbalances and inflation. During his last year in office Echeverría was forced to devalue the currency, the first change in the dollar-peso exchange rate since 1953. Devaluation immediately doubled prices for imported goods and generally raised all costs to consumers.

Devaluation was a major psychological defeat for the president. A lawyer by training, Echeverría did not have a firm grasp of financial matters. His spending programs, subsidies, and trade policies all cost much more than Mexico could afford. Even he finally acknowledged the end of the Mexican "economic miracle" when he replaced the long-term strategy followed since World War II. Instead of Stabilizing Development, he unveiled Shared Development, implying a redistribution of income in favor of the masses of poor Mexicans. His policies lacked coherence, however, and responded to political stimuli more than to economic logic.

In keeping with his impulsive, iconoclastic ways, Echeverría managed the presidential succession of the mid-1970s in such a way as to ensure the continuation of his policies. Perhaps recognizing the need for a firmer hand on the economic tiller, he imposed the candidacy of José López Portillo. A lifelong friend and associate, López Portillo was middle-aged and trained as an economist. He did not have a major reputation or strong following, so observers believed that Echeverría might try to influence him from behind the scenes. In the end, that did not happen, and López Portillo won his spurs and became president in his own right.

Death of the Revolution

As early as 1947 Mexican historian Daniel Cosío Villegas pronounced the revolution dead. His postmortem analysis was both nostalgic and pessimistic. He sympathized with the quest by the great reformers, the 1917 Constitution, and Lázaro Cárdenas to remake Mexican society along socialist, communitarian lines. He saw, however, that those goals had been abandoned by the post-Cárdenas presidents. Many of the social conquests of the 1930s were now lost. Since Cosío Villegas's statement, most writers have agreed that the revolution is dead.

Still, many policies, agencies, and programs enacted in the first years of the revolution—inspired by the blueprint of the 1917 Constitution—continued in effect through the Echeverría administration. Analysts believed that land reform, *ejidos*, nationalized subsoil rights, labor protection, free public education, elimination of public religious ceremonies, and a strong sense of national sovereignty were permanent achievements of the revolution. Any president, however negligent, corrupt, or venal, who threatened these icons of the past could expect immediate reprisals by the party, workers, peasants, and intellectuals.

Since 1976, however, Mexico has been governed by economist-presidents, men trained in orthodox and even neoliberal theory. They put private capitalists' interests ahead of the public welfare on the assumption that what is good for business is good for Mexico in general. Their positions have gradually become mainstream in the world of public finance, especially since the abandonment of socialist economics in communist countries after 1989. The last four presidents of Mexico have fit this pattern closely. Their policies have virtually dismantled the revolution.

The appearance of this remarkable generation of leaders was certainly not what Echeverría had in mind when he chose López Portillo in 1975. The candidate had served as secretary of the treasury and was expected merely to solve some of the economic problems then facing the country. He would then take charge of the Shared Development that Echeverría had initiated.

In fact, López Portillo and his successors abandoned the redistributive and populist approaches of Echeverría and instituted ones diametrically opposed to them. They rolled back the revolution by dismantling programs and institutions, privatizing public enterprises, ending subsidies, lowering tariffs, and shifting income even more toward capitalists and investors. If Alemán's generation had allowed the revolution to die, López Portillo's disposed of the body. Nothing in the 1917 Constitution was sacred anymore.

The economist-presidents did not need the army to enforce this radical shift in policy, as long as they had the full support of the bureaucracy and the acquiescence of the populace. The army served as a silent partner of the civilian elite and stepped in only when public order was disturbed by insurrection or terrorism. Despite severe suffering on the part of the masses since the late 1970s because of declining standards of living, uprisings have been few and manageable. The Mexican Army's total loyalty to the government has been unique in Latin America.

Despite the end of the revolution, civilian groups and political opponents have demanded and achieved more democratic procedures than ever before in Mexico.

Mexico's recent political history has included a gradual weakening of the PRI's power, brought on by greater honesty in elections and by declining public acceptance of one-party rule. Impetus for democratization came from both inside and outside Mexico. The historic unity of the party and its coalescence behind an official candidate finally broke down in the 1980s. Gradual liberalization of party rules gave birth to a number of leftist parties, and the PAN increased its popularity in the northern tier of states. Then the PRI itself split, with a reformist wing called the Democratic Current demanding internal changes in candidate selection. In 1988 these reformist groups ran a candidate against the PRI, Cuauhtémoc Cárdenas, son of the president during the 1930s.

In addition, world attention had begun to focus on Mexican elections, and for the first time its democracy seemed important for continued success in the economic realm. Neoliberal policies required cooperation by the industrial countries and by international financial institutions. News media, preference polls, and election monitoring by the opposition made it difficult to steal elections without adverse consequences. Although PRI carried the 1988 race by an unprecedently thin margin, electing a young economist named Raúl Salinas de Gortari, it lost the international opinion race by indulging in fraudulent practices.

Cuauhtémoc Cárdenas, son of President Lázaro Cárdenas, lost the presidential election of 1988 but won the mayor's race in Mexico City nine years later.

A foreign observer chats with Zapatista rebel soldiers in Chiapas, Mexico.

NAFTA, the economic integration treaty with the United States and Canada, constituted the centerpiece of Salinas's administration. Already his predecessor had begun reducing tariffs and eliminating import quotas when he led Mexico into the General Agreement on Trade and Tariffs (GATT). NAFTA went much further by stipulating a ten-year period for complete elimination of tariffs among the three countries of North America.

On January 1, 1994, the world awoke to news of a well-organized peasant rebellion in the southern state of Chiapas. It was led by the Zapatista Army for National Liberation (EZLN), named for Emiliano Zapata's famous guerrilla band of the 1910s. (See Chapter Fifteen.) The region had always suffered more poverty, government inattention, and landowner abuse than the rest of the country. The vast majority of the people in Chiapas were descended from Amerindians, and many still spoke native languages and lived in communal villages. Over the centuries, their lands and rights had been despoiled by outsiders, causing a legacy of bitterness and anger. The Zapatista movement sought to redress these ills once and for all by an armed uprising and a negotiated peace.

The EZLN revolt was timed to begin with the activation of NAFTA, which EZLN leaders believed would further erode their standard of living. The revolutionaries captured several towns and demanded that the government meet certain conditions before they would be liberated. The government overreacted by sending a huge contingent of soldiers into the region to suppress the revolt. President Salinas feared that a weak answer to the EZLN would frighten foreign investors; he did not realize that an overzealous answer would alienate the international community. The government's campaign against the Zapatistas dragged on for several months, exposing Salinas to accusations of both incompetence and brutality. Finally, he agreed to negotiate with the rebels, using Catholic leaders in the region to mediate. The talks dragged on for several years without reaching a satisfactory conclusion. Meanwhile, Salinas had to oversee the election of his successor.

In 1994 the government conducted the fairest election ever held in Mexico. The very fact that irregularities were found attested to the effectiveness of election vigilance. President Salinas had chosen Luis Donaldo Colosio, a reform-minded politician, to run for the presidency. In mid-campaign, however, Colosio was assassinated while campaigning in the North. Faced with the dissolution of the succession process, the president quickly chose another economist, also U.S.-trained, to run in place of Colosio. Ernesto Zedillo, at forty-three, was one of the youngest men ever to run at the head of the PRI ticket. With little popular support, he campaigned on the merits of the country's stability. He implied that a vote for any other candidate would plunge the country into further fighting and lead to economic chaos. Little did he know that at least one of these outcomes was virtually a certainty anyway.

Economic Upheavals

The Mexican economy has not prospered under the guidance of the economist-presidents. It is uncertain how much they are to blame for the country's troubles because these were also unsettled times for the world economy. Most presidents since 1976 maintained satisfactory levels of economic growth, employment, and consumption, yet they postponed necessary but unpopular adjustments until the ends of their terms, only to leave major crises for their successors. For example, Echeverría devalued the peso at the end of his term, while at the close of his term López Portillo defaulted on the foreign debt, imposed exchange controls, and nationalized the banks.

One of the most promising economic developments, the discovery of vast new oil reserves, yielded meager results for Mexico. Ever since the early twentieth century the country's abundant petroleum reserves had been known and partially tapped. After Cárdenas nationalized the industry, however, by incorporating production, refining, and distribution into Pemex, the major foreign oil companies pulled out, leaving Mexico unable to sell much oil abroad. Most Mexicans approved of the nationalization and believed that this resource should be preserved for development purposes and for future generations.

Between 1976 and 1980, however, exploration confirmed the existence of immense new reserves of petroleum, equivalent to about 5 percent of known oil reserves and 3 percent of natural gas reserves. These discoveries offered the opportunity to raise investment capital through foreign sales without sacrificing domestic consumption. The timing seemed propitious, too, because the OPEC production quotas between 1974 and 1979 boosted prices to exorbitant levels. López Portillo believed that Mexico could now have its cake and eat it, too. All this was possible without even joining OPEC, which would have violated Mexico's traditional sovereignty.

Culture in Mexico

Despite heavy influences—some call it "cultural imperialism"—from the United States and Europe, Mexicans enjoy a robust and rich cultural life.

Mexico's music blends haunting Amerindian melodies with African rhythms and European harmonies to achieve the distinctive *ranchera* sound. The *mariachi* or troubadour tradition, featuring waltzes and plaintive guitars, lives on in major cities. Along the border, the *ranchera* has teamed with country music to produce the Tex-Mex styles popularized by Selena and others. Persons familiar with musical traditions acknowledge Mexico's original contributions to the form.

Mexican art closely resembled Europe's until the early twentieth century. Then it boldly struck out on its own in the 1920s and 1930s. Modern art influences from Europe combined with nativist themes and public venues to produce spectacular arrays of mural paintings. Muralists received commissions to depict the country's great traditions, in light of the new revolutionary mythology. They chose government buildings and other public places, in Mexico City, Guanajuato, and Guadalajara in particular, in order to instruct the masses. The most stunning, perhaps, are Diego Rivera's murals in the presidential palace, showing all panoramic scenes from pre-Columbian times to the mid-twentieth century. In Guadalajara, Ministry of Interior murals by José Clemente Orozco re-created scenes of the Conquest and Father Hidalgo's rebellion. Whereas some artists imported Cubism and Impressionism, others resurrected the styles used by Aztec chroniclers and in Mayan glyphs.

During the revolution itself, novels portraying the bravery, cruelty, and great moral issues of the struggle emerged as a major literary genre. Authors like Mariano Azuela, Gregorio López y Fuentes, and Martín Luis Guzmán captured the drama of the era yet also revealed its contradictions and ironies. Their writings constituted a revolutionary school in the 1920s and 1930s. Later, more sophisticated voices, such as Octavio Paz and Carlos Fuentes, arose to reinterpret the national past and the character of the Mexican. The debate continued, in search of an elusive *Mexicanismo*.

During the 1930s Mexico also nurtured a film industry, using government subsidies and regulations limiting imported movies. By mid-century, Mexican studios churned out hundreds of films a year, featuring such stars as Cantinflas, Pedro Armendáriz, Dolores del Rio, Pedro Infante, and Jorge Negrete. The western movie, as in the United States, proved especially popular and durable. The industry still produces a respectable number of feature films each year, but they have not recaptured the popularity that they enjoyed in the 1950s and 1960s. One Mexican actor, Anthony Quinn, played in the original *Viva Zapata!* and managed to make a successful film career in the United States.

Last but certainly not least, Mexico proudly serves up a cuisine as distinctive and delicious as any in the world. Based upon native ingredients like maize, chili, avocados, tomatoes, and cacao, these dishes have become popular throughout the United States and Europe. It would be hard to imagine Mexico without its succulent and spicy dishes.

Born in 1911, Mario Moreno Reyes (better known by his film name, Cantinflas) entertained and charmed world audiences, as a bullfighter, comedian, and movie star.

The government began huge investment programs financed in part with new revenues from oil exports. Money was invested in manufacturing, improved farming, transportation, and infrastructure. López Portillo called this "sowing the petroleum," just as Venezuelan President Rómulo Betancourt had done. And for a time the strategy worked because the economy grew at tremendous rates between 1978 and 1981, buoyed by petroleum investments.

López Portillo did not regulate demand in the economy carefully enough, and inflation inevitably surged with the swelling GNP. By 1982 prices nearly doubled. Government spending also outstripped revenues, leading it to heavy borrowing abroad. In addition, the demand for imports soared, and he met balance-of-payments shortfalls with borrowed money. After all, petrodollars were being offered by international banks virtually interest-free, so it seemed too good to be true.

In 1981 oil prices began to fall, however, and Mexican export revenues dropped. Interest rates for borrowing suddenly shot up. Short-term investment capital began to flee the country. And as devaluation became inevitable, the bubble of prosperity burst. By early 1982 López Portillo had to suspend his government's policy of a fixed exchange rate for the peso, and the peso lost almost half its value on world markets. When the value continued to drop, López Portillo realized that he might not be able to service the foreign debt. In an extraordinary move, he announced that Mexico would suspend payment on the debt and take measures to prevent further capital flight. He decreed the nationalization of the banking industry, banned dollar-denominated accounts, and established a multiple exchange rate by which all transactions would have to be made. It was a financial debacle from which the country would require years to recover.

Miguel de la Madrid, López Portillo's successor, did not leave any unpleasant surprises for his successor, yet he carried out the boldest about-face in economic policy since the 1930s. In 1985, faced with unprecedented demands caused by the terrible Mexico City earthquake that year and further declines in petroleum prices, de la Madrid declared an end to the state-capitalism approach that had guided all of his predecessors. Henceforth, Mexico would follow neoliberal policies: balanced budgets, privatization of public enterprise, freer trade with the outside world, and elimination of most subsidies for consumers. Even the time-honored *ejidos* came in for alterations: Communal lands were allowed to be sold to private owners. The coming of neoliberalism overturned most of the revolutionary initiatives of previous decades.

De la Madrid's successor, Salinas de Gortari, maintained his orthodox policies. Salinas held the peso at an artificially high rate throughout his term, using short-term speculative capital from abroad to cover cash shortages. When the next president, Ernesto Zedillo, came into office in December 1994, he was immediately forced to devalue the peso in the hopes of moving toward freer market exchange of the currency. This move, long overdue, touched off one of the worst financial crises in the last half-century. Exchange speculators drove the peso down to less than a third of its former value, while the government spent all of its reserves trying to prevent the peso's fall. Meanwhile, the short-term funds that had kept the economy solvent evaporated overnight. The net effect was the massive impoverishment of Mexico.

By early 1995 most Mexicans found their real incomes reduced by up to half and bank credit unattainable. Bankruptcies multiplied, tens of thousands of workers were laid off, and major construction or expansion projects were canceled.

One consequence of Zedillo's approach was an economic shock program unveiled just as the administration completed its first one hundred days in office. This program contained all the familiar measures favored by the International Monetary Fund (IMF) during the previous two presidential terms: curtailment of government expenditures (9.8 percent less than 1994 levels), 20 to 35 percent higher utilities fees, and a 50 percent increase in the value added tax. These measures were designed to avoid inflationary currency emissions, public indebtedness, and higher interest rates (which in mid-1995 ran about 100 percent per year). To help Zedillo, U.S. President Bill Clinton put up a Treasury loan guarantee that, matched with IMF and World Bank credits, totaled $50 billion. This helped to cover Mexico's immediate debt obligations and restored confidence in the peso. By the time the two presidents met personally, in October 1995, Mexico's economy had stabilized and had begun a slow recovery from the crash. Both men hoped that sustained employment and development would vindicate the decision to form NAFTA.

The two presidents met again, this time in Mexico City, in May 1997, the first time in almost twenty years that a U.S. president had traveled to Mexico. Zedillo and Clinton could now point to solid economic gains in the previous eighteen months. For one thing, Mexico had paid off the 1995 loan ahead of schedule. The GNP was now growing at nearly 5 percent, and inflation (previously in triple digits) ran about 18 percent. Unemployment stood at low levels, reflecting the increased production capacity created by heavy foreign investment. For the time being, Mexico benefited greatly from its partnership with the booming U.S. economy.

The recovery did not, however, raise the standard of living of all Mexican workers. Per capita income was less than $4,000, having shrunk because of several years of austerity and recession. Disparities between rich and poor Mexicans, and between Mexican and U.S. workers, continued to grow. In that respect, the promises of the economist-presidents still had not been kept.

On the political scene, Zedillo reached an accommodation with the Zapatista guerrillas and gradually improved the electoral system, at the expense of the PRI. As a result, in July 1997 opposition leader Cuauhtémoc Cárdenas won the mayoralty of Mexico City, the second-most powerful job in the nation. His Democratic Revolutionary Party (PRD), meanwhile, attracted many progressive voters and politicians from the PRI. In addition, rival parties won more seats than PRI in the lower house of Congress. But at least PRI would hold on to the presidency until the elections scheduled for the year 2000.

Conclusions and Issues

As Mexico approached the twenty-first century, uncertainty abounded. Its future hinged on whether the great gambles of neo-liberal economics, reluctant democratization, and integration with Canada, the United States, and eventually the South American nations would pay off. The long-suffering farmers and workers had shown tremendous patience throughout the economic crises of the previous two decades. Many observers believed that the majority would finally give up on the PRI and decide to join the left (led by Cuauhtémoc Cárdenas) or the right, represented by PAN. National and local elections indeed showed growing victories for the opposition. Whether the left or the right would capture disaffected PRI voters remained the biggest question in Mexico's political future.

Discussion Questions

1. How can a revolution be institutionalized, as the name Institutional Revolutionary Party implies? When did the revolution die? Does rampant corruption explain how politicians can live with the contradictions between their words and their deeds?

2. The love-hate relationship between Mexico and the United States, begun in the 1840s, continues to the present. Which aspects of the relationship cause bad feelings? Which aspects resemble a partnership?

3. Why did Mexico's presidents increasingly come from the ranks of persons trained in economics after the 1970s, after a half-century of law-educated presidents?

Colombian Conundrum

The Assassination of Gaitán in 1948

Jorge Gaitán, accompanied by four friends, stepped through the door from his office into the street. They jostled one another getting onto the sidewalk. Then they headed right, toward a nearby restaurant. It was nearing one o'clock in the afternoon.

"*Oye, Jorge,*" said one companion, looking up at the taller Gaitán. "Now that you saved the colonel from going to the stockade, you can start running for president again. You know you're the only one who can beat the Conservatives! We named you as our candidate, and we'll do anything to make you win."

"I know, I know," answered Gaitán, "I appreciate your support. But I don't want to begin too soon. The election isn't going to be for two more years," he added, "and when the campaign starts, my life will be hell. Besides, I can't make any money with my private practice after I start running. Let's take it easy for a while. We'll take over when our time comes."

"Maybe," said his friend, "but the labor guys and the communists are real upset, Jorge. They backed you in '46 and took a lot of heat from the rich Liberals, and now the Conservatives are crawling all over them. They think you're an ingrate, Jorge. You need to get out from defending social-ism and the workers' republic."

Gaitán nodded as they strode down the street. It's hard being all things to all people, he thought.

"Plus," his friend continued, "the government used the Red Scare to bring our ambassador back from Moscow and is trying to kick the com-munists out of Congress. It may get violent if they do it!"

"Well, tell them to be patient," Gaitán responded. "We'll take care of them when we win. Anyone who loses his job can come to our headquar-ters, and we'll hire him. But tell the union bosses that we can't stand any general strikes or disruptions. That would just play into the hands of the

Conservatives. We want to show the people that the Liberal Party under Gaitán is the party of work, order, and prosperity. Strikes just don't help us right now."

"Say, Jorge, did the Foreign Office ask you to attend the Pan-American Union meeting? You know, where they're drawing up a new charter? That would be good publicity for you," said his friend.

"Hell, no, they don't want me anywhere near the meetings! They said it would be interference in national politics for me to attend. That's all right. I'm meeting with some student leaders who came to town to watch the show. They came from Argentina, Cuba, and Mexico. Maybe they can help us later on."

"I know you're anxious to get started with the campaign, and we will, in about six months. Trust me, our time will come!"

Gaitán threw his arm around his friend to reassure him. They pushed through a little crowd on the sidewalk. Gaitán smiled at passersby and wished them well. He was a celebrity, and he acted like one.

As they moved on, a shabbily dressed stranger stepped in front of Gaitán and pointed a pistol at him. Not saying a word, Gaitán turned aside as if to walk away. The man fired several shots, and Gaitán slumped against the wall of a building.

A companion ran to find a car to take Gaitán to a clinic, while two others grabbed the assailant and wrestled him to the ground. Onlookers screamed and cried openly, recognizing their hero on the brink of death.

An ambulance rushed Gaitán to a nearby hospital, where doctors fought to save him. He didn't survive long, however, and word of his assassination spread quickly.

With him died perhaps Colombia's greatest hope for achieving political peace and for mending the tears in the social fabric of the country. The anguish, rage, despair, and hopelessness that many felt in the wake of his assassination erupted among the people. The city turned into a battlefield, as rioters who blamed the Conservatives for Gaitán's death swept through the streets for days. Enraged Liberals broke into police stations to steal guns and ammunition. The *Bogotazo,* as it was called, shattered Colombia's image as a progressive, democratic nation. Bogotá, long called the "Athens of South America," had turned into a killing field.

Meanwhile, one of the foreign observers in Bogotá, Cuban student leader Fidel Castro, held talks with his counterparts from other countries. They believed that the Cold War did not concern them and might be used as a tool to support dictatorship in the Americas. They saw the *Bogotazo* as another indictment of capitalism, a sign that the working classes could stand no more. Social reform had to be enacted or else the whole continent could explode in revolution. Some, in fact, intended to make it happen.

La Violencia

The assassination of Jorge Gaitán on April 9, 1948, echoed like a curse through the corridors of modern Colombian history. The masses believed that some hidden conspirators, most likely the Conservatives, had taken away their leader. The Liberal Party bosses, not wholly supportive of Gaitán while he lived, found themselves without a credible candidate and unable to build a consensus. For years afterward, politicians would be measured against Gaitán, to gauge their ability to generate enthusiasm, to attract lower-middle-class voters, and to rise above the level of patronage deals and partisan bickering. Few compared favorably to the slain leader.

The country's elite, both Liberal and Conservative, may have felt relief that a champion of the people was eliminated from the scene, but they and all Colombians soon paid a high price for his death. The partisan violence that had begun to seep out onto the streets of villages, small towns, and cities now flooded the nation. It engulfed the country in the 1950s, smothering its tranquillity and claiming over a quarter of a million lives. No one escaped *La Violencia*.

The Conservative-led government clamped down in an attempt to control the rioting and killing. Censorship, summary arrests, and a permanent state of siege went into effect. After Gaitán's death, Liberals agreed to accept appointments by President Ospina Pérez, hoping that a show of cooperation with the Conservatives might lessen the partisan fighting in the countryside. This sharing harked back to

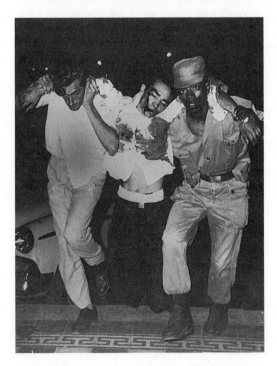

A soldier and a civilian assist a victim of La Violencia. *From the late 1940s until the 1960s, endemic violence gripped Colombia and left hundreds of thousands dead. Even in the 1990s, Colombia suffered the highest levels of crime and homicide in the hemisphere, a legacy of earlier violence.*

the administration of Carlos E. Restrepo (1910–1914), when the reformist Republican Union got minority party representation and other power-sharing measures included in the constitutional reforms of 1910. Those earlier reformers believed that this would help end the bloody wars that had racked the country during the nineteenth century, culminating in the War of a Thousand Days (1899–1902). (See Chapter Eleven.)

The new Conservative president, Mariano Ospina Pérez, attempted to keep Liberals in his cabinet, but he also used the army to harass Liberals. Under these circumstances, Liberal appointees broke with the president and resigned from their offices. Faced with hostility from Conservatives, they even refused to run a candidate for president in 1949 and abstained from voting. They charged that government partiality and police abuse made fair elections impossible. They were also in disarray after the death of Gaitán.

The new Conservative president elected in 1949, the fascistic Laureano Gómez, extended the state of siege and deployed the army and police against Liberals. Most of the killings were mutual acts of revenge committed by angry Liberals and Conservatives. In the supercharged partisan atmosphere of rural Colombia, killings begat more killings, and the violence continued its macabre escalation. Most of it occurred in rural villages and towns, rather than in larger cities, and local authorities who attempted to arrest perpetrators were targeted for reprisals. Protestants also suffered attacks because they were associated with the Liberals. In the end, nothing served to end the killing. After a slowdown in the mid-1950s, *La Violencia* surged back in the 1960s and 1970s, taking new forms and justifications, and has not ended even today.

Colombians have long argued that their country is distinct from the rest of Latin America, in part because of their long tradition of two-party political rule. Since 1910 they have enjoyed almost uninterrupted civilian, constitutional government. The military has remained in the barracks, with only one exception—when the army followed General Rojas Pinilla into power between 1953 and 1957. Moreover, except for Gaitán, Colombia had few populist leaders, none of whom created regimes like those of the Peróns, Getúlio Vargas, or Rómulo Betancourt.

Colombians called Bogotá the Athens of South America because of the democratic commitments of the leaders as well as the cultural sophistication of the country's elite. Educated Colombians enjoy debate and analysis in a republican framework, or what one historian called "the ideals of public life." They claimed that their Spanish diction and pronunciation were purer than any other in the hemisphere. Colombians believed that their system of federal government was among the most effective in the world. Finally, they believed that the moderation that they practiced in public affairs helped avert the civil wars and strife that plagued many neighboring countries.

Colombia is decidedly not a banana republic, yet it is not as atypical as the myth of exceptionalism suggests. During the nineteenth century it was one of the most strife-ridden countries in the hemisphere. And although it did not experience full-blown populism, Colombia witnessed truly terrifying episodes of insurgency in this century. With regard to Colombian exceptionalism, then, perhaps the most that can

Table 21-1 Colombian Presidents

Name	Years in Power	Born	Class	Urban Rural	Race	Ed	Age @ 1st/off	Mil?	Party	Foreign Influence	Died
Olaya Herrera	1930–34	1880	middle	R	wh	law	30	n	lib	Y	1937
López	1934–38 1942–45	1886	middle	R	wh	univ	48	n	lib	Y	1959
Ospina Pérez	1946–50	1891	upper	U	wh	eng.	57	n	cons	Y	1976
Gómez	1950–53	1889	middle	R	wh	eng.	22	n	cons	Y	1965
Rojas Pinilla	1953–57	1900	middle	U	wh	mil	53	Y	ANAPO	Y	1975
Lleras Camargo	1958–62	1906	middle	U	wh	univ	24	n	lib	Y	1990
Valencia	1962–66	1909	middle	U	wh	law	53	n	cons	Y	1971
Lleras Restrepo	1966–70	1908	middle	U	wh	law	26	n	lib	Y	1994
Misael Pastrana	1970–74	1923	upper	U	wh	law	26	n	cons	Y	
López Michelsen	1974–78	1913	upper	U	wh	law	54	n	lib	Y	
Turbay	1978–82	1916	middle	U	wh	univ		n	lib	n	
Betancur	1982–86	1923	lower	R	wh	law	40?	n	cons	n	
Barco	1986–90	1921	upper	U	wh	econ	40?	n	lib	Y	
Gaviria	1990–94	1947	middle	U	wh	econ	23	n	lib	n	
Samper	1994–98										

Source: *Encyclopedia of Latin American History and Culture* and authors' research.

be said is that Colombia's historical trajectory in this century has been very different from those of the other American republics.

The Conservative Era

The post-World War II Conservative administrations of Ospina Pérez and Laureano Gómez managed the economy reasonably well, overseeing solid growth in industry and agriculture. In the spirit of the era, they supported public ownership of key industries as a way to complement private enterprise. Ospina inaugurated a government-owned steel mill at Paz del Rio, Boyacá, and Gómez created a state petroleum industry, the Empresa Colombiana de Petróleos (ECOPETROL). They balanced their budgets, promoted exports, opposed strong unions, and welcomed foreign investors. Overall government policy favored the continued growth of import substitution industrialization (ISI). Given this record, it was unlikely that economic hardships played a major role in the violence because most adults had jobs or land to farm.

President Gómez accepted a U.S. invitation to send troops to fight in Korea, in the first military action of the United Nations. No other Latin American country did so. The Colombian armed forces supported the decision as a way to build morale, purchase new weaponry, gain combat experience, and broaden the scope of their mission. Also, Gómez wished to show his solidarity with the United States in the Cold War.

Despite their preference for free enterprise capitalism, the Conservatives instituted several social programs. In 1948 they created a profit-sharing scheme like that in Argentina, and shortly afterward they organized a rudimentary social security system. These social programs came too late, however, to win the president much support from the working class. In this respect Colombia was far behind most countries in the hemisphere, where social security began to be instituted in the 1920s.

The extent of Gómez's traditionalism became apparent when he proposed amendments to the Constitution that would expand presidential powers, centralize authority in Bogotá, and permit corporatist representation in the Senate, even by the Church. These reactionary politics alienated all but a few hard-core ideologues.

Because of the state of siege, the opposition of Liberals, and the growing defections in his own party, Laureano Gómez presided over what amounted to a civilian, quasiclerical dictatorship. Despite pressure from moderates within his party, he clung to power tenaciously and refused to step down. He closed Congress to end the attacks on himself, and he appointed an assembly to adopt his autocratic constitutional reforms. His opponents went on a virtual war footing.

The turmoil and bitterness that Gómez evoked, against the backdrop of rural violence, probably contributed to the heart attack that partly incapacitated him in mid-1953. Still clinging to power, Gómez tried to dismiss his chief of the armed forces, General Gustavo Rojas Pinilla, for allegedly conspiring against him. Rojas refused to step down, however, and instead deposed Gómez. It was Colombia's first military coup since the turn of the century and one that many Colombians supported in the hopes of ending the partisan strife that fed *La Violencia*.

General Rojas had not actively plotted to take the presidency; he merely led a junta into power. In the absence of anyone obviously better suited to take the office, however, Rojas decided to take charge. He quickly came to relish the exercise of power and to view himself as Colombia's savior in the dark days of political dissolution and violence. Amazingly, moderate Conservatives and virtually all Liberals welcomed the coup because Gómez had so clearly lost the capacity to lead.

The constitutional assembly that Gómez had impaneled now legalized Rojas's mandate, appointing him to serve as president until the end of Gómez's term in 1954. A year later, it extended the term until 1958. The public responded positively, hoping that his Government of the Armed Forces would end partisan fighting and restore order in the countryside. Rojas moved quickly to lift the most oppressive aspects of the state of siege and allowed Liberals in exile to return home. The Liberal Party recovered and soon collaborated partially with the government. Rojas apparently saw himself as a Colombian version of Spain's Generalissimo Francisco Franco, a firm, authoritative figure who would pacify the nation from above. Even though he never ran for election, he exhibited mildly populist qualities as well, promising to spread the benefits of progress to all classes of people.

Rojas created a government staffed largely by Conservatives, but he nonetheless welcomed the cooperation of Liberals and buttressed his authority with Church sponsorship. The general optimism that followed the departure of Gómez brought temporary respite from the violence, and Rojas took advantage to ease the severity of the state of siege. Still, he proved to be an arbitrary leader unused to the rough-and-tumble ways of civilian politics, and gradually the mood of the country soured and violence returned. In the end, he presided over a *dictablanda* (mild dictatorship), as Brazilians referred to Vargas's Estado Novo.

Rojas, probably imagining that he could become popular and win election as president, authorized women's suffrage in 1954. As it turned out, he did not hold elections during this period, and hence women did not vote until after his overthrow. He also carried out other initiatives designed to win popularity: He created a rival labor federation affiliated with Juan Perón's ATLAS in Argentina. He established a charity like Eva Perón's foundation and appointed his daughter, María Eugenia Rojas, to administer it. This foundation largely helped resettle refugees from the rural violence in urban centers. These programs ostensibly would shift power and income from the traditional oligarchy to the masses of Colombians.

These and other programs never paid off fully, however, because Colombian politics and sensibilities were so different from Argentina's. When he failed to win adulation through his actions, Rojas created a propaganda agency to foster his glory with pictures, busts, news clips, and admiring stories.

The economy seemed to boom at first, with high coffee prices, new investment by foreign firms, and deficit spending. One author called the general prosperity a "dance of the millions." It turned out to be a hollow boom fueled by temporary conditions that soon gave way to inflation. Moreover, the general relaxation of economic controls induced many public officials to enrich themselves.

In 1956 the violence surged again, and Rojas responded like an army officer, with raw force. This probably provoked only greater resistance on the part of rebels.

Meanwhile, the world market price for coffee, Colombia's major export, plummeted after 1955, causing major economic hardships. Rojas apparently decided that he needed to remain in office longer to accomplish the pacification and reconciliation he had promised, so he began seeking support for another term. At that point, Liberals and most Conservatives balked. Party leaders Alberto Lleras Camargo and Laureano Gómez met in Spain in 1957 to negotiate an agreement under which Liberals and Conservatives would share power in a restored civilian government. They then mobilized a general business strike to protest Rojas's attempt to continue in office, and they were joined by students and some unions. At the same time, they conspired with the army high command to remove Rojas. Rather than watch the country deteriorate politically and economically, the army sent Rojas into exile in May 1957.

National Front, 1958-1974

The bipartisan National Front, designed to replace Rojas, required full sharing of power between the two parties. The agreement was signed in the spirit of peaceful co-existence. In addition to dividing public offices between the parties (as had been done before), the new agreement provided for alternation of the Liberals and Conservatives in the presidency for four four-year terms, from 1958 to 1974. As the majority party, the Liberals occupied the presidency in the first and third terms. For the second and fourth terms, only Conservatives ran for president.

All high-level government posts, elective or appointive, including those of cabinet ministers and legislative and judicial bodies, were scrupulously divided between the two parties. Lower-echelon jobs, meanwhile, were converted to merit civil service appointments. This minimized the partisan conflict that fueled electoral competition and violence. Legislation in Congress required two-thirds majority to carry. In addition, the educational system was guaranteed a share of the federal budget. Finally, third party candidates were barred from elections.

The National Front largely accomplished what it set out to do: Restore civilian government to leaders from the traditional elites, diminish political conflict, encourage economic development programs, and defuse *La Violencia*. The first National Front president, Alberto Lleras Camargo, was a veteran Liberal who had served as president in 1945 and had enjoyed a good reputation afterward. He had taken the initiative of proposing the National Front to Conservative leader Laureano Gómez. Not required to boost his party at the Conservatives' expense, Lleras Camargo's 1958-1962 administration sought to restore peace and achieve some economic development.

Lleras Camargo helped set the policy agenda for the rest of the National Front presidents, if not exactly the tone of government. Studiously neutral, almost bland, Lleras Camargo cultivated the image of a healer. He took to heart the goals of the U.S.-supported Alliance for Progress, articulated in 1961, and positioned Colombia to become a showcase for democratic development. The army, while still patrolling the countryside, began carrying out civic action projects to help towns and villages.

Lleras Camargo also took up the old Liberal banner of agrarian reform and created an agency, INCORA, to make land and agricultural extension available to poverty-stricken rural families. Many believed that improved living conditions in the countryside would mitigate *La Violencia.*

The next three administrations continued programs launched by Lleras Camargo. In the late 1960s the government undertook a more vigorous program of economic development, entrusting planning to university-trained economists, engineers, and technicians. Government agencies and mixed public-private enterprises borrowed heavily to build up the infrastructure and expand national productivity. They also pushed to diversify exports, favoring flowers, bananas, coal, and nickel to lessen dependence on coffee. Industrial associations and producers' organizations played more active roles in policy formulation, too. After years of stagnation, the economy responded, producing something of an economic boom that lasted into the 1970s.

La Violencia did abate in the mid-1960s, and religious persecution also ended. In response, the government eased the state-of-siege measures and eventually ended them. A new threat arose, however, on the left. Marxist guerrilla forces, formed in the mountains and urban slums, attempted to destroy capitalism and foment world socialism. The success of the Cuban Revolution (see Chapter Twenty-Three) had inspired scores of similar armed movements in Latin America, including several in Colombia. Although never endangering the government, these guerrilla organizations persisted well into the 1990s and occasionally embarrassed authorities.

The National Front government also faced a serious challenge from an old adversary, General Rojas Pinilla. Rojas had returned soon after his exile and managed to win acquittal of charges of corruption filed against him. Rather than fade into obscure retirement, he founded a party, ANAPO, devoted to the principles and initiatives of his earlier administration. To the chagrin of traditional party bosses, ANAPO proved quite popular among urban lower-class and campesino voters.

As a candidate in the 1970 election, Rojas became a genuine populist, traveling about the country shaking hands and promising to redress the grievances of poor people. He criticized the oligarchy that had monopolized power and wealth for generations and promised to use government for the benefit of the masses. Because third parties could not participate, Rojas ran as a Conservative. Recalling the "dance of the millions" prosperity of his 1950s regime, many voters believed that he could deliver again and decided to vote for him.

Rojas stunned the traditional party leaders by coming within 1.6 percent of taking the 1970 election. The victor, Conservative Misael Pastrana, won by only a slim margin, so he made sure that ANAPO did not share in the spoils. ANAPO soon began to decline in popularity. Many followers were disappointed that Rojas did not fight the election outcome, which most believed was the result of government fraud. The M-19 guerrilla movement, which declared itself to be the armed wing of *Anapismo,* struck out on its own. ANAPO represented a continuing challenge to the National Front leadership.

Four years later, Rojas's daughter María Eugenia Moreno ran for president, on the ANAPO slate, after the National Front agreement lapsed. She received just under 10 percent of the votes, an indication that the party would not be able to mount a credible campaign for president again. Rojas himself died the following year. ANAPO gradually shifted toward the left, began espousing a socialist philosophy, and cooperated closely with the Communist Party. It suffered a thorough defeat in the 1976 by-elections and was reduced to insignificance. In 1978 it supported the Conservative, Belisario Betancur, for president.

Beyond the National Front

Liberal and Conservative leaders had decided in 1968 that the political climate was still too unsettled to return to fully competitive elections in 1974, so they amended the Constitution to phase out the bipartisan arrangements gradually. The presidential contest of 1974 was open to all parties, but the winner was obliged to share executive appointments equitably with other parties for one more term. President Alfonso López Michelsen decided to split cabinet posts six and six with the Conservatives and designated the defense minister as a neutral. Other practices of the National Front lingered as well. The Liberal Party, seemingly assured of winning elections for president by its larger voter base, continued the office sharing until 1986, when it reverted to exclusive party appointments, and then returned to bipartisanism in 1990.

By the 1970s philosophical differences among presidents had become less important than their personal styles. Contentious issues of the past, like Church-state relations, economic intervention, state and local autonomy, and property rights, no longer caused fights between the parties. Regardless of party affiliation, the presidents (all Liberals except for Pastrana and Betancur) had to struggle against new, powerful forces that jeopardized the integrity of the government. Drug merchants were turning Colombia into the narcotics emporium of the world. Violence at higher levels than anywhere else in the hemisphere had become endemic. And guerrilla bands, emboldened by Maoist and other extremist ideologies nurtured in the universities, resisted all attempts at eradication. These forces brought unsettled times to Colombia.

La Violencia did not disappear altogether in the 1960s; instead, it persisted at lower levels in several regions. In many places banditry and street crime overlapped with politically motivated offenses. The violence did not threaten the government, so it did not trigger permanent state-of-siege measures. Yet, there was a sense that society was ill and that civil conflict lay just beneath the surface tranquillity. It also hampered the suspension of state-of-siege measures. People began to barricade their homes and planned their lives around security measures. Tens of thousands of men were employed as private guards for homes and businesses. In short, the remnants of *La Violencia* kept the administration on the defensive, made life insecure for most citizens, and plagued state and local government in affected regions.

The violence heightened confusion and despair because of its ideological diversity after the 1960s. Many citizens who sympathized with the Cuban Revolution and regarded the United States as an imperialist nation lent their support to the guerrillas. The rise of the Catholic left wing, inspired by radical priest Camilo Torres, added moral weight to dissident movements of all sorts. After years of political activism, Torres joined the Army of National Liberation guerrilla band in 1965. When police captured and executed him in 1966, he became a martyr to the leftist cause. The ferment and diversity of these movements made suppression nearly impossible.

The Drug Trade

The narcotics industry also destabilized Colombia after the 1970s. At first, Colombian farmers raised marijuana ("Colombian gold") for export to the United States, shipping from La Guajira on the Caribbean coast. This did not remain profitable, so some traffickers began to refine and export cocaine from semiprocessed material imported from Peru and Bolivia. In the 1980s cocaine became popular in the United States and Europe, driving up the price and defying efforts to control it. Entrepreneurs in Colombia formed organizations, called cartels, by which they managed and financed the central and most lucrative parts of the cocaine business. In particular, they took over and expanded existing distribution networks in the United States, especially in New York and Miami.

Cartel agents operated refining laboratories in South America, where semiprocessed cocaine was purified for re-export. They also set up elaborate smuggling routes to the United States and Europe, corrupting officials throughout the Caribbean basin. They supervised overseas distribution networks. Finally, they oversaw money-laundering operations to hide the sources of their profits. It became a multibillion-dollar industry.

The major drug cartels operated in Medellín, Cali, and Cartagena—industrial and agribusiness centers where they did not attract too much attention. Medellín, for example, had 1.3 million inhabitants in 1975, of whom 200,000 were unemployed. In addition, thirty-two thousand women worked as prostitutes, and forty thousand families lived in shantytowns. Accordingly, the cartels found it easy to hire all the operatives they needed. Gradually, they assembled cadres of buyers, shippers, bankers, accountants, pilots, gunmen, chemists, and assorted underworld characters. The profit margins were so phenomenal that no expense was too great for the cartels. They corrupted Colombian officials with bribes and threats, assuring themselves of secure places to run their businesses. The cartel chiefs, many still young men, became legendary and outrageous figures. Some, like Pablo Escobar and Carlos Lehder, even nurtured political aspirations and ran for congressional office.

Many, perhaps most, public officials gave in to the terrible choice—cooperate or die—forced upon them by cartel traffickers. The public's respect for civil servants certainly began to decline. In 1978 presidential candidate Julio César Turbay Alaya's campaign promised a "moral crusade to stamp out corruption." Those who would not accept bribes were murdered by the cartels to intimidate others into cooperating. The cartels' favorite targets were prosecuting attorneys, judges, and police officials. A dramatic turning point was their 1983 assassination of the crusading attorney general, Rodrigo Lara Bonilla. After that the cartels became so entrenched that it

Pablo Escobar, wealthy and powerful head of the Medellín drug cartel in Colombia, eventually accepted a prison sentence in exchange for guarantees he would not be extradited to the United States.

seemed that only full-scale warfare could defeat them. Indeed, many cartels employed small armies of gunmen as guards and enforcers.

The sheer volume and profitability of the drug trade, and the corruption it spread, convinced hemispheric leaders to organize a coordinated attack against the cartels. The U.S. government took the lead, convoking inter-American meetings and financing programs designed to slow down the drug trade. The multifaceted program, dubbed the War on Drugs, itself consumed billions of dollars each year. It entailed the eradication of coca fields in Peru and Bolivia (where the raw material was grown), the destruction of processing labs, the interdiction of shipments, aerial surveillance in the Caribbean basin, espionage, suppression of money laundering, and the prosecution of distributors in consuming countries. These enormous forces at times seemed to rival the forces marshaled against the Soviet Union during the Cold War.

Colombian cooperation was essential for success in the War on Drugs because the coordinating centers were located and protected in its cities. Yet, attempts to bring the drug lords to justice unleashed terrible attacks against public officials. Literally thousands of federal judges, political candidates, district attorneys, police detectives, and prison officials were murdered in retaliation for operations against the cartels. Colombia's leaders also paid for the war with their own and their families' blood. For example, Liberal presidential candidate Luis Carlos Galán was murdered, apparently on Escobar's orders, for threatening to crack down on the drug industry. It was a terrible price to pay because Colombians did not even consume narcotics heavily. The government leaders recognized, however, the corrosive effects that the cartels had on society, public honesty, and politics, and many made immense sacrifices.

The struggle in Colombia became even more vicious when the cartels entered into deals with guerrilla groups. These deals developed after leftists began kidnapping and ransoming children of cartel bosses to raise money. The cartels responded by sending hit teams against the guerrillas in retaliation. Eventually, some cartels struck agreements whereby the guerrillas stopped kidnapping and served as mercenaries for the cartels. With plenty of cash and freedom of movement, the drug lords could offer attractive terms. Some cartels bankrolled guerrilla forces in exchange for occasional paramilitary cooperation. Cartel planes that before had been returning empty from the United States began carrying automatic weapons, grenade launchers, explosives, and sophisticated detonating mechanisms that they turned over to the guerrillas. From the standpoint of those fighting drugs, this development could not have been worse.

The Guerrillas

Rural guerrilla activity that had surfaced in the late 1950s in Colombia spread rapidly during the early years of the Cuban Revolution. Militant leaders, drawing on university students, disgruntled intellectuals, bandits, alienated peasant leaders, and the like, could attract hundreds of men and women to their ranks. The most powerful guerrilla group of the period was the Revolutionary Armed Forces of Colombia (FARC), founded in 1964. Urban guerrillas appeared in the late 1960s and were even more difficult to detect and suppress. The M-19 movement, begun in 1973, combined rural and urban guerrilla tactics. For many years it struck fear into the hearts of the citizenry.

The guerrilla movements terrorized the country, making the government look inept and repressive. The guerrillas accumulated cash and weapons easily and enjoyed great notoriety. Many leftist intellectuals and reformers sympathized with and helped the guerrillas. The revolutionaries' elaborate support units offered safe houses, weapons caches, medical aid, legal services, and escape routes. The guerrillas frequently carried out acts of social justice, so-called Robin Hood operations, to appear to be progressive friends of the people.

Throughout the 1970s the government battled the guerrilla forces without much success. Bank robberies, kidnappings, and hit-and-run attacks on military garrisons occurred constantly. The army and security services cooperated with their U.S., Brazilian, Argentine, and Chilean counterparts, constituting an informal counterinsurgency alliance. (See Chapter Twenty-four.) Right-wing generals at times threatened democracy in Colombia. Repression grew, and authorities invoked state-of-siege powers constantly. Student-police strife was almost constant. Critics spoke of a partial militarization of the country.

In 1979 and 1980 President Julio César Turbay Alaya's government was seemingly battling everywhere against urban guerrillas. In January 1980 the feared M-19 group raided an army arsenal, much to the embarrassment of the government. In the subsequent crackdown, authorities claimed that they captured fifty-six hundred weapons, fifteen vehicles, and one thousand uniforms. The danger was real.

By the 1980s everyone recognized that crime, drugs, and guerrilla activity were self-reinforcing, but they constituted a Gordian knot impossible to untie. The criminal organizations threatened or killed politicians who attempted to shut them down. The 1985 capture of the Justice Palace showed the extreme power and daring of these groups. M-19 staged the raid to force the president to negotiate, and the army responded with a massive counterattack. Scores of lives were lost, including half of the Supreme Court justices. The world looked on appalled, and the Colombian government lost even more credibility in its fight against violence and crime.

President Betancur managed to diminish the guerrilla challenge somewhat when he offered the rebels not only amnesty but also access to the political system. The FARC leadership accepted and in 1985 transformed itself into a party, the Patriotic Union. As a legal entity, it received considerable support from across the spectrum, from disaffected citizens to communist voters. Its leadership suffered, however, from systematic attacks by right-wing paramilitary groups. Then in 1990 President Virgilio Barco struck a similar deal with the M-19, which renounced violence and fielded candidates for virtually all offices in that year's election.

A partial solution to the drug cartel problem seemed to be found by Colombia's new president in 1990, César Augusto Gaviria. A pragmatic hard-liner determined to eliminate the drug industry, Gaviria offered a deal to the cartel bosses. On the one hand, he would continue to raid, arrest, prosecute, and punish narcotics traffickers to the full extent of his powers. He would also extradite persons wanted on drug charges in the United States. The image of Panama's Manuel Noriega locked in a Miami jail was still fresh in the public memory. (See Chapter Twenty-five.) On the other hand, he offered more lenient treatment to drug bosses who turned themselves in—no extradition, lighter sentences, and better prison accommodations.

Gaviria's gamble paid off. Cartel leaders began to surrender, including the notorious head of the Medellín cartel, Pablo Escobar. By the mid-1990s the drug bosses could no longer bribe and intimidate Colombian officials with impunity, and the industry lost some of its profitability and had to disperse to other countries. Drug-related violence fell, and with it political and petty crime declined as well.

Economic and Social Successes

Despite the terrible battles that Colombian presidents had to wage against the drug industry and the guerrillas, the economy performed remarkably well since the end of the National Front period. On average, the GNP rose about 4 percent a year in the period 1974–1995. When coupled with a reduced population growth rate of 1.8 percent, this economic expansion lifted most Colombians' standards of living significantly. This growth, moreover, occurred across the board, in mining, manufacturing, and agriculture. For a variety of reasons, the government had never intervened as fully in the economy as had other Latin American governments, and the private sector managed to adapt to the changing world scene. One analyst concluded that Colombian politicians and administrators shared some of the credit for managing the economy well.

Business associations have been especially powerful in Colombia's economy. The Colombian National Federation of Coffee Growers, formed in 1927, has managed to uphold quality and price levels for its product and to preserve its foreign markets. The National Association of Industrialists likewise has played a major role in expanding manufacturing. These and other groups negotiate with presidents from positions of authority.

Much of the economic growth of the last half-century was financed by capital owned by a small number of families. Colombia has witnessed a growing concentration of wealth, as has the rest of the hemisphere. Yet, several factors have ameliorated the situation. The appearance of new manufacturers, export businesses, and service industries spread the wealth beyond the traditional elite families. The drug trade also contributed significantly to the capital stock of the country, allowing new players onto the scene. And the fact that Colombian enterprises are distributed throughout a number of cities—Medellín, Cali, Barranquilla, Bucaramanga, and Cartagena, in addition to Bogotá—has meant that a broader business class has emerged in recent times.

A final factor mitigating the concentration of wealth has been the modest recovery of the labor movement since the 1960s. Colombian unions had traditionally been unable to defend their members aggressively and had operated as mere appendages of the Liberal and Conservative parties. Strong partisanship and the influence of the Church were held responsible for labor's weakness. The fragmented political left, meanwhile, could not help labor's cause. By the 1960s, however, several union federations became more independent and assertive. The high point of collective action came in 1977, when general protest strikes broke out in response to inflation and wage policies. Although the action was mild compared with strikes in the Southern Cone of South America, it did help to establish labor as a separate force to be reckoned with.

The 1991 Constitution, which replaced that of 1886, responded to growing popular pressures for reform and solutions to the nation's problems. It incorporated into basic law many of the sociopolitical trends evident since the 1950s. Largely the work of President Gaviria, it had been on the agendas of several of his predecessors. The new Constitution made senatorial elections nationwide, allowing grass-roots organizations greater access to candidates. It also decentralized authority by changing governorships from appointive to elective offices. Mayors have been popularly elected since 1988.

Rights of Amerindians in 1991 Constitution

Art. 10 That the native tongues and dialects of the country's ethnic [indigenous] groups are official languages—along with Spanish—within the territories occupied by these groups. That education in those territories will be, henceforth, bilingual.

Art. 96 That the definition of Colombian nationals includes members of Indian groups who share the country's borderlands; this being done in accordance with the principle of reciprocity as applied in official treaties.

Art. 171 That the Colombian Senate will contain an additional two senators [beyond the one hundred elected nationally] elected by the country's indigenous communities.

Art. 246 Indigenous authorities may exercise jurisdiction within their territories, in conformity with their own norms and procedures as long as these do not conflict with the Constitution and the laws of the Colombian Republic.

Art. 329 The formation of indigenous territorial units will be undertaken in line with the provisions of the Organic Law of Territorial Organization; territorial limits are to be set by the National Government and with the participation of representatives of the indigenous groups. Also, the reservations (resguardos) remain collective and inalienable property.

Art. 330 The indigenous territories will be governed by councils organized and regulated in accordance with the customs and practices of their own communities. These councils will exercise a variety of functions including: enforcing laws pertaining to use of the soil and settlement; designing policies and programs for economic and social development of their respective territories and in line with the National Development Plan; promoting and supervising state investment; keeping track of and distributing their resources; conserving natural resources; coordinating programs and projects developed by the different communities within the territory; collaborating [with the national government] in maintaining public order; representing the territories before the national government; fulfilling all other obligations stipulated by the Constitution and the laws.

Moreover, the exploitation of natural resources within these territories must not threaten the cultural, social, or economic integrity of the indigenous communities. In all decisions concerning such exploitation, the national government will facilitate the involvement of representatives of the affected communities.

The new Constitution barred extradition of citizens who surrendered to Colombian authorities—a measure that induced more drug lords to turn themselves in. Attempts were made to improve the shattered judicial system. The new Constitution confirmed the civil nature of marriage and freedom to divorce—a basic right for women. Finally, it declared the state to be neutral among the various religions, thereby ending official ties to Roman Catholicism. The overall outcome of these changes was a more open, decentralized, and democratic system of government.

Also symptomatic of the new social peace in Colombia was President Gaviria's appointment of a civilian minister of defense, the first in four decades.

In the half-century following World War II, Colombian society evolved and became more connected to the outside world. Regions once isolated and provincial in their outlook joined the national and even international scene. Colombia hosted important international meetings, such as the 1948 founding of the OAS, the 1966 formation of the Andean Common Market, and the historic 1968 Conference of Latin American Bishops in Medellín, which launched a wave of left-leaning Catholic reforms and activisim. During the 1980s Colombia pressed hard for peace negotiations in Central America, giving rise to the Contadora talks. In this light, the 1994 election of former President Gaviria as secretary general of the OAS recognized and reconfirmed Colombia's vital role in hemispheric affairs.

In the world of letters, Colombia moved to the center of the stage in 1982, when Gabriel García Márquez won the Nobel Prize in literature. His works, beginning with *One Hundred Years of Solitude* (1967) had already sold millions of copies in dozens of translated editions. Probably no other Latin American writer did as much as García Márquez to ignite the region's literary boom.

Gabriel García Márquez, who won the Nobel Prize in literature, is one of Latin America's most revered writers. An excerpt from his One Hundred Years of Solitude *appears on pp. 338–339.*

Except for García Márquez's work, however, Colombian culture was little known to the outside world. North Americans associated the country with Juan Valdez, a fictional farmer used in TV commercials to sell Colombian-grown coffee. Rather, bad news swamped outsiders' impressions of Colombia: Images of drug lords and guerrilla warriors crowded out more favorable images of the country. In one ironic case, in a U.S. best-selling novel, Tom Clancy's *Clear and Present Danger*, the United States mounts an illegal invasion of Colombia to wipe out a cocaine-producing operation. It was hardly an advertisement for Colombian tourism.

Conclusions and Issues

Colombia straddles two subregions of the hemisphere, the Caribbean basin and the Andean republics. Colombian diplomats, intellectuals, politicians, businessmen, and clerics provide leadership for many nations in both regions. Known to be profoundly conservative, Colombians have seldom been innovators in social or political policy. Many features of the last century seem to be preserved in today's society, as portrayed by Colombia's most famous novelist, Gabriel García Márquez. Its society is stratified, its reward system rigidly controlled, and its local affairs deeply familial.

Physical geography also kept Colombians more apart than together, reinforcing regionalism and the ways of the past.

The severe challenges faced by post-World War II administrations, in the form of endemic violence, guerrilla movements, and the narcotics industry, strengthened the Colombian elite's tendency to retrench and protect inherited values. This tendency was most pronounced during the period of the National Front, explicitly designed to preserve order. Since 1974, however, the Liberal Party, always more open to change, has dominated the presidency and managed a gradual democratization process. Meanwhile, sustained economic growth and improved standards of living fostered a more national outlook on the part of most Colombians. These changes, codified in the 1991 Constitution, are likely to continue into the foreseeable future.

Discussion Questions

1. What circumstances led the Colombian elites to acquiesce to a military government in 1953? Was Rojas Pinilla a caudillo, a typical dictator, or a populist?

2. How did the interparty cooperation of the National Front inhibit democracy? Did the national government respond adequately to the demands and pressures put upon it in this period? Has the elite adapted successfully to late twentieth-century realities?

3. How did the nation grapple with the challenges posed by the cocaine cartels and the guerrilla movements? To what extent is the drug trade a Colombian problem instead of a global problem?

Caribbean Basin Countercurrents

Michael Manley Speaks to Shantytown Voters

Standing on the bed of a flatbed truck, Michael Manley towered above the restless crowd of poor and sweating people in West Kingston, Jamaica. He gripped the microphone tightly.

"What GOOD is our bill of rights if you are unemployed? What GOOD is our cherished independence if the international companies steal our wealth? What GOOD do our public schools do if teachers go unpaid and students sit at their desks hungry?"

The crowd roared approval in refrain.

"We are like a colony still," Manley thundered, "still far from the Promised Land that my father and his generation bequeathed to us in 1962. The new colonialism does not rely on bullets or gunboats, but on bank loans and export quotas. This colonialism MUST end, just as British rule did a decade ago!"

"JO-SHU-A, JO-SHU-A, JO-SHU-A," the crowd chanted, recalling the biblical Joshua, a nickname the people had given Manley when he led the strikers against the Jamaican Broadcasting Corporation. Then he urged them to "March around this citadel of injustice called Jericho," reminding them of the great Hebrew general Joshua who delivered Jericho into the hands of the Israelites and ultimately led them into the Promised Land. So would Manley.

"Our People's National Party," he continued, "WILL win this election! And we WILL fulfill my father's dream of a strong, fair, prosperous, and autonomous Jamaica."

Manley stopped, his speech punctuated by cheering and applause. He knew how to work the crowd, especially using the old preacher's oratorical device of repetition. He wiped his brow with a big kerchief he kept in his rear pocket.

"We MUST offer a good life to the woman as well as the man, to the worker as well as the clerk and shop owner, all of them sufferers. And to build the New Jamaica, we need you, your families, your homes, and your children. To be Jamaican shall bring pride to our people."

"Too long we have relied on bauxite and tourism—we are like a banana republic. We must diversify, bring industry, create good jobs, and become self-sufficient."

Across the crowd hundreds of heads nodded, punctuated by "amens" floating up from many of his listeners.

"This will require hard work, but that work will produce a decent paycheck and a sense of justice. Jamaica will be strong again because of our people and because the message is change."

"These are troubled times in our region. The Great Powers seek to make us pawns in their struggles, while they drain our resources for their war-machines. Jamaica needs to look after her own interests, not those of the superpowers. Under our party, Jamaica will assume an important role in the Third World movement. We will use our combined voices as a chorus to win rights as debtor nations, for dominion over our territorial seas, and to avoid the divisive and irrelevant conflicts of capitalism versus communism. We know who we are: *JAMAICANS!*" Manley exclaimed.

"And we know what is good for our island and its beloved people. We must have government by participation. So, go vote NOW, vote PNP, and I will be your next Prime Minister. Honor our party and your country by casting your vote for the PNP. Power for the people!" Manley again exhorted the crowd.

He held up a carved scepter, a biblical rod of correction given, according to tradition, to his father by the Emperor Haile Selassie of Ethiopia himself. Manley ended the speech with the Rastafarian refrain:

"The word is LOVE."

As the cheering rose, a reggae band started up a popular protest song, "Let the Power Fall on I." Rastafarians in the front row threw their braided red, green, and yellow tams into the air to celebrate, and many started dancing as the rally broke up on a festive note.

Michael Manley's party won the 1972 election, and he served as prime minister until 1980. The prosperity that he promised never materialized, and the people grew angry. Later, however, he won election again, after a decade of probusiness austerity under Manley's rival, Edward Seaga. Manley's last term was cut short by illness, and he died in 1997, still a hero to the millions of poor Jamaicans who knew him as Joshua.

Storm Warnings Offshore

The Caribbean basin—embracing the Greater and Lesser Antilles plus Central America—has a distinctive history, quite unlike that of North and South America. Of the island colonies, only Haiti (1804—) and its neighbor on the island of Hispaniola, the Dominican Republic (1865—), achieved their liberty before the beginning of the twentieth century. So the history of the Caribbean since 1900 must begin with the struggles for independence.

Even after winning independence, however, the new Caribbean nations suffered intense meddling and control of their affairs by the major powers. Informal imperialism, as experienced by the recently liberated island nations, was especially degrading. One critic, a former diplomat in the region, referred to this imperialism as "jungle diplomacy." As Chapter Thirteen made clear, this region was especially prone to government by dictatorship and U.S. intervention. The epithet "banana republic," in fact, was a U.S. invention.

Central America received much the same treatment from the rest of the outside world, which approached its shores from the Caribbean Sea and valued its people mostly for their ability to produce bananas and coffee.

For these reasons, the Caribbean basin experienced more instability, corruption, violence, and outside meddling than did virtually any other region in the world. These factors also made the area fertile ground for revolution. Some major episodes—such as the Mexican Revolution, Sandino's movement, and the Cuban upheaval of 1933—have already been discussed in earlier chapters. The Caribbean basin appeared to be fractured by social fault lines and surrounded by political volcanoes.

After World War II, some reformers in the region decided to eliminate dictatorship by means of military coups. Some were merely out-of-power tyrants hoping to return to power. Many, however, were young, idealistic, and university educated, and they often came from middle-class families. These latter revolutionaries coalesced into a movement called the Caribbean Legion.

Figueres Revolution

In December 1947 José Figueres of Costa Rica, angry at the intention of ex-President Rafael Calderón Guardia (1940–1944) to run for office again, traveled to Guatemala, where the reformist president, Juan José Arévalo, had instituted a peaceful revolution. Figueres, known to all as "don Pepe," negotiated an agreement, called the Caribbean Pact, for promoting democracy in the region. Arévalo promised arms and military assistance so that don Pepe could overthrow the Costa Rican government dominated by Calderón. In exchange, don Pepe later promised that he would help other exile groups overthrow dictators in nearby Nicaragua, Honduras, and the Dominican Republic.

When the 1948 elections were annulled by Calderón's allies in Congress, don Pepe organized a rebel force at his farm in the south of Costa Rica and activated his military alliance. Immediately advisors and arms arrived from Guatemala, and Figueres then advanced toward the capital. Because Costa Rica had a small army, the rebels fought mostly against Calderón's communist supporters in the banana workers' union. The action, a civil war rather than a coup or revolution, lasted over a month and sacrificed about two thousand lives. Figueres's forces prevailed, and when they captured the capital they exiled the incumbent leaders.

Table 22–1 Caribbean Basin Dictators, Dynasties, and Revolutionaries

Country	Name	Years in Power	Born	Class	Urban Rural	Race	Ed	Age @ 1st/off	Mil?	Foreign Influence	Died
Guatemala	Ubico	1931–44	1878	upper	U	wh	mil	53	Y	Y	1946
	Arévalo	1945–51	1904	middle		wh	Ph.D.	41	n	Y	1990
	Arbenz	1951–54	1913	middle		wh	mil	31	Y	n	1971
	Rios Montt	1982–83	1926	middle		wh	mil	56	Y	Y	
	Cerezo	1986–91	1942	upper		wh	univ	32	n	Y	
	Rigoberta Menchu	Nobel laureate	1959	lower		ind	prim		n	Y	
Cuba	Batista Era	1933–59									
	Castro	1959–	1926	upper	R	wh	law	33	n	Y	
	Guevara	n/a	1928	middle	U	wh	med	31	n	Y	1967
Haiti	Duvalier	1957–71	1907	middle		bl	med	39	n	Y	1971
	Jean Claude Duvalier	1971–86	1951	upper	U	bl	univ	20	n	Y	
	Aristide	1991, 1994–64	1953	middle		bl	relig.	38	n	Y	

Dominican Republic	Trujillo Era		1930–61								
	Bosch	1909	1963	middle	R	wh	univ	53	n	y	
	Balaguer	1907	1960–63 1966–78 1986–96	upper		wh	law		n	y	
Costa Rica	Figueres	1906	1948–49 1953–58 1970–74	middle	R	wh	high sch	42	n	y	1990
	Oscar Arias Sánchez	1940	1986–90	upper		mes	univ	30	n	y	
Panama	Arias Era		1932–84								
	Torrijos	1929	1968–81	middle	R	mes	mil	39	y	y	1981
	Noriega	1936	1983–89	lower	U	mes	mil	47	y	y	
Nicaragua	Somoza Dynasty		1932–79								
	Ortega	1945	1979–90	middle	R	wh	univ	34	n	y	
	Barrios de Chamorro	1929	1990–95	upper	R	wh	univ	61	n	y	
El Salvador	Duarte	1925	1980–82 1984–89	middle		wh	eng.	64	n	y	1990

Source: *Encyclopedia of Latin American History and Culture* and authors' research.

Don Pepe insisted that his rebellion aimed only to restore democracy, but once victorious he and his reformist allies called a convention to write a new constitution. They began calling their regime the Second Republic, signaling the start of a new era. Adopted in 1949, the new Constitution established a decentralized state with stronger democratic safeguards than before. It created a number of autonomous agencies, outside of executive control, that would carry out broader social and economic policies than the previous state. Thus government became more intrusive yet less centralized. Women gained the vote, and elections came under the supervision of a Supreme Electoral Tribunal. Most surprisingly, the Constitution abolished the army and left law enforcement to a police agency. To a large degree, the Constitution legalized tendencies already under way during the previous administrations.

Far more dramatic than the new Constitution was the advent of a generation of young leaders in Costa Rica. The forceful and charismatic don Pepe amazingly declined to run for president and supported an ally, Otilio Ulate, for the first term. Then don Pepe ran for office in 1953 and won a stunning victory. Calling his movement the National Liberation Party (PLN), he ended the era of oligarchic control of the government and brought in principled, educated, and determined young men descended from the original Spanish families. They continued to run Costa Rica for decades. Don Pepe served out his first term from 1954 to 1958, and another from 1970 to 1974, and his collaborators served for several other terms. In fact, his son, also named José Figueres, won election as president in 1994 on the PLN ticket.

Figueres's collaborators did not hesitate to impose programs on the private sector if such programs benefited the majority of the population. Although entirely democratic in ethic, they believed in government providing a decent living for all citizens. Costa Rica came to rival Uruguay as the foremost welfare state in the hemisphere. The country had so little foreign investment, however, that this democratic socialization caused no adverse reaction from abroad. Instead, the modest profits from exports of coffee, cattle, timber, and bananas were spread around equitably and supported a contented, well-educated populace.

Figueres had been aided in his 1948 revolution by a number of exiles from other Caribbean states. After their success they called on don Pepe to help them, as promised in the 1947 Caribbean Pact. Figueres did allow them to assemble and train in Costa Rican territory, and he provided money and arms. He also founded the Institute for Political Education in San José, which published the prodemocracy journal *Combate*.

The Caribbean Legion's most dangerous enemy was Anastasio Somoza, the dictator of neighboring Nicaragua. The fact that anti-Somoza exiles were preparing to invade from Costa Rica provoked Somoza to a preemptive strike, thereby forcing Figueres to call a truce and bring the Nicaraguan exiles under control.

Next, the Costa Rican-sponsored exiles invaded the Dominican Republic, then under the dictatorship of Rafael Trujillo. This invasion failed, as did operations against Cuba's Batista and Venezuela's Pérez Jiménez. Soon the legion languished. The regimes that it opposed were too entrenched and well armed to be easily overthrown, and the United States pressured Figueres and others to stop promoting invasions. The U.S. government had begun fighting the Cold War and insisted on tight security in its private lake, the Caribbean Sea.

José "don Pepe" Figueres (center), architect of Costa Rica's Second Republic and champion of democracy in the Caribbean Basin.

Despite calling off the Caribbean Legion, Figueres continued to promote democracy in the region, supporting exiles and speaking out against tyrants. He harbored Rómulo Betancourt after his ouster from Venezuela in 1948. He helped Nicaraguans planning to assassinate Somoza. And he supported the production of print and broadcast material favoring democracy in the region. For a time, Figueres was a one-man campaign for democracy. He received good press from most outside observers.

Guatemalan Revolution of 1954

The people of Guatemala had tolerated one of the most oppressive dictatorships in the region, that of General Jorge Ubico (1931–1944). But, as World War II was about to end, Ubico stepped down and was replaced by an equally unpopular general. The new leader attempted to calm the populace with minor concessions, but the politically active middle class clamored for democracy. When the general rigged elections and declared himself the winner, two army officers formed civilian militias and removed him in a bloodless coup. They quickly formed a junta and scheduled new elections.

The surprise victor in the 1945 elections was a mild-mannered professor, Juan José Arévalo, who had lived in Argentina for over a decade, in exile from the Ubico regime. He was nominated by the junta because he had no ties to existing parties.

He also had a strong following among students, who emerged as the heroes of the movement against Ubico. His return was hailed as a redemption, and thousands flocked to the airport to welcome him. He was a tall, handsome, imposing figure, and he spoke forcefully and well about his plans for reforming the nation. He promised most of all to educate, to promote culture, and to improve the lives of the poor and downtrodden. He won the election by a landslide, in an outpouring of relief that the dictatorship was over.

Juan José Arévalo's ideas came from several sources. He had been deeply impressed by the administration of Franklin Roosevelt during the 1930s, especially by Roosevelt's forceful intervention in the economy and by efforts to protect common citizens from economic harm. Arévalo also embraced progressive aspects of Argentine society. Finally, he and other leaders were inspired by the Mexican Revolution. Mexico in the 1940s offered an appealing model to follow.

Arévalo quickly had legislation drafted to improve society. His social security law of 1946 instituted workers' disability insurance and maternity leave. Soon, a new Social Security Institute began enrolling employed persons for medical care and eventual retirement benefits. The 1947 Labor Law brought Guatemala up to date in workers' rights, at least workers in urban areas. Arévalo also experimented with land reform to help peasant farmers and peons become viable producers.

Arévalo's reforms, socialistic in character, did not sit well with landowners, industrialists, and foreign investors, especially the powerful United Fruit Company. Likewise, his tolerance of communist leadership in key labor and university sectors and appointment of the controversial Jacobo Arbenz as defense minister caused considerable unrest and provoked a number of attempted coups. Arévalo survived largely due to the army's obedience under Arbenz.

Arevalismo, as his program was called, received renewed stimulus under the next president, Jacobo Arbenz. Although just an army officer, Arbenz sought the good life by marrying a wealthy Salvadoran and using his position to acquire extensive plantations. He also aspired to lead his country, participating in the 1944 coups and serving as defense minister under Arévalo. Perhaps the most questionable act in his climb to power was the 1949 assassination of General Francisco J. Araña, his principal rival for the presidency. Arbenz won election by an overwhelming majority in late 1950, yet his record was tarnished by many questionable and brutal acts.

Arbenz achieved his electoral victory with a coalition not unlike that of the PRI in Mexico: His National Unity Party contained labor unions, public employee associations, peasant organizations, many military units, and a variety of splinter groups from across the ideological spectrum. Communists who had joined the government under Arévalo continued in the new regime, leading some to brand Arbenz himself a communist. In fact, Arbenz was a populist and a nationalist whose inspirations came from a variety of sources, including Arévalo.

With support from international banks and local capital, Arbenz promoted major economic projects. He attempted to reduce Guatemala's dependence on the United States. His most daring undertaking, however, was the 1952 agrarian reform act. This act nationalized large, uncultivated landholdings, which the government then distributed to small farmers. Former owners received compensation in twenty-

During the CIA-directed coup of 1954, foreign pilots dropped leaflets on Guatemala City. Their purpose was to frighten the populace and spur the army to overthrow President Jacobo Arbenz, which it did.

five-year government bonds. The new owners, mostly peasants, paid for the land in small allotments.

Among the major landowners who lost property under the law was the United Fruit Company (UFCO), which held a near-monopoly on banana exports, rail service, and shipping throughout Central America. UFCO encouraged the U.S. State Department to cooperate in a campaign to discredit the Arbenz government and perhaps replace it. Washington soon authorized the Central Intelligence Agency (CIA, 1947) to destabilize the Guatemalan government by conducting a campaign of propaganda and conspiracies. Eventually these efforts paid off in a coup orchestrated by the CIA. A rival army officer, Carlos Castillo Armas, staged a fake invasion from Honduras, after a propaganda blitz by the CIA that made Castillo Armas's forces appear more numerous and popular than they actually were. The army high command panicked and withdrew its support from Arbenz. Arbenz then resigned and fled into exile, and Castillo Armas became president.

The blatant U.S. intervention and the quick restitution of UFCO properties marked a counterrevolution in Guatemala. All of the programs and electoral reforms instituted since 1945 were canceled, and the country fell under full dictatorial control by the army. For the next two decades, few elections were held, and no elected president served out his term. Brutal repression, censorship, assassinations, ethnic warfare, and flagrant profiteering by high officials characterized Guatemala. Tragically, the army targeted Amerindian villagers among its enemies.

The attacks against Mayan peoples became so intense that as many as a million fled across the border into Mexico to survive. The plight of these refugees was dramatized in the feature film, *El Norte,* made in the 1980s. The ethnic war gained worldwide attention when thirty-three-year-old Rigoberta Menchu won the Nobel Peace Prize in 1992 for her courageous work on behalf of her fellow Mayas.

The only other Guatemalan ever to receive a Nobel Prize was Miguel Angel Asturias, for literature in 1967. Asturias lived abroad for many years, where he spread a pessimistic view of his country's political and economic systems. His major novels include *El Señor Presidente* (1946: a trilogy loosely depicting General Ubico's dictatorship), *Strong Wind* (1950: about the abuses of the United Fruit Company), and *The Mulatta and Mr. Fly* (1963: a story evoking the mix of native and imported cultures).

Since the mid-1980s, when President Marco Vinicio Cerezo began his term (1986–1991), Guatemala has lived under uneasy democratic governments. Guerrilla attacks, army coups, general strikes, and adverse international publicity plagued the country. Efforts to stimulate dialogues among the country's deeply divided peoples—the Maya majority, the European minority, the mixed groups called *ladinos*—brought some respite from war but did not immediately guarantee peace.

A dramatic breakthrough occured on December 29, 1996, when a peace treaty was signed between the government and the guerrillas, principally represented by the Guatemalan National Revolutionary Unity (URNG). A UN military observer team was sent in 1997 to help with the demobilization of the rebel forces and later that year thousands of Guatemalan refugees who had fled to Mexico began to return. Guatemala's 35-year civil war was finally coming to an end.

It is estimated that over 150,000 people perished in that brutal war, with as many as 50,000 unaccounted for and missing. Sporadic violence still punctuated the next several years. Late in April 1998, Bishop Juan Gerardi Conedera was murdered after the Roman Catholic bishop published a report on army abuses during the long civil war. Many thought the Bishop was bludgeoned to death with a cinder block to warn others not to investigate too deeply into the atrocities committed by the military.

Duvalier Dynasty in Haiti

Haiti, which occupies the western third of the island of Hispaniola, lived through an era even more tumultuous than did the neighboring Dominican Republic. Subjected to humiliating interventions in the 1910s and international ostracism throughout the 1920s and 1930s, Haitians had great difficulty forming stable governments. Moreover, their nation usually ranked near the bottom of the Latin American indices for political, economic, and social development. Few visitors realized the illustrious history of Haiti's people, who had overthrown a slave regime and European colonialism in the 1790s.

A populist government came to power in Haiti in 1946, one devoted to giving blacks a larger voice in government (previously dominated by upper-middle-class mulattoes). The new president, Dumarsais Estimé, sought to provide up-to-date services for poor Haitians, especially in labor relations, public hygiene, and education. He introduced Afro-Haitian culture into his public ceremonies instead of following traditional Catholic rites. When Estimé tried to rig elections to continue in power, however, the general who had installed him stepped in and took control. The country got along fairly well until 1956, when the army withdrew support from the president, and a heated succession campaign ensued.

François Duvalier, a public health doctor and intellectual long active in politics, had been instrumental in the collapse of government in 1956. He then ran for president in 1957 with the backing of the army, promising to bring calm and prosperity. Duvalier organized paramilitary forces to intimidate opponents and assure his victory. His campaign called for the political triumph of *Negritude,* a problack sentiment previously limited to literature and the arts. In reality it meant a return to dictatorship.

Inaugurated as president at the age of fifty, Duvalier had lost the idealism of his youth and ruled instead by terror and coercion. He did not allow organized groups to oppose him, and he declined to call elections. He exalted and manipulated popular culture, including the Afro-Haitian religion Voudon, which he used to win broad acceptance and to intimidate rivals. He also professed sympathies with black nationalism and African liberation movements.

In his consolidation of totalitarian powers, Duvalier cleverly pitted group against group, so that in the end he was the final arbiter. No one doubted, moreover, that death could result from disagreeing with Papa Doc, as he was commonly known. Indeed, a macabre cult of death attached to the paramilitary thugs known

François "Papa Doc" Duvalier (center), president and then dictator of Haiti from the 1950s until his death in 1971, relied on military and paramilitary support. On the right, U.S. envoy Nelson Rockefeller waves to onlookers.

as the *Tontons-macoutes* (bogeymen). It was widely believed that, through Afro-Haitian religious leaders loyal to Duvalier, the *Tontons-macoutes* had turned thousands of persons into zombies, suspended in a state of death-in-life. Myths like these enhanced the power and awe that Papa Doc exercised over most Haitians. The *Tontons-macoutes,* meanwhile, persisted well into the 1990s.

Sadly, Duvalier's earlier commitment to health and education evaporated after he gained power, and the Haitian people suffered terrible deprivations at the hands of labor brokers, sugar planters, corrupt police, and tax collectors. He converted the army into an ineffectual bureaucracy while forming a fearsome palace guard loyal to himself. He attacked and demeaned the Catholic church, allowing it to operate only as an adjunct of the state.

Papa Doc cast himself in the tradition of Haiti's black heroes. A 1964 publication proclaimed, "Dessalines, Toussaint, Petion, Christophe, and Estimé are five distinct Chiefs of State who are substantiated in and form only one and the same President, in the person of François Duvalier." In fact he represented the worst features of the Caribbean dictator. He wasted his tremendous authority and charisma on vain and petty adulation, combined with brutal repression.

In 1971 President-for-Life Duvalier died in office, and his son Jean-Claude (nicknamed Baby Doc) succeeded him. Jean-Claude had never taken his leadership role seriously, instead dabbling in university studies and living well in France. As a result Papa Doc had created a Council of State in the late 1960s to provide continu-

Poverty and unemployment led Haitians to strip their land (left side of the photo) of vegetation in order to farm and graze animals. Across the border (right side of photo) Dominicans left hilly regions in the original forest cover.

ity after his death. Baby Doc allowed the council to run Haiti for a time but soon asserted his influence by firing the chief advisors.

Baby Doc's major interest lay in economic expansion through trade. He courted the U.S. government and won approval to bring in more investors looking for cheap labor. Haiti's elite prospered under the new regime, but wages remained the lowest in the hemisphere. This trend continued under the Caribbean Basin Initiative (CBI) launched by U.S. President Ronald Reagan in 1983. (See Chapter Twenty-five.)

Jean-Claude Duvalier inherited his father's position but not his charisma, and he cared too little about his people to devote himself to their welfare. He married a wealthy socialite (significantly, from the mulatto elite) who spent lavish sums on entertaining and travel. His reign was characterized by cronyism, careless fiscal management, and tolerance for criminal activity. He had no interest in the intellectual pursuit of Negritude or African solidarity.

Government services and the economy stagnated under the Duvalier dynasty, and many things changed, largely for the worse. Population growth soared, taxing the infrastructure and natural resources of the country. Poor people took any jobs that opened, regardless of the pay, and those who could not find jobs cleared small plots of land to farm in the hills. Slash-and-burn cultivation devastated the environment, stripping the country of forest and eroding the fragile mountainous soils. The industrial growth induced by the CBI did not begin to lift the country out of its poverty.

Eventually public disgust with Baby Doc erupted in rioting and demonstrations, abetted quietly by the Catholic church and political activists. In early 1986 he decided that his position was untenable and accepted a U.S. offer to escape into exile. He took up residence in a Paris mansion and lived with his wife and retainers in opulence for the next decade.

In 1986 Haiti reverted to military government, which in fact consisted of an uneasy coalition of armed units, secret police, powerful businessmen, drug traffickers, and corrupt bureaucrats. Pressured by international opinion and rocked by their own instability, the military finally allowed free elections in late 1990. A leftist Roman Catholic priest, Jean-Bertrand Aristide, won and he took office in February 1991.

Aristide's first term was cut short by another military coup in late September led by General Raoul Cédras. This brazen usurpation of power in turn triggered a powerful international reaction led by the United States which imposed a strict economic embargo on Haiti. Thousands of Haitians fled on small, fragile boats bound for the U.S., provoking a crisis in this country which sought to return most of these impoverished exiles back to Haiti. The "boat people" became the focus of a national debate on immigrants for a time in the American press.

Meanwhile the U.S., along with the UN and OAS pressured the military to yield to Aristide and allow him to return. Faced with a possible U.S. military invasion, the Haitian generals yielded in late 1994 and fled the country. Ex-President Jimmy Carter went to Haiti to assist in making this important transition.

Aristide was accompanied by over 20,000 U.S. troops when he returned to his homeland in October 1994. They, along with troops from other member UN countries such as Canada, were there to ensure security and help in the transition to democracy by training an apolitical police force, helping rebuild rural roads, hospitals, and schools, and overseeing fair elections. Aristide himself ended his term in 1996 and was replaced in the presidency by René Préval, a close associate who won the election in December 1995.

Since then, conditions have not improved dramatically in Haiti. Political violence still punctuates the scene as rivals grapple for power. As the UN gradually shrank its presence to a few hundred peacekeepers and observers in 1997–98, violence erupted, as at Cap-Haitien in March 1997. It was so brutal that the UN observers had to be evacuated.

Panama in the Spotlight

No issue so focused Panamanian attention as the U.S.-run Panama Canal. Leased permanently to the United States in 1903 in exchange for protection when Panama separated from Colombia, the Panama Canal Zone became the major bone of contention between Panama and the United States. The canal was, in the words of one observer, "a body of water entirely surrounded by trouble." Twice the two countries had altered the terms of the original concession to benefit Panama (1936 and 1955 treaties), but these did not assuage Panamanian nationalist sentiment. Most Panamanians wanted the United States to provide them with more benefits and eventually turn the canal over to them. They regarded the canal as their natural patrimony. In 1964 students from Panama clashed with their American counterparts in the

The April 1964 flag riots in Panama were begun by U.S. Canal Zone students, who removed a Panamanian flag from its pole. Panamanians responded by desecrating the U.S. flag, touching off fighting that left more than two dozen dead.

Canal Zone, and the incident blossomed into full-blown riots that lasted several days. Twenty-six persons died in the fighting, and the two countries suspended relations.

The following year, the presidents of the two countries appointed negotiating teams to completely rewrite the terms of the canal concession, with an eye to eventually turning the canal over to Panama. They worked out a treaty package but had to shelve it due to political difficulties in both countries.

Panama held elections in mid-1968, leading to the inauguration of the populist veteran Arnulfo Arias on October 1, 1968. Arias had served before as president, in 1940–1941 and 1949–1951, and had been deposed by the military both times. In addition, he had probably won the 1964 election before the results were fixed. His return to the presidency reflected a broad desire among the electorate for change, plus a reluctance of the military to falsify the ballots. Arias quickly disappointed and angered powerful forces, however, and he was again overthrown, after only eleven days in office. A military junta took control of the nation.

After some jockeying for power among the top officers, Colonel Omar Torrijos emerged as head of state, a position that he held until his death in a plane accident in 1981. Like the Arias brothers in the 1930s, Torrijos ushered in new political players and reached out to unrepresented groups, especially small farm owners and workers. Over the long term his politics weakened the hold of the oligarchic families on the reins of government and made the national guard (renamed the Defense Force from 1983 to 1989) the arbiter of power. Torrijos decreed a constitution, a new labor code, lax banking regulations, replacement of the legislature with a council of municipal representatives, and greater government supervision of the economy. In many ways his regime paralleled those described in Chapter Twenty-three.

Torrijos did not believe that the United States had the will to intervene in the Caribbean region unless threatened directly, so he played power politics boldly. He secured Soviet aid, befriended Fidel Castro, helped the Sandinistas, and permitted increased drug traffic through the country. He also courted literary celebrities such as Graham Greene and Gabriel García Márquez. It was an impressive show.

Torrijos's major accomplishment, however, was obtaining new treaties to replace the 1903 Panama Canal Convention. In brief, he badgered U.S. presidents and diplomats long enough and persistently enough to cause them to take up the canal issue seriously. Eventually Torrijos and President Jimmy Carter signed new Panama Canal treaties in 1977. They pledged the two countries to a gradual transfer of operations until December 31, 1999, when Panama is scheduled to take full possession of the canal. The United States exercises a residual protective role after that date.

While the two countries bargained, the United States poured aid and loans into Panama, buoying the economy and allowing Torrijos to triple the government payroll. The country soon topped the ranks of nations in per capita debt, and the economy became distorted by easy money and graft. Drug traffickers paid officials in Panama for the right to land and refuel their planes, and banks profited from laundering their illegal money. Meanwhile, international money flowed into Panama to take advantage of low taxes and banking secrecy. This so-called offshore banking sector boasted assets of

U.S. President Jimmy Carter and Panama's strongman Omar Torrijos shook hands after signing the historic Panama Canal Treaties of 1977 that transferred the Canal to Panama by 1999.

over $30 billion by 1980. Yet, critics pointed out that the apparent prosperity of the Torrijos years was an illusion, built on loans, drugs, and a bloated bureaucracy.

After the treaties were signed, Torrijos stepped back from active leadership and encouraged a civilian puppet president to found the Revolutionary Democratic Party (PRD). The party gradually emerged from a shadowy existence to become a major force in the 1990s.

Conclusions and Issues

The Caribbean basin underwent great turmoil during the decades following World War II. In some regions, the struggles for independence spilled over into internal conflict after nationhood was gained. In others, campaigns for modernization of the economies created social tensions and pressures for reforms. Even Central America, long independent and relatively mature in its political evolution, experienced un-usually intense fighting over a variety of issues. Postcolonial and anti-imperial strug-gles continued for generations.

The countries that defied the United States—Guatemala, Cuba, Nicaragua, and Panama—found themselves under great pressure and often the targets of military in-tervention. The defiance did produce stronger national solidarity but often at tremendous costs in economic and human terms. For better or worse, the United States continued to regard the Caribbean basin as a private preserve and defense zone.

Discussion Questions

1. Costa Rica escaped the violence and instability that gripped the rest of Central America. To what extent was this due to don Pepe Figueres's leadership? How effective was the Caribbean Legion in curbing tyranny in the region?

2. Was the Arbenz government a threat to the United States? Was the CIA operation against Arbenz consistent with international law? Did the overthrow of Arbenz contribute to the civil wars of later decades? How did the overthrow fit into the context of the Cold War?

3. What mix of policies did Papa Doc use to retain power for life in Haiti? Could he honestly claim to be the heir of "Dessalines, Toussaint, Petion, Christophe"?

4. Was the United States right to give in to Panamanian demands for a treaty that would hand over the canal at the end of the century? If so, why? If not, why?

The Cuban Revolution and Its Aftermath

Fidel Castro Addresses the Cuban People in 1959

The black banner, with the date *26 de julio* scrawled in huge red letters, billowed in the wind and swayed out over the crowd gathered in the plaza. A half-million Havana residents and peasants (*guajiros*) waited to hear Fidel speak about the revolution on the anniversary of the famous 1953 attack on Moncada barracks. Only six months had passed since Fidel's forces had triumphed, and Cuba still pulsed with the excitement and expectation that revolution brings. The day was stifling, cooled only by an onshore breeze. Many people unbuttoned their shirts and fanned themselves with hats. A military band played marches in the background. Then the music stopped, and the crowd quieted.

Fidel strode to the podium and grasped the microphone. He was dressed in khaki fatigues and wore the beard that had become a virtual trademark of revolutionaries around the world.

"*Compañeros!*" he shouted. "*La revolución* is not our exclusive property, nor is it only here on this island. Our brothers in Latin America cannot fail to join us. They feel a part of our revolution and will defend it with us. We will not bow to the attacks and calumnies from abroad.

"We must rebuild our island in justice, providing a decent living for the workers and supplying more of our necessities here at home. Much of the island is owned by foreign corporations that have profited for decades. We must convince them to share the wealth with our people." Fidel paused, while the crowd cheered.

"Meanwhile, our government will undo the terrible wrongs committed by the dictator Batista! The corruption, spying, and lazy government have ended. Now public employees are servants of the people, who sacrifice so that everyone may live better. The army, that disgraceful parasite spawned by the dictatorship, is no more. Instead, we have the glorious revolutionary forces who fought for years in the Sierra Maestra mountains to liberate the people." Again the crowd erupted in "Viva Fidel! Viva la revolución!"

"Not all the evils of the past came from within. We must also purge the island of foreign leeches that suck our blood. The Mafia that ran casinos and whorehouses and lotteries and the drug rackets are being eliminated right now. They are not welcome, nor any of their *gusano* collaborators!" He raised and pumped his fist to show his anger.

"The people must recover what is rightfully theirs: homes, jobs, schools, hospitals, land to grow food, and basic human rights. We will give these things to the people, as their revolutionary right. From now on, children will be vaccinated and go to school. Teachers will be the philosophers of the nation. Doctors will work in clinics and hospitals, treating the poor and destitute. Our social security system will take care of the old and the sick. Our agriculture service will teach campesinos to grow more nutritious crops and to raise healthy animals. It is time for Cuba to belong to the Cubanos!" A roar welled up from the massed people below Fidel's platform.

"We hope to cooperate with the United States, our great partner to the north. That is where our forefather, the great martyr José Martí, lived and struggled to bring freedom to our island. And the Americans helped to lift the Spanish yoke, even as they enslaved us with the hated Platt Amendment." He shifted the microphone to his other hand.

"But we ask for American help as an equal, as a brother, not as a weakling. Cuba is strong with revolutionary spirit now and will not suffer demeaning treatment from imperialist powers anywhere. Cuba is now truly independent and will forever remain free: *Por una Cuba libre del imperialismo.*

"If the United States wishes to help the Cuban people and contribute to our crusade for social justice, then they must be willing to invest in Cubans and not just sugar mills. In our houses and clinics, not just the oil refineries. In our schools and roads, not just the power plants. In our shops and farms, not just in big banks. This is the foreign capital we need, to develop ourselves, not simply more investment that exploits our resources and people for the profits of the corporations!"

The crowd cheered, again and again, obviously ecstatic that one of its leaders would finally stand up to the Colossus of the North.

Castro took off his military hat and tossed it over the plaza. His brother Raúl did so, too, and soon the air was thick with flying hats. The atmosphere crackled with enthusiasm, hope, and energy. Castro continued to speak late into the night, with a stamina that became famous. He was articulate, attuned to poor people's aspirations, angry at the injustices of the past, and forceful in his promises to build a better society.

The massive rally marked the sixth anniversary of the start of Castro's movement to overthrow the dictator Fulgencio Batista. Called the "26th of July Movement," it consisted of a guerrilla campaign in the mountains, a strong urban resistance supported by labor and student leaders, and a lively propaganda effort directed toward the middle class and international opinion. Fidel won the battle on January 1, 1959, when Batista abandoned the island to the rebels.

Cuban Revolution

No hemispheric event of the past half-century rivals the Cuban Revolution in terms of impact on Latin American history and international relations. When Fidel Castro led his army into Havana on January 7, 1959, he inaugurated a new age in regional affairs. As the Cuban Revolution turned toward the left and became a Marxist movement, it undermined U.S. hegemony in the hemisphere and spurred the formation of scores of guerrilla forces. Castro himself became a hero and a model for millions of admirers around the world. To his enemies, by the same token, he represented a sinister force. Latin America would not be the same after his accession to power.

Cuba had enjoyed considerable prosperity under the early Batista administrations (strongman 1933–1940, president 1940–1944), but after World War II a malaise settled over the island. To be sure, the economy grew rapidly from tourism and exports, and political freedoms led to intense competition for public office. Cuban disquiet, rather, arose because of massive fraud in the public sector, stifling control of the economy from abroad (mostly the United States), and the growing power of gangsters and criminal bosses in the drug, smuggling, gambling, and prostitution businesses. The disparity between the liberal, egalitarian republic promised in the Constitution of 1940 and real events caused major dissatisfaction on the part of the middle class, intellectuals, and students.

Such was the turmoil in 1952 that Fulgencio Batista came out of his retirement in Florida to run for president and save the country. He promised to clean up politics and restore good government. When the prospects of his winning seemed questionable, he activated his contacts among army generals and simply seized power by force. He then settled in for another long turn at the helm of state. Batista's coup evoked widespread criticism and protest. University students were particularly enraged, claiming that the dictator had violated his own Constitution.

A lawyer and former activist at the University of Havana, Fidel Castro emerged as the leader of a conspiracy to overthrow Batista. Born in 1927 in Oriente province, Fidel had been raised on his father's sugar plantation. His father had emigrated from Spain after having served in the Spanish Army during the war of independence. Fidel's mother had been the family cook.

In 1945 Fidel entered the University of Havana, where he eventually earned a degree in law and gained a large following among student activists. He was tall, handsome, well spoken, and charismatic. In 1947 he launched his revolutionary career by participating in an unsuccessful invasion of the Dominican Republic. While in college he also joined the opposition Ortodoxo Party.

In the course of his travels in the region with other students, Castro had met with the Caribbean Legion group in Costa Rica and with other prodemocracy leaders. He was in Bogotá in April 1948 when Jorge Gaitán died. The violence and looting that followed left a deep impression on him.

When Batista took over the Cuban government in 1952, Fidel decided to mount an armed movement. With smuggled arms and underground contacts with labor unions and disgruntled politicians, Castro's band executed an assault on a secondary base in eastern Cuba, the Moncada barracks. The attack, carried out on July 26, 1953, failed. Many revolutionaries died, and the rest were imprisoned.

Castro used his trial as a forum to speak out against Batista and to establish his reputation as a revolutionary. His basic reformist, nationalist philosophy came out in a famous speech, "History Will Absolve Me," made from the defendant's docket. He called for an end to imperialism, dictatorship, oppression, and corruption, as well as the reinstatement of the 1940 Constitution. The trial proved so popular that the government suspended the proceedings and sent Castro and the other defendants to the Isle of Pines penal colony.

Revolutionary Goals

Fidel Castro enumerated the five revolutionary laws they would have broadcast by radio had they succeeded in capturing Moncada barracks:

The First Revolutionary Law would have returned power to the people and proclaimed the Constitution of 1940 the supreme Law of the land, until such time as the people should decide to modify or change it. And, in order to effect its implementation and punish those who had violated it . . . the revolutionary movement, as the momentous incarnation of this sovereignty, the only source of legitimate power, would have assumed . . . the legislative, executive, and judicial powers. . . .

The Second Revolutionary Law would have granted property, not mortgageable and not transferable, to all planters, sub-planters, lessees, partners and squatters who hold parcels of [160 acres] or less . . . and the state would indemnify the former owners on the basis of the rental which they would have received for these parcels over a period of ten years.

The Third Revolutionary Law would have granted workers and employees the right to share 30 percent of the profits of all the large industrial, mercantile and mining enterprises, including the sugar mills.

The Fourth Revolutionary Law would have granted all planters the right to share 55 percent of the sugar production and a minimum quota of forty thousand arrobas [bushels] for all small planters who have been established for three or more years.

The Fifth Revolutionary Law would have ordered the confiscation of all holdings and ill-gotten gains of those who had committed frauds during previous regimes. . . . Half of the property recovered would be used to subsidize retirement funds for workers and the other half would be used for hospitals, asylums and charitable organizations.

Furthermore, it was to be declared that the Cuban policy in the Americas would be one of close solidarity with the democratic people of this continent, and that those politically persecuted by bloody tyrants oppressing our sister nations would find asylum, brotherhood, and bread in the land of Martí. Not the persecution, hunger and treason that they find today. Cuba should be the bulwark of liberty and not a shameful link in the chain of despotism.

(*History Will Absolve Me* [New York: Lyle Stuart, 1961])

Upon his release in 1955, Castro traveled to Mexico, where he teamed up with other leftists and guerrillas. Ernesto "Che" Guevara, an Argentine physician and revolutionary sympathizer, joined Fidel Castro and his brother Raúl in what would become the core of a new insurgent force. They gathered weapons and money and studied guerrilla tactics with veterans of the Sandino movement in Nicaragua.

By the following year Castro had assembled a company-sized force, and they set out from Mérida, Mexico, for Cuba aboard a cabin cruiser named the *Granma*. They landed at Niquero, on the southeastern coast. Castro expected simultaneous uprisings to occur all over the island to support his invasion. The broader revolt fizzled, however, and Batista's army easily overcame Castro's small force, sending Castro, his brother, Che Guevara, and nine others fleeing into the Sierra Maestra mountains. Many of Castro's companions were killed or wounded in this inauspicious start.

During the next two years the revolution took root, grew, flourished, and finally triumphed. Castro's forces remained mobile at first, in classic guerrilla fashion, then became strong enough to create permanent camps. The local peasants lent support and began to enlist, while sympathizers from other countries joined as well. Castro set up a portable transmitter with which he broadcast his Radio Rebelde calling for insurrection. Foreign observers—visiting to assess the strength and nature of the movement—came away impressed with the ardor and progressive ideas of the youthful leader.

Fidel Castro, about thirty years old, photographed in the Sierra Maestra mountains, where his guerrilla forces challenged the authority of Bastista's army.

Fidel Castro was an appealing figure in his battle to overthrow the Batista dictatorship in the late 1950s, often being interviewed by the U.S. press and eliciting much sympathy from the American public. He turned into the longest lasting dictator of modern Latin America, still in power in 1998, forty years after seizing Havana and establishing a Marxist state.

Much of Castro's success depended on the readiness of many Cubans to support a change of government. Disgruntled employees, students, enlisted men, union members, teachers, and aspiring politicians jumped on the bandwagon and conspired with the *guerrilleros,* making it a truly mass-based movement. In addition, foreign sympathies favored Castro, who was seen as a fresh, honest, devoted reformer pitted against a corrupt dictator. His growing international reputation led the U.S. government to embargo arms shipments to Batista in early 1958, signaling a shift in allegiance. So, although the sides were somewhat lopsided in terms of troop strength, Castro's seven thousand soldiers had the advantages of public support, esprit de corps, battle readiness, and sheer momentum.

In December 1958 Batista ordered an all-out assault on Castro's mountain strongholds. Meanwhile, he promised to raise wages and hold new elections. Both efforts failed miserably. The public was not fooled, and government forces melted away when confronted with withering guerrilla attacks. When it became clear that the battle was lost, Batista and his high command fled the island with as much cash as they could scrape together.

Castro took seven days to march into Havana, consolidating his hold on power by appointing trusted lieutenants as military commanders in the provinces. He ordered the executions of thousands of Batista collaborators, especially those with military records. When he arrived in the capital, Castro was greeted with thunderous welcomes. He disarmed the population and put the irregular forces under the command of his revolutionary army, which his brother Raúl commanded. There was no doubt, then, that he alone controlled the destiny of the nation.

Besides eliminating the old regime through executions, exile, and expropriation, Castro set out to build a new society, one guided by nationalist and socialist principles. He spoke of the "new Cuban man," motivated by love of country and solidarity with fellow citizens, instead of by greed and self-interest. He set out to spread the wealth that had been noticeably concentrated in the hands of rich Cubans and foreigners. Castro spent heavily on school construction, nutrition programs, clinics, public health campaigns, housing, and literacy classes. He called his approach "humanism," which meant "government by the people . . . liberty with bread and without terror." Castro also set out to end Cuba's subservience to the United States. His foreign policy broadened to include interaction with all countries, not just the pro-U.S. allies. In all, it was a strikingly radical approach.

Castro had welcomed help from all sides during the revolution—he even received CIA money channeled through Costa Rica. The core of his coalition, however, was center-leftist in orientation. Some close associates, especially Castro's brother Raúl and Che Guevara, were Marxists who pushed to make Cuba into a communist state. They urged Fidel to join with the Soviet Union and oppose the United States on many fronts. They traveled to Moscow to confer with Premier Nikita Khrushchev, who defied the U.S. leadership in the world and sought to spread Soviet influence. Castro did not claim to be a communist himself until much later (December 1960), but his regime had a distinctly leftist quality from the beginning. He played a dangerous game in the Cold War environment.

By cutting off arms shipments to Batista, the Eisenhower administration had inadvertently helped Castro come to power. Early in 1959, however, the United

Cuban soldiers pinned down CIA-supported invaders on the Bay of Pigs beach (Playa Girón) in 1961, a major embarrassment for the Kennedy administration, which authorized this failed attempt to remove Fidel Castro from power.

States began trying to rein in Castro. Exuberant in his role as leader, Castro refused to cooperate and spoke of nationalizing the sugar industry, the most obvious remnant of imperialism and obstacle to socializing the economy. Other sectors were ripe for nationalization as well. Castro expropriated United Fruit, IT&T, Standard Oil, and other U.S. corporations, causing losses totaling billions of dollars. Soon, an international game of tit-for-tat broke out in which Castro defied the United States and the latter responded with ever-sharper sanctions. In April 1960 Eisenhower finally authorized the CIA to begin training a secret counterrevolutionary exile force in Central America.

The next few years witnessed many bitter confrontations between Cuba and the United States, confrontations that undermined U.S. leadership in international affairs and, in one instance, brought the world to the brink of nuclear war. Yet, paradoxically, the standoff with the United States strengthened Castro's hand and enhanced his fame. Young people and leftists all over the world emulated him by growing beards, wearing army fatigues, planning guerrilla movements, and denouncing the United States. Among sympathizers around the world, Castro and revolution were the future.

One flash point of this era was the Bay of Pigs invasion by Cuban exiles, in April 1961. The CIA, with Eisenhower administration authority, had recruited, trained, financed, and readied an assault force to overthrow Castro. Ostensibly an initiative of Cuban exiles, the assault was in fact a full-blown covert operation by the United States. Still poised to launch when John F. Kennedy was inaugurated, the force awaited its orders. Kennedy, not wishing to appear soft on communism, allowed the assault to go forward. At the last minute, however, he withdrew air support; thus the invaders landed virtually unprotected on the south side of the island. Castro's army, forewarned by spies in Miami, managed to capture the entire force and exposed its sponsorship by the CIA. Kennedy suffered a major humiliation in this incident and began seeking other ways to overthrow Castro.

Another flash point occurred the following year, when Kennedy blockaded Cuba in order to force the Soviets to stop installing intermediate-range nuclear missiles on the island. For several days a U.S.-USSR confrontation seemed imminent, until Khrushchev agreed to withdraw the missiles in exchange for a U.S. pledge not to invade Cuba. The Soviet Politburo removed Khrushchev from power several years after the crisis, and Kennedy's 1963 assassination had indirect links to the U.S.-Cuban confrontation. Castro, on the other hand, managed to dig in and fortify his position in the aftermath of the missile crisis. For the remainder of the 1960s, Castro allied himself more closely with communist leaders in Beijing and eastern Europe and undertook to spread guerrilla war throughout the Third World.

Ernesto "Che" Guevara

Che Guevara, who for a time served as a roving ambassador of revolution, coined a famous phrase in that era: "One, two, many Vietnams!" An Argentine born in Rosario in 1928, Che grew up in a family with aristocratic lineage but little wealth.

Despite his fragile health, Ernesto "Che" Guevara played an important role in early revolutionary leadership in Cuba. He commanded a division during 1958 and then served in the cabinet under Fidel Castro.

The eldest of six siblings, he suffered from asthma from the age of two. Like Teddy Roosevelt, Che fought to overcome his asthma with outdoor living, exercise, and a strong will.

When he was sixteen, the family moved to Buenos Aires, where Che studied at a leading high school and then went on to earn his degree in medicine in 1953. He was an excellent student throughout these years. In the meantime, however, Che had begun traveling in South America to gain a deeper knowledge of the world. He gained an empathy for the poor and sick of the region.

After his graduation, Che set out for even more distant lands, visiting Mexico and Central America. He met a number of leaders in exile who would eventually come to power in their respective countries. Of foremost importance were Fidel and Raúl Castro, who recruited him into their invasion on the *Granma*. One of the few survivors, Che made his way into the mountains to serve as medic and eventually commander. He, Fidel, and Raúl became close over these months. He earned everyone's respect by learning to cope with his asthma in the difficult terrain.

After the triumph of the revolution, Che became a Cuban citizen and headed the industrialization program that Fidel was pushing. He remarried and had four children in Cuba. Along the way he served as president of the national bank, minister of industry, and roving ambassador in search of foreign aid. Moreover, he served as a theorist of the revolution, especially regarding socialist economics and guerrilla warfare. His book on the latter became an instant best-seller all over the world.

Che on Guerrilla Warfare

We consider that the Cuban Revolution contributed three fundamental lessons to the conduct of revolutionary movements in America. They are: 1) Popular forces can win a war against the army; 2) it is not necessary to wait until all conditions for making revolution exist—the insurrection can create them; 3) in underdeveloped America the countryside is the basic area for armed fighting. . . .

The part that the woman can play in the development of a revolutionary process is of extraordinary importance. . . . The woman is capable of performing the most difficult tasks, of fighting beside the men; and despite current belief, she does not create conflicts of a sexual type in the troops. In the rigorous combatant life the woman is a companion who brings the qualities appropriate to her sex, but she can work the same as a man and she can fight; she is weaker, but no less resistant than he. She can perform every class of combat task that a man can at a given moment, and on certain occasions in the Cuban struggle she performed a relief role. . . .

"Know yourself and your adversary and you will be able to fight a hundred battles without a single disaster." This Chinese aphorism is as valuable for guerrilla warfare as a biblical psalm. Nothing gives more help to combatant forces than correct information. This arrives spontaneously from the local inhabitants, who will come to tell its friendly army, its allies, what is happening in various places; but in addition it should be completely systematized. . . . An intelligence service also should be in direct contact with enemy fronts. Men and women, especially women, should infiltrate; they should be in permanent contact with soldiers and gradually discover what there is to be discovered.

(*Che Guevara's Guerrilla Warfare*, translator I. F. Stone [New York: Vintage, 1968], pp. 1, 86, 101)

In 1965 Che disappeared from public view and spent months in the African Congo, applying his theories and training guerrilla leaders. The following year he returned to Cuba to launch another campaign, his most famous (and disastrous) exploit. He began to place soldiers in eastern Bolivia in order to spread revolutionary action among peasants and workers throughout South America. In 1967 he took personal command of the unit. His force was detected by U.S.-trained Bolivian Rangers, however, who tracked him down with sophisticated counterinsurgency equipment. They captured most of the *guerrilleros* and executed Che. The cycle of rural uprisings contracted noticeably afterward.

Global Impact of the Cuban Revolution

Castro's new role as a leader of anti-imperialist movements in the Third World paid off handsomely in money and prestige. The Soviet Union found itself obliged to subsidize the Cuban economy and supply all of the arms required by Castro's growing army. The cost was estimated at over $300 million a year. Meanwhile, Cuban defiance of the United States induced many other Latin American leaders to distance themselves from the United States and follow independent directions in foreign policy. The traditional U.S. political forum in the region, the Organization of American States (OAS), consequently lost influence. In the early 1970s rival leaders almost took control of the OAS in the name of ideological pluralism. Castro was definitely the inspiration for this rebellion against U.S. control.

The United States attempted to win back hemispheric influence in the 1960s through a carrot-and-stick combination of foreign assistance and military repression. In 1961 President Kennedy launched an ambitious, wide-ranging, and sometimes confusing program called the Alliance for Progress, designed to strengthen cooperation and mutual security among the republics of the Americas. The Alliance responded directly and obviously to Castro's revolution. It especially appealed to progressive leaders in Latin America who sought social and economic reforms

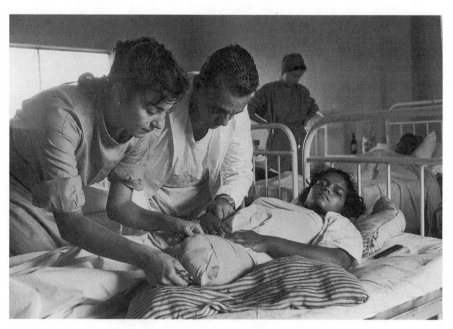

Two volunteers in the U.S. Peace Corps treat a patient in a Latin American clinic. The Peace Corps, begun in 1961, proved an effective way to give idealistic young Americans an intense overseas experience in developing countries.

within a democratic framework. Kennedy's program was widely hailed—perhaps naively, in retrospect—as a new beginning for Latin American-U.S. cooperation. For a time it gave the United States an opportunity to renew its leadership.

The military side of the alliance focused on the Caribbean basin, thought to be especially vulnerable to communist insurgencies. Working with military governments in Guatemala, Honduras, El Salvador, Nicaragua, and the Dominican Republic, the United States sponsored training and rearmament programs to combat guerrilla movements. Various strategies were developed, including civic action, counterinsurgency, jungle warfare, and police training. Modern, professional armies in the region were expected to respect normal civilian dissent while combating communist subversion. In fact, most regimes became more efficient dictatorships.

The struggle between military and insurgent forces escalated in the late 1960s, with the appearance of urban guerrilla movements in major cities. These may have been inspired by Castro's revolution, but they took entirely different approaches, relying on subterfuge, publicity, clandestine organization, and terrorism. Brazil's Carlos Marighella literally wrote the book on this style of warfare, which he pioneered. Called *The Mini-Manual of the Urban Guerrilla* (1969), Marighella's work stressed organizing secret, independent cells that could resist attacks by government agents. Urban guerrillas sought to provoke authorities into repression and abuse of the citizenry. They stopped short, however, of causing the government to unleash an all-out assault on the movement. Eventually the people would tire of the government and support a revolution by the guerrillas. This new challenge, impossible without the lead of Cuba, induced a wave of military takeovers in South America, to be discussed in Chapter Twenty-four.

By 1970 Castro's revolution had begun to falter and required a renewal. For one thing, the promise of a high-income, independent, industrial economy had failed, and the country reverted to its dependence on exports of primary goods (sugar, tobacco, nickel) in exchange for petroleum and manufactures. The Soviet Union subsidized Cuba heavily, causing accusations that Castro had merely traded one imperial sponsor (the United States) for another (the Soviet Union). To be sure, the general welfare of the population had improved measurably: Cuba's literacy, nutrition, schooling, housing, and health were among the best in the hemisphere by 1970. Yet, in some respects little had changed. No elections were held, old-fashioned machinery held down productivity, imported technology worked poorly in the tropical environment, and political control was as tightly centralized as it had been under Batista. Castro tried to raise morale (and deflect criticism) with a crusade to harvest ten million tons of sugar cane in 1970. The effort failed, and some Cubans began to lose faith in the regenerative power of the revolution.

Since the 1970s Castro has largely reacted to external stimuli and made small adjustments domestically. He maintained an active foreign presence in Africa during the period of decolonization but pulled back in the 1990s, with the end of the Cold War. He promulgated a constitution that set up a system of regional councils to spread power more broadly than the Communist Party had done. Yet, all high-level decisions and appointments continued to flow from Castro himself.

Dominican Intervention

In April 1965 twenty-four thousand U.S. armed troops landed outside of Santo Domingo, the capital of the Dominican Republic. They put down a rebellion and settled in for a year-long occupation. Some observers believed that the invasion prevented a revolution like Fidel Castro's from occurring. For better or worse, the United States would not allow a second communist government in the area.

The background of the invasion encompasses the regime of Rafael Trujillo, which lasted from the 1930s until his assassination in 1961. (See Chapter Sixteen.) The U.S. CIA had favored bringing down Trujillo because policymakers feared that if Trujillo continued in power a broader movement like Castro's would emerge. With financial aid and coaxing from the State Department, the Dominican political elite created a democratic government and held presidential elections in 1962. The winner was Juan Bosch, a fifty-one-year-old novelist and longtime conspirator against Trujillo. Bosch had founded an opposition party, the Dominican Revolutionary Party (PRD, 1939—), while in exile. For almost half of his life—twenty-three years—Bosch had lived abroad, waiting, planning, plotting against the dictator.

When Bosch took office in February 1963, he was an intellectual out of touch with local politics and overly sanguine about reforming the country. He immediately changed the name of the capital from Ciudad Trujillo back to its original Santo Domingo, then set to work on a constitution. The new Constitution, ratified in July, separated Church and state, legalized divorce, and set maximum expenditures for the armed forces. Another controversial measure transformed the massive Trujillo family holdings into state enterprises, a kind of instant state capitalism. Many businessmen and old families, hoping to buy the holdings cheaply, were angered by the move. As it was, bribery and influence peddling, rampant in the pre-1961 government, continued under Bosch.

The U.S. ambassador strongly supported Bosch, despite the latter's initial stumbling, but U.S. military attachés in the embassy did not, thinking that the leftists and communists in the PRD were a security threat. Only seven months into the new government, the top army general, Elías Wessin y Wessin, decided to remove Bosch. A staunch Catholic and anticommunist, Wessin y Wessin believed that Bosch would lead the country down the road to Marxism and dissolution. So Bosch went into exile again—not an unfamiliar move for the old battler—and the military assumed control.

The army installed a mild-mannered civilian, Donald Reid Cabral, to reverse course and sell off the Trujillo properties. He reinstated the Church-state alliance and ordered communists jailed again. Liberal aid and a bigger quota of U.S. sugar imports helped wealthy families gain control over the economy. Meanwhile, exiled opponents rallied to the PRD and plotted their return to power.

In November 1963 Lyndon Johnson succeeded to the U.S. presidency and devoted much more attention than his predecessor, John Kennedy, to domestic affairs. His advisor for Latin America policy, Thomas Mann, made it clear that U.S. business interests and national security would be his chief concerns. He would not automatically deny recognition to military governments and might in fact welcome them

Lyndon B. Johnson (President, 1963–69) sent troops into the Dominican Republic in 1965 to prevent what advisers claimed could become a "second Cuba."

if they followed pro-U.S. policies. The stick approach in the Alliance for Progress would definitely prevail over the carrot.

In the Dominican Republic, opposition to Reid Cabral was widespread, involving some army units, exiles, politicians, and leftist groups of many sorts. In April 1965 a revolt broke out among junior officers and quickly spread to slum districts in Santo Domingo. The bulk of the army remained loyal, under Wessin y Wessin's command, but street fighting threatened order in the city. When the U.S. ambassador could not give Reid Cabral any assurances about bringing in U.S. troops, Reid Cabral abandoned the country, and the rebels took the palace. A desultory artillery duel between Cabral's forces and the rebels broke out on the outskirts of Santo Domingo. At this point the U.S. ambassador called President Johnson and requested troops, which were ordered in almost immediately.

Johnson did not know if a communist takeover was imminent, but he believed that even the slightest hint of Marxism might undermine his position at home and his growing commitment to the Vietnam War. Therefore, he decided to intervene and freeze events in the Dominican Republic. On television he said, "The American nation cannot, must not, and will not permit the establishment of another communist government in the Western Hemisphere. . . . " Later it became clear that no communist threat existed and that the OAS had not given its prior authorization. The troop total reached twenty-four thousand, and the fighting soon ended. As in Guatemala in 1954, a reformist revolution that might have been was quashed by U.S. action.

After several months of negotiations, a civilian caretaker government was set up, and elections were scheduled for mid-1966. When the ballots were counted, a veteran of the Trujillo regime, Joaquín Balaguer, emerged the clear victor over candidate Bosch. A canny fifty-nine-year-old lawyer and statesman, Balaguer promised peace, stability, and jobs, and he managed to deliver, with generous help from the United States. Having lived in exile since 1963, he was seen as untainted by the revolt and invasion.

Balaguer's first three terms, lasting twelve years, proved successful, in part due to U.S. assistance, and the rancor of the past faded. Very gradual reforms modernized the capital, and high sugar profits trickled down among the people. The old part of the capital was restored for tourism, which peaked during the 1992 commemoration of Columbus's first voyage to the New World.

Balaguer stepped down from the presidency for two terms but left the PRD in control of the country. Party rivals were unable to transfer Balaguer's popularity to themselves, so the former president exercised power from behind the scenes. He stood for reelection in 1986 and managed to hang on through the mid-1990s, a remarkable case of political longevity. Bosch also remained active at the head of a new party but did not manage to win any elections.

Balaguer's principal opponent in 1994, former Santo Domingo Mayor José Francisco Peña Gómez, accused Balaguer of rigging the election. International observers there confirmed widespread irregularities. In the resultant crisis, Balaguer agreed to hold new elections with outside monitoring.

The 1996 election pitted Peña Gómez, who was ailing from prostate cancer, against Leonel Fernández, a young PRD figure whom Balaguer had groomed for his replacement. Surprisingly, Bosch, the perennial rival of Balaguer, also supported Fernández. The PRD swept the election, deemed fair by observers, and took office shortly afterward. Peña Gomez passed away in 1998.

Sandino's Revenge in Nicaragua

The longest family dynasty in modern Latin American history, that of the Somozas, came to an end in 1979, felled by a grass-roots revolution. The revolution was led by the Sandinista Front for National Liberation (FSLN, 1961—), which took its name from Augusto Sandino, whose guerrilla forces in the early 1930s stymied both the Nicaraguan and U.S. armies. Sandino had eventually been betrayed and murdered (see Chapter Fifteen), but some of his followers survived. Several Nicaraguan youths, inspired by these tales, named their liberation movement after Sandino. Unfortunately for them, Cold War tensions in the Caribbean basin made such movements targets for suppression.

Shortly after forming the FSLN, about twenty would-be-revolutionaries established a base camp in the mountains of northwest Nicaragua. A Sandino veteran, Santos López, introduced them to the terrain and taught them guerrilla strategy and tactics. For years the FSLN led a precarious existence, losing battles and soldiers but learning the skills of warfare. In 1963, for example, the FSLN recruited a peasant force that was devastated by the national guard. In 1966 it launched an urban guerrilla campaign and was again smashed by government forces. After each defeat the FSLN retreated into the mountains of the North to plan its next actions.

In the early 1970s the FSLN began to split into factions, more or less following the preferences of its leaders. One faction favored political action to raise money and arms for its rural colleagues. Another followed the pure route of the *foco* (small guerrilla operation) favored by Che Guevara. A third sought out workers and students for urban guerrilla activities. This natural split produced rivalries but also created a flexibility and resourcefulness not available before.

The FSLN also benefited indirectly from the 1972 earthquake that devastated Managua. The Somoza regime so bungled the rescue and relief efforts that it alienated most Nicaraguans. For example, Red Cross blood was withheld from clinics and later resold to foreign countries for profit. Moreover, high officials refused to move the capital—located in the most intense fault zone in Central America—because they owned most of the land there. The rubble where downtown Managua had stood, therefore, became a constant reminder of the profiteering that Somoza and his henchmen had indulged in.

From 1975 the struggle intensified on both sides, and the FSLN suffered major defeats and demoralization. Yet, the years of fighting, plus declining support for the corrupt regime, gradually led the international community to condemn Somoza and to call for a negotiated settlement. The United States, long a major backer of Anastasio (Tachito) Somoza, decided to withdraw aid in 1978 and to pressure him to leave office. Other countries, including Cuba, Venezuela, and Panama, sent arms and aid to the Sandinistas. Somoza refused to budge, however, and unleashed more terror against the guerrillas, completing the alienation of international observers and Nicaraguan elites. The end was near.

In the spring of 1979 even the OAS voted to urge Somoza to step down, and several countries severed relations with him to express their displeasure. The FSLN, having reached an agreement to coordinate its separate commands, then launched an all-out offensive. Its forces encroached on the suburbs of Managua and threatened Somoza's infamous bunker headquarters downtown. At this point the United States sent an emissary to convince Somoza to resign, and he finally agreed in July. He fled the country and took up exile in Paraguay, the guest of another dictator, General Alfredo Stroessner. The following year Somoza was assassinated by Uruguayan guerrillas.

The Sandinistas quickly consolidated their hold on the country and began to restore order. Some forty thousand to fifty thousand people had died in the fighting. Strikes and battles had knocked out a large share of the nation's industry. Perhaps 150,000 people crowded into refugee camps, and another 120,000 had fled into neighboring countries. Farms had been abandoned and roads destroyed. The cleanup alone loomed as a formidable job.

The provisional government was composed of a nine-person board with representatives of all the major revolutionary factions. The Sandinistas held a majority of the seats and naturally dominated its decision making. Their program reflected the coalition nature of the junta: They called for good government, land reform, nationalization of Somoza-owned property, higher pay and benefits to workers, encouragement of unionization, broader access to basic services, rent control, more schools, democratic procedures, equality for women, nonaligned foreign policy, and an overhaul of the army. The program was left of center but by no means Marxist.

Nationalization of the Somoza holdings sounded like a simple way to spread the benefits of the economy, yet it also proved divisive. The government immediately became a major landlord and employer by controlling 41 percent of the capital stock of the nation. Meanwhile, foreign and domestic businessmen decided not to reinvest profits until the long-term plans of the Sandinistas were clear. Thus their machinery and buildings gradually deteriorated in value, while the owners pushed production to the maximum to extract profits from their plants. As the value of existing private investment declined, the government share of ownership increased.

The Sandinistas immediately adopted a foreign policy featuring broader ties with communist bloc nations, especially Cuba and the USSR. They called this "ideological pluralism" and vowed to respect the rights of all political groups. In their zeal, however, they exercised some censorship and stifled critics. This shift in policy raised Cold War concerns in Washington.

The United States quickly recognized the Sandinista government and pledged $75 million to help rebuild the country. Very soon, however, relations cooled as the new government began paying off favors received from guerrilla organizations in neighboring countries and forged stronger ties with Cuba. The election of Ronald Reagan to the U.S. presidency in November 1980 further undermined U.S.-Nicaraguan cooperation. Reagan and Congress, pointing to Sandinista gun-running to Salvadoran guerrillas, canceled the aid program and vetoed loans from international banks. They cut the sugar quota and enacted economic sanctions.

A more direct threat soon emerged. The CIA began training counterrevolutionary forces (called the Contras) to harass or even invade Nicaragua. Many Contras were former national guard officers. Ronald Reagan supported this and other assaults, in what became a fixation for him. The Sandinista leadership had largely de-

Daniel Ortega led the Sandinista coalition during its years in power (1979–90), then attempted unsuccessfully to win election as president. Mural art like that in the background sought to inspire the people to support schools and education.

volved to Daniel Ortega by that time, and the young leader took up the challenge with vigor. A clandestine war broke out in Central America that for years defied mediation. (See Chapter Twenty-five.)

The Contra War sapped the vigor of the Sandinista revolution and starved the nation's recovery from the struggles of the 1970s. It kept the populace on constant alert and robbed the economy of labor and investment. In the end the Contra War also undermined the second Reagan administration because presidential advisors were implicated in illegal activities against the Nicaraguan government, the so-called Iran-Contra scandal. The sorry spectacle ended only when President Oscar Arias Sánchez of Costa Rica negotiated a peace agreement in 1987, for which he received the Nobel Peace Prize.

President Oscar Arias Sánchez of Costa Rica won the Nobel Peace Prize in 1987 for leading his neighboring countries into a regional peace treaty that year.

Conclusions and Issues

Throughout the Caribbean region, long-festering disputes among elites, grinding poverty, and anti-American feelings produced tensions of volcanic proportions. Cubans felt these tensions deeply and heeded the call to revolution in the 1950s. Fidel Castro proved a brilliant leader, able to elicit loyalty from followers while broadcasting an appealing message to the world. His guerrilla campaign in the Sierra Maestra in 1957 and 1958 served as inspiration to tens of thousands of young people desirous of change.

Once in power, Castro learned that he could not achieve as much as he promised, partly because the U.S. government and private investors exercised broad control over the island. He set about to free the island, angering the United States. He then struck a deal with the Soviet Union for economic and strategic aid. By 1960 Cuba had become the hottest spot in the Cold War.

Two confrontations in 1961 and 1962—the Bay of Pigs invasion and the Cuban Missile Crisis—nearly caused a war between the superpowers. When the crises subsided, Castro turned his attention to spreading guerrilla warfare throughout the Third World. A number of governments, and many would-be revolutionaries, took seriously the possibility of broad-based insurgencies led by communists. Established regimes and their military backers feared such an outcome, and revolutionaries welcomed it.

When instability in the Dominican Republic led to a civil war in April 1965, the U.S. government quickly sent a large force into the island to quell the fighting. Although not a full-scale revolution, the civil war might have led to more progressive elements coming to power. As it was, the United States stabilized politics and backed a figure from the Trujillo dictatorship, Joaquín Balaguer. Soon the new regime got on its feet and remained in control of the country until the 1990s, usually with Balaguer as president. Meanwhile, the knee-jerk invasion by the United States served warning to other leaders that definite limits existed. The gunboats were back under a new flag: the Truman Doctrine (containment of communism) instead of the Roosevelt Corollary (Caribbean security).

Yet another insurgency arose in the region—this one in the mountains and cities of Nicaragua. Invoking the cause of Augusto Sandino from the 1930s, young revolutionaries of the FSLN challenged the long dynasty of the Somoza family. For fifteen years the FSLN fought sporadically, unable to make progress against the U.S.-backed regime there. Finally, however, in the mid-1970s the tide began to turn, and Somoza went on the defensive. A tactical alliance among several guerrilla movements made it possible for the FSLN to surround and then capture the capital of Managua in 1979. The last Somoza president fled into exile and was assassinated shortly afterward.

The Sandinista government faced trenchant opposition from the United States, which launched a counterinsurgency force against it. The conflict finally ended in 1987, leaving the country more bankrupt than ever. The 1990s brought peace but continued political instability.

Discussion Questions

1. Why did the Cuban Revolution have such a powerful impact on international relations? How did the United States figure into the motives and drives of the Cuban revolutionaries? What could the United States have done to avoid the dangerous drift and confrontations of the 1960–1962 period?

2. The decision to invade the Dominican Republic in 1965 had local, hemispheric, and global calculations. How did they influence the outcome of the invasion?

3. The Sandinista movement, once in power, always walked a delicate line between revolution and reform. How did Cuba and the United States influence the path of the FSLN during the 1980s? How do the accomplishments in Nicaragua compare with those in Cuba?

The National Security States

1980s Military Investigation in Montevideo

A black sedan skidded around a street corner and braked sharply in front of a plain, two-story house on the outskirts of Montevideo, Uruguay. Its headlights switched off, and four large men, dressed in dark clothing, jumped out. They carried military-issue pistols. One ran to the rear of the house, and the other three positioned themselves in front. The one closest to the front door knocked, then kicked down the door, and all three rushed in with their pistols drawn. Screams pierced the night air, two shots rang out, and the man who had knocked on the door dragged a woman out by her hair onto the stoop. The other two brought out an older man and a boy, both at gunpoint. The man who had gone to the rear came to join them.

The man who had dragged out the woman released her hair, and she fell back, holding her scalp and crying. The man shouted at her, "Where is Díaz?"

"I don't know. He left a week ago," she cried.

The man grabbed her arm and twisted it behind her until she screamed. "I'll break this arm if you don't tell me! We know you saw him yesterday. We have your telephone tapped." The woman sobbed and shook her head "no."

One of the other men stepped forward. "We know you're lying," he said. "If you don't tell us, we'll take the boy and cut off his arms and legs. You'll never see him again. Do you want that?"

"No," the woman pleaded, "I can't tell you because I don't know. Don't hurt the boy, please. He doesn't know anything, I swear." Her eyes flitted back and forth between her captors, then fell on the terrified boy.

"Then tell us who else you saw yesterday," the first man said. "Everyone. If we find you are lying, we'll take the boy and the old man. And we'll take you to our headquarters. You have to give us twenty names for each of these two—otherwise you will never see them again."

"But I don't know anyone. I'm just a teacher," she sobbed.

The man twisted her arm more, and she cried out, "Stop, I'll tell you, but nobody did anything wrong. They're only my friends and relatives. They never broke any laws. Please don't hurt them."

"Talk fast, into this recorder, or I'll break your arm anyway. Quick!"

Sobbing, the woman began naming her brothers and sisters, her cousins, her co-workers, her aunts and uncles, her neighbors, her deceased parents, her godfather and godmother, her local priest. She grew hysterical as she spoke. The men taped her voice and prodded her when she slowed down. One of them spoke: "Come on, that's only thirty-five! Give us five more if you want to save these two!"

She shook her head in bewilderment and spoke the names of her supervisors, her babysitters, and a local grocer. Then the man released her arm, and she fell to the ground, sobbing uncontrollably.

The second man looked at the old man and the boy. "This didn't happen," he said. "You didn't see anything. If we hear that you spoke with anyone about this, you'll disappear. We have your house bugged and your car under surveillance. You cannot escape us or fool us. We have confessions from your neighbors, saying that you are helping the guerrillas. You are accomplices, and we could take you in right now. You have violated the National Security Laws and could be put to death. Your only hope is that we find Díaz and the other rebel outlaws by talking with the people you named. You better be absolutely silent about this or we'll come back, and then you'll be sorry!"

Finished, the four men got back into the car and drove away, leaving the stunned family members huddled on the porch of their home.

Their lives had been invaded, perhaps more forcefully than if their home had been bombed. They would never forget the night's visit by security police. It was the beginning of a nightmare, part of what the Argentines called the *guerra sucia* (dirty war) that military regimes throughout South America waged against their own citizens in the name of national security. Before it was over, tens of thousands of people died at the hands of police and military agents.

Beginning in the 1960s, a new type of military regime appeared in South America. These regimes, concentrated in the Southern Cone (Argentina, Uruguay, Chile, and Brazil) had much in common with one another, yet they bore little resemblance to traditional dictatorships in the region. Instead, the generals who led them were middle-aged career officers who preferred to remain aloof from politics, or in the words of some analysts, antipolitical. They tended to avoid the limelight and often remained anonymous. Most were army men, but several naval admirals took part as well. The few who stood out in public memory had frightening images and evoked fear in the citizenry. This generation of officers left a dreadful legacy of repression, torture, and death.

Table 24–1 Generals of the Late 20th Century

Country	Name	Years in Power	Born	Class	Urban Rural	Race	Ed	Age @ 1st/off	Mil?	Foreign Influence	Died	@ Age
Argentina	Levingston	1970–71	1920	middle		wh	mil	50	Y	Y		
	Lanusse	1971–73	1918	middle	U	wh	mil	53	Y	Y		
	Videla	1976–81	1924	middle	U	wh	mil	52	Y			
	Viola	1981	1924	middle		wh	mil	57	Y	Y		
	Galtieri	1981–82	1926	middle	U	wh	mil		Y	Y		
Brazil	Castello Branco*	1964–67	1897	middle	U	wh	mil		Y	Y	1967	70
	Costa e Silva*	1967–69	1902	middle	R	wh	mil	65	Y	Y	1969	67
	Médici	1969–74	1905	middle	R	wh	mil	64	Y	Y	1985	79
	Geisel	1974–79*	1908	middle	R	wh	mil	66	Y	Y		
	Figueiredo	1979–85	1918	middle	U	wh	mil	61	Y	Y		
Chile	Frei**	1964–70	1911	middle	U	wh	law	35	n	Y	1982	71
	Allende**	1970–73	1908	middle	U	wh	med	29	n	Y	1973	65
	Pinochet	1973–90	1915	middle	U	wh	mil	58	Y	Y		
Peru	Velasco Alvarado	1968–75	1910	lower?	U	mes?	mil	58	Y	Y	1977	67

*Participated in Italian Campaign during WWII

**Civilian presidents

Source: *Encyclopedia of Latin American History and Culture* and authors' research.

New Military Missions

Historians disagree over whether guerrilla movements arose in opposition to the military or vice versa. The 1950s witnessed several insurgencies in Latin America, and military planners in the United States and abroad devoted increasing attention to counterinsurgency strategies and jungle warfare training. On the other hand, many military dictatorships existed before serious guerrilla activity began. Some historians argue that tyrannical governments sparked the rise of armed opposition movements. Regardless of which came first, however, all analysts agree that the 1960s moved the struggle between these two forces toward a climax. In most cases the military won and established powerful dictatorships. By the 1990s Cuba was the only country in the hemisphere under revolutionary or Marxist leadership.

The new military regimes are often called the "national security states" because of their dedication to domestic order above all other goals. During the 1950s and 1960s, military planners, especially in the Southern Cone countries, began developing a new mission for their armed forces. The Cold War standoff between the United States and the USSR and the advent of nuclear weapons meant that the Latin American militaries would probably never become engaged in major armed conflicts. Instead, they saw armed insurgencies such as those in eastern Europe, Asia, and Africa as the most likely challenges to their institutions. Rather than face external enemies, in other words, they would most likely have to face internal threats to security. Therefore, they reorganized their defenses to ward off communist takeovers from within.

The new military doctrine, taught in the general staff colleges of Argentina, Brazil, Chile, and elsewhere, was derived in part from U.S. training programs. Tens of thousands of Latin American officers received training in the School of the Americas, located in the Panama Canal Zone until 1983. Gradually, not only the doctrine but also a solidarity spread among officers throughout the hemisphere, and a kind of inter-American military brotherhood developed. The armed forces invited one another to training programs, joint maneuvers, defense planning, weapons plants, and intelligence sessions. The common enemies of the new military were rural or urban-based Marxist insurgencies.

The national security doctrine further stipulated that the armed services had to go beyond military preparedness in their fight against communism. The best defense against communism was a well-run, prosperous country, in which every citizen had a job, a home, and a decent living. Unfortunately, many Latin American countries had corrupt and incompetent civilian leaders who unwittingly allowed communists to take over. Whether they called themselves "socialists," "populists," or "liberals," many of these civilian leaders represented a serious threat to stability, the generals argued.

It took only a short step in logic to conclude that in many cases the armed services themselves could run their countries more efficiently than could civilians. They had professional training, a sense of discipline, and a dedication to the national well-being. Once in power, the new military could boost economic development and pursue counterinsurgency programs without interference from civilians.

The populace would applaud their cool, competent management of the nation. Thus the Cold War scenario had a very peculiar impact on the missions of the Latin American military, broadening them to include nation building.

Argentina

Argentina had the dubious distinction of developing the first national security state. From the mid-1950s, that country's armed forces viewed civilian leadership and leftist politics as dangerous to the national welfare. In 1955 they overthrew the elected government of Juan Perón and installed a military regime that lasted three years. In 1962 they replaced the duly elected administration of Arturo Frondizi with one acceptable to the generals. After another flirtation with democracy, they replaced the civilian president with General Juan Carlos Onganía in 1966. He served four years and was followed by two other generals, Roberto Levingston (1970–1971) and Alejandro Lanusse (1971–1973). No one doubted that the generals ruled Argentina throughout the 1960s.

Each intervention by the army ratcheted up the level of confrontation between civilian and military elements. Students always protested takeovers, and the army responded by shutting down the universities. Unions struck against economic austerity measures that cut the income of workers, and the military outlawed strikes. The confrontations escalated in severity as the decade wore on. For example, the *Cordobazo* of 1969, a forty-eight-hour general strike in the industrial city of Córdoba, left a bloody toll of dead and wounded among protesters and police alike.

Meanwhile, writers and artists denounced censorship, and they suffered more repression and controls on expression. The military increasingly divided the citizenry into friends and foes. The latter constituted threats to the security of the state and were considered enemies.

By 1973 the level of confrontation between the government and opposition reached alarming levels. Labor federations routinely shut down the economy with general strikes. Several powerful guerrilla movements, operating in the major cities and some rural areas, kidnapped and ransomed foreign businessmen, robbed banks, and committed other acts of terrorism at will. The tension between the government and its citizens began to resemble a civil war.

Part of the reason for the impasse in Argentine politics was the persistence of a strong Peronist movement, accounting for about 25 percent of the electorate. The military had exiled Perón and prevented his party from running in elections, but it could not erase the loyalty that his followers gave him. No other party could win a working majority in Congress nor govern the country effectively without Peronist support. Yet the generals who had exiled Perón could not imagine allowing him to return. Perón represented the worst aspects of civilian politicians, those that the generals had vowed to purge. So they could not work with him, yet they could not govern without him.

For his part, Perón behaved as something of a spoiler from his exile in Madrid. He encouraged his followers to resist the military and did not allow them to form coalitions nor any other leader to emerge from the Peronist ranks. He did nothing to discourage the terrorist groups who operated in his name, especially the Montoneros, known as the "armed wing of Peronismo." Especially ominous was the 1973 merger of the Montoneros with another guerrilla group, the Revolutionary Armed Forces, into the single largest clandestine army in the hemisphere. The more chaotic Argentina became, the more likely it was that the army would have to call Perón back to save the country.

In 1972 General Alejandro Lanusse decided to deal with the Peronist dilemma once and for all. He opened negotiations with Perón to let him return and run for president if he would commit to ending the guerrilla warfare being waged in his name. Perón agreed, and a hastily called election allowed one of his aides to assume the presidency. El Líder's return to Argentina, after an eighteen-year exile, was greeted with savage battles among the various armed groups operating in his name. His plane had to be rerouted to another airport for security. It was an inauspicious sign.

Lanusse's gamble with Perón operated on two levels. If the aging populist could really end the guerrilla struggle, the Argentine army would be rid of its most formidable challenge in 170 years of national history. On the other hand, if he failed (and he was showing all of his seventy-eight years) he would be discredited among his followers and no longer able to prevent other leaders from taking strong positions in national politics. Either way, it seemed, the military would benefit.

Unfortunately for Lanusse, neither scenario played out. Instead, Perón proved quite successful during the year he served as president before abruptly dying of natural causes. He reduced inflation by browbeating unions and employers into signing a social pact under which wages and prices were stabilized and labor's share of national income was restored to 1950 levels. He succeeded in attenuating the guerrilla struggle, partly by stepping up counterterrorist operations, many of them illegal and brutal. The federal police seemed to be coordinating these efforts, called the Argentine Anticommunist Alliance (Triple A). Meanwhile, Perón spent his last months basking in the adulation he so craved.

Perón's third wife, María Estela "Isabelita" Martínez de Perón, elected vice president in 1973, succeeded her husband upon his death. In 1951 the army had vetoed Perón's attempt to have his wife Evita run as vice president, but this time the army acquiesced. Isabelita Perón became president in July 1974.

The army now faced what it saw as the worst of all worlds: a female commander-in-chief with little experience and less authority, intensification of the guerrilla warfare, collapse of the economic truce and development program, and constitutional limitations on the army's counterterrorist operations. The generals pressured Isabelita to allow them to respond vigorously, so she put her close advisor and confidant, José López Rega, in charge of antisubversive activities. Officially minister of social welfare, López Rega actually coordinated the Triple A campaign of surveillance, torture, kidnapping, rape, and murder of leftists, later known as the "dirty war." Government death squads unleashed horrors against the civilian population in order to crush the guerrilla organizations.

For more than a year and a half the military tolerated the awkward situation that Isabelita Perón created for them. Because Juan Perón had died while enjoying the full sway of his popularity, the military had to wait until Isabelita proved herself incapable of governing the country. By March 1976 Isabelita's regime was no more than a shell, so the army removed her and took power in the name of national security. The evolution of the national security state was nearly complete.

The generals who assumed power in 1976, men in their mid-fifties, had no intention of returning government to civilians until they had purged the country of communists, guerrillas, and leftist sympathizers. Their goal of purifying the country became a sacred mission, more profound than mere doctrine.

General Jorge Videla served for five years as head of the military government. He pulled out all the stops in the dirty war against the guerrillas. Although barbaric beyond all reckoning, it nonetheless succeeded after about three years. By then virtually no paramilitary group could resist the army's power, and few even attempted to do so.

The legacy of the dirty war, in suffering, psychic torment, broken families, and death, haunted Argentina through the 1990s. Estimates of the number of persons "disappeared" by the military alone run to thirteen thousand. Perhaps the real number was double that. No accounting can ever be made of the other human losses incurred in the dirty war. For many years afterward, *las madres* (the mothers) of missing persons paraded weekly in Buenos Aires's Plaza de Mayo demanding news of their loved ones. The story has been retold countless times in documentaries, feature movies, novels, and biographies. American audiences saw the worst aspects of the dirty war dramatized in films like *Only the Emptiness Remains* (1984), about the *madres,* and *The Official Story* (1986), about elite attempts to cover up complicity in the reign of terror.

Description of las Madres by U.S. Journalist in Buenos Aires

They would not go away, those pushy women circling the Plaza de Mayo silently, as if under water, photographs of their sons, daughters and husbands swinging on chains from their necks like good-luck charms. Sometimes the women would bear the photographs on placards; sometimes they would hold a snapshot delicately out in front of them between the index finger and the thumb, presenting unassailable proof to anyone who cared to look that the subject of the picture did, at one time, exist. Every Thursday the Mothers of Plaza de Mayo performed their half-hour ritual across the street from the presidential Pink House, and then dispersed for a week. But they would not go away. In many of the photographs the children posed formally, in dresses and coats and ties. In several, they looked saucy before the camera. That was in better days, before the subjects came to be counted among the *desaparecidos*: thousands, possibly tens of thousands of men, women and children who, as alleged enemies of the state, disappeared under the military government of Argentina in the late 1970s.

(Roger Rosenblatt, "Things That Do Not Disappear," *Time,* 123:74 [January 23, 1984], p. 74)

Las Madres marching in the Plaza de Mayo in Buenos Aires, protesting the "disappearances" of their sons and daughters during the dirty war.

The military did not succeed in its attempts to revive the economy. Inflation continued at high levels, unemployment soared, and the GNP actually shrank several years in a row. The principal reason for poor economic performance was the austerity program designed to wring inflation out of the currency before beginning privatization and expansion. Unfortunately, just when the Argentine economy showed signs of growing again, the 1980–1982 world recession hit and plunged the country into deeper trouble. The army had nothing to show for the previous four years of economic hardships except more of the same.

By 1982 the one best hope for the army to remain in power and salvage a modicum of dignity seemed to be a successful foreign conflict. Argentina began to test the waters regarding the Beagle Islands dispute with Chile, but that pitted Argentina against a formidable and determined regime in Santiago. Tensions also existed with Brazil over nuclear arms competition. But the two military regimes reached an understanding on their rival nuclear programs and on sharing hydroelectric sites along the Paraguayan border. Besides, no one believed that Argentina could win a real conflict with Brazil.

Instead, General Leopoldo Galtieri, who now commanded the army and also served as president, decided to invade the Malvinas (Falkland) Islands. These islands had been occupied by Argentina in the 1820s after independence but were seized by a U.S. naval vessel and then taken over by the British in 1833. From then on, they were administered as a crown colony by Great Britain. Argentina protested the seizure off and on, but the British refused to give up the islands. The islands had little economic or strategic importance by the 1980s but held a huge symbolic value to Argentines.

In April 1982 Galtieri's forces invaded the islands and managed to capture most of the land. Soon, however, the British counterattacked and waged a successful war on land, sea, and air. By early June the Argentines surrendered. Galtieri was sacked as commander-in-chief and president. The armed forces, discredited and defeated, stepped aside and held elections soon after the war. In 1983 a Radical Party leader, Raúl Alfonsín, took office.

Brazil

Whereas the Argentine Army took twenty-one years (1955–1976) to perfect its version of the national security state, the Brazilian Army did so much more decisively. It seized power in March 1964 and relinquished it only twenty-one years later, in 1985. In that long period of dictatorship, the army created the quintessential national security state.

The formulation of national security doctrine in Brazil began in the 1950s, at the Superior War College in Rio de Janeiro. There, intellectuals, planners, strategists, and generals mulled over the likely threats to Brazil's peaceful development.

General Humberto Castelo Branco led the 1964 coup in Brazil and served as president for three years. A moderate, he hoped to restore civilian government. Instead, hard-liners extended the military tenure until 1985.

They decided that internal forces would menace the state more than would external threats, and they concluded that a strong central state, with safeguards against subversion, and a solid economy would prove the most resistant to attacks.

As the 1960s began, however, two presidents, Jânio Quadros (1961) and João Goulart (1961–1964), seemed bent on undermining stability and the economy. Goulart, in particular, proved to be an inconsistent and thoughtless leader, vying for popularity without considering his actions. As a result, the economy took a nosedive, and public disturbances became more frequent. Goulart seemed to relish the agitation, mistaking it for adulation. The generals removed Goulart and began to stabilize the country before turning it back over to civilians.

Army Chief of Staff General Humberto Castello Branco led the army in overthrowing Goulart on March 31, 1964. A veteran officer with ample experience in many lines of military work, Castello carried out the coup with little problem. He turned down an offer of assistance from U.S. forces stationed offshore. He expected to govern as provisional president for a year or so, long enough to purge leftists and dangerous leaders from high positions. He thought that the 1965 presidential election possibly could be held on schedule.

With this plan in mind, Castello and his team removed about three hundred politicians and leftists from sensitive positions, taking away their political rights (a unique Brazilian process known as *cassação*) for ten years. Particularly visible figures were urged to leave the country. A number of people vehemently opposed to the coup went into exile in order to continue the fight against the army. Meanwhile, Castello turned the economy over to a team of fiscally orthodox managers, who instituted a painful austerity program to bring down triple-digit inflation. Congress continued to operate through this period, and a majority of its members accepted the coup as necessary.

This relatively benign plan unraveled quickly, however, and the temporary regime became permanent. The doctrine of the national security state held that a long, recuperative period was needed to immunize the nation against Marxism and instability. All civilians active before 1964 began to look like agitators. The economy did not respond as it should have. And the global scene took on more ominous tones as the Vietnam War deepened, Che Guevara stirred up revolution, and the United States invaded the Dominican Republic to keep out communists. Castello found himself leading a military regime estranged from its early civilian allies.

Many ranking generals decided that they could not turn over control to the politicians without a thorough housecleaning and reconstruction of the nation. They had plans for foreign investment, infrastructure projects, social reforms, constitutional amendments, and more. It would take a long time, and those who advocated permanent military government called themselves the "hard-liners." They represented a majority of the active generals.

Castello found himself outvoted among the generals. A broad purge of civilians got under way. Elections were postponed, politicians sidelined, and universities shut down. As this occurred, civilian opposition, especially from students and labor groups, escalated. Guerrilla groups arose in the country and linked up with outside revolutionaries.

For the next two decades five-star generals succeeded one another in power and presided over Brazil's destiny. The presidents all were in their sixties, most came from Rio Grande do Sul on Brazil's border with Argentina, and all had spent some time in the Superior War College, a strategic think tank. Most had some foreign training or duty tours. None was charismatic, and only Emílio Garrastazu Médici attempted to become popular. None tried to extend his own term beyond the five years provided by the Constitution. Even more surprisingly, all of the presidents made a point of holding regular elections for local and state offices, and they worked more or less cooperatively with the Congress. In fact, the number of persons who voted in elections rose more rapidly under military rule than during the preceding populist era.

Each army president had his own style, agenda, and coterie of supporters, which gave him a distinctive administration. Artur Costa e Silva (1967–1969) was a model hard-liner, ruling by decree and responding to opposition with harsh measures. Guerrilla warfare and terrorism mounted, and repression reached into all corners of society. Summary arrests and torture became common, and he closed Congress more than once due to so-called insubordination. He judged this internal war to be necessary in order to purge the nation of undesirable elements.

Costa e Silva suffered a stroke and was replaced by Médici (1969–1974), former director of the National Intelligence Service, a spy and repression agency. His selection signaled the desire of hard-line generals to root out and destroy subversives. Médici did so, cooperating with state police and the armed services intelligence branches. A wide array of paramilitary forces carried out a terrifying campaign against anyone suspected of subversive activity. The latest counterinsurgency methods were imported from the United States, but in Brazil they were applied without any regard for human or civil rights. Thousands of persons were seized and interrogated, many were tortured, and hundreds died in police or military custody. Brazil's dirty war in 1969–1972 actually preceded Argentina's.

Médici did attempt to improve his image by using public relations services. He appeared on television and tried to project a pleasant image. He pushed soccer and tried to take credit when Brazil won the World Cup matches in 1970. He expanded television service throughout the country with satellite relays. Finally, he took undeserved credit for a surge in economic activity after 1968, sometimes called the Brazilian Miracle. In fact, the rapid growth in production occurred after three years of shrinkage and was due to massive investments by foreign corporations. Profits from the surge benefited mostly the foreign investors, Brazilian businessmen, and middle-class managers. During this period Brazil's distribution of income became the most inequitable in the world among industrialized countries.

Médici did succeed in stamping out terrorism and guerrilla activity, though at a terrible cost to civil society, political freedom, and individual rights. Increasing numbers of voters cast blank or marred ballots to protest the lack of true representation. In fact, the disqualified ballots rose to 25 percent of the total and served as an indictment of his regime.

In 1974 Ernesto Geisel won the vote among the generals and became president. An administrative officer formerly in charge of the state petroleum corporation,

Edson Arantes do Nascimento, known all over the world by his nickname Pelé, took Brazilian soccer to its greatest heights in the 1970s—the world championship.

Petrobras, Geisel belonged to the group called Castellistas, followers of Castello Branco's moderate line. Determined to turn over power to civilians by the end of his five-year term, he took steps to democratize the country in preparation. He had to grapple with increasing public criticism of the military government and with challenges from Congress. He found himself most beset, however, by army hard-liners, who opposed any loosening of their control. He walked a difficult line, vigorously opposed by generals and civilians alike.

The greatest economic challenge that Geisel faced was the 1973–1974 oil crisis, under way when he took office, because Brazil's economy depended almost exclusively on energy generated from imported petroleum. The balance of payments tilted massively against Brazil, and Geisel took emergency measures to cope. He expanded oil exploration and authorized foreign companies to participate. He ordered three nuclear generators from Westinghouse. He pushed construction of the Itaipú dam, today the world's largest hydroelectric plant. The economy, meanwhile, entered a period of jagged ups and downs as it adjusted to expensive energy, rising inflation, shifting employment, and irregular consumer demand.

Geisel found himself criticized from an unexpected quarter in 1977 when U.S. President Jimmy Carter decried violations of human rights in Brazil. Irked by this censure and by a refusal by the U.S. Atomic Energy Commission to ship test fuel for the Westinghouse reactors, Geisel broke the twenty-five-year military alliance with the United States and signed a $10 billion deal with Germany for the transfer of advanced nuclear technology. Brazilian-U.S. relations later recovered but never were as close as in the late 1960s.

Geisel was unable to round up enough support for a civilian successor, so he chose a colleague willing to commit himself to continuing the democratization process (by then called *abertura,* or "opening"). General João Figueiredo governed from 1979 until 1985, when he turned the office over to civilians. Like his predecessors, Figueiredo avoided the limelight and served as caretaker. He disliked politics and public appearances, yet he never wavered from his commitment to *abertura.*

When his term expired, Figueiredo allowed Congress to select a civilian president. Protests that the choice should be made by general election were ignored. In early 1985 Congress chose a veteran politician from the center of the ideological spectrum, Tancredo Neves. The last votes necessary to give Neves a majority came from the Liberal Party, led by the little-known José Sarney. Sarney won the vice presidential nod in exchange for his support.

The final transition from military to civilian rule contained both high drama and pathos. On the eve of his inauguration, Tancredo Neves fell ill and was operated on for intestinal disorders. For ten days he fought off fevers and infections while Brazilians prayed for his recovery. And then he lapsed into a coma from which he never recovered. He was buried amid tremendous honors, regarded as a hero for having steered the country from military to civilian rule. The tragedy lay in his being denied a chance to preside over the restored democracy. Instead, Sarney took the presidential sash in 1985.

Chile

Chile's military planners and policymakers had long been concerned about the leftward drift of Chilean politics. Since 1958 a socialist doctor-politician, Salvador Allende, had enjoyed a growing reputation for leadership and coalition building among center-left parties and factions. He came close to winning the 1964 election and was thwarted only by a last-minute deal among conservatives and by U.S. aid to his opponents. Allende himself may not have been a threat, but the communists, socialists, Maoists, and others in his camp were certainly anathema to Chile's military authorities.

To the army, the salvation of Chile seemed to ride on the shoulders of the capable and popular leader of the Christian Democrats, Eduardo Frei (1964–1970). After winning with a campaign called Revolution in Liberty, Frei attempted to carry out major reforms in the economy, government, political system, and social institutions. He claimed that he could check the leftward trend of voter preferences by instituting progressive reforms. He enacted a land reform program and legalized rural cooperatives and unions. He "Chileanized" the foreign copper mining giants by making the government the principal shareholder in these enterprises. He brought down inflation rates and attracted substantial new foreign investment. Health and educational programs expanded substantially. In short, Frei accomplished a remarkable array of reforms that benefited the lower classes.

Many analysts believe that Frei's success was his undoing because increased services and benefits only whetted people's appetites and fueled rising expectations for more. By the same token, the rapid pace of change frightened conservative voters, who shifted their support from Frei's Christian Democratic Party to the National Party ticket, headed by former President Jorge Alessandri. In the 1970 election voters split three ways but gave a slim plurality (36.5 percent) to Salvador Allende. This important election attracted clandestine monies from foreign governments, including the United States and Cuba.

The Chilean military had a strong tradition of professionalism and disengagement from politics. Its last full intervention had taken place in 1924–1925, when the army took power, instituted social and constitutional reforms, and handed the presidency to a civilian. Since that time, Chile had enjoyed a reputation of solid democracy. After the 1970 election, however, the military became increasingly involved in politics, culminating in its coup d'etat of September 1973.

This usurpation of constitutional authority was one of the central and tragic moments of modern Chilean history, although it was not entirely unpredictable, given Allende's record between 1970 and 1973.

Even before Allende's inauguration, middle-ranking military officers plotted ways to discredit the president-elect and prevent him from taking office. The plot went awry, though, and resulted in the death of a high-ranking general. The plotters failed to derail Allende's inauguration and later revealed that they had been encouraged by the U.S. CIA. The U.S. government, meanwhile, continued to work against Allende, alleging that he constituted a threat to Western Hemisphere security.

Allende had not misled the voters during the campaign: He promised that if elected he would nationalize major banks and insurance companies, the copper giants, and the telephone and electric power industries. These involved two hundred of the largest firms in the nation, including most U.S.-owned companies. He also pledged to extend the vote to illiterates and to carry out a much bolder land distribution program. Finally, he would recognize Cuba and carry on friendly relations with all nations, including communist and socialist ones. Once in office, he began to effect these changes, using the constitutional means at his disposal as president. He also raised the minimum wage so that workers received a 50 percent increase in real income.

At first the citizenry and economy responded warmly to Allende's program, and it appeared that his "peaceful road to socialism" would succeed. Factory output rose when workers spent their larger share of national income on consumer goods. Congress approved the measures necessary to nationalize major sectors of the economy. In the April 1971 municipal elections, pro-Allende candidates won 50 percent of the votes.

By the second year, however, the scene changed considerably, and Allende had to struggle to keep his government on track. Opposition parties cooperated to block his measures, U.S. vetoes cut off international loans, and the economy began to contract. Worse, organizations of workers, employers, housewives, peasants, and other groups began to protest policies unfavorable to their interests. Public order dropped precipitously.

Leftist groups, including armed guerrillas who had supported Allende in the 1960s, began to carry out terrorist acts against conservatives and as a warning to the

During the 1973 coup, Chile's presidential palace, La Moneda, was strafed by fighter-bombers and gutted by fire from grenades and mortars launched against Salvador Allende, who perished in the attack.

military not to intervene. Throughout 1972 the level of violence escalated, drawing the army and police into counterinsurgency operations. Allende, meanwhile, carried on with his reforms, and he won support from 44 percent of the voters in the March 1973 congressional elections. Society had become increasingly polarized between those who supported Allende and those who did not. At best the country faced government gridlock; at worst, it would plunge into civil war.

In mid-1973 army Chief of Staff General Augusto Pinochet began to organize a coup against Allende. He chose his allies carefully and sidelined those he did not trust. When the time came, on September 11, 1973, Pinochet mobilized his forces and surrounded the presidential palace. After nearly a day of skirmishing and bombardment, the army stormed the palace, and Allende died in the fight, a victim of either hostile fire or suicide.

Pinochet ruled with a three-man junta for months before assuming power as sole head of state in June 1974. Throughout 1973 and 1974 the army and police carried out a drastic campaign to eradicate leftists. The most brutal and feared agency of repression was the DINA, an internal security organization. Tens of thousands of Allende sympathizers fled the country into exile. Thousands who stayed perished at the hands of the police, in torture chambers and in jails. Guerrilla groups in the mountains were pursued and soon eliminated. Political freedoms and civil rights, long the pride of Chile, virtually disappeared. The 1982 movie *Missing,* starring Jack Lemmon, dramatized some of these events for American audiences, as did later films like Isabel Allende's *Love in the Shadows* (1996).

Like the other national security states, Pinochet's Chile instituted censorship, citizen surveillance, and martial law. The Army closed universities and suspended political activity. A cloud descended over Chile. In fact, by 1976 all of the Southern Cone was under military rule.

Pinochet claimed that economic disorder had been a major reason for his coup, and he quickly set out to reorganize (and unsocialize) the economy. As in the rest of the region, Chile received a strong dose of austerity medicine to bring down inflation, break strikes, shrink government payrolls, eliminate subsidies, and raise taxes and fees for government services.

To accomplish these goals, Pinochet put the economy in the hands of persons trained in orthodox, free-market economics, many of whom held Ph.D. degrees from the University of Chicago. They attempted not only to revive free enterprise capitalism but also to prove that laissez-faire economics works in the real world. Critics came to call them the Chicago Boys because of their doctrinal zeal.

Chile experienced severe economic contraction from 1973 until about 1978, as credit dried up, companies large and small went bankrupt, and nationalized firms (except copper) were returned to their former owners. Income again became concentrated, and high unemployment was tolerated as a necessary by-product of the recovery process. From 1978 to 1980, however, the economy grew at robust rates, seemingly vindicating the Chicago Boys' approach. Then the 1980 recession struck and brought the economy to a standstill again. Finally, from the mid-1980s on the Chilean economy performed very well, fueled by strong capital flows from abroad, aggressive export promotion, a well-managed fiscal system, and investments in infrastructure.

In terms of repression, dirty war tactics, economic orthodoxy, anticommunist foreign policies, and conservative social policy, Chile's military regime resembled the other national security states. In one respect, however, it differed: Pinochet stayed in power for the entire seventeen years of military rule. He assumed the role of exalted leader and savior of the country, unlike his Brazilian and Argentine counterparts. He gave his regime the sacred task of purifying the citizenry and political system. He allied with the Catholic church (a staunch foe of Allende) and proclaimed divine sanction for his actions. Pinochet's was a one-man dictatorship.

The Elusive Character of Pinochet's Regime

General Augusto Pinochet Gives 1984 Interview to U.S. Journalist

The president greeted me with a flourish bordering on gallantry when I entered, extending his hand, then bowing low in traditional Spanish greeting; he complimented me on my "elegant dress." He had shed his military uniform for a dark blue suit, blue shirt with red tie, white socks and black shoes.... [Regarding civil unrest in 1983–1984, he said:] "The difficulties rising from the world recession created a restlessness here, since they significantly affected the economic situation.... The opposition used these difficulties politically, attributing them exclusively to the government. Their purpose, quite obviously, was to create a climate of agitation, of social trade-union effervescence in order to destabilize the government. But they were mistaken.... Let me tell you that I was formed as a military man. I am a military man. I have been a military man for more than fifty years. I have eaten my meals with my fellow army officers. I have lived with them.... [Regarding communists:] The Communist party works most effectively in developing countries, in poor and underdeveloped societies. Communism appeals to the idealism of the youth. Thus we have to work on two fronts: alleviate economic misery and at the same time point out to our youth the insidious nature of communism. This is not a dictatorship here: this is not a Nazi or Fascist society where you order the youth how to think. We in the government have tried to do things with full liberty.... Maybe we have given our youth too much freedom...."

(Patricia J. Sethi, in *LASA Forum*, XV:2 [Summer 1984], pp. 11–12)

A Chilean academic teaching in the United States wrote:

The Chilean regime is not Fascist.... It is also a serious mistake to characterize the Chilean regime as corporatist or functionalist.... It is also not correct to say that it is purely a military government.... The dictatorship is of the armed forces but not by the armed forces.... One should not exaggerate the degree of personal rule in Chile. Pinochet presides over a complex state, constituted by many institutions and organs, most with long trajectories.... The complexity of the historical Chilean state reduces arbitrary power, and the average citizen relates to his or her government for the mundane things of everyday life in largely the same way as before the advent of military rule. This contributes to the sense of routine "normality" that often characterizes authoritarian regimes and, paradoxically, helps to defuse opposition to the dictator.

(Arturo Valenzuela, in *LASA Forum*, XV:2 [Summer 1984], pp. 17–18)

According to his own Constitution, Pinochet was to step down in 1989. Because of his success in bringing about economic growth, however, he believed that the citizenry wanted him to remain in power. Therefore, he ordered a plebiscite in 1988: Should he step down or continue in power another eight years? When the votes were cast, a solid 55 percent opposed Pinochet's continuing in power, so he stepped aside and allowed elections for a civilian successor. In 1989 Christian Democratic leader Patricio Aylwin won a four-year term. Thus ended Chile's national security state. Pinochet retained his post as commander-in-chief of the armed forces, however, and continued to monitor politics from his army headquarters until 1998. Then he took up a seat he had designated for himself in the national Senate, despite protests from his opponents.

Uruguay

From early in the century, Uruguay gained an enviable reputation for having the most democratic politics and progressive social policies in the hemisphere. It was known as the Switzerland of South America. Even when partisan strife and economic difficulties beset the country in the 1960s, few observers believed that Uruguay could succumb to military dictatorship. The democratic tradition was simply too strong.

But three factors undermined democracy and plunged Uruguay into a military regime as repressive as those of the national security states of neighboring Argentina and Brazil. First, the stable, state-subsidized, egalitarian society—forged during the 1910s and 1920s under the leadership of don Pepe Batlle—had become unaffordable, given Uruguay's tiny economy. By the 1960s politics had degenerated into a fight for spoils in a quasisocialist economy. This widespread insecurity fostered a vicious scramble for public office to control government patronage for one or another special interest group. The entire focus of politics was on distribution, not production. Uruguay bankrupted itself and poisoned its civic culture in the process.

Second, in response to the escalating partisan conflict in Uruguay, dissidents formed guerrilla groups, and for the first time in generations terrorism appeared on the streets of Montevideo. The foremost guerrilla group, the Tupamaros, first appeared in 1963 and by 1967 enjoyed extraordinary success. The Tupamaros, named after an eighteenth-century Inca revolutionary, Tupac Amaru II (see Chapter One), combined well-planned military strikes with brilliant publicity stressing their pro-working-class acts. The already crumbling government put up an ineffectual resistance, while the army increasingly assumed authority. The resultant power vacuum in Montevideo worried the military leadership, especially at a time when rebel forces in many parts of the world were gaining the upper hand.

Third, Uruguay fell under military rule because of outside pressure. Brazil and Argentina, governed by army generals who campaigned to strengthen national security in the region, encouraged their Uruguayan counterparts to join them in exercising power. Uruguay's civilian leaders simply could not resist the pressure from within and without.

A spate of assassinations by guerrilla forces in April 1972 led the military to impose its will on civilian authorities. The army pressured the new president, Juan Bordaberry, and Congress to declare a state of internal war so that it could carry out a full-scale counterinsurgency operation. Civilians acquiesced, and the army soon achieved a number of important victories against the guerrillas. The president, meanwhile, became the virtual captive of the army, unable to moderate the growing struggle. The following year, when congressional leaders tried to rein in the military, the latter closed Congress, and the government became a military dictatorship. Bordaberry went along with the fiction that he governed. When his term was about to end in 1976, the military simply removed him.

The military established a regime in which its terrorism replaced that of the Tupamaros without any pretense of benefiting the working classes. In a little over a year, the military rooted out the principal leaders of the guerrilla organizations and murdered them. The military arrested, tortured, and killed large numbers of citizens in the process. The army used the same methods that had proven successful in Argentina and Brazil. By 1979 political prisoners made up 1 percent of the population (the highest ratio in the world), and another 17 percent lived in exile.

Uruguay's military regime did not produce a single leader like Pinochet of Chile. Its generals remained anonymous and unforgiving in their purge of leftists and opponents. They adopted neoliberal economic policies designed to prune government payrolls and reduce spending, and the economy sank deeper into stagflation. The general standard of living fell to pre–World War II levels.

In order to update the Constitution in 1980, the army conducted a referendum on a proposed constitution that allowed strong military participation in most aspects of government. Despite heavy spending by proponents of the proposed constitution, citizens voted it down by a wide margin, signaling their repudiation of army rule. Rebuffed by the vote, the army began a process of gradual democratization that culminated in the 1984 election of a civilian president, Julio Sanguinetti (1985–1989, 1995–).

Peru

Peru's government had wavered from right to center, and from dictators to populists, since the 1930s. The elite preferred autocratic regimes, elected or not, that could keep the Amerindian and mestizo masses under control. By most social and economic indices, Peru trailed far behind the rest of the continent. Political leaders, however, had little interest in reforms, much less in revolution.

Beginning in 1963, however, newly elected President Fernando Belaúnde Terry devoted more than just lip service to reforms in the Peruvian economy and society. An architect by training and pro–United States by temperament, Belaúnde set out to achieve some of the goals of the modernization program called for by the Alliance for Progress. The platform of his party, Popular Action, included land reform, improved tax collection, more housing, better farming methods, industrialization, schools, and so forth. Leading Peruvian analysts and foreign observers alike hailed Belaúnde's program as progressive.

The land distribution program focused mostly on the Amazon region, where colonists were supposed to start profitable farms. But virtually none was successful because of the lack of knowledge and investment. The 1960s feature film *The Green Wall* dramatized this experience. Meanwhile, huge plantations and ranches in the populated regions went untouched.

In the capital of Lima, Belaúnde undertook a public housing program to alleviate the suffering of hundreds of thousands of squatters who lived in shantytowns on the outskirts. The more he built, however, the more people migrated to the city, and the shantytowns became permanent fixtures in Lima.

Had Belaúnde succeeded with these and other initiatives, Peru would have been a different place. His plans were ambitious but ran head-on into the unwillingness of the elite to give up its wealth and privileges. Congress, meanwhile, watered down or blocked much of his legislation, and the economy stagnated, leading to higher unemployment. The enthusiasm that had greeted Belaúnde at first now turned to disaffection.

Peru's military leaders had given some thought to the changing nature of their national defense requirements in the Cold War. An army think tank, CAEM, had come up with a blueprint for a stronger economy and reinforced institutions, called Plan Inca. Still, the army had little stomach for meddling in politics. Its long history was studded with defeats at the hands of foreigners, and the periods in which the army had ruled the nation had been singularly unproductive.

The army found itself drawn into politics, however, by a dispute over petroleum rights in 1968. The International Petroleum Corporation (IPC), a medium-sized production and refining operation owned by Standard Oil of New Jersey, negotiated a contract with Belaúnde for partial nationalization. High-handed tactics by the company had long offended Peruvian nationalists, and Congress refused to ratify the contract. Scandalized by Belaúnde's inept negotiations and the company's attitudes, a high-ranking officer, Juan Velasco Alvarado, mobilized his troops and seized power. He immediately nationalized the IPC and renamed it Petroperu amid great public rejoicing.

Military strategists reasoned that they might counterbalance their poor historical record by presiding over a positive, constructive period at the helm of government. Because civilians had proven themselves unable to reform society and the economy, the army would do it for them.

General Velasco showed a certain flair for leadership when he assumed the role of president. No aspect of the country's life escaped his attention. One of his most popular undertakings was land reform throughout the country. He created a new agency to confiscate 350,000 acres owned by the U.S. firm operating the Cerro de Pasco copper mine. The miners themselves were invited to take up farming there to raise their standard of living.

The next phase of land reform targeted the coastal plantations of the North, where sugar and cotton estates had operated since colonial times. These were

General Juan Velasco Alvarado, president of Peru from 1968–1975, led the Peruvian Institutional Revolution that ousted President Fernando Belaúnde Terry and started Peru on a very nationalistic course. This included the nationalization of major foreign-owned properties and a popular and widespread reform program such as the expropriation and redistribution of land.

converted into communal farms to be operated by and for the workers. Union leaders assumed the lead in converting the businesses into cooperatives. In a short time they adjusted and produced solid profits for the unions. They were hailed as a great success.

The land reform agency then turned to other extensive highland estates, the backbone of the old landed elite. After they were expropriated, the lands were subdivided into self-sufficient smallholds, termed *minifundias* by the new peasant owners. This withdrew crops and animals from the market and resulted in food shortages in the cities. In all, land reform redistributed thirteen million acres, a creditable record.

Velasco then turned his attention to other sectors of the economy. He created an industrial development agency, Induperu, to stimulate greater production and self-sufficiency. Fishing fleets and fishmeal processing plants were converted to cooperative ownership under Pescaperu and continued to prosper for several years. Domestic banks and insurance companies were partially nationalized. Some of the mines, meanwhile, were consolidated into a public enterprise called Mineroperu. It enjoyed strong profits because of high world prices for minerals. Other industries taken over by the military were railroads, telecommunications, coastal navigation, and electric power.

In order to make his administration a true revolution rather than a mere stewardship of the economy, Velasco sponsored a program called SINAMOS, designed to build grass-roots participation and support for the army's objectives. Neither a party nor a publicity campaign, SINAMOS sought to create a new sense of citizenship among the common people. It envisioned self-help programs, literacy, voter registration drives, small-scale cooperatives, and public debate on the destiny of the nation. Government representatives formed community groups, which were then federated into local, state, and national associations. SINAMOS hoped to give Peruvians a sense of pride in their nation and of participation in the revolutionary process. Parallel institutions provided radio and press communications among the local and regional groups.

The regime tried to change people's prejudices by using new language in all government publications. The regime stipulated that the term indio, traditionally pejorative in Peru, would henceforth be changed to campesino, meaning "peasant." The shantytowns were to be renamed *pueblos jóvenes* ("new townships"). For a time the terminology seemed to catch on. The traditional monetary unit, *sol,* was renamed *inti.* Even traditional street names were altered to emphasize Peruvian themes. For example, Avenida Woodrow Wilson became Avenida Garcilaso de la Vega after a famous Inca chronicler.

To stress the innovative character of his government, Velasco forged an independent foreign policy as well. Eschewing the traditional Cold War alliance with the United States, he struck up relations with Cuba and China. He purchased a wing of MiG fighters from the USSR and another of Mirages from France. He declared that Peru would no longer abide by the orthodox rules of the World Bank and International Monetary Fund. He also took belligerent stances toward Peru's traditional enemies, Ecuador and Chile, by stationing troops and aircraft on the common borders. The United States, meanwhile, went along with Velasco, reasoning that he was not as hostile as Fidel Castro or Salvador Allende and could serve as a counterpoise to communist expansion.

For nearly five years General Velasco could do no wrong. His nationalized companies reported profits, inflation was down, export earnings were up, his popularity was high, and no one put up much opposition to the government. Foreign observers were fascinated with what Velasco called the Peruvian Institutional Revolution. Fidel Castro reportedly said that for the military to carry out socialist reforms was like firefighters starting a blaze in their own firehouse. The military regime was not Marxist, not repressive, and not bankrupt, either. It did not commit the terrible excesses of the other military regimes. Many began to tout this unique experiment as a model for other modernizing countries. To be sure, the army administered top-down change, but it seemed to work.

But in 1974 things began to go sour for Velasco. His own health faltered, and doctors amputated his leg. He became irritable with aides and colleagues. The SINAMOS program did not move Peru any closer to real participatory democracy, and some politicians now dared to criticize him for not holding elections. Even worse, the economic success stories of preceding years turned into debacles. In just a few years, the rich fishing grounds off Peru's coast turned barren due to long-term climatic shifts, and the fishing fleet had to be put into mothballs. World prices for minerals plummeted when the Vietnam War wound down, and Mineroperu began to post serious losses. Adjustments to wages and dividends angered workers, who began to protest. Layoffs provoked demonstrations.

Meanwhile, Petroperu had run short of crude oil to refine and issued contracts for international companies to explore for new fields. This seemed to violate the nationalist stance that the government had taken with IPC and caused considerable opposition. On the positive side of the ledger, though, companies found high-quality crude on the eastern slopes of the Andes.

Velasco, who had reveled in his early successes, proved inept in dealing with his failures. Poor health made it impossible for him to carry on the duties of president. An associate, General Francisco Morales Bermúdez, deposed him in 1975.

Morales could see that the ship of state was heavily indebted ($5 billion) and sinking, so he announced his intention of allowing more political participation. Implicitly admitting that SINAMOS had failed to generate public support, he began to govern more by decree and repression. With the economy sinking fast, Morales fired his leftist advisors and instituted a program of austerity to appease the international bankers. Peru began to resemble the other national security states.

Just as Morales executed this turn to the right in 1976, however, Velasco died. During the state funeral, hundreds of thousands of people paid homage to him and used the occasion to demonstrate against recent policy shifts. Protesters actually stole the coffin and proclaimed that the government did not deserve to hold his remains. Morales then changed direction again, hoping to win back support, but it was too late. By 1977 he announced that the military would remove itself from power as soon as a constitution could be adopted and elections held.

Young men and women recruited from Amerindian villages filled the rank and file of the Sendero Luminoso (Shining Path) guerrilla movement, whose power in Peru peaked in the 1980s.

Morales did not have Velasco's flair for leadership nor his faith in the destiny of the Peruvian revolution. His administration proved to be a major disappointment and only added to the army's reputation for mismanagement.

The Peruvian regime differed from the others. First, Velasco played a leading role, like Pinochet, but he did not have the staying power of his Chilean counterpart. Second, the economic policies that he followed were not orthodox (like Chile's and Argentina's), not heterogeneous (like Brazil's), and not purely socialistic, as some people claimed. In truth, the nationalizations seemed to be largely opportunistic moves driven by whim and public opinion polls, not guided by doctrine or by a carefully laid-out plan. Likewise, no sustained effort was made to transform popularity into lasting support for the regime, much less for the army. When Velasco exited, the whole experiment collapsed around him.

The army's retreat from power was fraught with irony. The army's *bête noire*, Haya de la Torre, won the job of presiding over a constitutional convention in 1978 for the purpose of restoring civilian rule. An election held in 1980 was won by Fernando Belaúnde Terry, the same man whom the military had ousted in 1968. He won by promising to undo the harm and distortions introduced by military rule. Although no strong guerrilla movement had existed prior to military rule, during Velasco's administration one of the most threatening and powerful insurgencies of all time arose in Peru—the Sendero Luminoso (Shining Path). Finally, like the Argentine army, Peru's was discredited by its assumption of power and left office largely in disgrace.

Conclusions and Issues

The national security states outlined in this chapter differed from earlier military dictatorships in a number of ways. They arose out of a tidal shift in defense missions brought on by the Cold War. They had programs and ideologies developed in army think tanks. They created formal structures of power and incorporated many officers into public management. They sought to clean up corruption and inefficiencies that had plagued civilian governments. They also tried to purge society of dangerous individuals, usually leftists who were politically active. In fact, the wave of terror against the citizenry has dominated our memory of that era. Even the relatively benign Peruvian regime did not escape accusations of abuse.

The national security states arose out of domestic politics in each country, but they also fit into regional and even global trends. The Cold War set the stage for defensive intrusions into government, while the Cuban Revolution and the Vietnam War hoisted warning flags against guerrilla movements. Internal rebellion certainly heightened the sense of peril among army officers and convinced them to act in concert to eliminate the danger. After the officers were in control, other demands kept them from renouncing power until they had worn out their welcomes. Finally, these were institutional governments, not the work of a single leader or a small group. Armies as organizations took power and later relinquished it. While in office, they often provided considerable stability.

Discussion Questions

1. To what extent were the changing military missions in South America a response to global events, as opposed to a response to internal events?

2. What roles did the new security doctrine prescribe for the armies of the region? The navies? The air forces? The police?

3. What forces eventually drove the military out of government? Were these physical, moral, intellectual, or social forces? What lasting impact did the military regimes have on the armed services as institutions?

Democratization and Conflict
since 1980

Clandestine U.S. Support for the Contras in Nicaragua

The Honduran major named Felipe leaned over to his American counterpart, Jimmy, and asked when the shooting would begin.

"Not long now, good buddy. We'll start lobbing grenades into their camp in about an hour. Then you and I hightail it out of here 'fore we get caught. We make it look like the Contras fired on them."

"What do 'hightail' mean?" the Honduran asked.

"It means 'get out,' 'scram,'" said the American officer. "We'll have a gunship drop in for us at 0800 hours. We don't want to leave any clues behind."

"These Contras don' treat us good. They think we cheap and bad soldiers 'cause we don't fight communists. We don' have no communists in Honduras, so why should we fight? But we like to help you 'mericans fight the Sandinistas."

"Those Contras are tight-ass bastards, all right," said the American. "They ran Nicaragua for so many years they don't know how to get along on their own. Lot of 'em went to Miami and learned about communism from the Cuban exiles. Now they're trying to whip the Sandinistas, 'cept they couldn't do it in '79, and they can't do it now, not even with our help."

"How come your government won't let you give guns to the Contras no more? Don' they want to kill the Sandinistas?"

"It's a long story, Felipe. President Reagan's been givin' 'em guns and money and a few Ranger advisors since '82. But we caught some flack from the liberals 'cause this ain't a declared war or nothin'. The president really believes in these guys, and he's gonna help 'em any way he can, even if Congress says we can't. So now Ollie North has to move supplies in through the back door, if you know what I mean."

"You mean Honduras is only a back door?"

"No, Felipe, you guys are like regular allies. 'Back door' just means how we get the guns 'n' ammo in without using government money, is all. This is a Cold War operation, and we're tryin' to keep the Sandinistas from spreading communism. You're the good guys."

"Yeah," Felipe said, "you treat us OK, givin' us jeeps an' tractors an' shit. I would like if some of the money you give the generals—how do you say it?—trickle down to us. We get great boots, but General Hernández, he buy a condo in Miami, and I don' even have a house."

"That's all right, Felipe," the American said. "If we keep the Sandinistas off guard enough they're gonna piss off their own people, and they'll kick 'em out. Then the old Somoza guys'll be very grateful, and they'll pay you off. Our job is to keep them Sandinistas on alert, mobilized, draftin' young guys, and shootin' at shadows. In fact, you could call this a shadow war more than a shootin' war.

"Fact is, some White House and intel guys are runnin' this, not the Pentagon jocks. Sometimes I think all we're doin' is tryin' to fool each other. Main thing, though, is to screw the Sandinistas good for talkin' to the Cubans and Russians."

"Sometimes I don' understand you gringos," Felipe said, shaking his head.

"Come on, buddy, time's up. Let's go kick us some Sandinista butt! *Geronimo!*"

"*Geronimo?*" thought Felipe as they jumped into their jeep.

The year 1980 marked a watershed in Latin America's modern history, the beginning of a difficult and tumultuous decade. The national security states of South America were on the defensive, with some tracking toward restoration of power to civilians. Most guerrilla operations had been shut down, and public opinion ran solidly against military government. Oil prices slumped, hurting producers Venezuela, Mexico, and Ecuador, but doing little to help the importing nations. Generalized inflation in the 1970s had pushed the interest indexes into double digits, making it difficult for Latin American nations to keep up payments on their burgeoning debts. Meanwhile, production slipped in the United States and Europe, signaling the onset of the worst general recession in fifty years. And Ronald Reagan defeated Jimmy Carter in the U.S. presidential election. Everything was about to change.

Recession and Neoliberalism

In the Southern Cone countries in the 1960s and 1970s, the army's ability to make the economy run smoothly and equitably was central to its justifications of the national security state. The Brazilian Miracle, the surge of growth in Chile, and sporadic good times in Argentina were supposed to make the loss of civil liberties palatable.

Yet, the military's economic performance turned out mediocre and was generally accompanied by a sharp concentration of income in the hands of the wealthy. In addition, military governments welcomed foreign investors and acquiesced to the demands of international bankers. Then, with the severe downturn of the early 1980s, remaining in power seemed even less advisable. In fact, the hard times of the 1980s hastened the retreat of the military from power.

Economists termed the 1980s a "lost decade" because the region's economies stagnated and sometimes shrank painfully. The average 1.2 percent-a-year rise in production did not keep up with population growth. In the 1980s the region experienced its worst recession in a half-century. Little new investment took place from either public or private sources. Capital—both physical and human—deteriorated from lack of care and upkeep. Industries failed to compete with more aggressive companies in Asia and retreated further behind protectionist barriers. Meanwhile, the international debts contracted in the 1970s continued to drain the economies of working capital. No wonder that development planners in Latin America could not overcome obstacles to growth. Theirs seemed a dismal science indeed, as an economist once called his discipline.

The economic crisis began with the 1980 recession in the United States and then spread to major trade partners, especially Mexico, Brazil, Venezuela, Peru, Colombia, and Chile. The Reagan administration took office in January 1981 and allowed the shakedown to continue, to drive down inflation and improve long-term competitiveness in the U.S. economy. This position led to further declines in international trade, bank credit, employment, and capital movement. Interest rates, meanwhile, remained high due to residual inflation and scarce capital. For Latin America, it was the worst of all worlds.

A generalized debt crisis swept the region in 1982, causing Mexico to default (see Chapter Twenty) and Brazil, Argentina, and Chile to experience severe hard-currency shortages. These in turn led to grave social and political problems. In Argentina, the crisis persuaded the military to invade the Malvinas (Falkland) Islands in hopes of diverting attention from hardships at home. After losing the war with Great Britain, they were obliged to relinquish power to civilian leaders. The fiscal emergency in Brazil nearly derailed the Figueiredo government's timetable for the return to civilian rule. In Chile activists organized protests, strikes, and press campaigns to force Pinochet out of office. They failed, and the general hardened his resolve to stay in power, by force, if necessary, until he could eradicate all threats of a Marxist revival. And in Mexico the economic crisis led to a debt moratorium, devaluations, nationalization of domestic banks, and a thorough overhaul of national policy. Other countries in the region shared the hard times and troubles.

The severity of the early 1980s economic crisis forced Latin American leaders to reevaluate their theories about the economy. Although no regime collapsed directly because of economic problems, they all were weakened by the poor performance. Except in Chile, the problems hastened the process of democratization. They also had a profound impact on general policy.

ECLA Doctrine from the Thirties to the Eighties

Some background helps in understanding the importance of the philosophical changes underway. Since the 1930s Latin American economists and planners had followed distinctive theoretical paths, somewhere between laissez-faire liberalism and full-fledged socialism. Many were guided by the ideas of John Maynard Keynes, the British economist whose ideas became widely accepted in Western Europe and the United States after World War II. Others derived their theories from experiments in Eastern Europe.

In general, the Latin economists preferred an expanded role for the state in decision making and even ownership, yet short of the total control exercised in the USSR and a few other communist countries. Government intervention in the economy usually took the form of multi-year planning, arbitration of labor disputes, investment in infrastructure, joint ownership of basic utilities, and close monitoring and regulation of money and credit markets. It was basically a hands-on style of government that gave politicians a great deal more influence than in laissez-faire capitalistic systems.

In 1948 a group of Latin American economists, led by Chilean Raúl Prebisch, formed a United Nations think tank to study development problems in the region and to propose integrated planning approaches. Called the Economic Commission for Latin America (ECLAC—the Caribbean was added later), it conducted a number of in-depth analyses of why Latin America kept falling farther behind the industrialized countries. They found that concentration on exports of raw materials and food had actually impoverished Latin countries, because over the long haul these commodities fell in price relative to manufactures. The only solution, they suggested, was to industrialize (*The Economic Development of Latin America and Its Principal Problems* [Lake Success, N.Y.: UN, 1950]).

Because Latin America undertook to industrialize long after the North Atlantic world had done so, it needed to create special conditions in order to succeed. First, market protection would be necessary until "infant industries" reached full efficiency. Second, countries with small populations should band together into common markets to help one another industrialize. Third, governments should promote manufacturing, through subsidies, infrastructure investment, easy loans, and other means. Finally, ECLAC economists said, during this time governments should tolerate inflation as an unavoidable by-product of development. Strict monetary controls to eliminate inflation could strangle the economic efforts. In all, these prescriptions, often labeled "structuralism," became ECLAC doctrine, and they were widely adopted throughout the region.

ECLAC policies also favored the working classes by advocating education and training, nutrition, housing, better wages, collective bargaining, and expansion of the domestic market for consumer goods. These social policies later came to be called "populist" because they could be used by politicians to garner support among the masses. At their core, however, these ECLAC policies related to the overall objectives of economic development, not political advantage.

The results of following ECLAC doctrine were quite damaging in the long run. Protected industries used inefficient machinery and methods while paying labor more than its value added. Members of urban unions, in particular, formed a labor aristocracy. Investors likewise reaped profits far out of proportion to their economic contribution. By the 1960s Latin America's industry could not globally compete yet wielded enough power to protect itself from competition. Latin America fell further behind the advanced economies of Europe, Asia, and North America.

In addition, because they had followed ECLAC prescriptions, most Latin American countries of the 1960s and 1970s were referred to as having "mixed economies" or "state capitalism." The governments exercised powerful tools of planning, regulation, and investment. Even the most right-wing governments often exercised full command over the private sector. Therefore, some regimes' economic policies contradicted their philosophical rhetoric.

By the 1980s the economies of the major countries had been through decades of turmoil and inconsistent leadership by government economists. ECLAC policies could no longer be defended. Meanwhile, dictators gave way to populists, who were succeeded by the military, which then faced severe crises and decided to restore power to civilians. In light of the confusing array of institutions, regulations, controls, and laws inherited from preceding regimes, many people began to favor a return to the simpler rules of laissez-faire capitalism. This approach, also supported by the Republican administrations and international banks in Washington, came to be known as "neoliberalism."

Neoliberal economics swept the region in the 1980s in response to the failed approaches of earlier decades. Neoliberalism appealed to people of all walks of life in Latin America. It promised, in the words of a U.S. politician, to "get the government off the backs of the people." It would extricate the politicians from private decision making and bargaining. Gradually the notion of free-market economics spread, gaining favor among a majority of policymakers, and it became a new orthodoxy.

The neoliberal doctrine consisted of several key principles. First, privatization would put government-owned enterprises up for sale to investors, domestic or international. Second, labor unions would negotiate contracts directly with employers, rather than through public mediators. Third, the maze of regulatory laws and rules had to be stripped away to allow entrepreneurs room to operate. Fourth, the free market required reduction or elimination of tariffs and quotas on foreign trade, floating rates for currency and relaxation of controls on capital transfers, free sale of land and other resources, and balanced budgets and alleviation of debt service. In short, neoliberalism prescribed running the economy in a businesslike fashion.

The coincidence of *apertura* (democratization) and the rise of neoliberalism in much of the region meant that most emerging democracies in the 1980s attempted to set in motion the new economics. This put them on common ground with the international banking community, with the major industrial powers, and with one another.

One especially promising result of the new economics was interest in regional common markets, attempted in the 1950s but abandoned in the 1970s. In the late 1980s several new regional organizations moved ahead: NAFTA, comprising the United States, Canada, and Mexico; Mercosur, including Brazil, Argentina,

Paraguay, Uruguay, and perhaps Chile; and the Andean Group of Colombia, Ecuador, Bolivia, Peru, and Venezuela. A 1994 summit meeting of the hemisphere's presidents pledged to move toward free trade in all the Americas by the year 2005. Plans for integration moved slowly, however, because of the halting recovery from the recession and the political costs of readjustment.

The Transition to Democracy: Peru

Democratization of Latin America moved forward quickly in the 1980s, first in the larger nations of South America and then in the Caribbean basin countries.

Peru underwent a transition to civilian rule in 1980 as the discredited army returned to its barracks in disgrace. The victor in the elections held that year was Fernando Belaúnde, whom the army had unceremoniously removed twelve years before. His Popular Action Party won a 45 percent plurality. Now sixty-eight years old and chastened by his failures in the 1960s, Belaúnde was no longer a populist nor even an advocate of the common people's interests. He avoided attacking the military and instead took office promising to continue the housecleaning begun by Morales Bermúdez, complemented by free-market economics.

Belaúnde emphasized economic recovery led by exports. This meant increased production for foreign markets so that Peru could earn hard currency and resume paying off the huge debt incurred by the military. It also meant hard work and austerity measures at home, which Peruvian workers were not expecting. Protests and strikes spread, in part because the world recession dried up markets for Peru's goods. Although not Belaúnde's fault, the recession could not be overcome by his free-market policies, which merely punished workers and consumers. Wealthy Peruvians moved their capital abroad for protection. Economic indices, meanwhile, went from bad to worse.

Privatizing land, or returning it to private owners, raised hackles among peasant leaders, members of rural cooperatives, and unions on big collective farms. Other state enterprises put up for sale languished on the auction block when no one stepped forward to buy them. Production slipped, and shortages grew unbearable, especially in the cities.

Belaúnde eventually appointed another cabinet to deal with the economic crisis, but he himself increasingly ignored the country's problems and spent his time hobnobbing with the Lima elite in private clubs and restaurants. In the mountains, moreover, a new guerrilla organization had begun to operate—the dreaded Sendero Luminoso (Shining Path).

Sendero had been founded by a university professor from Ayacucho, Abimael Guzmán, after he grew disaffected with Peruvian society and sought inspiration in Mao Tse-tung's China. Upon his return, Guzmán began to gather converts to his revolutionary philosophy and to organize them into clandestine cells. By the 1970s Sendero had perfected a mission and *modus operandi* that seemed invincible.

Like other guerrilla bands, Sendero built its command structure out of almost totally isolated cells, each one composed of leadership cadres, battle orders, weapons

Table 25-1 Leaders of the Democratization

Country	Name	Years in Power	Born	Class	Urban Rural	Race	Ed	Age @ 1st/off	Mil?	Party	Foreign Influence
TRANSITIONAL											
Peru	Belaúnde	1963–68 1980–85	1912	upper	U	wh	arch	33	n	AC	Y
Argentina	Alfonsín	1983–89	1926	middle	R	wh	univ	56	n	UCR	Y
Brazil	Sarney	1985–90	1930	middle	U	wh	law	34	n	Liberal	n
NEOPOPULISTS											
Peru	García	1985–90	1949	middle	U	wh	law	29	n	APRA	Y
Argentina	Menem	1989–	1930	middle	R	wh	univ	25	n	Peronista	n
Brazil	Collor	1990–92	1949	upper	U	wh	univ	30	n	n/a	Y
Peru	Fujimori	1990–	1938	lower	U	Asian	eng	52	n	n/a	Y
OTHERS											
Brazil	Cardoso	1995–	1931	middle	U	wh	Ph.D.	55	n	PMDB	Y

Source: *Encyclopedia of Latin American History and Culture* and authors' research.

caches, and regional assignments. Guzmán trained the first cell leaders and sent them out, and gradually these trained hundreds more, until every part of the country had Sendero representatives. Some cells operated in the cities, others in rural areas, always in isolation from one another. They communicated with controllers infrequently and only through highly secret channels. It was almost impossible for police to break into the general command structure.

The members of Sendero all had been trained in operations and doctrine, and their faith in Guzmán was absolute. Hundreds perished in suicide terrorist missions, and hundreds more died at the hands of police interrogators. Theirs was a faith as total as that of any religious fanatic. Women as well as men staffed the cells, and they penetrated all walks of Peruvian life. Their devotion to the cause and success in winning new recruits increased with the deteriorating political and economic situation in the country.

Gradually Sendero spread across the valleys and hamlets of highland Peru, clashing with and eventually displacing many local authorities. By the mid-1980s two-thirds of the highlands was under Sendero control, and their area expanded with each passing year.

President Belaúnde, who had dealt forcefully with guerrilla groups in his first administration, dispatched the army to defeat Sendero in the early 1980s. To his dismay, the army could not prevail against Sendero's superior tactics, nor could it gain the cooperation of peasants in areas under Sendero influence.

Even more disturbing, Sendero offered protection to farmers who produced coca leaves, the raw material from which cocaine is refined. Because coca production generated a lot of cash from the narcotics trade, fees and taxes collected by Sendero financed its arms and training programs. Sendero gradually became a state within the Peruvian state.

During his last two years in office, Belaúnde lost all the public support that he had enjoyed in 1980, and he left the dwindling powers of government in the hands of subordinates. The most that could be said is that he managed an election and a peaceful transition to his successor.

Argentina

Argentina changed to civilian rule in 1983, following the country's defeat in the Malvinas (Falkland) War. Army-supervised elections gave Raúl Alfonsín, leader of the Radical Party, 52 percent of the votes, compared to the Peronistas' 40 percent. The army had insisted that civilians not pursue judicial charges against officers for their actions in the dirty war or the Malvinas debacle. In fact, after in office Alfonsín did indict those who served in juntas since 1976 or held command posts during the war. Most of the country's highest-ranking officers retired or resigned, and the army was pared down to its smallest size in generations. Argentines were relieved to be rid of military rule but disappointed by the light sentences received by officers known to have committed atrocities.

Alfonsín took over a country devastated by economic mismanagement, internal repression, and a failed war mobilization. Citizen morale stood at an all-time low.

The new president had to make his way through a political minefield, and he did not escape unharmed.

To salvage the economy, Alfonsín reached agreement with the Peronistas and international lenders to carry out a general restructuring program with austerity measures, but also with some protection for the working class. Called the Plan Austral after the new unit of currency that it created, the program applied neoliberal prescriptions. Alfonsín's finance minister began dismantling myriad controls and regulations inherited from past regimes. He also cut wages, began privatizing public enterprises, and scaled back government spending on subsidies and salaries. The program succeeded in bringing down inflation and restoring the nation's credit rating, but it did not stimulate general growth, as planners had expected.

Meanwhile, members of a new generation of army officers began to abuse their power, kidnapping leftists and threatening politicians hostile to the armed forces. Many officers, doubting Alfonsín's will or ability to control the military, began new protests. His public authority plunged, and his party lost a critical election in 1987.

Alfonsín's last major initiative was a second economic plan, Austral II, intended to deepen the neoliberal policies recommended by his advisors. This plan, plus major capital investments and petroleum discoveries, got the economy growing again, but it was too late to save Alfonsín's presidency. The Radicals lost the 1989 election, and Alfonsín actually stepped down in disrepute before the end of his term.

Brazil

In Brazil residents welcomed José Sarney as president in 1985 and even anointed him with some of the sainthood that they had conferred on the deceased Tancredo Neves. Sarney's accession was met with optimism and good cheer after twenty-one years of military dictatorship. Although little known and representing the poor state of Maranhão in the North, Sarney nonetheless enjoyed a long honeymoon. He undertook to build a working majority in Congress because his Liberal Front Party was both new and small. He also continued the *abertura* process by freeing unions and employers to pursue collective bargaining and by allowing communists to operate legally for the first time in thirty-eight years. The electoral system was reformed to allow illiterates to vote, lower the voting age to sixteen, and select the president by direct ballot. Finally, in November 1985 Sarney oversaw municipal elections and the next year congressional elections, in which record numbers cast ballots and asserted their civic authority.

The army had exacted from Tancredo Neves the promise of a decree of amnesty for military officers accused of crimes while serving in official capacity. Sarney did not try to reverse this decree, and no reprisals were carried out. Those who fought the dictatorship did not approve of the amnesty and kept alive the memory of the military atrocities through books, memoirs, movies, and public testimony. A chronicle of the tortures and deaths, kept secretly by the archdiocese of São Paulo, was published later as *Nunca Mais* (*Never More*) and was soon translated into several languages.

The economy that Sarney inherited from Figueiredo was in disarray, so Sarney made reorganization a high priority. To be sure, the GNP had begun to grow again, and export earnings were strong, but the foreign debt, totaling over $80 billion, cast a pall over capital markets. In addition, a huge internal debt fed triple- and quadruple-digit inflation rates, which threatened to become hyperinflation—an uncontrollable upward spiral.

Moreover, economic ministers in the 1970s had devised controls and mechanisms that could be described only as baffling and counterproductive. For example, the Byzantine indexing system that was required to adjust for inflation consisted of dozens of separate indicators. One economist euphemistically called this system "heterodoxy" because it combined elements of classically liberal, Keynesian, and socialist approaches. In fact, it was an insoluble maze that choked off business initiative and foreign investment. Sarney could not decide how to proceed, so he kept advocates of both ECLAC and neoliberal doctrine in his cabinet.

In 1986 Sarney unveiled the Cruzado Plan, a heterodox scheme inspired by the Argentine Austral experiment. The president decreed a whole new currency, the *cruzado,* to replace the *cruzeiro,* which had circulated since 1942. To protect the *cruzado* from inflation, he ordered a freeze in prices and wages and went through the motions of reducing government deficits and making other adjustments. The government printed the new currency and then launched it with a major publicity campaign against inflation.

The Cruzado Plan proved enormously popular. Virtually everyone applauded the effort and wished it well, recognizing that Brazil could never attain economic maturity without a stable currency. Sarney went on television to exhort common citizens to cooperate by reporting any illegal price or wages increases. The feeling of empowerment that swept the nation stunned observers. One government economist believed that it was economic democracy at work. Soon tens of thousands of people donned badges calling themselves Sarney's Watchdogs and began monitoring price tags in stores and businesses of all sorts. For several months prices remained stable, and the country enjoyed a genuine euphoria.

Gradually, however, inflation began to creep back, and the government was powerless to prevent it. Indeed, public deficits fueled expansion of market demand. Other factors beyond government control also undermined price stability. By early 1987 Sarney was obliged to launch another package of reforms, the so-called Cruzado II, which included a suspension of interest payments on foreign commercial loans. This effort was met with more skepticism, and the resultant price stability lasted only a few months. Toward the end of his term, Sarney launched a third, desperate plan, introducing the *cruzado novo* currency (worth one thousand old *cruzados*) and a new list of economic measures. This plan barely slowed inflation at all. Sarney's once-brilliant image as a leader was tarnished beyond repair. His approval ratings sank into single digits by the end of his term.

Generalizations

The transitional governments of Belaúnde, Alfonsín, and Sarney, along with several others, had some common features. For one thing, all three men were veteran politicians in their fifties and sixties. None had military experience, but they had survived army regimes. Once in office, they reestablished constitutional procedures. They instituted free, direct elections and pluralistic, party-based decision making. They also began to apply neoliberal economic policies, although inconsistently. The plans that their advisors assembled had standard as well as unorthodox elements. They struggled with massive foreign debts, high inflation, pent-up labor demands, social inequality, and overregulated financial systems.

The transition presidents enjoyed one major advantage, however: the relaxation of international tensions that accompanied the decline of the Cold War. Internal and external military threats gradually disappeared (except for the Sendero in Peru). As a result the armed forces retreated into the background. Still, the civilians had difficulty making army officers accountable for their actions. Only Alfonsín managed to bring the worst offenders to trial, and as a result he suffered three unsuccessful coup attempts. In Brazil, Peru, and later Chile, the army enjoyed immunity from prosecution.

Neopopulism

Hidden among the many rationales of the national security states lay a frankly political motive: to eradicate populism. Military leaders believed that populists stirred up the masses, destabilized government, awakened appetites that they could not satisfy, and fomented crises so that they could solve them and become heroes. Army officers in their respective nations disliked Juan Perón, Getúlio Vargas, Juscelino Kubitschek, João Goulart, Arnulfo Arias, Haya de la Torre, Velasco Ibarra, Rómulo Betancourt, Belaúnde, and other populists. In most cases the dislike was mutual. The national security states were supposed to discipline their citizens so that they would not succumb to the deceptive appeals of populism. In fact, during the long years of military rule most of the populists either died or grew too old to run for office.

When the Brazilian military allowed exiles to return and run for office after 1979, however, three of their "most unwanted" populists campaigned and won major victories. Leonel Brizola, Goulart's brother-in-law and the most audacious foe of the army in the 1960s, formed a new party and ran for the governorship of Rio de Janeiro state in November 1982. He won handily and served with great flair and ability. Miguel Arraes, also a trenchant opponent of the 1964 coup, won a seat in Congress and then won the governor's race in Pernambuco in 1986. In São Paulo state, meanwhile, Jânio Quadros lost a bid for governor in 1982 but then won the mayoralty of São Paulo city in 1985, a position more powerful than most governorships. So the old populist magic still worked among many voters.

Other factors favored the return of populism. The electorates had grown rapidly since the 1960s, and literally hundreds of millions of new voters became eligible to vote and eager to participate. Many of the new voters had no direct memories of the classic populists yet were attracted by their legends. Vargas, Perón, Evita, Kubitschek, and others became even more celebrated in death than in life. Also, the electoral laws in most countries were altered to allow teenagers and illiterates to vote, and these people could be recruited by populist methods. A kind of "virgin voter" phenomenon occurred in which newly enfranchised persons proved especially receptive to populist appeals.

As it turned out, however, old-style populism was not a practical option for the redemocratizing nations of Latin America. None of the pre-military-era populists still alive managed to capture the presidency in Brazil. Arnulfo Arias's probable 1984 victory in Panama was simply erased by vote fraud, and he died four years later. Assad Bucarám in Ecuador, thwarted in his bid for the presidency, ended up supporting a relative, Jaime Roldós, for president in 1979. For two years, Bucarám and Roldós sparred for control, but then both died, and with them populism in Ecuador largely disappeared.

A different kind of populism arose in the mid-1980s, however, practiced by younger leaders. This neopopulism had many of the characteristics of the earlier version—appeals to nationalist sentiment, charismatic leadership, mass media blitzes, promises of reforms, and evocation of the common people's interests—but it differed in some key ways. Most important, neopopulists began to abandon the economics of government control and intervention. Instead, some cobbled together so-called heterodox approaches, whereas others embraced neoliberalism as the salvation of their countries.

The neopopulists were mostly very young, white, middle class, university educated, and well spoken. They had traveled abroad and were conversant in global issues. Like the classic populists, none had pursued a military career. In addition, whereas the earlier populists had avoided existing parties and instead formed their own personal organizations, a few neopopulists remodeled the old parties to fit their needs. Still, they addressed their appeals to the masses, usually on television, without acknowledging any intervening organizations. They posed as outsiders untainted by the corrupt politics of the previous generation, and they attacked the incumbent regimes mercilessly. Finally, the neopopulists were up to date in the latest media techniques, especially television and polling.

The neopopulists' pursuit of market-oriented, private enterprise programs alienated some of their institutional support. Unions, employee groups, business associations, and others repudiated the neopopulist leaders when they learned that they would no longer enjoy special protection. These groups had been lukewarm in their support anyway and quickly withdrew from the coalition. Many protested vigorously at the first signs of austerity programs.

The unorganized masses, on the other hand, saw the bold new policies as innovative and daring solutions to long-festering problems. In fact, the dramatic shifts in stance enhanced the neopopulists' charisma and reputation for leadership. Polls showed that neopopulists received the most support from among the poor who worked in the informal sectors—those outside the mainstream economy and most vulnerable to economic downturns. To be sure, the measures caused widespread suffering among the masses, and poverty rates at first soared. Still, the poor approved of the radical measures, believing them to be the harsh medicine needed for economic healing.

Peru

The first neopopulist, Alan García of Peru, fizzled before he could test the full possibilities of this approach. At age thirty-six the youngest president ever to serve in Peru, García was handsome and well spoken. Haya de la Torre had been his mentor, helping to groom him for power. García seized the reins of the Aprista Party after Haya's death, and he ran a first-rate campaign in 1985. It was the first time that APRA ever won a presidential victory. In essence García mixed interventionist, Keynesian initiatives with neoliberalism. At first they worked, pulling the economy out of the deep slump of the Belaúnde years. In time, however, the inexpert blending of policies began to fail, and García lacked political staying power to pull off an effective change of course, as the classic populists had often done. Within three years García became overextended, lost his public support, and lapsed into emotional burnout from overwork and tension.

García first announced an independent foreign policy, as had Haya and other classic populists before him. He recognized Cuba and worked to reduce U.S. influence in Central America. This played well with the public yet did not upset major power strategists unduly.

On the economic side, García rejected his predecessor's free-market, export-driven model. Instead, he implemented an anti-inflation package, raised wages, and blocked transfers of capital out of the country. He also refused to pay interest on the foreign debt in excess of 10 percent of export earnings. This unusual measure also pleased the public but alienated international bankers, who cut off further credit. The United States then suspended nonmilitary aid. García's policies blended ECLAC economics and expansion of domestic capitalism. Oddly, this unorthodox blend succeeded at first, sparking Peru's first two years of economic growth in a decade. Inflation, meanwhile, went down, giving hope that the economy had finally turned a corner.

But García's program faltered in 1987 because too many independent actors refused to go along: manufacturers, farmers, bankers, retailers, and workers. Shortages appeared as production in factories and on farms diminished. A serious trade deficit and shrinking currency reserves led García to announce that he would nationalize the banking system. This act sparked an explosion of protests and induced the opposition to coalesce into a single force. At the head of the opposition stood Peru's foremost novelist, Mario Vargas Llosa, an advocate of neoliberalism and leader of a conservative coalition that eventually took the name Fredemo Alliance.

By the late 1980s Peru was in the grips of a stalemate. García was incapable of initiating any new policy or of making the earlier ones work. He tried to regain support with *balconazos,* his famous impromptu speeches from the balcony of the presidential palace, but they had lost their appeal. His attempts to enact fiscal austerity measures worsened his declining approval rating. The economy groaned to a halt and shrank again for two years. García became a recluse, disappearing into the palace for days at a time.

Given the decline in public authority, the Sendero Luminoso became bolder and took total control of huge areas in the Andes and Peru's Amazon sector. It had very strong bases in the cities as well. Where Sendero was in control, its leaders performed all government functions, from collecting taxes to running the schools. In some Sendero regions, peasants noted a marked improvement in public services and safety. In other regions, however, peasants armed themselves or furiously resisted Sendero, which just as often employed outright terrorism and brute force to intimidate the inhabitants. Given the remarkable spread of Sendero, some observers questioned whether the army could win even an all-out war against it.

García was succeeded by one of Latin America's most colorful and strong-willed presidents of recent times, Alberto Fujimori. A middle-aged engineer of Japanese descent, Fujimori had never before dabbled in politics. But he became so disgusted with García's collapsing administration that he formed a new party, Cambio 1990, in late 1989. Made up of other professionals, small business owners, Pentecostal and evangelical Protestants, and middle-class discontents, Cambio 1990 entered the 1990 presidential race. Fujimori posed as the friend of the downtrodden and mixed-race majority (the Cholitos) and promised to end the rule by the white oligarchs (the Blanquitos). Amazingly, he came in second, with a quarter of the votes cast.

The runoff pitted Fujimori against Mario Vargas Llosa, thought by most to be the favorite. The well-financed Vargas Llosa preached doom and gloom, however, and the need to institute draconian austerity measures. Voters turned from the frightening rhetoric of Vargas Llosa to the more upbeat message of Fujimori.

Fujimori campaigned on the need to protect the citizenry against the ravages of more economic shocks. He spoke vaguely of dealing with the country's problems in a professional manner but did not outline specific measures. To everyone's surprise, Fujimori received over 56 percent of the runoff vote and was inaugurated in July 1990.

Fujimori quickly enacted austerity measures, which skeptics called "Fuji-shocks," of the sort that he had denounced during his campaign. One observer termed his reversal of policy "bait and switch." He put virtually all state enterprises up for privatization. He ended subsidies for staple foods, provoking a spike in price levels. He did, however, create a special program of aid to needy persons, and he gained a lot of media coverage giving out aid personally. Meanwhile, Fujimori seemed imperturbable and immune to pressures of all sorts.

Remarkably, the shock treatment began to produce dividends by 1991 when inflation came down into a manageable range and the recession abated. By 1993 the country began its first sustained growth in over two decades. Foreign credit was restored, new jobs appeared, business invested in new plants and equipment, and Fujimori's approval rating stayed surprisingly high. He also instituted health programs to alleviate epidemic diseases and improve the productivity of Peru's workers.

Peru's president, Alberto Fujimori, campaigned as an outsider who could defend the interests of the little people. A practical and articulate man, he convinced a majority that he could bring growth and equity to the nation.

Encountering adamant opposition from Congress in 1992, Fujimori mobilized the army and simply closed Congress until further notice. He accused it of obstructionism and corruption and began to rule by decree. He purged the judiciary of judges who blocked his reforms. He also proclaimed a state of siege so that he could carry on the war against Sendero, which still controlled a sizable portion of the national territory. The public did not protest these emergency measures because it believed that the president needed special powers to solve the economic and military crises facing the nation.

Sendero stepped up its attacks on the government after Fujimori closed Congress. Guzmán may have believed that Fujimori was more vulnerable because of his closure of Congress, or he may have acted because Sendero was losing its base in much of the highlands. Many peasant leaders had cooperated with Sendero merely because it was a lesser evil than the central government in Lima. Fujimori's successes in reviving the economy and reforming the administrative system, however, convinced many local officials to shift their allegiance back to the government. As they did so, they turned their arms against Sendero and drove it out of region after region. This reversal in the highlands may have motivated Guzmán's decision to attack the government strenuously.

The Sendero offensive of 1993 was met with a concerted military and publicity campaign, and at a critical moment Guzmán was captured by the authorities. This proved a major breakthrough because it decapitated the centralized command structure that Guzmán had maintained. For months Sendero drifted leaderless and by 1995 was clearly on the retreat. Guzmán, meanwhile, was kept under heavy guard in a prison island offshore.

Fujimori believed that he needed more than five years to complete the reorganization and stabilization of the country, so he held elections to choose a new Congress. When this new Congress convened, it dutifully changed the Constitution to allow Fujimori to be reelected. In 1995 Fujimori ran and won handily, beginning his second term with a renewed mandate.

Fujimori represented neopopulism at its most effective. A convincing speaker on television (where he hosted a talk show) and so unorthodox as to be appealing, he overcame voters' mistrust and became their savior. His reforms were neoliberal in inspiration yet required strong leadership reminiscent of the classic populists. Although he did use military force to close Congress, he claimed that his mandate came from the people and was exercised in their name.

Fujimori was less successful in bringing the oldest border dispute in Latin America to a successful conclusion. Peru and Ecuador had been squabbling over their border along the upper reaches of the Amazon River since independence in the early nineteenth century. Various border conflicts marked the dispute, and in 1941 finally erupted into a short but intense war between the two nations that threatened to break the united front that the United States desired from Latin America during World War II. The United States, along with Chile, Argentina, and Brazil, mediated a truce that resulted in the Rio Treaty of 1942. Peru not only won the border conflict in the field but also gained the lion's share of territory in the treaty. Ecuador eventually renounced the treaty, and another round of border conflicts began in the 1960s, culminating in Ecuador's armed occupation of parts of the disputed territory in January 1995. It couldn't have come at a worse time for Fujimori.

Essentially, Ecuador wanted unimpeded and sovereign access to the Amazon, and Peru stood in the way. The border in question lay in a remote section of the Andes called the Cordillera del Condor and the upper Cenapa River region. Ecuador had been modernizing its armed forces for more than a decade—especially after skirmishes in 1981 went badly for Ecuador—and in January 1995 Ecuadorean units pushed into the region to challenge Peruvian outposts. The Peruvian military, distracted by the prolonged war against terrorism, failed to dislodge the Ecuadorean troops and equipment, and a cease-fire was established.

In December 1996 Fujimori faced another challenge from an unexpected quarter. A small guerrilla group, the Tupac Amarus, seized the Japanese ambassador's residence during a reception, capturing scores of prominent foreigners and Peruvian authorities, including the president's brother. The hostage crisis lasted for four months, during which time Fujimori resisted pressures from various quarters and seemed to be paralyzed. Finally, in April 1997 he ordered an infiltration assault in which one hostage and all the guerrillas perished. The president received congratulations for the operation, and Peru seemed finally to be capable of managing terrorist threats.

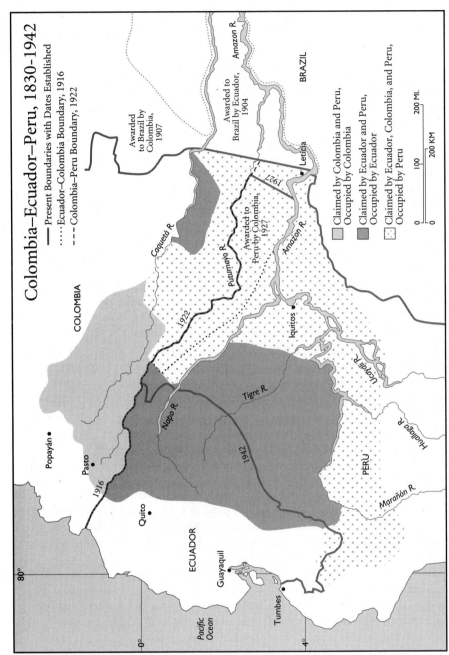

Colombia–Ecuador–Peru, 1830–1942

— Present Boundaries with Dates Established
······ Ecuador–Colombia Boundary, 1916
– – – Colombia–Peru Boundary, 1922

Claimed by Colombia and Peru,
Occupied by Colombia

Claimed by Ecuador and Peru,
Occupied by Ecuador

Claimed by Ecuador, Colombia, and Peru,
Occupied by Peru

200 KM

200 MI.

Awarded
to Brazil by
Colombia,
1907

Awarded to
Brazil by Ecuador,
1904

Awarded to
Peru by Colombia,
1927

BRAZIL

Leticia

1927

Amazon R.

Amazon R.

Caquetá R.

Putumayo R.

COLOMBIA

1922

Iquitos

Ucayali R.

Tigre R.

Napo R.

Huallaga R.

Popayán

Pasto

1916

Quito

ECUADOR

Guayaquil

PERU

Marañón R.

1942

Tumbes

Pacific
Ocean

80°

0°

4°

Source: John Lombardi, *Latin American History: A Teaching Atlas.* University of Wisconsin Press.

Brazil

The next neopopulist to appear, Brazil's Fernando Collor de Mello, began his term with a burst of glory, like García, but crashed even faster than his Peruvian colleague. The Brazilian electorate had grown so disenchanted with President Sarney and the major parties in Congress that it voted wholesale for nontraditional candidates. Out of more than a dozen who ran for president in the first-round election of 1989, the two top vote-getters were Collor, a virtually unknown figure from the small northeastern state of Alagoas, and Luís Inácio "Lula" da Silva, a metalworkers' union manager and candidate of the Workers' Party (1979–). Voters showed remarkable independence in repudiating the politicians who had weathered the military regime.

In the runoff election of December 1989 Collor managed to win a slight majority by using his superior financing and strong backing from the national media. He was a handsome, polished, well-spoken young man (forty when elected) who emphasized his distance from regular politicians by running almost without a party. Instead, he used a highly professional campaign staff to flood the media with his image, his shallow promise of national renewal, and his insincere devotion to the common man and woman. He claimed to be an outsider who cared about the *descamisados*. In fact, Collor came from a rich and well-connected family. He had grown up in Rio and Brasília, where his father served several terms as senator. The family owned a chain of newspapers and radio and television stations in the Northeast.

Collor stressed several points in his speeches. First, he promised to moralize public life and clean up corruption, which he personified as the "maharajahs" who controlled regional politics and lived in opulence. Second, he pledged to carry out neoliberal policies, including privatization, freer trade, and shrinkage of government programs. Third, he guaranteed an end to inflation, which he would kill off with a shock treatment. Yet, Collor's victory probably gained most from his appeal to youth over age, the modern over the old, and the fresh over the stale. It was largely a media-driven campaign during which Collor spent hundreds of millions of dollars to project an appealing image of himself.

The labor candidate, Lula, made a phenomenal showing, given the facts that his party was new and that he had not run for national office before. A plain-looking, bearded young man, Lula spoke directly and honestly about his years in union organizing, his program to increase workers' incomes and benefits, and his opposition to excessive foreign control of the economy. He stood frankly for having greater public regulation of the economy and for shifting income to working-class families. Many of his campaign aides were leftists and intellectuals who had suffered during the military regime.

When Collor took office in March 1990 he declared a bank holiday and initiated drastic reforms designed to sanitize the economy. He ordered banks to transfer funds in excess of about $1,000 into accounts that would remain frozen for eighteen months. This would "wring out" excess demand from the economy, he said, and thus dampen inflation. He launched another currency, the *cruzeiro*, worth the same as the previous year's new *cruzado*, which would not circulate. Because of the sharp contraction in money available to consumers, the new unit quickly rose in value domestically and abroad. The shock could not have been greater, and it took months for the economy to return to normal.

Collor also instituted price and wage controls in the name of the free market, saying that prices had to be pegged at the previous year's levels. A government team carried out a veritable blitz of reform measures, led by the thirty-six-year-old minister of economy, Zélia Cardoso de Melo. The team closed down agencies and ministries, laid off public employees, deregulated whole sectors of the economy, cut back spending, and overhauled the rules governing the banks.

Amazingly, the public not only accepted but also applauded these initiatives, in the desperate hope that the new president would truly eradicate inflation. The public believed that spiraling prices caused the greatest hardships to the greatest number and that only drastic, painful measures could stabilize prices. Congress followed suit and approved most of his program in the following months.

Collor's brash and daring assault on inflation suffered two major flaws. It was far too complex to be implemented knowledgeably by fiscal authorities at all levels, and it required drastic curbs on spending that the president simply could not carry out. Soon inflation began to creep back like a wounded bear, and it ate into Collor's approval ratings and effectiveness. Arrogant to a fault, however, he believed that he could prevail by sheer will power and personal energy.

Collor also took a calculated risk by inviting the United Nations to hold its second Earth Summit on environment in Rio de Janeiro. Scheduled for 1992, the summit attracted delegates from most countries of the world, plus tens of thousands of observers representing public interest groups. Brazil had been heavily criticized in recent years for deforestation of the Amazon rain forest and for abuse of native peoples. Collor had decreed an end to fiscal incentives for forest clearing and had set up huge Amerindian reserves, yet many environmentalists were skeptical at best. Collor hoped that by sponsoring the summit he could improve the country's image.

The Collor administration performed well and managed to counteract adverse opinion. By then the pace of deforestation had slowed, and Amerindian groups had become quite outspoken about their rights. Not all of the country's ecological problems were improving, to be sure, but Brazil's sponsorship of the summit strengthened the position of those committed to better policies.

Apart from the whirlwind economic program and environmental grandstanding, Collor's administration did little else of substance. He kept up an incredible flow of publicity from press conferences, media leaks, and impromptu appearances. He and his beautiful wife seemed to appear at every gala function in the country. He jogged, drove fast cars, flew a supersonic fighter plane, and traveled abroad as well. On the sly, investigators later revealed, administration officials were salting away tens of millions of dollars from bribes taken in exchange for favors and concessions to contractors. The administration's glitter concealed corrupt backroom deals.

Collor was certainly a neopopulist, albeit a short-lived one. His image gained him charismatic authority with the masses, especially among young and poor voters, who wanted desperately to believe in someone. He ran without party ties or obligations to major political factions. He made expert use of media specialists and pollsters to portray himself as the embodiment of a better future for Brazil. He promised reforms that would benefit the masses and break the power of the oligarchy. He polled especially well among new voters: the sixteen- to eighteen-year-olds, illiterates, and the rural poor.

Collor's term was cut short by impeachment in 1992, an unprecedented event anywhere in the Americas. Congress, spurred on by the press and growing public demonstrations, gathered evidence of bribe taking by Collor's personal secretary and opened a formal investigation. Congress had its share of scandals and was not known for political bravery, but when polls and citizen complaints began to flood Brasília, members of Congress saw their duty. Collor resisted until the end and refused to resign, so he became the only president ever impeached in the Americas.

In good populist tradition, Collor had chosen a virtual nonentity for his vice presidential running mate, Itamar Franco, from the interior state of Minas Gerais. An elderly bachelor who expected to coast through the administration with little to do, Franco was suddenly thrust into the limelight by Collor's impeachment. The new president served out the last two and a half years of the 1990–1995 term with dignity.

Itamar Franco assumed caretaker responsibilities and avoided major initiatives or disasters. Congress emerged from the impeachment with a great deal more authority, so the president worked closely with legislative leaders. The economy lapsed back into its triple-digit inflationary mode but performed reasonably well. The country marked time until an elected president could finally take office.

The 1994 election seems to have been a turning point in modern Brazilian history. It certainly put clear choices before the voters and resulted in decisive changes. A wide range of candidates ran in the November round, including the perennial populist Leonel Brizola. Lula again represented the Workers' Party, offering much the same platform as he had in 1989. He had solid backing from unions, students, the intelligentsia, and a portion of the middle class. A centrist candidate, however, Fernando Henrique Cardoso—a sixty-three-year-old sociologist and former senator—took an early lead in the polls. Promising neoliberal economics, concern for the poor, and a sane approach to the foreign debt, Fernando Henrique won over 45 percent of the first-round votes and was proclaimed the winner.

In fact, Fernando Henrique was elected largely on the basis of his economic stabilization program, implemented in July 1994 while he was serving as finance minister. By far the most carefully planned and executed effort of its sort, it required a new currency, the *real*, which was loosely pegged to the U.S. dollar. For months before the money circulated, businesses were obliged to record all of their transactions and accounts in a dollar-equivalent unit, as preparation for shifting to the *real*. The government built up $40 billion in hard-currency reserves to be able to withstand any run on the exchange rate. Finally, a huge publicity campaign preceded and accompanied the new currency, essentially brainwashing the population as to the steady value of the *real*.

The Plano Real, as the program was known, worked even better than its creators hoped. They had used all manner of coercion to prevent businesses and unions from increasing prices or wages before the plan went into effect, and afterward they remained vigilant against clandestine price hikes. In some cases the government authorized importation of cheaper foreign goods to drive down prices. The *real* began trading at about $1.10 in July 1994, and it remained at about that level for more than a year. The overall inflation during the first year, moreover, stood at less than 10 percent. It seemed nothing short of a miracle, the lowest price increases in decades. The public credited Fernando Henrique Cardoso with this success and accordingly elected him in November 1994 in the first round of voting.

The new administration took office on January 1, 1995, and continued to pursue neoliberal policies while keeping a wary eye on potential sources of inflation. One by one, public enterprises were offered for sale to private consortia, resuming the privatization begun under Collor and Franco. The economic performance of Brazil was truly remarkable, posting growth rates consistently above 4 percent a year through the mid-1990s. The foreign debt, meanwhile, had been reduced through rescheduling with the commercial banks. Although still large, it receded in importance due to overall expansion of the GNP.

Cardoso began making trips abroad after his first six months in office. He met with Southern Cone presidents to move negotiations ahead on Mercosur, the free trade zone embracing Brazil, Argentina, Uruguay, and Paraguay. He met with President Bill Clinton to update him on Latin American developments. He visited Europe, finally, where he conferred with business and finance leaders. Without doubt Cardoso enjoyed the greatest prestige of any president in Latin America in the mid-1990s. His re-election in late 1998 seemed assured.

Argentina

Like García and Collor, Carlos Menem in Argentina was a neopopulist. He so thoroughly dominated the political field that analysts began to compare his reign with that of Juan Perón nearly a half-century earlier. Born in the province of La Rioja in 1930, Menem rose through the ranks of the Peronista Party and achieved national prominence in the late 1980s as an outspoken critic of Raúl Alfonsín's policies.

In May 1989 Menem won an overwhelming victory on the Peronista Party ticket, and in July he took office five months early to try to contain the economic crisis. Inflation had made the peso worthless, and only dollars or other foreign currencies could be used for purchases. The GNP was one-sixth lower than it had been at the beginning of the decade, and unemployment had soared. Goods disappeared from supermarkets, crowds milled the streets, and the economy virtually stopped altogether. As a candidate, Menem had promised to carry out a classically Peronista program of raising wages, stimulating production with loans and subsidies, starting construction work to revive the economy, and postponing repayments on the foreign loan. These pledges appealed to the masses just as much as they had in the 1940s.

Once in office, however, Menem reversed his course and carried out a neoliberal stabilization program. Protests arose from the unions, public employee groups, and other sectors that had supported his election, but he ignored them. To cushion his program's impact on the very poor, he created the Federal Solidarity Program of direct assistance to the unemployed, a kind of safety net. He did everything possible to sustain his support from the unorganized masses who had voted for him.

Privatization of major state enterprises topped Menem's list of priorities. Most of these enterprises lost money, saddled the government with debt, and were political liabilities. Much of the capital needed for privatization had to come from foreign sources because Argentines preferred to invest abroad. By late 1993 virtually all of the public companies were at least partially owned by private interests, including the huge oil monopoly, YPF.

In 1993 the economy began to grow at a good rate, just in time to reinforce Menem's party in Congress and to elect delegates to a constitutional convention that would authorize a second term for himself. Menem kept up a vigorous schedule of traveling throughout the country, especially in the western region where he grew up. He drew significant support from the rural working class.

In 1995 Menem ran for reelection and widened his margin of victory. The economy was doing very well, he had survived a scandalous divorce, and citizens believed that they could rely on him to continue policies that favored them.

Menem, Fujimori, and Collor all defined a new strain of populism, one that brought forward many of the techniques of classic populism from the 1950s but that also adopted neoliberal economics and appealed to the unorganized masses.

Central America and the Caribbean

To the north of the equator, other events unfolded during the 1980s and 1990s, often closely monitored by or even driven by decisions in Washington. The CIA began training and arming counterrevolutionary forces (called the Contras) to harass and even invade Nicaragua. To contain the Sandinistas who had won control there in 1979, and thereby to keep Marxism from spreading, the Reagan administration unveiled the Caribbean Basin Initiative (CBI), a development program that offered low tariffs and investment money in exchange for cooperation with U.S. policy aims in the region. Nicaragua was not included in the CBI.

The fighting that centered on Nicaragua undermined peace to such a degree that neighboring countries, and indeed nations from around the globe, tried to induce the United States to end its sponsorship of the Contras. From these efforts, a new sense of solidarity swept the region, prompting plans for political and economic cooperation.

Sandinistas versus Contras

The Contra War was waged by former Nicaraguan National Guard officers and soldiers. Financed and supported logistically by the United States, they grouped in neighboring Honduras and occasionally Costa Rica and raided across the border into Nicaragua. Their purpose was to sap the vigor of the Sandinista revolution and to prevent the nation's recovery from the struggles of the 1970s. The war kept the populace on constant alert and robbed the economy of labor and resources that could have been used for investment. The Contra War was one of the more vicious episodes of harassment and manipulation sponsored by the United States.

To the Reagan administration, then locked in the final battle that would lead to victory in the Cold War during George Bush's term, the Sandinistas represented a potential Soviet-style client state in the Western Hemisphere, like Castro's Cuba. And the Cold War had been fought often brutally and relentlessly by the protagonists.

By 1980 Nicaraguan leadership had largely devolved upon the Sandinistas, in particular on Daniel Ortega. The young leader took up the challenge with vigor. He and his advisors announced that their revolution would provide the masses with a better life, including a higher standard of living, social justice, national dignity, and full civil liberties. Immediately sympathetic countries and organizations from around the world sent supplies, aid workers, technicians, and funds to rebuild Nicaragua. Despite the sometimes awkward policies of the government, this seemed to be a moderate revolution whose social and economic goals ought to be nurtured. Sympathetic foreign volunteers, often wearing casual 1960s clothing, were jokingly called the *sandalistas.*

The Sandinistas' leftist ideology and warm relations with the USSR and Cuba, however, concerned Nicaraguan businessmen as well as CIA analysts. The former were reassured that they would be free to continue their business operations as before, as long as they obeyed the new labor and economic laws. Most did so but

A Contra commander led the way over a grassy hill in northwestern Nicaragua in the early days of the conflict.

avoided investing any more capital than necessary to continue production. They also kept their profits in overseas banks in case the government tried to confiscate them. The general recovery was also hampered by the deep world recession of the early 1980s.

Ronald Reagan decided to take a tough approach to the Sandinista revolution, to force its leaders into line with U.S. security desires. He funded the Contras because their pressure could be increased at will to punish the Sandinistas. U.S. backing for the Contras was hardly a secret, and it soured relations between the two countries. Clandestine aid by the Sandinistas to leftist, rebel forces in El Salvador further fueled the Reagan Administration's determination to isolate the Sandinistas.

The Sandinista leaders, mostly young, proud, and seasoned in guerrilla warfare, resisted Reagan's pressure. Therefore, they formed militias to supplement their small army, and they prepared defenses against a possible attack by the Contras. Even children received military drilling, and the country went on a permanent state of alert.

President Reagan bribed the Honduran government to allow construction of a Contra base on the Nicaraguan border. U.S. forces also landed in Honduras and helped prepare the terrain for Contra attacks, and U.S. advisors accompanied most Contra operations. To finance the offensive, the Reagan White House gave the Contras a great deal of cash, much of which ended up in Swiss banks. None of the funds, however, could be accounted for publicly because they came out of the intelligence budget or slush funds. For Reagan, Nicaragua became an obsession: He called the Contras "freedom fighters" and compared them to the Minutemen in the American Revolution.

Reagan received a great deal of criticism for his Nicaragua policy, at home and abroad, so in 1982 he announced the CBI. Countries that qualified (by supporting U.S. policies, lowering tariffs, and allowing imports of machinery and raw materials) were eligible to receive aid plus investments from U.S. corporations. These projects were mostly factories where local workers assembled final products, like the *maquiladoras* in Mexico. The most common industries begun under CBI auspices produced finished clothing, usually located in free trade zones. Of the almost two dozen participating countries, the Dominican Republic, Haiti, and Guatemala received the largest amount of CBI investment. Congress excluded Nicaragua for political reasons.

Rising trade with island nations under the CBI also encouraged other enterprise. Tourism, always a mainstay of the Caribbean, bounced back and became a major factor in its recovery from the 1980s recession. U.S., Canadian, and European tourists visited by the millions, traveling mostly by plane and cruise ship. Offshore banking and data input services also grew in importance in the late 1980s.

In 1983 Reagan ordered the Pentagon to invade the tiny island nation of Grenada. This invasion, justified on the grounds that a Marxist coup put U.S. citizens in jeopardy, was analogous to Lyndon Johnson's invasion of the Dominican Republic eighteen years earlier, on a much smaller scale. Grenada was tiny in comparison and did not pose any security threat to the United States. The U.S. State Department elicited an invitation from several governments in the region to intervene in Grenada. The occupation accomplished its objective, but serious communications and logistical errors greatly embarrassed U.S. military officials.

The Reagan administration's policies in the Caribbean harked back to the era of gunboat diplomacy. Aid to the Contras violated international law, and a clandestine CIA attack on Nicaraguan port facilities even brought a World Court judgment against the United States. In 1984 Congress attached an amendment to the federal budget banning military aid to the Contras. Nevertheless, the administration continued to channel supplies and cash to the area, through surreptitious means coordinated by the staff of the National Security Council. In 1986 the ban was lifted, but by then information had leaked out about the illegal aid. These leaks led to the Iran-Contra scandal, indictments of high officials, and last-minute pardons by Reagan.

Interview with Ricardo E. Chavarria, Nicaraguan Official and Former Priest, 1983

At one time, five Sandinista ministers were priests, drawn to service by their struggle against the Somoza dictatorship.

I'm a sociologist. I was with my wife in the United States when our first child was born and the Sandinista People's Revolution was victorious. One thing became quite clear to us: we had to come back to Nicaragua to work and serve the people.... I'm a believer and a militant Christian. I'm a Catholic. Eight years ago, I was a priest.... I left the priesthood on January 10, 1976.... Why did I leave the priesthood? ... I should not continue to be a priest if I could not be really fulfilled alone.... Before the insurrection, when the Sandinista Front was struggling and suffering underground and I was working as a priest, I was invited to work with the Front. I took part in hunger strikes. I remember spending twenty-two days in a hunger strike with the mothers of political prisoners and so getting a number of our Sandinistas out of jail.... I also took part in student strikes. For me there was no alternative. Not to have done that would have been a betrayal—of the people, of my community, of my faith and of my priesthood....

(Teófilo Cabestrero, editor, *Revolutionaries for the Gospel* [Maryknoll, NY: Orbis Books, 1986], pp. 75–82)

The most heartening development in Central America was a series of meetings aimed at ending the Contra War and other hostilities in the region. At first these were called the Contadora Talks, named after the Panamanian island resort where they began. Representatives of Central American nations and several other nations took part, while the United States dragged its feet, not wishing to abandon its clients in Nicaragua. By 1987, however, with the Reagan administration nearing its end, the Central American talks led to an agreement that included a cease-fire and the bases for permanent peace. President Oscar Arias of Costa Rica (1986–1990) came up with an acceptable formula, called Esquipulas II after the Guatemalan town where it was initialed. Arias subsequently received the Nobel Peace Prize for his efforts.

In 1990 the Nicaraguan government held elections for virtually all executive and legislative offices in the country. The campaigns, very intense and competitive, attracted thousands of observers because they would test the ability of the Sandinistas to transform their government into a democracy. It would be a plebiscite on the revolution. The opposition candidate, Violeta Chamorro, won the election, and the parties that supported her gained a majority in the legislature. Daniel Ortega, head of the Sandinista government, passed the presidential sash to her peacefully late that year.

Despite the uneven impact of U.S. policy and intervention, the Caribbean basin emerged from the 1980s in relatively good shape. Moreover, several cultural and economic blocs coalesced or reemerged to seek better ways to promote economic development. The Central American Common Market, for example, which had lapsed into inactivity in the 1980s, took on new life in the 1990s. Moreover, the five participating countries plus Panama created the Central American Parliament, designed to resolve border and economic disputes and perhaps develop more uniform immigration and social policies. Integration proceeded in the Caribbean as well. The Caricom economic group, for example, which was formed in 1975, expanded its trade in the 1990s.

Narcotraffickers and Politics

The amount of drugs—mostly from Colombia—being shipped to the United States increased rapidly in the 1980s. (See Chapter Twenty-one.) The multibillion-dollar industry had complex roots. Colombian producers had for many years dominated shipments of marijuana grown along the Caribbean coast. The rise of cocaine consumption, however, required other sources. The raw material for cocaine was coca leaves, which were grown at intermediate altitudes in Bolivia and Peru. Local processors reduced the leaves to a paste and sent it north to Colombia by airplane. Elaborate factories in Colombia completed the refining, after which the pure cocaine was put onto airplanes for dispatch to the United States and other markets.

Most of the distribution of drugs in the United States was handled by U.S. criminal organizations. Their payments to Colombian suppliers, however, required special handling to evade detection and taxes. This process, called "laundering," took place mostly in banks around the Caribbean region.

The ratio between the price of coca leaves, a staple product in Bolivia, and the value of the refined product on U.S. streets was on the order of one to ten thousand, creating a huge potential for profits all along the way. As cocaine became more popular during the 1980s, the price rose even more, fueling the largest illegal industry in the world. This prompted President Alan García of Peru to state, partly in jest, that the cocaine trade was the only successful multinational industry ever created by Latin Americans. Mafia-like organizations called "cartels" sprang up in Colombian cities, where production, transport, refining, and financial arrangements were coordinated. For a time, the cartel in Medellín dominated the drug trade, but soon the Cali and Cartagena cartels joined in. They employed veritable armies of professionals to carry on the business. Their operations stretched down into Peru and Bolivia for raw materials, through Central America, the Caribbean, and Mexico for transport and money laundering, and finally to the United States and Europe for marketing.

The narcotics trade proved terribly destructive to many Latin American nations. The cartels controlled significant shares of the GNP in Bolivia, Peru, and Colombia, where they wielded enormous power in all branches of government. At least a dozen other nations were drawn into the narcotrafficking business. The cartel bosses bribed and intimidated officials, murdered rivals, bought and sold front companies, and introduced drug consumption everywhere they operated. They made alliances with guerrilla organizations, often trading weapons for raw materials or security services. In short, the narcotraffickers wreaked havoc throughout the region.

The United States invested considerable effort in curbing the supply of illegal drugs in the so-called War on Drugs. U.S. officials financed programs designed to end the growing of coca plants, for example. This sometimes went against the grain of local customs in Peru and Bolivia, where chewing coca leaves was as common as smoking tobacco in the United States. And U.S. policy goals were often confusing and even contradictory. For example, the CIA actually sanctioned some drug trade in Central America in order to help the Contras. In the end, the drug business seemed to plateau in the mid-1990s when demand in the consuming countries tapered off and when the national elites decided that they could no longer tolerate the cartels' most brazen activities and took steps to control them.

Panama

During the 1980s drug trafficking increased in Panama. Drugs had been smuggled through Panama at least since the 1940s, but in the 1980s both shipping and money laundering became major businesses there. The national guard (renamed the Defense Force in 1983) had usually had a hand in various illegal activities, especially drugs. When Colonel Manuel Antonio Noriega became head of the Defense Force in 1983, he oversaw arrangements by which the cartels sent drugs and money through Panama. Many lawyers, politicians, and bankers profited along with Defense Force officers. With all this activity came the increasing scrutiny of the U.S. government.

Noriega ruled Panama from behind a facade of constitutional government. He installed and removed several presidents during the time he served as commander of the Defense Force. He also ran something of an intelligence brokerage in the Caribbean region. He maintained contacts with the Cuban and Nicaraguan regimes while also exchanging information with the U.S., Honduran, and El Salvadoran governments. The fact that he also permitted a number of other illegal activities in Panama eventually gave him an unsavory reputation.

The United States found itself in an awkward position due to Noriega. George Bush, vice president under Reagan and then president from 1989 to 1993, had dealt with Noriega on an official basis since the 1970s and presumably found him

Panamanian strongman Manuel Antonio Noriega (1983–1989) shown giving encouragement to the troops under his command. After being captured and transported to the United States, he was tried and sentenced to 40 years in jail.

acceptable. By 1987, however, Noriega had become an embarrassment to the Reagan-Bush administration. Noriega had profited from drugs, helped furnish illegal weapons to the Contras, shared intelligence information, and now ruled Panama as a dictator.

In December 1989 President Bush authorized Operation Just Cause, a full-scale military invasion of Panama. The alleged purpose was to capture Manuel Noriega for prosecution in Florida on drug charges. In fact, the invasion boosted Bush's popularity by making him appear decisive, and it also diverted attention from the fact that the United States was largely responsible for Noriega's rule. It also allowed U.S. authorities to put the Panama Canal treaty implementation back on track. The invaders captured Noriega, and U.S. courts eventually tried and sentenced him to forty years in jail. In the meantime, the United States installed a caretaker government and launched a massive aid program to revive the Panamanian economy.

The aftermath of the 1989 invasion proved favorable to U.S. interests. State Department and military officials encouraged reforms and disbursement of aid in ways that stimulated the economy. Democratic procedures were adopted for revising the Constitution, eliminating the military, and adopting neoliberal economic policies. Finally, in 1994 the government held elections in which a former ally of General Torrijos, Ernesto Pérez Balladares, won the presidency. Promising to continue the neoliberal reforms and to protect democracy, Pérez Balladares presided over the final years of the 1977 treaties.

Cuba's Adjustment to Post-Cold War Politics

The 1980s had been particularly difficult in Cuba, due not only to the world recession but also to the decline and dissolution of the Soviet bloc. Cuba's economy had long since reverted to dependence on sugar and tobacco exports, sold at subsidized prices in communist countries. The economy was kept afloat by cheap petroleum and reexports from the USSR, as well as by Soviet credit to cover Cuba's imports. Economists calculated that Cuba cost the Soviets several billion dollars a year in the mid-1980s. Fidel Castro partially repaid the aid with a vigorous pro-USSR foreign policy and an active role in furthering the socialist cause in Africa. At one point Castro maintained thirty thousand troops in Africa.

Throughout the early decades of the Cuban Revolution Castro had resisted all pressure to democratize the country. He argued that the great advances that Cubans had achieved in health, education, housing, and nutrition far offset losses in political participation. He stated that Cubans enjoyed more civil liberties than under Batista and that true democracy required a decent standard of living, not an artificial system of politics. Finally, he said, the Cuban people were quite happy with his leadership, which in effect gave him legitimacy.

After his failure to achieve a symbolically important ten-million-ton harvest in 1970, Castro began to alter the political system somewhat. Without relinquishing personal control, he spread responsibilities more widely among persons who had worked with him throughout the 1960s. In 1975 he held the first Communist Party congress, which wrote a constitution that was ratified the following year in a plebiscite. The new system boasted a National Assembly of people's representatives, called Poder del Pueblo. A council of state, headed by Castro himself, naturally, was elected by the National Assembly. The degree of participation, however, barely increased because elections were run by party members.

Cuba's 1980s economic experience was, if anything, worse than the rest of Latin America's. The USSR capped aid to Cuba and intimated that Castro should find a way to earn his living by trading with the noncommunist world. By the time the USSR began its twin processes of *perestroika* and *glasnost* (economic and political liberalization) in the 1980s, Cuba was seriously out of step with its long-term ally.

Cuban leaders faced major political dilemmas around 1990. First, Castro, now sixty-four years old, was unable to repudiate communism and formulate a new regime, as the Russians had done, because of his history of opposing the United States. Ironically, the old anti-imperialism defined his country in juxtaposition to a colonialist power that no longer paid it much attention. Second, the huge and prosperous Cuban exile community in Florida stood on the sidelines waiting for Castro to die or be overthrown. If that happened, Cubans feared, their island would be swamped by exiles bent on reclaiming their lands and businesses. Exiles might cause a bloodbath or undo thirty years of revolutionary reform, or both. Unable to solve these predicaments, Cuba's leaders simply continued to behave the way they always had.

When the Soviet Union dissolved and its bloc of allies collapsed, Castro found himself cut off and isolated from most of the world. In the early 1990s only Cuba,

In 1997, Pope John Paul II met with Cuban Premier Fidel Castro to discuss increased religious freedom on the island. The following year the Pope paid a historic visit to Cuba to reinforce these understandings and to lessen Cuba's isolation by the United States.

Albania, Laos, and North Korea maintained the kind of closed, Soviet-style economy that had once prevailed among communist countries. Cuban economists, desperate to adjust to the end of Soviet aid, took small steps toward allowing private initiative and foreign currency transactions. Happily for Cuba, growing numbers of European and Canadian tourists took advantage of cheap prices and unpolluted beaches, providing some hard-currency income. Still, the economy sank to levels approaching those of the nineteenth century.

The election of a Democratic U.S. president in 1992 slightly eased pressures by the exile community to force Castro to leave power. Meanwhile, large numbers of refugees came across the Florida Strait each year, contributing to social and political problems in Florida. Washington instituted naval patrols to restrict flows of exiles and reached an agreement to return most to Cuba. U.S. leaders then settled back to wait for some change in Cuba. As public opinion changed, however, it became easier for President Clinton to relax the embargo.

By the late 1990s, however, world opinion mounted against the U.S. policies of economic embargo and nonrecognition. The European Union sued the United States in the World Trade Organization to block enforcement of anti-Cuban legislation. Pope John Paul II held a visit to Cuba in 1998 that exerted further pressures for normalization. Finally, hundreds of thousands of European and Canadian tourists voted with their vacations for normal relations with Cuba. And in so doing, they pulled Cuba's economy out of the slump caused by the withdrawal of Russian aid.

Conclusions and Issues

The 1980s brought turmoil and suffering to much of Latin America. Many nations were ravaged by wars, low-intensity conflicts, economic recession, and dislocations of people. The "dirty war" in the Southern Cone countries left tens of thousands dead, maimed, or missing.

The economic collapse of the early 1980s proved so severe that it induced a major shift in thinking by policymakers. They abandoned the approaches devised by the ECLAC in the 1950s and 1960s and turned to market mechanisms to drive economic decisions. A new orthodoxy emerged, called neoliberalism, which prescribed freer trade, privatization, and less government employment and spending and which dismantled decades-old intervention and regulation by public agencies. Perhaps the most beneficial impact of neoliberalism was its encouragement of more productivity from workers, businesspeople, and professionals.

The hardships suffered in the early 1980s also underlined the failure of the national security states that had swept over the region in the 1960s. Gradually, the military withdrew from government and allowed civilians to restore democratic administrations.

Democratization occurred fitfully, hampered by continued meddling by army officers, by an inexperienced generation of leaders, and by millions of new voters. Several patterns emerged in South America. For a time, populists who survived from the 1960s made comebacks. Then, managerial governments devoted to economic stabilization and democracy predominated. By the 1990s several countries had chosen neopopulist leaders, persons who used the old methods of vote gathering while insisting on neoliberal economic programs.

The Caribbean basin, meanwhile, survived an escalation of political violence sponsored by the United States. The decade ended in relative calm. The Contra War wound down in 1987, when belligerent and neighboring countries signed a peace accord. A new economic approach based on free trade and offshore manufacturing boosted some Caribbean economies.

Only in Panama and Cuba did the situation worsen during the 1980s. In the former, an impasse between Washington and the dictator Manuel Noriega led to an armed invasion that returned Panama to U.S. tutelage. And in the latter, Castro found himself isolated by the dramatic end of the Soviet Union and the breakup of its eastern bloc of allies. Unwilling to reform internally and unable to deflect hostility from the exile community in Florida, Castro rode out the 1990s in the hopes of finding some solutions to these dilemmas.

Discussion Questions

1. Were the neoliberal policies simply imposition of control from the economic superpowers, or were they necessary adjustments and restructuring to correct decades of erroneous and inefficient policies? Were the adjustments easy or hard?

2. Why do the major countries of South America seem to follow similar political paths? Did democratization suddenly "catch on" in the way that the national security doctrine did twenty years earlier? Were the new governments simply resurrections of earlier democracies, or had the rules of governance shifted since the 1960s?

3. Why did the Reagan administration concentrate so heavily on Central American affairs when the East-West confrontation and the security of Europe were at stake? Did its initiatives in the Caribbean basin hasten the fall of the USSR and end the Cold War?

Into the Twenty-first Century

The 1990s were generally positive years in Latin America, a time when civil unrest seemed to diminish, employment and standards of living rose, and the international scene favored the region. The largest insurgencies, led by the Sendero Luminoso in Peru and the Zapatistas in Mexico, lost their edge, and peace generally prevailed. Even the drug trade slowed somewhat in the 1990s, and cartel leaders pulled back from their alliances with guerrilla forces. As a backdrop, superpower tensions eased, and burgeoning global trade opened markets for Latin America's exports. The U.S. nonrecognition and embargo of Cuba remained the last vestige of the Cold War in the Americas.

U.S. President Bill Clinton made his first trips to Latin America in 1997, visiting Mexico, Costa Rica, and Barbados in the spring and South America in the fall. In San José and Bridgetown, heads of state from neighboring countries attended what amounted to minisummits. More ceremonial than substantive, these meetings sought to bolster feelings of hemispheric solidarity and enhance cooperation on tariff reduction, immigration, and narcotics suppression. In South America Clinton tried to advance the process of hemispheric trade integration, which had been a major goal of the Miami Summit of the Americas in 1994. A follow-up summit in April 1998, held in Santiago, Chile, saw the presidents reaffirm their commitment to the Miami agenda. Some solid advances were achieved at this meeting toward the goal of promoting a truly hemispheric trading bloc.

The economies of most nations seemed to hit a new stride in the 1990s, growing and providing more jobs and higher wages—the average growth in GDP was 4.1 percent between 1990 and 1994. Certainly, neoliberal policies unleashed potential energies in the private sector and attracted international investment to complement them. New capital formation created the highest demand for workers in decades. In addition, the economy of the United States came out of the 1991 recession and grew rapidly for years, stimulating exports from Latin America, which rose at about 6 percent a year.

The Zapatista revolt in Chiapas, Mexico, was put on hold during 1994 and 1995. In fact, the threat of violence had put the entire Mexican elite on notice regarding the consequences of failure of their plans. The Zedillo administration, after an ill-advised crackdown on the Zapatistas provoked an international outcry, held discontinuous talks with Zapatista leaders in the hope that the 1995 truce would become permanent. A massacre of peasants in Chiapas during Christmas week 1997 probably set back these talks and certainly tarnished the government's image. Chiapas became an upleasant reminder that the revolutionary goals of 1917, especially those to provide land for all who desired to work it, had not been fully achieved nearly a century later.

The armies in most countries remained quiescent and aloof from politics. Most officers active during the period of military regimes had retired, sometimes in disgrace. Only sporadic conflicts put armed forces on alert, such as a border skirmish between Peru and Ecuador, guerrilla attacks in northern Colombia, and conflicts between miners and Amerindians in the northern Amazon region. The long years in power had equipped the armies with enough firepower and mobility to respond quickly to these threats. In the case of the Peru-Ecuador War, Brazil convened peace talks in early 1995 and managed to steer them to conclusion.

Civil society took advantage of the military retreat from power to examine the bloodshed and injury of those years. In several Southern Cone countries, religious and judicial authorities published accounts of the persons who had died or been reported missing in the repression. The spirit of these accounts was conveyed by their Spanish title, *Nunca Más* (*Never More*). Intellectuals and politicians vowed to prevent the politics of hate and repression from ever reappearing in their countries. Feature films like *Death and the Maiden, The Official Story, Kiss of the Spider Woman,* and *Missing* also helped to keep alive the memory of the terror of those times. Foreign audiences learned much about the dark past of Latin America from these films.

Venezuela, long an exception to the militarist trends of the region, suffered several unsuccessful coups in the early 1990s, precipitating the impeachment and prosecution of President Carlos Andrés Pérez in 1995.

Latin America and the New World Order

The collapse of the Berlin Wall and the dissolution of the USSR in 1991 broke up the Eastern Bloc, ended the Cold War, and brought enormous changes to the world. Writers and politicians spoke of a "new world order," in which fears of a third world war and nuclear devastation abated. The United States and Russia disarmed missiles and decommissioned warships in an attempt to lower tensions and improve domestic affairs. In Latin America, these developments reinforced the retreat of the armed forces from involvement in politics because they were even less relevant to world peace.

The new world order also implied globalization of the region's economies. In eastern Europe former communist governments embraced freer market policies when they liberalized their regimes. The burgeoning industrial "tigers" of Asia— Japan, Taiwan, Hong Kong, Singapore, and South Korea—continued to capture growing shares of the global market, forcing competitive adaptation everywhere.

Even the Asian troubles of 1997 did not rule them out of the global economy. Within the Latin American nations, freer trade and more efficient production promised ways to increase standards of living and to reinforce the political freedoms recently acquired. Certainly the emerging consensus regarding free trade, privatization, and less regulation stimulated more production and trade in the region. Commerce among Latin American countries surged from $12 billion in 1988 to over $30 billion by 1994. A number of trade integration schemes in existence by 1998 helped this growth:

NAFTA—Mexico, Canada, and the United States
Mercosur—Brazil, Uruguay, Paraguay, Argentina, and Chile (associate member)
Andean Pact—Venezuela, Colombia, Peru, Ecuador, and Bolivia
Caricom—Trinidad/Tobago, Jamaica, Suriname, and others
Central American Common Market—Guatemala, Honduras, El Salvador, Nicaragua, and Costa Rica

The upshot was greater trade freedom and more competitive prices for consumer goods, plus broader markets for enterprising businesses. In the 1994 and 1998 Summits, the gathered presidents pledged to create a free trade hemisphere by the year 2005.

It was also noteworthy that inflation decreased since a high in 1991 and continued to drop. In 1994 only two countries, Brazil and Suriname, had triple-digit inflation rates, and Brazil stabilized its currency by mid-year. The decline of inflation also brought moderation of exchange rate fluctuations, helping the poorest consumers meet their basic needs. In 1997 Argentina, whose economy was long known for hyperinflation, had an annual inflation rate of less than 5 percent. These developments transformed the region into a major growth pole in the global economy. For example, the combined automobile markets of Brazil and Argentina had become one of the most lucrative and vibrant in the world.

The end of the Cold War released Latin American governments from the practice of suppressing parties on the left, especially the communists. In most countries, remnants of the radical left have emerged from clandestine existence to participate in elections, such as in Guatemala and El Salvador. They have not, however, prospered because of the generally moderate mood of the 1990s. Moreover, where large numbers of recently enfranchised persons became active, media hype, personality, and popular endorsements have proved influential.

Homogenized Latinos

The increased ease of travel, trade, and communications has permitted millions of Latin Americans to travel abroad, generally within the hemisphere. Latin businesspersons frequent Miami, New York, and Los Angeles and often maintain offices there, while tourists inevitably visit the amusement parks in Orlando and Anaheim. Meanwhile, North American tourists by the millions travel to beaches in the Gulf of Mexico, cruise the Caribbean and Panama Canal, and often visit South America as well. In many ways, these interchanges have overcome physical distances between societies and cultures.

By the same token, hundreds of thousands of Latin Americans have come to live in the United States, legally and otherwise. They swell the populations of Florida, Texas, California, and New York to the extent that immigration has become a hot political topic in those states. The national differences among these immigrant peoples are often enormous. For example, Haitians, Argentines, Guyanans, and Brazilians all speak different languages. Chileans and Guatemalans represent European and Amerindian cultures, respectively. Caribbean islanders and Mexicans may come from opposite sides of the Industrial Revolution. North Americans, however, rarely recognize such distinctions and regard them all as Latinos.

The travel and communications revolutions have allowed Latin immigrants to keep up ties with their countries of origin. Using phones, charter air service, Internet, overnight mail, money wires, and other innovations, they stay networked with families, friends, and associates. Emigrating from a country, then, no longer requires cutting links with home. Likewise, the Latin American countries do not necessarily lose the services and expertise of emigrants. And emigrants' cash remittances make substantial contributions to the national incomes of several countries in the region. Finally, more and more countries are recognizing dual citizenship.

Within the United States, of course, many millions of persons of Latin American descent live in their own Latino communities. Some of their ancestors lived on lands—from California to Texas—annexed by U.S. expansionism, while others immigrated in the nineteenth and early twentieth centuries. These descendants have Iberian names and may speak Spanish or Portuguese, but they think of themselves as Americans. These peoples often have little in common with recent visitors and immigrants. Yet again, some North Americans regard them as "all the same."

In fact, people of Latin descent from all sources now account for 15 percent of the population of this country, and that percentage is growing at a faster rate than those of most other minorities. Members of this community have reached high public office and lead major business organizations. They wield great weight in elections and support two national television networks. And they generate a growing share of the mass entertainment consumed in the United States. The U.S. Latino community will continue to grow in numbers and influence.

Thus, Latin peoples who in the past may have seemed foreign, distant, and even enigmatic have become neighbors and even celebrities. The popular Tex-Mex singer, Selena, enjoyed an enormous following throughout the nation. Their history, formerly taught as Third World studies or world affairs courses, has begun to blend into the history of the United States. The histories of Mexico, Cuba, Nicaragua, and Panama cannot be told without recounting the U.S. part played in their affairs, nor can those countries be written out of general U.S. histories. The separate histories of the peoples of this hemisphere, then, are beginning to coalesce into a common one.

Not only do Americans sometimes treat Latinos in the United States as if they were homogeneous, but also they subject them to prejudices and preferences fitting Euro-American views. For example, people of partial African descent who in

Colombia or Brazil may be regarded as white are considered blacks in this country. Persons thought handsome by Amerindian values are here regarded as plain. And forms of artistic expression from the Caribbean may be regarded as "primitive" in the United States.

Solving such prejudices and intercultural misunderstandings, faced in the past only by international travelers, is critical to the evolution of American society. Major problems faced in our cities—crime, environmental degradation, drugs, teenage pregnancy, and homelessness—have deep multicultural sources. Improvements surely require much greater sensitivity to the foreign backgrounds of many who are victimized by these problems.

Challenges for the Next Century

Three policy areas confront government leaders in Latin America, all of them legacies of the autocratic 1970s and 1980s. First, the dramatic concentration of wealth in the bank accounts and portfolios of the richest sectors, accompanied by a shrinking share of income in the pockets of the masses, threatens to polarize societies and suffocate economic growth. Crime, banditry, drugs, shantytowns, and homelessness have expanded largely because poor people could not afford to raise and educate their children under the military governments. The neoliberal policies of the 1990s cannot easily address the skewed distribution of income because they require less government intervention. In a laissez-faire environment, it may take decades before any market-driven equalization occurs.

The Mexican, Cuban, and Nicaraguan revolutions were fought in the name of *los de abajo* (the downtrodden). Social scientists now realize that the mere existence of poverty does not lead automatically to political upheavals. Still, continued growth of urban shantytowns, illegal peasant communities, "informal" businesses and workers, and Mafia-like crime syndicates can create an environment conducive to a major revolt from below, led by a charismatic or messianic figure. The best antidote to revolution may be overcoming the growing gap in living standards throughout the region. This dilemma has no easy solutions.

Second, strong feelings of nationalism inherited from previous generations must be tempered with an acceptance of global trends and integration into the larger world. Political leaders have always found nationalism to be an effective appeal to the masses. National interests are naturally the closest to the voters' hearts. The outside world, in contrast, seems to have no domestic constituency, no one to speak up for international policies. The last several Mexican presidents have faced this problem, attempting to justify signing international trade agreements—like GATT and NAFTA—after a long tradition of protectionism. Business people were not the only ones to protest these changes: The rebels in Chiapas believed that NAFTA would hurt their interests as well, and they chose to protest on the day that the agreement went into effect. The neopopulists of the Southern Cone also faced this problem because they had to betray legacies of developmental nationalism to open their economies to global competition.

Whether or not the end of the Cold War eliminates nationalism in world affairs, as some have predicted, remains to be seen. Relaxation of international tensions may ironically lead societies to turn inward and become more nationalistic. The late 1990s has witnessed the growing authority of multilateral organizations (like the UN, the World Bank, and the OAS) to assume ever-larger roles in international affairs. At the same time, regional consolidation is molding new entities in western Europe, North America, and eastern Asia. The Latin American nations need not join this trend, yet they may find themselves left out of the new world order if they do not.

Third, government leaders must continue to protect and strengthen the democratic procedures in place for choosing new representatives and for approving legal frameworks. Elections, plebiscites, judicial review, and constitutional rights have been restored throughout the region, but their continuance is not at all certain. The spread of peaceable conduct suggests that Latin Americans, like most other peoples, cherish security and predictability in their lives. Stable, representative government is the best way to attain these conditions.

None of these challenges will be easily met, yet they must be dealt with openly and boldly to protect advances already won in politics, economy, and quality of life. And much progress has been made by the generations who have arisen in Latin America since independence in the early 1800s.

Preserving Diversity

Trends toward globalization, homogenization, political integration, and the like will not erase the rich diversity of life, culture, and nature in Latin America. No other region in the world has experienced such a radical mixing of peoples on its soil as Latin America has. Its original inhabitants migrated from central Asia tens of thousands of years ago; over twelve million Africans were transported to the Americas as slaves; and many more millions emigrated from Europe and the Middle East. This coming together of the world's peoples constitutes a human experiment of great significance. If they succeed in building peaceful and prosperous societies out of this historic diversity, it will be a major achievement for humankind.

Not all of the immigrant peoples of Latin America have given up their traditions and cultures. Large communities of Jews, Japanese, Poles, Russians, Chinese, North Americans, and Europeans thrive in the region. Non-Iberian names abound among the presidents of Latin America—such as Galtieri, Fujimori, Geisel, Kubitschek, Bosch, Aylwin, Montt—attesting to the upward mobility of immigrants. The African contribution has been vast in culture, aesthetics, social interaction, and family life. And last but not least, the Amerindian peoples remain politically and culturally important in a number of countries. By studying contemporary Amerindian peoples we can understand a great deal about the deep past of our hemisphere. They, too, have interacted and risen to high positions in Latin America. Preserving and expanding this social and cultural diversity ought to be a major priority of national leaders.

To speak of the successful accommodation of so many distinctive peoples in the Americas is not to deny the existence of racism, discrimination, conflict, and separation based upon differences. Latin America has a long way to go to eradicate racial and ethnic problems, and in some countries they must first be admitted in order to be eradicated. That so many groups have already achieved peaceful co-existence augurs well for preserving diversity in the future.

Environmental diversity is also at risk in Latin America, and its conservation must be given top priority. From the steppe-like Altiplano of Bolivia to the steamy jungles of the Amazon, the region contains more biodiversity than any other on earth, especially in the plant kingdom. The world received from the Americas major food staples like the potato and corn; pharmaceuticals like quinine and ipecac; unique animals like the rhea and the llama; and tropical plants running into the tens of millions of varieties. No wonder that Darwin received his inspiration for *On the Origin of Species* (1859) after studying South America. The region is a veritable laboratory for botany, zoology, biology, geology, and most other sciences.

Naturalists have long been adamant about protecting the Amazon rain forest from clearing and burning, and with good reason. They now understand how interconnected the many regional environments of the world are, and they warn us against the loss of biological diversity. Lowland tropical forests on the west coast of Colombia, in Central America, on many Caribbean islands, and along Brazil's littoral have also been subject to a great deal of timber harvesting and clearing. Because those forests are less extensive than the Amazon, their ability to regenerate is limited. In all, Latin America contains approximately 70 percent of the world's remaining tropical rain forest.

Other locales are in jeopardy as well. Scientists have voiced concern for the coastal reefs and deep marine life of the Caribbean and the Pacific trenches. Even mountainous settings in Latin America have undergone drastic alterations due to human occupation. Central Mexico and the Andean highlands have lost most of their original forest cover. And as scientists in temperate lands have discovered, loss of habitat leads to the loss of animal species.

Humans have adapted to the extremely diverse lands of Latin America, most of which are still livable. The more important question, however, is whether economic activity can be sustained in these landscapes. Haiti's mountains may never again be cultivable due to clearing and erosion. The barrier reef of Belize may never again produce shrimp due to pollution. Farms in western Brazil may never again grow cereals due to leaching of the soils. North-central Mexico may never again raise cattle due to overgrazing in the past. And the Darien rain forest of eastern Panama may never again produce hardwoods due to overlogging. In short, human existence in these fragile environments may itself become impoverished because of mismanagement of the land.

The environmental dangers in tropical America influence and are influenced by the rest of the world. Latin Americans have caused drastic losses in species diversity by clearing rain forests. Meanwhile, industrial pollution in the Northern Hemisphere has depleted the ozone layer over Antarctica. As a result, people in southern Chile and Patagonia have elevated rates of skin cancer caused by excessive solar radiation.

Ecological concerns in Latin America go beyond the land's ability to sustain people. Changes in the rich and concentrated natural processes of tropical areas (most of Latin America lies between the Tropics of Cancer and Capricorn) may actually affect climate. Desertification has begun in some regions, rainfall has been reduced in others, and wind patterns have altered in yet others. Our knowledge of global climate is still so limited that we cannot say for certain what causes such changes or what outcomes will ensue. But certainly prudence suggests avoiding environmental impacts whose effects on nature are largely unknown.

Centennial Appraisals

Today, at the dawn of the twenty-first century, we look back and take stock of a century of change, just as our ancestors did in 1800 and 1900. Out of the confusion of people and events and evidence, we discern broad trends, critical moments, and dominant leaders.

Latin American observers in the year 1800 clearly saw time accelerate. They had witnessed a revival of Spain's fortunes under the Bourbon dynasty. That led to increased exploitation of American subjects by agents of the king and the pope. They noted the reorganization of Portugal's government under Prime Minister Pombal and its enforcement of new taxes and levies on Brazil. Many writers forecast that momentous change would result from the independence of the thirteen British colonies in North America and the massive rebellion of Africans in Haiti. They believed that people of the Americas would no longer tolerate the yokes of colonialism and slavery. And they were right.

Many educated Latin Americans had traveled to Europe and the United States in the 1780s and 1790s. They predicted that Spanish and Portuguese Americans would emulate those other societies. In the area of material civilization, they foresaw the spread of industry to the Americas, resulting in major increases in the productivity of its economies. New knowledge available in the liberal arts, sciences, and applied fields would permit Latin Americans to use more of their resources to improve their standard of living. Steam power, carbon steel, and high-grade ceramics would make life easier and more rewarding for people all over the world. International travel had become accessible to large numbers of well-to-do citizens, who could visit the far corners of the earth for business and study. And governments were listening more closely to the voices of their citizens, even those who labored with their hands and who expressed themselves in protests and riots.

The late 1700s were truly the beginning of an age of revolution in all facets of life: political, economic, intellectual, religious, and social. Latin America was almost immediately swept up in these changes.

Observers in the year 1900 could assess the outcomes of the multiple revolutions that had swept the western world in the previous century. Most of the former Iberian colonies had become independent nations in the 1810s and 1820s, following the example of the United States. All took steps to end the terrible trade in Africans and eventually abolished slavery itself. The new nations opened their borders and ports to foreigners, who brought manufactures, new businesses, railroads, scientific instruments, books, and other innovations. Native leaders took over from Europeans and forged national identities based on their own traditions and aspirations. Writers, painters, poets, sculptors, composers, and dramatists soon created national cultures for their homelands. These drew on European heritage and avoided Amerindian or African traditions, at the time thought to be inferior. Leading citizens built cities, factories, ships, railroads, plantations, and monuments to reflect their coming of age.

The nineteenth century had brought progress of a sort to Latin America. Exports of raw materials and food—nitrates, coffee, cacao, guano, sugar, hides, cereal, meat, nonferrous ores, industrial metals, timber, and much more—allowed Latin Americans to import the commodities thought to represent civilization in that era. Yet, these imports also harbored stowaway attitudes from Europe, like racism, disdain for the poor, evangelical religion, and materialism. These attitudes often clashed with centuries-old traditions in the region and produced conflict and upheaval. Social classes antagonistic to one another emerged, poor people lost touch with propertied families, and mass migrations brought in millions of outsiders and uprooted millions of natives. By the year 1900 mass society, with all its ills, had appeared in the larger cities of Latin America.

Today's centennial observers look back on an even more accelerated and tumultuous period of history. Revolutions continued, this time mobilizing those at the bottom—*los de abajo*—against the elites. In Mexico, Bolivia, Cuba, and Nicaragua, guerrilla armies of discontented workers and peasants overthrew established governments. In other places, movements from below narrowly missed becoming full-blown revolutions. Governments in the hemisphere, usually led by the United States, cooperated to prevent disturbance to the existing order, especially by revolutions. By the mid-twentieth century, the Cold War strengthened the resolve of American regimes to resist changes in the status quo. So an overarching theme of the past hundred years has been revolution versus repression.

The spread of modern technology and modes of production continued during the past century, allowing several Latin American nations to become fully industrialized. Mexico, Brazil, Argentina, Chile, Venezuela, and Colombia possess balanced economies, in which the primary sectors—mining, agriculture, and ranching—provide raw materials for and support laborers in the secondary or manufacturing sectors. Well-developed service enterprises in the cities allow for safe, pleasant, productive lives for workers and their families. Most governments provide a wide array of basic services to their citizens. Today Latin America ranks somewhere in the middle of the world's nations in terms of productivity and standard of living.

Latin American culture gained in stature and impact during the twentieth century. This was led by African-inspired music from the Caribbean, which swept the western world after the 1920s. Then Latin American novels became popular in the 1960s, creating an unprecedented publishing boom. Many nations excelled in sports, especially soccer, baseball, tennis, and volleyball, and won recognition in Olympic games. Meanwhile, sophisticated film and television production developed in Mexico, Brazil, Argentina, and Chile after the middle of the century. Even hybrid cuisines from Latin America—from tacos and plantains to feijoada and enchiladas—spread to the United States and Europe. World culture has certainly been enriched by Latin American contributions in the last century.

Recent trends in Latin America suggest that its people, institutions, governments, and cultures are coming to resemble those of Europe and the United States. Radio and satellite-fed television, global communications, multinational corporations, and mass travel have certainly produced a "modern" and westernized citizenry in the metropolitan areas. Nevertheless, in its smaller cities, in villages and rural districts, and in the vast expanses of deserts and savannas and rain forests, Latin America remains unique and distinctive. The diverse populations preserved in these areas, we may confidently predict, will continue to enrich life in the region throughout the twenty-first century.

Bibliography for Part Five

Almeida, Anna Luiza Ozorio de, *The Colonization of the Amazon* (Austin: University of Texas Press, 1992).

Bergquist, Charles W., et al., *Violence in Colombia* (Wilmington: SR Books, 1992).

Camp, Roderic A., *The Making of a Government: Political Leaders in Modern Mexico* (Tucson: University of Arizona Press, 1985).

Child, Jack, *The Central American Peace Process, 1983–1991* (Boulder: Lynne Rienner, 1992).

Clawson, Patrick L., and Rensselaer W. Lee III, *The Andean Cocaine Industry* (New York: St. Martin's Press, 1996).

Constable, Pamela, and Arturo Valenzuela, *A Nation of Enemies: Chile under Pinochet* (New York: W.W. Norton, 1991).

Cornelius, Wayne A., *Mexican Politics in Transition: The Breakdown of a One-Party-Dominant Regime* (San Diego: Center for U.S.-Mexican Studies, 1996).

Davis, Diane E., *Urban Leviathan: Mexico City in the Twentieth Century* (Philadelphia: Temple University Press, 1994).

Drake, Paul W., *Labor Movements and Dictatorships: The Southern Cone in Comparative Perspective* (Baltimore: Johns Hopkins University Press, 1996).

Drake, Paul W., and Eduardo Silva, eds., *Elections and Democratization in Latin America, 1980–1985* (San Diego: Center for U.S.-Mexican Studies, 1986).

Fleet, Michael, and Brian H. Smith, *The Catholic Church and Democracy in Chile and Peru* (Notre Dame: University of Notre Dame Press, 1997).

Gillespie, Charles Guy, *Negotiating Democracy: Politicians and Generals in Uruguay* (Cambridge: Cambridge University Press, 1991).

Gleijeses, Piero, *Shattered Hope: The Guatemalan Revolution and the United States, 1944–1954* (Princeton: Princeton University Press, 1992).

Guzmán Bouvard, Marguerite, *Revolutionizing Motherhood: The Mothers of the Plaza de Mayo* (Wilmington: SR Books, 1994).

Handy, Jim, *Revolution in the Countryside: Rural Conflict and Agrarian Reform in Guatemala, 1944–1954* (Chapel Hill: University of North Carolina Press, 1994).

Hunter, Wendy, *Eroding Military Influence in Brazil: Politicians Against Soldiers* (Chapel Hill: University of North Carolina Press, 1997).

Keck, Margaret E., *The Workers' Party and Democratization in Brazil* (New Haven: Yale University Press, 1992).

Kopinak, Kathryn, *Desert Capitalism: Maquiladoras in North America's Western Industrial Corridor* (Tucson: University of Arizona Press, 1996).

Loveman, Brian, and Thomas M. Davies, Jr., eds., *The Politics of Antipolitics: The Military in Latin America*, 3rd ed. (Wilmington: SR Books, 1997).

Lowenthal, Abraham F., *The Dominican Intervention*, 2nd ed. (Baltimore: Johns Hopkins University Press, 1995).

Martinez, Oscar, ed., *U.S.-Mexico Borderlands* (Wilmington: SR Books, 1996).

Middlebrook, Kevin J., and Carlos Rico, eds., *The United States and Latin America in the 1980s* (Pittsburgh: University of Pittsburgh Press, 1985).

Morris, Stephen D., *Political Reformism in Mexico* (Boulder: Lynne Rienner, 1995).

Nunn, Frederick M., *The Time of the Generals: Latin American Professional Militarism in World Perspective* (Lincoln: University of Nebraska Press, 1992).

Oppenheim, Lois Hecht, *Politics in Chile* (Boulder: Westview, 1993).

Orme, William A., Jr., *Understanding NAFTA* (Austin: University of Texas Press, 1996).

Palmer, David Scott, ed., *Shining Path of Peru*, 2nd ed. (New York: St. Martin's Press, 1994).

Pérez-Stable, Marifeli, *The Cuban Revolution: Origins, Course, and Legacy* (New York: Oxford University Press, 1993).

Potash, Robert A., *The Army and Politics in Argentina, 1945–1962* (Stanford: Stanford University Press, 1980).

Potash, Robert A., *The Army and Politics in Argentina, 1962–1973* (Stanford: Stanford University Press, 1996).

Quirk, Robert E., *Fidel Castro* (New York: W. W. Norton, 1993).

Reich, Peter Lester, *Mexico's Hidden Revolution: The Catholic Church in Law and Politics since 1929* (Notre Dame: University of Notre Dame Press, 1996).

Schneider, Ronald M., *Brazil: Culture and Politics in a New Industrial Powerhouse* (Boulder: Westview, 1996).

Sigmund, Paul E., *The Overthrow of Allende and the Politics of Chile, 1964–1977* (Pittsburgh: University of Pittsburgh Press, 1978).

Skidmore, Thomas E., *The Politics of Military Rule in Brazil, 1964–1985* (New York: Oxford University Press, 1988).

Spooner, Mary Helen, *Soldiers in a Narrow Land: The Pinochet Regime in Chile* (Berkeley and Los Angeles: University of California Press, 1994).

Vanden, Harry E., and Gary Prevost, *Democracy and Socialism in Sandinista Nicaragua* (Boulder: Lynne Rienner, 1992).

Walker, William O., III, ed., *Drugs in the Western Hemisphere* (Wilmington: SR Books, 1996).

Wickham-Crowley, Timothy P., *Guerrillas and Revolution in Latin America* (Princeton: Princeton University Press, 1992).

Wood, Bryce, *The Dismantling of the Good Neighbor Policy* (Austin: University of Texas Press, 1985).

Wright, Thomas C., *Latin America in the Era of the Cuban Revolution* (Westport: Praeger, 1991).

General Bibliography

Aguilar Camín, Hector, and Lorenzo Meyer, *In the Shadow of the Mexican Revolution* (Austin: University of Texas Press, 1993).

Atkins, G. Pope, *Latin America in the International Political System* (Boulder: Westview, 1995).

Atkins, G. Pope, and Larman C. Wilson, *The Dominican Republic and the United States* (Athens: University of Georgia Press, 1997).

Bethell, Leslie, ed., *The Cambridge History of Latin America*, 11 vols. (Cambridge: Cambridge University Press, 1985–1995).

Blasier, Cole, *The Hovering Giant: U.S. Responses to Revolutionary Change in Latin America* (Pittsburgh: University of Pittsburgh Press, 1985).

Bulmer-Thomas, Victor, *The Economic History of Latin America since Independence* (Cambridge: Cambridge University Press, 1994).

Burns, E. Bradford, *Latin America: A Concise Interpretive History* (Englewood Cliffs, N.J.: Prentice-Hall, 1986).

Burns, E. Bradford, *A History of Brazil* (New York: Columbia University Press, 1993).

Bushnell, David, *The Making of Modern Colombia* (Berkeley and Los Angeles: University of California Press, 1992).

Camp, Roderic Ai, *Politics in Mexico*, 2nd ed. (Oxford: Oxford University Press, 1996).

Camp, Roderic Ai, ed., *Democracy in Latin America* (Wilmington: SR Books, 1996).

Clayton, Lawrence A., *The Bolivarian Nations of Latin America* (Arlington Heights, Illinois: Forum Press, 1984).

Clayton, Lawrence A., *Peru and the United States: The Condor and the Eagle* (Athens, Georgia: University of Georgia Press, 1999).

Collier, Ruth Berins, and David Collier, *Shaping the Political Arena* (Princeton: Princeton University Press, 1991).

Collier, Simon, and William F. Sater, *A History of Chile* (Cambridge: Cambridge University Press, 1996).

Collier, Simon, Thomas E. Skidmore, and Harold Blakemore, eds., *The Cambridge Encyclopedia of Latin America and the Caribbean*, 2nd ed. (Cambridge: Cambridge University Press, 1992).

Conniff, Michael L., *Panama and the United States* (Athens: University of Georgia Press, 1992).

Conniff, Michael L., ed., *Populism in Latin America* (Tuscaloosa: University of Alabama Press, 1999).

Conniff, Michael L., and Thomas J. Davis, eds., *Africans in the Americas: A History of the Black Diaspora* (New York: St. Martin's Press, 1994).

Conniff, Michael L., and Frank McCann, eds., *Modern Brazil*, 2nd ed. (Lincoln: University of Nebraska Press, 1991).

Davis, Darien J., ed., *Slavery and Beyond: The African Impact on Latin America and the Caribbean* (Wilmington: SR Books, 1995).

Eakin, Marshall C., *Brazil: The Once and Future Country* (New York: St. Martin's Press, 1997).

Ewell, Judith, *Venezuela* (Stanford: Stanford University Press, 1975).

Ewell, Judith, *Venezuela and the United States* (Athens: University of Georgia Press, 1996).

Flick, Carolyn E., *The Making of Haiti* (Knoxville: University of Tennessee Press, 1990).

Hamill, Hugh M., ed., *Caudillos: Dictators in Spanish America* (Norman: University of Oklahoma Press, 1992).

Hart, John Mason, *Revolutionary Mexico* (Berkeley and Los Angeles: University of California Press, 1987).

Jaquette, Jane S., ed., *The Women's Movement in Latin America* (Boulder: Westview, 1994).

Johnson, John J., *Latin America in Caricature* (Austin: University of Texas Press, 1980).

Keen, Benjamin, ed., *Latin American Civilization: History and Society, 1492 to the Present* (Boulder: Westview Press, 1986).

Keith, Robert G., ed., *Haciendas and Plantations in Latin American History* (New York: Holmes & Meier, 1977).

Kicza, John E. ed., *The Indian in Latin American History: Resistance, Resilience, and Accultura-*

tion (Wilmington, DE: Scholarly Resources, 1993).

Klein, Herbert S., *Bolivia*, 2nd ed. (Oxford: Oxford University Press, 1992).

Knight, Franklin W., *The Caribbean*, 2nd ed. (Oxford: Oxford University Press, 1990).

Krause, Enrique, *Mexico, Biography of Power: History, 1810–1996* (New York: Random House, 1997).

Langley, Lester D., *America and the Americas* (Athens: University of Georgia Press, 1989).

Leonard, Thomas M., *Central America and the United States* (Athens: University of Georgia Press, 1991).

Lombardi, John V., *Venezuela* (New York: Oxford University Press, 1982).

Loveman, Brian, *Chile*, 2nd ed. (Oxford: Oxford University Press, 1988).

MacLachlan, Colin M., and William H. Beezley, *El Gran Pueblo: A History of Greater Mexico* (Englewood Cliffs: Prentice-Hall, 1994).

Maingot, Anthony P., *The United States and the Caribbean* (Boulder: Westview, 1994).

Meyer, Michael C., and William L. Sherman, *The Course of Mexican History*, 3rd ed. (New York: Oxford University Press, 1987).

Miller, Francesca, *Latin American Women and the Search for Social Justice* (Hanover: University Press of New England, 1991).

Morner, Magnus, *Race Mixture in the History of Latin America* (Boston: Little, Brown, 1967).

Moya Pons, Frank, *The Dominican Republic: A National History* (New Rochelle, NY: Hispaniola Books, 1995).

Murray, Pamela S., *Dreams of Development: Colombia's National School of Mines, 1887–1970* (Tuscaloosa: University of Alabama Press, 1997).

Nicholls, David, *From Dessalines to Duvalier: Race, Color, and National Independence in Haiti*, rev. ed. (New Brunswick: Rutgers University Press, 1996).

Palmer, David Scott, *Peru: The Authoritarian Tradition* (New York: Praeger, 1980).

Perez, Louis A., Jr., *Cuba*, 2nd ed. (Oxford: Oxford University Press, 1995).

Perez, Louis A., Jr., *Cuba and the United States*, 2nd ed. (Athens: University of Georgia Press, 1997).

Perez-Stable, Marifeli, *The Cuban Revolution* (Oxford: Oxford University Press, 1993).

Pike, Frederick B., *The United States and Latin America* (Austin: University of Texas Press, 1992).

Plummer, Brenda Gayle, *Haiti and the United States* (Athens: University of Georgia Press, 1992).

Raat, W. Dirk, *Mexico and the United States* (Athens: University of Georgia Press, 1992).

Randall, Stephen J., *Colombia and the United States* (Athens: University of Georgia Press, 1992).

Reis, João José, *Slave Rebellion in Brazil* (Baltimore: Johns Hopkins University Press, 1993).

Richardson, Bonham C., *The Caribbean in the Wider World, 1492–1992* (Cambridge: Cambridge University Press, 1992).

Rock, David, *Argentina, 1519–1987* (Berkeley and Los Angeles: University of California Press, 1985).

Rodó, Jose Enrique, *Ariel* (Austin: University of Texas Press, 1988).

Rodriguez, Linda A., ed., *Rank and Privilege: The Military and Society in Latin America* (Wilmington: SR Books, 1994).

Rouquie, Alain, *The Military and the State in Latin America* (Berkeley and Los Angeles: University of California Press, 1993).

Sater, William F., *Chile and the United States* (Athens: University of Georgia Press, 1990).

Schodt, David W., *Ecuador: An Andean Enigma* (Boulder: Westview Press, 1987).

Scobie, James R., *Argentina: A City and a Nation* (New York, Oxford University Press, 1971).

Shepherd, Verene, Bridget Brereton, and Barbara Bainley, *Engendering History: Caribbean Women in Historical Perspective* (New York: St. Martin's Press, 1995).

Simpson, Lesley Byrd, *Many Mexicos* (Berkeley, University of California Press, 1966).

Skidmore, Thomas E., *Brazil* (New York: Oxford University Press, 1999).

Stone, Roger D., *Dreams of Amazonia*, rev. ed. (New York: Penguin, 1992).

Tenenbaum, Barbara A., ed., *The Encyclopedia of Latin American History and Culture* (New York: Charles Scribner's Sons, 1996).

Torres Rivas, Edelberto, *History and Society in Central America* (Austin: University of Texas Press, 1993).

Weber, David J., and Jane M. Rausch, eds., *Where Cultures Meet: Frontiers in Latin American History* (Wilmington: SR Books, 1994).

Williams, Eric Eustace, *From Columbus to Castro: The History of the Caribbean, 1492-1969* (New York: Harper & Row, 1970).

Winn, Peter, *Americas: The Changing Face of Latin America and the Caribbean* (Berkeley and

Los Angeles: University of California Press, 1995).

Woodward, Ralph Lee, Jr., *Central America*, 2nd ed. (Oxford: Oxford University Press, 1985).

Wright, Winthrop R., *Cafe con Leche: Race, Class, and National Image in Venezuela* (Austin: University of Texas Press, 1990).

Yeager, Gertrude M., ed., *Confronting Change, Challenging Tradition: Women in Latin American History* (Wilmington: SR Books, 1994).

Zea, Leopoldo, *The Latin-American Mind.* Translated from the Spanish by James H. Abbott and Lowell Dunham (Norman: University of Oklahoma Press, 1963).

Glossary

Abertura/apertura: political opening or restoration of democracy by military government.

Agrarios: rural representatives in Mexico, including militias.

Amerindian: a contraction for "American Indian" which easily serves to distinguish Indian peoples of the American continents from Indians from South Asia.

Anarchists: activists, usually laborers, who opposed all forms of organized government.

Audiencia: judicial court in Spanish American colonies that possessed both judicial and legislative authority.

Aviadores: merchants who sold goods and loaned money to rubber tappers along the Amazon tributaries.

Barriadas: shantytowns in and around major cities in Latin America.

Beneméritos: prominent patriots from the Wars of Independence epoch; sometimes translated as "founding fathers."

Bossa nova: a jazz-influenced version of Brazilian samba music popular since the 1960s.

Bracero Labor Program: special entry visas for Mexican workers (and later others) to harvest crops and work in specific industries for limited periods of time.

Cabildos: city councils; _____ abiertos: open town meetings to deal with crises, largely associated with early wars of independence period. The term cabildo refers not only to the elected officials themselves—the *alcaldes* and *regidores*—but to the physical building where the council met.

Caciques: regional or local leaders whose origins date back to the Spanish conquest of the Caribbean, where "caciques" were native Indian chieftains. In the modern (era, the term carries) many meanings, all implying a leadership role in the community, region, or even nation. See caudillo.

Café com leite: Portuguese for coffee with milk; slang for informal arrangements for Brazilian presidents to alternate from the states of São Paulo (major coffee-growing region) and Minas Gerais (a dairy state).

Café con leche: Spanish for coffee with milk; slang for mulattoes in Venezuela, with light skin color.

Candomblé: Afro-Brazilian religion; also Macumba and Umbanda.

Carabineros: Chilean national police.

Caudillo: classically described as a "strong man" in Latin American politics and society. He possessed dictatorial qualities, came to power and governed often through the force of his personality, and could exist at all levels of Latin American life, from local or regional caudillos to national leaders such as Juan Manuel de Rosas of Argentina.

Centrales: sugar refining complexes, including factories and estates that were created by combining older mills and estates for greater efficiency. Built after the 1880s, most often associated with the modernization of the industry in Cuba.

Cholo: Hispanicized or urbanized Indian in Peru or Bolivia; Amerindian who has moved to an urban environment and works, dresses, and acts like the mestizo/white society in the towns and cities, or mines and plantations of his new environment. Can also refer to a lower-class mestizo.

Científicos: Mexican positivists from the era of Porfirio Díaz (1876–1911).

Comandante: military commander.

Compradazco: godfather/godmother relations, ritual kinship.

Conquistador: Spanish conqueror from the era of discovery and conquest.

Constitutional monarchy: a king, or monarch, whose powers are circumscribed and delineated by a constitution whose laws he/she must abide by.

Contras: anti-Sandinista group, supported by the U. S., in the 1980s, dedicated to the overthrow of the Sandinista government of Nicaragua.

Coronel: in Brazil, a rural boss (lit. colonel); from National Guard commissions distributed liberally in the nineteenth century.

Cortes: Spanish parliament.

Coup d'etat: a *golpe de estado* in Latin America, or, literally, a blow to the state. The overthrow of a government outside the normal, usually constitutional, provisions for passage of political power.

Criollo: a person born to Spanish parents living in the Americas. Creole in English.

Cristeros: passionate Christians who rebelled in the late 1920s against the secularizing tendencies of the Mexican Revolution.

Descamisados: the poor or rabble; from Spanish word for shirtless persons; used most often in Argentina.

Ejidos: traditional communal lands in Mexico owned largely by Amerindians; community land grants under the 1917 constitution.

Estancia: large pastoral estate, ranch in Argentina.

Estancieros: ranch owners.

Fazendas: large landed estates in Brazil.

Fazendeiros: estate owners in Brazil.

Foco: a guerrilla base, usually a small encampment in a rural area; an integral part of the theory of guerrilla warfare developed by Che Guevara.

Fueros: corporate privileges enjoyed by certain groups, especially the military and clergy.

Gauchos: "cowboys" of the wide spaces of Argentina and Uruguay devoted to cattle raising. Gaúcho in Brazil.

Grandeza: army's dream of leading Brazil into great-nation status in the 1970s.

Grito de Dolores: literally, the cry or shout of Dolores, the small village where the priest Miguel Hidalgo began the Mexican War of Independence with his call to arms and revolution from his parish church.

Guardia Nacional: National Guards, many created by the United States in Caribbean and Central American nations to promote stability and order.

Gusano: Cuban term, meaning worm, disparaging exiles after the 1959 revolution.

Hacendados: hacienda owners.

Hacienda: large, landed estate in Spanish America.

Huasos: Chilean cowboys.

Iberian: referring to Spain and Portugal, which occupy the Iberian Peninsula.

Import substitution industrialization (ISI): an economic growth strategy popular from the 1930s to the 1970s that promoted domestic industrialization.

Indigenismo: Indianism; a largely twentieth century movement to restore the Amerindian to prominence in the history and culture of countries.

Inquilinos: Chilean tenant farmers.

Junta: a committee; term often applied to governments that come to power through a coup or revolution.

Ladinos: creoles in Central America; white people in general.

Llanos: prairies and plains of southern Venezuela and Colombia.

Machismo: virility, strength, and power in the man; male dominance.

Magical realism: literary style of Latin American writers after the 1940s, in which fantastic events were portrayed realistically.

Maquiladora: a bonded frontier manufacturer, usually along the U.S.-Mexico border, that assembles components from abroad and exports finished products to the United States.

Mariachi: a typical musical group in Mexico, specializing in popular songs from the countryside.

Marianismo: special worship of the Virgin Mary; stresses obedience, loyalty, docility, faithfulness in women. Often thought as the oposite of *machismo.*

Maximato: the 1928–1935 period when Plutarco Calles dominated Mexican politics.

Mazorcas: gangs of thugs who enforced Juan Manuel de Rosas's rule in 1830s and 1840s Buenos Aires; by extension pro-Perón bands in the 1950s.

Mesoamerica: Middle America, comprising Mexico and Central America.

Mestizo: a person born in the Americas whose parents are of European and Amerindian ancestry. For example, the offspring of a Spanish conquistador and an Inca woman would be a *mestizo.* Hernán Cortés and his Indian mistress doña Marina were said to have produced the "first" Mexican mestizo.

Mexamerica: borderlands of northern Mexico and the southwestern United States.

Miscegenation: the mixing of racial and/or ethnic types. For example, an Indian wed to a Spaniard produced a mestizo, an act of miscegenation.

Mita: Indian tribute labor, associated with the forceful recruitment of Indian labor by Spanish colonial administrators to work in the mines of the Viceroyalty of Peru.

Montoneros: guerrillas in the mountains of Peru and Bolivia.

Mulatto: a person born of a union between white and black; see *pardo*.

Negritude: literary and intellectual movement that recognized the importance of African cultural heritage on the continent and in the Americas.

New World: North and South America, including the Caribbean.

Norteños: Mexicans from northern states.

Oncenio: the 11-year administration of President Leguía of Peru from 1919–1930.

Pampas: plains of Argentina and Southern Brazil, where cattle and agriculture thrive.

Parceiros: Brazilian term for tenant farmers.

Pardo: a person born of a union between white and black; the term is used interchangeably with *mulatto*. Could also mean simply someone of mixed racial background, with white-black origins.

Patria: fatherland, homeland.

Patronato Real: the arrangement between the Spanish Crown and the Roman Catholic Church which gave the Crown the right to exercise effective control over the Church in the Spanish American colonies, such as founding churches, appointing clerics, and collecting the tithe.

Pax britannica: a period of British preeminence in world affairs, roughly from 1815 until World War I.

Peninsular: a Spaniard in the Americas who was born in Spain; as opposed to a child born of Spanish parents in the Americas; see *criollo*.

Peon: a Latin American peasant. Much controversy exists on the exact definition of a peon but he was basically a person tied to the land by tradition and various institutions, some formal and some informal.

Populares: members of Mexico's principal political party, the PRI, representing civil servants.

Porfiriato: the period in Mexican history, 1876–1911, when Porfirio Díaz governed Mexico.

Porteños: citizens of the port city of Buenos Aires.

Precursors: refers to those leaders who, like Francisco de Miranda of Venezuela, preceded the independence movements.

Ranchera: popular music in Mexico from the early twentieth century.

Rancheros: small-scale farmers and ranchers in Mexico.

Resguardos: Indian communities of Colombia which owned their land collectively.

Rosistas: supporters of the great Argentine caudillo, Juan Manuel Rosas.

Rurales: rural police force created by Porfirio Díaz in Mexico.

Saladeros: plants for salting beef.

Sertão: Brazil's dry, inhospitable backlands.

Sierra: mountain range.

Soldaderas: female camp followers during the Mexican revolution.

Syncretized religion: in the Latin American context, where native Amerindian or African practices, beliefs, and forms of worship survived and were integrated into standard Christian doctrine and religious worship, producing often uniquely Latin American forms of worship.

Syndicalists: radical labor unionists who, often allied with Anarchists, sought to destroy all government.

Tenentes: rebel officers and cadets in Brazil who fought against the government from 1922 to 1930 and then served in the Vargas administration afterward.

Tribute: a form of tax paid by Indians to the State; could be in crops or labor.

Unitarios: political party centered in the city of Buenos Aires which favored strong centralized rule in Argentina.

West Indian: people from the West Indian Islands in the Caribbean; also Antilleans.

Zambo: child of a union between black and Amerindian.

Zapatistas: revolutionary group in the southern states of Mexico in the 1990s that took its name from the followers of Emiliano Zapata during the Mexican revolution.

Index

Photo Credits